Thunder Across the Swamp

The Fight for the Lower Mississippi, February 1863–May 1863

Thunder Across the Swamp

The Fight for the Lower Mississippi, February 1863–May 1863

Donald S. Frazier

State House Press
Buffalo Gap, Texas

Library of Congress Cataloging-in-Publication Data

Frazier, Donald S. (Donald Shaw), 1965–
Thunder across the swamp: the fight for the Lower Mississippi, February–May 1863 / Donald S. Frazier
p. cm.
Includes bibliographical references and index.
ISBN-13: 978-1-933337-44-9 (hardcover: alk. paper)
ISBN-10:1-933337-44-3 (hardcover: alk. paper)
1. Louisiana—History—Civil War, 1861-1865—Campaigns.
2. Louisiana—History—Civil War, 1861-1865—Naval operations. 3. Mississippi River Valley—History—Civil War, 1861-1865—Campaigns. 4. Mississippi River Valley—History—Civil War, 1861-1865—Riverine operations.
5. United States—History—Civil War, 1861-1865—Campaigns. 6. United States—History—Civil War, 1861-1865—Naval operations. 7. United States—History—Civil War, 1861-1865—Riverine operations. I. Title.
E474.1.F74 2011
977'.02--dc22

2011013923

State House Press
P. O. Box 818, Buffalo Gap, Texas 79508
325.572.3974
325.572.3991 (fax)
www.tfhcc.com

Printed in the United States of America

Distributed by Texas A&M University Press Consortium
800.826.8911
www.tamupress.com

ISBN-13: 978-1-933337-44-9
ISBN-10: 1-933337-44-3
10 9 8 7 6 5 4 3 2 1

Book designed by Deborah M. Lindberg

This work is dedicated to the memory
of three fine Louisianans:

William T. "Billy" Shinn,
his wife Marjorie "Margie" Shinn of Franklin,

and

Grady McWhiney,
a native of Shreveport.

Contents

Preface

"Give me Louisiana, A state prepared to share
That good old southern custom, Hospitality so rare"

Give Me Louisiana, *State Song of Louisiana*
Doralice Fontaine (1906–1981)

I remember my first encounter with Billy Shinn, and I owed the encounter to Grady McWhiney—and dumb luck. Sometimes, as the old saw goes, you'd rather be lucky than skillful.

Louisiana got my attention not because I had any particular affinity for the place or any real experience with the state, but because I was "led" there. I knew it as little more than the entity east of Texas that looked like a sock or a Christmas stocking. By the summer of 1989, I had finished my first year of graduate school at Texas Christian University in Fort Worth, Texas. That year, I clearly remember Dr. Grady McWhiney advising me to "do a Louisiana topic, you'll never regret it. The people there will love you and will be glad to help." My first trip to Louisiana—to New Orleans—had been two years previous on my honeymoon with my bride, Susan. I must admit, while I enjoyed the trip, I found that city a little disturbing, a little *too* mysterious, and a bit unsettling. People had been eager to help, to be sure, but mostly in separating me from my money. When “Doc” had advised me to venture east of the Sabine—professionally—I was skeptical. I was twenty-three years old when I gave in and headed back.

Research was different before the Internet, and you actually had to *go* to places to learn about them. I had read about battles along Bayou Teche in St. Mary’s Parish, so I *called* the library in Franklin, the seat of government, to inquire as to sources. The librarian directed me to William T. Shinn, a local land abstractor, real estate appraiser, and repository of local lore. In my first conversation with him, he invited me to visit his personal library. A few months, later I did.

What I discovered was an amazingly complete collection of research, resources, and memoirs of the Civil War in southwest Louisiana. I scheduled a second trip for later that summer—July 1989—along with a fellow graduate student, Robert Pace, who was pursuing a topic in Southern agricultural history. The Shinns invited us to stay in their home and to browse the books. This fine couple fed us, entertained us with local stories, and then gave us run of the study, with instructions to mark what we wanted copied and they’d see to it. The rest of the evening, and into the morning, was a time of happy hunting.

Then—magic. Instead of spending the next day at a copy machine, Robert and I had something of a *Shoe Maker and the Elves* moment. Billy had risen early and photocopied all of our selections while we slept. The Shinns were those kinds of Louisianans.

Doc had been right, and the spell had been cast. I wished I had finished this project before their passing: Billy died on July 1, 1999; Margie, Christmas Day 2004; Doc, April 18, 2006; all left legacies to advance the cause of history. Billy’s incredible library is part of the Young-Sanders Center in Franklin. Doc founded the McWhiney Foundation, which, among other things, owns and operates State House Press—the publisher of this book.

The generosity of Billy, Margie, and Grady were typical of the Louisianans I encountered in my wanderings across the Pelican State and helped usher in a long love affair between this native Texan and Louisiana. I have crossed its bayous, driven its highways, taken my pickup down turn rows, and traced long forgotten roads on maps. I have eaten a wide variety of its wildlife; I have savored po-boys at Domilise's and barbecue shrimp at Pascal's Manale, meat pies at Lasyone's in Natchitoches and cream pies at Lea's in Lecompte. I have developed a refined appreciation for excellent boudin. I have bellied up to its bars in Thibodaux and Alexandria and marveled at its daiquiri stands and strobe-topped donut stands in Houma. I have reveled at many a *fais do-do* and experienced large doses of *lagniappe.* I have mangled its French, butchered its place names, and confused its geography. It remains one of my favorite parts of America.

The people—oh, the people. Among the first to take an interest in my career was Judith K. Schafer at Tulane University. She introduced me to the more civilized parts of New Orleans, guided me through the special collections at her institution, and generally encouraged my endeavors. Arthur "Art" Bergeron, Jr.—among the foremost experts on the Civil War in Louisiana—was generous with his time and talent and was one of the readers on this book. He died way too young. Terry L. Jones, at the University of Louisiana at Monroe, has been generous with his encouragement. Patrick Hotard and Roger Busbice, both of Morgan City at the time I began this journey, showed me every kindness. Betty McGowen of Alexandria was keen to explain the environs of Cheneyville to me and to school me on the differences between cane fields and canebrakes, whereas Steve Mayeux of Cottonport gave me several needed boosts on my research and, what's more, waded through this manuscript and made it better. Gary D. Joiner at LSU Shreveport did as well. Roland Stansbury of the Young-Sanders Center in Franklin and Carl A. Brasseaux at the University of Louisiana at

Lafayette's Center for Louisiana Studies invited me to come and look around awhile.

Louisiana boasts an outrageously good library system. Not only are its finding aids intuitive and technologically remarkable, but it is also crewed by dedicated professionals. In particular, I owe many thanks to Eric Seiferth at the Historic New Orleans Collection, Elizabeth Sherwood at the Louisiana State Museum, Judy Bolton at LSU's Hill Memorial Library, and Charlene Bonnette of the State Library of Louisiana. Mary Linn Wernet at the Watson Library, Northwestern State University of Louisiana in Natchitoches, provided me with priceless assistance with maps.

There is, of course, the Louisiana posse—raconteurs all. Glenn Falgoust, Angela Falgoust, Andrew Capone, and his late wife, Judy; "Colonel" Chris Peña and the rest of the Fort Butler Foundation have proven to be boon companions in the field and at the table. John Folse, a Louisiana legend, has been kind to take an interest in my work.

I marvel at people's generosity. Martha Hartzog of Austin, Texas, has been free with her sources and advice on my Civil War journeys. Ed Cotham of Houston and Dr. Light Cummings of Austin College in Sherman, Texas, have both been encouragers. Four people sent me photos of their ancestors to use—Robert Brinkerhoff of Ada, Michigan; William Molineux of Williamsburg, Virginia; Ronnie Atnip of Bonham, Texas; and William J. Kelly of Tucson, Arizona. Thank you.

This work had benefitted from the contributions of a cloud of scholars and archive managers. Trans-Mississippi historian Jeff Prushankin of Pennsylvania State University, Abington, read the manuscript and made a slew of great recommendations. Anne J. Bailey, a fellow McWhiney student, recently retired from Georgia College and State University and now a resident of Cleburne, Texas, was a reviewer as well and pencil-whipped these pages. Vernon Williams of Abilene Christian University offered up some sources, as did David Ward of the Edsel Ford Library at the Hotchkiss School in Lakeville, Connecticut, and Jerry Don Thompson at Texas A&M International University in Laredo, Texas. Clifton Hyatt at the United States Army Military History Institute, Corey Black at the Naval Historical Foundation, and Catherine Rokowski at the University of West Virginia were patient and efficient when running down a long list of photo requests. Thank you all.

Then there are the editors. Sylvia Frank Rodrigue copyedited this work—and those of you who know me understand what a chore that can be—and made wonderful suggestions that improved the book. Claudia Gravier Frigo served as project manager for this title and has proven, paradoxically, patient and persistent. Her eye for design and her eye on the calendar mark her as a true professional. Amy Smith and Robert Pace have been boosters all along the way. I read most of this manuscript aloud to Robert while on a long road trip. His is the genius behind the *Louisiana Quadrille* series. Thank you, my publishing family, for pushing this project along, sending it out to readers and evaluators, and for services before and after this book hits the shelves.

A great deal of appreciation must be showered upon my immediate family as well. Susan, Kay, and Sarah have been kind to not mind (at least outwardly) the fact that I was spending long days with dead people in my own little world upstairs in my office. I'm back, at least for a while. Also—the trip the girls and I took to Louisiana will remain one of my most cherished memories.

Working at McMurry University has also helped get this book completed. A generous Sam Taylor Fellowship from the United Methodist General Board of Higher Education and Ministry paid for, in large part, the photos and illustrations in this book. The administrators, staff, and colleagues at school have helped as well. In particular, Judy Surles, LaRue Williams, Dixie Hoover, Rob Sledge, and Joe Specht played a part, as did Gary Shanafelt.

Clearly this has been a work of massive collaboration. From the double-blind reviewers to the archivists, buffs, professors, students, friends, fellows, and philosophers who have lent a hand—God bless you all. The mistakes that remain, the suggestions overlooked or ignored, and the failures of my insights or scholarship reflect my own weaknesses and no failing of yours.

Soli Deo Gloria.

1

The Key

"The news in general are very good for our cause and many think the war will soon close."

Private Samuel Amsler

Company G, 4th Texas Cavalry

Christmas 1862 was a truly remarkable holiday for twenty-one-year-old Samuel Amsler. The young cavalryman, a son of Swiss immigrants, had seen amazing things that year: He had joined the Confederate Army, campaigned in New Mexico under General Henry Hopkins Sibley, survived battles at Val Verde and Glorieta, and traveled more than two thousand miles. He had covered the last few hundred miles, across the vast expanse of western Texas, on foot. After months of adventure and privation, Amsler's command had been so stricken that he and his fellow soldiers went home in the summer to recuperate for several months. Amsler had returned to Cat Spring, a German settlement in Austin County.

Back at camp near the village of Cypress, northwest of Houston, Amsler saw nothing that fall that topped his previous experiences. Military routine and discipline returned to his regiment as it drilled, both mounted and on foot, in the fields surrounding their sprawling tent city. New recruits arrived to replace the fallen. As the year slipped away, no active campaigning appeared imminent. Slightly bored, he found himself anticipating a festive observance of the holiday with his old friends, expecting Christmas to be the highlight of what had been a tame return to service for a seasoned veteran of Sibley's Brigade.

Instead of sleeping in and enjoying a holiday frolic in camp, as planned, officers awakened Amsler and his comrades at 3:00 AM on December 25. The bleary-eyed cavalrymen shuffled onto train cars awaiting them at the railway siding, leaving the horses in their pastures. After a five-hour trip of only two-dozen miles, the troops disembarked at the Houston depot, formed a column, and paraded before welcoming crowds on Main Street, crossing Buffalo Bayou near Allen's Landing. "All the town people crowded the side walks to get a look at Sibley's Hell Hounds," he wrote, "who made a terrible noise cheering and whooping with all their might."[1]

Christmas in town was festive enough for Amsler. After disturbing the city's peaceful holiday, the Confederate troops tramped a few miles beyond it to Harrisburg, where they stacked their arms and dropped their equipment near the railroad tracks leading to Galveston. Federal forces had occupied that city for two months, but the rumor spread that something new was afoot. "General Magruder is in Houston and many believe he is going to take Galveston again," Amsler reported. Even so, the holiday season demanded to be observed. "We . . . went back into town," he added, "and had our Christmas to our notions and I must say I enjoyed myself very well."[2]

Days had passed since that memorable occasion, and it became clear Amsler's understanding of the strategic situation on the Texas coast had been prescient. On January 1, 1863, Major General John Bankhead Magruder called into action the men of the 4th Texas Cavalry—including Amsler's Company G—ordering them to concentrate with other Confederate forces near Galveston. Risky travel on the darkness-draped tracks resulted in a midnight collision between trains carrying the 7th Texas and the 4th Texas

Major General John Bankhead Magruder came to Texas from Virginia after running afoul of Robert E. Lee. He showed himself to be an innovative and creative commander at the Battle of Galveston and reversed the tide of Union victories in the western Gulf of Mexico. He also provided inspiration to Confederate commanders in Louisiana.

Courtesy of the collections of the Louisiana State Museum.

cavalries to their destination at Virginia Point across the causeway from Galveston Island. The accident critically injured two Texans. It seemed an unfair fate for men full of élan, the survivors of so many battle horrors. The crisis and resulting delay, as the soldiers untangled themselves from the wreckage, also derailed carefully laid plans for Sibley's Brigade to participate in the battle at Galveston.

Therefore, Magruder sprung his attack without the 4th and 7th Texas, pouncing on the Union garrison and fleet at Galveston before dawn. By the time the 4th Texas Cavalry entered the streets of Galveston, dawn was breaking and the battle was in full fury. "This accident hindered us so much that the battle had already begun before our regiment reached the city," Amsler wrote. "[We] could see the flash of the cannons very plain for it was about four o'clock in the morning. . . . We marched in, the big cannons making a terrible noise all the while; the balls and shells reaching nearly every part of the city [and] ruining some of the finest houses I ever saw," he recalled. Within a few hours, the fighting had ended. The Confederates were victorious, thanks to the timely arrival of cotton-clad gunboats.[3]

In the aftermath of the fight, the young soldier walked through the debris-littered streets, the crunch of shattered glass under his feet, enemy prisoners under his guard. "I wish you could have seen them," he scrawled to his parents. "They are a fine set of men and as well equipped as they could be. They say that the war will not last long any more."[4]

Amsler believed he would not remain in Galveston. "Our brigade will leave here maybe in a day or two," he predicted on January 6, 1863. "I don't know how long we will stay in Texas. It is said that General Sibley is waiting for his brigade in New Iberia, Louisiana." Amsler was correct. The brigade commander was operating along the west bank of the Mississippi River, anxiously awaiting a reunion with his men, whom Magruder had diverted to participate in his recent great attack. Much remained to be done east of the Sabine River, and Confederate commanders wanted the Texas veterans to lend a hand.[5]

Delays, however, would plague Confederate efforts. Increased shelling from enemy vessels and threats of Union landings kept the troops hovering near the coast. Instead of heading for Louisiana, Amsler and his comrades built fortifications near Galveston and awaited a renewed Federal attack, which never came. Eventually the threat faded, and the command drifted back to its base near Cypress. Departure plans remained sketchy. "I can not tell you yet how long it will be before we start to New Iberia but I think we will not go before we get our winter clothing which is said to be nearly ready for us in Houston," Amsler reported on January 18. "The news in general are very good for our cause and many think the war will soon close."[6]

News of the victory at Galveston even buoyed Confederate spirits in New Orleans. "A report was circulated that the Texans had recovered Galveston, sunk some Federal vessels and captured others," wrote Julia LeGrand, a resident of the city's prestigious Garden District. "This was believed by Confederates and hooted at by Unionists. Bets are passed but I feel no humor in such things." When the *New Orleans Era,* a Unionist newspaper, ran accounts of the fight, residents of the Crescent City settled their wagers. LeGrand ruminated on the news. "This fight has made a profound and awful impression on me," she confided in her diary. "It was bold, it was glorious! I can imagine our men, on their insecure crafts, stealing out into the bay under cover of darkness; the suspense, the surprise, the desperate, bloody struggle, the contending emotions of fear and hate, the confusion, the triumph, and last of all, the horrible explosion." She hoped that this blow might convince the Federals to end the war. "Ah, when will they let us go in peace and such things cease!"[7]

With all that had transpired over the past year or so, the news was trending toward the positive for hopeful Confederates. By early 1863 Southern armies held firm against Federal forces in Virginia, Tennessee, and Mississippi. Even in Louisiana and Arkansas the earlier losses of territory and men had stabilized, and energetic Southern commanders had returned confidence to the troops. In short, the Confederacy had quit losing the war, but winning remained a distant goal.

Since the eleven Southern states had seceded two years before, the course of the war generally had generally weighed against the aspirations of an independent Confederate States of America. There had been peaks and valleys: The Battle of Shiloh had been hard fought and nearly won. General Robert E. Lee had ably defended Richmond but had failed to invade the North, nearing disaster at Antietam. General Braxton Bragg had invaded Kentucky but had failed to rally any secessionists sympathizers. He had eventually retreated while a Confederate army shattered itself against Union defenses at Corinth, Mississippi. Much of Arkansas, too, lay under Federal control. Clearly events were coming toward a point of decision.

For Northerners and Southerners alike, hopes for success increasingly rested on who controlled the Mississippi River. To that end, Confederates had failed miserably. Federal armies and navies operating in the Mississippi valley had initiated a spurt of success in early 1862 that lasted until midsummer. Union forces had collapsed resistance from the Ohio River past the mouth of the Arkansas and beyond Memphis while ships, men, and cannon from the Gulf of Mexico had gobbled up New Orleans and sped unchecked to Vicksburg. The fortified bluff had refused to yield—unlike Forts Henry and Donelson, Forts Jackson and St. Philip, Fort Pillow and Island Number 10—and thus Vicksburg alone had destroyed Northern hopes of an early end to the insurrection, at least in the west. The Union navy above Vicksburg kept watch on

the Confederate position, but Northern forces below the bluff had fallen back to Baton Rouge.

Then had come the awful battle at Baton Rouge. General Earl Van Dorn, the Confederate commander at Vicksburg, realizing the hour for a counterpunch had arrived, had ordered General John C. Breckinridge to follow the Federals south. Some five thousand Confederates had sallied out of their positions in Mississippi and had congregated at Camp Moore, just across the state line in Washington Parish, Louisiana. At dawn on August 5, 1862, fourteen regiments of Alabamians, Mississippians, Kentuckians, Tennesseans, and Louisianans had crashed through the fog into seven Federal regiments fanned out across the northern and eastern edges of the town of Baton Rouge.

The battle had been brief and violent. Anticipating the arrival of the ironclad CSS *Arkansas,* the spirited Rebels had driven back men from Connecticut, Vermont, Maine, Massachusetts, Wisconsin, Michigan, and Indiana. The Union commander, General Thomas

The Battle of Baton Rouge, fought on August 5, 1862, stopped the forward progress Union forces had made toward seizing the Mississippi River after their stunning capture of New Orleans the previous April.

The Historic New Orleans Collection, accession no. 1947.9.

Williams, had fallen dead near the town's Magnolia Cemetery, and the Union line had broken in several places. A counterattack by Colonel James W. McMillan's 21st Indiana and Captain Ormand French Nims's 2nd Massachusetts Battery had stalled the Confederate advance, while Colonel Nathan Augustus Monroe Dudley of the 30th Massachusetts had reorganized the Union line. Colonel William Cahill of the 9th Connecticut had rallied his command and nearby regiments and then led them back to prepared fortifications nearer the river. This respite from the Rebel attack had allowed U.S. Navy guns to check the Confederate assault. The *Arkansas* never arrived, and the Southerners had withdrawn at 10:00 AM, unable to deliver the killing blow. Around four hundred men had fallen on either side.

Both sides had given up ground. Breckinridge had led his army twenty miles north. Stopping at Port Hudson, Louisiana, he had ordered his men to dig at a critical bend on the Mississippi River, following directives from Van Dorn. The first spades had hit the dirt by August 19, and the fort that had emerged atop the muddy bluff secured a 140-mile stretch of river northward to Vicksburg. The Federals, meanwhile, had fallen back to safer ground at New Orleans to dream of strategies for taking the Rebel-held positions.

Major General Richard Taylor brought tenacity and creativity to the fight in Louisiana and carried with him the hopes of the Confederacy to "baffle the enemy in his designs on the Mississippi Valley." He did—for a while.

Library of Congress.

That fall, both armies had jostled for control of the approaches. Confederate Major General Richard Taylor had arrived to organize a defense of the west bank in southern Louisiana and actually had cleared much of the Union control from the area. He and his staff had established repair shops,

Lieutenant General John C. Pemberton had a large task before him when he took command of the Department of Mississippi and East Louisiana. The cultivation, improvement, and feeding of the Confederate garrisons at Vicksburg and Port Hudson consumed him.

Library of Congress.

arsenals, supply depots, and munitions factories across the state. While Taylor had ensured a plentiful supply of shoes, wagons, salt pork, and pickled beef, he still hoped to become self-sufficient in arms and ammunition. Taylor had also overseen the creation of inland boat yards. These modest affairs would be important to transform his growing fleet of bayou transports into ersatz men-of-war. At Vicksburg Taylor had conferred with Lieutenant General John C. Pemberton, the new commander of the Department of Mississippi and East Louisiana, and had stressed the importance of controlling western Louisiana in order to feed Confederate troops in the Mississippi valley and beyond. Pemberton had agreed.[8]

President Jefferson Davis had placed a great deal of confidence in Taylor. He had written to Louisiana governor Thomas Overton Moore, declaring hopes that the new commander would "baffle the enemy in his designs on the Mississippi Valley." Davis had expected cooperation between the Confederate commanders at Vicksburg, Port Hudson, and west of the river. At the time Taylor had believed that the recapture of New Orleans would be the ultimate solution to safeguard the Mississippi, but that goal had only been wishful thinking—to this point.[9]

The Federal invaders had instead baffled the defenders. By November 1862, after having sparred with the Confederates for weeks, the Union army under Brigadier General Godfrey Weitzel had swept through the Lafourche District. A three-pronged invasion had penetrated into the heart of the region, scattering Confederate forces at the Battle of Georgia Landing. Only the tardy arrival of the U.S. Navy into Berwick Bay had allowed the Rebels to evacuate most of their troops, covered by the guns of the CSS *Cotton.* This boat's sturdy defense of Bayou Teche as well as logistics problems caused by tens of thousands of refugee slaves clustering around the Yankee columns had stopped the Union's forward progress.

Confederate President Jefferson Davis knew what lay at stake on the lower Mississippi—his home and those of his kinsmen lay in that war zone. He struggled to find a solution for how keep it from Federal conquest.

Library of Congress.

Taylor, having grasped the implications of this Union success, had urged Pemberton to send reinforcements. Taylor believed he only needed a few hundred reliable troops to help stop the damage occurring to his command. But Pemberton had been too stingy: "Under existing circumstances, I cannot send a regiment unless of vital importance," read the responding telegram. "In which event I will do my best." Clearly Taylor had been more concerned about Pemberton's supply lines than the commander of the Department of Mississippi and East Louisiana himself had been.[10]

A few weeks later Weitzel had hamstrung Taylor's capacity to harass the Lafourche District. Taking Federal gunboats and soldiers up Bayou Teche in early January 1863, Weitzel had destroyed the *Cotton* before returning to Brashear City to consolidate gains along the Lafourche. From Fort Butler at Donaldsonville, to the camps around Thibodaux, to the batteries and emplacements along the lower Atchafalaya, the United States had reasserted its authority.

These changes had coincided with Federal war planners' renewed emphasis on the region. Major General Benjamin Butler, the first commander of the Department of the Gulf and the principal designer and implementer of Federal policies in Louisiana, had tackled several tough issues of land and labor. In addition to securing the region, he had also helped to craft a national response to the reality of forcibly emancipated slaves. His plan for introducing wage labor to Union-controlled plantations and farms served as a national model. Further, Butler had included black regiments in his army, showing a way to incorporate this manpower pool into the military ranks. A savvy politician and strategic thinker, Butler had hoped to follow up his success by expanding his modest enclave with an invasion up Bayou Teche into the interior of Louisiana and Texas.

Major General Benjamin Butler proved himself to be a competent military thinker but a shrewd and brilliant political mind. He introduced the nation to the idea of black soldiers fighting for their own freedom but ran afoul of Federal machinations.

Library of Congress.

He never had the chance. President Abraham Lincoln responded to demands by angry New Orleanians and foreign consuls by recalling Butler and replacing him with another Massachusetts soldier, Major General Nathaniel P. Banks, as the head of the 19th Army Corps. Banks had been told to cooperate more extensively with Major General Ulysses S. Grant, who was operating south of Memphis on the Mississippi. To the north, Confederate forces had done much to frustrate Union ambitions against Vicksburg, and by the end of 1862, Federal troops had made an unsuccessful assault against the Rebel lines at Chickasaw Bluffs, adding to their list of failures. The Union army had fallen back, establishing a sizable base upriver on the Louisiana shore at Lake Providence and Milliken's Bend.

President Abraham Lincoln believed the capture of the Mississippi was key to Union success in the war but fretted over how to accomplish this task. He turned to a succession of Massachusetts's political generals to help him find a way.

National Archives and Records Administration.

Despite the blood and treasure expended, victory had eluded Union arms. Now Banks and his twenty thousand men posed a clear threat in Louisiana, but the army remained inert between Baton Rouge and New Orleans. Some rumors suggested these troops were bound for an invasion of Texas. Instead of sparring with the Rebels on the Mississippi, why not starve the Confederate army into submission by cutting off its supplies at the source? In addition to cattle, Texas cotton could then flow unimpeded to northern factories. The Union's October 1862 capture of Galveston had been a critical first step. At the same time, General Butler had proposed "to . . . cut off the supplies of cattle for the rebel army from Texas via Opelousas and New Iberia . . . this coming winter." Now, his replacement would handle the chore.[11]

Baton Rouge. Lieutenant Colonel David Hunter Strother, a well-known illustrator under the penname "Porte Crayon" depicted the capital of Louisiana as a hive of military activity and the forward base for Union troops operating on the lower Mississippi.

West Virginia and Regional History Collection, accession no. 95.30.125.

Banks had also brought the horrors of occupation to Louisiana. He had sought to crush the spirit of rebellion. "Believe me, there is but one remedy," observed George Hughes Hepworth, a Union officer in New Orleans. "It is to conquer these people by an irresistible force, [and] persist in the war at all hazards and costs, until the victory is complete." The will of the Federal government, Banks had affirmed, must be imposed on the secessionists "with a hand of iron." This New Englander had also hoped to destroy slavery, and suggested that half of the invading troops stay behind as settlers to impose a dose of U.S. nationalism on the local Southern population. "Here is the chief source of trouble," he had declared. "The State flag is first; the national flag is nowhere."[12]

Taylor had fully appreciated the implications of the Federal invasion of Texas and Louisiana. He was fighting for a way of life that was threatened with extinction. With stakes this high, he had urged Pemberton to shake loose some cannon and regiments to help secure the vital supply lines to the Mississippi valley. Taylor had needed men and artillery in forts on the Red River, the Atchafalaya River, and Bayou Teche. The Pennsylvania Confederate had again refused. "I am utterly unable to afford you any assistance in the way of re-enforcements," Pemberton snapped. "I regard the defense of this valley of much greater importance than that of West Louisiana, and have an inadequate force to unsure successful accomplishment of the first object." Eventually, in late January, Pemberton had sent over a handful of men with experience handling heavy guns—a squad from the 3rd Maryland Battery, three companies of the 31st Tennessee Infantry, and the Louisiana Crescent Artillery—fewer than three hundred men. Taylor could not believe his superior's short-sightedness. Where did Pemberton think his groceries were coming from?[13]

Major General Nathaniel P. Banks arrived in Louisiana with instructions to cooperate with other Union armies working to take control of the Mississippi River. This goal proved more complicated than he anticipated.

Cartes de visite, Lincoln's Army Civil War Virtual Museum.

The beef cattle industry provided many of his meals, as anyone traveling through east Texas could have told him. The number of Texas beeves heading east during the first two years of the war was impressive. In more peaceful times, this industry had routinely sent tens of thousands of cattle to eastern markets annually. For example, in 1856 thirty-four thousand cattle had swum across the Sabine River heading toward New Orleans and another fifteen thousand had crossed the Neches River, traveling on the main cattle trails like the Atascosito Road, to Lake Charles, Louisiana, before fanning out toward Opelousas, Washington, St. Martinville, Franklin, and New Iberia. By 1860, census figures had counted three million cattle in Texas, and Confederate military planners had viewed this herd as a potentially inexhaustible supply of rations. In 1861 Texan cattle had traveled a long way to feed the Confederacy—twenty-five thousand head of Lone Star beeves made it to Richmond, Virginia—but more would be needed. In addition to livestock on the hoof, thousands of barrels of pickled beef—each bearing two hundred pounds of meat—left Texas and Louisiana plants routinely. The availability of large salt deposits near New Iberia and throughout Texas helped the packing industry.[14]

As the war lengthened, Confederate planners had became more intentional in their approach to Texas beef cattle. On April 2, 1862, Commissary General Lucius B. Northrop had appointed George W. White as "agent in the State of Texas for the commissary General of the Confederate States in the purchase of Bacon and Hogs and of Beeves." White had employed drovers and had organized drives sending thousands of animals east to Louisiana. He had instructed his men to compensate livestock owners with Confederate notes. Meanwhile, naval approaches to the beef road from Texas, vulnerable to raiders and landings from the Gulf of Mexico, had been fortified. Gun emplacements had risen up on the coastal plain near Lake Charles and other saltwater approaches to southern Louisiana.[15]

Most war planners believed the upcoming campaigns of 1863 might determine the outcome of the war. Clearly Vicksburg and Port Hudson would have to fall to collapse Rebel national ambitions. Getting at either town would prove difficult for the Federals. The twin citadels kept open a Rebel supply line from the

Trans-Mississippi that continued to nourish Southern hopes and fill the bellies of the Confederate garrisons. The mouth of the Red River poured into this gap, and down it flowed the agricultural bounty of three states—Louisiana, Arkansas, and Texas. As a result, the banks that channeled the muddy drainings of millions of American acres became among the most critical geography on the continent for the outcome of the war. The east bank held the forts, the west bank helped feed them. Arkansas corn, Louisiana hogs, and Texas cattle sustained the men behind the cannon at the posts holding the line. If Union forces dove into this stretch of the Father of Waters, then the flow of rations would fail, the forts might topple, and the hopes of the Confederacy would flag.

Texas Cattle Drive. Texas beef became a mainstay of the Confederate river garrisons, especially the army at Port Hudson. Protecting this supply line became critical to maintaining Confederate control.

John A. Kouwenhoven, Adventures of America, 1857–1900: A Pictorial Record from Harper's Weekly *(New York: Harper and Brothers Publishers, 1938).*

With control of the Mississippi's west bank clearly a key to victory or failure for the Confederacy, much rested on the ability of Rebels in the Trans-Mississippi to defend their country and keep open these lines of supply. The Louisiana waterways would assume an unprecedented importance. For the Federals, eliminating or neutralizing the Rebel presence in the Pelican State was emerging as an important component of success in their Mississippi Valley Campaign.

Confederates, on the defensive in Louisiana, needed the Texans to push back against the Union juggernaut then forming. But politicians west of the Sabine River, facing an imminent (or even a potential) Union invasion from the Gulf of Mexico,

remained reluctant to weaken their own forces in favor of operations on the Mississippi. Therein lay a stalemate. Until Banks sent his troops toward a particular military target, Confederate forces remained locked in place. Like Pemberton, Texans could be stingy as well.

The strategic catharsis resulting from the victory at Galveston had been key to Southern hopes. The Confederate success in retaking Texas's most important city had precipitated several weeks of military reversals in the western Gulf of Mexico, with the Union navy losing five ships—*Westfield, Harriet Lane, Hatteras, Morning Light,* and *Velocity*—as well as the 250-man garrison marooned on Galveston's wharves. If Banks had ever seriously maintained thoughts of exploiting the Union beachhead in Texas as a feint or a more serious threat against the Vicksburg and Port Hudson supply lines, his options were now limited. Unlike elsewhere in the South, Confederate forces in the Trans-Mississippi were regaining ground previously lost to the Federals. This victorious turn allowed Texans a chance to relax for the moment.

Banks also understood what had been lost at Galveston. He described the collapse of the Union toehold in the western gulf as "the most unfortunate affair that occurred in the department." If they had held Galveston, Federal troops could have maintained a credible and imminent threat to Texas. "It would have held a large force of Rebel troops in the vicinity of Houston, enabled us to penetrate the territory of Texas at any time," he wrote, "or to concentrate our forces on the Mississippi."[16]

Magruder's victory at Galveston confounded President Lincoln as well. Perhaps he had been too rash in dismissing Butler as commander of the Department of the Gulf. Changing his mind on January 23, 1863, Lincoln told Secretary of War Edwin M. Stanton, "I think General Butler should go to New Orleans again." By removing Butler, however, the politicians had wounded the Union officer's ego. "He is unwilling to go, unless he is restored to the

General Butler as the cleanup man. President Lincoln began having second thoughts about replacing General Butler with General Banks and hoped he could convince the former commander of the Department of the Gulf to return to the task of conquering Louisiana and capturing the Mississippi. He could not.

National Archives and Records Administration.

command of the Department." Lincoln suggested that Butler might once again coordinate efforts on the Mississippi while Banks might invade Texas with the greater portion of his army. "The whole must be so managed as to not wrong, or wound the feelings of General Banks. His original wish was to go to Texas; and it must be arranged for him to do this now. I think we can not longer dispense with General Butler's service." A week later Butler arrived in Washington to discuss the proposition. He turned it down.[17]

Rebel victories and Yankee dithering provided Taylor the opportunity he had been waiting for: the chance to launch a great offensive against the Union forces despoiling his native Louisiana. The best way to hold their stretch of the Mississippi and its attending supply lines was to maintain the strategic momentum and force the Federals to remain on the defensive. He also had a larger vision. If Galveston could be recaptured, then why not New Orleans? Certainly, Taylor assumed, he could use Magruder's tactics against Weitzel's isolated outpost at Brashear City and retake the Lafourche District.

Although he had the opportunity, Taylor lacked the number of troops necessary to fulfill his ambitious plan. A small brigade of Louisiana infantry under the command of Brigadier General Jean Jacques Alfred Alexandre Mouton camped at the Bisland Plantation,

General Banks landing at Baton Rouge. General Banks staged his army at Baton Rouge with plans to press on, up the Mississippi, to glory. The Confederate fortress at Port Hudson, though, proved to be a nearly intractable problem.

Harper's Weekly, *author's collection.*

near Centerville in St. Mary's Parish. This thousand-man force had been bested in the Lafourche District, and now it included many conscripts among its number. The command had excellent artillery, however, including three Louisiana batteries and guns from a Texas battery. Two cavalry units, numbering around seven hundred men total, operated in the area as well. General Sibley commanded about seven hundred infantry and three hundred cavalry east of the Atchafalaya, operating out of the village of Rosedale. Between these two positions lay a small fort at Butte-a-la-Rose, a modest, muddy hillock in the middle of the swamps, blocking passage along the Atchafalaya with fewer than four-score gunners and riflemen. Fewer than three thousand Confederate troops camped in the fields south of the Red River. Taylor needed more men, and he looked to Texas to provide them.

2

Reconnaissance

"Shout 'Harriet Lane!' into the ears of the rebels."

Admiral David Dixon Porter
Commander, Mississippi River Squadron

By February 1, 1863, Major General Richard Taylor chafed from the dawdling of General Henry Hopkins Sibley's Brigade. He blamed Major General John Bankhead Magruder for not speeding the brigade along to Louisiana after the Battle of Galveston. Wounded by Taylor's insinuations, Magruder, the commander of the District of Texas, New Mexico, and Arizona, shot back, "it is very difficult in times like these for truth to overtake error." He defended himself, telling Taylor, "You do me an injustice in holding such an opinion. The use of a portion of Sibley's brigade in the attack on Galveston caused no delay in its departure." To bolster his point Magruder forwarded Colonel James Reily's report, which argued that a lack of equipment and funds, poor weather, and hazardous roads had conspired to keep Sibley's Brigade from starting on its way.[1]

As Reily explained, Sibley's Brigade faced shortages of everything—clothing, provisions, weapons, and transportation. In addition, it was effectively bankrupt. Its funds were in New Iberia, but Reily had to purchase supplies in Texas. No one seemed willing to extend credit. In short, he could do little until someone arrived with a cash box. When the money arrived in mid-January Reily went to work hiring wagons, mules, and teamsters. "Now that funds are in hand new life and energy are imparted to all," he wrote to his commander, General Sibley. "We shall march with all practicable speed." He announced that five companies had already started for Louisiana, and more would follow. He also crowed a little about their recent victory. "Your brigade comes to you with increased renown," he wrote, "determined to win laurels as fresh and brilliant on the banks of the Mississippi as they gathered in Galveston and Galveston harbor."[2]

Reily still had to contend with the weather, which had turned miserable. "This portion of Texas has been flooded with the most immoderate rains," reported the colonel, "flooding the whole country and rendering the roads almost impassable and every stream swimming." He was a victim of the season. "It is to be a hard and

The Battle of Arkansas Post. The attack on Fort Hidnman from January 9 to 11, 1863, marked the renewal of the northern end of the campaign to capture the Mississippi. A Union combined arms assault carried the fortress and captured thousands of Confederates, mostly Texans.

Library of Congress.

Admiral David Dixon Porter commanded the Union fleet north of Vicksburg and worried about the best way to approach the Confederate position without endangering his gunboats and transports. He had lived in New Orleans as a child and grew up with foster brother David G. Farragut in the household.

Library of Congress.

difficult task to report the brigade at New Iberia," he stated. "In such weather, on such roads, and with our transportation we are doing all that can be done." The majority of Sibley's Brigade would not head for Louisiana for several more weeks.[3]

Once he understood the situation, Taylor, though known for his firmly held opinions, backed away from this argument. "Although I supposed you had detained Sibley's brigade," he wrote, "I did not speak or even think of your actions harshly." He also sent along reluctant congratulations: "Your glorious achievement at Galveston has found no admirer warmer than I." Taylor had more pressing issues to face.[4]

Throughout January the Federal army in northeast Louisiana had grown more fearsome. In the first week, troops under Major General John A. McClernand left their base at Milliken's Bend and, with the aid of Admiral David Dixon Porter's ironclads, captured Fort Hindman at Arkansas Post on the Arkansas River on January 11—the same day the *Alabama* destroyed the *Hatteras* off Galveston. Nearly five thousand Confederate troops, mostly Texans, surrendered with the fort and boarded transport for a deadly five-month stay in Federal prison camps in Illinois and Ohio. Victorious, the thirty thousand veteran

Union troops returned to the Vicksburg area and reoccupied their camps on the Louisiana riverbank, north and west of the Vicksburg fort. There they stockpiled tons of rations, equipment, and ammunition. By the last week of the month, thirty thousand more troops arrived under Major General Ulysses S. Grant, who assumed command of the Union effort to take Vicksburg.

Major General Ulysses S. Grant eventually took command of the Federal Army operating against Vicksburg. He discovered it to be no easy task.

Library of Congress.

The growing Union army busied itself with various projects designed to keep the troops in good condition and to maintain pressure on the Confederates. The direct approach—attempted by both naval siege and army assault the previous year—had failed. Grant's soldiers now resumed work on a canal across De Soto Peninsula, which General Thomas Williams had started the previous May. Engineers also eyed digging a cut that would connect the Mississippi via Lake Providence in northeastern Louisiana to the tangle of bayous west of the mighty river and provide an all-water bypass route. Naval officers, meanwhile, sought to take advantage of the maze of bayous east of the river and gain access to the Yazoo River and come against Vicksburg from that angle. Grant fidgeted, eager to attack the Rebels, and the ominous army at Milliken's Bend stirred to life under his command. Even so, reducing well-chosen Confederate position would continue to confound Union war planners and consume men, money, and matériel for months.

Colonel Charles Rivers Ellet was a dashing, twenty-year-old medical student before the war and then an assistant surgeon with the army. He rode the reputation of his famous engineer father, Charles Ellet Jr., into high rank and command of the USS *Queen of the West.*

Naval Historical Center.

In New Orleans the accelerating tempo of the battle for the Mississippi forced Julia LeGrand to make plans to leave the city and travel to her sister's home near Hempstead, Texas. A newspaper announcement made it clear that time for leaving grew short: "An order in the Yankee *Delta* made known to us that those 'enemies' who wished for passports and had registered, should come in person to receive them," she wrote on February 3. A male friend of the family offered to help on this errand. "He came over directly after breakfast to tell me . . . that he would deliver our note to some of our rulers and extort a passport if possible." LeGrand appreciated the help navigating the military government bureaucracy. "The Federal rulers here are less accessible than the most august of sovereigns, and even if one is admitted they send him from one to another until his patience is worn out, each official seeming to emulate the last in rude behavior," she recorded. If the Confederacy lost control of the Father of Waters, LeGrand realized she might be cut off from her kinsmen in Texas for the duration of the war. All she lacked was a way to get out of New Orleans.[5]

Indeed, the climax of this mighty campaign appeared imminent. Admiral Porter, after consulting with Grant, decided to test the Confederate defenses. He ordered a twenty-year-old officer, Colonel Charles Rivers Ellet, to dash south with the ram USS

Queen of the West on a bold foray against the Confederate supply vessel *Vicksburg,* which was tied up under the protecting guns of its namesake fortress. Porter wanted Ellet to show no mercy. "It will not be part of your duty to save the lives of those on board," he instructed "They must look out for themselves." He also ordered Ellet to fire balls of flaming pine tar into the woodwork of the vessel to "make a fine finish to the sinking part." Porter wanted to send a message to his enemies and to avenge the debacle at Galveston. They "may think themselves lucky if they do meet the same fate meted out to the *Harriet Lane.*" For months Porter had lived aboard the *Harriet Lane* as head of the mortar squadron under Captain David G. Farragut during the capture of New Orleans. He knew its men and officers; he mourned their loss. "Think of the fate of that vessel while performing your duty," he demanded, "and shout *'Harriet Lane!'* into the ears of the rebels."[6]

Major General Carter Littlepage Stevenson, a Virginian, led a division of troops to reinforce Vicksburg in December 1862 and served as the garrison commander there, following the edicts of Lieutenant General John C. Pemberton, the commander of the Department of Mississippi and East Louisiana.

Library of Congress.

With Grant operating on Vicksburg from the north, and Major General Nathaniel P. Banks idling to the south, Taylor had plenty to worry about. In early February, though, his chief concern was maintaining communications with Confederates on the east bank of the Mississippi River and keeping open the flow of cattle, corn, sugar, and hogs to Major General Carter Littlepage Stevenson, commanding at Vicksburg, and Brigadier General Franklin Gardner, in charge at Port Hudson since December. The 240-mile span of river between these posts had to be kept clear of Union forces or the entire Confederate scheme on the Mississippi would fall apart.

Taylor's first serious threat arrived February 2, 1863. As instructed, Captain Ellet led the USS *Queen of the West* away from the rest of Admiral Porter's fleet and snuck past the Rebel batteries. After ramming the Confederate gunboat *Vicksburg*, the Union raider sprinted downriver, prowling between the Rebel bastions and threatening to nibble away at their supply lanes while gathering valuable intelligence about the strength and location of enemy gun emplacements. The *Vicksburg*, badly damaged, stayed afloat. Rebel

The USS *Queen of the West* ramming the CSS *Vicksburg*. When Colonel Charles Rivers Ellet took his boat past the guns of Vicksburg, he lingered long enough to rough up the Confederate gunboat *Vicksburg* before dashing downstream to safety.

Naval Historical Center.

shore batteries did their best to strike the ship, but the *Queen of the West* proved too evasive.

The Union ram began gathering prizes almost immediately. Fifteen miles below the mouth of the Red River, the *Queen of the West* surprised and captured the steamboat *A. W. Baker,* which had been running upriver empty after having unloaded supplies at Port Hudson. Shortly after making prisoners of more than a half dozen Confederate officers and placing aboard a guard, Ellet spied another Rebel steamboat. The *Queen of the West* fired a shot across the bow of this startled newcomer, the *Moro,* which caused her to heave to. On board were fifty-five tons of salt pork, five hundred live hogs, and a large quantity of salt, all of which had been bound for General Gardner's command.[7]

Major General Franklin Gardner, born in New York City, had ties through his mother's family to Louisiana. A West Point classmate of Ulysses S. Grant and career officer, Gardner married the daughter of former Louisiana governor Alexandre Mouton. His father-in-law would lead his state out of the Union; Gardner and his brother-in-law Alfred Mouton would lead Confederate armies defending this decision.

State Library of Louisiana.

The Confederates along the Mississippi banks received word of this intruder several hours later. General Sibley, from his headquarters at Rosedale, reported the interloper was "an ironclad, but is arranged along Magruder's plan, with cotton bales." Although he did not entertain hopes of destroying the *Queen of the West,* he did hope to recover some of the captured steamboats. "I have ordered

Brigadier General Christopher C. Augur, West Point graduate, Mexican War veteran, and commandant of the U.S. Military Academy at the outbreak of the war, proved himself a competent battlefield commander. Severely wounded at the head of his division at Cedar Mountain, he recovered sufficiently to command a Union division in Louisiana under Major General Nathaniel P. Banks. He survived the war but nearly died in an altercation with a rowdy African American ex-con outside his New York City home in August 1886.

Library of Congress.

a company of cavalry and one section of artillery . . . to attempt the recapture of the boats, which at last accounts" he wrote, "were lying near the river banks and but slimly guarded." His men were unsuccessful.[8]

Meanwhile, Ellet turned his vessel back upstream, prowling for more victims. At a landing just upriver, the *Queen of the West* destroyed more than twelve tons of cornmeal awaiting shipment to Port Hudson. When his ship once again reached the mouth of the Red River, Ellet ordered his vessel to turn to port and hunt along that waterway. His instinct was correct, and the steamboat *Berwick Bay* and its cargo of two hundred barrels of molasses, ten hogsheads of sugar, forty bales of cotton, and fifteen tons of flour became forfeit to the U.S. Navy. Short of coal and having encountered no more quarry in a fifteen-mile scout up the Red, Ellet directed the *Queen of the West* back to the Mississippi. When the three captured steamers could not keep up with him, he had them burned. By February 5 he was just below Vicksburg and once again among friends, having completed the first of what he hoped would be many daring raids.[9]

Brigadier General Thomas West "Tim" Sherman graduated from West Point in 1836, performed heroically in the Mexican War as an artillery officer, and led U.S. troops in the land-sea capture of Port Royal, South Carolina, in 1861. He went west and served in western Tennessee and northern Mississippi, before taking command of the Union garrison at New Orleans.

Library of Congress.

Far to the south, General Banks renamed his force the Army of the Gulf and readied it for action. Steady veterans of regular three-year enlistments composed half of his command while militia serving nine-month tours made up the balance. "These privates, when they are Americans, have a sad and hopeless look, as if their hearts were aching for home, as I have no doubt they are," observed Julia LeGrand of the soldiers disembarking in New Orleans. "The Irish and Germans look very different, I think; they look as if they never had any home." Banks organized his command into four divisions under the leadership of West Point-trained officers: Major General Christopher Columbus Augur, 1st division, and brigadier generals Thomas W. Sherman, 2nd division, William H. Emory, 3rd division, and Cuvier Grover, 4th division. Banks distributed the veteran regiments among his militia units to provide stability to the green troops.[10]

The Army of the Gulf explored ways to compromise the Confederate position at Port Hudson. While the *Queen of the West* raided Rebel supply lines, General Emory's forces began an extensive reconnaissance of the Atchafalaya Basin waterways from their base in the Lafourche District. This scouting served three

Brigadier General William H. Emory had a reputation as a brilliant and meticulous topographical engineer. He served in mostly supporting roles in the army after his graduation from West Point in 1831, but he led a division during the campaigns for Louisiana. Officers and historians credit his handling of the 19th Army Corps at the Battle of Cedar Creek, Virginia, in October 1864 as preventing a Union disaster.

Library of Congress.

purposes. First, Sibley and his forces, overestimated as being some three thousand men strong, posed a potential threat if they descended Bayou Grosse Tête, passed through Bayou Goula, and fell upon the still-uncompleted Fort Butler at Donaldsonville. Second, if a route could be found connecting the Mississippi to the Atchafalaya—perhaps along Bayous Sorrell, Gross Tête, and Grand River—then an army might be able to bypass Port Hudson and gain its rear or link up with Grant and completely avoid the fort. Perhaps Port Hudson would never need to be assaulted; perhaps it could be ignored. Third, the navy could cut the fort's supply line, starving it, by running more gunboats past Vicksburg while light draft vessels from the south slipped up the tangle of inland bayous.

Emory's scouts met with mixed results. Logjams and driftwood rafts rendered impossible any vessel's approach from the south, so an amphibious operation seemed unlikely. Federal cavalry rode up the Mississippi's west bank until they encountered Sibley's pickets, whom they engaged in a spirited skirmish near Indian Village. The Rebels rode away, which led the Union horse soldiers to believe they intended no mischief on that front, at least not before Fort Butler was completed and armed. Perhaps troops could be safely passed overland via this route, moving through Rosedale to Simmesport, if Sibley's Brigade could be driven away, then they could board steamers to run past the batteries at Vicksburg. If that plan worked, Banks could join his army to Grant's and operate in the Mississippi interior.

Brigadier General Cuvier Grover was too young to have participated in the Mexican War, but he did serve on the western frontier in the 1850s. He developed a rivalry with a fellow officer, Henry Hopkins Sibley, which he would carry with him in the Civil War. He earned a reputation for being an aggressive and capable officer in Virginia and transferred to Louisiana to lead a division—and to square accounts with his old nemesis.

Library of Congress.

Based on this new perspective and wanting to be certain his intelligence was correct, Banks decided to make an amphibious reconnaissance in force in mid-February. Convinced he could ascend the Atchafalaya River with his Berwick Bay flotilla to cooperate with the *Queen of the West* and choke off Port Hudson, Banks directed the USS *Kinsman* and USS *Diana* to make a deep penetration into the basin. Five transports bearing three thousand men would accompany the two gunboats. These troops were to take a close look at the Confederate fortress at Butte-a-la-Rose, the principal obstacle to controlling this waterway, and capture it if possible. "There are many obstacles to overcome," he wrote, "but I believe we will be successful. It will enable us . . . to cut off supplies by the Red River and communicate with the forces below Vicksburg."[11]

Banks also wanted to dispose of the Rebel regiments lingering in the area. He ordered Brigadier General Godfrey Weitzel at

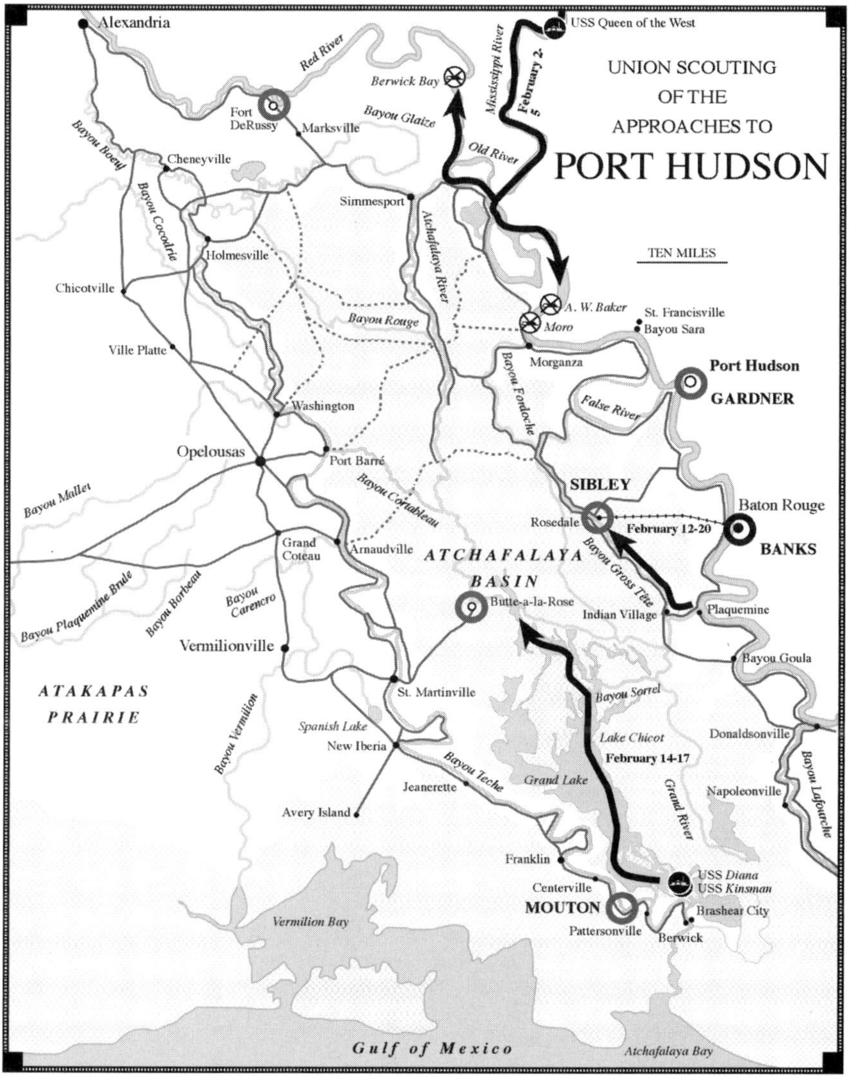

Brashear City to load a portion of his brigade onto two transports and, escorted by gunboats *Estrella* and *Calhoun,* to bypass Brigadier General Alfred Mouton's forces at Bisland by traveling up the Atchafalaya River to land at Grand Lake. Weitzel's men were then to head southwest on foot, through the town of Franklin, and capture or scatter Taylor's Rebel army by arriving in its rear. Only the lack of more transports kept Banks from sending more men.[12]

Coordinating the efforts of these various expeditions proved to be a nightmare. General Emory moved two brigades north to the Indian Village to continue his reconnaissance in force against Sibley at Rosedale, but he realized that all possible means of communication to the west, deeper into the Atchafalaya Basin, would be impossible due to five miles of driftwood rafts. Emory had no way to coordinate his efforts with Weitzel, so both columns would have to work independently and hope for the best. Steamers working eastward from Berwick Bay also confirmed this finding. Undaunted, Emory, the prewar explorer, remained determined to find a way through. Similarly, Banks remained hopeful. "If the attempt to cut the enemy's communications and sources of supply with the west succeeds—as I believe it will," he wrote, "we shall move from Baton Rouge on his rear at Port Hudson, and, cutting his communications with the east, compel him to surrender or give us battle on our own grounds." There was, of course, the problem of topography. Banks added an aside, "unless the natural difficulties . . . turn out to be insurmountable."[13]

Steamboats tied up at Baton Rouge. These and other transports would move the Army of the Gulf as it campaigned in Louisiana.

State Library of Louisiana.

Following Emory's orders, Colonel Halbert E. Paine took his brigade on a reconnaissance in force up Bayou Grosse Tête. Paine's soldiers moved into Rosedale unopposed, and he ordered work crews to clear the bayou of obstructions so that supply vessels could follow. General Sibley had quit the area the day before. From this new vantage, Paine believed U.S. troops could reopen the railroad to Baton Rouge and facilitate communications with General Grover's Division there. Paine was optimistic about what he found. "The roads near Rosedale I found excellent, and the country is very fine and high and dry," he reported. He recommended a foray to False River, opposite Port Hudson, to see if the route was usable all the way to the Red River. He did not get far. Across the Mississippi River at Port Hudson, General Gardner struck by ferrying a brigade of troops across the river, discouraging the Federal movements. Paine withdrew.[14]

At Brashear City, Weitzel had doubts about Banks's complicated plan. Although he was a subordinate in Major General Augur's Division with orders to obey, the outspoken Cincinnati German let his views be known in a letter to his immediate superior. "I judge

Baton Rouge Waterfront. The steamboat *Empire Parish, left,* served as the field headquarters for Major General Nathaniel P. Banks in his operations around Baton Rouge.

State Library of Louisiana.

from my instructions, and what I heard while in company with you and the other generals, that your object is to gain possession of Butte-a-la-Rose, and, if possible, capture the force on the Teche," Weitzel wrote, accurately summarizing the plan. "In all honesty and candor I do not believe the present plan to be the proper one." The entire Atchafalaya region was notorious for snags and sandbars, as Weitzel well knew. Before charging forward into the tangled swamp, he wanted to make sure there would be no hidden surprises, natural or otherwise. A boat stranded aground would be a disaster.[15]

Weitzel wondered, too, where Sibley had gone. Reports arrived from Emory's expedition that the Confederate troops at Rosedale had disappeared; at almost the same time, spies brought word that the Rebel general had given the Federals on the Mississippi the slip and was reunited with his old command, reinforcing the Confederates west of the Atchafalaya. "We have ample proof," Weitzel continued, "that by this time the whole of Sibley's Texan brigade is somewhere in the Opelousas country, either . . . to act as a reserve to General Mouton's force, or at Alexandria to hold the Red River." United, Sibley's Texans and Mouton's Louisianans would outnumber Weitzel's Federals. The Texans alone, Weitzel knew, were certainly capable of springing an ambush on either Union boat column as they navigated the treacherous waters of the Atchafalaya Basin.[16]

Instead, Weitzel urged that Emory's command quit hacking at the obstacles on Bayou Grosse Tête and relocate, with all their transports, to Berwick Bay. Thus reinforced, Union forces there would be sufficient to pin Mouton to his works while fending off any of Sibley's attacks. The Federals could then sweep the Rebels from the region and capture Butte-a-la-Rose as a matter of course. "I believe these to be the true and only correct plan of the campaign," Weitzel concluded, "and hence these views are submitted."[17]

General Augur found Weitzel's objections to be reasonable and therefore chose a middle course. He was not sure that the garrison at Brashear City was large enough for the two expeditions Banks had ordered. Augur set aside the planned operation against Mouton. He also decided against sending transports with the *Diana* and *Kinsman*. Instead of an amphibious assault on Butte-a-la-Rose, the expedition would be a scout. After reconnoitering the Confederate battery, the two steamers were to continue searching for a passage to Emory's men at Indian Village. Augur's plan fell well short of Banks's ambitious riverine offensive. The commander of the Department of the Gulf now mulled Weitzel's observations on the terrain and enemy disposition.

The general held a meeting of his division commanders at his headquarters in New Orleans. "After dinner there was a council of war to discuss the expedition up the Atchafalaya to take Butte a la Rose and open communications with Grant," staff officer Lieutenant Colonel David Hunter Strother wrote. "Augur advised a flank march around Port Hudson eastward . . . and Emory said he would prefer a direct assault on Port Hudson. Both these generals were evidently opposed to the Atchafalaya movement and suggested impossible and futile movements instead." These old regulars wanted to bash Gardner in a traditional attack or even a siege, even though the opposing numbers would be nearly equal.[18]

Brushing aside such bloody thoughts, Banks set aside his military role and attended business more to his liking. The former politician entertained guests and managed the ongoing reconstruction of Louisiana. Brigadier General George F. Shepley, the state's military governor, arrived to discuss politics. "He spoke with admiration of Judge Beverly Tucker's book, *The Partisan Leader,* as a prophetic work and generally remarked how much more far seeing were the Southern statesmen and Southern gentlemen than were the northern," observed Strother. The book in question was a novel written in 1836 by a prominent law professor at William and Mary. General Banks agreed with the author's assessment. "The truth is that the Northern people were too busy getting rich to study statesmanship," Strother recorded. The discussants noted that the best minds in the North disdained public service and politics in favor of commerce while Southerners were "men of power and sagacity, natural leaders of people. Ambitious and unprincipled, but still strong men." Northern politicians, Strother noted, "were either paltry thieves with no more capacity than to invent petty tricks to plunder the Treasury or fanatical ideologues bent on turning the government into a machine for carrying out their silly and impracticable conceits."[19]

Another newcomer, George H. Hepworth, came calling at Federal headquarters in New Orleans around this time. A chaplain with the 47th Massachusetts, Hepworth wanted to take an active part in the recruitment and mobilization of black troops. General Banks commissioned him as a lieutenant in the 4th Louisiana Native Guards and assigned him the task of visiting the various plantations behind Union lines and investigating the efficacy of the free-labor system recently implemented. After visiting some seventy-five estates along Bayou Lafourche from Donaldsonville to Thibodaux, the officer returned a promising report. "I am confident that the plan is not only satisfactory to the planter and the negro, but also it really affords to the black man an experience

Brigadier General George F. Shepley, a native of Saco, Maine, worked as a lawyer before the war. Major General Benjamin Butler appointed Shepley military mayor of New Orleans; when that city fell in 1862, he then elevated Shepley to governor of occupied Louisiana. *Library of Congress.*

which will do much to fit him for the freedom for which he is destined if the war continues," Hepworth wrote. "I think the negro understands this himself. I have talked with several thousand, and I find them far more intelligent, and better aware of the positions of affairs than I have been led to expect."[20]

At Confederate headquarters in Alexandria, Taylor thought little of politics. Realizing that the Federals were probing his defenses, the general focused entirely on his field operations. The presence of Union warships marauding between Vicksburg and Port Hudson would end supply shipments from the Red River and would shortly spell doom for Confederate hopes of a coordinated defense of the Mississippi. He would see the same results if the enemy were to gain control of the Atchafalaya, which would also allow them access to the Red River. Taylor faced another fearsome scenario: If the *Queen of the West,* a big cottonclad ram, passed down the Atchafalaya and united with Banks's forces at Berwick Bay, the outcome would be disastrous for the Confederates. Union ships would free the combined Federal flotilla and control the Atchafalaya Basin, rendering

USS *Queen of the West* became one of the most famous, and infamous, vessels on the Mississippi in the early weeks of 1863.

Naval Historical Center.

him, his supplies, and his army useless to Confederates east of the Mississippi River.

Controlling the west bank of the Mississippi was crucial to supporting Port Hudson and Vicksburg, and domination of the southern Louisiana bayous was key. But the 240-mile length of Rebel-controlled river also had to be kept clear of enemy warships. The Confederate general ordered his most powerful gunboat, the CSS *Webb* at Alexandria, to hunt down the *Queen of the West* should it venture forth again and to stand ready to descend the Atchafalaya if needed to repulse any movements against Butte-a-la-Rose.

The *Webb* did not have long to wait. After five days' rest Ellet made another sortie toward Old River. On the night of February 10 the *Queen of the West* left the Union positions on the Mississippi's west bank below Vicksburg, and this time the ram had company. Along for the raid were a captured Rebel supply ship, the one-hundred-ton steamboat *De Soto,* and a coal-laden barge to fuel the ships, allowing Ellet to extend the incursion's length and range. Two days later, the *Queen of the West* once again made its way up the Old River and reached the mouth of the Atchafalaya. Ellet ordered the *De Soto* to remain behind while he proceeded down this river, testing it as a possible means of communicating with Banks's army at Berwick Bay, as Taylor had feared. Six miles downriver, Ellet intercepted twelve Rebel wagons moving along the Atchafalaya's banks. A shore party destroyed them.

Turning about after this brief foray, he steered toward the *De Soto,* intending to patrol the lower Red River. At the junction of the Atchafalaya and Old River, the *Queen of the West* found more plunder. Confederates at Simmesport had abandoned seventy barrels of government beef, and the Union sailors destroyed them. Sighting another Rebel wagon train heading away from the town, this same shore party managed to capture just one straggler, a vehicle loaded with ammunition. After these successes Ellet ordered his ship back to the Old River for the night and a reunion with the *De Soto.* He suffered his only casualty en route, on the evening of February 12, when gunmen fired from the levee, sending a bullet through a Union officer's knee. Union officers refused to believe the shots came from Confederate snipers or pickets, and instead claimed the assailants to be local planters and thus exempt from the considerations offered to legitimate enemies. "I waited until morning, and then returned to the spot from which we had been attacked," Ellet wrote matter-of-factly. "All of the buildings on three large adjoining plantations were burned by my order." Having exacted his revenge against enemies real or imagined, Ellet took the *Queen of the West* up the Old River to the Red River, then up that waterway to the mouth of the Black River, halting there for the night.[21]

The Confederates scrambled to respond to Ellet's raid. That same day, the steamer *P. E. Bonford* arrived at Alexandria from Jefferson, Texas, carrying 320 men of the 1st Texas Sharpshooter Battalion to duty east of the Mississippi. These newcomers boarded the CSS *Webb* and the *Grand Duke,* now bound for the mouth of the Red River—and a fight. The steamer *Archer,* with a squad of the 3rd Maryland Artillery manning a pair of field pieces, left the Confederate position at Warrenton, Mississippi, with companies B, C, and I of Colonel W. M. Bradford's 31st Tennessee Infantry aboard, hoping to locate the *Queen of the West.*[22]

The Federals sent reinforcements as well, unknown to Ellet. Admiral Porter ordered Lieutenant Commander George Brown to take his ironclad, the USS *Indianola,* past the Vicksburg batteries on the night of February 13. Leaving around 10:00 PM, the vessel made it past the Rebel guns without a hit, being under fire for only about twenty minutes. Brown had crewmen show two red lights on the starboard side of his vessel as he passed the Union pickets, below the town, before anchoring about 1:00 AM. He would move cautiously downstream toward the Red River over the next few days to rendezvous with the *Queen of the West.*[23]

USS *Indianola* passing the guns of Vicksburg. When the *Queen of the West* succeeded in getting by the Confederate batteries at Vicksburg, Admiral David Dixon Porter decided to send down USS *Indianola* as well to cause as much mischief as possible against enemy supplies lines operating along the Red River.

Naval Historical Center.

Ellet's luck seemed to continue the next morning. Unaware of the welcomed approach of the *Indianola,* the young officer continued his solo mission on February 14. Fifteen miles further up the Red, the *Queen of the West* surprised and captured the *Era No. 5* with forty-five hundred bushels of corn and a dozen or so Confederate soldiers on board. From these prisoners he learned that three sizable boats lay just a few miles upstream, tied to the bank with their boilers cold. Ellet knew of the rumors of a Rebel fort nearby as well. "I decided on an effort to capture them, intending to return if I should find the battery at that point too strong," he wrote. As daylight began to fade, he left his coal barge and the *Era No. 5* behind while he took the *Queen of the West* and the *De Soto* on reconnaissance.[24]

At dusk, Ellet spotted signs of his next victims. "The dense smoke of several boats rapidly firing up could be seen above the trees as we approached," he wrote. As his boat rounded a point in the river, he found a surprise—the four 32-pounders of Fort DeRussy. "The rebels opened on us . . . the moment we came into sight," he reported. "The guns were in a fine position, and, at the third shot, I ordered . . . the pilot to back the *Queen* out." Instead, the vessel backed into the opposite bank, stranding itself aground. "The position at once became a very hot one," Ellet wrote. In moments, Taylor's men succeeded where Vicksburg had failed. After thirteen rounds struck the vessel with little effect, a single round from an aging 32-pounder cut the steam drum aboard the Federal vessel. Ellet ordered the vessel abandoned. "Nothing further, of course, could be done," he wrote. Sailors dumped the vessel's cotton bale armor overboard as makeshift life rafts as they floated downriver, away from the enemy guns, to safety. Most of Ellet's crew escaped. Some floated to the *De Soto* while others ran onto shore, headed downriver on foot, and boarded the *Era No. 5*. Meanwhile Confederate soldiers completed the capture

The **USS *Indianola*** carried an impressive battery of two 11-inch Dahlgrens forward and two 9-inch Dahlgrens aft, powerful additions to the vessels intent on blockading the Red River.

Naval Historical Center.

Luck ran out for the **USS *Queen of the West*** when it faced the guns of Fort DeRussy on the Red River. A critical hit on its steam apparatus forced the crew to abandon the grounded vessel or die by scalding.

Warren Daniel Crandall, Isaac Dinision Newell, History of the Ram Fleet and the Mississippi Marine Brigade in the War for the Union on the Mississippi and its Tributaries: The Story of the Ellets and their Men *(St. Louis: Society of Survivors, 1907).*

of the Union menace as darkness descended. With two ropes attached, Rebel steamers hauled the incapacitated *Queen of the West* to Alexandria for repairs.[25]

Calamity now replaced Ellet's earlier good fortune. A dense fog that night caused the *De Soto* to clip the bank, ruining her rudders. After drifting for fifteen miles, the survivors aboard that stricken boat transferred to the *Era No. 5,* and Ellet ordered the *De Soto* and his coal barge burned. He steamed toward the Mississippi as jettisoned corn from his captures bobbed in the Red River, marking his flight. The fog nearly compounded the disaster the next morning, shortly after the *Era No. 5* entered the Mississippi. "The pilot," wrote an increasingly exasperated Ellet, "ran the *Era,* a boat drawing less than 2 feet of water, hard aground, actually permitting her wheels to make several revolutions after she had struck."

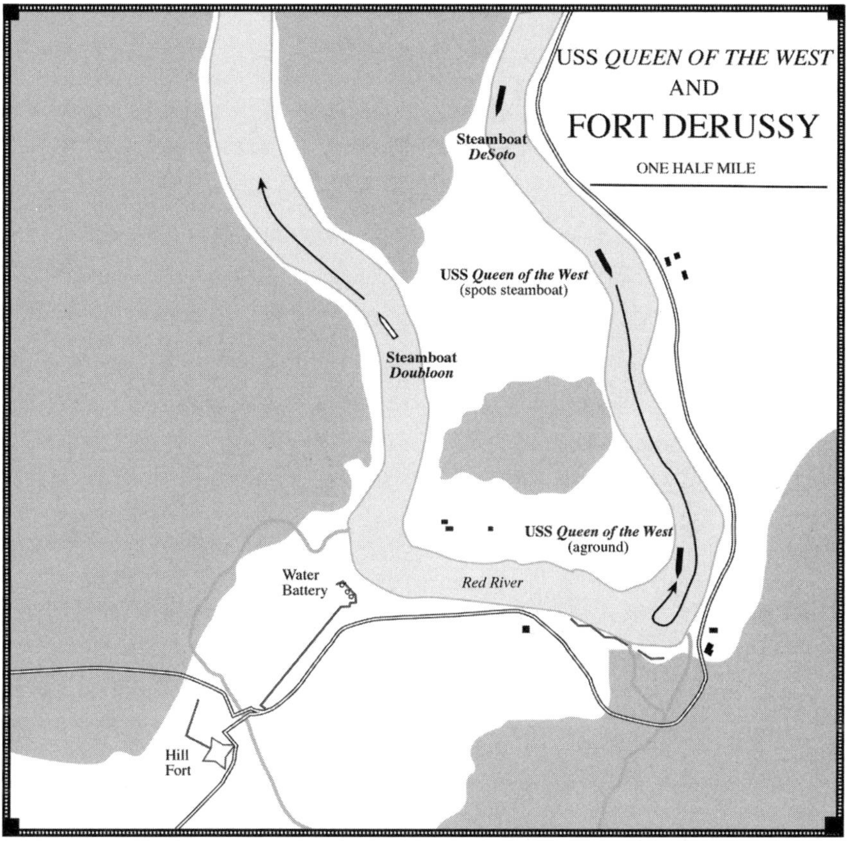

After several desperate minutes, the crew managed to get the vessel underway again.[26]

Ellet and his men knew they were in danger. The *Webb* was not far behind them, and it pressed hard for the Mississippi to try to run down the *Era No. 5* and its swashbuckling crew. "Knowing that the rebels would lose no time in pursuing," Ellet wrote, "I pushed on . . . through the fog." Help was just a few miles ahead. The spectral USS *Indianola* emerged from the mists. The *Era No. 5* came to near that vessel ten miles below Natchez, Mississippi.[27]

Not ready to admit defeat, Ellet hailed Lieutenant Commander Brown and convinced him to follow the *Era No. 5* on a risky venture back up the Red River. The ironclad *Indianola,* Ellet reasoned, would make short work of Fort DeRussy as well as the *Webb,* undoing most of Taylor's efforts. "I had not gone 3 miles when a break in the fog disclosed a steamer rapidly moving upstream about a mile ahead," Ellet wrote. It was the *Webb,* and it seemed determined. "I at once rounded to, and caused the whistle to be blown, to warn Captain Brown of her presence." Lookouts on the *Webb* sighted the looming silhouette of the *Indianola,* and its commander ordered his vessel turned around, unwilling and unprepared to tangle with the iron monster ahead. Ellet had escaped. After prowling around the mouth of the Red River for the next few days, the *Era No. 5* left the area and headed to the Union lines south of Vicksburg so that Ellet could explain himself to Porter. Lieutenant Commander Brown, left alone, took his lumbering ironclad up the Mississippi as well, making only two knots an hour against the river's heavy current.[28]

Porter raged when the news arrived. "Had the commander of the Queen of the West waited patiently, he would, in less than twenty-four hours, have been joined by the *Indianola,*" he wrote to the Secretary of the Navy Gideon Wells. "This is a serious disappointment to us all here, as we calculated certainly on starving out the garrison at Port Hudson by merely blockading the mouth of Red River. My plans were well laid, only badly executed." He feared that the remaining ironclad might be in danger. "The *Indianola* is now there by herself. Whether the commander will have the good sense not to be surprised, remains to be seen."[29]

For the Confederates, the mere presence of the USS *Indianola* created fear. The ironclad was home to nearly 150 men protected by three inches of armor. Two 11-inch Dahlgrens fired from gunports in the bow and forward broadsides of the vessel, while two 9-inch Dahlgrens fired from aft and stern. Four big engines drove the vessel, powering two paddlewheels and two screw propellers. Similar in size and armor to the more famous "Cairo class" river ironclads, the

Indianola was a formidable vessel. If Taylor's navy could not slay this Union water dragon, calamity would surely follow.

Even with this reversal of Confederate fortunes, the contest remained far from being settled. The Mississippi, the mouth of the Red River, and the interconnecting network of bayous were not completely blockaded. "You have doubtless learned from General Gardner that I have succeeded in throwing several cargoes of supplies into Port Hudson since the first [enemy] boat passed Vicksburg," Taylor wrote to Lieutenant General Pemberton. "He was probably in great need of them. I have several boats loaded for him, which will go out, taking our gunboat." The presence of the *Indianola,* though, clearly complicated Confederate strategy.[30]

Additional threats accumulated. In addition the *Indianola,* north of the Red River, Union gunboats operating out of Brashear City continued prowling the Louisiana waterways around Grand Lake, probing for Confederate weaknesses. The USS *Kinsman* and the USS *Diana* paddled north up the Atchafalaya toward Old River on their scout toward Butte-a-la-Rose. The steamers explored every inlet on the east side of the Atchafalaya Basin, hoping to find a secret passage to Emory at Indian Village and a way to coordinate the efforts of the various Union expeditions, but to no avail. Undeterred, they worked their way past Chicot Pass, Lake Chicot, and the log-filled mouth of Bayou Sorrell, then they headed back into the main channel of the Atchafalaya River. They paused where the river split into two routes around the swampy rise of Cow Island. The Rebel works at Butte-a-la-Rose commanded the rejoined channel just beyond this obstacle. On February 16, two days after the *Queen of the West*'s misadventure at Fort DeRussy, this naval probe pushed its luck as well. "I attempted to get the *Diana* within sight of the fort," reported 1st Lieutenant Frank W. Loring, Emory's aide-de-camp and personal representative on this expedition. But the skipper of the *Diana* refused, and the other boat moved ahead alone. "The

Kinsman went the northern passage," he added, "drove in five pickets and was stopped by sharpshooters."[31]

Taylor had anticipated this move on the part of the Union navy and had laid an ambush for the snooping gunboats. Confederate troops from Colonel Henry Gray's 28th Louisiana Infantry peppered the Federal steamers with small-arms fire from the woods and banks while four pieces of heavy artillery, manned in part by the Bull Battery of CSS *Cotton* fame, discouraged them further. The *Kinsman* found itself in trouble. "Her decks were swept in ten minutes by our sharpshooters posted on both sides of the river," Taylor crowed. Cruising up the Atchafalaya to Old River would prove tougher than Banks had hoped. Chastened, the two gunboats backed away from Butte-a-la-Rose, but at least now they could report exactly how many guns and muskets the Rebels had on hand at the swampy outpost.[32]

Foreshadowing his future plans, Taylor gave a hint to Lieutenant General Pemberton as to what he hoped would lay ahead for the Union navy. "We could have captured the boat had our men the means of pursuing her," he claimed, adding, "these means are now rapidly preparing, and I hope before many days to give a good account of the Yankee fleet at Berwick Bay." The Confederate general would no longer wait for the enemy to come to him. With the gift of the *Queen of the West,* Taylor would take the war to them. This plan would be welcomed by Jefferson Davis, who was waiting for good news from the West. "The condition of affairs in Mississippi and Louisiana excites continued anxiety," he wrote on February 19. "Nothing has been heard of the plan proposed, and which should have been executed before this date, for the recapture of the city of [New Orleans]. You will have observed the success of the gunboats in passing the batteries at Vicksburg. They will destroy a necessary navigation unless they can be captured."[33]

Fate would lend Confederate ambitions a hand. A week later, on February 23, the USS *Kinsman* met a humble fate unbefitting a warship. While patrolling Grand Lake with a company of the 114th New York Infantry on board, the vessel hit a snag forward of its starboard wheelhouse. Leaking badly, the gunboat turned around and steamed back to the docks at Brashear City. All those aboard bailed energetically against the rising water below decks. As the *Kinsman* neared its base, the skipper headed for the flats below the wharves, hoping to beach the steamer. He managed to ram the bow onto the muddy shore in three feet of water, allowing most of his passengers and crew to escape. The soldiers and sailors attempted the bring the vessel's stern to the riverbank, but the ship continued to fill with water. The *Kinsman* slipped backward into nearly one hundred feet of water and sank. The Federals had lost yet another gunboat, adding to the discouraging tally of the past six weeks.[34]

3

USS *Indianola*

"Thus we regained control of our section of the Mississippi."

Major General Richard Taylor
Commander, District of West Louisiana

Major General Richard Taylor, feeling bold after his recent successes, decided to expand his naval triumphs by taking on the much-feared Yankee ironclad threatening his lines to Port Hudson and Vicksburg. If he could capture the *Indianola,* he would be able to protect southern Louisiana from naval invasion, at least for the near future. If Confederates instead had to sink the *Indianola,* the most potent threat to Mississippi communications would be gone. He turned to his trusted lieutenant, Major Joseph Lancaster Brent, to bring in the enemy boat. "I was absolutely amazed at the order as I had no idea or expectation that I would be assigned to such a duty," Brent wrote. "I had absolutely no experience with Mississippi boats, or naval affairs." Before the war Brent, a Baltimore native, had worked as a California attorney. But the self-taught commissary and ordnance expert had all he needed: sound judgment and Taylor's confidence. Seasoned boatmen and combat veterans would handle the rest.[1]

This would be Major Brent's finest hour, and he planned well. On February 19, the artillery chief traveled to Fort DeRussy aboard the now-CSS *Queen of the West,* and met up with the *Webb.* He called for volunteers. A twenty-man squad from the 3rd Maryland Artillery, recently serving field pieces aboard Vicksburg-area supply boats, offered to lend a hand. One hundred and thirty men from the garrison of Fort DeRussy turned out to serve as sharpshooters and gunners on the expedition, including troops from the 1st Texas Sharp Shooter Battalion; companies B, C, and I of the 31st Tennessee Infantry (East Tennessee mountain boys); and the Crescent Artillery. He had enough riflemen but was short of deck hands and stokers, so he requested that local planters loan their slaves for the job. When they refused, he simply impressed the slaves who had been assigned to work on Fort DeRussy. "It was a curious feature of the war that the Southern people would cheerfully send their sons to battle," recalled Taylor in his memoirs, "but kept their slaves out of danger."[2]

Major Joseph Lancaster Brent was a Maryland-born lawyer who immigrated to California in 1850 at age twenty-four. His lucrative law practice allowed him to buy a modest ranch in present-day Glendale, and he began a rise in politics. At the outbreak of the secession movement, Brent helped raise a pro-southern militia company, the Los Angeles Mounted Rifles, but he sold his property and headed east at the outbreak of war. After serving on Major General John Bankhead Magruder's staff in Virginia, Brent accompanied Major General Richard Taylor to Louisiana, where the Marylander-turned-Californian proved himself to be resourceful, capable, and versatile.

Courtesy Special Collections Room, Glendale Public Library, Glendale, Calif.

After spending two days gathering boats and men, Brent began his hunt for the *Indianola*. He addressed the assembled crews at dawn on February 22. "I told the men that I was a stranger to them, as they were strangers to me," he wrote. "I preferred to make them no promises beyond assuring them that I would carry them where the enemy was, and then attack him, and therefore if there were any present who did not have the stomach for the certain fight into which I would lead them, they had better express their disinclination to go." As he spoke, Captain James Mangum, Brent's adjutant, brought his attention to the fact that it was George Washington's birthday. "I concluded by saying that the sun just risen seemed to bring us a good omen," Brent continued, "the birthday . . . of the Father of our Country, and that the freedom and liberty for which we were now battling were just the same as he battled for in the Revolutionary days; and I prayed that God might bless our efforts as his had been blessed." The men broke ranks, boarded the boats, and prepared for action.[3]

Brent's flotilla paddled down the Red River, heading for the Mississippi, expecting to meet the enemy at the confluence. Instead, the Rebels first encountered the crowded steamer *Dr. Batey,* coming up the Red River from Port Hudson. Loaded with sharpshooters from Colonel William R. Miles' Louisiana Legion and the men and guns of Boone's Louisiana Battery, this vessel fell in behind the Rebel rams and joined the search for the *Indianola.* Once in the Mississippi, Brent ordered the *Queen* to hove to at the Acklen Plantation to obtain wood and ask about the location of his enemy. The plantation's slaves, assuming this collection of boats must be Federal vessels, willingly shuttled wood aboard, "profuse in their tenders of service to the Union people, as they believed us to be," Brent recorded. He and his men had watched as, all along their journey, groups of slaves often lined the levees and banks of the Mississippi, assuming they were Yankee gunboats, hailing them and begging to be carried off behind northern lines. He continued, "What an enormous advantage the friendship of the blacks gave the Union forces, was very apparent, and could not have been bought with money."[4]

The next day, Brent's navy arrived at Natchez and learned that the *Indianola* was only a few hours upriver. The major ordered his crews to train on their guns for the rest of the day, knowing that the morrow would require them to be proficient in their use. As dawn broke on February 24, Brent led his boats slowly upstream to New Carthage, Louisiana, sixty miles downstream from Vicksburg, where lookouts had spied the *Indianola* ahead, stern on, coal barges lashed to its sides to protect it from ramming, and cotton-bale armor stacked on its decks, beating its way slowly upstream.[5]

Major Brent knew his limitations, and he decided to keep hidden and attack after sunset. "He determined to attack in the night, to diminish the chances of the enemy's fire," Taylor wrote. "It was certain that a shell from one of the eleven or nine-inch guns would destroy either of his boats."[6]

Once engaged, the work would have to be done swiftly. Brent planned carefully. At 10:00 PM, he ordered the *Queen* to attack with all available speed and the *Webb* to follow close behind. The *Dr. Batey* and the tender *Grand Era* would stay behind, lashed together, and offer what small arms assistance they could.

USS *Indianola* as cottonclad. Cotton bales were easy to come by, and boat commanders, even aboard ironclads, used them as ersatz armor.

Louisiana Office of State Parks, Department of Culture, Recreation, and Tourism.

CSS *Queen of the West* as cottonclad. Confederate commanders had great ambitions for their captured war-ram and used what they could to make it safe from Union cannon fire.

Naval Historical Center.

Lookouts on the *Indianola* spied the oncoming Confederate flotilla, and Lieutenant Commander George Brown ordered his men to their stations, cleared for action. As he turned the vessel around in the darkness of a moon-shrouded night, the ungainly *Indianola* moved with the current and crowded in close to the east bank of the river, its coal barges jutting out past its bow like two pontoons and covering its sides just short of the wheelhouse. Brown ordered his boat to reverse engines, backing up the Mississippi toward friendly lines while facing the enemy. He and his men were just fifteen miles from safety.[7]

As planned, the *Queen* struck first at full steam, smashing through the coal barge and hammering into the port side of the *Indianola* between it and the river bank. Iron plate crumpled inward from the shock as Union sailors tumbled among their guns. Brent ordered the *Queen* to back away, but the vessels remained locked together. "In this position our sharpshooters opened fire on every light and crevice," he reported. Even so, being jammed together with the enemy ironclad might prove disastrous. Soldiers of the 1st Texas Sharpshooter Battalion engaged the enemy sailors while the *Webb* took its turn.[8]

The *Webb* did not have as clear a shot at the enemy and struck a glancing blow along the starboard side after meeting the *Indianola* bow-on. As the Confederate ram passed alongside the wounded Union boat, Yankee fighters unleashed their forward battery of 11-inch Dahlgrens at close range but fired a movement too soon, missing their speedy enemy and only carrying away the *Webb*'s bow railing. Seconds later the protecting coal barge exploded into splinters and cinders as the *Webb* churned through it, cutting its lashings and setting it adrift before careening off the wheelhouse. Below the gun deck, the violence of the collision dismounted the *Indianola*'s engine, and its groaning machinery and clattering gears ground themselves to a halt, frozen in mechanical death. The collision did spin the *Indianola* away from the *Queen of the West,* allowing the Confederate vessel to free itself, reverse its engines, and proceed full steam upriver. Behind it, the coal barge on *Indianola*'s port side filled with water and sank. Both Rebel vessels schemed for a second pass. The *Webb,* rejoined by the *Queen of the West* astern the *Indianola* came about. Now the powerful Mississippi River current would add momentum to their next run.[9]

Brown realized the danger. The damage done to his vessel combined with the heavy current made the ironclad unmanageable, and the destroyed coal barges no longer covered the boat's sides. He ordered his sluggish beast, its paddlewheels useless but its screw propellers still turning, to reverse its engines and move forward, downstream, then turn around to face its attackers, but it barely answered to its controls. Slowly, laboriously, the *Indianola* heaved around, once again covering its vulnerable stern from the Confederate rams upstream, and presenting its heaviest battery to the enemy.

Gunners and riflemen continued the fight while engineers worked to get the vessel under control. "At this time, the engagement became general," Brown reported. Behind him, marksmen aboard the cottonclads *Dr. Batey* and *Grand Era* peppered bullets into the ironclad's gun ports and vision slits while soldiers operating field pieces did what they could against its armored hide. The Union men still worked their guns, too—dodging bullets and splinters—but in the darkness most of their massive shots fell wide of the mark.[10]

Brent plotted his second run. The enemy had managed to once again make this a head-on joust, so the Confederate commander decided at another tilt at the enemy. Once again *Indianola*'s heavy guns fired, and again they missed, both rounds hurtling across the water on either side of the Rebel ram. The *Queen of the West* collided with the bow and sheered away alongside its enemy's starboard side while both crews exchanged small arms fire. Brown strode the decks of his vessel, directing its movements and the gunnery of its cannon. "He stood upon the hurricane deck, swept by volleys of musketry, grape, and canister shot, looking out for the rams, giving orders to his pilots, and with his revolver firing upon the pilots of the enemy," an admiring crewman later noted. The *Queen of the West* headed downriver, quickly turned around, and maneuvered for a third run. The two Confederate rams had established their rhythm—the *Webb* still posed a threat from above while the *Queen* would make a quick turn and another run from below, this time with the *Indianola*'s stern exposed.[11]

Brown faced a dilemma. His crew, too few to man both forward and aft batteries, had to choose which Confederate vessel posed the greater threat. The gunners left their pieces trained on the *Webb* and scrambled down the length of their boat to run out the stern guns to bear on the *Queen of the West*.

The Union gunners were too late. The *Queen of the West* closed fast aiming at the tender aft of the *Indianola*. It hit to the rear of the starboard wheelhouse with an eruption of dust, sparks, and smoke, crushing the ironclad's wooden frame and loosening its giant sheet of casemate armor. This punch staggered the *Indianola* and carried away its rudder, opening its hull to the river. It also nearly ruined the *Queen of the West.* "She was for some time almost unmanageable," Brent reported. Cotton bales used as armor, five hundred pounds or better in weight, had tumbled off the boat's sides, and the violence of the repeated impacts wrecked its machinery. The Confederate ram reversed its engines, now grinding noisily from being jarred out of place, clumsily backing downstream and churning brown water into the wound in the *Indianola*'s side.[12]

As the *Queen of the West* pulled away, Union gunners on the two rear 9-inch Dalgrens shot a ball of fire, white hot iron, and a furnace wind through the vessel. When the smoke cleared, witnesses saw devastation. The first iron shell into the ram "carried away a dozen bales of cotton on the right side," Brent reported, shearing three tons of cotton like corn off a cob, cascading bales into the river. The other round entered from the left front and traveled the length of the *Queen,* diagonally, smashing men and guns. The round mangled two men and wounded four others, "be-spattering our deck and even the pilot house with blood and pieces of human flesh," Brent recalled. The shot exited the boat's right rear in an explosion of cotton bales, sending another five tons or more spinning into the river.[13]

The grievously wounded ram nearly rolled over on its port side. "Owing to the displacement of weight," Brent continued, the *Queen of the West* suddenly careened to the left, as if she was about to turn over. One of her wheels was much the most raised out of the water." The engineer cut the engine as the crew rushed to push cotton bales off the port side into the river. The gunboat righted itself and the engines started anew, but the vessel now rode bow high. Despite this, "they were able to bring her round very slowly," Brent added. "She was brought up by her gallant commander for a further charge."[14]

Sailors aboard the *Indianola* knew that their boat, too, had been badly damaged. This latest demolition had not only compromised the hull but it had also spun their boat back around, so the jagged

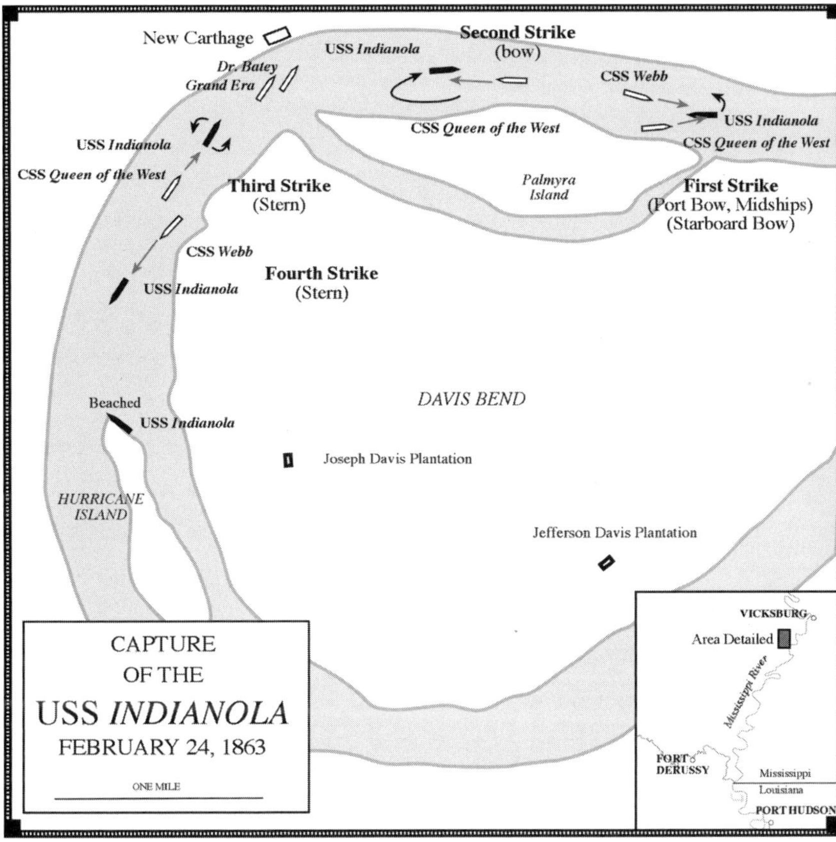

wound now faced upstream—and the *Webb*. As water oozed in, sailors and marines looked out the gun ports with dread as the other Rebel ram charged toward them. The *Webb*'s aim was true, and it struck next to the same spot the *Queen* had hit, completing the ironclad's destruction. Iron plate sloughed off into the water and smashed timbers gave way. River water gushed into the hole and filled the engine room as the Confederate vessel rode up and over the gunwales of the Union craft. "The sharp bow of the *Webb* penetrated as if it were going to pass entirely through the ship," Brent reported. Its forward momentum finally spent, the *Webb* backed away, leaving most of its bow in the wound. Even so, the Confederate ram backed up for a third run, despite water pouring in from a gash two feet long and eight inches wide. One more blow might be all the *Webb* could make before its frame buckled and its bow collapsed from the punishment.[15]

Brown knew that *Indianola* was done. He ordered his vessel out of action. As the *Webb* bore down for its third blow, Union sailors hailed their tormentors then lowered their flag, and the CSS *Webb* sheered off. The *Indianola* had fallen, at the cost of about a dozen men killed, wounded, and missing. The *Dr. Batey* pulled alongside and readied to board the Union vessel before Brown surrendered a second time.[16]

State pride shone through as news of the victory spread. "Although it was the first battle in which these gallant men . . . had been engaged, they fought like veterans and tigers," a Knoxville, Tennessee, newspaper crowed. "Too much praise cannot be awarded these brave East Tennesseans for their naval tact and chivalry." General Taylor hailed the triumph as well: "Thus we regained control of our section of the Mississippi, and by an action that for daring will bear comparison with any recorded of Nelson or Dundonald."[17]

Brent nearly did not live to hear these accolades. As the *Queen of the West* pulled even with the captured ironclad, the Confederate commander of the expedition leaped from the command deck to the top of the *Queen*'s cotton bale armor in his hurry to reach the Union vessel. He landed on a bale that had been jarred loosed by combat, and it rolled beneath his feet. Brent slid twelve feet to the deck and landed hard on his leg in a seated position, with his booted feet over the side. "The displaced bale, weighing over four hundred pounds, followed me in my fall," he later wrote. The bale struck the officer in the back and vaulted him violently into the river, his binoculars and pistol thrown from his body. "I struggled to the surface with great difficulty, scarcely able to use my left leg." Gasping and sputtering, Brent treaded water between the two vessels, in danger of being crushed between them or dragged into the wheel of his own vessel. No one heard him yelling above the steam whistles, triumphant cheers, and clattering machinery. A slave coal heaver finally noticed the soggy Rebel and threw him a rope. "I presented a most undignified and woeful appearance," he remembered. "I was without hat or cap, my uniform was sodden and dripping with water, and I limped and stooped and no doubt excited . . . the impression that I was drunk."[18]

Brent's gunboats had done their work too well over the course of the hour-long battle, and he had to act fast to save his capture. He ordered lines secured to the sinking ironclad and ordered it towed to the Mississippi side of the river to avoid the boat's falling into the hands of Major General Ulysses S. Grant's army on the Louisiana shore. As the vessel plowed its way across the river, it filled with water. Confederates maneuvered the boat onto a sand bar near Hurricane Island, but to all observers the *Indianola* appeared a total loss. The Union ironclad lay crippled and inert within two miles of the home of Joseph Davis, the brother of the president of the Confederacy. Unsure of how to proceed with their crippled capture, southern officers dawdled as they sought instructions. Time flitted away.

Now fortune favored the Federals. Luck visited Admiral David Dixon Porter the next day when a plan already set in motion yielded unintended fruit. Earlier on February 24, the admiral ordered workers to construct a faux ironclad using timber and a barge. This target vessel was designed to uncover Confederate gun positions at Vicksburg and test how they responded to another boat passing by. On the night of February 25, the fake gunboat drifted past the Vicksburg batteries contested and struck, but still afloat, while Union spotters counted muzzle flashes and noted the positions of the enemy guns. The next morning, an infantry patrol found it beached below Vicksburg south of De Soto point. "She has a square turret forward, with a mock cannon projecting toward the bow from within," a Union lieutenant reported after he discovered the odd contraption beached near his position. "Smokestack made of flour barrels, wheelhouse, etc., covered all over with thick coat of tar." Smudge pots in its fake stacks gave the appearance of a real gunboat under steam. Workers noted the nature and size of the damage, then pushed the unarmed, unscrewed vessel back into the current assuming it would sink just off shore, its mission complete. Instead, it drifted lazily with the current.[19]

Confederate scouts, a few miles downstream, spied the toothless monster and reported that the racket heard the night before from the guns of Vicksburg was due to Porter running another gunboat past the batteries. The Confederate flotilla hovering around Hurricane Bend was in no shape for another showdown with a Yankee ironclad. Spooked by rumors of Federal efforts to recapture their prize, and panicking at the reports that made Porter's barge appear to be another dragon heading to devour the battered Rebel gunboats,

Destruction of the *Indianola*. This newspaper image shows the *Indianola* being scuttled to keep it from being recaptured by a newly arriving Union gunboat while the Confederate boats flee. The threatening ironclad turned out to be a fake, and the destruction of the *Indianola* less than total.

Naval Historical Center.

Brent ordered his boats to retreat to the Red River. *Queen of the West* collided with *Grand Era* in the rush, nearly sinking it. Rumors and reports continued to swirl like the eddies of the river flowing around the *Indianola*'s hulk. The Confederates left behind to secure and salvage the wreck, unsure about how to proceed, destroyed the ironclad on orders from Major General Carter Littlepage Stevenson, commanding the works at Vicksburg.[20]

Lieutenant General John C. Pemberton had mixed reactions about the entire incident. He reported the affair to his superiors in Richmond, taking the opportunity to cast some aspersions on Major Brent and his flotilla. "Confederate fleet abandoned the *Indianola* on approach of what was supposed to be a turreted iron-clad," Pemberton telegrammed. "I am not satisfied that is was a gunboat, but have no intelligence yet. *Indianola* was blown up." The Rebels had held the captured vessel for two days. Meanwhile, the

Wooden Dummy. Admiral David Dixon Porter, as shown in his sketch, ordered a decoy ironclad crafted from lumber and barrels to float by the Vicksburg batteries. He had no idea it would survive the trip to even better effect.

Naval Historical Center.

Mississippi River's current beached Porter's target dummy a couple miles upstream.[21]

Pemberton did not seem to care that the ironclad had been lost to southern ambitions; his men needed rations and the elimination of the *Indianola* from the river supply route had reopened the flow of groceries. The general sent a dispatch to Taylor requesting help. "As you are in command of the operations on Red River, you can do this command and myself a great favor if you will take immediate steps to have forwarded all the beef possible, or bacon or salted pork," he wrote. "In this respect, general, no greater service can be done to country than in hurrying forward these supplies."[22]

On March 4, 1863, a Confederate cavalry scout arrived at the banks of Hurricane Bend and beheld a surprising sight. *Indianola* still lay on the sand bar, half sunk but intact. The demolition team had failed. Both Pemberton and Taylor claimed salvage right. Most of the boat's usable battery appears to have gone west of the Mississippi and would serve again in the hands of Confederate gunners. Richmond awarded control of the *Indianola*'s hulk to Pemberton, who hoped to raise the boat and put it back in action. He never did.[23]

4

Passing Port Hudson

"I am sick of hearing my officers talk of
cotton-clad boats and impregnable rams."

Admiral David G. Farragut
West Gulf Blockading Squadron

Sweeping away the Union naval threat allowed Confederates on both sides of the Mississippi River to once again assist each other. The men of the 1st Texas Sharpshooter Battalion boarded the *Nina Simms* to complete their journey to Port Hudson. The steamer *Robert Fulton* followed a few days behind, loaded with rations for Vicksburg.[1]

The newly open Rebel stretch of the Mississippi allowed the Confederacy to send across help for Major General Richard Taylor in the form of more brass, not troops. Lieutenant General Edmund Kirby Smith and his family finally completed a journey begun more than a month before. After marking time in Mobile, the sojourners had traveled to Port Hudson, where they had taken a steamer making a regular run between the fort and Alexandria. Assigned to command earlier in the year, Kirby Smith arrived on March 7 to assume control of the entire Confederate Department of the Trans-Mississippi. He was a logical choice—with West Point and Mexican War credentials as well as excellent service in East

Tennessee. "It was advisable to supercede Holmes," Taylor confessed. "[Kirby] Smith, from his training and services, seemed an excellent choice."[2]

The two officers had little time to get acquainted before the new commander left for an extensive inspection of conditions in Arkansas. Taylor knew him only by reputation. At thirty-eight years old, Lieutenant General Kirby Smith was a spectacle-wearing scholarly type, and he was devoutly religious. His graying beard and receding hairline made him appear much older. The notoriously high-strung Taylor, a year his junior, had dark hair and flashing eyes, was a stickler for discipline and order, and had a reputation for being occasionally profane and a keen skill in imaginative cussing.[3]

Lieutenant General Edmund Kirby Smith, a Floridian born to native Connecticut parents, graduated from West Point in 1845 and won laurels and promotions for bravery in the Mexican War. He served on the Texas frontier in the 1850s and refused to surrender Camp Colorado to secessionists, offering to fight it out instead. Despite this, he soon resigned his commission and threw in with the Confederacy, earning accolades, and more wounds, fighting in Virginia, Tennessee, and Kentucky. His success on the battlefield earned him promotion to lieutenant general and command of the Department of the Trans-Mississippi. He arrived just in time to face a major Union offensive.
Library of Congress.

Taylor urged his new boss to remain true to the ultimate goal of retaking New Orleans. Kirby Smith was more concerned with doing what he could to aid Vicksburg and Port Hudson. On the latter goal the two men agreed, and Taylor requested that Kirby Smith order reinforcements to move out of Arkansas. The general promised to study the problem, and he headed to Little Rock himself to assess conditions there before issuing the orders. Taylor, who had hoped for more immediate action, knew that very little had been accomplished in the northern reaches of the Trans-Mississippi, even though it had enjoyed the lion's share of men and matériel. Tension crept into this new partnership. "The substance of Louisiana and Texas," growled Taylor, "was staked against the shadow of Missouri and Northern Arkansas."[4]

Whether Kirby Smith agreed or not, Louisiana would take on even more importance in the coming days. By March 1863 New Orleans hosted thousands of U.S. sailors, and the masts of Admiral David G. Farragut's fleet formed a forest of wood and canvas along the city's waterfront. At the St. Charles Hotel in the New Orleans French Quarter the commander of the Federal fleet in the western Gulf of Mexico met with General Nathaniel P. Banks to talk about the naval component of operations on the Mississippi. The loss of the *Queen of the West* and the *Indianola* aggravated the wounds the sailors' pride had received on the coast of Texas two months before. Federal ship officers fumed. Once again, Rebel audacity had embarrassed the U.S. Navy. "At this news Farragut took fire," wrote Lieutenant Colonel Richard B. Irwin, Banks's assistant adjutant general. "Between him and the impudent little Confederate fleet . . . there stood nothing save the guns of Port Hudson." Instead of relying on Admiral David Dixon Porter to send gunboats downriver in ones and twos, Farragut would take part of the mighty West Gulf blockading squadron up the Mississippi. He planned to run past the batteries of Port Hudson with his mighty oceangoing capital ships, put an end to the petty steamboat give-and-take, and close the mouth of the Red River.[5]

Farragut asked Banks for the army's assistance in moving his fleet past the Confederate citadel. "Banks, whose movements were retarded and to some extent held in abeyance," Irwin reported, "promptly fell in with the Admiral's plans, and both commanders conferring freely, the details were soon arranged." The army and navy must show courage. "Iron gunboats are well enough," Farragut urged, "but give me a crew of iron hearts."[6]

Admiral David G. Farragut was sixty-two by the time he found himself back in New Orleans—where he lived as a child—as part of an invading armada. He had seen much in his lifetime, including naval combat against the British in the War of 1812 that left him wounded and a prisoner. At the outbreak of the Civil War, Federal authorities figured him to be past his prime and offered him trivial assignments in the Navy Department. His foster brother, David Dixon Porter, knew better, and lobbied for Farragut to lead the naval forces in the Gulf of Mexico. His successes there put him on a course that would lead him under the guns of Port Hudson.

Library of Congress.

Farragut was clearly losing patience with the war's tempo. He wrote to Porter, his counterpart above Vicksburg, that he had "learned by the secesh papers that two of your vessels had gone down the river and had been captured by the enemy's guns and riverboats, thus putting it out of your power to prevent the supplies from Red River to Port Hudson." He was also troubled by "the evils arising from having an ironclad, the *Indianola,* to act against us." Therefore, Farragut decided he would personally recover control of the situation, in a subtle chiding of Porter. "I determined to attempt to pass the batteries at Port Hudson, come up, destroy or recapture the boats you had lost," and succeeding where Porter had failed, "blockade Red River."[7]

In New Orleans, Banks and Farragut held a dinner party and looked forward to the work ahead. After opening a bottle of champagne, the admiral addressed those assembled. "We have more men and more resources than these traitors and five times as much money," he declared. "We must beat them in the end, but we must do it by poking them, butting them wherever we see them." He was especially irritated by the success of the Rebel gunboats from Galveston to the Red River. "By God," Farragut declared, "shall a United States ship of war hesitate to go in and destroy a dozen of these wretched Mississippi steamers? I am sick of hearing my officers talk of cotton-clad boats and impregnable rams. They should pitch in and destroy them."[8]

He knew that his proposal to pass the batteries at Port Hudson was personally risky, and apparently Banks pointed out the danger, too. "What matters it, General, whether you or I are killed are not," Farragut responded. "We came here to die. It is our business and must happen sooner or later." His bravado was followed by a very simple view of how the war should end. "We must fight this thing out until there is no more than one man left," Farragut roared, "and that man must be a Union man." Lifting his flute of champagne, the admiral added, "Here's to his health."[9]

Others southerners took advantage of the return of Rebel control of the Mississippi as well. In Alexandria the family of James Hewitt—refugees from their home near Donaldsonville—boarded the *Mary T.* for a dash downriver. This wealthy sugar-planting family had three sons in the Confederate army, including Richard, a lieutenant in Colonel William Miles's Louisiana Legion. "When my husband collected sufficient quantity of provisions he offered them to the Government for the relief of Port Hudson," wrote Clarissa Hewitt. She insisted on going along in hopes of seeing her son. "The trip . . . was made safely, without any incident worth recording, she scribbled in her diary as Port Hudson loomed into view."[10] She could not imagine the maelstrom she was so naively entering.

Downstream, on March 12, 1863, General Banks reviewed his army in Louisiana for the first time near their camps at Baton Rouge. In addition, the sailors of Farragut's fleet stood in formation, covering the battlefield of the previous August in a grand military display. "The new regiments, with some exceptions, showed plainly the progress already attained under the energetic training and constant work of their officers," Irwin wrote. Lieutenant Colonel David Hunter Strother agreed. "The display was fine," he wrote, adding a jibe at the horse-mounted crews from the ships by writing, "I expected to see some of the navy men fall into the ditch but they all got over safely."[11]

There was cause for concern, however. "The troops are very green and not in very good condition," Strother noted of the mostly nine months volunteers. He also noted the tension between white and black troops. "Some drunken white soldiers assaulted the Negro soldiers and there was a brickbat fight," he wrote. "The introduction of the Negro soldier only complicates the confusion and inefficiency of our army composed of green troops. The white soldiers won't do anything now except make the Negroes work for them. They are more exacting and brutal than the masters were originally."[12]

USS *Hartford*. Farragut's flagship was a large screw sloop-of-war bearing twenty 9-inch Dahlgrens, a pair of 20-pounder Parrots, and a pair of 12-pounder smoothbores, and a crew of three hundred.

Marshall Dunham Photograph Album, Mss. 3241, Louisiana and Lower Mississippi Valley Collections, LSU Libraries, Baton Rouge, La.

Helmsmen, USS *Hartford*.

Marshall Dunham Photograph Album, Mss. 3241, Louisiana and Lower Mississippi Valley Collections, LSU Libraries, Baton Rouge, La.

The next morning, this Union observer had a chance to observe one of Louisiana Native Guard regiments and to speak to its commander. "[They are] a fine-looking set of men and doubtless capable of being made good soldiers," Strother noted. "They will drill with any white regiment, are vigilant on picket duty, are good night owls, are very docile, and obey orders without thinking or questioning." He wondered if the same could be said for the temporary regiments from New England.[13]

Within days Banks's 19th Army Corps concentrated at and around Baton Rouge. Brigadier General Thomas W. Sherman kept his division at New Orleans while Brigadier General Godfrey Weitzel stood fast at Brashear City. Three divisions—Major General Christopher Columbus Augur's, Brigadier General William H. Emory's, and Brigadier General Cuvier Grover's—numbering nearly fifteen thousand men moved on upriver to within twenty miles of Port Hudson and set up camp.

Farragut readied his men as well. With him came an impressive array of oceangoing warships including his powerful flagship,

USS *Albatross* began its career as a merchant vessel, launched at Mystic, Connecticut, in 1858. The U.S. Navy purchased the ship, put aboard, seven cannon, and eventually assigned it to the Gulf of Mexico.

Library of Congress.

the twenty-four-gun screw sloop USS *Hartford.* A ship similar in size and power, the USS *Richmond,* glided upstream, along with a smaller but very potent screw sloop, the USS *Monongahela,* bearing five heavy guns including a monstrous 200-pounder rifle. The elegant but aging USS *Mississippi,* an eleven-gun side-wheel steam frigate, paddled alongside these young warriors—the oldest had only been at sea for five years—and rounded out the major combatants under Farragut's command. A number of gunboats were on hand, including the three-gun screw steamer USS *Albatross,* the side-wheeler USS *Genesee* with seven medium-weight guns, and the "ninety-day gunboat" USS *Kineo* with five guns. Farragut also brought up six mortar schooners to shell Port Hudson as he made his run. The lumbering ironclad USS *Essex* and the sturdy little steamer USS *Sachem* just in from the Texas coast would shepherd these bomb ketches.

Farragut carried with him a dispatch from Banks to Major General Ulysses S. Grant. The commander of the Department of

USS *Richmond* was a new and well-armed sloop-of-war at the beginning of the Civil War. This photo shows the ship anchored off Baton Rouge in early 1863.

G. H. Suydam Collection, Mss. 1394, Louisiana and Lower Mississippi Valley Collection, LSU Libraries, Baton Rouge, La.

the Gulf sent word that he was looking for ways the two Union armies could cooperate. Port Hudson, Banks had decided, remained the key to the Mississippi after all, and he urged Grant to send him troops to help subdue that post. An additional Federal corps would doom the Confederates in the Louisiana fort. The triumphant army could then head north and finish off Vicksburg. Of course, there remained the troubling question of how exactly Grant would get these troops to Banks, but the logistics could be worked out.

The coordinated plan of the army and navy seemed simple. While Banks's foot soldiers probed the enemy works at Port Hudson, Farragut would shell the place with mortars. With all signs pointing to a land assault and with lead and iron raining upon the Rebel fort, the four big ships and three consorts would make a dash upriver past the enemy guns. As he had done before, running the batteries below New Orleans, Farragut ordered the smaller ships lashed alongside the three large screw sloops. The USS *Mississippi* would make the run alone. Farragut announced he would steam ahead in

Crew at quarters, USS *Richmond*. This photo shows some of the 250 sailors and marines on board in position to service their broadside battery of 9-inch Dahlgrens.

G. H. Suydam Collection, Mss. 1394, Louisiana and Lower Mississippi Valley Collection, LSU Libraries, Baton Rouge, La.

"the gray of the morning" of Sunday, March 15, giving Banks time to shift his troops into place. In the late afternoon of Friday the 13th, "the gallant fleet steamed out of sight behind the bend just as the sun went down," Strother remembered. "Just after dark we saw signal rockets from the enemy thrown up."[14]

Although he may have been tempted, Banks refused to turn his feint into a full-scale attempt on Port Hudson. "I urged him strongly to march directly on Port Hudson," Strother recorded in his diary. "He said if he had ten thousand more men he would attack." Banks did not intended to try an assault. Instead, his army would launch a diversionary raid as planned, and perhaps, as Lieutenant Colonel Irwin observed, gain "some facility of movement, some knowledge of its deficiencies, and some information . . . as to the topography of the unknown country." Banks ordered all of his artillery, including the newly minted 1st Indiana Heavy Artillery—created from the veteran and capable 21st infantry regiment—to concentrate on the Rebel guns closest to the river.[15]

USS *Genesee* only arrived at New Orleans on March 7, 1863, just in time to lend a hand against Port Hudson.

G. H. Suydam Collection, Mss. 1394, Louisiana and Lower Mississippi Valley Collection, LSU Libraries, Baton Rouge, La.

USS *Monongahela*, a smaller screw sloop-of-war, was launched in the summer of 1862 at the Philadelphia Naval Yard, commissioned on January 15, 1863, and sailed immediately for the Gulf of Mexico to reinforce Admiral David G. Farragut's operations on the coast and up the Mississippi.

Naval Historical Center.

Banks's prudence may have been necessary. Behind the earthworks, Brigadier General Franklin Gardner mustered nearly fourteen thousand men. Along the river, twenty-two large-bore guns loomed from behind embrasures, and fire rafts and bonfires lay ready to illuminate the Mississippi should any attempts to pass the fort be made at night. The Confederates were ready for just such an attack, and Banks's army was still learning how to soldier. He had also received reports that a Rebel relief force sat between Port Hudson and Vicksburg for just such a contingency, and that more Southerners were coming from Mobile and points east. Unfounded rumors floated that troops from the Army of Northern Virginia had arrived to fall upon the Union flank. "The object of this movement was to make a diversion during the passage of the fleet, and not to make an attack with the expectation of carrying the works,"

USS *Mississippi*, shown here off Baton Rouge, was the old salt of the West Gulf Blockading Squadron. The twenty-two-year veteran had seen action in the Mexican War, opened Japan to foreign trade, patrolled off China, and had been around the globe several times. The ship, with her signature side wheels and heavy broadsides, played a significant part in the capture of New Orleans.

G. H. Suydam Collection, Mss. 1394, Louisiana and Lower Mississippi Valley Collection, LSU Libraries, Baton Rouge, La.

Mortar Boat of Farragut's Fleet, like the one pictured here, bombarded Confederate Mississippi River fortifications wherever Union forces encountered them.

Massachusetts Commandery Military Order of the Loyal Legion and US Army Military History Institute.

Banks reported. "The hope of the naval and land officers was that [the fleet] might run the batteries with as little firing as possible. No decisive encounter with the enemy was anticipated."[16]

The *Mary T.,* paddling down the Mississippi with a cargo of supplies, headed directly into the gnashing gears of war, which were turning once again. As the steamer approached the Confederate works at Port Hudson, its passengers realized their poor timing as they watched the drama unfolding below the Confederate fort. "We felt the signs of excitement, for when we got in sight of Port Hudson it was evident that the Federal gunboats were getting into line for [an] approaching battle," Clarissa Hewitt recorded. "The Captain felt a hesitation about landing, but we were too anxious to see Richard, so after a consultation decided to risk it."[17]

The crew of the *Mary T.* hailed at the landing, calling forth gangs of Confederates scrambling down the well-worn road to meet it. At the head of the mass of men was a young officer with orders to wave the paddle wheeler away from the clearly

USS *Essex*, converted into an ironclad from an Ohio River ferryboat, ran past the Vicksburg batteries on July 22, 1862, hunting for the CSS *Arkansas*. Afterward, the powerful gunboat joined in the fight at Baton Rouge on August 5 and served along the lower Mississippi.

State Library of Louisiana.

dangerous situation, but the skipper insisted on landing his cargo. The landing lay within range of the rifled cannon on the bows of the Federal warships. Amid the chaos of unloading, Clarissa Hewitt recognized the soldier as her son. "The Captain disobeyed the order . . . enabling us to have these precious moments with our dear boy," she wrote. As the afternoon faded into evening, the Hewitts bade their son farewell and went back aboard the *Mary T.* for a stealthy attempt to pass upriver before the coming battle. But they had tarried too long.[18]

A steamboat stood little chance of survival under the guns of Farragut's fleet. The *Mary T.,* its lights doused and blankets held up to block the light of its engine fires, tried to creep away as darkness descended so that they might ride out the battle in a nearby creek. Union gunners probed the darkness for the little steamer. "Had one of them struck our frail wooden steamer it would have been instantaneous death to all and complete destruction," gasped Hewitt. The Union, firing from extreme range, never managed a clear shot at the Rebel paddle wheeler. "I shall never forget the terrors of it, and not until we were safely around the bend of the river in front of Port Hudson did we realize the extent of our own danger, and how narrow an escape we had made."[19]

The presence of the Confederate vessel may have influenced a change in Federal plans. On the afternoon of March 14, Farragut became convinced that the enemy had discerned his intentions, so he decided to launch his attempt to pass the guns of Port Hudson that evening, about four hours earlier than he had told Banks. The reports from the army indicated the proximity of enemy reinforcements, and his lookouts certainly reported the landing of more supplies for the garrison. Naval observers counted four Confederate steamers at the landing, which jibed with the number of boats that had recently worked over the *Indianola*. The presumed presence of Rebel gunboats—perhaps the quartet of *Queen of the West, Webb, Nina Simms,* and *Dr. Batey*—added a juicy target for the navy.[20]

Fatigue Detail. This photo shows several of Farragut's ships off Baton Rouge. Sailors in the foreground have cut and stacked wood to fuel the steamers.

G. H. Suydam Collection, Mss. 1394, Louisiana and Lower Mississippi Valley Collection, LSU Libraries, Baton Rouge, La.

Banks, meanwhile, had gone to bed for the evening, but he would not sleep for long. "At half past eleven I was awakened to hear and see the bombardments by the mortar boats and the fleet running the batteries at Port Hudson," wrote Strother. "The noise and pyrotechnics were sublime, like the flashes and reverberations of a grand thunderstorm. We could see the shells slowly circling from the boats to the town. Through the glass you could see the bombs like red moons in the air." The *Hartford,* covering the *Albatross* to its port side, lead the acolumn, followed in like manner by the *Richmond* and the *Genesee,* then the *Monongahela* and the *Kineo.* The USS *Mississippi* followed in the rear. The infantry of the 19th Army Corps served mostly as spectators the navy's show.[21]

Almost as soon as the warships came into sight of the Confederate guns, signal rockets streaked skyward. Round after round of gunfire began churning the water around the Union vessels. Bonfires of pitch and logs erupted along the eastern bank, casting a lurid glow across the water as the oily smoke blended with that from

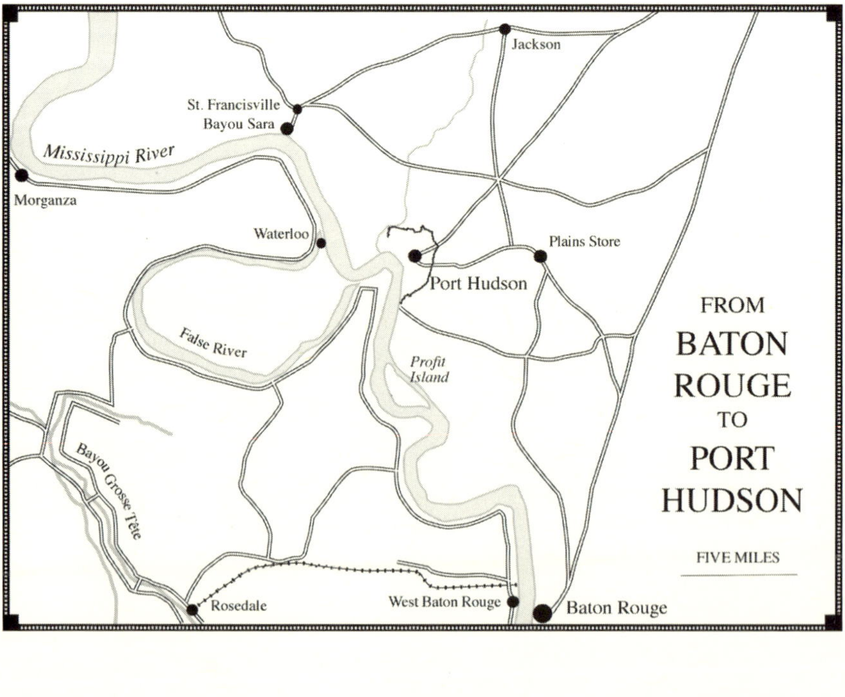

The run past the guns. The artist shows Farragut's fleet making its run past Port Hudson. The USS *Richmond* appears in the foreground. Notice two vessels, presumably USS *Hartford* and USS *Albatross*, have made it safely.

Harper's Weekly, *author's collection.*

Port Hudson Defended. The artist in this piece shows the attack from the Confederate angle. Notice the mortar fleet and USS *Essex* and USS *Sachem* firing in the background, smaller vessels shielded from the fire as they make their run, and USS *Mississippi* ablaze at the end of the battle line.

Harper's Weekly, *author's collection.*

the cannon. The *Hartford* and the *Albatross* passed by gracefully, but the current pushed them into the banks opposite the Confederate guns. After a few tense minutes, the duo came free, scarred and bruised, but still underway.

Behind them, the rest of the fleet steamed into trouble. The *Richmond* and the *Genesee* pushed ahead but had to slow their pace to avoid colliding with the *Hartford* and the *Albatross* while they freed themselves from the bank. Confederate cannon scored hit after hit on the ships as the head of the naval column untangled itself, but eventually the *Richmond* and the *Genesee* increased their speed and passed the worst of the danger. Then disaster struck. A large-caliber round passed through the *Richmond*'s engine room, severing key plumbing on the steam engine and leaving that ship and the *Genesee* drifting helplessly back down the river with the current. Once again the pair had to endure the Rebel gauntlet, this time in reverse.

Third in line, the *Monongahela* also faced a crisis as round shot wreaked havoc with its machinery while to its left the *Kineo* took a hit to its steering, causing both vessels to curve toward the port side and run aground. Under fire and desperate, Union sailors cut the *Kineo* loose. As it drifted back down stream, its crew grappled its larger consort and reversed its engines to help pull the *Monongahela* back into the current. Its rescue complete, the nimble gunboat cast off and drifted downriver, out of range. The vessels spent nearly an hour under heavy fire and suffered severely. The *Richmond* and the *Genesee* passed the crippled *Monongahela,* which was drifting backward, and the Union warship appeared doomed. Damage from gunfire had nearly killed *Monongahela*'s commander by carrying away the bridge. Another round overheated a bearing in the ship's machinery, causing its engines to fail.

Last in line, the *Mississippi* seemed destined to successfully join Admiral Farragut as the roiling smoke and the confusion ahead disguised its approach. These same factors, however, caused the *Mississippi*'s pilot to run it aground on a shoal very near where the

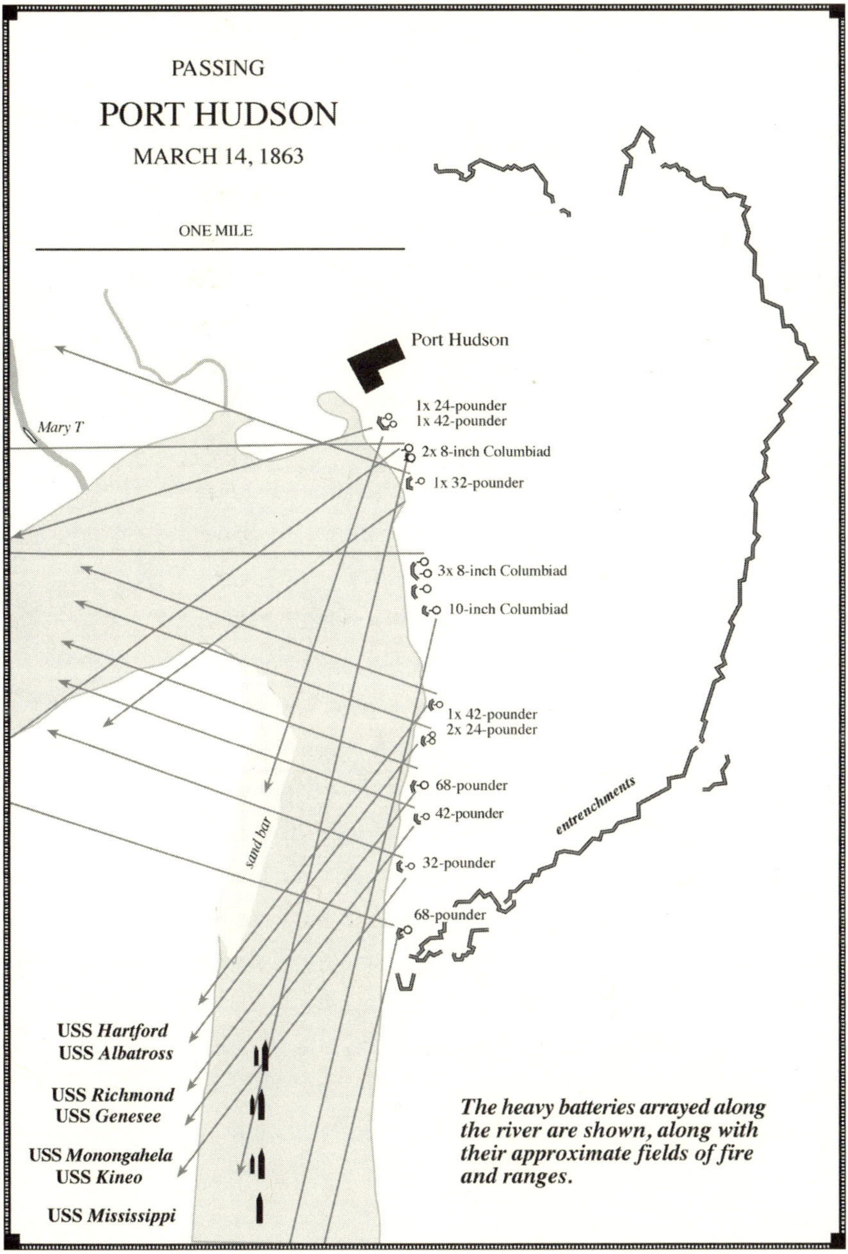

Monongahela and the *Kineo* had met with difficulty. When Gardner's gunners began running short of targets as the other vessels fell out of action, they turned their attention to the heretofore-unnoticed steam frigate. For more than half an hour, a score of heavy cannon threw nearly one hundred rounds at the *Mississippi,* knocking it to pieces as it labored to back off of the sandbar. The ship's commander gave in to this relentless pounding and ordered the living and wounded moved off the ship. Crews set it afire. Three hours later the *Mississippi* had burned enough to lighten its weight on the shoal, and it floated free and headed back downstream, dying.

The strong current of the Mississippi had complicated Farragut's run, but in the end, it may have saved most of his fleet. Four of the seven Union ships drifted back into friendly lines, battered, disabled, smoldering, leaking, and awash in blood and splinters. The *Monongahela,* mangled by enemy shot, shell, and grapeshot, may have even struck its colors and surrendered in the middle of the fight, but it floated to safety amid the chaos before the Confederates could secure it.[22]

Farragut's attempt had all the makings for yet another nautical disaster. "I could see a red light in the direction of the river which illumined the clouds above," remembered Strother. "This light had been slowly drifting southward down stream and was accompanied by flashes followed by heavy booming of guns and rolling explosions." As the fire swept to each battery aboard the *Mississippi,* it caused still more explosions as ammunition cooked. As the derelict ship drew nearer, Banks was nearly sick. "The General paced to and fro in great perturbation," Stother added. "Seeing the certainty that one of our first class ships was burning, he concluded the others had been sunk and the fleet beaten." Banks also made sure that he bore no blame in the disaster. "He said the Admiral had been rash and headstrong," Strother wrote, "and that the whole matter was at his door." Banks dispatched orders for the army to retreat to Baton Rouge.[23]

As the general and his staff fretted over their next move, the *Mississippi* signaled its end. "Just then the whole western horizon was lit by a red flame, vast and widespreading," recorded Strother. "In thirty seconds the breathless silence was broken by a roar, pealing and long continued, which made the earth tremble. Then utter darkness followed. There was the ship's magazine."[24]

The next morning after a largely sleepless night for him and his troops, Banks learned the particulars of the previous night's fight. The *Mississippi* had passed into history, and four of the vessels were pummeled but still at hand. The *Hartford* and the *Albatross* were missing; a dispatch arrived later in the day announcing that, although still beyond communication, both vessels had passed Port Hudson safely. With his courage restored, Banks rescinded the retreat order and directed his army to spend the rest of the day scouting the enemy works. After several hours of skirmishing and a handful of casualties, the Union army near Port Hudson stood back. After resting for a day, Banks ordered his generals to lead the army back to Baton Rouge on March 16.[25]

USS *Mississippi* Ablaze. This dramatic painting by Edward John Packbauer (1862–1948), a German-born artist, gives a deck-level view of the action, with USS *Mississippi* clearly in trouble. It reflects the chaotic nighttime conditions of the attack and even faithfully reproduces the smoke-rings' characteristic of black-powder-era cannon.

Library of Congress.

Even if the Federals could not get at Gardner's Confederates, they could certainly play havoc with local livestock as they trudged back to camp. "The soldiers plundered without restraint, keeping up a skirmishing fire all around on pigs, poultry, and cattle," observed Strother. "The whole land was covered with blood, guts, horns, hair, and feathers." The 19th Army Corps behaved more like a shambling mob than the U.S. Army, and little order remained as Augur's, Emory's, and Grover's Divisions marched back to Baton Rouge. "The discipline was very bad," Strother continued, "mules and horses were taken everywhere, and some houses wantonly robbed."[26]

Lieutenant George H. Hepworth, a native Bostonian and Congregationalist preacher, came to Louisiana as a chaplain with the 47th Massachusetts Infantry, but he soon took an assignment to investigate and report on the condition of slaves and freedmen in the state.

Photo from his book, The Whip, How and Sword; or The Gulf-Department in '63 *(Boston: Walker, Wise, and Company, 1864).*

As the army passed, Lieutenant George H. Hepworth happened upon a distressed plantation owner. His slaves, long gone, had left the cane in the field, where it had withered in the frost; his barns and larder lay bare. The Southerner approached the officer to ask for some relief from the government. Hepworth explained that the laborers could only return as paid apprentices, and that the horses and mules now served the U.S. Army. "They are paying a heavy price for the luxury of rebellion," the Yankee confided to his notebook.[27]

"I must carry on my plantation," the Louisianan demanded, determined to make his case.

"Why must you?" the Federal responded.

"Why must I? Because if I don't, I can't pay my debts."

Hepworth deflected this argument. "Well, suppose you do not pay your debts. What of it, sir?"

"What of it?" sputtered the planter. "What of it, sir? Why I shall starve, and all my family will be reduced to poverty. Three years ago, I was worth a million; now not a picayune."

This was the opening the Massachusetts preacher needed. "Exactly," Hepworth scolded. "What, pray, does the United States Government care, whether you—who for two years have stood in opposition to it—are worth a picayune or not? If you are a beggar, put it down as the legitimate result of rebellion." Hepworth recorded the exchange in his notebook, writing "that man voted for the act of secession . . . gave five thousand dollars to the cause, and pledged his life. Now he is willing to take . . . oaths of allegiance for the sake of a few mules and teams."[28]

Union camps at Baton Rouge. The Federal army bivouacked around the Louisiana capital surrounding the town in villages of white canvas, including this collection belonging to the 3rd Brigade, Augur's Division.

G. H. Suydam Collection, Mss. 1394011, Louisiana and Lower Mississippi Valley Collection, LSU Libraries, Baton Rouge, La.

Crevasse on the Mississippi. One of the easiest ways to deny enemy troops access to a region was to cut the Mississippi levee and allow the area to flood.

Harper's Weekly, *author's collection.*

Back in Baton Rouge, Banks reflected on his army's first outing and did what he could to ensure that history would give praise and blame to the right parties. "I took lunch with the General, who seemed pleased with the manner we had escaped from what he now thought was a rash and unwise movement," Strother wrote. For his troops, the affair had been a rude introduction to soldiering. As they filed into their camps, a Louisiana thunderstorm burst upon them, flooding their campgrounds and most of their tents. "Thus endeth," reflected Strother, "the first campaign of the Army of the Gulf."[29]

While reforming his army at Baton Rouge, Banks dispatched a brigade to the west side of the Mississippi River. The men were to pass along bayous Grosse Tête and Fordoche to False River, opposite Port Hudson, to see if they could spot the two missing Union ships. What they discovered instead was that Confederate saboteurs had opened the main levee holding back the Mississippi from the lands east of the Atchafalaya in several places, and the resulting crevasse had allowed several feet of water to flood much of the country.[30]

Union scouts renewed their investigation of how to move the army overland along that sodden route to bypass Port Hudson and reach Simmesport. Guided by a Creole prisoner who had formerly resided in that region, two companies of Federal cavalry divided into several parties, each of which took a different direction through the flooded country, leaving the infantry behind. When one group discovered the Rebel steamer *Hope* in False River, loaded with six hundred barrels of molasses, they set fire to the vessel and its

Flooded road. Union troops looking for a way around Port Hudson along the west bank of the Mississippi discovered the region underwater, a change from just a few weeks before.

Rossiter Johnson, Campfires and Battlefields: An Illustrated History of the Campaigns and Conflicts of the Great Civil War *(New York: Bryan, Taylor and Company, 1894).*

contents. On a deserted plantation nearby, the horse soldiers found a barrel of gunpowder, one hundred hog-heads of sugar, a dozen barrels of molasses, and twelve hog-heads of corn. This too went up in flames. At the outlet of False River, the Yankees destroyed one thousand barrels of molasses and a machine shop at Hermitage Landing, as well as a large granary with fifteen thousand bushels of corn, a drug store and its contents, the post office, and several outbuildings. Several large columns of smoke marked the route these troops had taken.

Confirming that the route was now quite impractical for a large army, and content with their destruction, the cavalrymen turned back. With them came a column of plunder that included 100 horses, 85 mules, 100 beef cattle, 20 wagons and carts, 40 plantation wagons, $10,000 worth of copper, 183 hogsheads of sugar, and 200 barrels of molasses. They were also escorting some 375 freed slaves, among whom were 200 men who, according to the *New York Evening Post,* "came into camp at various points for protection, and were suffered to return to the brigade." No one on this expedition spotted Farragut or his ships.[31]

To even casual observers, the much-ballyhooed invasion by General Banks to southern Louisiana appeared to be a bust. Newspapermen began thinking that it was a major blunder and believed Banks to be a coward. "The grand 19th army corps has moved out of its entrenchments, looked at Port Hudson, and moved back again; this too with a terrified enemy watching and fearing an attack," wrote a correspondent for the *Springfield* (MA) *Republican.* "There is no use longer deceiving the public, for the Banks expedition is a failure. Much as I admire Gen. Banks I am forced to admit that he is not the soldier I judged him to be nor the general this department needs."[32]

The journalist could not understand why the Army of the Gulf had not stormed Port Hudson when they had the chance. "His total failure to cooperate with Admiral Farragut in the reduction of that stronghold, when the admiral was periling his whole fleet and daring a rain of iron hail, speaks in thunder tones of indecision or want of courage on the part of the general," the scribe hissed. "I suspect the obstacles to be overcome, the risks of battle and fear of defeat tended to weaken his courage and determination to assist in opening the river."[33]

The writer pined for the old days under Major General Benjamin Butler. "A large portion of the army is dissatisfied and have lost confidence in their commanding general," the reporter continued. "The universal sentiment is, let Ben Butler come back—he will let us fight. It is no venture to say that the removal of General Butler was the gravest blunder of the war. Millions have been spent on the Banks expedition, and yet Gen. Banks with 50,000 men does not hold as much territory as Gen. Butler did a year ago with less than 10,000. If the government had given Butler 20,000 more six months ago he would have taken Vicksburg and opened the river. With rebellion to crush . . . we need an iron will and arm." The indecisive days of March had left many in the Union army in a surly mood.[34]

Within days of Farragut's disappearance upstream, a soldier at Fort Butler in Donaldsonville fished a corked wine bottle out of the Mississippi River. Inside he found a note from the wiley old salt, stating that the *Hartford* and the *Albatross* were safe with only one dead and five wounded. The two ships passed the mouth of Red River and pressed on toward Vicksburg. They needed a few more ships just to be sure, and they hoped to get them from Porter—he clearly knew how to get gunboats past Vicksburg. In short order Port Hudson would starve.

5

Taylor's Offensive

"It will not be long until someone gets hurt."

Colonel James Reily
4th Texas Cavalry

The struggle along the Mississippi River had hurtled toward a showdown, and the opening rounds of the final contest appeared to be days away. Although the USS *Hartford* and the USS *Albatross* were not the most efficient vessels for patrolling against steamboats, their presence in the gap between Port Hudson and Vicksburg meant trouble for the conveyers of Confederate supplies.

When word spread that Admiral David G. Farragut had pushed on to Vicksburg instead of immediately blocking the Red River, Confederate commissary officers, including Lieutenant Colonel William A. Broadwell in Louisiana, moved quickly to transport Trans-Mississippi supplies to the east side of the Mississippi. On March 17, 1863, four paddle wheelers from Jefferson, Texas, built up steam at Alexandria to make the run to the forts. The steamboats *Charm, Texas,* and *Frolic* had already started down the river while *Falls City, Louisville, Starlight, General Hodges,* and *Nina Simms* idled near Fort DeRussy, waiting for confirmation that the Yankee ships had passed. In the following days, seven steamboats—*Louis d'Or, Trent, Drover, Red Chief, Indian No. 2, T. D. Hine,* and *J. H. Tucker*—carrying corn, salt, beef, bacon, flour, and sugar as well as live hogs and beeves, joined the steady stream of supply vessels heading toward Port Hudson and Vicksburg. Meanwhile, the *Mary T.* ran back up the Red River to take on another cargo. Droves of Texas cattle that had been kept in pastures around Opelousas and Alexandria started heading toward the river, where cowboys would help the animals swim across. One herd of seven thousand animals headed across Louisiana toward a crossing point at Rodney, near Port Gibson, Mississippi.[1]

The stockpiles grew, ton after ton, bushel after bushel, and Department of Mississippi and East Louisiana commissary officer Major George L. Gillespie's optimism blossomed. "This supply will place the commissariat in better condition, I believe, that it has ever been before," he proclaimed in a report to headquarters at Jackson. "If the Yankee ships can be prevented from cutting off our communication with . . . Texas, I have but little doubt that the great energy of Colonel Broadwell, with my own exertions here, will soon give us a supply that will enable us to stand a six months' siege." Recent history had convinced him that the Confederates must cherish every morsel.[2]

The Federals had allowed one last window of time for Confederates to supply Vicksburg and Port Hudson. To the north,

Transporting Cattle across the Mississippi. Confederates carried cattle driven in from Texas across the Mississippi in a variety of ways, including barges lashed to river steamboats as depicted here.

Harper's Weekly, *author's collection.*

Major General Ulysses S. Grant appeared to be stalled while trying various schemes to put his army on favorable ground in Mississippi. To the south, Major General Nathaniel P. Banks appeared to be stymied at Baton Rouge and snarled in the log-chocked bayous along the eastern margins of the Atchafalaya Basin.

Nevertheless, the Confederates knew that either one of these two Federal armies might soon find a solution to its dilemma and that Farragut would not allow the Red River to remain open indefinitely. The outcome of the Mississippi Valley Campaign seemed foregone if the Confederates allowed their enemies time to consider the challenges of besieging both forts. Quick action might prevent this dire outcome.

Lieutenant General Edmund Kirby Smith, having completed his tour of Arkansas, was returning to Alexandria to render his opinion on how to proceed, and strategists working in the Trans-Mississippi for the past seven months under trying circumstances

Cattle Swimming. Confederate drovers swam herds across the Mississippi as well.

Scribner's Magazine, *author's collection.*

awaited his pronouncements. Major General Richard Taylor, a onetime protégé of General Thomas J. "Stonewall" Jackson and an aggressive warrior in his own right, had already formed a plan. No matter what Kirby Smith declared, Taylor intended to take the offensive. He would, as Jefferson Davis had asked him, "baffle the enemy in his designs on the Mississippi Valley." For months the dysfunctional Department of the Trans-Mississippi had muddled along without systematic communications among district commands, and the languid leadership of General Theophilus Holmes had left Taylor largely on his own. Lieutenant General John C. Pemberton had been little help. Now rumors indicated that the newcomer—Kirby Smith—seemed as smitten with Arkansas as his predecessor had been.[3]

Taylor, blessed with a surfeit of initiative, was used to doing much with little, and he had accomplished a great deal in the absence of direction—or interference—from his superiors. The commander of West Louisiana was ready for bolder action. He remembered that his father, General Zachary Taylor, had turned back a Mexican army of fourteen thousand with fewer than six thousand American volunteers, backed by good artillery, at the mountain pass of Buena Vista. The son knew he could equal that feat, for Banks was certainly inferior to General Antonio López de Santa Anna, and the constricted avenues of Southwest Louisiana created conditions similar to the narrows of *La Angostura* in 1847 and the Shenandoah valley in 1862. Taylor had studied one campaign at his father's table and had watched the other from his horse's back. Now he was ready for the biggest test of his life.

The sharpest spears in Taylor's arsenal were the inelegantly remodeled steamboats of his ever-growing navy. His little flotilla, moored in the Red River, included the ram *Queen of the West* and its unarmed tender the *Nina Simms.* The ice breaker-turned-ironclad-slayer *Webb* bolstered this squadron but was undergoing repairs at Alexandria. Rebel shipwrights and carpenters at Washington,

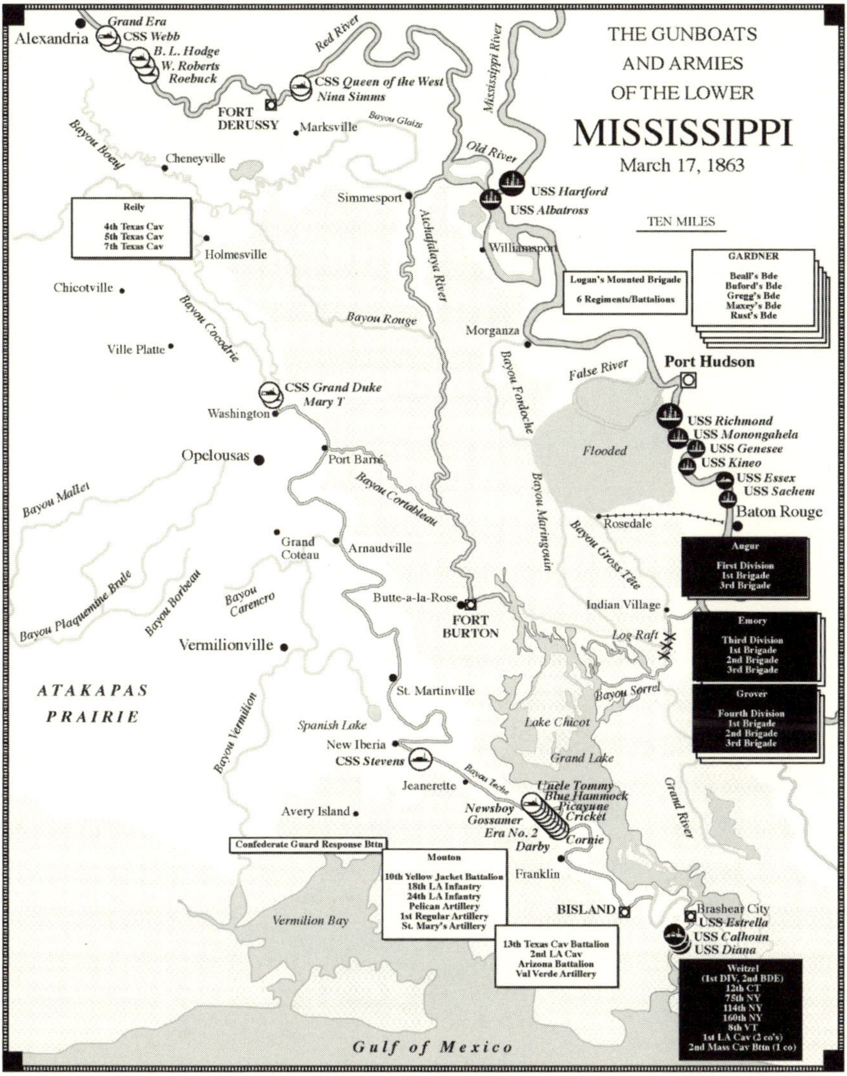

Louisiana, were converting the lightly gunned *Grand Duke* and the *Mary T.* into cottonclad fighting platforms, much like the victorious vessels at Galveston. The Southern craftsmen "had fitted these boats for the purpose of ramming and sinking the enemy, or capturing them with a large force of shooters," wrote Lieutenant Edward T. King, "the cabins being taken off and her machinery and the upper works being well protected by cotton bales solidly encased in wooden boxes." Other vessels available for carrying wood to fuel the fleet included the *B. L. Hodge,* the *Roebuck,* and the *W. Roberts.* Taylor's commodore was Captain Edward W. Fuller, who was still recovering from his January gunshot wounds on the *Cotton.*[4]

Further down on Bayou Teche, Taylor's squadron was also growing. He had the small unarmed side-wheelers *Cricket, Cornie, Blue Hammock, Picayune, Darby,* and *Uncle Tommy,* and the larger sternwheelers *Newsboy, Gossamer,* and *Era No. 2.* Two miles below New Iberia at the Olivier plantation, Orange Grove, crews worked steadily to transform the cottonclad gunboat *Hart* into the ironclad CSS *Stevens,* named for Lieutenant Henry Kennedy Stevens, the former executive officer of the CSS *Arkansas* who had been killed on board the *Cotton* in January. When finished *Stevens* would be a dangerous boat, boasting 32-pounders fore and aft, and a 24-pounder in each broadside, all protected by three-inch railroad iron. She would probably equal anything else afloat in Berwick Bay.[5]

Franklin, on Bayou Teche. Alfred R. Waud, famous Civil War-era illustrator for publications including the *New York Illustrated News* and *Harper's Weekly,* provided iconic images of the war in Virginia and Pennsylvania. After the war he spent much of his time touring other battlefields. He sketched the waterfront of Franklin, Louisiana, about 1871. The artist depicted the construction of a bayou steamboat, giving an idea of what techniques might have been employed as Taylor converted similar vessels into gunboats in early 1863. The St. Mary's Parish courthouse is visible in the left background.

The Historic New Orleans Collection, accession no. 1965.45 i, ii.

Taylor's longer term prospects looked promising. Confederate Navy lieutenant Jonathan H. Carter oversaw the development of a navy yard in Shreveport, where work was underway on a new ironclad ram, the CSS *Missouri,* as well as a half-dozen submarines along a design that would be made famous by the CSS *Hunley* at Charleston. Crews were already dismantling the cottonclad *Grand Era* to cannibalize its engine and machinery for these projects. When these warcraft became available, Taylor's little navy might be able to successfully slug it out with the heaviest Union warships downriver.[6]

Even though the majority of Taylor's vessels were lightly armed compared to those of their Union opponents, Major General John Bankhead Magruder had proven at Galveston that riflemen could do great service as boarders and that even the most powerful ships could be taken by humble yet daring cottonclads. The Federals understood this threat, and rumors of just such an attempt began to surface. In late February, when an informer came into Union lines near Plaquemine with news of Rebel plans, he warned of more ship-borne audacity. "Boarding steamers or other naval vessels was

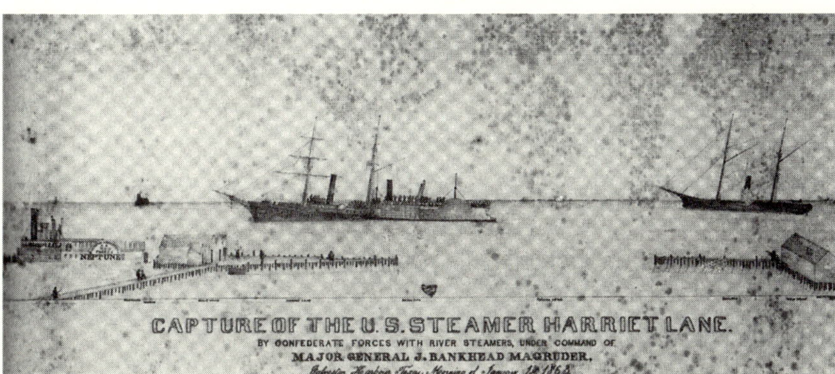

CSS *Bayou City* ramming the USS *Harriet Lane*. The Battle of Galveston and the success of "cottonclad" gunboats loaded with riflemen had a profound influence on Major General Richard Taylor's plans for an offensive against the Federals in Louisiana. The swamped CSS *Neptune,* also pictured, suggested some of the tactic's limitations.

George W. Grover Papers, Galveston and Texas History Center, Rosenberg Library.

the mode to be adopted by the Confederates," he warned, "and that before many weeks we should most certainly hear of more losses." Taylor likely had a boarding in mind when he had ordered the attacking flotilla hunting the *Indianola* to include the cotton-clads loaded with troops.[7]

Taylor's navy was already strong enough to make one or two more jabs at the enemy. Perhaps with enough luck and the element of surprise, he might be able to take on the *Hartford* and the *Albatross* when they returned to the mouth of the Red River. Then, he reasoned, the *Webb* and the *Queen of the West* could run down the Atchafalaya and rendezvous with the rest of his navy. Aided by the timely arrival of the Red River flotilla, Taylor's gunboats and transports on Bayou Teche, led by the CSS *Stevens, Mary T.,* and *Grand Duke,* would carry troops as boarders and conduct a land and river assault on Brigadier General Godfrey Weitzel's base at Brashear City.[8]

Within a few weeks, Taylor believed, he would finally be able to launch a coordinated attack that would not only keep open the supply lines to Port Hudson and Vicksburg but also crush the Union army in the Lafourche District. By mid-April, no later than May certainly, his army would be gazing across the Mississippi at the spires of New Orleans. Banks—and Farragut—would leave or at least fall back for a showdown in the Crescent City.

Repairs to Taylor's best boats after the bruising *Indianola* fight progressed slowly, however, and a sufficient number of reliable boarding crews would be difficult to find. A stroke of good fortune had returned the men of the Crescent Artillery to Taylor's district. In 1862 these New Orleans artillerists had served as the crew of the CSS *Louisiana* during Farragut's run past the lower forts, and they had surrendered when Forts Jackson and St. Philip fell. Once paroled and exchanged, they had reorganized in Mississippi before coming across the river to Taylor. The *Queen of the West* had been brought down by a shot from a gun they served, and they had also worked the guns of the *Webb* against the *Indianola*. The men of the Crescent Artillery were perhaps the best troops available for the job Taylor planned, but they numbered fewer than fifty in number.

Taylor's other soldiers might volunteer to serve as boarders for an attack against Union gunboats, but Brigadier General Alfred Mouton's Louisiana infantry regiments—heavily restocked with conscripts—had no experience in the matter, and their reliability under such hazardous conditions might be questionable. Taylor needed men who would show the pluck of the Texans at Galveston. Fortunately for his ambitions, the horse marines that had captured the *Harriet Lane* had finally started toward Louisiana.

The Texas vanguard began arriving in the Alexandria vicinity on March 17. General Henry Hopkins Sibley's Texans had entered Louisiana along three routes. At the end of January the first section, four companies of the 4th Texas Cavalry, had moved away from its camps near Hempstead and marched through Nacogdoches, Texas, before heading eastward to Louisiana. The two other groupings from that regiment—three companies each—staggered their arrivals

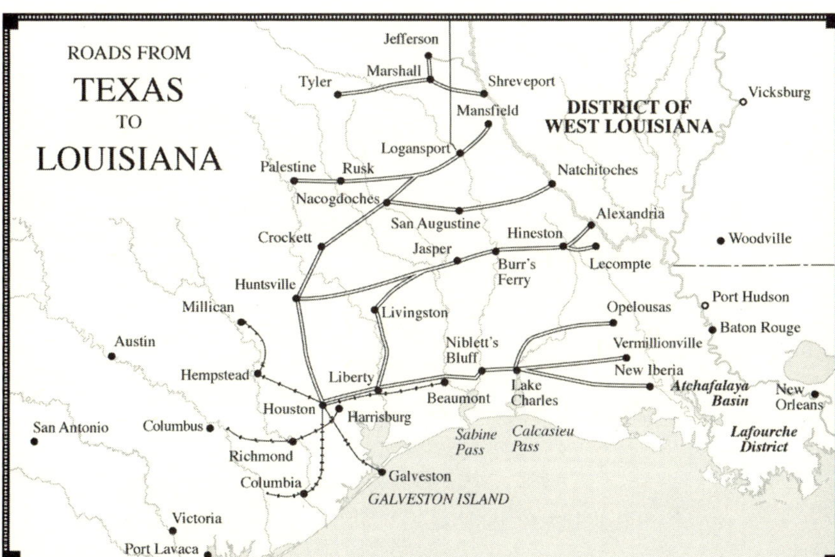

over a month, skirting Alexandria then marching down the Bayou Boeuf Road to Cheneyville. Private Samuel Amsler, in the rear of the 4th Texas Cavalry, had passed through Crockett before writing in German at Jasper that "our destination is now Opelousas." His travels had been educational: "I never had any idea of the amount of pine in Eastern Texas until now." The 5th Texas rode in two battalions a week apart and reunited at Natchitoches before moving south again. The 7th Texas took a southerly route and arrived at Cheneyville from the west. For nearly a month the brigade strung itself out over hundreds of miles, moving in staggered intervals as transportation and supplies became available.[9]

Colonel James Reily, commander of the 4th Texas Cavalry married into the family of Henry Clay, was an officer in the army of the Republic of Texas, one-time law partner to Thomas Jefferson Rusk, a diplomat to Russia, and well-connected Houston politician before the war. He was wealthy, dashing, and had a charming wife and daughter. *Author's collection.*

Colonel James Reily and his staff passed along and ahead of these columns en route, and preceded it to a reunion with General Sibley near New Iberia, where he had been for the last month. Shortly after arriving in the region, Reily wrote the editor of the *Houston Tri-Weekly Telegraph,* "Since our arrival, a new spirit has been infused in the department. The defensive policy has been abandoned. It will not be long until someone gets hurt. We trust to give a good account of ourselves."[10]

The trip had not been easy. Thousands of hooves and the butcher-knife tires of hundreds of wagons had churned the narrow roads into dust, and deluges had converted the dirt into mud. "With the exception of rain, mud, and high water we had comparatively a 'good time,'" wrote Private William Randolph Howell of Company C, 5th Texas Cavalry. "Several nights our tent was flooded . . . and frequently we crossed swimming streams."[11]

To Howell, the ride from East Texas into western Louisiana felt monotonous. "We found nothing but a huge body of pines woods, with an occasional fertile section situated on a pretty little stream," he wrote. When the troops finally made the descent into the valley of the Red River, many marveled at their new surroundings. "I never have in any country seen anything equal to the taste and elegance displayed by the wealthy of some portion of the state in beautiful dwellings, flower garden hedges, and in the style and arrangement of negro cabins," remarked Howell. "On nearly every place can be seen a large sugar mill filled almost with sugar and syrup and you must know we soldiers were given access to as much as we could devour."[12]

Private John W. Watkins, Company B, 5th Texas Cavalry, came from Marlin in Falls County. He missed the campaign in New Mexico but would get his share of combat in Louisiana.

Martha Hartzog, Austin, Texas.

As Sibley's Brigade trundled through East Texas, the men faced the realities of soldiering among friends and strangers. Some faithfully executed otherwise obnoxious duties. "I can write you but a short letter this time," wrote Private John W. Watkins of Company B, 5th Texas Cavalry, to his wife. He was a clerk from Waco, and his recordkeeping skills had landed him the acting role of sergeant major for the company. "I have to detail a court martial for the trial of one of our boys for the disgraceful offence of having illegal intercourse with a mule."[13]

Others enjoyed sentimental pursuits and the hospitality of the towns through which they passed. "Went to the concert today and saw all the young ladies of Crockett," wrote Sergeant Alfred B. Petticolas of Company C, 4th Texas Cavalry. The performance included a living tableau. "The girls [represented] the various states of the Confederacy in various attitudes," the sergeant continued. "For instance, Texas had a six-shooter, Mississippi was loading her musket, Louisiana had on black, one hand held a handkerchief and both were uplifted in a supplicating attitude. Maryland was in chains and dressed in mourning. South Carolina had a gun leveled." The evening ended with various vocal performances, he wrote. "The singing was rather monotonous—they seemed determined to make up in quantity what they lacked in quality."[14]

Not everyone in East Texas was as patriotic or as glad to see the troops passing their way, especially those who lived on isolated homesteads in the piney woods. Sibley's Brigade had a voracious appetite, and families along its line of march often found themselves impoverished after it had passed. At cabin after cabin where he tried to buy provisions for his regiment, Sergeant Petticolas met with suspicion and fear. "It is really distressing to see how afraid the citizens are of the soldierly," he wrote. "They frequently hid their bacon and their corn and everything eatable for man or beast." The conscription act had also made these residents wary. When they saw the troops coming up the road, many took to the woods "for fear that they will be pressed."[15]

For many of the Texas Confederates, the Sabine River was their Rubicon. "We crossed the border this morning and are now on the Louisiana side of the river," wrote Sergeant Ferdinand Boesel, a German in Company G, 4th Texas Cavalry, on March 19. "With longing we look to the opposite, beloved Texas bank. . . . Who knows if we will ever see that dearest soil again?" Sergeant Petticolas had a similar rumination. "I thought, too of my past, about the Merciful Providence that had shielded me from danger thus far, upon my vicissitudes since the war began, and while I thought I gazed upon the rolling river that marks one boundary of the state of my adoption, and upon the Louisiana forest trees upon the other." He undoubtedly remembered his many adventures in New Mexico: his close brush with disaster at Glorieta Pass, his suffering mule at Val Verde, his friend Bill Onderdonk getting his tongue shot off, the slow agonizing death of young Abe Hanna along the Santa Fe Trail, and the retreat through the mountains. "I sat for a good while on the banks . . . reflecting on the war, its probable duration and whether or not I would live to recross the Sabine," he scribbled in his journal, adding "and how many of us will be left . . . to manure the soil of Louisiana."[16]

Colonel Tom Green, 5th Texas Cavalry, was a veteran of the Battle of San Jacinto, the Battle of Monterrey, and several fights with Comanches while serving as a Texas Ranger. During the Civil War, he performed bravely in the New Mexico Campaign, but his reputation suffered because of speculation that he was a drunk. He helped repair his image by behaving boldly at the Battle of Galveston.

Author's collection.

As these reinforcements arrived, Colonel Tom Green left Major Denman Shannon in charge of his regiment, which was gathering at Natchitoches. The colonel dashed ahead to General Taylor's headquarters seeking guns and orders, and his troops followed at a more leisurely pace. Rumors buzzed through the column that the Texans might be needed for special duty. "There is a gunboat expedition fitting out at Alexandria, and [they] are calling for volunteers to man it," wrote Watkins on March 20. "Colonel Green is there now and I have no doubt has offered himself and his regiment for that service. If so we will all try another water fight and I can only hope we may be as successful as we were before."[17]

The soldier's instincts proved correct. Green sent orders detailing Major Shannon and 120 men for duty aboard the *Webb.* Watkins, still technically a private, saw his sergeant major duties expanded to include acting adjutant general for the detachment. When the detachment arrived at Alexandria, they found the gunboat undergoing repairs and laid up until mid- to late April, by most estimates. Confederate officers instead hustled the Texans to Fort DeRussy to defend that point while awaiting the *Webb*'s arrival. They joined the men of the 11th Louisiana Battalion, the Bull Battery, and the Crescent Artillery, as well as the 150 reluctant volunteers of the 1st Louisiana State Battalion.

Here the soldiers learned the particulars of their mission: two Federal ships had made it past Port Hudson and needed to be captured. "Our officers are fixing up the *Webb* and the *Grand Duke* for the purpose of capturing the Yankee boats," Watkins wrote. Having been damaged in the attack on the *Indianola,* the *Webb*'s bow was now being reinforced. Rebel planners needed the ram to be capable of staving in the sides of a large ship like the *Hartford.* Nearby troops from the 7th Texas waited for their turn aboard the *Grand Duke.*[18]

At Fort DeRussy Watkins fretted at the delay and feared that the calendar was against them. "Before we can get our boats ready the Yankees will either have more boats between our forts," he prophesized, "or will try to run those they have in here."[19]

The majority of Sibley's Brigade turned south, away from the Red River and toward New Iberia, and detachments left almost daily during the last week of March. As Sibley's men made their way deeper into Acadiana, they discovered an environment unlike any they had seen in the war so far. Much of the population spoke patois

French. Sugarcane fields, with two-foot-deep furrows, covered the countryside. Ancient oaks lined the roads, with Spanish moss flowing in long beards from their branches. Unlike New Mexico and most of Texas, here water was abundant, and knotty cypress trees towered above numerous black swamps. Even cemeteries appeared different, with large tombs resting above ground because of the high water table. To many of the Texans, Louisiana seemed like a foreign country.

Along the route, many Louisiana citizens showed great enthusiasm for the reluctant Texan reinforcements. "The people met us with open arms," wrote Private Henry Wright of Company F, 4th Texas. "In every town we passed through, they lined the streets and greeted us with waving flags and handkerchiefs. Many of them carried lunches and baskets of flowers which they lavishly bestowed upon all who wished for them." The road-weary Texans, unhappy they were even in the state, spurned much of the hospitality. "A great many of our men, who had gone through an arduous campaign the year before and others who had been drawn from their homes with great reluctance paid but little attention to the flowery offerings," noted the soldier. "But when lemonade and cakes appeared on the program, they were ready enough to take an active interests."[20]

Despite the occasional warm reception, many of the Texans distrusted the Cajun population of the countryside. "I suppose you would like to hear something about the citizens of this frog eating country," Watkins wrote home from Fort DeRussy. "Nine out of ten are French and speak the French language, and I believe that a majority of them are our enemies." Private Thomas Reade Roots of the 4th Texas echoed this sentiment, writing, "The Louisianans don't like Texans, but prayed for a few more when they found the Yankees coming."[21]

Sibley's Texans feared the Louisiana climate as well. "We are going into a very sickly country and to one where there will be a great deal of hard fighting," wrote Howell to his sweetheart. "It is very certain many of us will never again see Texas if we remain among those Louisiana swamps for any length of time. . . . We can only hope that the move is for the good of our glorious Confederacy." Private Theophilus Noel of Company A, 4th Texas Cavalry, had bad memories of his first Louisiana bivouac. "Think of our boggy, water camp ground," he wrote. "Doing so bring[s] on rheumatic pains."[22]

Before these reinforcements could be used against the enemy, Taylor and his officers first had to reequip the Texas brigade and turn it into an efficient military organization. The troops owned fine horses but had arrived with few other military assets. Half of the Texans reached New Iberia unarmed while the balance carried inadequate weapons; ordnance officers labored to eliminate the deficiency. Sibley's men quickly emptied the stocks of small arms at the New Iberia arsenal. Taylor, fretting over the lack of discipline within the Texans' ranks, reestablished brigade routines with frequent drills and dress parades.[23]

The government provided their weapons, but the individual Texans helped themselves to local lagniappe—a "little something extra"—from the surrounding country. Blackberries abounded. "The vines . . . ran up in the bushes and trees so that one could sit on a horse and gather all you wished," wrote one private. "So many of the men became sick with diarrhea that the doctors objected." Nearby plantations also provided delicacies to supplement the government fare of beef and corn bread. "Sugar was so plentiful that hundreds of hogsheads were left exposed to the weather," noted one Rebel. "When a man wanted any, he would break in the head of one, shovel out a sack full and go on his way leaving the rest to be wasted." Local rum also made its way into the brigade mess, and soldiers quaffed cups of the potent elixir as they gambled on horse races. "Green Louisiana rum, made of sour molasses," Noel noted, "warranted two doses to make a man fight his mother-in-law's remembrance."[24]

Brigadier General Alfred Mouton, son of Governor Alexandre Mouton, graduated from West Point in 1850 and was a classmate of Union Brigadier General Cuvier Grover. Mouton did not stay long in the army and returned to southwest Louisiana where he tended his family's business affairs. When the war came, Alfred received a colonel's commission to lead the 18th Louisiana Infantry. Grievously wounded at the Battle of Shiloh, he returned home to Lafayette to recuperate. He earned promotion to brigadier general and did his best to keep the Federals out of the sugar parishes but eventually gave up the Lafourche County and fell back to positions on Bayou Teche.

Alexandre Mouton House Museum, Lafayette, La.

Taylor needed to mold his two small Rebel armies into one cohesive fighting force capable of roughing up Banks's army. Brigadier General Mouton, Taylor's trusted subordinate in the Lafourche Campaign the previous year, had led his practically autonomous army of nearly two thousand veterans since August 1862. The arriving mounted command of General Sibley had also been an autonomous army when it fought through New Mexico the previous year. Both of these Rebel commands had gained expertise in independent action but had little experience in cooperative enterprises. Now the men would have to trust each other; the officers would have to cooperate.[25]

Their living arrangements did not help the effort to blend the armies. Soldiers of the two Confederate brigades rarely interacted with each other in their camps. The organizations bivouacked nearly ten miles apart, with the Texans camping near Centerville and Mouton's men at the Bisland fortifications, closer to the Federals at Brashear City. As the Texans drilled and paraded and dined on rum, blackberries, and sugar, the officers from the Louisiana regiments passed by their camps on their way to fashionable dances at Madame Porter's impressive plantation home on the Irish Bend of Bayou Teche. "All the natives had been quartered in the barns and sugar houses," Noel bellyached, "while we poor private solider[s], trash from Texas, were sent out in the swamps."[26]

Brigadier General Henry Hopkins Sibley was a native of Natchitoches, Louisiana, but descended from colonial Massachusetts Bay settlers. He made the army his home after graduation from West Point in 1838, serving in the Seminole War, the Mexican War, and on the Texas and New Mexico frontier. The conical "Sibley Tent" was his invention, patterned after Comanche teepees. When the war came Sibley took a brigadier's commission, led the disastrous New Mexico Campaign, and then defended himself against charges of dereliction. He went to Louisiana to serve under Taylor but did not always agree with his boss. *Library of Congress.*

Like the men they led, Sibley and Mouton differed greatly, although both had been born in Louisiana and trained at West Point. Sibley was married to a New Yorker and was a Mexican War veteran, recognized for dash and bravery. On the plains of Texas, Sibley had turned inventor, styling a new military tent after Comanche teepees. The Confederacy had made him one of its earliest generals because of his varied military record. Most importantly, Taylor had named Sibley commander of forces east of the Atchafalaya in late 1862, and he had served capably from his base at Rosedale against Federal probes and later against the gunboat incursions. Sibley outranked Mouton. With the levees on bank opposite Port Hudson and the surrounding country flooded, Sibley and his command were free to move to the Teche to join the growing army. Taylor named him commander of forces south of Red River in anticipation of the coming campaign. Colonel Reily continued to lead the Texas brigade.

Mouton and Sibley's military reputations and social status also differed. During the war, General Sibley had developed a reputation for his strong personality, his heavy drinking, and his poor conduct of the New Mexico campaign. Even so, Private Noel of the 4th Texas described this grizzled leader as a "high-minded, noble, valorous, and gifted officer." He was a professional soldier and the grandson of the famous explorer and naturalist Dr. John Sibley, who raised him, but whose exploits had not translated into family wealth. Sibley was also largely without political connections.[27]

Mouton, by contrast, had always lived in privilege and had left the old army just months after finishing his education at West Point. The thirty-two-year-old had grown up on the banks of Bayou Vermilion at *Ile Copal,* his family's mansion, and he had admired and idolized his father, who served as one of Louisiana's senators and as its governor. Born the son of planters and politicians, Mouton was not destined to be an anonymous and underpaid Indian fighter. Instead, he had returned home to a plantation of his own, carved from his father's estate, and he married and amassed his own fortune while he amused himself by raising racehorses. His had also watched with interest as his father led the Louisiana Secession Convention in 1861.[28]

There were other differences between the commanders besides pedigree. Sibley was from Natchitoches, in upcountry Louisiana. Mouton was Acadian, a gentleman, and reserved by nature. He tended to obey orders when issued and did not challenge Taylor's plans or reasoning. Sibley, on the other hand, freely offered his opinions to his superior.

Not surprisingly, Sibley and Taylor soon soured on one another. Sibley declared that the Confederate position endorsed by Taylor at

Bisland and held for half a year was patently indefensible. While the fortified line took advantage of the narrowest strip of land along lower Bayou Teche and allowed a small force to block a larger one, Sibley argued that the Federals could turn the position from Grand Lake. He believed a better location might be where Bayou Teche diverged from the main roads at New Iberia. An earthwork in the vicinity of Spanish Lake might serve the same purpose of "channeling" the enemy but also allow the Rebels a line of retreat. This idea of Sibley's was a purely defensive strategy that would leave St. Mary's Parish susceptible to Federal raids, so it was unacceptable for political reasons and because it did not suit Taylor's temperament. The commander of the District of West Louisiana ignored Sibley and stuck to his original plan, with a forward position at the Bisland fortifications, perfect for launching his land and bayou offensive to regain the lost LaFourche District. This crack in command harmony promised ill for the future.

Oblivious to the friction between Sibley and Taylor, Colonel Green led his portion of the 5th Texas Cavalry through Franklin, Louisiana, anticipating an imminent advance toward the enemy. Before Banks could concentrate his army—which Taylor believed was scattered from Baton Rouge to New Orleans, and from Bayou Grosse Tête to Berwick Bay—the Confederates hoped to retake Brashear City, flank the 19th Army Corps, and move back into the LaFourche District. Taylor needed all of his forces as far forward as possible in preparation for his offensive, and hurried forward as many as possible.[29]

Mouton had been at Bisland for four months. When the Federals chased him out of the LaFourche District and into the Bayou Teche region the previous November, he had planned to hold the Teche region as long as possible, and his Confederates had spent those intervening months fortifying their position. Engineers had designed a redoubt on the bayou's south bank, five miles upstream from its junction with the Atchafalaya at Pattersonville. Dubbed

Fort Bisland—the nearby Confederate encampment sat upon Thomas Bisland's Fairfax Plantation—the redoubt boasted two 24-pounders that commanded the bayou. Soldiers and slaves also built a line of works that extended one thousand yards away from the Teche with the ends anchored in the surrounding swamps. The deep furrows and unharvested sugar cane in front of the works provided further obstacles to advancing enemy infantry.[30]

Taylor considered Mouton's Louisiana infantry to be the most reliable part of his command. In the course of its faithful service, this little army had indeed endured much. Two of Mouton's Louisiana units, the 18th Creole Infantry and the 24th Crescent Infantry, first smelled gun smoke at Shiloh. Three additional foot units— Lieutenant Colonel Valsin Fournet's 10th Louisiana "Yellow Jacket" Battalion, Colonel Henry Gray's 28th Louisiana Infantry, and the 12th Louisiana Confederate Guards Response Battalion at Avery Island encompassed the whole of Taylor's infantry. Supporting these understrength regiments and battalions were the shotgun-wielding partisans of Colonel William G. Vincent's 2nd Louisiana Cavalry, experienced in scouting and skirmishing.

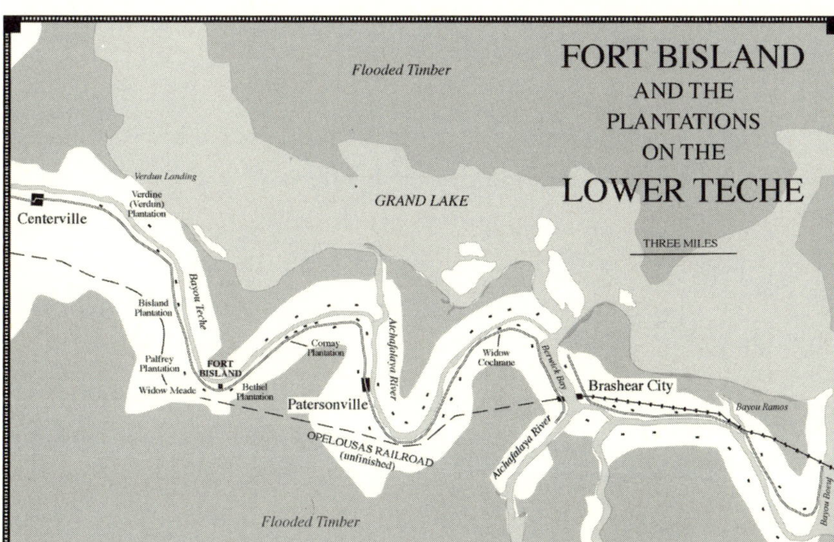

Three artillery batteries, Captain Oliver J. Semmes's 1st Regulars, Captain Florian Cornay's *St. Mary's* Cannoneers, and Captain Thomas Faries's Pelican Artillery, had also seen combat. Conscripts or veterans, willing or reluctant, these men were Louisianans and must surely be capable of fighting for their homes.[31]

By contrast, Sibley's three regiments, in the course of their far different military career, had displayed a number of peculiar contradictions. They had fared badly in New Mexico—the brigade had almost disintegrated—but the exhausted, prideful men brought by hand five captured cannon through the arid mountains back to Texas. These units arrived mounted and carried cavalry designations, yet everyone knew they would fight dismounted as infantry. If fortune turned against them here, as it had in New Mexico, would these strangers abandon Louisiana to the invader?[32]

Evidence suggested they would not as there were other Texans at hand that had already bled on behalf of the Pelican State. Sibley's men joined Colonel Edwin Waller's 13th Texas Cavalry Battalion and would operate and be associated with this command through most of the war. In addition, they would be reunited with the only trophies of the New Mexico adventure—the guns of the Val Verde Battery, already in Louisiana for the previous three months. There were other men from west of the Sabine River operating along the bayous. The skilled partisans of Lieutenant Colonel Philemon Herbert's Arizona Battalion passed for Texans, even though most of these scapegraces hailed most recently from Tucson and Mesilla. They had served with Sibley from Rosedale the previous winter; now these troops were closest yet to the enemy, and they picketed the no-man's land between Pattersonville and Berwick Bay.

Taylor both admired and disparaged these newcomers. He described the Texas officers as "bold and enterprising" and the rank and file as "hardy frontiersmen, excellent riders, and skilled riflemen . . . fearless and self-reliant." They lacked any form of discipline, however. The Texans "discharged their duty as they liked and when they liked," he wrote. "On a march they wandered about at will, as they did about camp, and could be kept together only when a fight was impending. When their arms were injured by service or neglect, they threw them away, expecting to be supplied with others. Yet with these faults, they were admirable fighters."[33]

While Taylor gathered his army and navy, the citizens of Louisiana caught up in the war tried to make the best plans that they could. Clearly the war would continue on for months, perhaps years, and they needed to prepare for their futures. In Alexandria, James Hewitt kissed his wife goodbye and decided to make a risky journey into the Federal-held Lafourche District to salvage what he could of his private property at his home near Donaldsonville, Crescent Plantation. He was a New Yorker, married to a Kentuckian—a cousin of Major General Grant—and his home had remained intact so far. The Confederates had seized his boats for the public good, and he had supplied food and supplies at his own expense for the Rebels at Port Hudson. Hewitt knew that before long U.S. agents would seize his house, free his slaves, and declare him an enemy of the government.[34]

He had to be stealthy. The sugar planter approached his home from the rear, hoping to enter unseen. Once he was back on familiar ground, Hewitt assembled his more than one hundred hands. "He . . . told them that when the Federals took possession of the place they would be given their freedom," Clarissa Hewitt wrote in her diary. "If they wanted to go with him, he would take them to Texas where he would give them work and treat as he had always done, but they would still be slaves." The choice divided the assembly. Men with families, women with children, the very old and the very young all decided to go with Hewitt. Groups collected all the wagons, draft animals, and harnesses they could and assembled a refugee train that he could lead around Donaldsonville toward Bayou Grosse Tête, behind Plaquemine and Bayou Goula to Rosedale and

Morgnaza beyond. Only fifteen half-grown boys remained on the place. Clarissa described the evacuation: "It is a strange sight to see these trains of wagons and negroes going through the country often with only one member of their master's family, and not infrequently there would be only a woman . . . seeking safety wherever she could find it. In most cases it was in Texas."[35]

6

USS *Diana*

"She was a terror to all the region."

Captain Joseph C. Terrell
13th Texas Cavalry Battalion

On the afternoon of March 20, 1863, a spy made his way across Berwick Bay and into the Union camps at Brashear City. He had wandered amongst the Confederates, posing as a mentally challenged man, until finally they shooed him away as simply too ignorant to press into service, telling him to "apply to the Yankees, who needed just such men as himself." He had done just that, rowing across Berwick Bay to report a fascinating tale to Brigadier General Godfrey Weitzel. Taylor, it appeared, planned to reinvade the Lafourche country with a combined force of infantry, cavalry, artillery, and a powerful combination of gunboats. The blow could fall at any time. If this man could be believed, the Rebels would bring to bear twice as many troops, cannon, and boats as the Federals had at hand.

Weitzel, feeling exposed and vulnerable in his outpost at Brashear City, acted upon this new intelligence immediately. "There is no question that [the spy's] timely arrival has saved the entire brigade from annihilation," wrote Corporal Rufus Kinsley, Company F, 8th Vermont. After dark, crews dismantled their heavy guns and loaded them and the regimental supplies and equipment onto 115 train cars. The next morning, March 21, Weitzel redeployed his entire command at the rail crossing of Bayou Boeuf, a sluggish stream that defined the eastern margin of Tiger Island, putting nearly ten miles between his infantry and Brashear City. "We were here," Kinsley continued from these new camps, "waiting with open arms to receive a rebel flotilla which is on its way hither from Red River . . . attacking us in the rear at Brashear City, while the forces on Teche were to engage us in front." With luck, Weitzel's move would cause Taylor to swing at thin air.[1]

Both sides now raced for the strategic initiative with the fate of lower Louisiana, and perhaps control of the Mississippi in the balance. The first to launch its offensive might very well win the round in Louisiana. Weitzel, a Union officer familiar with the region, had already spent months trying to destroy Brigadier General Alfred Mouton's army. He commanded some of the Federal regiments that had been in southern Louisiana the longest. On several occasions his men had skirmished with the meager Rebel forces in the Lafourche District before driving them out the previous October. Since that time, Union sympathizers among Louisiana's steamboat men had taught gunboat captains the area's intricate web of waterways and had kept Weitzel abreast of the movements of Major General Richard Taylor's army and the number of vessels being built, modified, or commandeered. Recent news was troublesome: these bayou boat men corroborated the spy's report. The Rebels were plotting a major offensive.

Weitzel knew his position would be the logical target. The Cincinnati German had already proposed that the 19th Army Corps, instead of operating close to Port Hudson, should launch a wide raid west of the Atchafalaya River. His sources of intelligence suggested that the bulk of Major General Nathaniel P. Banks's Federals should concentrate at Brashear City, send one column up Bayou Teche to pin the Southerners under Brigadier General

Brigadier General Godfrey Weitzel was born in Germany, raised in Cincinnati, and graduated second in his West Point class of 1855, showing great promise as an engineer. His first assignment was to improve the defenses of New Orleans. At the outbreak of the Civil War, Weitzel was in Washington D.C., and served as part of President Abraham Lincoln's bodyguard during the inauguration. He came to Louisiana with Major General Benjamin Butler and soon grew to be his most trusted field commander clearing the Lafourche parishes of Confederate forces in the fall of 1862.

Library of Congress.

Mouton at Bisland while another Union column, embarked on transports, could bypass the Confederate position by traveling up the Atchafalaya and Grand Lake—a variation of Banks's intended move in February. But this time, Weitzel wanted to use every resource in the Army of the Gulf's inventory and attack with overwhelming strength. He believed that a powerful amphibious expedition, landing in the vicinity of Franklin some twelve miles to the rear, would be able to block the Rebel line of retreat and fight off any counterattacks, whether by the oft-mentioned General Henry Hopkins Sibley or by any other troops Taylor might have at hand. The Confederate army in Louisiana, Weitzel believed, could be destroyed.[2]

General Banks recognized the merit of Weitzel's plan. He was tired of flailing away at Port Hudson from the south, and like his soldiers, he could read the newspaper accounts that ridiculed the army's efforts so far. Banks needed a victory, so he prepared for what would be the greatest gamble facing his army and, if successful, the greatest coup of his career. Eager to follow the new plan, Banks arranged to leave a strong garrison in New Orleans and a holding force at Baton Rouge before he ordered the remaining troops to concentrate at Brashear City on Berwick Bay. Of his four divisions, two and a half would move to Bayou Teche.[3]

Major General Henry W. Halleck was the general in chief of all Union armies. Credited with being a superb organizer, planner, and administrator, he lacked personal creativity and failed to appreciate it in his subordinates.

Library of Congress.

The stakes were high. An approach through the heart of Taylor's command would accomplish three objectives. First, Banks's army would fight their way up Bayou Teche and then march to Opelousas, destroying Taylor's army in the process and thereby removing it as a threat to Union lines of communication during operations on the Mississippi River. Second, the Federals would also pinch off several enemy overland supply routes. Third, once Taylor disappeared, Banks could either cooperate with Major General Ulysses S. Grant against Vicksburg or conduct his own operation against Brigadier General Franklin Gardner at Port Hudson.

Banks had some uninvited help as he planned this bold campaign. Brigadier General Daniel Ullmann was en route to New Orleans with orders from Major General Henry W. Halleck to raise a brigade of four black regiments. Although Banks had been supportive of the effort to recruit black men, he was inclined to reestablish the plantation labor system first. Ullmann, however, carried a blanket authority to enlist black men for the army by almost any means. Banks was concerned that the brunt of Ullmann's recruitment would be done in pacified areas—not from among the newly freed

Brigadier General Daniel Ullmann was a New York lawyer who led the 78th New York Infantry in campaigns in Virginia until his capture at the Battle of Cedar Mountain. After time spent in Libby Prison, he returned to Union lines with an idea: Slaves in the occupied South should be organized into disciplined and well-regulated commands of combat troops. Lincoln sent him to Louisiana to test his theories.

Library of Congress.

populations—since workers on plantations and army depots were easier to gather. Before Ullmann's recruiting efforts undid the economic craftsmanship of the reworked plantation system, Banks needed to find and provide fresh blood. Perhaps these new soldiers could be recruited from among the soon-to-be-freed slaves of the Teche country.[4]

On March 25, Banks ordered Brigadier General Cuvier Grover to move his division from Baton Rouge by steamboat to Donaldsonville and then to march them down Bayou Lafourche to Thibodaux. At the same time, Banks told Brigadier General William H. Emory to move his command via steamer to Algiers, then to send his men by rail into the Lafourche District. Both commands were to move on to Tiger Island in preparation for crossing Berwick Bay at Brashear City and invading the Teche country. Brigadier General Thomas W. Sherman's Division would hold New Orleans while Major General Christopher Columbus Augur would hold Baton Rouge with a brigade and a half. Banks gambled that Gardner would not sally out from his works at Port Hudson; if he did, presumably the Union fleet at Baton Rouge could beat him back. Knowing he would need more boats, Banks took the additional precaution of requesting that the navy dispatch two Galveston veterans, the gunboat USS *Clifton* and the small screw steamer USS *Sachem,* to Brashear City. These vessels would reinforce Lieutenant Commander Augustus Paul Cooke's three gunboats in case the reported Rebel steamers attacked before Banks could assemble his army. But the *Sachem* never arrived; it had sprung a leak and returned to New Orleans for repairs.[5]

Resting a bit easier now that reinforcements were on the way, Weitzel remained vigilant, armed with crisp intelligence of Taylor's intentions. Having moved his brigade back to Bayou Boeuf on March 21, and while awaiting the arrival of Grover's and Emory's Divisions, he kept Lieutenant Solon A. Perkins and his Company B, 2nd Massachusetts Cavalry Battalion, on hand to scout the country across Berwick Bay. He stationed several hundred men at an infantry garrison in Brashear City as an early warning picket. Weitzel also created an independent company of Massachusetts cavalry under the command of his trusted aide, Lieutenant Pickering Dodge Allen, to gather intelligence in the area in an attempt to smoke out any plots among the locals to aid the Rebel move. The gossip persisted. "The story goes that Mouton had had planned to send a column down . . . and cut us off from New Orleans, while his armored gunboats, the *Webb* and the *Queen of the West,* should beat our mosquito fleet and shell us out of Brashear City," wrote Captain John William De Forest of the 12th Connecticut. "As Banks is now threatening Port Hudson with the mass of his troops, it was important to evade every chance of disaster in his rear, and so we retired upon this new line of defense."[6]

The rumor of a Rebel offensive even circulated among Banks's staff in New Orleans. "Weitzel thinks Sibley intends to attack him, not knowing Grover and Emory are behind him," wrote Lieutenant Colonel David Hunter Strother. "I do not myself think Sibley is such a fool, but rather think he is making a demonstration to cover his retreat and gain time, or to attract attention from some other proposed movement of the enemy."[7]

West of Banks's headquarters and across Berwick Bay, the Texas and Louisiana horsemen were certainly active. When Union troops crossed the bay to forage or reconnoiter the enemy, they were certain of a fight. Weitzel also heard rumors of Rebel steamers scouting the approaches to Tiger Island. Something was afoot in St. Mary's Parish, and Weitzel wanted to know what was happening. He ordered Cooke's three gunboats, loaded with infantry riflemen, to prowl the waters of Grand Lake to make sure he was not caught unawares. The Confederates tracked these movements, and couriers reported the activity back to their officers around Bisland.

Lieutenant Commander Augustus Paul Cooke came to Louisiana aboard his ship USS *Estrella*, taking command of the flotilla of gunboats at Brashear City after the death of Lieutenant Commander Thomas McKean Buchanan in the fight against the CSS *Cotton*.

Courtesy of the Massachusetts Historical Society.

Both sides strained to learn what the other was doing, and the tension led Taylor to lose his temper. On March 26 what had become something of a routine occurrence—the approach of a snooping Federal gunboat—took on extraordinary meaning. "General Taylor happened to be to front when the pickets came running in with the gunboat alarm, and it made him mad," wrote Texan private Bill Davidson. The general addressed the troops at hand. "When gunboats come up those small rivers, instead of running off, capture them!" he demanded. He wanted to turn these machines against their former owners, adding to his strength while diminishing that of his enemies. Taylor turned wrathfully to the officers of the 2nd Louisiana Cavalry. "If you cannot do it, I will send men who can." Taylor later penned, "It is curious to recall the ideas prevailing . . . about gunboats. It was popularly believed that the destructive power of these monsters were not to be resisted," and he likened the gunboats' use of heavy-gun fire against skirmishers and sharpshooters to "snipe-hunting with twelve-pounders." Taylor ordered the 13th Texas Cavalry Battalion to replace the 2nd Louisiana at Pattersonville. "Old Dick was as [mad] as a wet hen that day," remembered Davidson.[8] The shamed Louisianans gave way to Texans.

When Major Hannibal Honestus Boone arrived at Pattersonville with his Texas battalion the next day, two women requesting

Brashear City Gunboats. A contemporary drawing showing the gunboat flotilla in Berwick Bay, including USS *Calhoun* to the left, USS *Kinsman* in the center, and USS *Estrella* to the right. The *Kinsman,* one of the more seasoned boats and crews in the region, hit a snag and sank on February 23, 1863.

Harper's Weekly.

Major Hannibal Honestus Boone led the 13th Texas Cavalry Battalion in most of its fights, earning this warrior from Hempstead, Texas, an enviable reputation.

Author's collection.

passage to New Orleans came to see him. Major Boone, Captain Joseph C. Terrell of Fort Worth, and a squad of soldiers escorted the women under a flag of truce to the village of Berwick, opposite Brashear City, where they awaited the arrival of the Yankee envoy. The Federal gunboat *Diana* glided across the bay, and the steamer's skipper, thirty-one-year-old Acting Master Thomas Lombard Peterson, a Cape Cod sailor, exchanged salutations and conferred with the Texas cavalrymen. Peterson agreed to take the women to New Orleans.[9]

Then the meeting between the two officers devolved into a glorified schoolboy shoving match. "I have been under the impression that, when a man put on a military uniform, and donned the garb of a soldier, he intended to fight," Peterson is reported to have said.

"I have thought it that way myself," responded Boone.

Peterson continued the badgering. "You Confederates don't practice that. I've been over . . . several times to try you, but at the bursting of the first shell you all stampeded."

Boone would have none of it. "You have never stampeded me or my men, yet."

"You are a new man, then, just come in?" Peterson asked.

"Yes sir, I have just come in today," the Texan answered.

Peterson had his opening. "Well, you mean to say that you are something better than you've had there before?"

Boone would not rise to the bait. "No sir, I mean to say nothing of the sort. But," Boone added, "I'll tell you what I mean, and that is that you can't stampede my men with one shell—nor a dozen shells—only that and nothing more."

Peterson took the women on board and turned to one of his officers, saying, "I will come over soon and see whether they fight as well as they talked," in a voice loud enough for Boone to hear. "Come ahead," the Texan yelled back, "we'll try and interest you." The *Diana* then reversed its engines, and Boone, Terrell, and their escort headed back up the bayou toward camp.[10]

Boone was a twenty-nine-year-old native of Tennessee and lawyer from Hempstead when he enlisted in the 2nd Texas Mounted Rifles in 1861. After his initial one-year enlistment, Boone had joined Colonel Edwin Waller's Battalion as a second lieutenant, rising through the ranks to major and second in command. Waller was gone much of the time, leaving the hard-fighting Boone in charge. Since the disaster at Bonnet Carré, he had earned a reputation for

USS *Diana*. This sketch by an officer on the USS *Clifton* is perhaps the only reliable image of this vessel uncovered to date. The drawing shows a partially armored, ocean going sidewheeler with twin funnels and iron covering its vulnerable machinery and steering apparatus.

Nestell Collection, Nimitz Library, U.S. Naval Academy, Annapolis, Maryland.

hard riding and harder fighting, and he wanted to redeem the reputation of his unit and restore honor to his friends and neighbors in arms. He would soon have his chance.[11]

Back across the bay at Brashear City, Peterson tied off the *Diana* but kept the boat's fires alive, for his business for the day was not finished. On the afternoon of March 27, the *Diana* took on a small contingent of riflemen. Peterson ordered deck hands to lash two barges behind the boat then paddled about a half dozen miles up the Atchafalaya River and hove to at the landing of the Cochrane plantation. After tying off and pulling the barges to the bank, Union officers produced a bill of sale for the inspection of the estate's widowed mistress, then ordered their crews to relieve the woman of her last year's sugar crop. Sugar was in great demand in New Orleans, and this contraband of war was a tempting target for gunboat commanders and their crews, since any resulting prize money would be theirs to divide. In the past, while making the rounds of lower Grand Lake, the mouth of Bayou Teche, and the lower bends of the Atchafalaya, certain gunboat skippers occasionally stopped near the sugarhouses of local plantations to conduct business, sometimes legal, sometimes illicit.

Instead of stepping aside and allowing the Yankees to take her crop, Mrs. Elizabeth Cochrane declared the document to be in error. Very quickly some of the infantry assigned to the boat began firing at Confederate horsemen hovering nearby. With the verbal sparring match with the Texan fresh in his memory, Acting Master Peterson sensed a trap. He ordered the twenty or so hogsheads of sugar already taken aboard to be abruptly off-loaded, and then he ordered the boat's whistle to recall the soldiers and sailors scattered on the grounds of the plantation.

The whistle could be heard for miles across the cane fields, but Boone and Terrell already knew what was occurring. They had not made it halfway back to camp when "the Major and myself turned back hearing from one of our scouts that the [*Diana*] was coming up the bayou on a stealing expedition," Terrell wrote. "She was a terror to all the region." Couriers rode back to hurry forward reinforcements from the Texan camp while the two officers, the pickets, and an accompanying squad of troopers rode toward Cochrane's plantation.[12]

Lieutenant Solon A. Perkins, a bookkeeper from Lowell, Massachusetts, led one of the most reliable Union cavalry companies in Louisiana.

Massachusetts Commandery Military Order of the Loyal Legion and US Army Military History Institute.

Peterson had barely retrieved his men before the Texans arrived, and the navy man hurried his gunboat to Brashear City. He reported the number of Rebels they had seen prowling about and told of the close call at the widow Cochrane's, and Weitzel responded immediately. He summoned Lieutenant Allen, his aide-de-camp, and put him in charge of a reinforced picket guard of seventy infantrymen who crossed the bay to scatter the insolent Texans. As soon as they landed, Boone's Texans opened fire on the foot soldiers from several hundred yards away.[13]

The Federal company scattered across the fields in skirmish order and began an hour-long running battle with the mounted Texans. "We drove them two miles, and fired a good many shots, without any one being hurt," Lieutenant Allen wrote. "They numbered fifteen or twenty mounted men, and kept at a very long range."[14]

The *Diana,* after delivering Lieutenant Allen's infantry detachment, returned to Brashear City and then ferried Lieutenant Perkins and his cavalry company to help in trying to catch the elusive Texans. The aggressive Union horse soldiers followed them

Lieutenant Pickering Dodge Allen had a reputation for being a reliable scout and dependable soldier. Brigadier General Godfrey Weitzel came to rely on this cavalryman from Salem, Massachusetts, to serve as his eyes and ears at the front.

Massachusetts Commandery Military Order of the Loyal Legion and US Army Military History Institute.

closely, and Boone and his men prudently withdrew. A few well-placed Rebel shots caused the aggressive Federals to slow their pursuit. As Perkins directed his troopers to keep up the pressure on the retreating Texans, a bullet crashed through his horse's head, and the lieutenant and his dead mount tumbled to the ground. Dusting himself off, he mounted another horse behind one of his troopers, noting that several of his men were in similar circumstances. A glance up the road revealed not only that the small cluster of Texans was getting away but also that hundreds more seemed to be boiling out of Pattersonville and forming up to offer a fight. Perkins ordered his bugler to sound the recall, and the Yankee cavalry trotted back to the covering lines of their infantry, pursued themselves by several hundred Texans. The Yankees retreated steadily through the cane fields and down the road to the welcoming, puffing, looming, *Diana.* Both sides claimed success in this affair of outposts. Terrell reported one dead Northerner and another wounded; Perkins claimed five Texans as prisoners.[15]

After the skirmish Weitzel, though aware that Banks and the bulk of his army were heading his direction, remained concerned about the possibility of a Confederate attack before help could arrive. He urged his gunboat commanders to remain vigilant and continued his naval patrols against the threat of waterborne

Confederate incursions. The three remaining gunboats at Berwick Bay—especially the nimble and partially armored *Diana*—kept busy. Many of the army-provided sharpshooters aboard these gunboats enjoyed the diversion of the daily reconnaissance outings but resented risking their necks to accommodate the navy's sweet tooth. In order to curb any plundering while on patrol, or poor decisions that Peterson might make because of the lure of personal remuneration, General Weitzel ordered Lieutenant Allen to post himself in the pilothouse of the *Diana* to keep watch over Peterson's route. "Fearing that this officer was inclined to be rash," Weitzel wrote, "I sent Pickering with him to see that my orders were not exceeded."[16]

Sugar Plantations on Bayou Teche. Alfred R. Waud drew this scene in 1871, showing a bayou steamer making its way toward a plantation sugarhouse. The magnificent home stands to the right, the cabins of the laborers line up along the bank. These self-contained agricultural/industrial complexes abounded in the region and were rich targets for extortion, smuggling, and even plundering during the war.

Historic New Orleans Collection, accession no. 1965.65.

Along the oak-lined banks of Bayou Teche, Waller's Texans watched the *Diana*'s comings and goings. These soldiers remained eager for a continuation of the previous day's gunfight. They also wanted revenge. The horsemen still felt the humiliation inflected by Federal gunboats at Bonnet Carré more than six months before, when they had lost their mounts, weapons, and reputation. Now they were prepared and impatient to settle this old score. With them were the guns of the Val Verde Battery and the muskets, shotguns, and pistols of Lieutenant Colonel Philemon Herbert's Arizona Battalion. As their camp still buzzed about the dustup with the *Diana* at the Cochrane sugarhouse, the Texans decided to lay a trap at the mouth of Bayou Teche in case the vessel decided to press its luck and return to finish the job they had interrupted.[17]

At noon on March 28 the *Diana* built up steam to make a patrol and to investigate several rumors of aggressive enemy activity. Reports indicated that a Rebel steamer had dashed out of the Teche and up the Atchafalaya to Grand Lake. Another rumor was that Rebel infantry and artillery were taking positions on the sizable island formed by the Atchafalaya River, Berwick Bay, and Grand Lake, which was sometimes marked as Pine Island on Federal maps. This reconnaissance mission, like so many in the previous weeks, was to steam up Berwick Bay and into Grand Lake, turn to port into the channel of the Atchafalaya, and then proceed as far as the mouth of Bayou Teche to investigate the gossip before turning about and retracing the route. As added protection, twenty-nine riflemen of the 12th Connecticut and forty men from the 160th New York loaded on board. "The affair was looked upon as a sort of picnic," wrote Captain De Forest of the 12th Connecticut, "and several officers volunteered to join it."[18]

That afternoon passed without much activity. As on the day before, the Federal patrollers saw the usual Confederate horsemen at Berwick City and watched them gallop to cover as expected. And, as was their custom, several Rebels had ridden along the banks of the Atchafalaya to Bayou Teche to spread the alarm among the Confederate forces upstream. Nothing seemed unusual to Peterson, who steered the *Diana* up Berwick Bay and into the tricky waters of Grand Lake. As ordered, he then ordered a left-hand turn to port and descended the Atchafalaya to the mouth of Bayou Teche.

Here, Peterson made a fatal error. Instead of turning the *Diana* around and heading back into Grand Lake and into the northern neck of Berwick Bay, as instructed, he decided to continue down the Atchafalaya past Pattersonville. After consulting with his officers and crew, he decided to make another call at Cochrane's plantation, approaching from above this time. Lieutenant Allen had seen the Rebel activity on the bank and had fought them the day before, and now he furiously demanded, "What will you do if you are suddenly attacked by a Rebel battery?" Peterson responded, "I can blow any six of their batteries to pieces." The *Diana*'s commander confidently ordered the boat to proceed.[19]

The Rebels lured him on. At 2:00 PM, as the *Diana* churned the waters in front of Pattersonville, troops on the upper deck reported Confederate cavalry and a few pieces of artillery in the cane fields moving toward the Atchafalaya. Lieutenant Allen again urged Peterson to reverse his path, return to Grand Lake, and avoid a fight. Instead, the commander of the *Diana* ordered his 30-pound Parrot to pivot and run out to starboard and shoot at the horsemen. The crew pulled the lanyard and hurled a shell at the enemy that exploded in their midst.

This round had unexpected consequences. Unseen by the Federals, nearly three hundred Texans were already in position, and the guns of the Val Verde Battery were ready to rake the river with crossfire. The Rebels responded with a storm of gunfire that swept the bow of the *Diana,* killing the crew of the big pivot cannon while volleys of canister from the field pieces shredded any unprotected machinery or woodwork. Pipes and cables critical to the vessel's control began to fail. One of these antipersonnel blasts killed the vessel's third in command, Acting Master's Mate George Dolliver of Cape Cod, Massachusetts, spattering his viscera on the deck.[20]

Acting Master Peterson appeared shocked by the aggressive Southern response. Before he could react, Peterson reeled from his position in the pilothouse, crying "Great God! They have killed me!" before falling lifeless to the deck, victim to a Texan bullet through his heart. Quickly thereafter the gunboat's executive officer, Acting Master's Mate Thomas G. Hall, fell with a bullet through the chest and lay unconscious, bleeding to death. Acting Master's Mate Henry Weston Jr., assumed command. He knew the stern of the boat was vulnerable and cannon rounds could soon strike the rudders and machinery, so he ordered his gunners to return fire and directed the boat pilot to turn the steamer around so that its cannon-tipped bow would face the enemy. The *Diana* would have to back down the Atchafalaya toward Brashear City.[21]

The Federals faced huge disadvantages. Bullets, fragments, and round shot eventually severed the boat's wheel ropes, making the vessel unresponsive to its controls. Hundreds of bullets poured through gun ports and portholes, cutting down many naval gunners

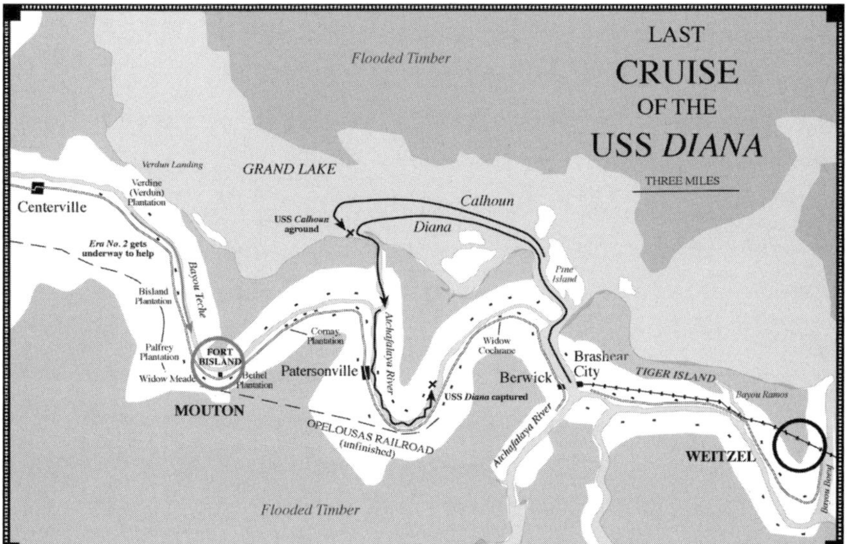

and sending others for cover. The infantry abandoned their exposed firing positions, seeking cover from the onslaught. Officers urged their men to fight back but fell dead or wounded as soon as they exposed themselves. James McNalley, an engineer aboard the boat, took a bullet to the head while communicating with the helm.[22]

The Federals' fire caused minor distraction for the Texans. Captain Terrell considered himself lucky. Just minutes before the opening of this fight, he had made a horse trade, swapping his animal and $250 Confederate for what he considered a better mount. "The horse I traded off had his leg shot off and the one I traded for, hitched close to me, was not hurt," he wrote home. Two other animals fell from shell fragments, but no Rebel soldiers were injured.[23]

As the *Diana* crept out of range, Rebel gunners switched to solid shot and exploding shell, and the rate of destruction increased. A round from a 6-pounder skipped off the boat's armor and crashed through its pilothouse, making it untenable and carrying away the wheel. Other rounds penetrated the engine room, maiming and mangling as they bounced among the crew and severed the steam escape pipe, enveloping the boat in a cloud of scalding vapor, making accurate return fire impossible, and turning the engine room into a scalding hell. A cannon round cut the forecastle captain in half at the ribcage while another carried away the legs of Boatswain's Mate Robert Crawford. A fragment slammed into the head of Captain Josiah Jewitt of the 160th New York, leaving him bloodied and paralyzed and the infantry on board without direction. Amid all the mayhem, Lieutenant Allen attempted to rally the soldiers and crew.[24]

The thumps of heavy gunfire could be heard at Brashear City, nearly a dozen miles away. Captain Meltiah Jordan of the USS *Calhoun* received permission from Commodore Cooke to investigate, and he ordered his vessel to raise steam and his crew to assemble onboard. The gunboat hurried away from the docks without a local pilot, since he was aboard the *Diana.* Instead of heading up the Atchafalaya, Jordan led the *Calhoun* up Berwick Bay to Grand Lake, assuming that the *Diana* would be somewhere on the route as it had been ordered. He was wrong. To compound the problem, when the *Calhoun* made its port turn from Grand Lake into the Atchafalaya, it ran aground. Its crew was unfamiliar with the vicissitudes of the route.[25]

The noise of battle had also attracted Rebel boats. On Bayou Teche crewmen aboard the steamer *Era No. 2* stoked their fires. A sortie by the Confederate transports might lend a hand by bringing on reinforcements.

The crew of the *Calhoun,* growing worried lest they be caught in this vulnerable position by the Rebels, tried desperately but unsuccessfully to free their vessel. After sending an officer with a boat back to Brashear City for assistance, Captain Jordan tried every measure he could think of to get the boat off of the snag, but to no avail. He dumped thirty tons of coal, his extra anchors, chain, ammunition, and provisions to lighten the boat, but nothing worked.[26]

At Brashear City, Weitzel fumed as he telegraphed his embarrassing situation to General Banks in New Orleans. "I ordered the *Diana* by the Grand Lake route to make a reconnaissance," the message read. "Instead of taking the route I ordered, for some unaccountable reason they went by the Atchafalaya, right in the teeth of the enemy." He also had to report the danger facing the *Calhoun.* His only other gunboat, USS *Estrella,* unknowingly steamed forty miles away, where Berwick Bay met the Gulf of Mexico, standing by to escort steamers loaded with supplies. "Just hurry on the [1st] Indiana [Heavy Artillery] battery with ammunition, and I am all right," Weitzel wrote, "even if they get all my boats."[27]

News like this caused quite a stir at the St. Charles Hotel. A reporter for the *Boston Traveler* loitered at his usual place in the lobby, eager to pick up news from the front, when he noticed a stir among the usual hangers-on. "The loyal men and our officers observed considerable jubilation among the rebels assembled there, who stood together in knots of half a dozen or more, whispering some terrible tale," he recorded. Weitzel's dispatch had been leaked from the personnel on the Algiers to Brashear City railroad all the way to Banks's own aides.[28]

Back along the banks of the Atchafalaya, the Texans continued shadowing the *Diana* for nearly three hours, tearing it to shreds. Firing from prone positions, they shot at any target of opportunity. "The upper works were riddled like a sieve from stem to stern," wrote one Union survivor. "Every berth was cut to splinters. Chairs, tables, knives and forks, books, broken glass and china,

Interior, St. Charles Hotel. This immense structure in the New Orleans French Quarter had served secession organizers in 1861. When the Federal army arrived it became the headquarters for the occupiers, and first General Butler, then General Banks, held court in its rooms, halls, and parlors.

Frank Leslie's Illustrated Newspaper, *March 28, 1863, Courtesy of the collections of the Louisiana State Museum.*

shattered panels, blood-wet beds, and pools of gore—and the dead and wounded—were everywhere." Texan captain Terrell reported, "even six-shooters were used with great effect." Lieutenant Allen, already cut on his left hand by a shell fragment, a pistol ball to the thumb, and unsuccessful in his efforts to get his riflemen to return fire or the sailors to man the *Diana*'s guns, took a rifle bullet in the back that passed behind his left shoulder blade and into his arm. Acting Master's Mate Weston realized that they had been in the grinder for nearly three hours but had only made about three miles of progress toward safety, and he looked to the pilot, a Louisianan named Dudley to do what he could to get them out of danger.[29]

This veteran boatman did his best. The *Diana* zigzagged backward down the Atchafalaya like a punch-drunk boxer while its enemies trotted alongside on the bank, pouring fire into the boat with little fear of retribution. Without controls to guide it, Dudley resorted to using the boat's two side-wheels to back it down the river. On the relatively protected starboard side, he clung to an exterior ladder that led down to the engine room. From this precarious spot Dudley called orders through the hatch as to which wheel to reverse in turn to keep the boat from grounding, keeping an eye on its progress. He and his crew had just settled into a rhythm when a solid shot cut the ladder in two, hurling the pilot into the water. The *Diana* was now flailing blindly in reverse, and its passengers were hopelessly demoralized. Weston, its third commander in as many hours, was running short of options.[30]

Without guidance and with a strong sea breeze pushing across the boat from the port side, the *Diana* ran aground at the first hard curve of the river, backing into the bank opposite its attackers. The crew and accompanying infantry, largely leaderless, surrendered the vessel. Some jumped over the starboard side to escape. Most simply awaited the coming Texans. Rebel bullets, shot, and shell had killed, wounded, or maimed more than a quarter of the nearly 120 Federals on board. The rest were now prisoners.

The Rebels were quick to claim their prize. Many of the Texans, upon seeing the vessel strike its colors, let out a Rebel yell and swam across the Atchafalaya to climb aboard their prize. A soldier from Fort Worth was to first to reach the *Diana,* and he climbed up a tree to get access to a window he could crawl through. Instead, he recoiled in horror: a stricken Federal had been laid on one of the boat's beds, but another round had cut him to pieces, and now his body was "mixed up with feathers by one of Sayers's six-pounders," Terrel wrote. The Rebel captain and Colonel Waller rowed a skiff to the boat. "She was much cut to pieces and thoroughly peppered," he wrote. "I do not exaggerate when I say there was not three feet square on the port side of the boat that was not struck by our small arms." The deck was ghastly. "I hope never again to witness a sight like that," he wrote, "covered with the dead and dying, and many wounded." Union lieutenant Allen, grievously wounded, attempted to surrender to Waller. "Damn your sword," the colonel responded, "I want to raise steam here!" Allen snarled back, "I hope the man's arm may be palsied who helps you."[31]

The young New Englander was horrified by his fate. He later wrote home that "the fight on the Diana was a very hard one. We were surrounded by a force of several times our own number, consisting of six companies of Texas rangers (Waller's battalion), two Arizona cavalry companies, one battery of field pieces, and two companies of the Twenty-Eighth Louisiana Infantry." He thought he was familiar with this crowd. "The Texas sharp-shooters . . . are the same desperados who boarded the *Harriet Lane* off Galveston," he wrote mistakenly. "They are a disorganized mob, under no military discipline whatever, paying no regards to the orders of officers but fighting and roaming at their own pleasure. Some of these fellows carried immense bowie knives, two and three feet long." Allen had one fact correct: "It was the same body of desperados who were driven into the swamps by our troops sixty miles above New Orleans last August."[32]

The Texans looted the boat. One soldier picked up a fiddle from among the wreckage, carried it over his head as he swam back to the bank, and climbed onto a limber of the Val Verde Battery. Putting the instrument to his cheek, the soldiers began sawing out *Dixie* as he danced on the limber chest. Triumphant boarders took the boots off the dead bodies of Peterson and Hall, while others took the boat's clock and raided its commissary. The slain captain's coat pocket contained five hundred dollars, which quickly vanished. "I now feast on good coffee," wrote Captain Terrell. Yankee infantrymen had ruined most of the small arms on board by bending their barrels, but the Rebels made an unusual and valuable haul—bulletproof breastplates worn by some of the crew.[33]

The Texans reflected on the day's fight, and the death of Peterson, whom many had met just two days before. "He was a good officer and bravely died at his post," wrote Davidson. "Like a great many of our own officers, he had too high an estimate of his own importance. From this time on, gunboats ceased to be an object of terror to our brigade."[34]

The *Era No. 2* arrived moments later, and its skipper began planning how to haul the *Diana* back up the Teche to Fort Bisland.

Sugar Plantation in Louisiana. These slave cabins as sketched by Lieutenant Colonel David Hunter Strother housed hundreds of people whose lives would be forever changed by the columns of blue uniformed soldiers marching past.

David Hunter Strother, Drawings and Sketches, The West Virginia and Regional History Collection Holdings, West Virginia University Libraries Acc. No. p.95.30.127.

Captain Terrell rounded up a crew of firemen, engineers, and a pilot from the Confederate boat and the prize crew came aboard the *Diana* and repaired the steering. Just before sunset, the *Diana* was once again under its own power. By midnight it was safely within Confederate lines.[35]

At almost the same time, Sibley's Brigade began arriving on the lower Teche. Colonel James Reily of the 4th Texas declared, "We are here in fine health and spirits and in the vicinity of the enemy." He was also mindful of the calendar, and the import of the day. "The Val Verde battery celebrated our arrival and the anniversary of Glorieta by capturing the gunboat *Diana*."[36]

Unsurprisingly, the crew of the stranded *Calhoun* was not jubilant. The firing had ceased, but there were certainly enemies close by. Although the Federals on board could not have known it, only about eight densely wooded and swampy miles separated them from the *Diana* and its Rebel captors. As the day faded into evening, some of the survivors of the *Diana* disaster hailed Acting Master Jordan from shore. The story they told made him and his crew frantic. An hour after midnight, the USS *Calhoun* backed off of the obstruction and once again floated free. Jordan ordered his boat to hurry back to base, where it arrived safely at daybreak on March 29.[37]

7

The Back Alley

"The Teche country was to the war in Louisiana what the Shenandoah Valley was to the war in Virginia."

Captain John William De Forest
12th Connecticut Infantry

The loss of the USS *Diana* may have changed the strategic balance on Bayou Teche, but along the Mississippi the Confederates faced an increasingly dire situation. The Red River would once again be blockaded unless Rebel gunboats could perform another brown water miracle as they had against USS *Indianola.* When Admiral David G. Farragut took the USS *Albatross* and the USS *Hartford* past Port Hudson two weeks before, on March 14, he had proceeded upriver to communicate with the land and naval forces around Vicksburg. Finding Admiral David Dixon Porter away—he was directing an expedition on Steel's Bayou, well above Vicksburg—Farragut told Porter's staff that he wanted two rams and an ironclad to run past the Confederate batteries at Vicksburg and reinforce his two-ship squadron of awkward oceangoing vessels with two nimble gunboats in order to seal off Red River. Even the veteran sailor was wary of what the CSS *Webb* and CSS *Queen of the West* might do to his *Hartford* and *Albatross* in the confines of the narrow waterways. Without waiting for permission from Porter,

Captain Henry Walke—the officer in command of the vessels anchored off Vicksburg—authorized another dash past the guns, but he could not spare an ironclad.[1]

Hearing of Farragut's request, Colonel Charles Rivers Ellet again sprang into action. At 4:30 AM on March 25, the youngster led the rams USS *Lancaster* and USS *Switzerland* through the gauntlet of Confederate batteries. Although Rebel cannon riddled the *Switzerland* and sank the *Lancaster,* the daring young soldier made it through and rendezvoused with Farragut to help block the Red River with his remaining battle-scarred vessel. Admiral Porter sent along his congratulations, despite being peeved that he had not been consulted on the operation. "Your service at Red River will be a godsend," Porter wrote to Farragut. "It is worth to us the loss of the [USS] *Mississippi* at this moment and the severest blow that could be struck at the South. They obtain all their supplies and ammunition in that way. It is death to these people."[2]

USS *Switzerland* passing Vicksburg, March 25, 1863.

Naval Historical Center.

Porter also made a dig at Ellet in his dispatch to Farragut: "In relation to the *Switzerland,* keep her with you, and please make the commander understand that she is under your command, or [Ellet] will go off on a cruise somewhere before you know it and then get the ship into trouble." The commander of the Mississippi squadron wanted to make sure that this impetuous young offer did not gift another boat to the Rebels. "She is a formidable ship as a ram, but I would never expect to see her again if she got out of your sight."[3]

Four days later, on March 29, 1863, Major General Ulysses S. Grant's army lurched into motion. After a month of seeking a route around Vicksburg from the north and east, Grant had given up and ordered his juggernaut to march south along the Mississippi River's Louisiana shore to gain fresh positions at New Carthage and Hard Times Landing. From this new spot Grant's foot soldiers would be able to operate in several directions. They could rendezvous with Admiral Porter's fleet, should he run all of his boats past the Vicksburg batteries. The Mississippi Squadron and its transports could then ferry Grant's army across the river to operate against Lieutenant General John C. Pemberton. The transports could also carry the army south, to Port Hudson, and Vicksburg might be ignored altogether.

On April 1 Admiral Farragut, having run past Rebel batteries at Warrenton and Port Gibson, Mississippi, hove to at the mouth of the Red River with the *Hartford, Albatross,* and *Switzerland.* The Red River was now clamped shut, starting the starvation process. The wily old sailor festooned his giant flagship in ersatz armor designed to foil ramming and boarding; he wanted the *Hartford* to avoid the fate of both the *Harriet Lane* and the *Indianola.* Crews fastened a bunting of chains from the bowsprit, draped it to the lower yards, which had been dropped to deck level, and fastened it again at the stern, creating a steel net intended to tangle attacking boats some twenty feet from the side of the *Hartford.* Should a fast-moving ram pass this defense, its stabbing bow would meet a ring of cypress logs suspended from the sides of the ship, just at the waterline. In the event that a steamer with troops came alongside, nets, hammocks, and rolled sails formed a breastwork at the rail that would provide a fighting position for *Hartford*'s crew to resist an attempt to board.[4]

Farragut had anticipated Major General Richard Taylor's plan, but the Texan volunteers for the Red River naval expedition still idled at Fort DeRussy, awaiting their ships and game for the fight. They were aware that that the odds had changed. "The Yankee boats (3 in no.) are blockading the mouth of this river and as soon as our boats are ready we will proceed to that place and attack them," Private John W. Watkins wrote. "With what success I am unable to say, but have every confidence in the expedition. The *Duke* is fitted up as a gunboat, and the *Webb* as a ram. Other boats will accompany us and everything will be done up shipshape." While communication with the rest of General Henry Hopkins Sibley's Brigade had been unreliable, the troops at the fort had heard about the capture of the *Diana* and it helped build their confidence for the task ahead. Watkins wrote his wife, "I suppose you heard of the capture of a yankee gunboat near Berwicks Bay by Cols. Waller and Herbert, which eclipses anything that has ever been done before. They went out in skiffs and small boats and boarded her."[5]

While awaiting their gunboats, the detachments from the 5th and 7th Texas helped Taylor with some unpleasant chores along the lower Red River. "There are about two hundred conscripts in this parish who are dodging about to keep out of service," Watkins noted. "There is a detachment of our brigade now hunting them up and turning them over to the commander of this post." Another Texan put it a little plainer, accusing the detachment of the 7th Texas for "sloshing around after Jayhawkers."[6]

Farragut reopened the Red River—briefly—to reestablish contact with his vessels below and with Banks and his army. On April 6 Farragut's three-vessel armada traveled downstream to just above Port Hudson. The following day, his secretary, Lieutenant Edward C. Gaubadan, disembarked on a covert mission, floating by the fort in a camouflaged skiff under cover of darkness, bearing news and dispatches. Near midnight, two signal rockets spiraling skyward from the USS *Richmond* confirmed his safe arrival. This errand complete and with his intentions now clear to Union forces around Baton Rouge, Farragut headed back upstream to clamp shut once again the mouth of Red River.

Confederate scouts had watched the Yankee warships depart the Red River and had signaled that there might be time to move another load of supplies down to Port Hudson. Two steamers loaded with food sped onto the Mississippi River. In the lead, the *J. D. Clark* bore a commissary officer with orders announcing that a large shipment of Texas cattle were coming on a later boat. The gamble failed. Farragut's vessels ran headfirst into the steamboats, intercepting the *J. D. Clark* but missing its companion, which scooted back up the Red River. The Yankees eviscerated and dismembered the captured side-wheeler, hauling out its engine and machinery before sinking what remained of the boat. The Mississippi once again closed to Confederate shipping.[7]

In New Orleans, Lieutenant Colonel David Hunter Strother speculated on why the campaign to capture the Mississippi was taking so long when the Union had been so close to success just a year before. He marveled at Northern leadership and how the nation's politicians made military decisions. "We are informed that the Mississippi is not to be opened until the Pennsylvania Central and the New York Railroad and the Illinois Central (which are having a good business in transportation) shall be satisfied," he wrote. "That the aims and objects of the war, its conduct and its conductors, are matters of traffic and have been since the commencement there can be no doubt." Cynicism gripped the staff officer. "This is faithful valor bought and sold."[8]

Corruption and war profiteering also clouded the issue. Lieutenant George H. Hepworth jotted his disgust in his notebook. "There are another class of persons thrown to the surface by the war," he wrote. "I mean the vampires." The Massachusetts chaplain estimated that the costs of the war had ballooned to five times what it should be. The men he called cheaters should be dreaded and hated. "They have souls so small," he sneered, "that the angel's microscope will hardly discover them."[9]

Nearby, Julia LeGrand hoped to be rid of all the Yankees and still longed to be heading for Texas. One of her friends, Mary Harrison, received two letters from her aunt, Ellen Ross Reily, wife of Texas colonel James Reily. Both missives came from Franklin, Louisiana, near Fort Bisland. Mrs. Reily "is there with Sibley's army, and that army is mostly composed of 'Texans,'" LeGrand wrote. She and her circle hoped to move west soon and looked forward to being "under the protection of some of our people." LeGrand and her siblings were natives of Maryland; now most of her family lived west of the Sabine River. "They are Texans now, wearing her colors, bearing her lone star banner, and we have a foothold still in this desolated Louisiana," she wrote. Armed with a passport, LeGrand hoped to accompany her friend through the Union lines to Franklin. "She then fell to begging us to go out with them," LeGrand wrote, "promising us a warm welcome at her aunt's and a splendid time." Her timing could not have been worse.[10]

Julia LeGrand felt trapped in Federal-occupied New Orleans and hoped to leave the city and join her relatives in Texas.

Kate Mason Rowland and Mrs. Morris L. Croxall, eds., The Journal of Julia Le Grande, New Orleans, 1862–1863 *(Richmond: Everett Waddey Company, 1911).*

Brashear City, between the Crescent City and Franklin, began to swell with Union reinforcements. The USS *Clifton* arrived on the first week of April, and its guns covered the town. "Bad news was the first things that greeted us," Marine private Henry O. Gusley reported. "One of our steamers, the *Diana,* had been captured by the rebels." Among the slain or missing were some of his old shipmates from the USS *Westfield,* lost at the Battle of Galveston three months before. "The bodies of her captain and executive officer had been recovered," Gusley wrote. The marines of the flotilla at Berwick Bay served as an honor guard. "We buried them in a beautiful orange grove, close by the town."[11]

While Grant started his movement in northern Louisiana, the Army of the Gulf flowed away from its various encampments on the banks of the Mississippi, taking a little over a week to reassemble near Berwick Bay. Brigadier General Godfrey Weitzel's Brigade returned to Brashear City. Lieutenant Commander Augustus Paul

USS *Clifton* had been a ferryboat between Brooklyn and New York before the war. By the Teche campaign, the gunboat was a battle-scarred veteran of the capture of New Orleans, the attack on Vicksburg, the Battle of Baton Rouge, the capture of Galveston, the attack on Port Lavaca, and the Confederate recapture of Galveston.

Naval Historical Center.

Cooke's gunboats and the newly arrived 1st Indiana Heavy Artillery continued to keep Rebel scouts at a distance on the west bank of the bay. The five-gun USS *Arizona,* a side-wheel ocean steamer and one-time blockade runner that had only been in Union service for a month, paddled in from the Gulf of Mexico by way of Atchafalaya Bay, reinforcing the flotilla and replacing the lost *Diana.*

Brigadier General William H. Emory's Division detrained in a field at the railroad crossing of Bayou Ramos, near the middle of Tiger Island, and filed out into stubbly cane fields to make their tent city. One soldier, Private Edmund Miles of Company F, 41st Massachusetts Infantry, marveled at the country he had just passed through. "Here and there we met houses deserted by those who had joined the Rebel army," he wrote to his wife. "I could not but feel sorry for those deluded ones who had left such nice homes, and for all I know their all to go and fight against their best friends, and try and overthrow the government which had vouchsafed to them such property in the past." The Louisiana climate and countryside had smitten the Bay State soldier, and he believed he would be happy living there since his enemies had forfeited the privilege. "If only I had my family here and owned one of these places," he sighed, "how happy should I be."[12]

Brigadier General Cuvier Grover's Division moved into dusty camps at the railroad crossing of Bayou Boeuf at the eastern margin of Tiger Island, four miles from the rest of the Federal army. The soldiers received orders to divest themselves of all extra gear and baggage and to store it in vacant warehouses alongside the tracks. On April 8 Major General Nathaniel P. Banks moved his headquarters from New Orleans to Brashear City, following the tracks of the Opelousas and New Orleans Railroad.

A two-regiment brigade of garrison troops stayed behind to occupy strategic points in the Lafourche District. A soldier in one of these regiments, Private Andrew Sherman of the 23rd Connecticut, guarded the railroad at Boutte Station, where mosquitoes and the humid, stifling heat were his most formidable enemies. "One evening, when these insects were unusually troublesome, and while walking my beat with my musket in the most comfortable position possible, General Banks and one or two of his staff suddenly appeared," he wrote. "I at once brought my musket to a present arms . . . punctuated with a violent stroke of first one and then the other of my hands at the mosquitoes, which seemed to be taking a most contemptible advantage of my preoccupation with my distinguished visitor." The general understood the man's predicament. "Never mind about presenting arms, my boy," Banks told him. "Make yourself as comfortable as possible." The relieved soldier watched as the officer and his entourage moved on, "all the time . . . slapping right and left to escape being eaten alive by the busy insects."[13]

On the morning of April 9 Banks announced to his staff, "I will make this campaign and go home." Many of his officers agreed that

USS *Calhoun* had been a notorious Confederate privateer and blockade runner until captured by the Federals in early 1862. The vessel proved equally formidable in service of the Union.

Naval Historical Center.

the war was not going as it should, and perhaps a break at home might give them some perspective. "The attempt to conquer the rebellion in its present condition is simply absurd," asserted Strother. "We cannot exterminate eight millions of people and occupy a territory one half larger than the whole loyal states." There needed to be a change of tactics, something to convince the Southerners to give up willingly. A carrot to go along with the stick. "There must be a radical change of policy that will effect the Southern people themselves . . . enabling them to return to the United States as free citizens," Strother added. "At present the Government offers them nothing but subjugation, ruin, and death whether they yield or fight us to the bitter end." Perhaps a dramatic military gesture followed by an offer of reconciliation would end the fighting.[14]

USS *Estrella* was a swift, English-built merchant ship captured while violating the blockade in 1862. Commissioned into the U.S. Navy, the vessel went to Louisiana, seeing action against CSS *Cotton* in late 1862 and early 1863. Lieutenant Commander Augustus P. Cooke used *Estrella* as his flagship at Brashear City but lamented its clumsiness in the narrow bayous in the region.

Marshall Dunham Photograph Album, Mss. 3241, Louisiana and Lower Mississippi Valley Collections, LSU Libraries, Baton Rouge, La.

Aboard the *Clifton,* Private Gusley could feel the tension building at Brashear City. He described the town as a "small, neat place," and the country all around as "beautiful meadows and lawns, rich fields and shady woods. The lover of picturesque and romantic scenery would find a paradise here . . . it is a fine place to spend a life in." Still, he knew the beauty would soon be tarnished: "War casts a gloom over all, and it looks as if it will leave its imprint pretty heavily here." Carpenters on the *Clifton* added an additional cannon to the vessel and knocked together gunner shields of iron and cypress logs to protect the crew from small arms. "Things look as if something desperate is about to take place," Gusley observed.[15]

Boston merchant **Edward B. Hall** came to Louisiana as a lieutenant in Company B, 26th Massachusetts Infantry in the army of Major General Benjamin Butler. Hall left his garrison duty post to take command of Company F, 1st Louisiana Cavalry and face off against the Confederates on the Teche.

Courtesy of Denis Gaubert, Thibodaux, Louisiana.

At ten o'clock on the morning of Thursday, April 9, the Federal invasion of the Teche country began. General Weitzel's infantry brigade, composed of the 12th Connecticut; the 75th, 114th, and 160th New York; and the 8th Vermont, crossed first, carried over Berwick Bay by the gunboats *Estrella, Calhoun, Clifton,* and *Arizona.* Once across, he asked staff officer Captain John B. Hubbard to see personally what lay ahead, giving him command of his three cavalry companies and Captain Edmund C. Bainbridge's Battery A, 1st U.S. Artillery. Lieutenant Solon A. Perkins and his Massachusetts horsemen trotted forward, followed by companies A and B of the 1st Louisiana.[16]

This last unit included some tough characters recruited from the rougher parts of New Orleans. Lieutenant Hepworth counted twenty-seven different nationalities among the 1st Louisiana troopers, some hailing from China, Hungary, Germany, and Peru. "Could you sit by the side of each for an hour, when the right mood was on him, he could tell you stories more like fiction than reality," he noted. "There are those who doubt their value as troops on the field." Some believed these men to be little more than foreign mercenaries, with little devotion to the national cause. Hepworth observed one characteristic that would make them useful in the campaign ahead: "implacable hatred of the rebels. They will fight like tigers . . . they will commit any depredation, and every conceivable one, on the foe."[17]

These Federal ruffians clashed with the Rebel pickets near Pattersonville and found that even more Rebel cavalry—probably Colonel Edwin Waller's Battalion backing the Arizona Battalion—were still there in force, as expected. After getting a good idea of the enemy strength, Hubbard and his skirmishers returned to the rest of the army. While Hubbard reported to Weitzel, Perkins

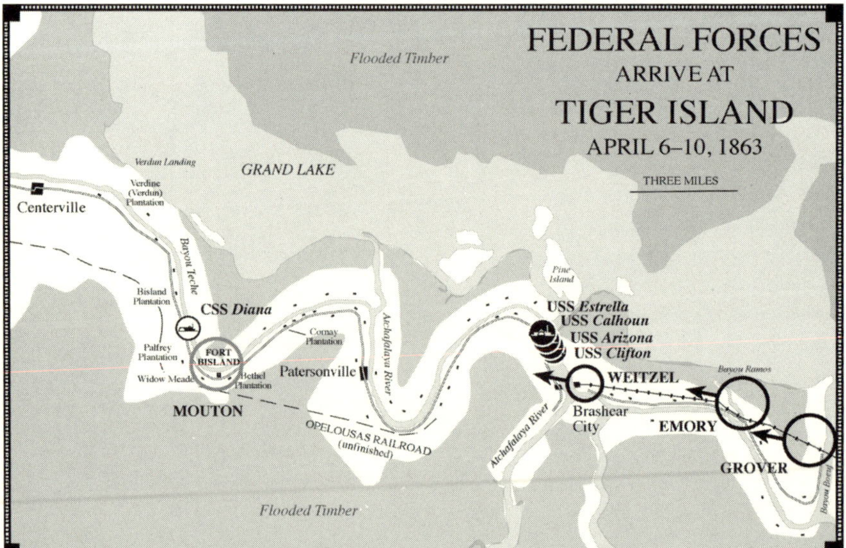

Union Troops in Baton Rouge. These Union troops would soon be engaged in the great battles for control of the Mississippi. The steamer *Sallie Robinson* is at the landing at the foot of Main Street.

Massachusetts Commandery Military Order of the Loyal Legion and US Army Military History Institute.

and the Federal horse soldiers were to keep the Confederates completely baffled as to Union intentions and to screen the movements of the army.[18]

Weitzel's infantry deployed in line of battle among the houses and gardens of Berwick City, with skirmishers thrown forward some three hundred yards. Lieutenant William H. Root of Company B, 75th New York, had been up since midnight getting his troops ready, crossed, and in line; they also drew skirmish duty. He made the best of the situation. "There was some of the most splendid berries along a fence . . . where I was, and I proceeded to fill my stomach to my satisfaction with the delicious fruit," he wrote home. After returning to the regiment to retrieve some mail, he was back on the picket line "to fight musketoes the rest of the night."[19]

The gunboats continued ferrying Union soldiers across Berwick Bay through the day and into the next morning. As the last of the men of Weitzel's Brigade stepped ashore, the first elements of Emory's Division huddled on the decks of the gunboats.

First came Colonel Timothy Ingraham's 1st Brigade, including the 4th Massachusetts and the 110th and 162nd New York. The soldiers of Colonel Halbert E. Paine's Brigade landed next, as the men of the 8th New Hampshire, 133rd and 173rd New York, and 4th Wisconsin walked down the gangplanks to dry ground. By late afternoon Colonel Oliver P. Gooding's Brigade was ashore, and the 31st, 38th, and 53rd Massachusetts as well as the 156th and 175th New York moved into position in the growing line of battle. As night fell, all four brigades had formed and were ready for war in the cane and corn fields on the western shore of Berwick Bay. The arrival of the 1st Indiana Heavy Artillery, the 1st Maine Battery, the 6th Massachusetts Battery, the guns of the 18th New York, and the regulars of Battery F, 1st U.S. artillery, completed the command.

Grover's division spent April 9 and 10 moving from their bivouac at the far side of Tiger Island to Brashear City. They could not be loaded onto the transports and gunboats as easily, for this was not just a ferry ride for them. Instead, they had to load in preparation for a day-long journey ending in an amphibious assault. This would take a little more time.

Bayou Boeuf Station. "Porte Crayon" as well as the rest of the Union army moving into position at Brashear City passed over this bridge.

David Hunter Strother, Drawings and Sketches, The West Virginia and Regional History Collection Holdings, West Virginia University Libraries, Acc. No. p. 95.30.142.

Captain John William De Forest, from his position on the west side of Berwick Bay, contemplated the campaign ahead. "The Teche county was to the war in Louisiana what the Shenandoah Valley was to the war in Virginia," he wrote. "It was sort of a back alley, parallel to the main street wherein the heavy fighting must go on. . . . There the resemblance ends, for the Teche country is a long flat, hemmed in by marshes and bayous, which, as everybody but a blind man can see, is a very different thing from a rolling valley bordered by mountains." Every one of the Federals posted in those battle lines knew why they were there—to baffle the enemy's designs in the lower Mississippi valley. "It was necessary to destroy the army of Mouton, or, at least, to drive it northward as far as possible," De Forest concluded, "in order to incapacitate it from attacking New Orleans."[20]

8

The Advance

"Roll your drums, flaunt your banners,
and advance to the battlefield."

Lieutenant Colonel David Hunter Strother
Topographer, 19th Army Corps / Army of the Gulf

Although Major General Richard Taylor did not yet realize it, Major General Nathaniel P. Banks had beaten him to the punch: the Federals, not the Confederates, had started the offensive in south Louisiana. On April 9, Rebel couriers raced up the banks of Bayou Teche, raising clouds of dust behind them. This spring was turning out to be unusually dry in south Louisiana, and the rich dark soil churned to powder with little coaxing. The couriers' news crackled like electricity through each of the Rebel camps: Yankees had crossed Berwick Bay. Word reached Taylor while he was on his way to Butte-a-la-Rose to coordinate the preparation of Captain Edward W. Fuller's ram and cottonclad flotilla for its descent down the Atchafalaya River and against Union positions. The first dispatch to reach him announced that the U.S. Army had "crossed a small force from Brashear City" and had driven back the pickets in that area. Figuring this was another of Brigadier General Godfrey Weitzel's probes, Taylor continued on his way. The next missive was more foreboding: "the enemy was in force at Brashear and was crossing troops." At this, Taylor headed back toward Camp Bisland. He also sent riders to gather his scattered commands.[1]

Although Taylor was unworried about Brigadier General Alfred Mouton's men, who were neatly gathered at Camp Bisland, General Henry Hopkins Sibley's men were scattered from Pattersonville to New Iberia, nearly sixty miles away. Breathless riders on lathered horses spread the news up the road, urging the Texans to move immediately to Camp Bisland. "We were ordered on by all available speed," wrote Sergeant Alfred B. Petticolas, Company C, 4th Texas Cavalry. "The wagons to follow at leisure." Nearby, Captain Julius Giesecke, Company G, 4th Texas, echoed the news, learning of it that evening. "We received orders by an express to report at the command at once," he wrote. The troops set out after dark and pushed hard for the front, fifty-two miles away.[2]

Taylor arrived at Camp Bisland on April 10 and met with his generals. Taylor instructed Sibley to lead all of the Texans forward and to send Colonel Tom Green with the 5th Texas to reinforce the troops at Pattersonville and to ascertain enemy intentions and delay their advance. Mouton would reinforce and expand the camp's defenses. Taylor also sent riders to Butte-a-la-Rose with the news and with orders for Fuller and his four boats—the *Queen of the West,* the *Nina Simms,* the *Grand Duke,* and the *Mary T.*—to pass down Grand Lake and cover his left flank. Taylor was too late to use his fleet for an offensive, but he would certainly use it to ambush any boats the Federals sent upriver.[3]

At his headquarters at Pickney C. Bethel's Plantation, Mouton would have to move fast. In the months he had been encamped at this bend of Bayou Teche, his engineers, aided by local slaves and the troops of his brigade, had strengthened an earthwork—Fort Bisland—that commanded the bayou and could hold four guns, and already counted two 24-pounders among its weaponry. On the bayou's east bank his men had constructed a line of entrenchments that ran along the edge of a wooded swamp and commanded broad

cane fields. Later, his troops had erected a line of breastworks west of Fort Bisland, protecting his winter bivouac but leaving the re-doubt exposed three hundred yards forward of the line. During the campaign to destroy the CSS *Cotton,* Mouton had ordered a new line of works on the bayou's west bank, a half mile forward, leaving the fort a half mile behind its left on the bayou's bank. Now he needed to refresh and repair that line as well as build a corresponding fighting position—nearly one thousand yards long—on the east bank, anchored in the woods fringing Grand Lake. In the fading light of day, two engineers began laying out the works.

After dark, Rebel soldiers made the rounds of the plantations near Fort Bisland. As they knocked on the doors of the main house, they heard murmuring voices and hurried footsteps inside. Once the doors opened, these troops presented their requisition orders to the house slaves and their owners and then went back to the slave quarters, roused the slumbering families, and ordered them to get dressed. Candles and lanterns flickered to life, babies cried, and men and women protested, but by morning a column of black men made its way to the Confederate camp. "By the most strenuous efforts," Mouton reported, "negroes were collected during the night."[4]

While the soldiers at Fort Bisland laid out their lines on April 10, the cavalry near Pattersonville spent the day fighting. Major Hannibal Honestus Boone and Captain James Belvarde Pope January led the 13th Texas Cavalry Battalion and four companies of the 5th Texas Cavalry in a daylong skirmish with the cavalry and infantry of Weitzel's Brigade. The Southerners learned nothing new of the size or scope of the invasion. The Texans reported that, behind the screen of Federal infantry and cavalry, the enemy appeared to be in no hurry. To further obscure the situation, a fog settled in and transformed the combatants into phantoms and shadows. That evening, Colonel Green led half of his regiment and five companies of the 7th Texas Cavalry to the front, ready to take his turn at the enemy, and relieving their tired comrades.[5]

What the Texans could not see through the skirmishers and the fog was the seemingly interminable loading of Brigadier General Cuvier Grover's Division at Brashear City. The three brigades of the 4th Division, 19th Army Corps, crowded onto four large steamers

Captain James Belvedere Pope January commanded Company A, 13th Texas Battalion and had already fallen into enemy hands at the Battle of Bonnet Carré in September 1862. Life in the field was hard for the fifty-year old.

Special Collections, Victoria College.

and three sizable gunboats—the *Estrella,* the *Calhoun,* and the *Arizona.* In addition to thirteen infantry regiments, three artillery batteries loaded on the boats, with all their horses, vehicles, and equipment, and were packed into position where they could land rapidly and deploy quickly if needed. This careful coordination took time—hours more than expected—and the Federal naval expedition slipped behind schedule.

Despite the sluggishness of his departure, Grover was delighted at the possibility of laying into an old nemesis. "Sibley used to run against me in the old army," he told Lieutenant Colonel David Hunter Strother as the two watched the troops loading. "There was a sort of rivalry between us. Now, for me to catch him would be too rich."[6]

From his headquarters at Brashear City, Banks scribbled a quick note to Major General Ulysses S. Grant informing him of this raid but reminding him the original plan to take Port Hudson was still on and reinforcements were still needed. The present operation would rough up Taylor's army at Pattersonville, destroy their depots at New Iberia and the salt works nearby, and occupy Opelousas. "This is the limit proposed," Banks wrote. "We do not intend to hold any portions of this country, as it weakens our force, but will at once return to Baton Rouge to cooperate with you against Port

Lieutenant Colonel David Hunter Strother was a well-known artist under the pseudonym "Porte Crayon" and contributed to several publications. A captain in the 3rd West Virginia Cavalry, he took a promotion and went adventuring in Louisiana.

Massachusetts Commandery Military Order of the Loyal Legion and US Army Military History Institute.

Hudson." Banks asked Grant to give him a month. "I can be there easily by May 10," he added. "We will endeavor to establish communication with Admiral Farragut near Bayou Sara, but the opening of the levee opposite Port Hudson may make it impossible. If so, we will communicate with you freely, by way of New York, as to our progress." The general signed the dispatch, sealed it, and placed it in a dispatch case. An officer would carry the missive on the long roundabout tour of the country, from Brashear by rail to New Orleans, then by ship up the east coast of the United States, then by telegraph and courier across the nation, back to Memphis, and down the Mississippi to Grant. Weeks would burn by before delivery.[7]

The next morning, April 11, the Federal army advanced in earnest, leaving behind the banks of Berwick Bay. Weitzel, with his right flank covered by the USS *Clifton,* commenced a steady and systematic push, preparing to skirmish with the Rebel cavalry all day long. The Texan horsemen took positions to impede the Federals. "Saddled up early, proceed to within two miles of the enemy . . . at the bay," Private William Randolph Howell scribbled in his dairy. "Halt and send forward skirmishers." These Confederates received help when General Sibley arrived with the 4th Texas Cavalry, having finally assembled his old brigade accordion-like all the way from New Iberia. By various rushes and ruses, these horsemen would spend the day trying hard to see what the Yankees were hiding and buying time for their comrades upstream.[8]

Weitzel's Brigade started later in the day, heading away from their camps of the last two nights about noon, after the fog of the morning had burned away. "We had orders to fall in at 12 o'clock [meridian] and strange to say we moved forward promptly at the time," Lieutenant William H. Root of the 75th New York penned. Weitzel took his line of battle, ordered the men into columns of fours, then marched them in parallel lines along the west bank of Berwick Bay. The 8th Vermont, 75th New York, and 12th Connecticut took the lead, skirmishers deployed ahead of the brigade and within supporting range of the Union cavalry, while the 160th and 114th New York followed, the USS *Clifton* gliding on the water nearby. The soldiers advanced steadily and deliberately. They had time.[9]

Brigadier General William H. Emory's Division followed Weitzel's Brigade. The soldiers marching near the head of Emory's column watched Weitzel's men as they occasionally deployed in line and probed the enemy to their front. Small clusters of Confederate horsemen scampered just out of range, exchanging shots with the two companies of Union cavalry and their supporting infantry skirmishers. When the Federals suspected they were near a Rebel strongpoint, they unlimbered the guns of Captain Edmund C. Bainbridge's battery and fired a few rounds into it. As they advanced, the *Clifton*'s guns went into action at least once, driving away Colonel Green's Texas cavalry when they appeared to be ready to make a stand.[10]

Five miles into the march, as Emory's spectator-column moved past modest homesteads, they watched the enemy bring out a battery of 6- and 12-pounders—most likely the Val Verde Battery—and unleash a salvo from the relative shelter of a large sugar house, far

Private George R. Harrington of Windham, Vermont, enlisted in Company H, 8th Vermont on March 2, 1862. He survived the Teche Campaign, although he was wounded during later service in Louisiana. At the end of the war he was driving wagons for the regiment.

Collection of John Gibson, Potomac, Maryland.

in advance, to the right of the road. The projectiles spiraled through the ranks of Weitzel's skirmishers and continued on through Emory's massed infantry. "One of their shells entered the chimney of a house, another buried itself in the trunk of a tree by the side of the house, while a third struck a residence two or three yards in advance," observed Sergeant Frank Flinn of the 41st Massachusetts. "The shell exploded in a closet, scattering the china, pots, pans, and victuals in every direction. Fortunately, not a man was either killed or wounded." Bainbridge's Battery A, 1st U.S., and the 6th Massachusetts Battery unlimbered and returned the fire, driving away the Confederate artillery.[11]

If the Texans could have seen beyond Weitzel's and Emory's march, they would have spied undeniable evidence that this movement was indeed an invasion. Banks moved his headquarters. "The tantara of drums and bugles sounded agreeably to me this morning," wrote staff officer Lieutenant Colonel Strother. "War is a business as natural to man as hunting squirrels or tilling the soil. Roll your drums, flaunt your banners, and advance to the battlefield. War is a joy and glory of our race." Soldiers and orderlies packed the tools and possessions of the headquarters of the Army of the Gulf and loaded them onto the steamer *Laurel Hill.* It paddled across Berwick Bay and landed the general and his entourage onshore.[12]

The terrain for the day's steady, grinding, long-ranged gunfight proved challenging to an orderly advance. It started four miles

Lieutenant Squire E. Howard of Jamaica, Vermont, enlisted as first sergeant of Company H, 8th Vermont. He won the Medal of Honor in the fight against the CSS *Cotton* in January 1863 while serving as a sharpshooter aboard USS *Calhoun*. At the height of the battle, he volunteered to carry a message to comrades on shore, an act credited with saving the gunboat from capture. Promoted to lieutenant, he served in that capacity during the Teche Campaign. Wounded later in the war, Howard recovered and led his company as its captain.

Collection of John Gibson, Potomac, Maryland.

wide at Berwick Bay and required every one of Weitzel's men to cover the ground in skirmish order and thus conceal the movements of the army behind. The troops moved northward along the edge of Berwick Bay, which turned west-southwest at the Atchafalaya River. The river's curves would define the northern margin of the field until the waterway made its great sweep to the northeast some six miles in. Meanwhile, the line's southern edge rested on the coastal swamp, clearly defined by the berm of the New Orleans and Opelousas railroad and angling in and narrowing the field. The further Weitzel pushed along the bayou, the more compact his line became. When the Atchafalaya swept northeast, Weitzel anchored his the right of his brigade on the riverbank—across from where Rebels had captured the *Diana* a week and a half before—and wheeled his line to within a mile of Pattersonville. Just beyond lay the mouth of Bayou Teche, the route Banks's army would follow into the interior of Louisiana.

The cane fields through which the skirmishers maneuvered, the proximity of the coastal swamp, and the curve of the Atchafalaya provided an opportunity for Sibley to peek behind the blue curtain. He ordered one of his best officers, Captain Jerome B. McCown—the same man who had helped lead the lancer charge at the Battle of

Val Verde—to lead a party through the swamp on the Confederate right and work its way beyond Weitzel's left to determine the enemy troop strength. As a Mexican War veteran and longtime Texas Ranger, he was a natural choice. Sibley trusted McCown to know exactly how to work behind enemy lines. Unexpectedly, however, the expedition ended in disaster. Captain Giesecke in Company G, 4th Texas, recorded that McCown, "having imbibed too freely, fell from his horse during a retreat." Federals quickly captured the forty-three-year old warrior and several of his men.[13]

After a rugged day of skirmishing the Texans withdrew and yielded Pattersonville to Weitzel's troops, who entered the town around five o'clock that evening. The Army of the Gulf marched about a mile beyond the village, curved left along Bayou Teche, before bedding down. They were now in control of the bayou's mouth and just five miles east of the Rebel works at Fort Bisland. Its work done, the USS *Clifton* backed away from the army in the darkness. The vessel continued to Brashear City for the campaign's next phase.[14]

This was the first campaign for many of Banks's men, and for many it was also their first time a long way from home. To these

USS *Clifton* approaching Bisland. A Union naval officer's interpretation of the confusing tangle that were the battlefields of Southern Louisiana.

Nestell Collection, Nimitz Library, U.S. Naval Academy, Annapolis, Maryland.

New Yorkers and New Englanders, Louisiana appeared exotic. "The Teche country has been likened to the Garden of Eden," remembered Lieutenant Elias P. Pellet of the 114th New York. "It is certainly the garden of Louisiana. The woods, beautiful with grey moss, which adorns every tree; the magnolia in full bloom—thousands of wild roses, which spread our pathway on either side—seemed like the fairy land of some olden tale."[15]

In this unfamiliar terrain, Federal troops readied their camp for the night. Some eager soldiers dismantled every fence they could find to build camp fires while others saw to their own comforts. Dr. Harris Beecher, an assistant surgeon with the 114th New York, remarked on the soldiers' evening rituals. "The banks of the river were lined for miles with men bathing, watering horses, and filling their canteens," he remembered. "By 9 o'clock they had cleaned themselves from dust, partaken of their suppers and were lying

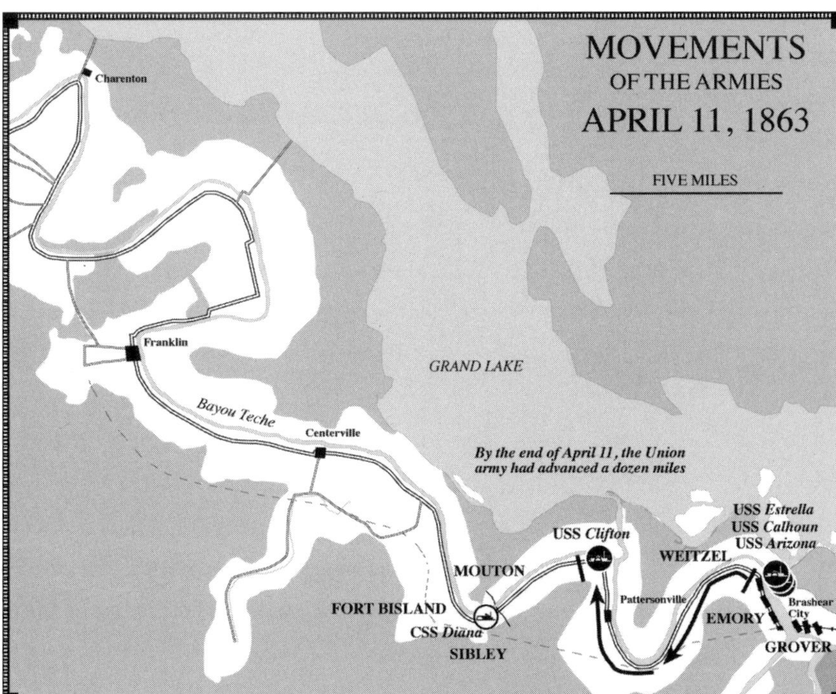

over the ground, rolled up in their blankets, fast asleep." But not all the soldiers were able to sleep so easily, despite their exhaustion. The campsite was marred by one disadvantage: the scattered carcasses of Texas horses and mules, killed in the fight with the *Diana* nearly two weeks before, littered the field. The smell kept many of the troops from having pleasant dreams. "From bundles of blankets would now and then proceed a curse," wrote Beecher, "or a call upon the commissary to 'remove those rations of meat.'"[16]

Private Paschal Prescott Shores of Granby, Vermont, served as a private in Company K, 8th Vermont. He survived the regiment's Louisiana campaigns only to be wounded and fall into Confederate hands at the Battle of Cedar Creek, Virginia, in October 1864. He later died from his injuries.

Collection of John Gibson, Potomac, Maryland.

Upstream from these slumbering Yankees, the Confederates remained frenzied. The Louisiana infantry and gangs of slaves had spent all of April 11 moving mounds of their native soil. Nearly a half-mile forward of the existing works, soldiers and slaves erected a chest-high earthen barricade on the east bank of the Teche The resulting structure, Redoubt Number 2, was described as a "log house filled with earth." It boasted a five-foot-deep moat and anchored the left of the Confederate line on the edge of the swamps and woods surrounding Grand Lake. This new line pivoted off of the previous year's works at this point, like two legs of a caliper. Redoubt Number 2 stood just nine feet ahead of the original works; the new right of the line lay a half mile forward of the old entrenchments.

Now Mouton's breastworks east of Bayou Teche cut a dark gash across the cane fields in a gentle arc. Engineers realized, nearly too late, that the line of works built the previous year needed to be adjusted for better fields of fire. The new fort at its left terminus, Redoubt Number 2, could cover the entire front and lob shells into the Federal right.[17]

General Mouton had few men to cover such an extensive fieldwork, nearly a mile long. Captain Florian Cornay's St. Mary's Cannoneers had a section of two 12-punder howitzers that augmented Captain Thomas Faries's Pelican Artillery and their mixed battery of two 3-inch rifles, two 12-pounder howitzers, and two 6-pounders. Three infantry units—the 18th Louisiana "Creole" Regiment, the 24th "Crescent" Regiment, and most of the 10th Yellow Jacket Battalion—supported the guns while the 7th Texas Cavalry provided a mobile reserve.[18]

Though the Confederates could have used more men on that front, the deeply furrowed sugarcane fields in front of their works favored defense. Much of the previous year's crop had not been harvested. "The cane had stood all winter, consequently it was frosted and shriveled," Private Felix Robert Collard of the 7th Texas wrote. "It grew eight or ten feet high and when the wind would strike it and blow it down it would elbow and straiten up, a tangled mass. A dog could hardly get through it." Officers sent details from their units to trample and cut the cane for three hundred yards in front of the works to give them better fields of fire.[19]

Confederate preparations continued through the night. Workers hurried to finish the shorter line on the west bank. Half as long as its counterpart on the east bank, this earthwork incorporated the unfinished railroad embankment on the far right, forming a 120-degree angle. Troops behind the berm could sweep the field and pour an oblique fire into the advancing Federals' left flank. Other troops cleared and enlarged the drainage ditches that ran through the sugarcane fields, using split cypress fencing rails to shore up the sides into natural trenches. With their flanks secured by impassable terrain, the Rebels also built additional redoubts and lunettes on their line. Gunners made ready the two 24-pounders into Fort Bisland.[20]

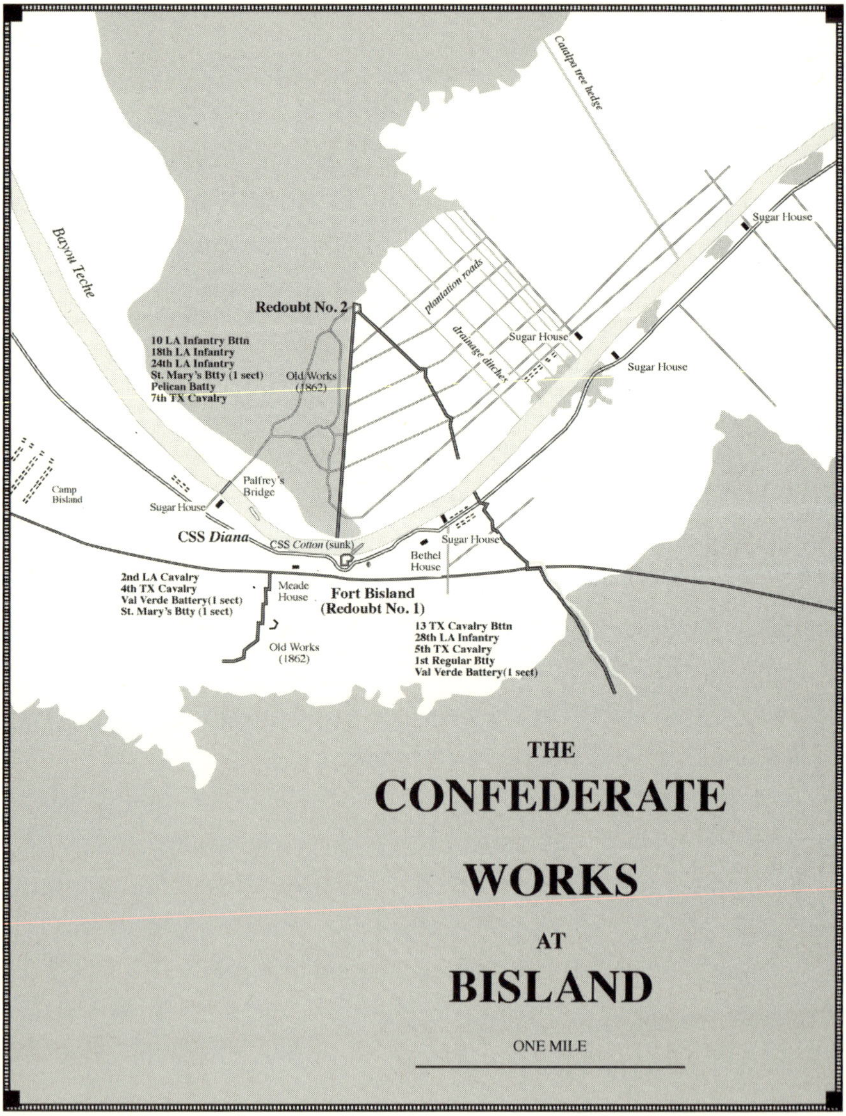

The Confederates concentrated much of their army behind these works. General Sibley—in command west of Bayou Teche—concentrated Captain Oliver J. Semmes' 1st Regular Battery near the bayou so that their four 6-pounders and two 3-inch rifles could cover the road and bank. Captain Joseph Draper Sayers commanded two sections of the Val Verde Battery in an elevated redoubt with gun ramps for his two 6-pounders and two 12-pounder howitzers on the far right, behind the railroad embankment. The 28th Louisiana Infantry took its place in line between these two concentrations of cannon. The 5th Texas Cavalry and Colonel Edwin Waller's Battalion moved behind the berm and into the woods to hold the Rebel right. The 4th Texas Cavalry and the 2nd Louisiana Cavalry constituted a mobile reserve near Fort Bisland, along with a section each of St. Mary's Cannoneers and the Val Verde Battery.

"On the Bayou Teche" by Alfred R. Waud. This view of Bayou Teche shows good examples of plantation bridges, barges, and a small steamer underway in the narrow confines of the waterway.

Historic New Orleans Collection, Accession no. 1977.137.5.8.

Sugar House and Refinery, St. Mary's Parish by David Hunter Strother. The agricultural-industrial complex astounded Union troops as they crossed Berwick Bay and moved up Bayou Teche.

David Hunter Strother, Drawings and Sketches, The West Virginia and Regional History Collection Holdings, West Virginia University Libraries, Acc. No. p.95.30.145.

The battle-scarred *Diana* waited in the bayou, around a bend and out of sight. Lieutenant T. D. Nettles of the Val Verde Battery commanded the vessel, and he had prepared it to edge out of the tree cover to fire, then draw back behind a bend with block and tackle to reload. If needed, he could also move downstream and slide into the center of the nearly mile-long Rebel line. Nettles understood that the *Diana*'s powerful 30-pound Parrot rifle needed to command both banks of the Teche as well as the bayou road.[21]

Both sides were now in place, and the next few days might determine the control of western Louisiana, and with it, the Mississippi River.

9

Counting Cannon

"Delightful task, to move up to be shot at."

Lieutenant Elias P. Pellet
114th New York

Major General Nathaniel P. Banks finally had his full army in motion. In the dark, foggy morning of April 12 his soldiers, bleary eyed from lack of sleep, shuffled into their ranks. Miles away at Brashear City, Brigadier General Cuvier Grover's armada had left the docks a few hours before sunrise to proceed with their great envelopment. The flotilla was a day behind schedule, but at army headquarters at Pattersonville Banks remained unaware of Grover's delay. Although the night before Banks had been certain Grover and his division were already underway, it was not until two o'clock that Sunday morning, April 12, that the division—on board the gunboats *Calhoun, Estrella,* and *Arizona,* and the transports *St. Mary, Laurel Hill, Quinebaug,* and *Southern Merchant*—started its journey up Berwick Bay, through Grand Lake Pass, and into Grand Lake. The *Clifton,* having escorted Brigadier General Godfrey Weitzel's troops to the Pattersonville area, had arrived at Brashear City around midnight and picked up Grover and his staff.[1]

Grover's delay was understandable. The space available on the transports and gunboats had been insufficient, and it took navy

Lieutenant George N. Carpenter of Northfield, Vermont, enlisted as the sergeant major of the regiment, but he earned promotion to lieutenant in Company C by the time of the Teche Campaign.

Collection of John Gibson, Potomac, Maryland.

men a day to round up flatboats and barges to accommodate all of the men, horses, wagons, artillery, and supplies in Grover's command. When the division—nearly eight thousand men—had finally squeezed into their tight berths, the flotilla embarked. A thick fog descended, however, and the advance ground to a stop. They had to wait until visibility improved, which was not until 8:00 AM. Finally underway again, the vessels churned north, up the bay, on their grand flanking maneuver. Assuming that Grover was already twelve hours into his movement and on schedule to land later that morning, Banks directed the army at Pattersonville to follow the course of Bayou Teche until they found the enemy. Weitzel had his men on the road by 8:30 AM, by which time Grover was barely underway at Brashear City. The great envelopment was no longer synchronized.

For the soldiers in the ranks of Weitzel's brigade, marching along the Teche, this was familiar ground. They had been in this neighborhood just three months before. Far to the front, the sound of skirmishers and supporting artillery began to crackle and thump but the rest of the column traveled in relative peace. "Until mid-afternoon nothing occurred to interrupt the steady

Colonel Arthur Pendleton Bagby Jr., led the 7th Texas Cavalry and was a veteran of the New Mexico Campaign and the Battle of Galveston. He was also a lawyer, a West Point graduate, the son and namesake of a famous Alabama politician, and had served at Fort Chadbourne on the Texas frontier before the war.

Library of Congress.

tramp of men and horses, and save the rattle of equipments and the low word of command, there was nothing to break the silence of the march," recalled Lieutenant George N. Carpenter of the 8th Vermont. "It was a lovely Sunday, and the eye of the imaginative soldier was free to wander over the slowly changing landscape and take in all its varied beauty." Few, if any, among that Union army, knew what waited ahead.[2]

Behind Weitzel's troops, the men in Brigadier General William H. Emory's Division had not been idle. The night before, the fifty-five-foot steamer *A. B. Seger* had ferried the 175th New York, part of Colonel Oliver P. Gooding's Brigade, to the east side of the Teche. They landed about a mile above Pattersonville at a place known to locals at Lynch's Point. This regiment shook out skirmishers and probed ahead, hurrying to keep even with Weitzel's line progressing on the bayou's west bank.

This thin blue line advancing across the fields looked like trouble, and Rebel scouts rode back to Brigadier General Alfred Mouton's headquarters to tell him of this development. The general responded by sending a courier to the leader of three hundred men of the 7th Texas Cavalry. "Colonel Bagby . . . was posted at this point with his regiment and ordered to check the enemy's advance by every means in his power," Mouton reported. The Texans mounted their horses, received their instructions, and filed past laborers working on the entrenchments. Colonel Arthur Pendleton Bagby's three hundred soldiers set out against the coming Federal army.[3]

West of Bayou Teche, General Henry Hopkins Sibley responded to the Union advance as well, ordering his men to prepare an ambush. Colonel James Reily's 4th Texas Cavalry and Colonel William G. Vincent's 2nd Louisiana thundered up the road to try to set as many traps as possible. Coordinating their efforts with Colonel Bagby on the bayou's east bank, these troops took positions about six hundred yards ahead of the earthworks near a large sugarhouse. From that spot, detachments could move ahead, harass enemy soldiers, and attempt to lure them into range of their Enfields. If the Federals cooperated, they would find themselves assailed from both their front and right flanks as Bagby's men joined the action from across the bayou. Should they come in force, Reily would then lead his troops in feigned flight back into the works. Then the combined guns of Major General Richard Taylor's whole army, as well as the *Diana* lurking behind the bend, might shred any impetuous Yankee pursuit. At the same time, two additional companies moved out from the right side of the Rebel works. Company C, 5th Texas Cavalry—the Grimes County Rangers—joined the New Braunfels Germans of Company B, 7th Texas, and the "Davis Guards" of Company B, 4th Texas, to work around the left side of the Union advance.[4]

Large clouds of dust thrown up by Reily's advancing Confederates caused some skittish Union scouts to scurry back and report that the enemy was coming in force. Weitzel repeated the news, bringing forward General Banks and Brigadier General William H. Emory, who rode ahead to personally reconnoiter the route and react to this unexpected development. The officers scanned the fields ahead through binoculars but spied only a few Confederate cavalry jostling the sugarcane. Convinced by what he saw, Banks turned his horse around, remarking, "There are no enemy in front, we will advance the army, gentlemen."[5]

Soldiers from the 8th Vermont, among others, took advantage of the brief stop. They marveled at the plantations and columned mansions that dotted the fields of corn and cane, "where for generations the proud old southern families had dwelt in luxuriant ease," Carpenter opined. One of these homes had been hit by a cannon ball. "Passing close to one of these houses about noon, the soldiers discovered it had just been deserted by the inmates, who in their hasty flight had left a nice hot dinner smoking on the board," Carpenter continued. "The path of a cannon-shot was traced directly across the room. So the boys, thinking it a pity to let a good dinner spoil, fell out and took it in."[6]

The Federal army, returning to motion, cleared a point of woods and emerged onto another broad agricultural plain of corn and cane fields. The men knew the well-entrenched Confederates waited somewhere beyond those acres. But they did not know whether the enemy waited in the fields as well, and clouds of dust from earlier in the day led many to prudently fear an ambush in the dense growth. Weitzel directed his brigade to file to the left in their columns then, facing right, deploy into line. The 12th Connecticut led the way and became the left side of the brigade—and of the entire army. The 160th New York and the 75th New York followed, and the 114th New York and 8th Vermont followed last. Brigadier General Halbert E. Paine deployed to Weitzel's right, filling the space between his brigade and the Teche. From left to right, the 173rd and 133rd New York filed in first, with the 8th New Hampshire and 4th Wisconsin closest to the stream. The guns of the 6th Massachusetts and Battery A, 1st U.S., rumbled behind the center of this line. Emory's two other brigades, those led by Colonel Timothy Ingraham and Colonel Gooding—less the regiments committed to the east bank—made second and third reserve lines.

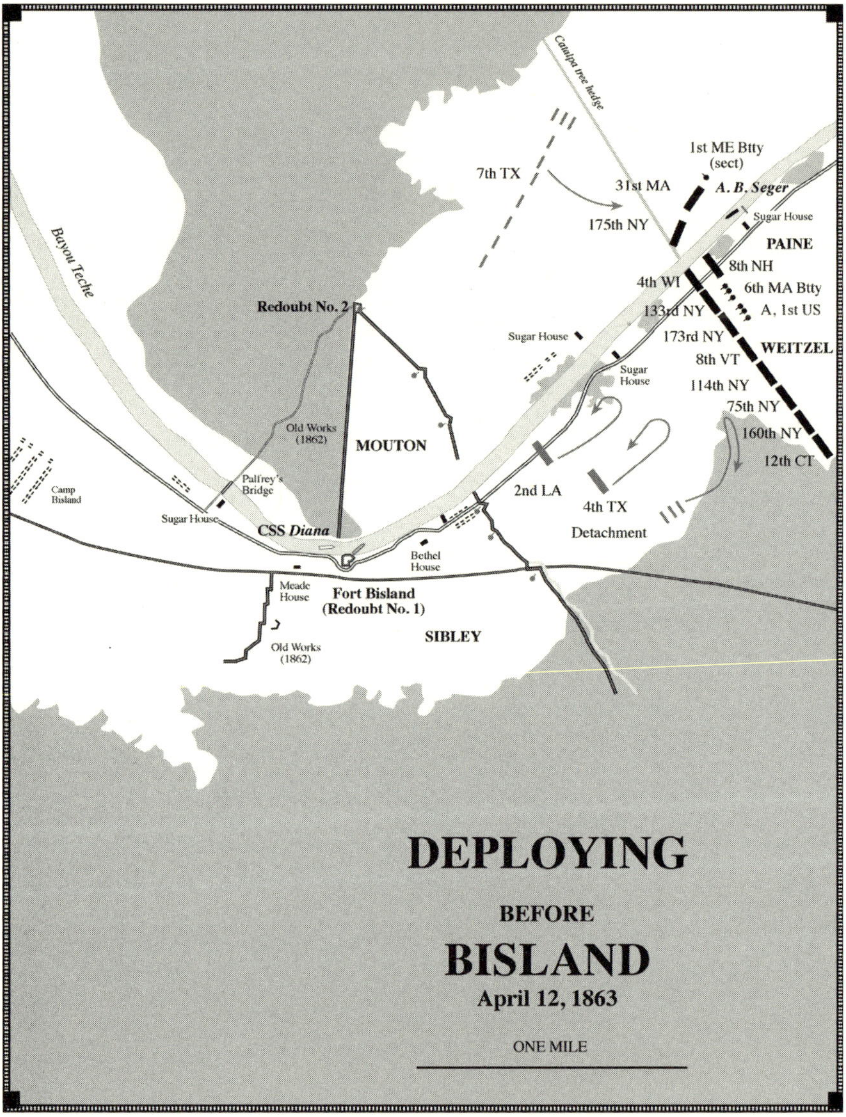

The fear of Confederates lurking in the woods and fields proved well founded. As Emory deployed his troops, Banks rode up with his staff and bodyguards. Several hundred yards away in the woods, to the left, a handful of Rebel sharpshooters could not pass up the chance to fire at such a tempting target. "Half a dozen muskets . . . discharged, and the bullets went whistling past and

Colonel Timothy Ingraham was a fifty-year-old New Bedford merchant before the war. He enlisted as a captain in the 3rd Massachusetts "Minute Men," a ninety-day regiment, and helped destroy the Gosport Naval Yard in Norfolk, Virginia, before serving in garrison at Fortress Monroe. He returned to Boston and then joined the 18th Massachusetts Infantry as its lieutenant colonel, serving in the defenses of Washington and on the Peninsula of Virginia but without seeing action. He left that unit in August 1862 to take command of the newly formed 38th Massachusetts headed for Louisiana.

Massachusetts Comandery Military Order of the Loyal Legion and the US Army Military History Institute.

between the Generals," wrote Sergeant Frank Flinn. One of the nearby orderlies tumbled from his saddle, shot through the heart. Emory wheeled his horse and, in a flash, pointed to the woods and yelled to his escort, "after them men; there are but five or six of them or we would have had more shots." The blue coats thundered toward the woods, but by then the quarry had flushed.[7]

In the early afternoon, the Federal line once again came to a lurching halt. Ahead, near the bank of the bayou and partially sheltered by a large sugarhouse, stood a barely visible Rebel line of battle. This, then, was the cause for all the dust. "They appeared ready to receive us," noted Flinn. Mounted Confederates moved unconcerned across the furrows of the field and along the bayou road, scanning the Union line, just out of rifle range. Banks's infantry stood still but called for their cavalry to come forward and chase these Rebels away. After watching the Federal army for a few minutes, the Confederate riders turned their mounts, spurring them into a lope, and folded in with the troops near the bayou. "Suddenly, the two Rebel regiments drawn up in line of battle disappeared," Flinn recalled, "and in a few moments after the dense cloud of rising dust marked the course they were retreating."[8]

Brigadier General Halbert Paine had been a Milwaukee lawyer before the war. He led the 4th Wisconsin Infantry when it came to Louisiana with Major General Benjamin Butler and had helped capture the Lafourche County. His capable leadership earned him to promotion to brigadier just prior to the Teche Campaign.

State Library of Louisiana.

Major Harai Robinson arrived at the front of the line with his two hundred or so Union cavalrymen just in time to see the enemy retreating. It was more than he could bear, and he ordered his troops after them. Buglers sounded the advance, and the Union horsemen thundered down the road in pursuit. Bagby's Confederates on the east bank had hoped for such a move, and from positions along the bayou they began peppering the Federal column as it galloped past. The bullets brought down a few horses, but their riders emerged unscathed. "Volley after volley was fired," Flinn observed, "but of all the firing, not a man was touched." Robinson recalled his troopers and moved out of range.[9]

The Federals responded to Bagby's volleys by reinforcing their forces on the east bank. The 250 inexperienced soldiers of the 175th New York had been exchanging shots with the Texans all morning, but they could do little more. They had failed to push the Rebels from their positions on the west bank, and Bagby's men now harassed the troops on the opposite bank. The *A. B. Seger* ferried over the 31st Massachusetts and Lieutenant John E. Morton with two guns of the 1st Maine Battery to try to drive away this nuisance.

Two companies of the 7th Texas, under cover in a cane field, moved in close to scout the Federals as they disembarked. "The enemy was unloading a steamboat of some kind of troops," wrote Private Felix Robert Collard. "The two companies kept concealed behind bushes and turn row weeds, but finally had to expose themselves when within six hundred yards of the steamboat." Lookouts on the gunboat spied the Texans and relayed word to the troops on shore. Lieutenant Morton, having just reached dry ground with his section of the 1st Maine Artillery, put his two 12-pound howitzers into action.[10]

Little time passed between the flash of Morton's cannon muzzles and the resulting explosion among the Confederates. "A piece of shell the size of a man's hand, struck one of the men . . . just above the belt," Collard observed. "All of his abdominal viscera were hanging over his knees." The soldier looked at his comrades—stunned—then at his own guts. "My God!" the soon-to-be dead man said in amazement, "would you look at that." A second round whistled past the Rebels, bursting behind them. A soldier had been riding forward at just that instant, having filled all the canteens of one of the companies. The horse bolted forward, dropping its rider, and jangled toward the Federals with the saddle rolled beneath it and more than two-dozen canteens slapping its withers and flanks. "I caught him with the bridle," continued Collard. He held him long enough for the rider to come and claim him, who arrived with "his eyes sticking out like yearling's horns." The Texans withdrew with alacrity to the safety of the woods beyond the sight and effective range of the New England gunners.[11] With the Texans in retreat and its troops delivered, the *A. B. Seger* left. Obstructions in the Teche blocked any further passage upstream, and engineers would soon have a pontoon bridge connecting both banks, so the boat relinquished its role as a ferry.

The quick-thinking and well-equipped Federals had foiled Confederate attempts at ambush, and had refused to be suckered into a headlong pursuit into the deadly embrace of the artillery studding the Rebel works. Apparently Banks would not fall for tricks that might have bamboozled Comanches and Mexicans back in Texas. Reily's men had "engaged the enemy for a while, and then broke in confusion back to our lines, hoping to draw the enemy on," wrote Private Bill Davidson, a Texan, "but they were too cautious to be caught in that trap."[12]

Major Robinson, now safely back behind Federal lines, reported that he had glimpsed the *Diana* around a bend in the bayou. Officers carried the intelligence to Banks, at the time supervising a repair crew working to repair a plantation bridge to the east bank and another crew clearing obstructions in the bayou. The general was intrigued by this news. He walked up the road and over to the bank to get a closer view, soon attracting a clump of fellow gawkers. "From a rising ground, the masts of our former staunch little gunboat *Diana* was seen with a large rebel flag flying, nearly a mile distant," Flinn remembered. "Everyone wished to take a good look at her," he added. Soon staff officers and other headquarters personnel clumped together, sharing binoculars and commenting on the sight. As they watched, a flash and puff of smoke, followed an instant later by a loud report, proved that they, too, had been spotted. The whirring and whistling of a 30-pounder Parrott round grew louder as it approach the general and his party. The bolt buzzed overhead, "plunging into the ground beyond with a thud," Flinn added, "that no doubt sounded musically to every ear."[13]

Relieved to have been shot at without effect, the cluster broke up, only to hear the report of another cannon, off to the right, from across the bayou. This shot whistled over them diagonally, smacking a bank of earth near the road and sending two lounging soldiers hurrying for cover. Banks and his aides quickly moved away, realizing that these shots had not been an accident.

While the two armies teased each other near Fort Bisland, Confederate scouts brought news from the shores of Grand Lake to Major General Taylor at his command post at Bethel Plantation.

The gallopers had spied at least one gunboat and several transports ascending Grand Lake and heading around and behind the Confederate lines. Taylor had anticipated this move, to be sure, but handling the next few hours would be a delicate business. He dispatched the 2nd Louisiana, horses lathered from a day of skirmishing, and two of Captain Florian Cornay's reserve guns—a 12-pounder and a 6-pounder—to the Verdun Plantation on the east bank. The plantation lay four miles back from the line, at the point where Bayou Teche curved closest to the shores of Grand Lake. Here these Louisianans would take the road to the Grand Lake landing and observe the fleet's movements, ascertain the flotilla's size, and oppose as best they could any attempted landings. Once his soldiers determined where the Yankees would come in, Taylor could prepare a proper response. Certainly, he assumed, Captain Edward W. Fuller and the Southern gunboats were at

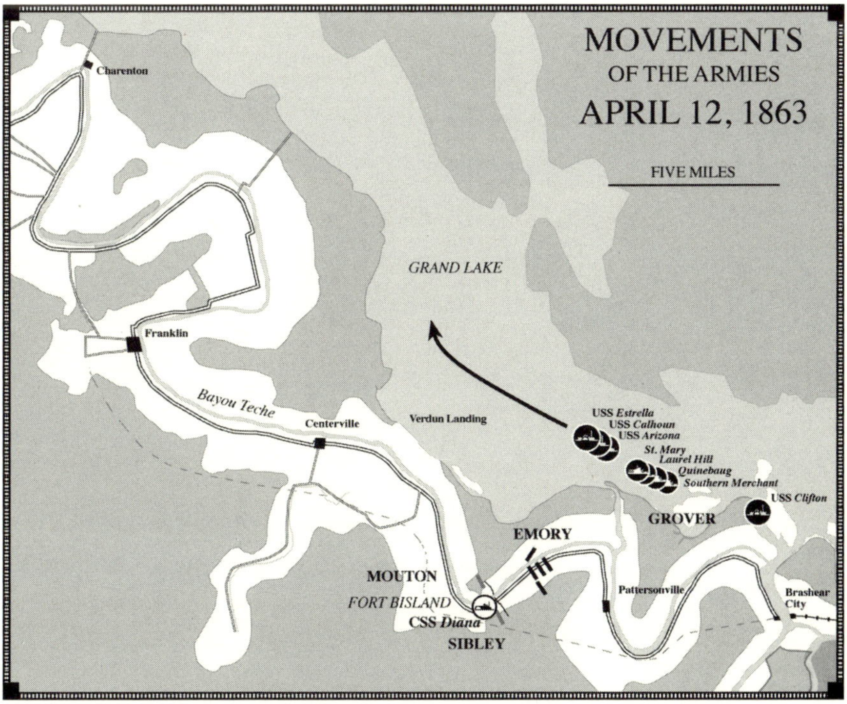

Butte-a-la-Rose by now. They could launch a slashing counterattack tomorrow. Meanwhile, Taylor would deal with the enemy to his front. With luck he could keep Banks busy around Fort Bisland long enough for the Rebel fleet to upend Union plans.

To Banks, the Rebels were acting peculiarly, almost inviting an attack. Taylor seemed to *want* him to butt against the works around Fort Bisland. Perhaps the Rebels had discovered Grover's Division en route, Banks mused. Had most of Taylor's army already retreated to safety, leaving behind only a rear guard and the *Diana?* The thought then settled in: Were they concentrating their troops to attack the Grand Lake column as it landed? What if they *did* attack Grover with both their land and naval forces while he was alone and unsupported? Banks and his army might be defeated in detail. The situation presented a conundrum. If, on the other hand, Emory and Weitzel stormed the Fort Bisland line too soon, the Confederates might fall back too soon, and escape before Grover could close the trap. If, however, they were trapping Grover instead while Banks dawdled, any delay in attacking the fort might lead to a Union disaster. After conferring with his generals, the commander of the Army of the Gulf decided it was time to see what the Southerners were hiding.[14]

Banks sent Weitzel's Brigade forward, giving them the honor of drawing the first Rebel fire on the bayou's west bank. At 3:30 PM, the Federals moved in a line three regiments across. The 75th New York was on the right, the green troops of the 114th New York took the center, the 12th Connecticut on the left, with the 160th New York and 8th Vermont following behind. The 6th Massachusetts Battery followed behind the infantry. "Delightful task, to move up to be shot at," wrote Lieutenant Elias P. Pellet of the 114th New York. "Targets on which the enemy might try his skill at gunnery." General Weitzel watched through his field glasses as his men moved forward on their "errand of discovery." The troops pushed through a field of growing sugarcane.[15]

Weitzel's soldiers found it difficult to cross the cane field's deep furrows and tangled crops, which were almost tall enough to conceal the regiments. "The fields through which we marched were covered with a growth of sugarcane," scrawled Dr. Harris Beecher, an assistant surgeon with the 114th New York, "and so dense that it required the most fatiguing labor for the men to push their way through." Soldiers jumped from row to row, leapt ditches, and crowded through openings. "Wading through mud holes beneath a scalding sun, the boys toiled on stopping every few minutes to reform the line, which necessarily became broken for it was impossible to one man to see more than half-a-dozen of his comrades at a time," described Beecher.[16]

The soldiers of the 12th Connecticut suffered as well. "The Brigade advanced," wrote Captain John William De Forest, "prostrating or climbing fences, and struggling amid horrible labyrinths of tangled sugar cane." He likened the experience as three times worse than sprinting diagonally through a mile-long cornfield. "Imagine yourself," De Forest continued, "tired and breathless as you are, and you will form some conception of what it is to move in line through a cane field." The soldiers tried different techniques. "At first you valiantly push aside the tough green obstacles; then you ignominiously dodge under or around them; at last you fall down with your tongue out. The ranks are broken; the regiment tails off into strings, the strongest leading; the ground is strewn with panting soldiers; the organization disappears," wrote the captain.[17]

After spending the afternoon in tortured progress, the troops emerged into an open area where the cane had been cut or trampled. "The cane once passed, stragglers began to come up and find their places," De Forest continued. "The ranks are counted anew while advancing, and we once more had a regiment." At last the troops could see the enemy works. "Before us lay a long and comparatively narrow plain, bounded by forests rising out of the swamps, and decorated by a long, low, earthwork, a third of a mile ahead of us, barely visible to the naked eye," De Forest described. "Away to our right were two half demolished brick sugar-houses." A cloud of dust, raised by the 2nd Louisiana Cavalry as it retired toward Verdun landing, was the only activity visible. "Otherwise the scene was one of perfect quietness and silence, and desertion."[18]

The Rebels waited patiently before announcing their presence at such a grand array of targets. "Presently a wreath of smoke curled into the air," Pellet remembered. A fraction of a second later the gun's report sounded, followed closely by the whir of an incoming 12-pounder solid shot. The round zipped past the cringing infantry and through their accompanying battery, splitting open the two lead horses of one of the Massachusetts limbers, scattering trace chains and harnesses through the air before bounding into the cane beyond. For inexperienced soldiers, this was a gruesome introduction to war. "This was plainly seen by the entire regiment," Pellet wrote, "and for an instant the line wavered."[19]

Then the Confederates opened fire with their cannon along the entire line. On the bayou's east bank Mouton's aide, Lieutenant F. C. Loret, reported that "The fire was opened by Lieutenant Felix Winchester of the Pelican Battery, who was in command of one section of Parrot's guns, causing the enemy who had landed at Lynch's Point, in order to attack our left, to change the position of their battery as often as three times in the course of an hour." Within minutes, smoke shrouded the Rebel earthworks on both banks, punctuated by flashes and blasts from more than twenty cannon. The Rebel fire also foolishly revealed the locations and caliber of their guns.[20]

Confederate skirmishers in front of the Bisland fortifications hurried to their entrenchments, certain the Federals would try to advance. "'Here they come!' was shouted down our line as skirmishers came running in and jumping over the works to their position behind them," recalled Private Theophilus Noel of the 4th Texas. "In a moment the graveyard sound of the minie bullets as they flew hissing over our heads reassured us they were coming." The Confederate riflemen did their best at long range and the steady work of their cannon cheered them on. "Then! Then!" Noel recalled, "but a moment more and bang! boom! boom! sounded the well known thundering voice of the [Sibley] Brigade's idol—the Val Verde battery, on our right."[21]

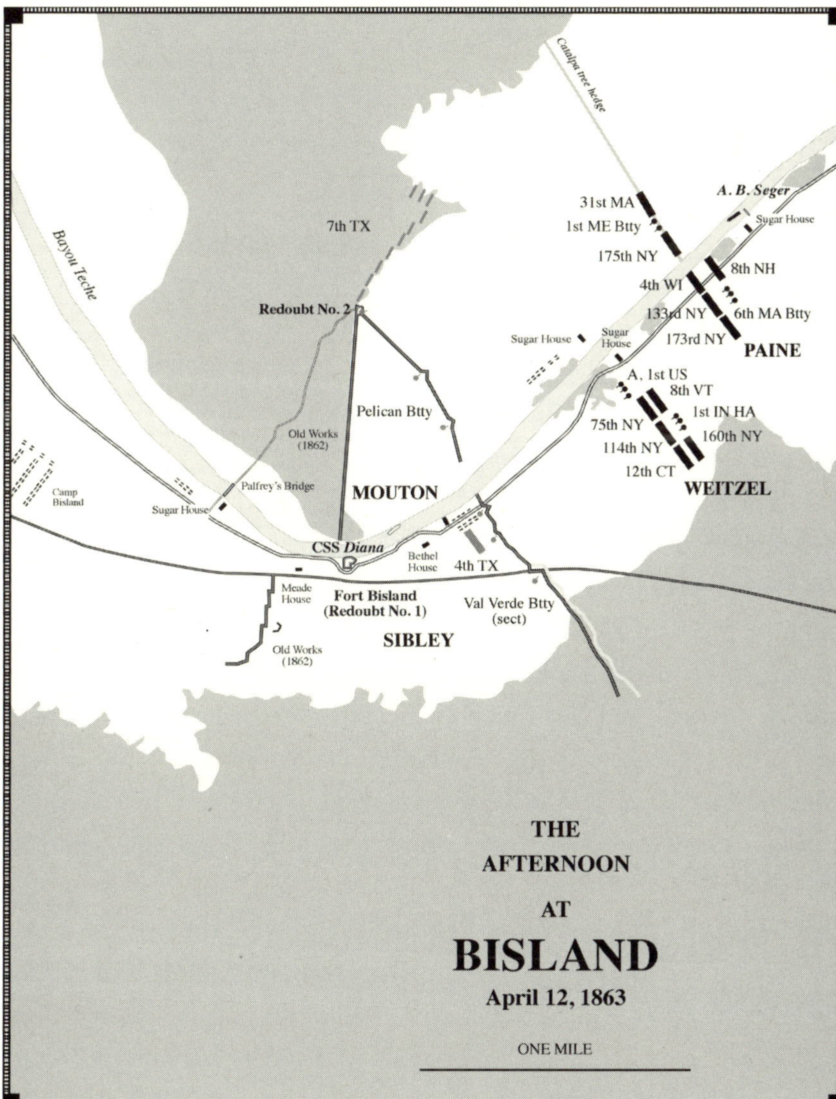

Colonel Stephen Thomas, 8th Vermont Infantry was a factory owner in West Fairlee before his commission and led the 8th Vermont during the Teche Campaign. He would earn not only the command of a brigade as a result of his conduct in Louisiana, but he would also earn the Medal of Honor in a hand-to-hand encounter later in Virginia.

Collection of John Gibson, Potomac, Maryland.

The rapid barrage of the combined Confederate guns addled the Federal columns. "It was a trying ordeal for the Green Mountain boys," recalled Carpenter of the 8th Vermont. "The air was full of deadly missiles of every description—shells, solid shot, grape, and even pieces of railroad iron, and the earth was plowed in every direction as the huge projectiles buried themselves in the ground, throwing the dust and dirt over the men." As this regiment wavered, Colonel Stephen Thomas rode in front to rally his men. "Steady men! Stand firm! Remember old Vermont is looking at you today!" he screamed. "We've been in the field a long while, boys, and this is the first time we have had a chance to begin the work we were sent here to do. Steady old Vermont!" The officer trotted his horse along the regimental front, repeating his admonishment that their home state was watching. A wit in the ranks called back, "Hope Vermont won't see us in such a scrape again."[22]

Weitzel's men had accomplished their task, luring the Confederates into revealing their positions. Now they were merely spectators and targets. "Shot and shell now rattled around us like hail, but the position of the enemy being known, our labors, for a while, were suspended," Pellet wrote. Upon reaching a drainage ditch, officers called out the order, "Lie . . . Down!" Subalterns and sergeants echoed the command.[23]

20-pounder Parrott Rifles. The Union army in the Teche Campaign included a dozen of these hard-hitting guns.

Library of Congress.

Some of the veterans of the 12th Connecticut remained unmoved by the spectacle. "Of a sudden, *bang, bang, bang* roared an unseen battery, and *jiz, jiz, jiz* screeched the shells over our heads," observed Captain De Forest. "The shelling didn't hurt us a bit, and consequently did not scare us much, for we were already accustomed to this kind of racket, and only took it hard when it was mingled with the cries of the wounded."[24]

The Federals moved their artillery forward from the rear of the army to answer this long-range insult. The massive 20- and 30-pounder Parrotts of the 1st Indiana Heavy Artillery trundled into position a few dozen feet behind the 114th New York lying in the ditch. The multitalented Hoosiers heaved their guns into place, sighted their barrels, and began drilling rifled shells into the Confederate positions. The big guns rattled the ribs of the nearby New Yorkers and scattered debris onto them. "Not infrequently," Pellet complained, "pieces of copper, bits of plugs and fragments of broken shell would fall thickly around us, and we were almost in as much danger from our own guns as from those of the enemy."[25]

Captain E. C. Bainbridge's battery of U.S. Regulars galloped ahead of where the 8th Vermont waited. Witnesses watched its captain "riding alongside the foremost gun, dressed in spick and span uniform, and lashing the horses with his rawhide as though life depended on every leap they made." The limbers wheeled their guns into position, making deep furrowing arcs in the soft soil. As soon as the first cannon had been manhandled into place, Bainbridge jumped off his horse and sighted the piece. His four 12-pounder Napoleons and two 3-inch rifles were soon in action.[26]

30-pounder Parrott Rifles. Notice the stack of ammunition, giving an idea of the size of projectile this awkward-looking cannon fired. These pieces are in a fortification with vent hole and muzzles covered.

Library of Congress.

As the artillery duel continued, the 12th Connecticut remained steady and still. "The shells hummed and cracked and fought each other in flights over our heads," observed De Forest, "dotting the sky with little globes of smoke which marked their explosions, and sending buzzing fragments in all directions."[27]

The 8th Vermont rose to its feet, its officers barking at the soldiers to move into closer support of the battery. "It requires nerve at any time to charge under fire and do valiant execution," Carpenter mused. "It is quite another thing to face unprotected the murderous hail, and to stand hour after hour and silently wait, for there is nothing to bind the eyes to danger or sustain the sinking spirit." Colonel Thomas moved ahead on horseback, leading his men. As he did so, another rider galloped forward, reining to a hard stop alongside Thomas, amid a splash of dirt clods and dust.

1st Indiana Heavy Artillery. A battery deployed in the field presented an impressive array of men, animals, and vehicles.

Andrew D. Lytle Collection, Mss. 893, 1254, Louisiana and Lower Mississippi Valley Collections, LSU Libraries, Baton Rouge, La.

The newcomer, one of Weitzel's staff, brought orders for the colonel to dismount and to not expose himself needlessly to enemy fire. "Colonel Thomas sends his compliments to General Weitzel," the officer responded, using the third person, respectful of military etiquette, "and begs to inform him that he didn't come down there to get off his horse for any damn Rebel."[28]

As they moved forward, the green regiment began to take casualties. A shell burst over the 8th Vermont, and a large piece shot straight down with, according to a witness, "a queer fluttering sound." Hit on the top of his head, a corporal dropped to the earth like a feed sack. Another fragment hit a soldier on his lower leg. As the injured man rolled around on the ground clutching his limb, his captain came to assess his wound. Finding no blood, the officer declared him "a lucky man, and would be pensioned for life." But he had not seen that the iron shard had shattered the man's femur. The soldier would lose his leg, and infection would later take his life. There were also casualties among the 75th New York. "The Rebels made some very good shots at our battalion," reported Lieutenant William H. Root. Nearly a dozen men had been hit or killed.[29]

The Federal artillery suffered as well. Bainbridge's regulars tangled with three Rebel targets, including a pair of 12-pounder

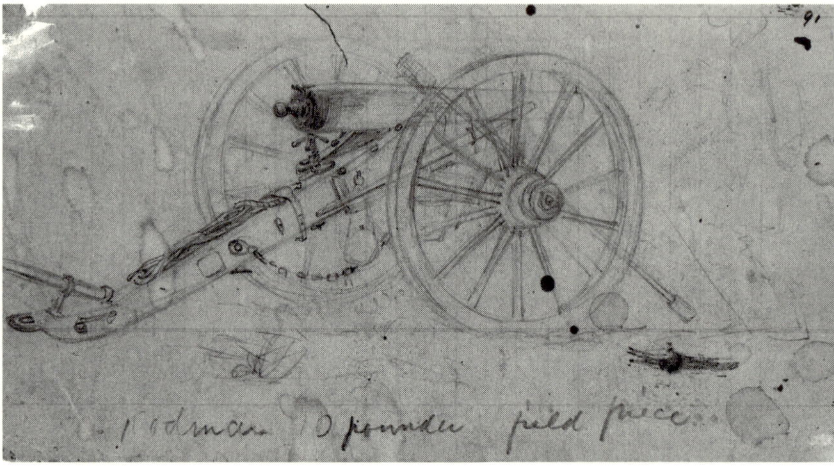

A 3-inch Ordnance Rifle. A lighter but robust cannon that provided good range and nice hitting power.

Library of Congress.

howitzers from the Pelican Artillery on the east bank, the *Diana* in the bayou, and the pair of 24-pounders dead ahead. Before long, one of his limbers had been smashed. Confederate projectiles also killed the horses and riders of a second limber. By the time he ended the attack against the enemy at Fort Bisland, Bainbridge would lose four killed and five wounded, as well as fifteen of his horses.[30]

A 12-pounder Napoleon. This smoothbore cannon served as the mainstay artillery on most Civil War battlefields and were quite versatile.

Library of Congress.

The artillery duel continued until that evening, when the majority of the Federals withdrew, as General Emory reported, "out of the range of the enemy's grape and canister and allowed to take a good night's rest." The men of the 12th Connecticut received their orders as a young aide to

Captain Samuel Gault, a Boston bookkeeper, led Company K, 38th Massachusetts Infantry, and kept a journal of his time in the Teche Campaign.

Historic New Orleans Collection, Accession no. 1995.42.

General Weitzel galloped up, bellowing "Colonel, double-quick your men out of range, double quick." The veterans were incensed. "Run? Be shot if I would run or let a man of my company run," hissed De Forest. "The regiment, hearing the command, had faced about and was going to the rear at a pace which threatened confusion and panic." The captain rushed to the head of his company, sword and arms outstretched, and brought his men under control and back to a normal pace. The rest of the unit followed their example, and "the regiment moved off in a style which we considered proper for the Twelfth Connecticut."[31]

Captain Samuel Gault of Company A, 38th Massachusetts, was a conscientious diarist. He sat down to pen what he had seen that day. "Heavy artillery fighting going on," he scratched. "A splendid fight going on directly in front of us. Could see the Rebel steamer plainly—our whole force finally fell back and we rested for the night in an old cane field. A severe days work." April 12 had been a trying day for the Boston soldier, and he concluded his entry by summing up the charms of the campaign so far: "hard marching—hot weather—miserable ground."[32]

Banks had his answer; the Confederates were still there. For nearly three hours he and his officers had scanned the enemy line from horseback while they watched the fight. Binoculars and telescopes had revealed a smudge of dark earth, banked to chest high, with troops behind it. Then, of course, the Rebel guns had revealed themselves. The movements of his batteries had allowed him to track the enemy artillery as they followed the Union limbers across the cane field with their fire.

The Confederates had remained at Fort Bisland in force, but why? Perhaps Grover had turned back—after all, Banks had received no word of his progress and, according to the planned timetable, he was past due. Banks resigned himself to the fact that he probably would not know where Grover was until he heard the sound of his guns. Perhaps the stiffening resistance along Bayou Teche indicated that Taylor did not fear an enveloping move because he had a surprise of his own. Or perhaps the Confederates simply had not discovered Grover's flanking move. Whatever the case, Banks was sure that the enemy was before him, in force and determined to remain so. Tomorrow, he reasoned, he would keep the Confederates busy as long as possible, giving Grover enough time to complete his mission. If he had not heard from his subaltern by midafternoon, he could safely assume that Grover had miscarried his task. Banks would then attack Fort Bisland with a frontal assault. It would be good training for his tenderfoots.

10

The Long Night

"To retreat without fighting was...to abandon Louisiana."

Major General Richard Taylor

Major General Nathaniel P. Banks did not know just how difficult Brigadier General Cuvier Grover's passage had been. At 11:30 AM, as the Federal artillery had started trading shots with the defenses at Fort Bisland, the USS *Arizona* had grounded near Cypress Island, just three miles from Verdun's landing and about the same distance from its destination, the Shell Road landing at Cypress Point on Madame Porter's plantation. The Shell Road was the most direct route to the Irish Bend on Bayou Teche and the town of Franklin beyond. For four hours the Federals struggled to get the vessel free before they gave up and left it to its fate. The rest of the flotilla steamed beyond Cypress Island and toward the target, mindful of the shoal-laden waters.

The armada arrived at its destination, dropped anchor, and discovered another surprise. "A reconnoitering party, under Lieutenant Fiske, 1st Louisiana Volunteers, was at once landed in ships' boats and the road and landing thoroughly examined," wrote Grover. "In about two hours this party returned, finding the road utterly impassable for even infantry, the lake from some cause having overflown the greater part of it." The delays had at least allowed the general to catch up with his division, but he had hoped it would have been ashore by now. With time zipping by, and operating literally in the dark about the region's geography, Grover knew he had to find a landing spot soon. He ordered the *Clifton* to steam along Grand Lake to find another beachhead. But Grover was not able to land his troops that night, and there would be far more distance between him and Banks than either of the generals had anticipated.[1]

Since midafternoon on Sunday, April 12, Confederate colonel William G. Vincent and his mixed band of Redland and Creole horsemen had shadowed the movements of the Union fleet, flitting from plantation road to landing, byway to levee, to get a glimpse of the enemy boats, but the miasmic swampland made scouting difficult, and the hazy dark lines of water and cypress trees in the bogs made discernment difficult. The swarthy, diminutive, bespectacled colonel—a former New Orleans auctioneer—shepherded his men closely, keeping Major General Richard Taylor updated as best he could. Vincent had no doubt that the Federals would land, but he could not predict where they would stop. As the hours passed, Vincent had received reports of Federal movements, which he had dutifully forwarded to General Taylor, his riders loping toward the distant rumble of artillery at Fort Bisland.[2]

Earlier in the day, Taylor had sent a galloper to Butte-a-la-Rose. "Banks was pressing Taylor hard and courier after courier arrived," recalled Lieutenant Edward T. King, a Confederate officer with St. Martin's Rangers at Fort Burton. Near shore, the *Queen of the West* lay idle at the Rebel redoubt with the transport *Nina Simms,* awaiting the arrival of the *Grand Duke* and the *Webb.* Captain Edward W. Fuller, the wounded hero of the CSS *Cotton* and one of the most-feared Rebel gunboat commanders, knew the timing was wrong. He badly needed those steamers, but the Yankees had forced the issue and he was not in a position to respond. He also needed sharpshooters and boarders—as Major General John Bankhead Magruder had used at Galveston—to serve aboard the *Queen of the West* and the

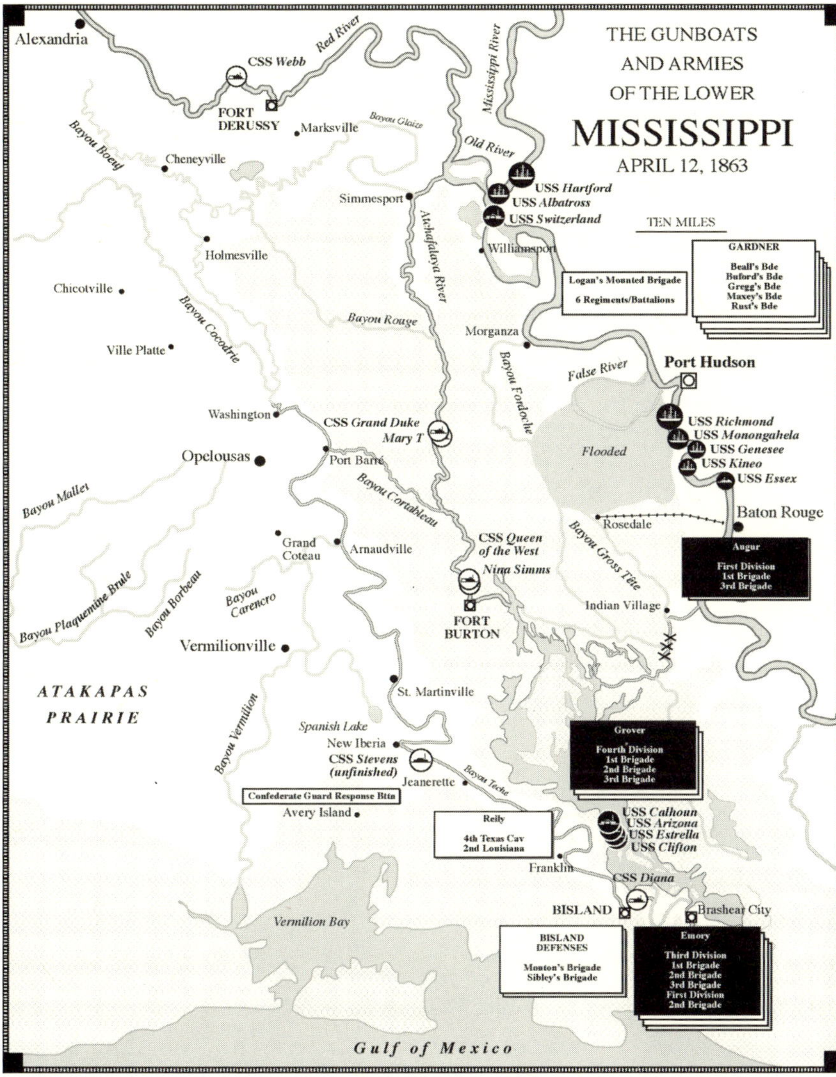

Simms. The *Mary T.* and *Webb* would in theory be bringing their own troops from Fort DeRussy. "To carry out his plan, he needed plenty of men," King continued. "These General Taylor had promised to furnish him."[3]

Events had now overcome these tidy plans, and the gunboat warrior decided to act. "Captain Fuller . . . got out of patience and decided to wait no longer, but go down on the *Queen of the West* and take the transport *Nina Simms* to get the men promised him," wrote King. The Rebel officer made a dramatic gesture for the benefit of his crew and the sixty or so men of the 3rd Maryland Artillery on board as sharpshooters. "I am going down with the *Queen of the West* and the *Nina Simms* to sink the Union fleet or drive them into the Gulf!" Captain Fuller thundered. The two-boat flotilla weighed anchor and followed the torturous course of the Atchafalaya River, heading toward Chicot Pass and into the relatively open water of Grand Lake. Fuller's goal was Charenton, where he hoped to find additional riflemen. "I remonstrated against it, but he paid no attention to me and left, leaving orders for me and Lieutenant Forgerty to have our guns, ammunition, and everything ready to put on the *Mary T.* and *Grand Duke* as soon as they landed," King wrote. Fuller also left clear orders that these vessels should join him as soon as possible, no matter the weather or conditions. His boats could wreak havoc on the Yankee flotilla if they arrived in time, and he was determined to prowl around until he found the enemy, even if he had to travel all the way to Berwick Bay.[4]

Just two hours after Fuller had departed, the Confederate steamers *Mary T.* and *Grand Duke* arrived at Butte-a-la-Rose. King delivered his instructions. "I rushed aboard and delivered the orders to the captains and informed them we were ready and would soon have everything aboard," King remembered. Certainly they would catch up with Fuller, the *Queen of the West,* and the *Nina Simms.* "They paid no attention to the orders and said they would not go until morning. Forgerty and I begged them to go, but they refused." Therefore, Fuller was seemingly into this battle alone and in the growing darkness.[5] He had acting rashly in looking for a fight. He would certainly find one.

The enemy Fuller was eager to massacre lay crowded and unsuspecting on their transports off of Hutchin's Point. Colonel Vincent's riders had finally caught sight of the Federal landing at dusk on the Shell Road leading to Cypress Point, but the enemy had turned back. Then, a second, more accurate report arrived, stating that the Union fleet was hovering off Hutchin's Point as dusk turned to night. Although the Confederates had spent a difficult time keeping abreast of the enemy movements throughout the day, at last a destination seemed to be clear. The roads of Duncan McWilliams's plantation appeared to be the invasion route. Riders immediately left Vincent's side, bearing dispatches for Taylor.

The Federals crowded aboard the steamboats felt stranded and alone in the blackness of Grand Lake, surrounded by the eerie sounds of a Louisiana night. The Federal soldiers had been packed tightly into every conceivable space among the various transports, and the journey from Brashear City had seemed interminable. They had come aboard the four steamers, four gunboats, and various barges with the understanding that their voyage would last only a day; then the delays began. Many men had been on board for a full day before the boats even left the docks. When the USS *Arizona* was grounded off Cypress Island, the weary troops had to stand by as the soldiers aboard the gunboat offloaded via barges and climbed onto other already overcrowded vessels. The soldiers of Grover's Division spent the rest of that day, into the night, packed tightly on board.

The weather and cramped quarters had made the trip nearly unbearable. "By daylight, we sat . . . under a blazing hot sun, under which we almost popped out on the deck like kernels of corn on an iron plate," reported Corporal James K. Hosmer of the 52nd Massachusetts. Many of the men were dangerously close to the boats' machinery as they tried to make themselves comfortable enough to doze. Men had to lay their heads upon the chests of comrades; some lay with their feet higher than their heads; and others learned to tolerate the odd leg or arm jabbing them in the ribs. "By night, we tried to sleep," Hosmer added, "with the plunging piston within reach of the hand." He ended up snoozing atop a row of muskets, only to awake sore and stiff, the impressions of rifle bands and barrels deep on his aching hide.[6]

The *Arizona*'s mishap posed another potential problem. Grover's protecting gunboat screen was reduced to three until the *Arizona* could be floated again. At least that many Confederate gunboats were known to be lurking nearby. If the Confederate boats moved among the transports before they could unload, the Federals would be murdered. "We were crowded," wrote Major Thomas McManus of the 25th Connecticut aboard the *St. Mary.* "We were packed just as close as the squares of hardtack in the bread barrels, closer than sardines in a box. So close we didn't have room to sweat." Though the vessel was made to carry at most five hundred passengers, twenty-five hundred—three regiments of infantry as well as the men and horses of a battery—had crowded on board. "We had to hold our haversacks that contained three days rations of sheet-iron biscuit and salt pork on our heads. The decks were covered with a solid mass of humanity."[7]

That evening, the first of Vincent's couriers arrived at Fort Bisland, bringing Taylor information that the Federal flotilla—reported as being up to five gunboats, a half-dozen transports, and barges loaded with troops—had gone past Verdun's landing and had moved out of sight on the other side of Cypress Island. Indications were that they were heading for a landing, probably at Cypress Point about three miles up the shore, where they could take the Shell Road to Irish Bend and Franklin and close off Taylor's escape route. Later incoming gallopers, though, reported sighting the Yankees at Hutchin's Point, six miles beyond Cypress Island and about twenty miles north-northwest of Banks and his army. If these reports proved true, then the Yankee amphibious effort was a lot deeper behind Confederate lines than perhaps would prove prudent.

General Taylor believed this to be good news and decided to strike. While his hoped-for offensive against Brashear City and the Lafourche country may have been upended by Banks's advance, Taylor might still recover the strategic initiative. He ordered the 2nd

Louisiana and Captain Florian Cornay's guns to fight the Federals as they came ashore—wherever that proved to be—and withdrew the two 12-pounder howitzers of the St. Mary's Cannoneers in Redoubt Number 2 to help. He also instructed this force to keep him apprised of the situation so that he could coordinate his reaction. Meanwhile, his army stayed at Fort Bisland.

As couriers heading for Vincent disappeared in the dark and foggy distance, Taylor's tactical mind-set mirrored his strategic vision, and he put into motion a plan that he hoped would turn the tables on Banks's encroaching army. He borrowed a page from the Virginia school of Yankee thrashing. He would attack with almost his entire army in the morning. He laid out his plan to Major Joseph L. Brent, his chief of ordinance and artillery, and Major William Levy, his adjutant and inspector general. The concept was simple. Using the cover of the early morning fog, General Henry Hopkins Sibley as senior brigadier would lead his veterans on the bayou's west bank in an aggressive assault on the enemy lines as they were rousing from their slumber. At the same time the *Diana* would dash forward at full steam and scurry down the bayou to penetrate and enfilade the Yankee lines, and Brigadier General Alfred Mouton would overrun the meager Union forces facing him on the east bank. Taylor knew he was ordering about three thousand men to wrangle perhaps three times as many.

Audacity and success, he argued, would unhinge Banks and his campaign. If they were attacked in front and on their flank before dawn, the Federals would tumble backward in chaos, Taylor believed, masking their batteries and confusing their reserves. If they held on, Sibley's men and the *Diana* could press the advantage. Mouton's men would sweep away the enemy to their front and then swing to the bayou bank and enfilade the entire enemy position on the opposite side of the Teche. The fog and dim light would also allow for a safe retreat, should the Confederates need it. Taylor strongly believed that an aggressive assault at Fort Bisland would succeed in rolling up Banks and his forces and cause the enemy's amphibious force in Grand Lake to withdraw from their beachhead in reaction. Then, Taylor would close the trap.

Thinking on an even grander scale, Taylor hoped Fuller might arrive in time, too, compounding the disaster to the Union cause. Fuller's gunboats could fall upon the withdrawing amphibious column. If Sibley managed to seriously injure Brigadier General Godfrey Weitzel's and Brigadier General William H. Emory's commands, then Grover might be left alone and exposed, hemmed in by Taylor's army and Fuller's squadron. The future seemed ripe with possibilities. The whole of the plan, of course, depended on crisp execution, complete surprise, and tactical enthusiasm. Taylor left Brent and Levy to explain the move to Sibley while he tended to the details of destroying the Federal flanking column. He crawled inside his ambulance and headed north toward Franklin to attempt contact with Fuller and his gunboats.

After seeing their boss on his way, Brent and Levy came to Sibley's headquarters at a little after nine o'clock that night to explain Taylor's plan. Sibley listened politely. When the two majors had finished, he told them why the plan would not work. He simply did not have enough time to organize such an audacious attack. When Taylor's officers insisted, he agreed, but reluctantly. Brent and Levy left; Sibley did nothing—at least not right away.

Meanwhile, General Taylor had issued orders and had sent couriers galloping into the night. "When all was quiet, I rode up to Franklin, thirteen miles distant, to see to my rear," he wrote. One messenger pressed on to New Iberia with orders to have the arsenal, machinery, and supplies there packed up and removed to safety. Another dispatch rider carried orders for Lieutenant Colonel Franklin Clack at Avery Island to move his small command to Butte-a-la-Rose and there cooperate with Fuller and the rest of the Confederate fleet. With so many variables in play, and with only a hopeful understanding of where his scattered forces might be and how they might work together to blunt this Yankee offensive, Taylor was prepared to gamble. "To retreat without fighting," he wrote, "was . . . to abandon Louisiana."[8]

Colonel Vincent met General Taylor in Franklin around midnight and reported that there had been no Federal landing yet. Meanwhile, Lieutenant William Smith arrived with two guns from the Val Verde Battery, bringing together a force capable of contesting, but not defeating, a landing. As the small force assembled, Vincent pondered the question as to where exactly the blow would fall. He would have to divide his small command. Part of the 2nd Louisiana Cavalry, Captain Cornay's two six-pounders of the St. Mary's Cannoneers, and two companies of Lieutenant Colonel Valsin Fournet's 10th Yellow Jacket Battalion concentrated near Charenton, a Chitimacha village, to oppose the landing that must certainly come. Vincent took the balance, including the better part of his regiment as well as Smith's guns, toward Hutchin's Point.

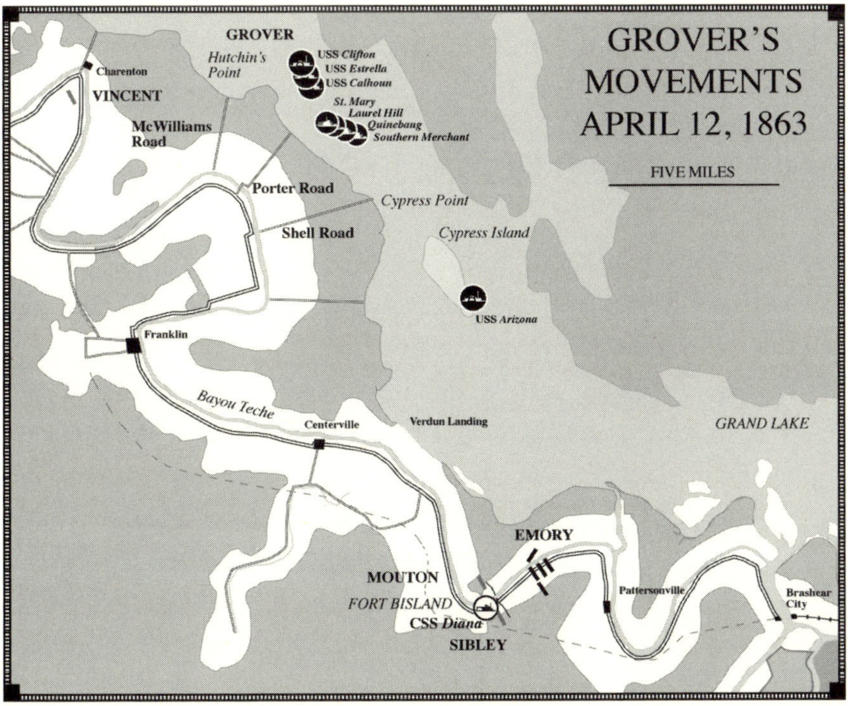

At Fort Bisland, little happened as the night wore on. The Confederates there had already assumed the positions they would start in on the following day. On the east bank of Bayou Teche—Mouton's side—Redoubt Number 2 on his far left held two 12-pounder howitzers of the St. Mary's Cannoneers while Colonel Arthur Pendleton Bagby's men of the 7th Texas lay in their lines beyond and in front. To the right of Redoubt Number 2, some four hundred yards distant at the apex of this chest-high earthwork, the two 3-inch rifles of Lieutenant Felix Winchester's section nosed over the dirt. The 18th Louisiana Infantry stood along the line left of this point all the way to Reboubt Number 2 in extended order, roughly one man per yard. The men of the 24th Crescent Regiment stood in similar intervals to the right for four hundred yards until it met the left flank of the 10th Yellow Jacket Battalion—greatly diminished through detachments—that held the line for another hundred yards to the bayou's bank. There, Lieutenant J. R. Winchester stood by with two 12-pounder howitzers of the Pelican Artillery. The twin 6-pounders of Lieutenant S. R. Garrett's section from the Pelican Artillery remained in reserve, ready to rush to whatever point was threatened.

On the west bank of Bayou Teche—Sibley's side—Lieutenant John Barnes of the 1st Regulars positioned his two 6-pounders between the bayou bank and road. A crew from the St. Mary's Cannoneers served two large 24-pounders inside Fort Bisland just beyond the road to their right, supported by two more 6-pounders of the 1st Regulars on its right, putting six guns in a space of less than one hundred yards on the left of Sibley's line. The 28th Louisiana supported next in line in the works, its men in open order like their comrades across the bayou, and filled the interval between their position and the intersection with the railroad embankment, three hundred yards away. Lieutenant John A. A. West placed his two 3-inch rifles at this critical angle, pointed to sweep diagonally across any Yankee advance, supported by a nearby 12-pounder and

6-pounder of the St. Mary's Cannoneers. The dismounted Texans of Colonel Edwin Waller's Battalion and the 5th Texas Cavalry lined up behind the railroad berm in closer formation; three of the five guns of the Val Verde Battery held the far right of the Rebel line where the earthen bank entered the woods bordering the swamp.

Four hours passed before Sibley sent a courier relating the details of Taylor's plan to Mouton's headquarters. Arriving at around one o'clock in the morning, Sibley's messenger delivered both Taylor's instructions and his own note about why the scheme was impractical. Sibley, though, was a soldier, and he would follow his orders. Mouton, too, would need to support the attack however he could.[9]

Mouton, however, was not feeling aggressive, and apparently he did not believe Sibley intended to make much of an effort. What Mouton had seen during the day had rattled him, and he sent a scout to investigate what he would face in the morning. "At night, I sent out my adjutant, Captain Louis Bush, to reconnoiter the position, force, and dispositions of the enemy," Mouton wrote. Bush's report convinced Mouton that there were simply too many Yankees for Taylor's bold scheme to have any chance of success. Based on Bush's description, Mouton believed Redoubt Number 2 would be the focus of the Federals' energy on his side of the bayou. He decided to make them pay dearly to take it, but he was not going to order his men to dash out from behind cover in the hopes that they could scare the Federals away.[10]

Mouton sent dispatches to his regimental commanders to make adjustments to their positions. "I directed Colonel Bagby with his regiment to take position in front of the entrenchments, about 500 yards in advance, on my left flank, in a copse of woods bordering on the lake," Mouton wrote, "with orders to hold the point at all hazards."[11]

That night, Bagby's 7th Texas Cavalry posted to the far left of the line, ahead of the works. They would occupy a line almost at a right angle to Redoubt Number 2, along the edge of the woods, flanking the field through which the Federals must approach. The Texans improved their positions. Private Felix Robert Collard of Company G, 7th Texas, wrote that "a sugar cane field of six-hundred acres" fronted his position, and that "outside this field there was a fence of cypress rails; outside of the fence a ditch for drainage purposes." The soldier threw down the fence, then deepened the drainage ditch, throwing the soil on top of the rails to make a hasty earthwork for men lying prone or crouching, "each man," sighed Collard, "as it were, digging his own grave."[12]

Sergeant William A. "Arlie" Carlton, Company H, 7th Texas, enlisted in Crockett and earned promotion to first sergeant in the New Mexico Campaign. He was among those on the Confederate left at Bisland.

Courtesy of Ronnie Atnip, Bonham, Texas.

All along Bayou Teche the Confederates spent a damp, humid, restless night. Several buildings between the opposing lines at Fort Bisland had caught fire during the day's engagement and, as one Texan observed, continued to flame up "fierce and hot toward the sky." As fog settled over the battlefield, men from the 24th Louisiana on the east bank added to the arson, igniting a cluster of slave huts and a sugar house to deny cover to an advancing enemy. Those Rebel soldiers fortunate enough to avoid some type of extra duty lay in the mud and water of the trenches with bayonets fixed, preparing for close action in the morning. Mosquitoes from the neighboring swamps added to the unpleasant conditions.[13]

Across the fields from the Rebel lines, the Union army slumbered as best it could, while the commanders of the 19th Army

James W. Connelly, 1st Indiana Heavy Artillery lived in Rockville before he entered the ranks of Company H, 21st Indiana Infantry as a lieutenant on July 29, 1861. Earning promotion to captain on January 1, 1863, he served the newly designated 1st Indiana Heavy Artillery during the Teche Campaign. *State Library of Indiana.*

Corps studied the terrain and the Confederate position and discussed their strategy for the coming day. Their biggest threat was the *Diana,* and it would be a priority on the morrow. Next in order of Rebel dangers was their artillery, estimated to be a third fewer guns than the Union had brought and of much smaller caliber. Colonel James W. McMillan's Hoosier infantry-turned-heavies, the 1st Indiana Heavy Artillery, worked four 30-pounder Parrotts, four 20-pounder Parrotts, and a pair of 3-inch Ordnance rifles. They would aim for the *Diana.* Captain Albert G. Mack's 18th New York would use its four 20-pounder Parrotts for the same purpose. Once the gunboat was out of action or destroyed, these behemoths would rake the Rebel field pieces until they fell silent, then the infantry could do its work.

On the morning of April 13, Banks and his officers agreed, the Federal infantry brigades would deploy as they had before. West of Bayou Teche, Weitzel's five regiments would hold the left of the line, and Colonel Halbert E. Paine's four regiments would fill the area between that brigade and the bayou on the west bank. Supporting these foot soldiers would be the regulars of Captain Edmund C. Bainbridge, Battery A, and Captain Richard Duryea, Battery F, 1st U.S. Light Artillery, each with four Napoleons and two 3-inch rifles. Captain William Carruth's 6th Massachusetts and their four

6-pounder Sawyer rifles and two 12-pounder howitzers would be in action as well. Colonel Oliver P. Gooding would cross to the east side with his three remaining regiments and the four 6-pounder rifles of Lieutenant Eben D. Haley's 1st Maine Battery and take command of that side of the bayou. These reinforcements would join the forces already there and concentrate on Mouton's line. Colonel Timothy Ingraham's three regiments would constitute the reserve of Banks's army.

Henry McMillan, 1st Indiana Heavy Artillery, enlisted in Indianapolis, joining Company B, 21st Indiana Infantry as a sergeant on July 24, 1861. Promoted to lieutenant after the Battle of Baton Rouge in August 1862, he served as the regimental adjutant during the Teche Campaign.

State Library of Indiana.

The day's plan was simple. Federal artillery would begin as soon as it was light enough to see and clear enough to pick out targets, given the foggy nature of this country. They would pummel *Diana* first, then they would destroy the Confederate field pieces. This bombardment would be conducted systematically so as to cripple the Rebel army one piece at a time. After the enemy army had been maimed, the infantry would move forward—more than likely in the afternoon—paying special attention to both of the Rebel flanks in a classic double envelopment. Banks wanted to keep the Southerners in place long enough for Grover—wherever he was—to land, take position, and then herd them into the waiting trap by cutting off their line of retreat.

Even with this clear plan and tidy summation, Colonel Paine remained nervous, and his Federals near the bayou were restless

Silas Bates, 1st Indiana Heavy Artillery, of Martz, enlisted in Company I, 21st Indiana Infantry as a corporal on July 24, 1861. He remained with the unit after its conversion to the 1st Indiana Heavy Artillery. Service in Louisiana would eventually earn him a commission and captain's bars.

State Library of Indiana.

all night. The colonel observed a key position to his front, and while most of the army withdrew for rest, he ordered the veterans of the 4th Wisconsin to move forward and occupy the cluster of buildings and trees near the bank of the Teche. "The sugarhouse, with the negro cabins and grove of shade trees near it, covered a position," reported Paine, "the occupation of which by one party or the other in the morning promised to be of great moment." He also took another precaution. He ordered skirmishers to line the bayou's bank in case the *Diana* did not follow the script and attacked them first. These riflemen could clear the boat's decks while the Union artillery fashioned a response. Even with these precautions, Paine could not rest easily, so he reinforced this lone forward regiment with three additional companies of the 8th New Hampshire Infantry and one of the three companies of cavalry on hand. The officers in the 4th Wisconsin shared his concern. They could hear the movement of troops to their front. "Apprehending that they might be engaged in preparation for an attack at daybreak, I forwarded a note to General Emory," Paine wrote.[14] Emory noted Paine's apprehension but showed little concern.

Even so, Paine remained nervous. On his front, near the 4th Wisconsin, the company of skirmishers ahead of the regiment tangled with mounted Confederates for much of the night, muskets and pistols popping in the fog near the Teche, but fading for long pauses, only to be renewed at intervals. The Rebels, it would seem, were probing the Federal line.

Federals on the bayou's east bank also did not trust the Rebels to wait for the hammer to fall. The 31st Massachusetts maintained a strong skirmish line well forward of the line of catalpa trees where most of the men of that regiment and the 175th New York had bedded for the night. At 4:00 AM, these troops fell in, along with the howitzer section of the 1st Maine Artillery on their side of the Teche, just in case the Confederates tried something daring.

As the dark hours crept by, fog once again shrouded the area, making the early morning feel spooky and sinister, amplifying noises, and causing the men on both sides to be edgy. Though the unseen sun brightened the eastern sky that Monday morning, April 13, the fog remained and cast a surreal gloom over the verdant cane fields. The groggy Federals of Weitzel's Brigade and Emory's Division rubbed their eyes, rose from their muddy beds, and tended to the needs of the morning.

Soon the pickets came back to the line and reported that the Rebels were on the move. The staccato popping of small arms became a general, unbalanced rumble near the grove of trees and sugarhouse. The Confederates were making an advance against the 4th Wisconsin, as Paine had anticipated. The Federals scrambled to face the coming challenge.[15]

Indeed, Sibley had followed Taylor's orders, and his Confederates advanced to the attack. However, he had not put his heart into the effort. The men moving toward the 4th Wisconsin were a few companies of the 28th Louisiana, determined to simply roust the Northerners from the trees. In the bayou the *Diana* made a tardy appearance, gliding toward the attack, later than anticipated and in poor shape to cover the Louisianans' advance. Its commander, Lieutenant T. D. Nettles of the Val Verde Battery, had been carried

Sugarcane. Left in the field, this dense vegetation could turn into a tangled mess.

Author's photo.

off the boat in the night, dangerously ill. Captain Oliver J. Semmes of the 1st Regular Battery had taken over and led the vessel into action, anxious to make up lost time.

On the east bank, the twin 6-pounders of Lieutenant Garrett's section from the Pelican Artillery and the two 12-pounders saw the attack underway and began pummeling Paine's brigade from its right front, as did the six Rebel guns directly to its front on the west bank. With this rude wake-up, the already edgy Paine grew panicky and requested that two 20-pounder Parrots from the 1st Indiana heavies be brought forward.[16]

As the fight gained momentum, Mouton—in accord with orders for a dawn attack—merely sent pickets forward to find the Federals on the east side of Bayou Teche. These Rebel scouts rolled out of their entrenchments and began probing the enemy by seven o'clock, then a reinforced line of skirmishers from the 18th and 24th

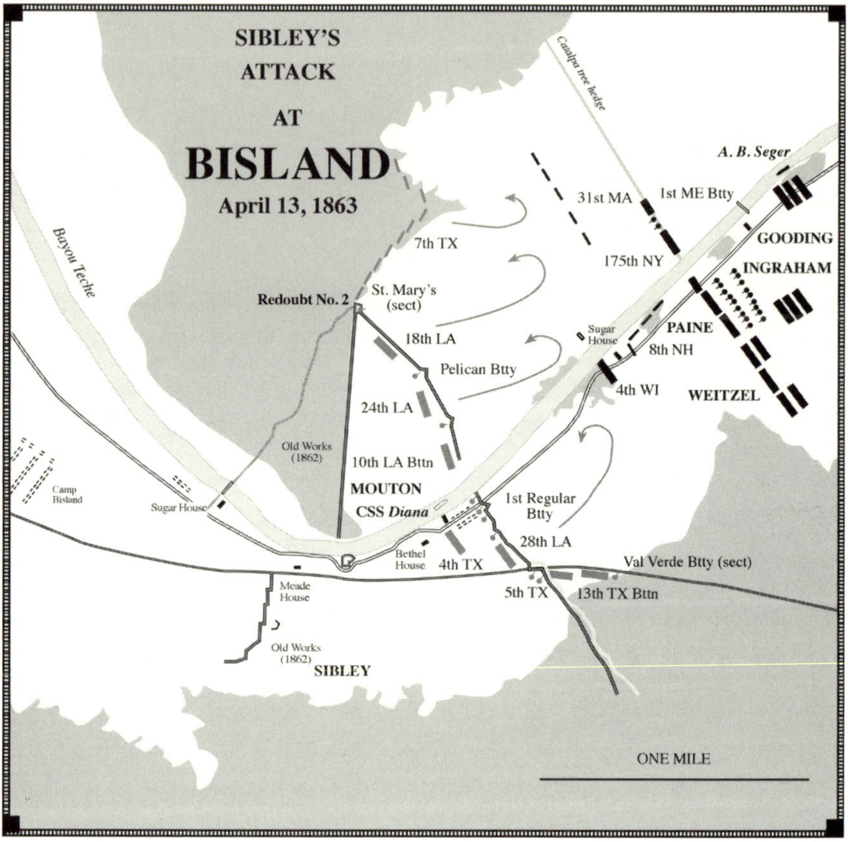

Louisiana and 7th Texas moved about five hundred yards ahead of their works through the fog, listening to the erupting racket from the west bank, across the Teche, and steadily up their own line. As these squads stepped closer to the enemy, and the sky faded from black to gray, they could make out the vague shapes of fellow Rebels moving along the opposite bank.

Then, just as quickly as the combat had accelerated, it fizzled. A few dozen minutes into this noisy demonstration, the Rebels lost their enthusiasm. After a half hour of blind shooting from their artillery in the works and on the *Diana,* and the sloppy, awkward advance of the 28th Louisiana in the haze, the Southerners on the west bank withdrew to their trenches. Mouton hesitated, then ordered his east bank men to do likewise. The attack had been loud and impressive but not terribly lethal and Union commanders shrugged off the Confederate advance as an affair of outposts. This pinprick was the sum of Sibley's efforts. While he had followed Taylor's orders as military discipline had demanded, he had also proven his opinion to be correct—that the attack was impractical. Brent and Levy, stunned, rode up the bayou road to report to their general, intercepting him just as he was arriving at Fort Bisland to investigate the progress of his surprise attack. Taylor could not have known it would be over by 7:45 AM. He could not help but believe that his own subordinates had sabotaged the attack.[17]

Sibley's tepid effort infuriated Taylor. "The supineness of that officer . . . and the positive declaration of the impracticability of carrying the plan into execution for want of time frustrated the scheme," raged Taylor, "which I am satisfied would have accomplished the most favorable results if actively attempted." With his best move fumbled, Taylor had to reconsider his strategy, taking into account the relative strengths of his various units and positioning them accordingly. Taylor would keep Mouton as commander on the east bank of Bayou Teche and Sibley as commander on the west bank, but he would keep Sibley under his personal supervision.[18]

11

Bisland

"Green was assured that there were
no places on our line particularly cool."

Major General Richard Taylor
Commander, District of West Louisiana

Drums, bugles, and shouts marked the awakening of the Federal army, the early morning skirmish serving notice that the workday had begun. Now fully roused, the U.S. troops in the cane fields formed into their lines of battles and prepared to implement Major General Nathaniel P. Banks's plan. The thudding of hooves, the rattle of chains, and the rumble of limbers and caissons marked the progress of their artillery. On the far right of the west bank line, Battery A, 1st U.S., moved in to support the supposedly beleaguered 4th Wisconsin, and they arrived in time to watch the Confederates withdraw. The rest of Colonel Halbert E. Paine's Brigade, including the remaining men of the 8th New Hampshire as well as the 133rd and 173rd New York, moved beyond the grove of trees to hurry the Rebels along. Behind them the men of Captain Albert Mack's 18th New York Battery, with quirt and spur, urged on their horses as they, too, reported for duty to Colonel Paine on the right of his line. With the Confederate attack obviously spent, and in anticipation of the day's work, officers instructed their men to burn the

Crews drill with a pair of 20-pounder Parrott Rifles from the **18th New York Battery.**

Massachusetts Comandery Military Order of the Loyal Legion and the US Army Military History Institute.

slave cabins in the grove of trees to create a smoke screen so that the newly arrived cannon could start their work against the *Diana.*

Far to the rear, Captain Samuel Gault of Company A, 38th Massachusetts, had spent a relatively quiet night with his regiment. In the darkness, he had listened as workers laid an improvised pontoon bridge of sugar coolers—long troughs for refining the juice of crushed cane—and planks across Bayou Teche, allowing easy support of the east side. He rose early to survey the engineering marvel, which he knew his regiment would soon use, and he heard the dust-up about a mile to his front, along the bayou, near a column of smoke that began spiraling toward the sky. He pulled his diary from his haversack. "Up at daylight," Gault wrote hastily. "At 7 AM, first shot fired." He soon found himself, his company, and his regiment in line and awaiting orders.[1]

As more and more guns joined the opening fracas, Colonel Oliver P. Gooding ordered the 38th Massachusetts to cross the pontoon bridge and move into position along the catalpa trees.

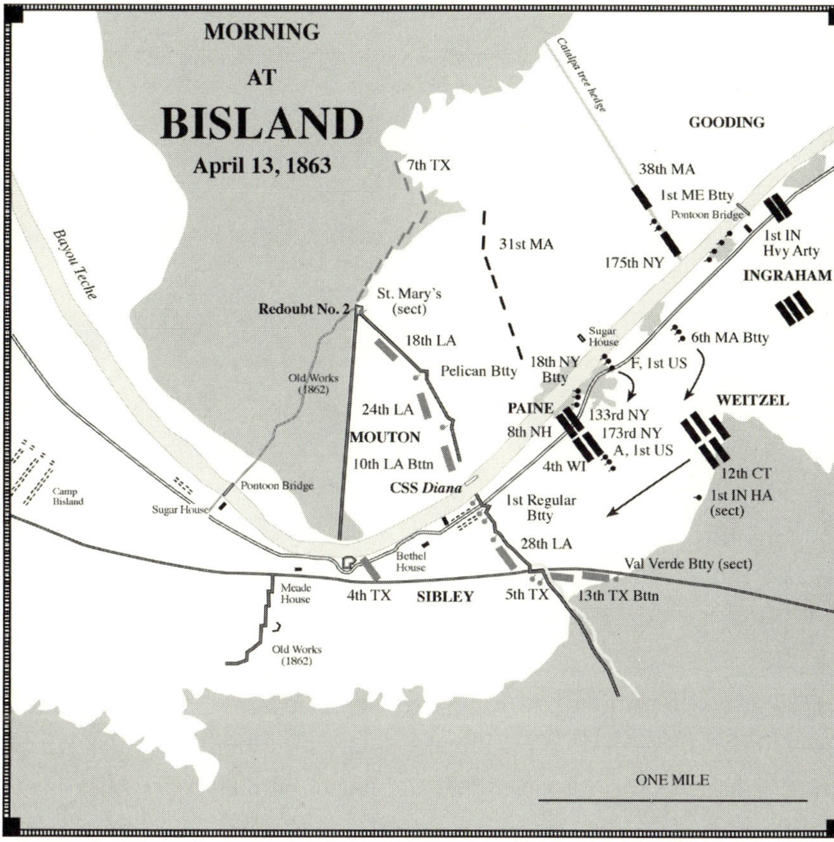

As the column hustled across the thirty or so yards of bridge, the 30-pounder Parrott on the *Diana*'s bow tried to interrupt the procession. Many of the troops arrived on the east bank wet, having been splashed by near-misses from the Parrott and other guns that had picked up the cause. Before long, the pontoon bridge sagged. One of its floats was damaged or had been poorly installed and was rapidly taking on water.

The *Diana* would enjoy this long-range target practice only briefly. While the gunboat sniped at the Bay State men on the distant bridge, Brigadier General Richard Arnold, Chief of Artillery of the 19th Army Corps, plotted its destruction. He personally placed two 30-pounder Parrotts of the 1st Indiana Heavy Artillery on the extreme left of the Union line, planning to strike the *Diana* broadside as she moved along the Teche. The other heavy guns took positions where they, too, could damage the steamer. Pairs of 20-pounder and 30-pounder Parrotts took positions on the bayou's banks near the pontoon bridge, from where they could fire down the bayou and into the vessel's bow. In all, between Mack's and Colonel James W. McMillan's batteries, ten heavy guns were now dedicated to the *Diana*'s destruction. For a time the gunboat might use its 24-pounders and 30-pounder rifle to annoy Paine's men on the near bank, or Gooding's troops moving in the distance, but before long it would be engulfed in a storm of iron.

At half past nine o'clock, the two 30-pounder Parrotts of the 1st Indiana Heavy Artillery bucked into action, directing their missiles toward the muzzle flashes of the *Diana*'s guns. This task—firing at an oblique angle across the entire front of the Union line on the west bank, at a target some two thousand yards away—required skilled marksmanship on the part of the Union gunners. The first two rounds hit near the boat, but the third and fourth rounds hit the target squarely. The shots penetrated the railroad iron protecting the engine room and exploded. Shell fragments severed a steam pipe, crippling the gunboat's ability to propel itself. At that point, every gun designated for the task began firing at the stricken steamer. Union snipers in treetop perches and riflemen of the 4th Wisconsin and the 8th New Hampshire peppered the *Diana* with bullets.

Some of these projectiles missed their mark, buzzed past the boat, and carried all the way across the field into the woods beyond it, striking other targets. "In the early morning, some of the enemy climbed moss-covered cypress, away down the bayou, armed with high powered rifles," recalled Private Felix Robert Collard of the 7th Texas Cavalry, laying in front of Redoubt Number 2. "[They] were so far away that we could not hear the reports. . . . The balls would strike the timber just in our rear like hailstones.

Colonel Oliver P. Gooding of Indiana had enlisted as a lieutenant in the 10th U.S. Infantry at the outbreak of the war, but he took command of the newly formed 31st Massachusetts Infantry early in 1862 as it left for Louisiana with Major General Benjamin Butler.

Massachusetts Comandery Military Order of the Loyal Legion and the US Army Military History Institute.

Directly one struck Lt. [James] Cunningham, of my company, piercing the right lung."[2]

With the *Diana* fighting for survival, the pontoon bridge was now rendered relatively safe. Colonel Gooding crossed to the east side of the bayou and ordered skirmishers of the 31st Massachusetts to probe the woods on the Rebel left and uncover the Confederate positions. After moving forward a few hundred yards, these two companies ran afoul of Colonel Arthur Pendleton Bagby's Texans, hunkered low behind their fieldworks and firing steadily. The Federals, cautioned by the discovery, fell back to their regiment. Based on this new knowledge, Gooding prudently ordered that the entire 31st Massachusetts be deployed as skirmishers from the bayou to the woods so that they could discover any other surprises that might be lurking.[3]

Visibility improved as the morning slipped away, and the battle's noise began to reach a crescendo. One Texan observed, "the firing was so brisk that one could scarcely discern any pause whatever." Even as the *Diana* shuddered under the repeated blows of Union bolts and shells, the Rebel 24-pounders near the Teche's west bank began to strike at the riflemen of Paine's Brigade, aided by a pair of Pelican Artillery 12-pounder howitzers on the east bank. The Northern foot soldiers ended their participation in this increasingly hostile fight and took cover in drainage ditches. They did their best to keep low as artillery—friendly and hostile—crisscrossed their position with smoking, buzzing, and hissing projectiles in a duel of heavy iron. This rumble was between the artillerymen.[4]

Private Judson Brinkerhoff enlisted from New York City in August 1862 at age twenty-two, joining Company B, 133rd New York Infantry. Before he left for Louisiana, he made sure and had his picture taken. The reverse of this image reads "To Lizzie, from her Husband Judson Brinkerhoff, Sept. 8th, 1862, time 15 min of 5 o'clock, place 714 Greenwich Street, N. [Y.] C."

Courtesy of Robert Brinkerhoff, Ada Michigan.

Private Judson Brinkerhoff of Company B, 133rd New York and the rest of his regiment received orders to lie down as rounds pass through their ranks from the east bank of the Teche. "Their cross fire upon us," he wrote his wife, "done [the] most damage." Before he could hit the ground, a shell burst above the regiment, wounding a man standing just behind him in the knee, and another in the hip. A blast of canister also whipped through the ranks. "Our second sergeant had his right eye carried right out of his head," Brinkerhoff added. "He was laying within two feet of me at the time."[5]

As the *Diana* failed, the Federal artillery kept pressuring the vessel and also began to pound the Confederate earthworks on both sides of the Teche. Captain Mack's 18th New York Battery shifted its fire a few degrees to the right, letting up on the *Diana* in order to bombard the Pelican howitzers on the east bank, just beyond the gunboat.

Major Richard T. Brownrigg served as the commissary officer for Sibley's Brigade. He was a veteran of the New Mexico Campaign and a capable soldier.

Confederate Veteran.

Many heavy rifles of the 1st Indiana did likewise. Captain William Carruth moved the 6th Massachusetts Battery to the center of the Union line, alongside Captain Edmund C. Bainbridge's Battery A, 1st U.S., and engaged the rifles and 6-pounders of the Confederate 1st Regular Battery in a head-to-head duel, outnumbering the Southerners twelve guns to six. By midmorning, the artillery mayhem had become a general fight.

As the volume of fire increased, many rounds bounded well beyond the entrenchments. The soldiers of the 4th Texas Cavalry, held in reserve near the earthwork of Fort Bisland, took casualties from artillery rounds that went long. "We were placed in a sort of fortification close to the Teche and near the gunboat *Diana,*" wrote Sergeant Alfred B. Petticolas, "and so we got the benefit of the shelling." A squad of brigade staff officers, riding toward Sibley's headquarters, presented Union gunners with a tempting target. "It was while crossing the plain of fire, coming to my assistance, in company with other officers, that Maj [Richard T.] Brownrigg was struck by a cannon ball," Sibley wrote, "which crushed his leg and killed all the other officers, four in number, except Maj. Tom Ochiltree, who barely escaped the same fate." Brownrigg, the quartermaster of the 4th Texas Cavalry, had been an Austin lawyer, a secretary to the Texas secession convention, and a signer of the Texas Ordinance of Secession. Ochiltree rushed to his aid, carrying him to the porch of Bisland Plantation nearby. Brownrigg died an hour later. This one shot from a Yankee cannon gutted Sibley's logistics command.[6]

Just ahead of the 4th Texas lay the 28th Louisiana, also shaken by the bombardment. "The troops . . . were raw," wrote Major General Richard Taylor. "As shot and shell tore over the breastwork behind which they were lying, much consternation was exhibited, and it was manifest that an assault, however feeble, would break a part of the line." Taylor decided to make a grand—yet perilous—gesture to encourage his men. He mounted atop the works, coolly rolled a cigarette, put it to his lips, lit it, and calmly puffed as he strode down the length of the regiment. One of the Louisiana officers, Captain Robert Bradford, was inspired by his war chief's actions and offered to climb a nearby tree to get a better look at the enemy. "I gave him my field glass, and this plucky youngster sat in his tree as quietly as in a chimney corner," Taylor continued, "though the branches were shot away." Taking heart, the men of the 28th Louisiana stood to their task.[7]

At the far right of the line, even the normally unflappable Colonel Tom Green sent word that "his corner was uncomfortably hot." Taylor left the 28th Louisiana, headed toward the Texans, and surveyed the situation. He quickly agreed with the colonel. The Val Verde Battery had been hit hard and its commander, Captain Joseph Draper Sayers, was severely wounded. Major Joseph L. Brent ordered the guns withdrawn. Satisfied that he had done all he could, Taylor assured Green that "there were no places on our line particularly cool, and that there was nothing to be done but submit to the pounding."[8]

Across the bayou, forty-six-year-old Major Gustav Hoffman, a New Braunfels German with the 7th Texas, tried to steady his men as they endured the cannonading, unable to respond. "Hoffman went about in the old field in front of the men, picking and eating strawberries," wrote Private Bill Davidson. "When a shell would burst among them . . . the old fellow would say, 'Tut, tut, tut, boys, dat ish noting.'"[9]

Joseph Draper Sayers was a young officer thrust into a desperate fight at Bisland. He would later be governor of Texas.

Texas Civil War Museum UDC Collection.

Despite the helplessness of the infantry, the Rebel gunners fought back gamely. On the east bank, Lieutenant Felix Winchester, who commanded the two rifles in the center of Brigadier General Alfred Mouton's line, directed most of his fire at the 1st Maine Battery and the Federal cavalry on the east bank, though he took an occasional shot at Paine's Brigade, far away to their right. Lieutenant J. R. Winchester, commanding the howitzers on Mouton's right, switched targets often, his gunners serving their pieces on their knees, taking whatever cover they could from the poorly finished earthworks. All the Confederate artillerists conserved their ammunition against the possibility of a general assault by the Union infantry.

The fight had not gone as General Taylor had planned, and by midmorning he received a note from the *Diana.* His hope for the center was crippled. Taylor rode to the edge of the Teche to establish the extent of the damage. When he arrived, he realized he was in serious danger. "She was lying against the bank under a severe fire," he remembered. "The waters of the bayou seemed to be boiling like a kettle." The Commander of the District of West Louisiana hailed the boat. "An officer came to the side of the boat to speak to me, but before he could open his mouth a shell struck him and he disappeared as suddenly as Harlequin in a Pantomime."

He learned that Captain Oliver J. Semmes, the boat's commander, needed to back the vessel down the Teche and out of action in order to effect repairs. Taylor reluctantly agreed.[10]

By late morning, the Federal artillery ganged up on troublesome Confederate strong points so that the Union infantry could make their move. Battery F, 1st U.S., and the 18th New York moved to support Paine's Brigade, and they funneled their shots at Mouton's guns of the Pelican Artillery. The found the 3-inch rifles of Lieutenant Felix Winchester's section to be especially troublesome. "Concentrating all their fire on the battery, that brave and gallant officer mounted the parapet," wrote Louisiana Lieutenant F. C. Loret, "appealing to his brave and gallant men, whose valor had several times been tested." Felix Winchester, exposing himself to the incoming shot and shell, addressed his men. "Boys," he yelled, "they are trying to silence your guns, let them know that you never were silenced."[11]

Between 10:00 AM and 11:00 AM, the Federal infantry on the west bank advanced, each regiment packed into columns of divisions, for their approach to the Rebel works. "The whole army, three lines deep—a fine martial spectacle—advanced slowly through the canefields," witnessed Captain John William De Forest of the 12th Connecticut. "Marching in my preferred position, in the front rank of my company and next to the regimental colors, I felt myself to be an undesirably conspicuous person, as we came out upon the open ground in view of the enemy." The Rebel artillery began to open up. "It is a grand thing to take the lead in battle, but all the same it is uncomfortable," recorded De Forest. The first shot, aimed at the colors, hit the ground eighty feet ahead of the captain, "threw up the ploughed soil in a little cloud, leaped a hundred feet behind the regiment, and went bounding off to the rear." The captain turned to his soldiers. "'That's bad for the fellows behind us,' I said to my men, with that smile which a hero puts on when he makes the best he can of battle, meantime wishing he were home."[12]

A second round came closer. "The next shot struck within thirty feet of the line, and also went jumping and whistling rearward," De Forest continued. "They were evidently aiming at the colors, and that was nearly equivalent to aiming at me." The captain knew the next Rebel cannon ball would get him. "'You'll fetch him next time,' I thought grimly; and so, doubtless, thought countless others, each for himself."[13]

The Union artillery coordinated with this move, placing their guns to smother the fire of any Confederate artillery still showing some fight. Battery F, 1st U.S., moved to the left, unlimbered its guns in the center of the Federal line, and began pounding at any likely targets, shifting aim along the entire length of the works. The 12-pounder rifles of the 1st Indiana moved up and joined in. The 6th Massachusetts also moved to the left, taking a new position near the woods, where they could fire at the Texans holding the Rebel right. Bainbridge's men stood fast, but trained their guns against targets near the bayou. The counterbattery fire shook the Rebels. "Our own batteries . . . evidently shook the nerves of the enemy's gunners," wrote De Forest, "for their next shot screeched over the colors and first struck the ground far in rear of the regiment, and thereafter they never recovered their . . . dangerously accurate range."[14]

As had happened before, the infantry regiments were ordered to lie down while the artillery snuffed out any resurgent embers of Confederate resistance. "I never knew that order to be disregarded on the field of battle," quipped Captain De Forest, "not even by the most inexperienced and insubordinate of troops, unless they were already running." The prone soldiers made use of the deep furrows of the cane field and listened to the Federal cannon. "The loud metallic spang of the brass howitzers, the dull thud of the iron Parrotts, and the shrieking and cracking of enemy shells made up a *charivari* long to be remembered."[15]

Skirmishers scooted out from the flattened regiments and moved ahead to scout the enemy trenches with their rifles. The addition of small arms was not welcomed by the Federals laying in the open. "This drew the Rebel musketry and made things hotter than ever," complained De Forest. Well-intentioned officers told the troops to lie low. "We did the best we could with the cane hills, wishing they were bigger." The captain took advantage of his inactivity and relatively comfortable position to grab a quick bite of hard tack. "As I lay on my side behind one of these six-inch fortifications, chewing" he remembered, "several balls cut the low weeds which overhung me."[16]

The Federal army also advanced on the east side of the Teche. The seven companies on hand of the 31st Massachusetts deployed as skirmishers, moving in a long, undulating line toward Mouton's works. The left end got within musket range of the breastworks, but the Federal line curved back toward the center of the field, and the right end folded back as it cautiously neared the woods. Confederates deployed in the ditches in front of the fortifications kept the Yankees tied down for the next three hours, and Bagby's Texans kept the right end of that regiment away from the woods. As the 7th Texas stubbornly defended its ground, Colonel Bagby received a painful wound in the arm, but he remained in command.

Taylor's little army had passed its first challenge. Barraged for hours, battered and bruised, his troops had held fast and showed courage when the Union infantry had advanced. As Taylor took stock of his situation, unwelcome but not unexpected news about Brigadier General Cuvier Grover's amphibious operation kept arriving from Colonel William G. Vincent's command. Taylor understood that control of the strategic initiative had slipped from his hands, but now he needed to buy time so that he could reposition his army in a safer place. He could not abandon Bisland, yet—he needed to wait for the cover of night. With luck he could still slip away, concentrate against Grover, and with the help of the gunboats destroy that wing of Banks's army. Taylor simply needed a little time. The general sent orders to Colonel James Reily for his regiment to mount up, head toward this new threat beyond Franklin, and delay the enemy as long as possible. The Texans responded enthusiastically, glad to be back in the saddle and out from under the enemy artillery.

The morning's fight had begun to wear on the Union troops as well. At noon men all along the Union line headed to the rear for more ammunition. The artillery duel that had begun at first light slackened at midday but would continue for the rest of the day. The batteries that had been firing since sunup withdrew to refill their ammunition boxes, accounting for any abatement in the roar. Resupplied and refreshed, the combined guns of Battery F, 1st U.S., and the 18th New York began sweeping the banks on both sides of the Teche. Before long, the two most troublesome Rebel batteries were silent, and by early afternoon the Federal infantry rested easier.

The weight of the U.S. guns pounding them with shot for more than five hours had injured but had not destroyed the Confederate artillery. The batteries on Mouton's side of the Teche, the object of close Union attention, stood bruised but not broken. The rifle section had lost one dead and three wounded, and their horses had been cut up, with nine dead and six injured. The howitzers on the far right of Mouton's line, despite all the fire, counted but two men wounded. They had, however, lost a limber and twelve horses, crippling the mobility of the two guns. Enemy fire had wounded four men in Lieutenant S. R. Garrett's section, but by the end of the day the Federals had killed or injured fourteen of his horses—more than half of his animals.

On the far right of the Confederate line, the Val Verde Battery, too, had been punished. Two men lay dead, and eleven more left the fight wounded, reducing the strength of the battery by a quarter. A similar grim ratio faced the battery's animals; ten mangled horses littered the ground where their handlers had dropped them from their traces.[17]

Major Silas T. Grisamore, the quartermaster for the 18th Louisiana, had spent most of the morning behind the Confederate lines, but he took the opportunity at midday to survey the line of battle. He reported first to General Mouton who, as he had done for most of the morning, stood exposed behind the incomplete breastworks near Redoubt Number 2. "As I was standing near General Mouton, Col. Bush, and his aides, a minie ball came whizzing over us and," he wrote, "passing between two soldiers heads who were eating from the same plate, buried itself in a post at their side." Mouton, unfazed, continued scanning the enemy lines with his telescope.[18]

Twenty-six year old **Corporal Albert Wilkerson** had enlisted in Company F, 5th Texas Cavalry back in San Antonio. He served in New Mexico and at Galveston before facing the enemy again in Louisiana.

US Army Military History Institute.

Continuing his errand, Grisamore crossed over to the west bank of Bayou Teche. As he walked over the Confederate pontoon bridge and back to Fort Bisland, he noticed General Sibley and his staff taking refuge under a corn shed near the Palfrey Plantation more than a mile away from the fighting. "The contrast I made between him and that of our gallant Mouton," Grisamore wrote in his memoirs, "will be left to the imagination of the reader."[19]

On the bayou's east side the 31st Massachusetts had shot away all of its ammunition by early afternoon and requested to be relieved, reporting that the enemy works could be taken easily. The 38th Massachusetts came forward as the 31st moved to the rear, less one dead and five wounded. Gooding used the lull and the time bought by his skirmishers to bring forward the rest of his brigade from the west bank. When the two remaining sections of the 1st Maine Battery crossed, a caisson plunged off the slippery planks of the damaged, sagging pontoon bridge and into the water, its load of ammunition lost to the battle. The 53rd Massachusetts, the 156th New York, and the two companies of the U.S. 1st Louisiana Cavalry made it across without incident. Gooding deployed his men with the 38th Massachusetts front and center in skirmish order, facing the left of Mouton's line, and the 53rd behind them and to the left in support, also in skirmish order. To the right and rear, the 156th New York would serve as reserve while moving obliquely into the woods to extend the line to the right; the 31st Massachusetts would help if needed. On Gooding's left, the 175th New York would support the 1st Maine Battery opposite the Rebel right and close to the bank of the Teche.

This was the first fight for all of these regiments, and the men were noticeably anxious. "We commenced to advance and I kept looking up and down the line at the men's countenances to see how they stood it," wrote First Sergeant Charles W. Kennedy of Company I, 156th New York. "Most of them looked pale but determined but a few were shakey in the knees and I could see they were actually sick with fear, and these too were some of those who had been loudest in their brags before they had been put to the test."[20]

William Parker, III, a twenty-seven-year-old carpenter from Quincy, enlisted in company I, 38th Massachusetts, serving as its first sergeant during the Teche Campaign.

US Army Military History Institute.

In a brief lull in the violence, Mouton and his men could see the gathering threat, and they prepared to receive the attack. The general ordered the 6-pounders of Lieutenant Garrett's section from the Pelican Artillery moved from the right of the line, nearer the

Teche, into position between Redoubt Number 2 and Lieutenant Felix Winchester's rifles. If the Yankees advanced, they would face these guns dead ahead while also being shot at on their right flank by Bagby's Texans and on the left front by Felix Winchester's pair of 3-inch rifles.

Just after noon, Banks arrived at a decision. With his batteries refreshed with full limber chests and the Confederates cowed, Banks ordered the entire line forward in a general advance, but he gave Brigadier General William H. Emory full discretion as to how bold a move to make. Banks had reason to be indecisive. He, unlike Taylor, had received no word of the whereabouts of Grover or even if that officer's errand had been successful. If Banks pushed too hard, Taylor might escape before the Federals sprung the trap. There was also the nagging suspicion that the Confederates were playing a game of their own. If Banks entangled himself in the works at Fort Bisland, and Taylor held him off, any Rebel surprises from its gunboats or troops up the Atchafalaya River might result in a full-fledged Union disaster. On the other hand, if he did not push Taylor and the Confederates successfully concentrated against Grover, they might defeat the Army of the Gulf in bits and pieces. Banks had already accumulated a few smudges on his military record in Virginia and editorial criticism from his feint at Port Hudson; in this campaign he could afford to be cautious. To hedge his bets, he would let the unassailably venerated Emory make the final decision.

As the cannon renewed their steady booming across the open fields along the Teche, Emory passed the burden of decision to his most trusted subordinate, Brigadier General Godfrey Weitzel. The Cincinnati German quickly decided that the Confederates had been beaten down or could be routed, and he moved to turn their right flank to prove his hypothesis. He ordered his veteran 75th New Yorkers to push into the woods on his left, move behind the Opelousas railroad embankment, and push from behind the Rebel lines.

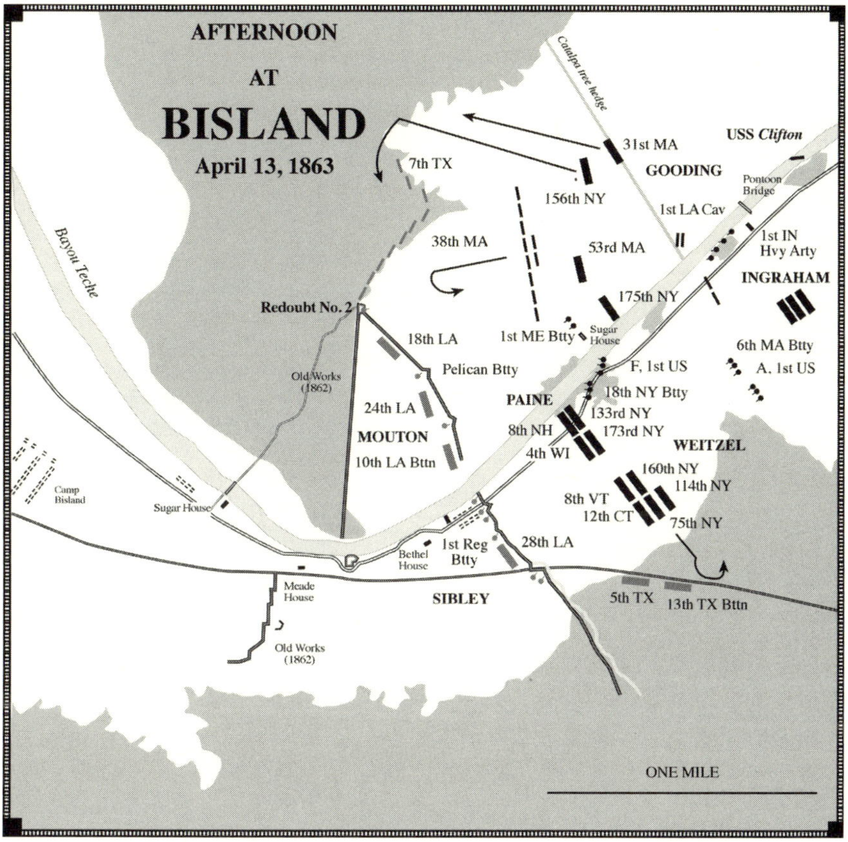

The unit's commander, Lieutenant Colonel Willoughby Babcock, rode to meet with Colonel Elisha Smith of the nearby 114th New York and to let him know that he was "going to see what was in there." Babcock left some advice. "He advised Colonel Smith to cause his men to lie down, as they would be in the line of the enemy's fire," wrote Dr. Harris Beecher, the regiment's assistant surgeon. "This judicious order was given, and the boys hugged the ground between the rows, or screened themselves behind a few scattering trees or stumps."[21]

Progress was more difficult for the 75th New York than either Weitzel or Babcock had anticipated. "The briers and bushes were almost impassable," wrote Lieutenant William H. Root of that regiment, "though we moved in single file. After working along an hour or so and getting the regiment all broken up we came out of the swamp about twenty rods from where we went in." Deciding that the effort was futile, officers ordered the men to move back out of the trees and to re-form.[22]

The Confederates, hearing the thrashing about of the nearby 75th New York, decided to discourage the Yankees. "The thickest storm of rifle shot whizzed by and over us that I ever was in," wrote Root. Unscathed by this volley, the New Yorkers took cover and fell prone. The men of Colonel Edwin Waller's Battalion and the 5th Texas raised a Rebel yell and continued to fire, but they aimed too high for the Yankees just in front. Instead, the bullets traveled on, hitting anonymous targets down range. "Several shots took effect on the 114th N. Y. a few rods in our rear." Root noted. They had been warned.[23]

Lieutenant Colonel Willoughby Babcock of Oswego led the 75th New York during the Teche Campaign. He had been through three regiments, each transfer leading to a raise in grade, to achieve that position.

Massachusetts Comandery Military Order of the Loyal Legion and the US Army Military History Institute.

Despite their precautions the 114th New York took casualties. "The rapid rattle of musketry in the forest was terrific, while a shower of hissing, singing bullets poured over," remarked Dr. Beecher. "It was at this time that most of those in the regiment, killed or wounded . . . were struck, while lying defenseless on the ground." The regiment lost nearly a dozen men from the unseen fight ahead of them.[24]

Colonel Elisha Smith, of Norwich, led the 114th New York. The Battle of Bisland would be the regiment's first fight.

Massachusetts Comandery Military Order of the Loyal Legion and the US Army Military History Institute.

For the next few moments the fighting raged loudly and impressively with volleys and yells, but the battle was not particularly lethal—neither side being able to see the other through the brush and swampy canebrake. "Nothing could be seen a rod ahead, though we fancied we could hear the Rebs talking in front of us," Root commented. "No sooner was the firing commenced than it was answered and for a few minutes the bullets fairly rained around us." The young lieutenant urged his men to load and fire, then watched three of his soldiers fall, just ahead of him, from the Texans' fire. Then it was his turn. "A spent ball hit me fair in the arm above the elbow and numbed it and made a sore spot," he reported to his parents in a letter. He was now one of the seventeen of the 75th New York hit by the enemy.[25]

The noise and violence on the left shocked and concerned the Federals. "The Union troops were startled by that most hideous of modern war cries, known as the rebel yell," wrote Sergeant George N. Carpenter of the 8th Vermont, who was about one hundred yards from the fight. "This was the first time the Vermont boys had heard that fiendish sound, and it is not too much to say that they were appalled by it for a moment, and thought their time had come to be wiped out." Even General Emory grew concerned. "Hearing a fusillade to the extreme left of the line, supposing it was an attempt to turn our left," Emory reported, "I [ordered] up the reserve, or such portion of it as might be necessary to check this movement." But after this dramatic though blind exchange, the skirmish petered away to nothing.[26]

Having watched the progress of the day, and mindful of the other parts of his complicated plan, Banks signaled to his commanders that the time for the big push had arrived. Weitzel, unsure how to proceed after his tangle in the woods, rode over to his right to discuss strategy with Colonel Paine. "He notified me that if I would advance to the assault, he would conform his own movements to mine," Paine wrote. The colonel saluted, then he rode to each of his regiments to deliver their orders. They would advance on a compact, two-regiment front, with skirmishers from Company D, 4th Wisconsin, leading the way. When they reached the last few score yards, the entire brigade would rush the works at the double quick. "They responded with loud hurrahs," Paine continued. The colonel rode ahead of his command and signaled the advance. The skirmishers trotted forward, followed a minute later by the brigade, rising in unison from the ditches and furrows of the field. Forming their ranks, the regiments stepped out smartly. The sound of rifle fire came from their front.[27]

Then, just a few paces into the advance, an officer galloped up from behind, and the brigade lurched to a stop. "We had proceeded a but a short distance when one of General Weitzel's staff officers overtook me with a request . . . that I would delay the attack," Paine wrote. Weitzel still had some reservations about what he was heading into, and he had asked for clarification from Banks. Paine ordered his men to return to their covered positions. As they fell back, he came across a dying soldier, one of his skirmishers. He recognized him as a recent addition from Wisconsin who had arrived the night before. "During the two minutes which elapsed after the brigade left the ditches and before it returned, this recruit was killed," Paine wrote. "Poor boy, he died lamenting that he had had no opportunity to fire a shot."[28]

Lieutenant Colonel William L. Rodman left his business and his home in New Bedford to serve as an officer in the 38th Massachusetts Infantry. He led the regiment during the march up Bayou Teche.

Massachusetts Comandery Military Order of the Loyal Legion and the US Army Military History Institute.

While the troops on the Union left fell back after their false start, Emory ordered his Federals to push on Mouton's front across the bayou. As the fight in the canebrake crackled to a close a mile away to his left, Colonel Gooding ordered his brigade forward to press the Confederates at Redoubt Number 2. Lieutenant Colonel William Logan Rodman of the 38th Massachusetts, mounted and riding behind his battle regiment, called out "Guide Left! Forward," which officers and sergeants echoed along the line. He ordered his two reserve companies—in line of battle to support the skirmish line ahead— to fix bayonets. "I think I am justified in describing the advance as elegant," Rodman reported. He was proud of his tidy command and pleased by the proper spacing his nine months volunteers kept while on the advance, even in the face of growing attention from Rebel gunners. His skirmishers moved forward, bounding and leapfrogging, closing the distance to the enemy. [29]

Facing the Bay State men, Mouton's men knew what to do. The 18th Louisiana and Garrett's battery opened fire on the thin Federal line as the men stepped gingerly through the bent and tangled cane stalks. "The fire, which had been incessant all day, was much increased at this moment," Rodman wrote, "and several of my men were put *hors de combat.*" Shots from Felix Winchester's guns whizzed into the left reserve company at eight hundred yards, clipping Captain Gault's leg clean off—he soon bled to death—and killing one and wounding six others, including a soldier with a severed arm. When another round came from in front, the 38th Massachusetts's color bearer dropped the national flag; his head had been carried away by the cannon ball.[30]

Rodman urged his men onward, and the regiment regained its composure and lurched forward. "Officers and men, on learning that the order was to advance into the enemy's works, from the first regarded themselves as a forlorn hope, but hesitated not to advance boldly," he wrote. "Every step in their advance revealed more and more the strength of the Confederate works, which were found to be vastly more formidable that was suspected in the morning."[31]

The Confederates ground away at the 38th Massachusetts with artillery and added their rifles to the mayhem when the advancing Federals were within a quarter mile from the works. From his vantage point in Redoubt Number 2, Lieutenant Loret observed, "The enemy . . . attempted to storm our works, but our boys received them with such gallant discharge of musketry and artillery, twice cutting down their colors."[32]

About five hundred yards ahead of Redoubt Number 2, the 38th Massachusetts reached the spot where Bagby's Texans had been waiting. With the Federals just fifty yards away, the Texans chose their targets. "We lay in the trenches with rifles on the loose bank of earth," remember Private Collard of the 7th Texas. Officers moved up and down the line, admonishing the riflemen with "Hold your fire, boys, until they get close enough. Don't two of you shoot the same man—kill the man directly in front of you. Don't overshoot—try and hit the top button of their breeches."[33]

Then the Texan officers unleashed their soldiers. "Damn em! Get em!" they shouted as the troops opened fire. "There was not a man of us but who could shoot a squirrel's head or tail off, as we chose, or hit a deer running through the woods," boasted Collard.

"When the smoke cleared, not an enemy could be seen, only an arm or leg kicking out of that cane stubble." The Yankees, stunned, dropped back to reform. "The enemy charged again . . . just giving the Confederates time to reload," continued Collard. Rodman eventually gave up the attack and ordered his men to fall back and take cover among the ditches, stumps, and stubble of the field. "There were many hair breath escapes during the fight," one Massachusetts private reported, "and as the shells flew thick and fast our boys must have got a pretty fair idea of the stern realities of war." The 38th Massachusetts lost six dead and twenty-nine wounded that day. Although it was the heaviest loss of any Federal unit on the field, considering the weight of ammunition thrown at the regiment, it was fortunate not to have lost many more men.[34]

The 156th New York, meanwhile, came up on the right of the 38th Massachusetts and prepared for their first taste of combat. "Whiz, whiz went the bullets round our ears, and down ducked the heads of nearly every officer and man in the regiment," reported First Sergeant Kennedy. "It was perfectly natural for the first fire and was done almost without knowing it but I can't tell you how it made me feel." The sergeant, determined to set a good example, set his jaw and refused to bob his head. He shouted to his troops, "Hold up your heads men!" At that moment, a bullet struck a soldier nearby, the unit's first combat casualty.[35]

The New Yorkers began to sidle to their right and into the margins of the swamp just as the 38th Massachusetts withdrew in near panic, nearly carrying the 156th New York with it. "The enemy encouraged by the falling back of the Mass[achusetts] men cheered and poured in volley after volley," Kennedy continued. "We emerged . . . into a perfect hail of bullets." Two more soldiers went down within arms' length of the sergeant, one an officer with the company, shot through the head. "There was some confusion, the [Massachusetts] men going back double quick, the bullets were flying thick, the officers of the company gave no order and for a minute it looked as if the men were going to run away," explained Kennedy.[36]

At this crisis point, the officers and sergeant steadied the New Yorkers' jangled nerves. Sergeant Kennedy, waving his kepi and rifle in the air, moved ahead of his company and shouted, "Staten Islanders, come on!" His gesture had the desired effect. "I could have faced a battery vomiting grape shot just then," he wrote home in a letter. "The boys rallied in a minute. . . . There was no more wavering or fear after that, the decisive moment had been seized and everyone fought like a lion." Unbeknownst to the Confederates, the reenergized New Yorkers continued to work their way around the margins of the swamp and away from the heaviest of the enemy fire.[37]

The Union advance on both sides of Bayou Teche sputtered out in the face of stiff Confederate resistance. Clearly Taylor's army was still in place and capable of a vigorous fight, and Banks agreed to hesitate for a while longer. The cannon continued, and after the excitement on each end of the line, most of the men in the ranks spent the rest of the afternoon as spectators. "The battle of Camp Bisland was an artillery duel . . . with a dash of infantry charging, heavy musketry on either flank, and a dribble of skirmishing along the whole line," observed Captain De Forest. Some Union foot soldiers, recumbent between cane rows, used their positions to study artillery projectiles passing overhead and ciphering the equations and ratios of bullets fired to wounds inflicted. "Lying on the earth, they could watch on a grand scale the graceful curves described by shot and shell in their swift aerial passage, and criticize to their hearts content the display of the gunner's skill," wrote Carpenter. "Their ears soon learned to distinguish the peculiar sound made by different kinds of missiles, and they were enabled to make some approximate estimates as to the number of balls that miscarried where one did execution." Doing the math, these soldiers soon calculated their odds of dying. Carpenter explained, "A man may base his chances of life on the fact that, in a battle, so many balls are wasted that a soldier cannot be killed until the enemy has discharged at him a weight of lead equal to his own."[38]

On the east side of the Teche, near the woods, the retreat of the 38th Massachusetts left one Federal alone behind a tall stump, cut off from his regiment and closer to the Texans than to his own comrades. Sitting behind the trunk, which had been cut off at about the height of a man, he loaded his rifle and waited for a target, determined to do what he could despite his precarious situation. "He couldn't get away, or some of us would kill him," observed Collard. This trapped Yankee, though, could make the Confederates worry. "The fellow behind the stump shot my comrade, Jap Caldwell, through the head," Collard wrote. The Texan returned fire, "but it was like shooting at a fox squirrel laying behind a limb." Twenty minutes later, the Yankee ventured another try. "He shot Lewis Lee in the back of the left hand, shattering the wrist, the same ball striking the right arm and shattering the right elbow," Collard remembered. A nearby Rebel declared that he would end this Yankee menace, and he fired and missed. The enemy reloaded and shot another Texan in the throat, breaking his jaw.[39]

This lone New Englander had become dangerous, and all along the Rebel line soldiers tried their luck but missed him. A soldier known only as "Jack of Clubs" crawled over to Collard and whispered, "That fellow is killing your men." The two conferred and arrived at a solution. They would send a request down the regiment for the high-powered hunting rifle Quartermaster Sergeant Jim King used for sniping. "If it will carry to the center one hundred yards, I could kill him from where I am," Jack of Clubs continued. The soldier crawled off, then returned with the rifle. "You'd better wipe that gun out," Collard advised, "it has been shot so much today." Jack of Clubs thanked him for the advice, rolled onto his back and, using spit and shirttail, ran a patch down the muzzle. He loaded the rifle and crawled back to his previous position with his company. "Every once and a while I peeped over the bank of earth, listening for the crack of Jim's rifle," Collard recalled.[40]

A few minutes passed during which neither the Texan nor the New Englander fired. Then Jack of Clubs took his aim and knocked down the Yankee. "The first thing I saw was the bottom of that fellow's feet—he went over backwards," Collard wrote. "Jack came crawling back with Jim's gun, saying 'Oh God damn him, I got him.'" Looking out across the field, the two Texans could see Federals hunkered further off in the distance. "Keep them fellows off me and I'll see what he had in his canteen," Jack told Collard. The sharpshooting Rebel crawled up to the Yankee corpse, took off his canteen, uncorked it, and drank from it, waving it over his head. "By this time the enemy had discovered him and was cutting dirt all around him," Collard recalled. Returning triumphantly, Jack of Clubs had almost reached the works when a bullet found its mark. "He sprang erect and with one jump he was over in the trench," Collard wrote. The minie ball had struck a glancing blow and broken three of Jack's ribs. "I know what was in that canteen," Collard concluded, "because I sampled it then and there."[41]

Garrett's section of the Pelican Artillery took advantage of Rodman's withdrawal to reset their guns. Lieutenant Garrett ordered that one gun be moved into Redoubt Number 2, and he led the other 6-pounder back to the position he held earlier in the day, on the right of Mouton's line. From there his gunners resumed firing steadily into Gooding's Brigade, this time at the guns of the 1st Maine. Near dusk, a round came whistling in from across the bayou to their right and front, smashing the gun and mangling a crewman. "A solid shot . . . cut the tire and felly of the right wheel of the carriage, instantly killing Acting Gunner Private Joseph Landrey," reported Captain Thomas Faries, "who, with his hands on the elevating screw, was in the act of aiming the piece."[42]

Banks had pounded the Rebels all day and had tested their flanks. Men had died—some dramatically—but his army had not forced the works. His day of skirmishing had won him a clear idea of how the Confederates had been deployed and where they might be vulnerable. Yet he still had not heard from General Grover. His semaphore teams had been wig-wagging throughout the last two days, and his scouts had witnessed the ascension of Grand Lake by the gunboats and transports the day before, but they had passed beyond range and were now behind Rebel lines. Banks had no way of knowing how well his subordinate was doing at his assigned task.

Banks faced a dilemma. Only about an hour and a half of daylight remained. Should he order another general advance by his infantry? Could his nine months men even carry the enemy works? After all, the Confederates still showed plenty of fight. He wrestled with the dilemma of groping about in a tactical battle while dependent on strategic factors now beyond his control. If his men attacked now, would the assault still be premature? He might be sending his troops to a needless sacrifice that could be avoided if Grover did his work well. On the other hand, the Rebels might scatter and get away without someone in place to catch them as they ran. Banks knew he would certainly not catch the Texas horsemen.

Worse yet, what if Grover had met with disaster? Would not a reverse at Fort Bisland compound the debacle? At best, could a victory at Bisland overcome the reversal of a defeat upstream? Though Banks felt confident of success, he remained prudent and tortured. He sent word to Weitzel and Emory to stand their ground for a little longer unless a clear advantage presented itself.[43]

At 4:00 PM, the arrival of the USS *Clifton* exorcized the demons tormenting Banks. As couriers and aides hurried about the Union headquarters, a huge 8-inch shell arced overhead from well beyond the pontoon bridge and burst above the Rebel lines, announcing the gunboat's arrival. A wig-wagged message revealed that Grover was ashore and moving ahead against light resistance. Banks's plan—really Weitzel's—was working as anticipated. Banks relayed the news to Weitzel and Emory who, with their mission now to simply keep the Rebels in place, ordered their men to hold fast; there would be no further attacks that day. They would fall back to a safer distance that night, leaving pickets at their farthest line of advance.[44]

On the Union right, though, some of Colonel Gooding's men were already in motion for what would be the last dust-up of the day. Despite having had his advance blunted and the 31st and 38th Massachusetts shot up, Gooding had already committed his reserves, the 156th New York, to the fight, and they had made progress—disappearing into the swampy woods beyond his clear control. The colonel sent the re-formed 31st Massachusetts in after the New Yorkers, hoping they had found a way around the Confederate flank.

Private Collard had already been through much that day, but when the soldiers of the 156th New York began beating the woods to his left, the Texan turned to face the new threat. He reloaded his Enfield, but his bullet stuck fast halfway down the barrel. He had fired so many times that day that his rifle was fouled and unworkable. As he worried with his weapon, a round cut past his right arm, "a flesh wound," he wrote. "I felt for my pistol, which had slipped out of the scabbard sometime that day." Totally unarmed, the Texan jumped to his feet and dove behind the cover of a felled tree. "Just as I fell over, whack! he took the log," Collard wrote. He realized he was the object of someone's attention. "I got the end of my gunstick against a limb, and succeeded in pushing the bullet down." The Texan figured his assailant would soon follow. "If he did," Collard added, "I aimed to shoot the gunstick through him."[45]

The men of the 156th New York did keep coming, and the Rebel left began to unravel. "We kept advancing, taking advantage of the stumps of trees and inequities of the ground till we finally got near enough to make a rush on the woods where the rascals lay hid," Sergeant Kennedy wrote. Mouton quickly responded to the threat. He sent a rider across the Teche to hurry forward any reinforcements available from Green, since his flank no longer appeared threatened. Major Hannibal Honestus Boone responded by sending about half of Waller's Battalion. Mouton also ordered a company of the 18th Louisiana to shift to the left and help the 7th Texas.[46]

As the advancing New Yorkers worked their way up the flank of the Texas regiment, the Louisiana reinforcements ran headlong into the Federals, finding themselves almost immediately smothered by their superior numbers. "I could hear my comrades saying 'I surrender, I surrender,'" Collard wrote. "I remained quiet until good dark and crawled off." While making his escape, he saw the movements of a soldier ahead of him. "I dropped on my knees, covering him with my rifle," Collard added. "Up with your hands, I have the drop on you," yelled the private. When the soldiers emerged from the shadows, arms erect, Collard saw that he "had captured one of my own Majors." The Texan officer asked about men still behind, then directed Collard toward safety at Redoubt Number 2.[47]

In the growing darkness the 156th New York and the 31st Massachusetts stopped their advance, happy to have dislodged the troublesome Texans and content to spend the night in their newly won positions and to count their prisoners. "Some of them were awfully frightened when they crept out of the bushes and two or three of them begged us not to kill them," wrote Sergeant Kennedy. He and several other Federals marched more than seventy Texas and Louisiana captives to the rear. "In my judgment, two hours more of daylight would have enabled me to turn the enemy's left flank," reported Gooding, "and witnessed the triumphal entry of my troops into his works."[48]

The battle ended. As the last light faded, the Federals left a strong skirmish line in place, with some soldiers within two hundred yards of the Rebel works, but they withdrew the bulk of their troops to positions far to the rear. Occasional shots rang out as both sides settled down for the night, but clearly the decisive portion of the contest would come in the morning. At the end of the day, Southern cannon and small arms killed forty Northerners and wounded nearly two hundred more. The Federals herded scores of Confederate prisoners to the rear, and another hundred or so Louisianans and Texans lay dead or wounded behind their works.

The Confederates remained far from whipped. That night, Taylor remained upbeat about his outgunned army's performance. "Night brought quiet," he wrote. "The force at Bisland was in fine spirits. Protected by the breastworks, we had suffered but little; and the *Diana* was expected to resume her position before morning." Taylor clearly believed that Banks would be drubbed and that if the Yankees attempted to force his works, they would be slaughtered. Although he had not heard from Reily, Taylor was unconcerned. He made plans for the next day's fight, penning "No news seemed good news, for I would have ample time to provide against a debarkation north of [Hutchin's Point]."[49]

12

The Landing

"We skirmished around all day but nothing definite came of it."

Captain Julius Giesecke
Company G, 4th Texas Cavalry

For the other part of Major General Richard Taylor's little army, April 13 had been a long day as well. The Confederate war chief had placed great faith on two cavalry regiments and the equivalent of an infantry battalion and two artillery batteries to hold off three Union brigades supported by as many gunboats—USS *Arizona,* USS *Calhoun,* and USS *Estrella*—for an entire day. Remarkably, they had.

The Louisiana terrain helped. "The difficulties of landing at this, as well as at all other adjacent landings, are very great for boats of any considerable draft," reported Brigadier General Cuvier Grover. "No transport of any considerable capacity was able to go nearer than 100 yards of the shore." Frittering away valuable time, the Federals struck upon the idea of making a floating pier out of the barges and using their shallow draft vessels as lighters. At dawn on April 13, as Sibley's and Mouton's Confederates made their lackluster attack at Bisland, Federal troops began moving ashore above Franklin.[1]

The Landing. Artist James E. Taylor painting this fanciful scene of Grover's Division coming ashore. There are too many Confederates and they are too well armed; the Union flotilla includes ironclads and the landing appears to be well coordinated. The reality was a little too chaotic to make a nice canvas composition.

Rossiter Johnson, Campfires and Battlefields: An Illustrated History of the Campaigns and Conflicts of the Great Civil War *(New York: Bryan, Taylor and Company, 1894).*

While some soldiers trundled down the makeshift pontoon bridge, Brigadier General William Dwight's infantry brigade loaded into oar boats and rowed to a landing on the western shore of Grand Lake, seizing a beachhead. The U.S. 1st Louisiana Infantry scrambled onto the *Clifton*'s boats and went ashore first, aided by the covering fire of the gunboats, which shelled a heavy fringe of woods and a stout fence that bordered an open field near the water. Colonel Richard Holcomb ordered two companies of skirmishers to fan out and move toward the plantation road, which led away from the lake and toward Bayou Teche, while the rest of the regiment formed a reserve to await developments.[2]

The troops soon made contact with the Confederates. As the Federal soldiers advanced, Colonel William G. Vincent's dismounted cavalrymen opened fire from the woods on their front

Colonel Richard Holcomb of Granby served as major in the 13th Connecticut before taking a promotion to command the 1st Louisiana Infantry formed in August 1862. He led them ashore in their first combat near Franklin, Louisiana. Holcomb and his men did not get along, and the colonel died under suspicious circumstances two months later.

Salmon Brook Historical Society, Granby, Connecticut.

and right, as did the two guns from Lieutenant William Smith's section of the Val Verde Battery, sited directly across the road and firing at the transports beyond. "The skirmishers continued to advance in good order," wrote Holcomb, "notwithstanding the galling fire of the enemy." The colonel ordered the rest of the regiment to form a line of battle to the left of the road, facing south, as shells from the gunboats began to pass overhead toward the two Rebel guns, inadvertently endangering his men. "I ordered the regiment to fire a volley and charge into the wood, which they did in good style," Holcomb continued. The 6th New York—Wilson's Zouaves—was the next regiment ashore. "The enemy opened a battery on the transports, and riddled the upper works of the high decked Mississippi steamers with grape and canister," wrote regimental historian Gouverneur Morris. "The Sixth was quickly tumbled out of its transports in front." The unit formed up on the bank of Grand Lake and advanced toward the Rebels. "These woods were stiffly held, and the Sixth marched forward steadily as was its wont, firing and cheering."[3]

The Rebel Louisianans and the Texan artillerists soon found themselves outnumbered and overwhelmed. With the U.S. Navy rapidly finding the range on the road, and more and more Union infantry moving around their right and threatening to cut off their line of retreat, Vincent's Confederates fell back. They had killed just one of the invading Federals and had wounded three others.

Brigadier General William Dwight was a West Point graduate who resigned from the army to follow a career in manufacturing in Boston and Philadelphia. He led the 70th New York Infantry in the Peninsula Campaign where he fell, seriously wounded, into Confederate hands. He recovered, and on his exchange, received promotion to brigadier general and was transferred to Louisiana. He proved to be an aggressive and capable officer. *US Army Military History Institute.*

Behind Dwight's brigade-sized advance, the rest of Grover's Division made their ways off the transports and onto land. "It was not my intention to expose a large force to the view of the enemy until the whole division was in readiness," wrote Grover. "I ordered General Dwight to keep the body of his troops under cover of the wood."[4]

The Federals had forced their way past the first obstacle with little effort, and next they tramped through the swampy woods and fronted the cleared fields of the McWilliams plantation beyond. Here they encountered Vincent's reunited force, his regiment and Smith's guns drawn up in line of battle, reinforced by two additional guns—Captain Florian Cornay's section of the St. Mary's Cannoneers—and the two companies of Lieutenant Colonel Valsin Fournet's 10th Yellow Jacket Battalion. The Federals of the U.S. 1st Louisiana held their position on the edge of the woods, soon joined by the 26th Maine as well as the 6th and 131st New York. Although they outnumbered the Southerners by better than three to one, they were outgunned by the Rebel artillery.

The Union navy executed its orders expertly. Having unloaded its cargo of Union infantry as well as General Grover and his staff, the USS *Clifton* churned the brown waters of Grand Lake and headed south for Brashear City and its trip up Bayou Teche to Major General Nathaniel P. Banks, destined to be the harbinger of dramatic and exciting dispatches. The USS *Arizona,* lately arrived after having shaken loose its muddy shackles, patrolled to the north and east of the landing site, vigilant against any Rebel incursions. The USS *Estrella* and the USS *Calhoun* continued their duties as transports but claimed priority for landing troops, in case they needed to clear the deck—and guns—for action.

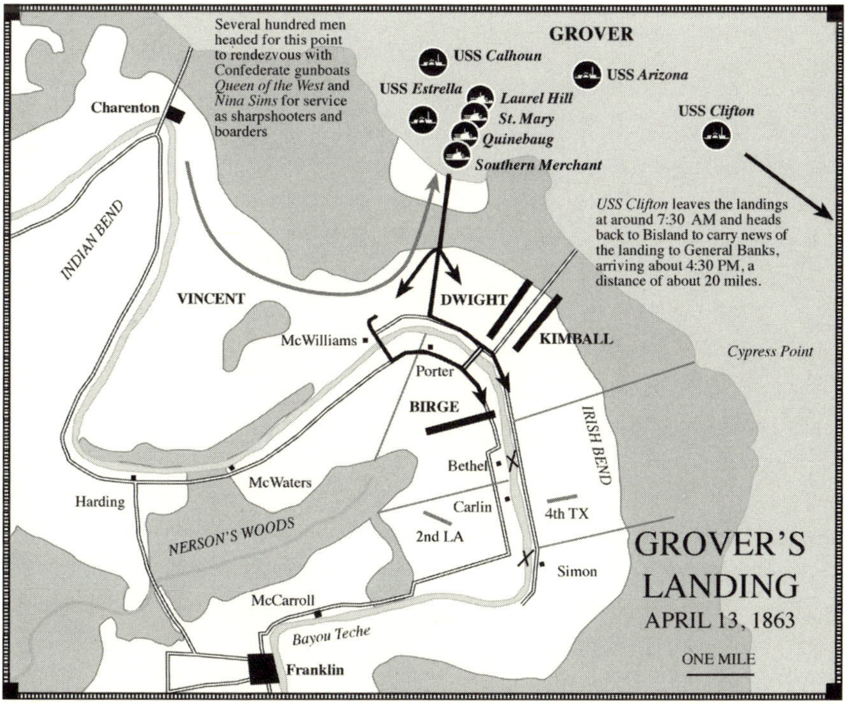

General Dwight, now on shore to command the advance, ordered the 6th New York to send skirmishers across the field to the southwest to find and engage the enemy while he dispatched Captain Richard Barrett's company of Louisiana cavalry toward the southeast, to seize the junction of the plantation road and the east bank road. Vincent's men responded by firing upon the Union horsemen. Smith's section of the Val Verde Battery paid them special attention while the Yellow Jackets tried to turn the Union right. To counter this move, Dwight ordered Captain Henry W. Clossen's Battery L, 1st U.S. Artillery, and the 131st New York infantry regiment to move forward and seize the bridge while the balance of his command shadowed the Confederates, moving toward their left.

As the Union soldiers moved steadily but prudently toward the bayou, they learned that four plantation bridges over the Teche were vital for both armies. The bayou made a large curve to the east, called Irish Bend by steamer pilots. Four plantations edged the bayou's east side. The McWilliams plantation was along the north edge of the bend, Alexander Porter's Oaklawn Plantation was on the northeast edge, Bethel's plantation was south of Porter's, and Simon's plantation was on the southeast and south. Various owners farmed the fields on the bayou's west side. All the bridges were extensions of lanes separating the various farms.

Across these bridges—inside the bend—the terrain looked deceptively simple. A dense swamp and canebrake formed by Bayou Yokely dominated the interior about a mile back from the Teche's west side, and plowed fields curved alongside the bayou's banks. Cutting across the neck of Irish Bend lay a forest called Nerson's Woods, also fronted in places by a dense canebrake. The strength of Yankee numbers would easily win the day.

As Dwight's command divided, Vincent's Rebels faced increasingly long odds. Outnumbered and in danger of being bypassed and cut-off, the Louisianans withdrew southeast toward the Teche, moving to disengage, cross the bayou, and cover the approaches to Franklin. Cornay's gunners took position at the McWilliams bridge at 10:30 AM to cover the retreat then aided in its partial destruction. Dwight's Federals moved them along, blue skirmishers pushing past the buildings of the McWilliams plantation a few hundred yards behind their foe.

By late morning, the first of the four bridges lay in Federal hands. Clossen's Battery, the 131st New York, and Barrett's Company B, 1st Louisiana Cavalry, positioned themselves around the "T" intersection of the eastern bayou road and the McWilliams road, commanded the partially destroyed bridge over the Teche, and spilled across to the west bank road. The next objective, Porter's bridge, lay a little more than a mile to the south, and additional reinforcements, five companies of the 41st Massachusetts, marched up from the landing site.[5]

Even though Vincent's force had fallen back, additional Confederates had apparently arrived and began to contest the progress of Dwight's troops. At a little past noon, the leading elements of the 4th Texas Cavalry, Companies C and F under Captains Charles Carroll Linn and James Murray Crossen, had galloped to capture and destroy Porter's bridge. These troops from Fort Bisland began tearing up planks and setting fires as soon as they arrived.[6]

Dwight had responded with like force. By 11:00 AM he had ordered a section of Battery L, 1st U.S., and two sections of Battery C, 2nd U.S., to shell the Texans. He also ordered Barrett's cavalry and the 131st New York to move south along the Teche's east bank and to sweep away the eighty or so Texans bent on vandalism. The move had the desired effect. Sergeant Alfred B. Petticolas was among the Confederates dismantling the bridge when the alarm sounded. "All at once an infantry regiment was reported in 400 yards of us," he wrote. "We retreated precipitately to the main command about a mile." The advancing Federals captured Porter's bridge and put out the Rebel's fires at the cost of a single artillery horse wounded. Colonel Nicholas Day of the 131st New York ordered the slaves at Porter's plantation rounded up to repair the damaged structure and to fix the McWilliams Bridge. Meanwhile, new orders arrived directing him to send half of his regiment and Barrett's cavalry on to the third bridge—Bethel's—a mile and a half downstream.[7]

Vincent's Confederates had already leap-frogged over to set Bethel's bridge afire and had destroyed Simon's bridge on their way back to Franklin when additional reinforcements arrived. At 1:30 PM Vincent's retreating troops met the rest of the 4th Texas, which had just arrived from Fort Bisland. Although the situation at the bridges seemed dire, the Federals had not pursued, and the Louisianans were eager to confer with the newcomers to plan a course of action. The greatest danger, all agreed, was that the Federals might realize that there were two routes to Franklin—the bayou road from the east and the New Iberia Road from the north.[8]

The Federals, though unfamiliar with the confusing geography, were astraddle a significantly strategic intersection at the McWilliams bridge. If they took the road to the right, following the Teche counterintuitively upstream to the west-southwest, they would first pass through the northern extension of Nerson's Woods, less than a mile away, and almost immediately find a narrow lane through the woods and across the interior swamp at the McWaters plantation. Passing that path, it was too poor to admit the passage of large amounts of men and horses anyway, and continuing on up the west bank of the Teche would take the Federals west-southwest until the bayou took an abrupt, almost acute angle turn to the right, north-northeast. Near this point the vigilant Federals would notice a road named Harding Lane heading to the left, cutting across the neck of the Irish Bend. This road ran west of Nerson's Woods, through the swamp and cane, and it crossed Bayou Yokely at the only bridge over that tactical impediment. Harding Lane, then, was the short cut route between Franklin and New Iberia. If the

Northern soldiers discovered it, Taylor and his entire army would be caught; the most strategic junction in the campaign would be that inauspicious-looking junction of Harding Lane and the bayou's west bank road, two miles north of Franklin. This would be the choking point that would throttle Taylor's army.

There was another route into Franklin. If the Federals moved to their left after crossing the McWilliams bridge, moving to the south-southeast down the west bank of the Teche and following the current of the stream, they would eventually make a sweeping right-hand turn at the southern shoulder of Irish Bend and head west-southwest toward Franklin until they reached that town. This was the more logical route to Franklin because it followed the course of the Teche and was the more intuitive way toward the village, but it was about a mile longer. It was also open, with clear visibility almost the entire way, with the exceptions of the swamp in the middle of Irish Bend and Nerson's Woods.

What the Federals could not see was abundantly clear to the Confederates. Vincent summoned Captain Cornay, who was native to the region, to explain the geography to Colonel James Reily. After a brief description, all agreed that the enemy must be lured into taking the more obvious route down Bayou Teche. "It was determined to invite the enemy, by attacking him, to follow us down the bayou toward Franklin and prevent, if possible, his occupying the road to New Iberia through Harding's Lane," wrote Cornay. "Colonel Reily at once ordered me to retake position at Simon's Bridge and have the bridge repaired if possible." The Louisiana artilleryman ordered his guns turned about, and they rumbled back toward the enemy. By 3:00 PM, slaves from Simon's plantation had repaired the span.[9]

To the north, the Federals were busy repairing Bethel's Bridge. When Smith's section of the Val Verde Battery arrived, Cornay ordered them to shell the Yankees to discourage their industry. "The enemy opened with brisk firing . . . from the other side (west side) of the bayou," reported Colonel Day. Lieutenant John Rodgers arrived with the four guns of Battery C, 2nd U.S., to support the outnumbered New Yorkers, and together they held the Confederates at bay. The smoldering and contested span was unoccupied by either side. "A warm skirmished ensued," wrote Private Theophilus Noel of Company A, 4th Texas. "This should have been classed as a battle."[10]

Colonel Reily led the 4th Texas across the bayou at Simon's Bridge, formed a line of battle and began sweeping north across Bethel's fields. Both sides were only occasionally visible to each other in the cane and corn fields, and both groped around trying to gain advantage. Cornay's guns moved to his extreme left to form a crossfire with Smith's guns to the west and began sending shot and shell in the perceived direction of the enemy. "We were unable to learn the strength of the Yankees," penned Captain Julius Giesecke in his journal. "We skirmished around all day but nothing definite came of it." The Federals were not as blasé. Rebel bullets and shells—mostly fired blindly—wounded three men of the 131st New York and killed another. The Union troops had not been able to respond. "We found by this day's experience," reported Colonel Day, "that our pieces were very defective and exceedingly short of range."[11]

As these advance regiments skirmished, the rest of Grover's Division used the bulk of the morning to unload. There were ominous signs brewing for the Federals at the crowded beachhead. To the north, on the horizon, spotters in the hurricane decks of the transports reported seeing the unmistakable smudges of smoke from steamer funnels. All hands aboard the Union gunboats knew that the Confederates possessed a formidable fleet. Many feared that it might descend at this critical moment, when the army was most vulnerable, and bring about an amphibious disaster heretofore unparalleled in the history of the nation. "During the afternoon the smoke of the enemy's steamers was discovered in the distance, apparently in Lake Chocot, coming down," reported Lieutenant Commander Augustus Paul Cooke, the commander of Banks's navy. Yet, throughout the day, the foe did not come. The Yankees aboard the *Arizona, Calhoun,* and *Estrella* continued their tasks as required, but nervous hands held binoculars and telescopes trained to the north at the fringe of green topped with columns of gray smoke—the swampy labyrinth that harbored the Confederate dragon. They felt the absence of the *Clifton* acutely.[12]

By mid-afternoon Colonel William King Kimball moved forward with the second brigade of Grover's Division. "We filed off on our march on a road leading through a dense wood of tall live oak and low palmetto, a number of the wounded of the enemy were carried by us to the rear, having been picked up where the skirmish of the morning had taken place," wrote a soldier in the 41st Massachusetts, "then over a road which divides two extensive sugar plantations, the one on the left owned by Mme. Porter employing about three hundred slaves; the one on our right owned by Mr. McWilliams and about the same extent." As the New Englanders marched by, the plantations' slaves crowded the fences along the route. "Crowds of negroes dressed in their best thronged the road, using the most extravagant expressions of welcome, for they seemed to have some kind of an instinct idea that our coming was in some way or other to better their condition." The men of the 12th Maine, 24th Connecticut, and the 41st and 52nd Massachusetts moved onto the grounds of Porter's plantation.[13]

After a brief pause, Kimball ordered a portion of his brigade into the fight. Troops from the 41st Massachusetts deployed across the bayou and headed toward the sound of the guns further south, hoping to outflank Reily's Texans by moving down the west bank. The Confederates noted the shift and hurried across the Teche on Simon's Bridge. Cornay's guns rattled across to take a new position holding the bend in the bayou road on the west bank while the mounted Texans moved west across Carlin's Field to their left,

Colonel William King Kimball of Paris, Maine, started the war as Lieutenant Colonel of the 12th Maine Infantry and came with Butler's command to Louisiana. He replaced Colonel George Shepley as commander of the regiment upon his superior's promotion to military governor of Louisiana. Kimball led a brigade in the Teche Campaign.

Massachusetts Comandery Military Order of the Loyal Legion and the US Army Military History Institute.

then turned and headed north along the fringes of Nerson's Woods to get at the enemy flank. "We advanced about a mile . . . when the rebel cavalry were discovered in groups near a wood which skirted a field of two or three hundred acres, then under cultivation," wrote one Yankee. "Two companies from our regiment were sent out as skirmishes; quite a brisk firing was kept up between the two lines, but the sun going down the rebels retired to their cover."[14]

The appearance of so many additional troops convinced Reily's Texans that the time to leave had arrived. As Kimball's skirmishers descended the bayou's west bank road, the Texans gave up the fight, abandoning Irish Bend to the enemy but hopeful that the Federals would perceive this to be the route to the rear of Taylor's army. Across the bayou, men from the 131st New York destroyed the now uncontested third bridge and then withdrew behind friendly lines at Oaklawn for the night. Kimball's Brigade withdrew from their forward positions as well, retiring to Porter's Bridge where the men made makeshift camps in the furrows of a massive cornfield.

Near sunset, with the heavens threatening rain, Colonel Henry Birge moved his troops forward past Kimball's Brigade, crossing the Teche to deploy in the fields beyond it, and moved fatefully south along the west bank, assuming the front line of Grover's Division and taking Reily's bait. When the 13th Connecticut crossed Porter's bridge it marched down along the bayou road, eventually forming a line of battle to the left of the lane and anchored on the Teche. Colonel Edward L. Molineaux deployed the 159th New York to the right of the New Englanders, and Birge's last two regiments, the 25th Connecticut and the 26th Maine—after having served with Dwight's Brigade for most of the day—deployed in successive lines behind the New Yorkers. Eventually, the 3rd Brigade of Grover's Division held the ground between the tip of the wooded swamp at the source of Bayou Yokely all the way to Bayou Teche, and they held their positions while watching as the Texans disappeared into the dusky distance toward Franklin. Across the bayou some of Kimball's men formed a picket line east of the stream to extend the Union line all the way to Grand Lake. Grover's systematic deployment was complete. It had taken all day to unload and move about three miles while Banks had been battering away at Taylor's army ten miles southeast—fifteen by road—at Bisland.

13

Escape

"Grover had stopped just short of the prize."

Major General Richard Taylor

A heavy downpour drenched both armies as darkness fell on April 13, and the Rebels retreated through the deluge. Colonel James Reily ordered the dismantling of the foot bridge behind the McWaters plantation across Bayou Yokely, and he posted pickets from the 2nd Louisiana along Harding Lane to keep that critical route open. The balance of the Confederate troops moved along the west bank bayou road, through Franklin, and halted at Carline's plantation, a mile and a half beyond the town, within communication range of Fort Bisland. "We then learned that the Yankees had stormed our redoubts three times and that it would be impossible for us to hold our position," wrote Captain Julius Giesecke. "From below at Bisland yet came the rumbling sound of our big guns," observed Private Theophilus Noel, "which plainly told us that all was not quiet there." Reily rode on to headquarters at the Bisland Plantation to deliver the day's news. "At 9 PM appeared Colonel Reily," wrote Major General Richard Taylor. The soaked Texan reported that the enemy had landed at Hutchin's Point in undetermined but superior strength and had taken Bayou Teche. He thought Franklin was still in Rebel hands, but if the Northerners pressed their advantage, they would arrive in the town that night.[1]

The Confederate army lay trapped. "Here was pleasant intelligence!" sneered Taylor. "There was no time to ask questions." After having defended the works successfully all day against Major General Nathaniel P. Banks, Brigadier General William H. Emory, and Brigadier General Godfrey Weitzel, Taylor was shocked by the bad news from the north. The Rebel war chief now had to make a decision—the time for hoping for a grand, coordinated counterstroke had passed—and he needed to save his army. "I hoped to cut my way through, but feared the loss of my wagons and material," Taylor noted. He called his aides together and began making rapid-fire decisions. Taylor directed General Alfred Mouton to withdraw from the left bank of the bayou, start the artillery and trains to Franklin, and follow with the infantry. Colonel Tom Green with his cavalry was to form the rear guard; Semmes was told to hurry his repairs and get the *Diana* to Franklin by dawn.[2]

Taylor now hoped that, by some stroke of luck, the widely scattered and jealously shepherded elements of his great offensive might providentially converge at just the right point and dramatically smash the Yankee invasion. After leaving Major William Levy in charge of executing the evacuation, Taylor rode up the bayou road with Reily to see the situation personally. When he arrived at the Confederate camps near Franklin, he was dumbfounded. "I found the men sleeping and the trains parked, though the enemy was so near at hand," Taylor wrote. "The camp was aroused, the troops were ordered under arms, and Reily left to move up at once, with his trains following." The exhausted soldiers moved to their task, thankful that at least the rain had ended.[3]

The Confederate commander proceeded up the road with his aides. At 2:00 AM the small cavalcade entered Franklin, its brick streets shiny from the recent downpour that had turned the night steamy. Taylor described the settlement as being "as silent as the

The Gates House, later called the **Mathew Bell House,** stood near the middle of Franklin. Built in the 1850s by Alfred Gates, it reflected the style and taste of this important sugar parish town.

Library of Congress.

grave." Once the Rebel officers determined that the town was free of Federals, they continued the personal reconnaissance along the New Iberia cut-off road and into Harding Lane. "Beyond the last houses . . . a faint light from some camp fires could be seen," Taylor recalled. "Were the Federals in possession of the road?"[4]

Taylor moved cautiously forward and finally, to his relief, he determined that the troops were Confederates. Lieutenant Colonel Franklin Clack's Confederate Guards Response Battalion had made its way from the Avery Island salt works and was heading toward Fort Bisland. They had camped for the night, unaware of the proximity of the enemy or the danger they faced.

Taylor, glad to see this band of comrades, asked Clack to roust his men and shake them into a skirmish line. Together, the general and the small 12th Louisiana Infantry Battalion confirmed that the bridge over Bayou Yokely on Harding Lane remained unscathed. The Confederates continued their scouting in the pitch black through the bulk of Nerson's Woods, across the McWaters plantation north of the swamp, and across McKerall's fields to the south. When they emerged from the far edge of the forest, the sight they beheld amazed them. Just over a mile away lay Brigadier General Cuvier Grover's entire division, their campfires glowing orange. "It was a wonderful chance," a thankful Taylor remembered. "Grover had stopped just short of the prize. Thirty minutes would have given him the wood and the bridge, closing the trap on my force."[5]

While the divided Yankee armies slept at Irish Bend and opposite Fort Bisland, Taylor's officers executed a skillful withdrawal. Between 9:00 and 10:00 PM on April 13, General Henry Hopkins

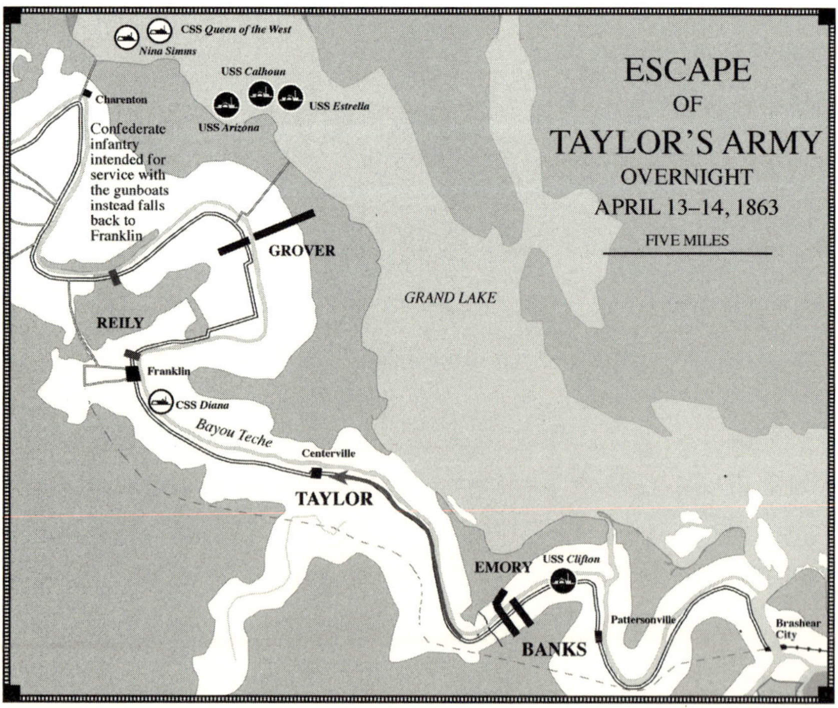

Sibley organized the supply wagons and ambulances full of the wounded, starting them north toward Franklin and New Iberia. Next, Colonel Henry Gray's 28th Louisiana and the remainder of the St. Mary's Cannoneers withdrew from their west bank positions at Fort Bisland, marching silently up the road toward Franklin. Brigadier General Mouton followed with the rest of the Bisland command, crossing over from their hard-fought positions east of the Teche and joining the caravan headed north. Green and his 5th Texas Cavalry, joining up with Colonel Edwin Waller's 13th Texas Cavalry Battalion and the 3-inch rifles from the 1st Regular Battery, brought up the rear. Their two 24-pounders remained in the shell-torn and blood-defended works, and an upended 12-pound Napoleon with a smashed axle lay in a ditch by the railroad embankment. Lieutenant Minos T. Gordy of the St. Mary's Cannoneers lamented the loss. "I hated to part with it," he reported. "It had done good service, and was the best piece in the field, in my opinion." Remarkably, the Rebel evacuation took nearly four hours to complete, and none of their blue-clad enemies sleeping just a mile away impeded their progress.[6]

Sibley's plans for evacuating the sick and injured seemed reasonable. He loaded the steamer *Cornie*—a onetime salt boat from Avery Island but more recently an ammunition transport from the New Iberia arsenal—with the army's disabled men and issued orders for the boat to proceed up the Teche as far as Franklin. Taylor meanwhile would see that transportation would be at hand in Franklin to transport the wounded overland around Grover's Division.[7]

Not surprisingly, Federal pickets had heard some of the midnight commotion in the Rebel lines. "At 11 o'clock on the night of the 13th . . . Colonel [John W.] Kimball, of the 53rd Massachusetts, heard the enemy making preparations for evacuating his entrenchments," wrote a Union soldier. "The movement of the artillery and baggage wagons, packing and nailing of boxes, and drivers cursing their mules, could be distinctly heard by the advance

Arlington Plantation, or the Old Baker Place, was a Greek revival landmark near Franklin, rising a few miles south of the town and fronting Bayou Teche. Built in the 1850s by a wealthy, slave-owning mulatto named Euphrazie Carlin, it undoubtedly attracted the attention of the various soldiers passing by its front gates.

Library of Congress.

pickets of Colonel Gooding's brigade." The Yankee officer hurried to report the sounds to Colonel Oliver P. Gooding in command of the brigade, and that officer in turn sent riders to General Banks's headquarters. Nevertheless, continued the soldier, "no special movement was made in pursuit of the enemy until early next morning."[8]

On the west bank Colonel Halbert E. Paine also heard some noise. An officer startled the brigade commander awake just after midnight, shaking him out from under his makeshift blanket, a purloined carpet. The pickets reported hearing vehicular movement behind the Confederate works. Paine crept up to the picket line to listen for himself. "A careful inquiry failed to satisfy me

Colonel John W. Kimball, a scythe manufacturer from Fitchburg, was an officer with the 15th Massachusetts Infantry during the infamous disaster at Ball's Bluff, Virginia, which destroyed half the regiment and led to formation of the U.S. Congress Joint Committee on the Conduct of the War in 1861. At Antietam, the regiment again lost half its men. After this second debacle, Kimball resigned as lieutenant colonel to take command of the nine months 53rd Massachusetts as it readied for service in Louisiana. The veteran officer heard the Confederates evacuating their works at Bisland in the middle of the night of April 13, 1863. His superiors decided to ignore his report until first light.

Massachusetts Comandery Military Order of the Loyal Legion and the US Army Military History Institute.

whether a general evacuation or only a transfer of guns was in progress," Paine wrote. The Wisconsin colonel sent a messenger back to Emory then returned to his rug in the mud.[9]

Therefore, despite the dutiful reports of the Union soldiers assigned with the task of watching the enemy, Taylor's Confederates slipped away unmolested. "At midnight an aide of General Sibley rode up and ordered me to load up and remove back to New Iberia as rapidly as possible," wrote Major Silas T. Grisamore of the commissary department. "Having my train already loaded, I was soon on the march." In the dark hours that followed, the Confederate Army in Southwest Louisiana was in full retreat, and the first hints of panic began to appear. Wagons passed through Franklin and continued up the New Iberia Road, along Harding Lane, and across Bayou Yokely toward safety, the teamsters remained tense and edgy until reaching the intersection of the bayou road at the top of Irish Bend.[10]

At a residence in Franklin, a distraught doctor shook awake a pair of slumbering Texans. Sergeant Alfred B. Petticolas and Private Thomas Reade Roots, having spent the day skirmishing with the Federals, had taken note of the threatening weather and had ducked into a house where a sick comrade was convalescing so that they, too, could spend the night in dry comfort. They found themselves awakened suddenly at 3:00 AM. "I got up, saddled my horse, and went to Franklin," Petticolas wrote. After asking where he could find his regiment, he received the erroneous information that they were with the others heading up Harding Lane toward New Iberia. "With great difficulty [we] went up the New Iberia Road blocked as it was with vehicles of all sorts, the baggage trains crowding through," he noted. The retreat swept him along, away from his comrades.[11]

With his army's withdrawal underway, Taylor turned to the task of holding the Yankees at bay long enough for his troops to escape. He ordered the 4th Texas to form into line of battle in the fields of McKerall's plantation, about a mile and a half northeast of Franklin, and he told other troops to assemble there as well. Colonel William G. Vincent's 2nd Louisiana arrived, less the troops assigned to the various outposts and picket lines. The two companies of Lieutenant Colonel Valsin Fournet's 10th Yellow Jacket Battalion arrived. Both of the units filed into line on Reily's left. Clack's 12th Battalion, newcomers to the fight, took their place as skirmishers in advance of the line. Captain Florian Cornay also arrived and posted one section of his St. Mary's Cannoneers on the bayou road and the other in the center of the battle line. Lieutenant William Smith's two Val Verde guns received different orders, and they continued on into Franklin then turned right up the New Iberia Road. They would protect the head of the retreating column. Just before dawn, Taylor ordered this small army forward, across the three hundred yards of plowed fields to the strip of Nerson's Woods that separated the McKerall estate from the Carlin Plantation beyond.

Not everyone found the rendezvous as easily. Petticolas and his companion were surprised to learn that they had gone the wrong direction. "At last, about sun up, we reached the forks of the road where the cut off and the bayou road from Franklin came together again," Petticolas continued. "Here we did not find the Regiment and found that they were on the bayou road and expecting a fight." Petticolas and his companion then made a logical conclusion and turned right at the intersection, following the road along the bayou's west bank. They did not know they were heading straight for the rear of Grover's Division. "I started down the bayou road and having traveled some two miles was halted at a picket guard under command of a Louisiana Cavalry Captain who informed me that I could go no further down that road," continued the astonished Texan, "and kept me and Roots with him to strengthen his picket." The two wayward Texans adjusted to their new status and took their place on the line as the eastern horizon turned from black to gray.[12]

At Hutchin's Point, sailors in the U.S. Navy had also spent an uneasy night. They had watched the smoke from steamers—presumed enemy boats—the entire previous afternoon until daylight ceased and the rains fell. Then the haunts appeared at night in the form of boat's lights that drifted southward along the northern reaches of Grand Lake. These were certainly enemies, and to many aboard the Union gunboats, they seemed to move with the fluid grace of a hunter stalking prey. "I had the midwatch, the fires were banked. Abut 2 o'clock I saw two lights as if on boats, up the lake, and they were moving," wrote Acting Third Assistant Engineer George W. Baird from his vantage aboard the USS *Calhoun*. "I . . . told the officer of the deck, but he was a phlegmatic old fellow and was not enthused." Faced with this rebuff, the young sailor could do little else but watch the lights slowly drift closer. "At 4 I was relieved and I turned in, thinking I had overrated the importance of those lights." He hadn't.[13]

14

King of the Swamp

"I would rather see the devil than that boat."

Captain Edward W. Fuller
CSS Queen of the West

The creeping light of dawn on April 14, 1863, ushered in the day that would determine whether or not the richest part of the Confederacy would remain a part of the Rebel nation or once again fall under the authority of the United States. The first few daylight hours would determine the fate of Major General Richard Taylor's Confederate army. Thousands of muskets and rifles held by work-worn hands would deliver the answers, and the gaping maw of big-bore guns, snug in their carriages on the decks of wooden gunboats, would also have their say.

At just a few minutes after 5:00 AM, the boatswain's mate on the USS *Calhoun* bellowed, "All hands to quarters!" The lookout had spotted the lights aboard the CSS *Queen of the West* and the *Nina Simms;* the fading darkness had at last yielded its secret. "I was so sleepy I waited a moment to see if there was any excitement," wrote Acting Third Assistant Engineer George W. Baird. "I heard the cable slipped and then a gun fired; then I was got out in a hurry. The engine was going ahead slowly; day was breaking." It appeared that two Rebel gunboats were heading forward in headlong attack.

One was a black ram armored with cotton bales, and the other was a steamboat that, if the Confederates were true to form, would be loaded with riflemen. Acting Master Meltiah Jordan, eager to avoid a Galveston-style catastrophe, began to turn the *Calhoun* away from the danger.[1]

The skippers of the other two Yankee boats, however, were game for the fight. "I could see the *Arizona*'s beam working," Baird continued, having scrambled to the *Calhoun*'s hurricane deck for a better look. He saw the *Arizona* glide by on his port side, heading in the opposite direction. As a growing cluster of officers gathered, leaning on the railing to peer into the gloom, they noticed another Federal vessel moving forward on their starboard side to challenge the Rebel threat. "Why, even the *Estrella* is headed toward the enemy," one of their number called to the *Calhoun*'s commander. Jordan responded by ordering his vessel turned about and heading back up Grand Lake, taking his place behind and between his consorts, in an open V, heading toward their duty. Below him, on the bow, the crew of the 30-pounder Parrot readied their gun and raised it to its maximum elevation. In the distance lay the two enemy targets, a white steamer and a sizable black warship.

If these Yankee sailors had known the predicament faced by the Rebel commander facing them, they might have relaxed. Captain Edward W. Fuller had led his two-boat flotilla all the way from Fort DeRussy to the landing closest to Charenton to take on troops in the dark hours after midnight, only to discover that Taylor had ordered a full retreat and the Confederate steamers were on their own. If troops had been on their way to board the vessels, they never arrived. Realizing that the Federal invasion had upended the plans for a bold strike against the Union base at Brashear City and that the U.S. fleet was actually very close by, Fuller prudently ordered his vessels to turn about and run back toward Chicot Pass. Then came an unwelcome shuffling sound of mud sliding along the bottom of the warship. In his haste, the pilot had run the *Queen of the West* onto a sandbar; the tide had turned during the night, and his chosen path was too shallow for the heavy vessel. Fuller ordered all hands to work on freeing the ship.

The lightening of the eastern sky revealed to the Confederates that fate had ruled against them. Not only were they aground, but they were soon to be within visual range of the enemy fleet, just three miles distant. "There is the damned *Calhoun,*" Fuller said. "I would rather see the devil than that boat." The *Queen of the West*'s bow swung toward the leftmost of the oncoming Union gunboats—the *Arizona*—now fully awake and making its way up Grand Lake. Within moments Federal shells began to claw toward Fuller's ram, still out of range but closing.[2]

On board the *Estrella,* on the left of the Union naval arc, Lieutenant Commander Augustus Paul Cooke assumed that the Rebel ram would make a dash to cut one of its assailants in two, as it had done to the *Indianola.* "The black steamer pointed toward the *Arizona* as though she were going to ram her," he reported. But when the *Queen of the West* did not attack, Cooke seemed perplexed. He attributed the lack of response to superior Union gunnery: "Our firing was so rapid and accurate that she did not advance." He had no way of knowing that he was facing a largely helpless foe.[3]

The 30-pounder on the *Calhoun*'s bow aimed at the ram from about three miles away, and the Confederates' luck evaporated. "I did not see the shot, but I heard it fired, heard its flight, and its landing on the *Queen,* its explosion, and the rush of steam that followed," Baird recalled. One of the first rounds to hit the Rebel steamer, perhaps the first fired from the *Calhoun,* struck high on its target and plunged through the roof of the casemate. The exploding shell cut a major steam pipe and caused a fire in a ready magazine, and the flames spread to the cotton bales stacked around the machinery and protecting the engines. "Captain Jordan . . . pointed

Destruction of the Queen of the West. The USS *Estrella (left)*, the USS *Arizona (right background)*, and the USS *Calhoun (right)* surrounding the dying CSS *Queen of the West* as its Confederate crew abandons the burning boat. The *Nina Simms* is shown making a run for it in the background.

Harper's Weekly, *author's collection.*

his vessel to run down the black stranger," Cooke noted, "but she was now seen to be on fire from the explosion of our shells and was soon wrapped in flames fore and aft."[4]

The first battle of the day belonged to the U.S. Navy. The *Nina Simms* turned and fled up Chicot Pass, abandoning the stricken ram and its men to their fate. The *Arizona* pursued. Fearing another Rebel bayou ambush—one of his enemy's favorite nautical tricks—Cooke ordered his signal officer to wigwag a recall to the ambitious gunboat. "It is probable Commodore Cook feared that the *Arizona* might fall into a trap similar to that in which the *Diana* fell, if she attempted to pursue the [*Nina Simms*] into the bayou to which she retreated," an observer reported. The skipper of the Arizona complied. Meanwhile, the *Queen of the West* burned fiercely.[5]

The Confederate crew and the men of the 3rd Maryland Artillery jumped from the doomed ram and did their best to escape to the shore, which was four miles away. "All of our boats were now lowered to pick up the crew of the burning steamer who were clinging to cotton bales all around her," reported Cooke. The Northern sailors fished ninety men from the waters of Grand Lake; about thirty others drowned or burned. Captain Fuller survived, having now outlived two of his commands, but he received more injuries—this time, severely scalded feet—to add to the gunshot wounds he had sustained in January while commanding the CSS *Cotton.* "One of the boats approached a bale of cotton, to which were clinging a white man and two negroes. The white man called out, 'I am Captain Fuller; save me,'" a newspaper account related. "He and the contrabands were got in the boat, when the captain soon discovered another cotton bale with a paymaster hanging to it. He called the attention of our men to it, and they secured the paymaster." As the Rebel ram blazed, it grew lighter and eventually floated free from the sandbar. It drifted several miles down Grand Lake in a crescendo of fire before exploding. After the first guns had opened that morning, it had taken the U.S. Navy just two hours to obliterate the *Queen of the West.*[6]

Baird questioned some of the Rebel prisoners and gained a new appreciation for Taylor's plan. "It was learned later that these . . . vessels were on their way to Berwick Bay to capture or destroy the *Calhoun* and *Estrella,* exactly as had been done to the *Westfield* and *Harriet Lane* in Galveston Bay on the 1st of January," he wrote. "They had the *Diana* ready to help; they did not know that the *Clifton* and *Arizona* had reinforced us; they did not expect to find us in the open waters of Grand Lake. They had taken the *Queen* from us, and she was the strongest ship they had." The hopes for a repeat of Confederate naval success now lay amid the smoldering, sputtering, waterlogged remains of the *Queen of the West,* which Union wags now dubbed the "King of the Swamp."[7]

15

Irish Bend

"Thus it was that the 'glorious victories of Louisiana' of which we heard so much ado about in the Northern press were gained."

Private Theophilus Noel
Company A, 4th Texas Cavalry

Unaware of the naval calamity at Grand Lake, Major General Richard Taylor focused his efforts on April 14 on tricking the Federals to make sure his army had time to slip away and his fleet to pounce. At McKerrell's plantation, in the subdued predawn light, Taylor ordered his troops to proceed cautiously forward, across the plowed fields. He anticipated that the enemy was in the canebrake trees at the field's far end. Lieutenant Colonel Franklin Clack's skirmishers advanced unopposed, navigating east toward a canebrake with dense trees flanking it north and south. The soldiers plunged into the half-mile wide strip of woods to the South, anticipating an engagement. Instead they found that the trees merely sheathed a lateral lane connecting the McWaters plantation on the north shoulder of Irish Bend with the bayou road to the south. Following this lane north, they also discovered a fence separating the path from the edge of the canebrake, and the swampy mass of Nerson's woods beyond. Heading into the trees, the Rebels found the footbridge over Bayou Yokely dismantled. Runners reported these findings and this terrain while Clack continued his reconnaissance. Taylor urged his men forward. Captain Florian Cornay ordered his guns to stop at the edge of McCarroll's field in a position to shell the southern woods if necessary and cover the advance. Cornay's men endured a tense period of waiting before Clack sent back the news that the enemy was not yet at hand.

Remarkably, Brigadier General Cuvier Grover's Yankee division remained camped in the fields beyond, and its officers had not even bothered to secure Nerson's Woods, the key terrain in Irish Bend. Delighted, Taylor directed Colonel James Reily to lead the Confederates forward to seize the woods and canebrake and

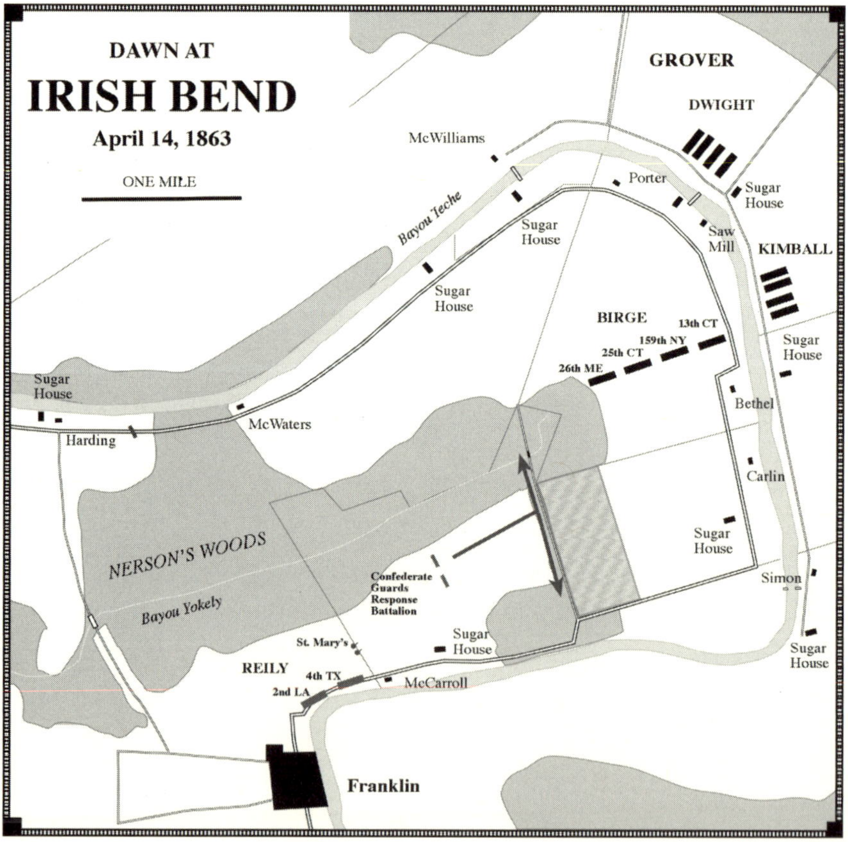

to prepare a defensive position. "The line was ordered forward by Colonel Riley, he riding ahead leading his column steadily on," reported his aide, Captain Andrew Jackson Scarborough. "The artillery was left a mile back." Reily and Colonel William G. Vincent ordered their troops to dismount, picket their horses under cover, and push into the trees and thickets to wait there—concealed—until Clack found the enemy.[1]

The wait would be short. After the one hundred men of the Confederate Guards Response Battalion emerged from the other side of Nerson's Woods, crossed a heavy rail fence, and thrashed their way through a fringe of sugar cane beyond, they arrived at an open area on the edge of Carlin's and Porter's fields and found what they were seeking. Before them lay three Federal brigades and their attending artillery, breaking camp and deploying road columns and skirmish lines as it advanced. Taylor had won this leg of the race—just barely.

Grover's Division had indeed stirred to life, its men having risen early to complete their journey to Franklin. Although Colonel Henry Birge's 3rd Brigade had been the last to arrive the night before, it had been posted the farthest forward. Now they continued the course they had started upon—the one Reily had apparently convinced Grover was the best route to Franklin the day before. Birge and his men were erroneously leading the division away from the more strategic course along the northern edge of Irish Bend. Instead, the Federals were tramping into a Confederate ambush.

Reily, sensing his luck, began giving instructions to his staff. "On ascertaining the position of the enemy, he ordered me to bring up the artillery, and reported to Major General Taylor the strength and position of the enemy," Scarborough continued. The Confederates would make their stand at Irish Bend. The Texans and Louisianans held favorable ground. Their front measured about a half mile, with woods anchoring each flank—north and south—like a "U" with a tree line and standing cane field filling the quarter mile gap between. A stout cypress fence and ditch ran the entire length, providing a ready breastwork. Nerson's Woods, on their left, provided great concealment and jutted out another half mile perpendicular to the line, but the swampy margins of Bayou Yokely deep within would discourage any enemy attacks from that angle. In the center, beyond the margin of the standing cane field, lay a cut cane field—part of the Carlin plantation. A rectangular copse of trees—a quarter mile north to south, a half mile east to west—provided cover for that end of the line, and ended at the levee of Bayou Teche. There were few options for any oncoming Federals but to go straight at the Confederate line.[2]

Colonel Henry Warner Birge of Norwich, Connecticut, served as an officer in the 4th Connecticut Infantry but left that regiment to come to Louisiana in command of the 13th Connecticut Infantry, but orders arrived placing him in charge of the defenses of New Orleans. His performance in that role led him to command of a brigade that he saw savaged at the Battle of Irish Bend.

Cartes de visite, *Lincoln's Army Civil War Virtual Museum.*

The 387 men of Colonel George Bissell's 25th Connecticut on Birge's skirmish line would be the first to make contact. They had little inkling what lay concealed in Nerson's Woods and beyond, but had had risen before daybreak to find out, half the regiment had screened the front and right flank of Birge's brigade while the balance formed a reserve. In the morning darkness they had

Colonel George Bissell received a commission from the governor to lead the 25th Connecticut Infantry during its nine months' service in Louisiana. He performed capably and returned the regiment to Hartford in August 1863 after having seen heavy fighting at Irish Bend and Port Hudson. State officials described the regiment as "One of the best of our nine months regiments . . . it has won for itself a high and lasting reputation."

US Army Military History Institute.

very deliberately advanced down the bayou road, passing the wreck of Bethel's Bridge, as they made their way along the southern shoulder of Irish Bend, toward Franklin. Soon they closed in on Simon's Bridge at the road's great right turn. Sharp-eyed soldiers in the right flank companies dutifully reported seeing Rebels climbing over the fence at the far end of the fields. Officers gave permission to fire upon the enemy. The Federal skirmish line wheeled around, pivoting on its right, and advanced, pushing to within two hundred yards of the wood and canebrake line. At the same time the 25th Connecticut's five reserve companies also changed fronts. They formed a line of battle, advanced a short distance into Carlin's field, and lay on the rain-softened soil to await developments. From this vantage point the reserve companies watched as their skirmishers advanced toward and into the standing cane, chasing Clack's Confederates.

Captain Scarborough heard the sporadic firing from Birge's skirmishers as he led the Confederate cannon into position. "By the time I returned with the artillery the battle had fairly opened all along the line." Reily, his forces now committed made sure to create a warm surprise for the advancing Federals. "The colonel coolly distributed his men, after which he dismounted, sent his horse some 200 paces to the rear, and walked up and down the line cheering his men," Scarborough added.[3]

Colonel Birge fed troops into the fight slowly, assuming the butternut phantoms were merely pickets. He ordered Lieutenant John I. Rodgers to unlimber a section of his Battery C, 2nd U.S., guns behind the 25th Connecticut's reserve companies and near Carlin's sugarhouse, with orders to probe the woods more than twenty-two hundred yards away. The Federals wanted the shake

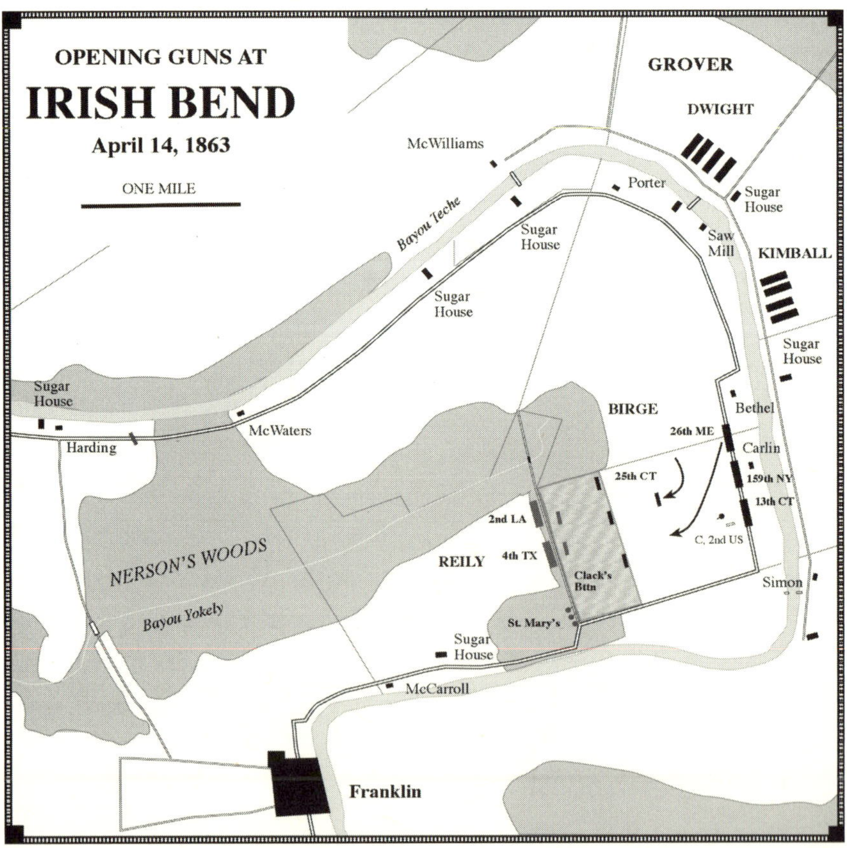

the trees to see what might fall out. "While advancing through the canefields," . . . reported Lieutenant Henry Hill Goodell, the regimental adjutant, "the troops heard the cry, 'Attention battalion! Take Aim. Fire!' and immediately the woods seemed to spring to life while a perfect storm of canister, grape, and Minnie balls were rained down upon our ranks." The Nutmeggers attempted to return fire against their concealed enemies, but could only aim and fire at the flash and smoke. Casualties among the Yankees mounted. "Men began to be carried out pretty rapidly," added Goodell. Next Birge sent in the 26th Maine, who pushed over the fence bordering the eastern edge of Carlin's field then headed across the cane stubble toward the fight. "Across the field they go, just as though they are on dress parade, arms at right shoulder, giving no heed to the buzz and zip of the Rebel bullets," wrote Private Eldon D. Maddocks of that regiment. They fell in with the left side of the companies of the 25th Connecticut.[4]

Behind the sheltering screen of woods and out of Birge's sight, the Confederates in McCarroll's field also sent more men into the fray. First two, then four Rebel guns emerged, beating Rodgers and his Union regulars more than a mile away in the contest for speed of deployment. Private Theophilus Noel of the 4th Texas, just returning to his command after being lost the night before, watched as the limbers and cannon sped by on his right. "Our battery dashed by us at full speed," he wrote. Reily had ordered the move based on what he saw in Carlin's field, and the battery commander had to catch up. Confederate captain Cornay reported, "I had just left my battery to see General Taylor for further orders when, hearing my artillery in motion on the public road, I hurried to assume command and took it in position at . . . the road leading to Simon's Bridge." Within minutes Cornay had all four of his guns on the right of the Confederate line and poured rounds into the left front of the Union infantry and at the cannon beyond. "I opened fire upon the enemy with solid shot at about 1,500 yards with my six-pounder, and soon with spherical case and howitzers with shells at 1,400 yards," he continued. He was soon joined by the lone gun of Lieutenant Minos T. Gordy's section, which had been up all night after leaving Fort Bisland. "The five guns played upon the enemy's lines a terrific connonade, and I think with good effect."[5]

Reily ordered all of the Confederates present to sneak to the edge of the trees, take positions behind the fence bordering the standing cane field, and lay down a base of fire that would sweep the field. Noel took a poetic view, writing "the deadly sound and clash of arms broke the stillness of the morn. It was but a few moments until the engagement became general." Clack's skirmishers, meanwhile, continued their individual gun battles, holding their ground in the southern copse of woods against the Yankee skirmishers. The Confederates were almost invisible to the Federals, and the advance of the 25th Connecticut fell into confusion as the scattered soldiers lost sight of each other in the dense cane and began to fall from Rebel bullets. Private George Schubert, a German immigrant, wrote "I must say that we wonder ourselves how so many of us got out of it without being shot." The baffled skirmishers followed their instincts and dropped to the ground, but they were within dangerously close range of the concealed Southerners in the cane at the edge of Carlin's field to their front and as well as those along the margins of Nerson's Woods to their right and the copse of trees to their left.[6]

Having pinned the enemy skirmishers, the Confederates' next task was to tackle the 26th Maine advancing in good order across the open field. Birge had ordered the Mainers and the Connecticut reserves to move forward and sweep across Carlin's field in line of battle in an attempt to drive off what he believed was simply a strong enemy skirmish line. Now they also had to rescue the advanced companies of the 25th Connecticut. Anticipating close work in the dense cover, Lieutenant Colonel Philo Hersey ordered his troops in the 26th Maine to halt, fix bayonets, then rush forward toward the cane field at the double-quick, amid a crescendo of bullets and canister rounds. "The 26th sprang forward with the determination to drive the Rebels from their stronghold," Maddocks continued. "The Rebel fire was so strong that the advance was checked, and the order came to lie down." The time was just past 6:00 AM, and now the better part of two Union regiments lay prostrate and pinned by Confederate rifles.[7]

Too late Birge realized he had stumbled onto more than a thin line of pickets. "It became evident that the enemy were in strong force," he reported. He sent a courier to Grover's headquarters for instructions and ordered Lieutenant Rodgers to put into action as many of his guns as possible. Four rifled pieces joined his two other guns near Carlin's sugarhouse, at the bend in the bayou road. As the gunners awaited clarification of the battle before them, they lobbed an occasional shell toward Cornay's guns. As word arrived that the 25th Connecticut and 26th Maine might be in trouble, a section of that guns, led by Lieutenant Theodore Bradley, limbered up and advanced across the furrowed fields in support of the skirmish line. They deployed in line to the left rear of the 26th Maine, about five hundred yards from the enemy. "In complying with this order the section was under fire of the enemy's guns," Rodgers reported, "but fortunately their shell burst over."[8]

With this extra muscle on hand, Birge once again ordered Hersey's 26th Maine to pick themselves up and to push against the enemy line. "Again came the order," Maddocks remembered. "Every man leaped to his feet, with that yell known the world over as the Indian war-whoop." The Southerners answered the gesture with a ragged volley from their hidden firing line, prompting the New Englanders to fall back to earth. The Confederates had pinned down the 26th Maine. "In this place the regiment remained, loading and firing for an hour or more," Maddocks continued, "until every cartridge was gone and they could do no more."[9]

For the next sixty minutes the battle continued as a close-range firefight, with both sides firing blindly. The muskets and rifles of the 4th Texas and their Louisiana allies methodically killed eleven and wounded nearly fifty New Englanders. Lieutenant Colonel Hersey received a bullet in his shoulder. The men of Maine shot thousands of rounds into the canebrake, splintering the rails of the fence beyond and sending miniè balls zipping through the trees hiding their enemies but with little effect.

Corporal James W. Gates, Company A, 25th Connecticut, enlisted for nine months and fought his way across Louisiana in the Teche Campaign before returning to his home town of Hartford in August 1863, his service complete.

US Army Military History Institute.

The 25th Connecticut did their best as well. The men in the reserve battalion loaded and fired as best they could while laying prone while the men of the regiment's five companies on skirmish detail hugged the earth and kept their heads down, low crawling toward any available cover. The intensity of the firefight was bewildering; for most of these soldiers serving out nine-month enlistments, this was their first battle. Casualties began to mount. One soldier observed that a lieutenant in the regiment had taken a bullet though the blouse and hat but remained unharmed. When a nearby comrade was wounded, the lucky officer carried the man on his back as he searched for medical aid. The eager lieutenant did not get far before he laid "him down again because another bullet has struck the poor fellow, inflicting a second and mortal wound."[10]

The rest of Grover's Division soon learned of the scuffle at the head of the column. Corporal James K. Hosmer of the 52nd Massachusetts was in Colonel William K. Kimball's 2nd Brigade, at the far end of the division, and he had been enjoying the Louisiana morning in comparative safety as his regiment ambled down the bayou road toward the sound of the guns. "As we sweep along the road toward the firing, the day each minute becomes more and more beautiful," he wrote. "We come, at last, into full view of the scene. We halt in the road; and leaning against a fence . . . the whole combat is visible to us." He noted the placement of batteries, the "bodies of infantry, in long dark lines, moving upon an open field in front of a wood." He also observed that "in the lines are gaps, which may be caused by moving over rough ground, or by the plunge of shot and shell."[11]

Hosmer and other observers watched as Federal casualties began to trickle out of the canebrake. Anticipating some injuries, Grover's medical officers had designated Carlin's sugarhouse as the field hospital, but the cart path leading to it quickly became filled with the stricken. "Ambulance men, with stretchers, are hurrying across the field to a sugarhouse in the rear," Hosmer wrote. "On each stretcher is a wounded man, and the number of these makes it certain to us that the engagement has reached the sad dignity of a pitched battle." The corporal noted that along the dirt lane that crossed Carlin's field came "a stream of wounded men on stretchers, or supported by comrades. I am close by, and can hear the talk of a sergeant, bloody but able to walk, who is glad he has had a chance to do some service." One regimental surgeon moved out of the rapidly filling building to work outside, beneath the shade of a tree. "Close where he stands, on his back, stiff and stark, dead, a tall broad-chested man, with closed eyes. I look, too, upon the ghastly head of a young lieutenant, who is dying," wrote Sergeant Major Henry M. Whitney, 52nd Massachusetts. "They make a pile of leg and arms, feet and hands," he wrote. "You would better not look at such things if you are about to expose yourself to the probability of contributing to the ghastly pile."[12]

Twenty-two year old **Private Nathan T. Warren** left his farm in Northampton and joined Company C, 52nd Massachusetts on October 2, 1862, to serve for nine months. He died of disease a little shy of nine months later in Baton Rouge, Louisiana.

US Army Military History Institute.

The Confederates, too, began to suffer. Rodgers's rifles had been keeping up a steady, long-range drumbeat for the first hour of the fight, and the Confederates were unable to respond with their short-range 6-pounders and 12-pounder howitzers. Eventually bolder skirmishers from the 25th Connecticut crept to within small-arms range on Cornay's left and began picking off his crewmen. "After awhile the enemy's skirmishers came up under cover of a ditch to within 150 yards from my position," Cornay reported. "They poured a heavy fire on my men." Fretting over this turn of events and noticing that Clack's men, to his left, could cover a withdrawal if necessary, Cornay wheeled his horse around for permission from General Taylor to remove his troops. "At this moment my horse was shot from under me," he continued. "Procuring another I rode toward the center where I met Colonel Reily and asked his advice.

An unidentified member of **Company F, 52nd Massachusetts,** veteran of fierce fighting at Irish Bend.

Courtesy of Denis Gaubert, Thibodaux, Louisiana.

He me told to try and occupy a new position and communicate the fact to General Taylor. I rode back to my command and ordered it to the rear." Cornay took his men out of the fight and repositioned them on the edge of McCarroll's field. He had lost eleven men killed and wounded as well as thirteen horses. He left behind the battery's wreckage—two caissons and a limber—in the southern patch of woods.[13]

For the Federals the removal of Cornay's five guns was a hopeful development. General Grover trotted forward to Birge's Brigade to assess the situation. He saw two regiments pinned by what appeared to be an equal number of enemy troops, and he had managed to drive away the Rebel guns. Perhaps, Grover thought, the enemy just needed to be pushed harder. Here was a chance to brush aside what he thought was little more than a remnant of the force from the day before and seize the road junction at Franklin, trapping Taylor. He directed Birge to deploy the rest of his brigade and to carry Nerson's Woods by assault. Birge saluted and then sent riders to his last two regiments, the 159th New York and the 13th Connecticut, to order them to turn from column formation into a line of battle and take their places in Carlin's field.

With the decision settled, Grover next rode over to Lieutenant Rodgers and helped him deploy his cannon to greatest effect. The general personally placed two of Battery C's remaining guns on either side of the bayou road, firing along the route of that byway and into the woods beyond. These two guns, he predicted, would cover the advance of the 13th Connecticut. He would not let a thin line of Rebels deny him his glory.

But Grover could not see that the Confederate confidence was waxing, not waning. At this critical point Taylor received happy news. Colonel Henry Gray's 28th Louisiana was coming across McCarroll's field, heading toward a position on the Rebel left, arriving after a brisk nighttime march from Fort Bisland. Unknown to the Federals, Taylor had been reinforced. Once in position on the swampy margins of Bayou Yokely, Gray was to lead his column through the dense woods and along the northern periphery

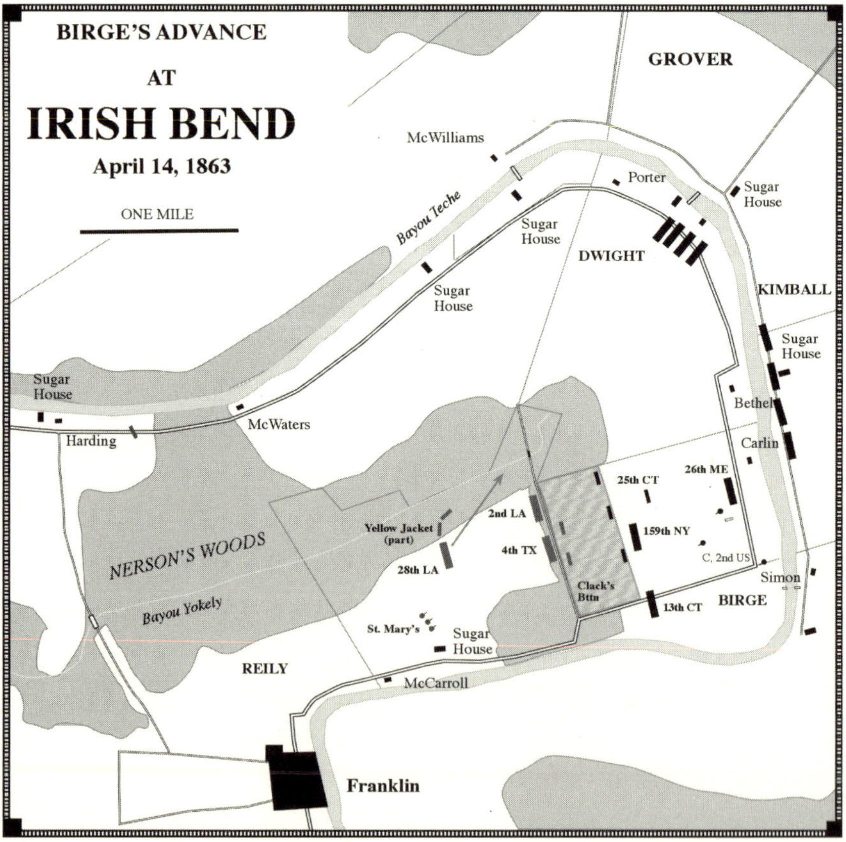

of Carlin's field. From his forested vantage point, he could enfilade the right of the Union line and wreak havoc with their advance. The Confederates moved energetically to set their trap and had just taken position—unseen—when the next wave of Yankees came into view.

Grover and Birge, convinced that this was but a minor holding action by two battered Rebel cavalry regiments, were impatient for this fight to be concluded, and they anticipated that the last regiments of the 3rd Brigade would finish the job. Colonel Edward L. Molineux led his New Yorkers into their inaugural battle and angled toward the left of the still-prone 26th Maine; the 13th Connecticut moved even further left to fill the space between Carlin's field and the Teche, a front of about 150 yards. Another courier carried dispatches directing Hersey's regiment out of the fight. The Maine men rose up and started for the rear as the 159th marched

Battle of Irish Bend. This image from *Frank Leslie's Illustrated Newspaper* gives an accurate depiction of the battlefield—woods on right and left forming a *U* with a cane field in the middle backed by trees. The Federals clearly blundered into an ambush.

Frank Leslie's Illustrated Newspaper, *author's collection.*

through them. The Mainers had lost more than a quarter of their three hundred men, and they were happy for the New Yorkers to take their turn.

Colonel Edward Leslie Molineux, born in England, lived most of his life in Brooklyn and was not yet thirty years old when he took command of the 159th New York and led them to Louisiana to take part in the Teche Campaign. He and his regiment would contribute much blood in capturing the Mississippi.

Courtesy of William A. Molineux, Williamsburg, Virginia.

Colonel Molineux and his men faced a difficult task. "We advanced in good style over a plowed cane field in line, passing over the 26th Maine, who were lying down," wrote Lieutenant Edward Duffy of the 159th New York. Then they began taking hits. Lieutenant Colonel Gilbert Draper, astride a magnificent horse, made a tempting target. He and his mount fell dead, hit multiple times. The regiment steadily moved closer to the enemy, eventually catching up with the skirmishers of the 25th Connecticut hunkered down after creeping to the cover of the cane at the far edge of the field. "Several of our men fell in the advance. Reached within pistol shot of the fence and wood where the enemy was concealed. Scarcely one could be seen while they poured a most effective fire on us, but we steadily advance 'till ordered to lay down," reported Duffy. The regiment now foundered like its predecessors, but they were within much closer range of the enemy.[14]

The 159th New York had entered a meat grinder: the Confederates enjoyed an almost perfect defensive position from which they could fire a steady and close-range fusillade. For the New Yorkers the trial became desperate. Lying on their chests and bellies in the dense cane, unable to see where the bullets were coming from, was bad enough. Additionally, however, the men were exhausted. None of Grover's Division had eaten breakfast. Molineaux's men had moved at high speed across the killing zone of the open field in full marching order, knapsacks and greatcoats included. "It took a little time to catch fresh wind and unburden ourselves of our heavy load," Duffy continued. This line of discarded baggage marked their farthest advance. "We could not have stopped at a more uncomfortable place, for the enemy gave it to us hot and sweet, while we did not have a chance to see them."[15]

After being buffeted for several minutes, the 159th faced a genuine crisis. Colonel Molineux knew he could not ask his men to simply lie there and take it, and he searched for an opportunity to strike back. When he supposed that the Rebel fire was slackening, he took it as a sign that his own regiment had bloodied the enemy. Seizing his chance, the colonel rose up, ready to lead his men forward in a final rush to take the fence. "Molineux, perceiving his opportunity, as it seemed, was in the act of uttering the command 'Forward' when a bullet struck him in the mouth and he fell, painfully wounded," wrote a Union staff officer. The charge was nearly stillborn; the regiment's second-in-command as well as its adjutant were both dead, and its colonel was thrashing in pain on the ground. The control of the 159th New York passed to a captain, who bravely picked up Molineaux's cause. "At the word the men sprang to their feet, but before the command could be carried out, suddenly came the crises of the battle."[16]

What the New York colonel had sensed was not a slackening but a gathering. At about 7:30 AM Colonel Gray and his 28th Louisiana played their hand brilliantly. Raising a yell, the Confederates fell on the right and rear of the trapped skirmishers of the 25th Connecticut. "Suddenly, there was a terrific yell and 1100 men rushed in on our flank and began peppering us well," wrote Lieutenant Goodell. "I have heard men speak of a hail storm of bullets but I never imagined in before . . . the way the balls whistled and zipped among the cane stalks and ploughed up the ground around us was truly astonishing." All around the young officer, soldiers writhed from fresh wounds. "[Private Jonas] Holden fell by my side pierced by three balls," he wrote, adding a "sergeant lost his leg, my first corporal had a ball pass through both jaws, cutting off his tongue. There is scarcely a man in the regiment but what has a bullet hole in come part of his clothing, and some have two or three." One Connecticut Yankee rolled on his back, clutching his chest after a hard blow, feeling

Colonel Molineux wounded. The commander of the 159th New York fell with a painful wound to the mouth and jaw. He recovered in New Orleans and returned to command the regiment two months later.

Courtesy of William A. Molineux, Williamsburg, Virginia.

for a wound. Instead he found his metal tobacco box mangled inside his shirt pocket, but his life intact. Nearby, a German immigrant clutched the earth and pleaded with the almighty. "We had to stay in a pretty bad crossfire," Private Schubert wrote to his wife, Sophia. "The bullets flew around us just like raindrops. I though of you and prayed to god that he might spare me for your sake."[17]

Gray's charge rolled up the 159th New York as well. "They came out of the wood through the cane to the rear of our right flank, and right on top of us," Duffy gasped. The New Yorkers broke and ran. If they had waited for an order, Duffy concluded, "we no doubt would have layed there 'till every man of us was shot." Gray's Rebels moved in and among the Yankees on the right of the regiment, in some cases killing men at point-blank range, manhandling others as they rose from the dirt, pushing them to the rear as prisoners.[18]

The Confederates closed in for the kill. Reily ordered the 4th Texas Cavalry to advance, starting with the right and rippling to the left. Clack's men remained in the copse of woods near the road, reforming on the Confederate right. The destruction of Birge's brigade seemed assured.

Grover could not believe what he saw unfolding before him. The 26th Maine was withdrawing in some confusion, and now the 159th New York and many of the 25th Connecticut were routing out of the standing cane. Drivers and gunners from Lieutenant Bradley's section of Battery C, 2nd U.S., moved fast to limber their guns and save them from the enemy advance. Right behind them was a line of Rebels who seemed to be sweeping the field clear of Federals. Birge's 3rd Brigade was obviously whipped. As the commanding colonel tried to stop the flow of men, a Rebel bullet killed his horse—a gift from the governor of Connecticut—tossing Birge to the ground. He had lost control of the fight. Grover sent a young officer with orders for Brigadier General William Dwight to bring up the 1st Brigade and rescue the situation.[19]

Despite appearances, not all of Birge's 3rd Brigade had been whipped. Lieutenant Colonel Alexander Warner continued leading forward the five hundred veterans of the 13th Connecticut, oblivious to the disaster befalling the other three regiments from the 3rd Brigade because of an intervening screen of woods. As his troops listened to the commotion erupting a few hundred yards to their right, they assumed they heard the sounds of victory and quickened their pace. The New Englanders made their way through the southern patch of trees in advance, along the bayou road. Beyond the trees to their right front lay the small three-hundred-yard cane field in front of the presumed Rebel position, but the looming forest directly ahead was strangely quiet. Warner called forward a

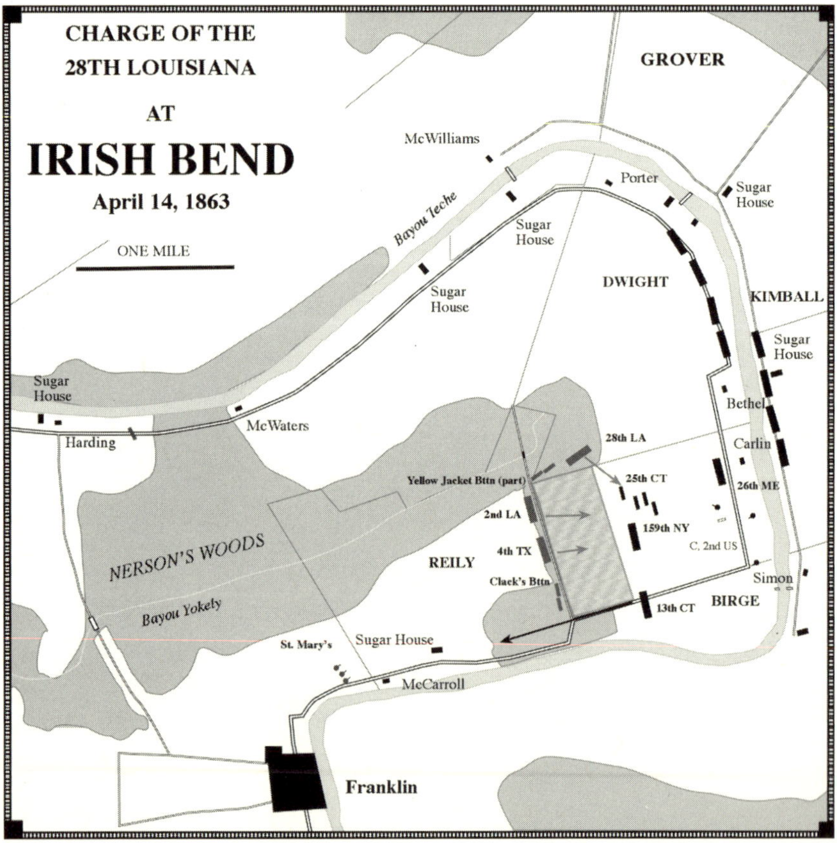

detachment. "In this thin strip of woodland the regiment halted and Company A commenced employing as skirmishers to feel the enemy in front," Captain Homer B. Sprague of Company H confided in his diary. "This deployment was very slowly executed."[20]

The men advanced in their intervals through the trees, but Warner was growing impatient, and he ordered the rest of the regiment to follow soon afterward. "With a brisk and steady step the Thirteenth moved up in solid line close on the heels of our skirmishers," remembered Captain Sprague. They passed around the Confederate right, through the position vacated by the Confederate artillery, and into McCarrol's field beyond. "The instant we began to emerge from the belt of trees and entered the freshly plowed field that now intervened between us and the enemy, a rapid fire greeted us." Clack's men began peppering the Yankees from front and right flank, while the Connecticut skirmishers responded in kind. "The Thirteenth, though startled, did not retreat, but continued advancing with as much precision as if at a review," Sprague wrote.[21]

The ensuring combat was brief. Warner ordered his veteran soldiers to perform a trademark maneuver in which the battle line advanced while firing. "We had used it at Labadieville," remembered Sprague. "It seemed the spontaneous action of the regiment, and it wonderfully supports the courage of the men." Hours of drill had trained these Nutmeggers how to coordinate and how to maneuver with awkward muzzleloaders, and now their training yielded great results. "From the gleaming rifles of our advancing line, there poured a steady stream of lead, every man loading and firing three times a minute, and the twenty or thirty shots a second making with the answering fire of the rebel line a prolonged and tremendous roar," Sprague continued. "It had no cessation."[22]

Clack's hundred men would exact payment from the bold Yankees. As the 13th Connecticut moved ahead, Confederates in front and to their right began to kill them. "Fifty of our number fell in the first two or three minutes," Sprague observed. Then he too was hit while waving his sword overhead, urging his men on. "The ball struck the end of my sword hilt and split on the sharp edge of the guard into many pieces, some of which tore through the side of my right wrist and hand," he wrote. "One small piece was buried in my face near my left eye, three or four fine pieces in my little finger and four or five in my right arm half way between the wrist and elbow." It took a moment for the shock to sink in. "The blood pattering in [my] face, and a numbness in the disabled hand, first apprised [me] that I was wounded," he wrote. "The wound bled profusely . . . I bound a handkerchief round it and continued with the company through the fight."[23]

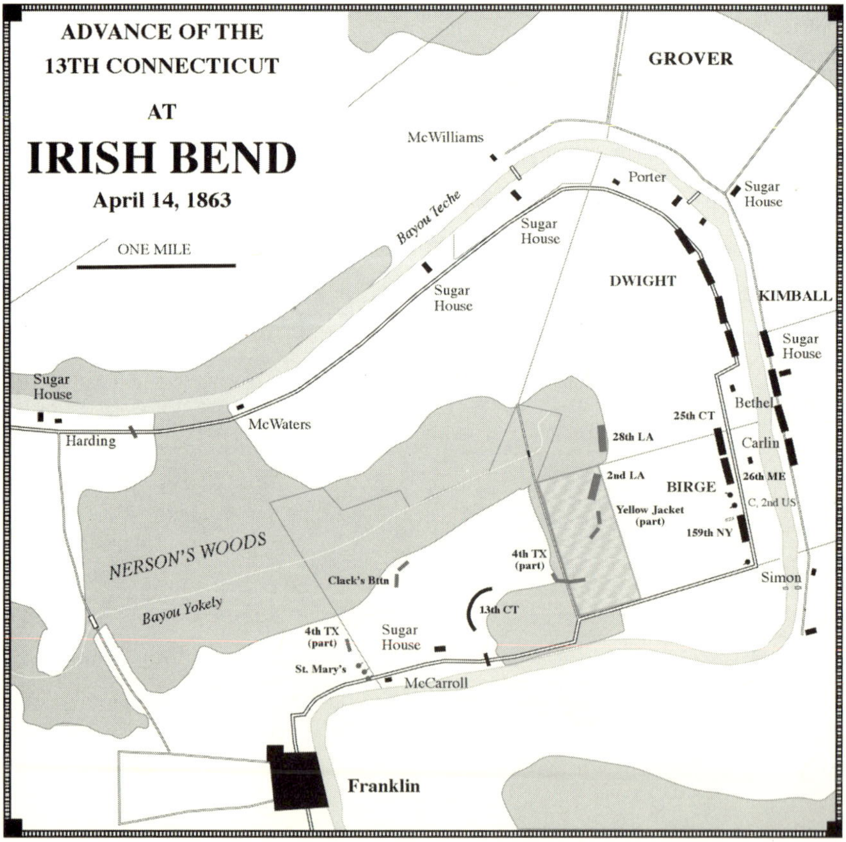

The 13th Connecticut continued forward forcing the Rebels in front to flee to the rear and halfway across McCarroll's field. The exuberant Federals lurched forward to claim their prize. "It is impossible to describe the enthusiasm of the men at this moment," Sprague remembered. "Our men were firing irregularly, whenever they caught sight of a retreating rebel." The Northerners surged over the leavings of the St. Mary's Cannoneers and found to their delight that the Rebels had left behind their battery flag. It had been a gift from the women of Franklin, whose homes lay just a mile away.[24]

Warner began barking commands to regain control of his regiment. "Battalion, halt! Cease firing!" he bellowed. Three companies on the right, though, continued to load and shoot. The colonel, enraged, rode to that end and berated the men. "What does this mean, I ordered you to cease firing!" he demanded. "Colonel, do you see those men in gray?" came the response from one of the company commanders. The 13th Connecticut had inadvertently come upon the right flank of the 4th Texas Cavalry just as they were moving forward from their positions in support of the attack of the 28th Louisiana. Victory against the 159th New York had confused the Rebel line almost as much as victory over Clack's Battalion had scrambled that of the Federals.[25]

Reily, unaware that the Federals were gaining ground on his right and rear, ordered his men along the tree line to rise up and push forward to complete the destruction of the enemy regiments to their front. As Reily moved along the line, yelling words of encouragement, a Yankee bullet found its mark but from an odd angle. "The fatal ball struck him in his left side striking the spine," remembered Scarborough. "I was near him when he fell helpless." The staff officer ran to the colonel's side and dragged him into a safer and more comfortable position. "In about 5 minutes he recovered sufficient to speak. He was cool and collected," wrote Scarborough. Reily directed Major George James Hampton to take command of the 4th Texas Cavalry. When Scarborough attempted to carry him from the field, Reily protested. "Captain, I am mortally wounded, and must die soon," he said. "The enemies numbers are greatly superior to ours; I don't wish one man to be taken from the field to carry me off. Let me die on the battlefield."[26]

The unexpected appearance of the 13th Connecticut behind them tripped up the Rebel assault. Half of the 4th Texas—already advancing on the orders of Reily—found itself completely surprised. The veterans of Val Verde, Glorieta, and Galveston gave way. "The Yankees succeeded in gaining a position from where they could fire on our right flank," wrote Captain Julius Giesecke of Company G. "That moment was terrible and we were whipped and badly scattered." The regiment, now leaderless, unraveled. Authority fell to Major Hampton, "who was so busy trying to light his pipe while his horse was prancing round at a furious rate that he did not recognize that he was in command," recalled Private Noel of Company A. "I always shall believe that he was as badly scared as I was." About half of the regiment routed into and beyond McCarroll's field and remounted their horses to make their escape while dozens of steedless Texans in the trees, including Giesecke, surrendered. With Clack's men falling back and nearly half of the 4th Texas in retreat, Cornay and his five guns were now vulnerable. He ordered his men to limber the guns, and he rode to the rear to find Taylor and seek instructions.[27]

From the perspective of the 13th Connecticut's Lieutenant Colonel Warner, it appeared as though *his* unit was the one in greatest danger. He knew a battery of guns was just ahead. In addition, the five fugitive companies of the 4th Texas had now mounted and, realizing that the danger had passed, wheeled and reformed in the open acres of McCarroll's field. The Texans who remained in cane field had now turned to face the Union threat. "At this moment the bullets commenced coming thicker from that quarter, and some even came from a direction obliquely in rear of the right of our regiment," Sprague observed. "This sprinkling of shot was fast increasing to a shower, and again the rallying rebels began to annoy us in front." Clack's men had recovered and were renewing their fire at the Federals as well. "The alarming truth flashed upon Warner's mind that the Confederates had turned our right, as we had turned theirs, and had actually got in our rear!"[28]

The 13th Connecticut had been lucky, but it was now in a bind. "What shall I do?" Warner asked his officers. He looked to the rear, hoping to see a courier from Birge, and fretted, "they have given me no orders. Why don't they send me orders?" Nearly half an hour had passed since he had gained his position, and the confusion in the rest of the brigade now left the 13th Connecticut an orphan, to make the best fight it could on its own. Warner, "who manifested the greatest anxiety and perplexity," according to Sprague, feared a mounted counterattack on his left down the road simultaneous to a Rebel move from his right. He strengthened both flanks, sending his skirmishers toward the bayou while three other companies formed at right angles to counter any moves from the cane field to the north.[29]

Both sides had flanked each other. Despite the Yankee thorn in their side, however, thus far the Confederate assault had carried the day. Colonel Vincent's 2nd Louisiana Cavalry, the two companies of Lieutenant Colonel Valsin Fournet's 10th Yellow Jacket Battalion, and Gray's 28th Louisiana had poured over the fence and from the edge of Nerson's Wood, driving back the Federals in great confusion. The ragged Rebel line advanced through the canebrake and emerged in the fields beyond, a great reversed *Z* with Gray's infantry forming the top and the rest of the Louisianans forming the shank. The remaining Texans, forming the bottom, had drifted away to the right rear, eager for a shot at their surprise Union visitors.

Having played its best move, the Confederate attack now tottered to a stall, with its immediate task accomplished, its ranks tangled, and the enemy unexpectedly on its own flank. Leaderless, the question of command and control had not been settled. Colonel Reily had died back in the woods, so tactical direction passed to Colonel Vincent, but he had been hit in the neck. None present knew who was next in line. Until the chain of command could be reestablished, the Confederates milled around, watching as the majority of Birge's 3rd Brigade moved out of effective range. They could also see Dwight's 1st Brigade moving forward.[30]

The Federal commanders appeared shocked and disgusted by this setback. "As I moved forward the scene in the open field before me was embarrassing," Dwight recounted. He and Grover consulted quickly, and the 1st Brigade received their instructions, Dwight wrote, "giving the necessary directions to stretch them well to the right so as to outflank the rebel force which, by its flank fire, was so distressing the brigade in front of me." Meanwhile Colonel Kimball's 2nd Brigade would move down the road, make a right-hand turn, and deploy into line as well. This time Grover would attack the Confederates simultaneously, using twice the number of troops that he had previously ordered.[31]

Dwight's men had observed the growing battle and immediately grasped the situation. "Birge was a good soldier and had a good brigade, but as he pushed forward, the error of the plan of attack exposed itself," observed an observer in the 6th "Wilson's Zouaves" New York, on Dwight's extreme right. "Birge's left was too far south and his right entirely in air was enfiladed from the woods that flanked it. The further he advanced the worse became his position, and finally his unprotected right being ground up, his brigade gave way . . . leaving the grounds well dotted with quiet or writhing men in blue. This did not auger well for success, but General Grover was a fighting man first, last, and all the time."[32]

Now Birge's 3rd Brigade had clearly run out of fighting power. Grover, keenly aware that he had blundered into an ambush, ordered the stricken 3rd Brigade to fall back and reform. Birge, astride a fresh mount, rallied his three mangled regiments in the rear of Carlin's field. As they sorted themselves out, Birge sought news of his fourth regiment, eventually gathering that Warner remained well in advance. Birge and his aides galloped to the rescue of the imperiled 13th Connecticut, his former regiment.

From their advanced position, Warner's New Englanders weighed their options. One captain offered the commander his advice. "Colonel," he said, "if you ask me, I say wheel round to the right and charge bayonets on their flank; or charge strait ahead, and then swing around and take them in rear." Another captain requested a charge on Cornay's battery, now out of action in the dead zone between the armies. While brave and well-intentioned,

this bold advice would have been risky at best. Grover had already blundered by assuming the Confederates to be a mere rear guard. Warner and his men had no way of knowing what else might lie beyond McCarroll's plantation, and they did not know what might be lurking on their immediate right. For all they knew, Taylor might have hoodwinked Major General Nathaniel P. Banks and assembled his entire army to destroy Grover's Division.[33]

Welcome relief arrived, galloping down the bayou road out of the southern woods, ending the debate among Warner and his commanders. "Colonel Birge rode up and communicated orders to fall back to the grove or till we met the supports which General Grover had ordered up," wrote Sprague. "We retired slowly and sullenly across the ploughed field, many of the soldiers refusing to turn from the enemy and marching in the backward step, as dreading a wound in the back." Sprague was among those walking backwards, describing himself "much disgusted at retiring when I thought we ought to be advancing, as I then and there took occasion to say in pretty decided terms."[34]

Warner and Birge knew they remained in danger, even after crossing the open ground to the shelter of the grove. The Confederates swarmed behind them, sending occasional shots after the retreating Yankees. Warner also thought he saw Rebel cavalry on the move and heard orders being given indicating a mounted charge. It was a *ruse de guerre.*

"I screamed so loud that my voice was heard by every Yankee and every Confederate on the other side," Noel boasted. "'Clear the road for the cavalry!' which was re-shouted in an instant by . . . the men near, as only well-scared men can shout." The Confederate private believed the enemy held a special dread of Texans. "The Yankees . . . had been told that they were going to face the terrible New Mexico–Texan Sibley brigade of ferocious Rough Riders," Noel boasted.[35]

Warner, spooked, ordered his regiment to turn at the edge of the woods and face the enemy. "We halted, fixed bayonets and awaited their onset," wrote Sprague, "but they did not come." After the imagined danger had passed, Warner directed his exhausted men to lie down and for the 13th Connecticut's trophies—sixty prisoners and the silk Confederate first pattern national flag of the St. Mary's Cannoneers—to be taken to the rear. The New Englanders unfixed their bayonets and swapped long-range and largely ineffective shots with the Confederates in McCarroll's field and Nerson's Woods, happy for the lull in the fighting. To their front they watched as Cornay moved his guns to safety and redeployed them into battery, ready to shell their position. Birge ordered his men to fall back and rejoin the rest of the brigade. Their battle was over.[36]

Taylor had now spent two anxious hours fighting the Yankees, and his watch read 8:00 AM when new arrivals buoyed his spirits. Brigadier General Alfred Mouton arrived to report that Fort Bisland had been evacuated without loss, Colonel Tom Green had established a rear-guard ambush near Centerville, and the CSS *Diana* would arrive within minutes. In addition, the 18th and 24th Louisiana Infantries and the 7th Texas Cavalry were also close at hand. Taylor ordered Mouton to take command of the battle and to form a second line on the edge of Nerson's Woods at the west end of McCarroll's field and on the outskirts of Franklin—the last stand before Grover would be in position to capture the road to New Iberia. In this new position, the Confederates would have clear fields of fire and could slaughter the battered Federals as they came across the plowed ground. Taylor had achieved a brilliant tactical and strategic success. By using the advantage of interior lines, he had successfully withdrawn from a superior force at Bisland. Now Taylor concentrated the bulk of his army against Grover's men. The puffing arrival of the *Diana* added to the sense of security.[37]

At the eastern edge of Carlin's field nearly two miles away from Mouton's line, Grover had no idea what might come next, but he prepared as best he could. Dwight's 1st Brigade dressed its two battle lines. The 6th New York held the right end of the first line, and the Albany men of the 91st New York held the left end. Behind them the 22nd Maine held the left, the 131st New York held the middle, and the 1st Louisiana held the right end of the second line. Lieutenant Bradley's section took up a new position on left of the second line, joined by another section from Battery C, 2nd U.S., and together the four guns renewed their pounding of the Rebel positions. The cannon . . . "cracked away rapidly," observed Gouverneur Morris of the 6th New York. "The smoke-grimed gunners worked at their pieces until they fairly jumped with the recoil." Birge's rallied regiments filed to their left and formed up to the right of the 13th Connecticut, and the brigade was whole again, extending to the left of Dwight's line. Kimball's 2nd Brigade struggled in behind Birge, accompanied by Captain Ormand French Nims and his 2nd Massachusetts Light Artillery. A soldier in the bloodied 26th Maine quipped that Kimball's men were "so tangled in a tall thick and thorny blackberry hedge . . . [lost] more blood in that way than in fighting with men." Grover saved Captain Henry W. Clossen's regulars of Battery L, 1st U.S. Artillery, as a mobile reserve.[38]

Mouton knew that the fight in Nerson's Woods and along the cypress fence was over, and he had already ordered the Confederates there to fall back in stages while he covered them. The dismounted men of the 4th Texas and 2nd Louisiana moved out first. "The secret was out—a retreat was ordered," Private Noel wrote. A Texas officer yelled to his men, "Get your horses as quick as hell will let you!" The troops fell back through the woods and across McCarroll's field while the Louisiana Infantry in Nerson's Woods guarded them from attack. "Going at the double quick for better than a mile, we reached our horses just in time to return to the front." Mouton motioned Cornay's guns into new position near the McCarroll sugarhouse. The *Diana* moved forward on the bayou to keep Birge's and Kimball's men off balance.[39]

The 28th Louisiana, the two companies of the Yellow Jackets, and Clack's Confederate Guards Response Battalion had already been bruised and pummeled, but they held the trees as long as possible. One stalwart was Captain Robert Bradford of Jackson Parish, Louisiana, a commander of Company F, 28th Louisiana. He was the young man who had asked Taylor for his binoculars while under fire at Fort Bisland and had coolly climbed a tree in front of the earthworks to show his courage. He also led by example at Irish Bend. According to a Louisiana cavalryman, Bradford had been hit three times already, "one ball entering behind his right ear, passing around and lodging behind his head; one ball passing through his right side; and one through his left hip. For an hour after, this gallant officer was still leading his men." Bradford and his comrades would have to hold Grover long enough for the mounted regiments to join Mouton and establish a second line.[40]

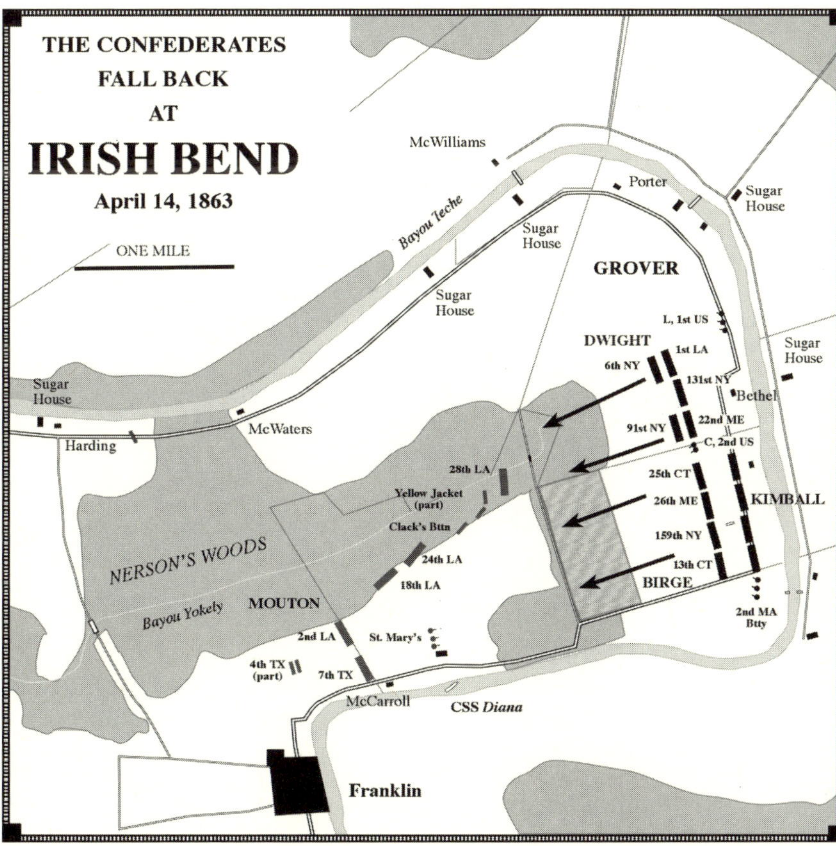

Grover ordered his division to advance on this new two-brigade front at 8:30 AM. The 91st and 6th New York Regiments moved forward but soon took fire from Confederates hidden in the trees at the head of Bayou Yokely. The 6th New York refused its flank then headed at an oblique angle toward the position—held by the Confederates of the 28th Louisiana—opening a gap in the line. General Dwight sent a staff officer to dress the New Yorkers to the left and to close the interval. "But the Sixth didn't seem to be inclined that way," reported Morris. "There was a heavy fire in front, and the regiment returned it savagely, and charged the timber in good order and with great vigor." The Confederates gave ground. "When the Sixth . . . broke fiercely into the woods, which were well marked with shot and strewn with bodies," Morris continued, "the whole Confederate line gave way and scuttled off as fast as it could." Rebel colonel Gray lost a few dozen men as prisoners in his escape. Dwight's entire brigade lost two killed and thirteen wounded in the advance.[41]

The fight on the right. A painting by James E. Taylor showing the Battle of Irish Bend from the right of the Federal line. The Confederate troops opposing them would have been the 28th Louisiana, and the trees behind Nerson's Wood.

James E. Taylor, artist, in Rossiter Johnson, Campfires and Battlefields: An Illustrated History of the Campaigns and Conflicts of the Great Civil War *(New York: Bryan, Taylor and Company, 1894).*

For the Federals, it seemed as if the once-solid Rebel resolve had suddenly turned to jelly. In just about half an hour the Confederates had been driven back from their positions. Grover and his officers were jumpy, however, and they cautioned the Union soldiers as they continued the advance. Colonel Birge moved across the ground he had lost earlier, but this time he ordered Rodgers's guns forward to shred the woods with canister from new positions just sixty yards away. "After a number of discharges the infantry entered the wood," wrote Rodgers. "There was no more artillery firing during the day." Birge felt relieved. "Little or no resistance was offered by the enemy," he sighed. Captain Sprague noted that "this time the rebels retreated along their whole front, and we penetrated into the woods."[42]

The 3rd Brigade moved to the far edge of the southern woods, and Birge scanned the line of trees beyond McCarroll's plantation for the enemy. "On reaching the opposite ground beyond he was discovered in line with artillery, supported by infantry and cavalry, on rising ground about 1,000 yards distance," Birge reported. Grover would not send his troops across this potential killing ground. He ordered Birge to withdraw to the middle of the woods, reform his brigade, and wait.[43]

Grover also ordered Dwight to halt in Nerson's Woods and to look to his right, as there might be another Rebel surprise from that angle. "The character of the wood and of the ground on our right flank made it difficult, if not impossible, to tell what the enemy was doing in that direction," Dwight reported. "The constant reports from my front in a great deal confirmed . . . that the enemy were massing their troops on our front and right for the purpose of making an attack." Birge added to the skittishness by reporting enemy troops in the trees bordering Bayou Yokely on the northern periphery of McCarroll's field. What the Federals actually saw was probably the Louisiana infantry falling back, and the mounted regiments forming up to cover the retreat.[44]

As if to emphasize the futility of continuing on this line, the Federals listened as incoming rounds from big-bore cannon ripped the air and crashed through limbs and branches. "The rebel gunboat *Diana* on the bayou on our left kept pitching shot and shell into the woods where we were, knocking the dirt upon us, breaking the trees over our heads, and dropping pieces of shell in our midst," Sprague remembered. The 13th Connecticut sent two dozen skirmishers to try to pick off the Rebel gunners while the rest of the regiment hunkered down under what cover they could find. Behind them the men of Battery C, 2nd U.S. Artillery, had hoped they were through for the day. They were not. "I was . . . annoyed by the fire of the gunboat, several of her shells (30-pounders) falling among the teams," he wrote, "but fortunately not exploding." The harassing fire from the gunboat and the mysterious movements of enemy troops was enough to convince Grover that he could go no further. He ordered his division to hold their ground. It was now just short of 10:00 AM, and Grover was beaten.[45]

The entire division idled. "Hours pass, and we remain in line," Corporal Hosmer remembered. "We cook, eat, and sleep." The men in Kimball's Brigade watched as escorts herded the Confederate captives down the bayou road. "Prisoners come by in squads—sometimes five or six, sometimes twenty or thirty; some in gray, some in blue, some in faded brown," Hosmer continued. "Once in a while, there is an intelligent, good-looking face; more often the features are unintelligent—the brutish face of that deteriorating class, the white trash."[46]

Hosmer also visited the nearby makeshift hospital. "It was a bloody strife. Within half a dozen rods of our line lie, of one New York regiment, the wounded colonel, the dead lieutenant colonel, adjutant, and other officers and men. I go over and see the writhing wounded, and the hospital attendants laying out the dead. An Irish private lies close by the strait young adjutant, whose face is reverently covered; not far off is a rebel, covered thick with his own gore. Before death go down all distinctions and animosities," he wrote. The violence and chaos of the surgeons' work seemed at odds with the day. "It is a perfect summer day—an almost cloudless sky with a cool sweet wind coming from the woods where the rebels had been hidden; the woods green and fresh and innocent, as if they were only a haunt for fairies."[47]

Just about two miles away, at the far edge of McCarroll's field, the men of the 4th Texas and 2nd Louisiana continued to keep the Federals at bay. "Holding our position until the infantry had made good its escape," Noel remembered, "our line broke by single file to the right and in a few moments 'nary a rebel' was to be seen confronting the dastardly cowards who thought but a short time

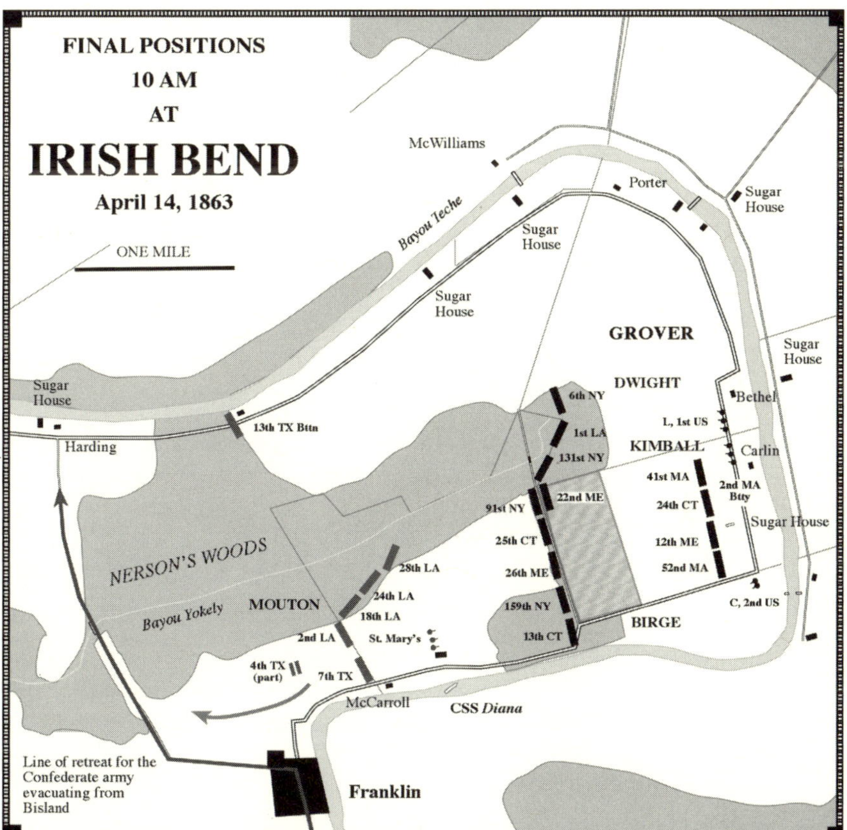

before that they had 'Dick Taylor's army bagged.'" Only the *Diana* remained engaged, sending an occasional shell toward the Federals to keep them under cover and out of the fight while a remnant of the Confederate army spent the next few hours doing its best to look more dangerous than it was. The effort was needless. The fight at Irish Bend was over.[48]

The battle had been a three-hour infantry scuffle at close range, and casualties were high. With three hundred men hit, Colonel Birge's Brigade was down by more than a quarter, leading one Federal to note "the Texas Rangers, of whose marksmanship and fighting qualities we had so uncomfortable an experience . . . seem to be represented here for the loss is heavy." The most bloodied was the 159th New York, with twenty-nine of its men killed, seventy-one wounded, and twelve captured. "The victory was ours," claimed Duffy, "though the regiment had paid dearly for this, their maiden fight." Lieutenant W. Frank Tiemann of that regiment considered the whole affair to have been botched. "The fight at Irish Bend . . . was a needless murder of our troops," he wrote to the wounded Colonel Molineux. The 25th Connecticut, in the fight the longest, suffered next with nine dead and eighty-two wounded. "There was very few of us that had no bullet mark about his clothes or body," observed Schubert. The 26th Maine lost sixty-eight soldiers killed or wounded. Private Maddocks penned, "the enemy saved their fire until [we] almost reached them and then mowed them down as the British were served at Bunker Hill."[49]

Even the venerable 13th Connecticut had suffered, losing fifty-three men, seven killed outright. "Glorious yet mournful at best, is death on the battlefield," remarked Sprague, still nursing a sore hand and wrist from his wound. "Happy he, whose brain is instantly darkened by the missile crashing though it, or whose life gushes away in a crimson torrent! But sadder than words can tell is the fate of him who lingers hour after hour in agony, and then dies. The usual consolations of the last hour are wanting; the soft hand; the last kiss; the cooling draught that quenches the mortal thirst;

Major Thomas Peck Ochiltree, the red-headed, ambitious son of influential Texan William Beck Ochitree of Jefferson, started the war as a sergeant with the 1st Texas Infantry in Virginia. He joined Brigadier General Henry Hopkins Sibley's staff in the summer of 1861 as an aide-de-camp and assistant adjutant general, serving in the first part of the New Mexico Campaign. Ochiltree had a horse shot out from under him at the Battle of Val Verde; Sibley sent him back to Virginia bearing dispatches and news of the Confederate victory. Promoted through the officer grades to major, Ochiltree had a near-death experience at Bisland and watched five of his fellow staff officers from Sibley's Brigade killed by a single artillery round. He arrived in Franklin, Louisiana, to discover that the 4th Texas Cavalry had been severely cut up in the fighting around Irish Bend and the army's retreat was falling into chaos. He reported to General Richard Taylor and lent a hand. *Library of Congress.*

the whisper that bids the soul look heavenward while the earthly eye is growing dim." Instead, the brief Battle of Irish Bend had been a vision of brutal anguish. "No angel graces or heavenly charities there," he noted, "but yells, curses, groans, the rattle of musketry, the shrieks of shot and shell, the earth ploughed by iron projectiles, the air rent with explosions, the roll of ponderous wheels crushing all beneath them—a hell on earth!"[50]

There were casualties, too, among the Rebels, who had "fought handsomely," as one Union officer grudgingly conceded. Of the one thousand or so engaged, more than one hundred had been taken prisoner with a like number killed or wounded. Most of the injured fell into Federal hands. "Thus it was," observed Noel, "that the 'glorious victories of Louisiana' of which we heard so much ado about in the Northern press were gained."[51]

The Confederates carried with them the body of Colonel Reily. Major Hampton had directed that the colonel, who was paralyzed and dying in Nerson's Woods, be carried to McCarroll's plantation to get him out of the fight. There, "he had breathed his last on that bloody battlefield above Franklin that enabled our little army to make safe their retreat before . . . Banks' thieves," Captain Scarborough reported. "I carried the body of the hero to Franklin." There the officer encountered a staffer from Sibley's command coming up from Fort Bisland. "Meeting Major T. P. Ochiltree, I was ordered by him to lay it out in the courthouse, which I did. I know enough of Colonel Riley to know him to be a high minded honorable gentlemen, a good officer, and as brave as the bravest."[52]

The little skirmish with the heavy losses left an impression on the participants. "This battle is known among men as Irish Bend," mused a soldier in the 26th Maine. "It does not make much of a figure in history, because only a division was present and not all of that fully engaged, but it was sharp, obstinate and bloody . . . and was truly a battle as Gettysburg or Shiloh."[53]

16

The Retreat

"Oh, we've found the scoundrels again."

Brigadier General Godfrey Weitzel
Second Brigade, First Division, 19th Army Corps

As Louisiana and Connecticut skirmishers fired the opening shots of the Battle of Irish Bend, Union troops opposite the Confederate works at Bisland made a shocking discovery. "The colonel in charge of the pickets, a greenhorn of some nine-months regiment, distinguished himself by an exhibition of the minimum of native military genius," scrawled Captain John William De Forest of the 12th Connecticut. "Early in the morning he reported to Weitzel that the enemy had vacated their position." When questioned as to how he had come upon this intelligence, the officer responded by saying, "I heard their artillery going off about two o'clock." Furious, Brigadier General Godfrey Weitzel asked the colonel why he had not informed him of this occurrence. "Why, General, I thought you wanted them to clear out," came the innocent reply. "I didn't want to disturb you after such a hard day's work."[1]

The news rippled through the ranks at dizzying speed. Brigadier General William H. Emory ordered a portion of his command to fire into the breastworks to make sure that they were indeed vacant. No one shot back. The Federal riflemen responded by rushing the works in a victory spasm, and all along the lines national and regimental flags raised above the parapet, the symbol that the glorified ditches of Fort Bisland now belonged to the United States. General Weitzel knew instinctively that the retreating Rebels must be pursued—closely—and he ordered his brigade into column formation and onto the road. It would be a long day. Within moments of sunrise, the far-off thumping of artillery revealed that the armies had renewed the battle and that Major General Richard Taylor had given Major General Nathaniel P. Banks the slip. He had at least a six-hour head start.

"Thus collapsed the plan by which we were to stick like a burr to the enemy and pitch into his rear whenever he should attempt to force his way through Grover," De Forest lamented. "Sling blankets and shoulder arms was the order now." Banks had to make up for the time squandered during the night. It would be an uneven race. "Texans on horseback," noted DeForest, "can travel faster than Yankees on foot." Weitzel's men, preceded by the various cavalry companies at hand, took to the road, fully aware that the enemy had gained a sizable lead in this cross-country race.[2]

While the vanguard of Banks's army swung into swift-moving march columns and moved rapidly through and beyond the enemy works, other Union troops took the opportunity to tour the captured entrenchments. "Upon entering the works the scene on every hand gave the fullest evidence of bloody work the day before," wrote a reporter along on the expedition. "Their unburied dead were lying around on all sides. Within an area of fifty feet thirty horses lay dead on the field." He also mentioned a Rebel gun lying upended in a ditch; it was Lieutenant Minos T. Gordy's 12-pounder. The Confederates had left a good deal of war matèriel. "Large stores of all kinds of ammunition and some Enfield rifles, and a few small arms, were found in the works, having been abandoned by the enemy," the reporter continued. Near the big siege guns the writer found the "remnants of a hasty meal . . . scattered around near the cannon."[3]

They encountered a large amount of battle damage. "In one place the earth-works were torn up by a bursting shell, and the earth in many places was very much plowed up by the iron missiles of death," the journalist continued. As the Federal regiments took their places on the road to Franklin, a cheer rippled along the column as the soldiers passed the contested ground in turn. "The wildest enthusiasm prevailed among our troops as they entered this rebel stronghold [and] beheld the fearful effects of the two days' struggle."[4]

The victory felt cathartic for many of these first time soldiers. Banks had carried the day, the Southerners had gone, the day was won. Surely Brigadier General Cuvier Grover would close the trap and complete the triumph, and the Richard Taylor's Confederate army would be destroyed. As the tail of Weitzel's brigade moved up the bayou road, Emory directed his regiments to fall in behind

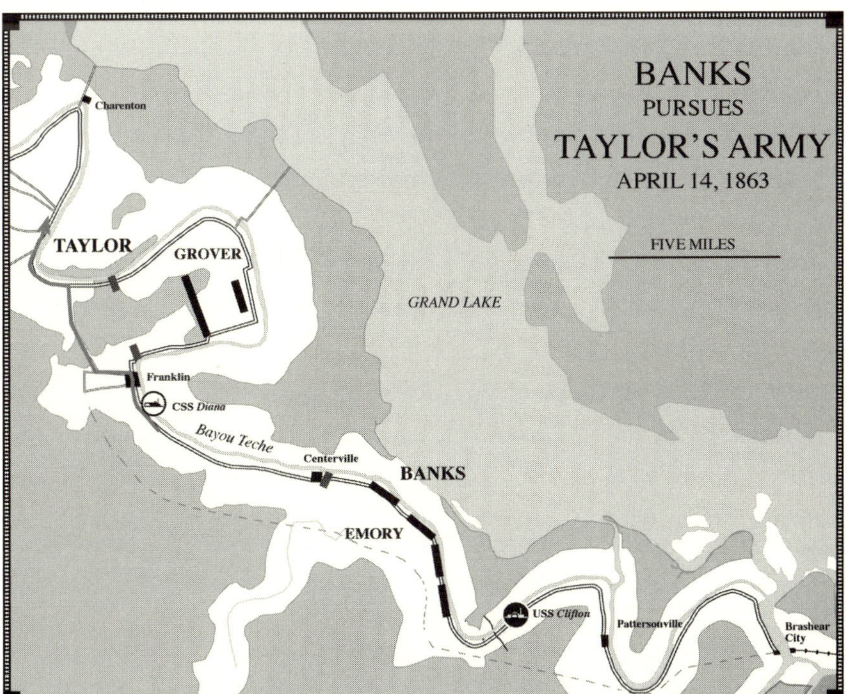

them and follow at a more leisurely pace. If Grover did his job, there would be little need to hurry, these rookies reasoned. The veterans of Bisland believed they merely needed to round up prisoners at this point.

Weitzel knew better, and urged his men up Bayou Teche at a steady gait, the flush of victory giving them new energy. Many, glad to have survived such a noisy and ominous fight, now looked at war as a great lark with ample opportunity to enjoy themselves in an alien land. The weather was beautiful, the scenery striking. "The Teche has, with much truth, been called 'The Garden of Louisiana—the Paradise of the South,'" wrote Dr. Harris Beecher, assistant surgeon of the 114th New York. "It has indeed been doubted whether, in the whole South . . . could be found more fertile plains, more elegant mansions, more wealthy inhabitants, a more lavish expenditure of money, in gardens, outbuildings, and fences, a larger amount of slave property, that was seen by our troops." This treasure trove of privileged lives now lay at the mercy of the U.S. Army. "The planters, for the most part, left their valuable acquisitions upon the advance of the patriot army," Beecher continued, "either from fear of the Yankees, or from love of the Confederacy."[5]

As the advance continued, some soldiers slipped away from the jolly columns and began to mill around in the yards of the homes lining the road. As soon as one soldier violated the sanctity of private property, others also took license. At first in ones and twos, but eventually in whole squads, Federal troops plundered the stately houses, helping themselves to the contents. Before long soldiers rejoined the ranks laden with a variety of items, from poultry to plates, treasures to tools. "One was seen with a large and elegant clock upon his back, while another was trudging along with a family bible under his arm," remarked Beecher. "One misguided soldier [attempted] to carry off an *anvil* on his back."[6]

The restraints of law and civilization unravel easily in war. Men who had seen friends killed or maimed and those relieved to have cheated death thus far released the tension of the previous days in a crescendo of looting and vandalism. There was no studied purpose or pattern. As the booty got heavy, the troops abandoned the items taken earlier in favor of some new item that caught their fancy in houses further along the route. "The road in the rear of an army is often found encumbered with books, furniture, china ware, portraits, ladies' apparel, farming utensils, and every portable thing that possibly can be imagined. Oftentimes a soldier can be found . . . indulging in the breaking of mirrors, and pianos, and the most costly furniture," Beecher lamented. "Men of such reckless dispositions are frequently guilty of the most horrible desecrations and have been seen . . . in the full robes of a Catholic priest [or] ornamented with the regalia of a Free Mason, while they marched through the dust, with guns upon their backs."[7]

Weitzel's column, bogged down with loot, also became mired in a swell of former slaves eager to move with the army, wherever it might lead, toward freedom. "At every plantation, the road would be lined and the fenced covered with grinning black faces, men, and children, courtesying and bowing, singing and dancing—all attempting to express their joy all at once," Beecher wrote. The Year of Jubilo was at hand. "Most of them would have their bundles all ready to leave their homes, and fall in with the troops marching along. It required the most strenuous exertions to keep the army from being clogged with thousands of negroes," reported Beecher.[8]

Weitzel had no time to attend to the looters at the rear of his column or to the jubilant former slaves. His mounted vanguard seemed nervous. Major Harai Robinson, Banks's chief of cavalry, had provided Weitzel with Lieutenant Solon A. Perkins's company of mounted troops. These men scouted the approaches to the village of Centerville while Weitzel advanced the skirmishers of his lead regiment, the 8th Vermont's Company H. The rest of his brigade received orders to halt, taken by many as an invitation to break ranks, break into houses, or loll about on the lawns as the minutes ticked by. At the column's head, bugles directed skirmishers to move one way or another, but then signaled that they had evidently found something. The unmistakable call of "rally on the reserves" brought the soldiers of Company H scurrying back to their regiment while the Union cavalry edged ahead and the six guns of Captain Edmund C. Bainbridge's Battery A, 1st U.S. Artillery, crowded the road.[9]

The serious business in the brigade's van did little to dissipate the carnival atmosphere in its rear. A tangle of men rushed from the door of one plantation house, laden with jam and jellies from the cellar, answering the call of the distant bugle and looking to find their place in line. Their comrades, observing from the roadside, began chiding them with the taunt, "Rally on the preserves!" Troops from the 114th New York surged into that house and neighboring homes, hoping to harvest a few of these portable delicacies themselves. "Every man in the regiment had his fill of preserved oranges, and citrons, and pears, and figs, and melons, and every

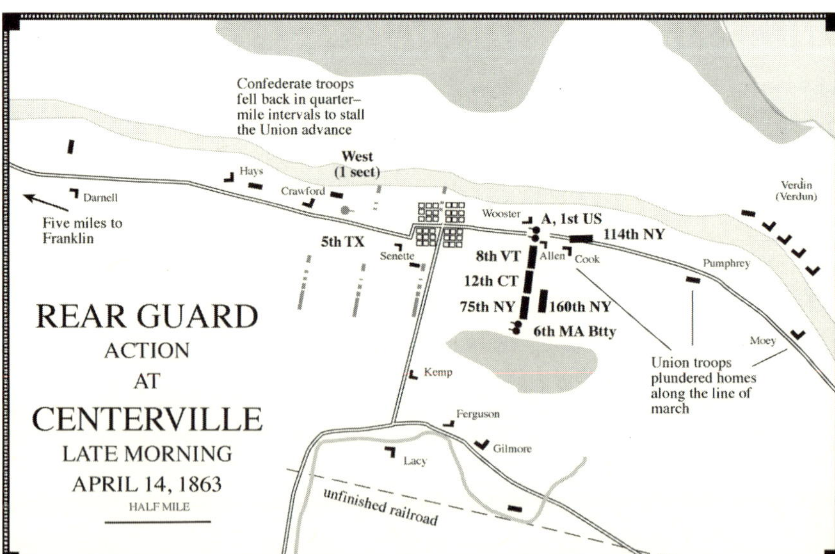

Lieutenant John A. A. West of Semme's 1st Regular Battery helped Colonel Tom Green and his Texans delay the Union pursuit.

Louisiana Historical Association Collection, Tulane University.

variety of jams and jellies," Dr. Beecher observed. "The capacity of that house for preserves was greater than that of the men."[10]

The realities of war soon intervened. Unbeknown to the vandals in the rear of Weitzel's column, but soon apparent to the men in the front, the Confederates had not simply run away. Colonel Tom Green had been falling back at intervals to keep the Federals from shuffling unfettered up the road. The wiley Texan occasionally hid his troopers behind buildings and cover, and their sniping forced Weitzel to deploy his advance in a deadly tedious game of hide-and-seek. Just past Centerville, Green's Texans and the two 3-inch rifles of the 1st Confederate Battery made a serious stand. "Here I masked my pieces, and Colonel Green deploying his cavalry to check the enemy's sharpshooters, I awaited the advance of the enemy's main column," reported Confederate lieutenant John A. A. West.[11]

West's opening salvo shocked Weitzel's brigade. "Suddenly there was a loud report of a cannon, and a ball went ricocheting down the road," wrote an officer in the 114th New York. "Oh, we've found the scoundrels again," Weitzel bellowed, ordering the men off of the road and into line of battle. Lieutenant West seemed proud of his work as the Yankees scrambled for cover, and he ordered his gunners to find a fatter target. "Finding one of their batteries crowded together within a narrow space of the road, I directed my fire upon it," he reported. The missiles created havoc, crippling a caisson and wounding two of its horses as well as a half-dozen men.[12]

Weitzel's troops recoiled,. then the great blue army began to pulse and swell as regiments peeled off of the road and headed into the surrounding fields. In minutes the entire advance brigade puffed out into a mile-long front. A second Union battery—Captain William Carruth's 6th Massachusetts Battery—took its place on the left of the Yankee line and began hunting for West and his Rebel artillerymen among the buildings of the plantations above Centerville, probing each likely hiding spot with several rounds of white-hot iron. Weitzel could not be sure, but he hoped that perhaps this was the last stand of Taylor's army. It was not.

Colonel Green ordered his Confederates to fall back at intervals of five hundred yards, keeping his enemies guessing and forcing Weitzel to keep his men deployed, slowing his advance. The Federals at Centerville could not see, but could plainly hear, the echoes of battle at Irish Bend. Maddeningly, the boom of artillery had slackened as the morning wore on. Either Grover had triumphed, or Taylor had given him the slip. Either way, Green's delaying tactics frustrated Weitzel and his attempt to finish the campaign.[13]

In fact Taylor used the time purchased by Green at Centerville and the fallen Colonel James Reily at Irish Bend to try and save the vehicles and supplies of his escaping army. He grew frustrated by the pace of the retreat. A few miles ahead, his gray column lurched and stopped, started again and stalled again, on its way north, in an accordion-like jam of vehicles, men, and animals as they passed through Franklin and headed down Harding's Lane. Taylor, having just seen to Brigadier General Alfred Mouton's battlefield deployment at the McCarroll plantation, turned his attention to logistics. As the last of the wagons pulled through town, the general ordered General Henry Hopkins Sibley to move to the head of the column, prevent straggling, and "select a suitable camp for the troops and wagons, and to report to me the selection which he had made of camping ground for the night." With that chore delegated and enemy forces on the Teche above and below Franklin, Taylor commanded that all steamboats tied up at the town be destroyed. Around noon, the transports went first. Pitch and turpentine sped the destruction of the *Newsboy,* the *Gossamer,* and the *Era No. 2,* with explosives finishing off the machinery.[14]

Two miles away, behind Grover's battered line at Irish Bend, Corporal James K. Hosmer of the 52nd Massachusetts remained a spectator, an impotent part of the failed Union strike force now dealing with the wreckage of battle. Signs of the destruction of the Rebel steamers billowed up in the distance long before the distant rumble of the death-blasts. "In the course of the day, up into the blue, calm, sky go mighty columns of smoke, with deep reports," Hosmer wrote, "the explosions of rebel gunboats and

Centerville, on Bayou Teche. Alfred R. Waud sketched the Bayou Teche village looking downstream, the town on his right. Confederates lurking among the buildings managed to delay the pursuing Federal columns coming up from Fort Bisland.

Historic New Orleans Collection, Accession no. 1965.83 i–v.

transports . . . blown up by their crews as they flee." These small victories provided some consolation to the weary, wounded and dying from the early morning battle.[15]

One piece of business Taylor left unfinished was the fate of the Confederate sick and wounded. The steamer *Cornie* had arrived safely at Franklin with its cargo of disabled soldiers from Bisland, but now it waited, tied to a dock, its human cargo on board. Through some miscommunication, promised transportation had not arrived nor were their hands to unload the vessel. The streets were empty, and not a single wagon remained to receive the casualties. Taylor had left the supervision of this task to General Sibley. Instead, that officer contradicted his orders, and on his own initiative had apparently sent the wagons up the road to safety. Instead, Sibley hoped that the *Cornie* might continue its humanitarian journey up the Teche and slip by Grover's Division unmolested. Amid the confusion, the steamboat idled at the docks in Franklin, the fate of the wounded uncertain. To compound the problem, medical attendants appeared with sick and wounded Rebels from Franklin and Irish Bend, loading them on the *Cornie* as well.

With Weitzel approaching from the south, and Grover's men still looming to the east, the wounded and invalid Confederates became one of the last portions of Taylor's army heading toward safety. With time short and panic growing, General Sibley directed his officers to hoist a hospital flag on the boat and take the *Cornie* past the Federals upstream. Before the small paddle wheeler had proceeded far, Captain Oliver J. Semmes aboard the CSS *Diana,* his boat still harassing Grover's Division, hailed the *Cornie* and had a counsel with its skipper, shocked at its foolhardy and potentially disastrous mission. Reluctantly, one of Sibley's officers ordered the *Cornie* back to Franklin, its eighty wounded and ill Confederates, two Federal prisoners, and four armed guards onboard seemingly abandoned. When the *Cornie* arrived back at the dock just after noon, the town was in a state of chaos. U.S. lieutenant Pickering

Dodge Allen, wounded and captured along with the *Diana* when it was taken by Colonel Edwin Waller's men a little more than two weeks before, simply walked off the *Cornie* and mingled with the crowd—entirely unmolested by the few Rebels remaining around the center of town.[16]

Remarkably, Grover remained frozen in place. Weitzel, though, advanced relentlessly and the Confederates moved fast to save the remnants of their army and to avoid being trapped between the two portions of Banks's army. General Sibley sent word to Green to quit his game and to hurry his command through Franklin and across the bridge at Bayou Yokely. East of Franklin the Confederate soldiers who had fought so well at Irish Bend, as well as Mouton's brigade at McCarroll's plantation, turned right onto the Harding Road and headed north, joining the exodus out of town. Private Felix Robert Collard of the 7th Texas, just arrived from Bisland, observed the arrival of these weary troops along with the wreckage of their battle. "As we entered Franklin, Riley's and Vincent's regiments joined us, bringing the dead body of Colonel Riley and bringing Colonel Vincent, who was shot through the neck but was still alive," Collard wrote. For the battered men of the 4th Texas it was a glad reunion as they once again rode alongside the other regiments of Sibley's Brigade and learned of the part each had played in the violent last two days. "They too had covered themselves with glory," wrote Private Theophilus Noel. "Banks's whole army had confronted them for nineteen long miles, and only advanced as Green and his brave boys would allow them." Green and his mounted troops clattered across the Bayou Yokely Bridge just after 1:00 PM. convinced they must be the last to the Confederates in the area. Lieutenant West moved his guns into position to cover the span while soldiers prepared its timbers for burning. With luck the Federals would find only its charred remains, and the swampy waters of Bayou Yokely would check their advance.[17]

Green and his men were too eager, Confederates still remained in Franklin. Captain Semmes, knowing that his boat, too, was probably doomed as the Teche would grow to shallow to allow it passage further on, held his position opposing Grover until a rider from General Mouton ordered him back to Franklin. The crew dutifully reversed the engines and took the battle-scarred cannon-boat back to Franklin, satisfied in the knowledge that the mere presence of the steam-driven huntress had buffaloed Grover and had protected the Teche, at least for a short while.

Despite his diminishing chance of escape, Semmes took the vessel a little downstream to check on the Yankees coming up from Bisland. He fired a few shots, hoping to slow Weitzel's advance; he certainly made an impression. "One solid shot struck in the road and bounded over the left of our company without hurting any-one," wrote Lieutenant William H. Root of the 75th New York. Knowing that the pursuing columns coming from the direction of Fort Bisland would arrive in Franklin shortly, Semmes ordered the pilot to run the *Diana* back upstream and into the bank a little above and opposite the town, its bow pointed toward Grover's line of advance. After efficiently arranging the steamer's ammunition in the magazine, the crew dashed turpentine and oil on its decks before leaving their vessel for the last time. Semmes set a slow match and scrambled overboard. He was the last to leave.[18]

A half mile away, Sibley ordered another pyre to be lighted. While the gunners of Lieutenant West's section covered their work, soldiers applied torches to the bridge over Bayou Yokely. The flames took hold in a smoky billow, and the final work of the rear guard was complete. But Sibley had blundered. He had not heard from Semmes, and Mouton, his staff, and a rear guard remained in position east of Franklin hoping to recover Semmes and his crew. A quick-thinking staff officer galloped off to warn Mouton, who hurried his troops over back roads to the burning bridge. "The enemy were in a position and threatened to cut-off our retreat," the

Acadian general reported. "I succeeded in eluding their pursuit and extricated the troops from a very perilous attitude . . . and saw every man file over a burning bridge in the rear of the village, myself and my staff crossing when it was almost entirely consumed." Semmes and his gunboat crew were on their own, as were the wounded aboard the *Cornie,* now uncomfortably close to the burning *Diana.*[19]

These two fires marked the Confederates' concession of the battlefield. As the flames spread across the woodwork of the Bayou Yokely Bridge and the CSS *Diana,* the leading elements of Weitzel's Brigade arrived at Franklin, under a mile away. "They entered . . . the streets of one of the largest and prettiest villages in western Louisiana," wrote Dr. Beecher. "As the flags were unfurled, and the bands commenced to play, the foot-sore and weary soldiers were infused with new energy . . . the whole patriot army presenting an imposing spectacle to the astonished citizens of Franklin."

At nearly the same time, fire reached the Rebel gunboat's magazine, and the resulting explosion served as the death knell for the hopes of the Confederacy in southwest Louisiana. "Scarcely had they advanced a few squares into town, before a stunning, deafening crash was heard," Beecher observed. "The earth quivered with the violence of the concussion, and the air was filled with a sulphurous cloud, and flying sticks and debris. The *Diana* was no more."[20]

Federal lieutenant Perkins and his scattering of mounted troopers at the head of Weitzel's column scoured Franklin for any Rebel stragglers, but one of the first soldiers they encountered was Lieutenant Allen of their own army. "Three or four of Perkins' cavalry passed through; I took a revolver from one them and let them go by," he wrote. "I then returned to the [*Cornie*]." Allen, although wounded, went to settle a score. Walking up to the *Cornie,* remarkably unharmed by the detonation of the *Diana.* Lieutenant Allen demanded that its skipper surrender the boat. "Take charge of her sir, and hoist your flag upon her," was the Confederate response. Made a prisoner when the Rebels took the *Diana,* he had now captured a boat of his own. "Was I not very fortunate in getting away from the secesh?" he wrote home, adding, "I received better treatment than their prisoners ordinarily received from us."[21]

Moving on, the U.S. cavalry made a big catch. Captain Semmes and his men arrived too late to cross the Bayou Yokely Bridge. They had set out to find another crossing, but Perkins's troopers rode them down and captured them. "Thus," hissed Taylor in a report, "by the unjustifiable and careless order of General Sibley the escape of Captain Semmes and his crew . . . was prevented."[22]

For Confederate officials in the Trans-Mississippi, this utter reversal of fortune came as a shock. Just days earlier, these same leaders had anticipated hearing of a major victory over the Federals at Brashear City, delivered by the men, cannon, and boats of General Taylor's intrepid army. Now Lieutenant General Edmund Kirby Smith arrived back in Alexandria after his long visit to Arkansas just in time to face calamity. He did not realize Taylor was already on the run, but the time-delayed reports he read were ominous enough. Dispatches poured in to headquarters, detailing the shift of Banks's army to the Teche and the news of Major General Ulysses S. Grant's movements west of Vicksburg. Kirby Smith hoped this news meant Union forces might have given up their Mississippi Valley Campaign. With Federal forces probing the interior of northeast Louisiana and the southern portions of the state, Kirby Smith believed that the enemy had shifted its target away from the Mississippi River and was converging toward western Louisiana, a potentially positive outcome from the changed strategic situation and a move that would save Vicksburg and Port Hudson. Kirby Smith was wrong, however. The Confederates in Louisiana were simply in the process of being overwhelmed while Grant remained focused on Vicksburg.

17

The Pursuit

"We plunged deeper and deeper into the heart of Rebeldom."

Corporal James K. Hosmer
53rd Massachusetts Infantry

As Major General Richard Taylor's army scrambled north, the Confederate regiments continued to lose men, and its officers reorganized their commands. Brigadier General Alfred Mouton, his uniform singed from his dash across the burning bridge, came upon Colonel Tom Green around 2:00 PM on April 14 and directed him to take charge of the cavalry while he reorganized the infantry. "I collected and reorganized as rapidly as I could the shattered fragments of my own brigade," Mouton wrote. The rendezvous for the night was the Grevemberg Plantation, just beyond Bayou Cypremort near Jeanerette. For most of Taylor's army, arriving at that destination would mark the ending of one of the longest days of their lives—nearly twenty hours of fighting and retreating over the course of twenty-five miles. They had eaten little, and the trains with rations pressed on to New Iberia, another ten miles away.[1]

The day had also been hard on the Rebel fleet that Taylor had so carefully assembled in the Atchafalaya Basin's maze of bayous. He now faced hard choices. After the destruction of the *Queen of the West,* the *Nina Simms* had sought to escape and met the *Mary T.* and the *Grand Duke* as they were groping their way toward Chicot Pass, too late to make a difference. The leaderless flotilla instead turned back to the cover of the four guns at Butte-a-la-Rose, where the navy learned the news of the fights at Fort Bisland and Irish Bend. The *Grand Duke* pressed on to carry word of the reverses to the forces gathering at Fort DeRussy, and the *Mary T.* and the *Nina Simms* turned about to keep vigil for the arrival of the pursuing Union fleet.

When *Grand Duke* reached the Red River, the news of the disaster on the lower Bayou Teche and Grand Lake fell hard on the men from General Henry Hopkins Sibley's Texas Brigade who were

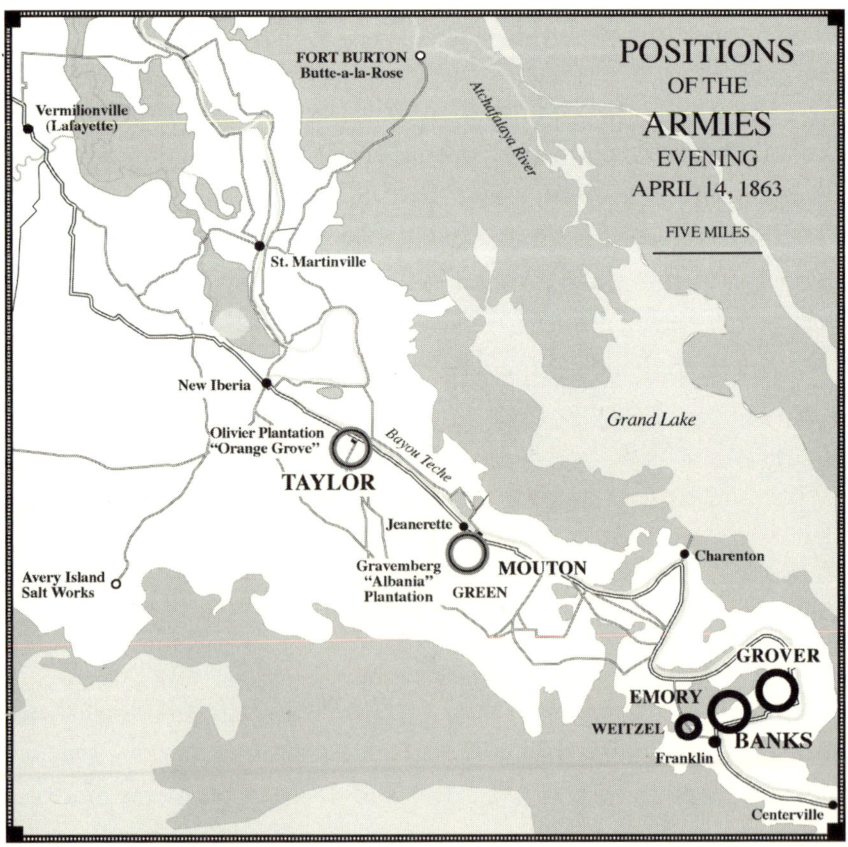

idling at Fort DeRussy. "Here I am yet, still waiting," scribbled Private John W. Watkins to his wife, adding "I have bad news to write. They have surrounded our brave boys and left them no chance of escape unless we can get to them in our boats, which we will try to do."[2]

Across southwest Louisiana, all the effort Taylor had put into creating an army and navy to "baffle the enemy in his designs on the Mississippi Valley" had come to naught. Retiring in the face of the enemy now not only placed his command in danger from attack and pursuit but also imperiled it with confusion and panic, the evil companions of retreat. Among the Confederate infantry and horsemen, steamboats and wagons, the retreat along the Bayou Teche

Albania Plantation. Charles Francis Grevemberg completed this palatial home in 1842, the centerpiece of a 6,500-acre sugar plantation down Bayou Teche from Jeanerette. The farm produced 475 hogsheads of sugar in 1860; three years later it served as the bivouac of Richard Taylor's defeated Confederate army. This Adrien Persac painting of Albania is from 1861, just before the dark days descended upon this region.

State Library of Louisiana.

toward Jeanerette and beyond turned into a nightmare. Vehicles and refugees clogged the road, and fright spread through the ranks. "Ten thousand rumors were afloat throughout the army," wrote Sergeant Alfred B. Petticolas. "The panic became the greater the further the men got from the enemy." Although out of immediate danger from Federal troops, Taylor's army might destroy itself by simply unraveling.[3]

As the general moved up the column from the rear toward the front, he could not believe what was happening to his command. He had successfully pulled it from the jaws of Major General Nathaniel P. Banks's trap, but it was now disintegrating on its own, even after fighting so bravely. Why were they not holding together, stopping for the evening in orderly wagon parks, caring for their animals, and maintaining the discipline of their troops?

Taylor immediately learned who was to blame: Sibley. The officer he had put in charge of these issues had simply disappeared, leaving the retreating army to fend for itself. "I was much surprised to find late in the afternoon that [my] order had not been complied with; that General Sibley was not with the command, but had taken a different road from that of our troops, and that the men were straggling without order over the whole line of march," Taylor wrote. He sent gallopers to locate Sibley with demands that he do his job. Rethinking that decision, Taylor took charge himself "and endeavored to collect the stragglers."[4]

The pursuing army experienced its own frustrations, and would gain little new ground that day. As the Federals troops deployed past Franklin, they found that their quarry had slipped away. They learned too that the construction of a new bridge over Bayou Yokely was unlikely to be completed in the remaining daylight. "We entered Franklin, a town of three thousand inhabitants and many rurally beautiful residences," wrote Lieutenant Colonel David Hunter Strother of Banks's staff. "A stern-wheeler filled with Confederate wounded was our only capture." The commanding general moved his staff into one of the larger homes and established his headquarters there. Banks issued orders for his subordinates to lead their troops to suitable campgrounds and to rest them for the remainder of the day. Colonel Oliver P. Gooding's soldiers, marching up the east bank of the Teche from Fort Bisland, drove before them a large herd of cattle that would serve to feed the army that night. The men would need their strength in the morning. "The General is much chagrined at the failure to capture the army of Taylor and Sibley, but we will march rapidly on New Iberia tomorrow," Strother continued. "We have clearly thrashed these people and the Battles of the Teche will tell well in the history of the war."[5]

The Union veterans of the Battle of Fort Bisland camped in the fields beyond Franklin. Brigadier General Godfrey Weitzel's men stopped near Bayou Yokely on the New Iberia Road, and Brigadier General William H. Emory's men turned right and headed toward McCarroll's field and Brigadier General Cuvier Grover's Division. There the soldiers at last learned what had happened to the other part of the plan. "Why General Grover, after driving the enemy away in confusion at the Battle of Irish Bend, should content himself to quietly encamp, in the middle of the day, near the battle ground . . . is one of the questions that probably never will be answered," Dr. Harris Beecher remarked. "Yet the humblest private in the ranks saw the situation, and chafed under his restraint." Some were inclined to be charitable. "Although we failed in taking the whole force," wrote Lieutenant William H. Root of the 75th New York, "no little has been accomplished as it is."[6]

The men of Grover's Division meanwhile moved back toward Carlin's field and set up camps near the scene of their fight. Officers formed fatigue details while some of the soldiers scoured the surrounding farms for livestock and others tended the wounded and the dead. "Toward night, I go down the cart path to the actual field, and see the broken muskets, the scattered knapsacks and clothing, the furrows where the enemy lay, the bloody pools where the dying fainted, the burial parties, and the piles of distorted corpses lying by the trenches just dug to receive them," Corporal James K. Hosmer wrote. "I cast a farewell glance at the fence, along the rails of which the rebels had rested their pieces in the morning . . . at the group burying the dead, a rebel prisoner standing at the elbow of the sergeant in charge, giving him the names of a pile of the enemy about to be interred, then we marched off."[7]

The Union field hospital, busy throughout the day and into the night, was lighted by just a few candles and lanterns and was seriously undermanned. "Quite a number of dead lay at one door, and a pile of legs, feet, arms, hands, beside the bloody table where the surgeons are still amputating," wrote Captain Homer B. Sprague of the 13th Connecticut. "Nothing to be heard but cries, groans, entreaties. It really seemed as if nobody cared for the sufferers, so few were there to assist them." After seeing to the care of the wounded of his unit, the officer returned to his camp, "sick at heart of war and all its surroundings."[8]

That evening, Taylor received an overdue visitor at his headquarters between Jeanerette and New Iberia. General Sibley arrived looking sickly, pale, and pathetic. He claimed to be incapacitated and wanted to travel ahead of the retreating army until he could regain his health. "Which request I granted," Taylor reported curtly. He believed that the damage created by Sibley's "illness" might prove irreparable. "Thus commenced the scattering and straggling of our troops," Taylor remembered. Sibley had already faced charges over abandoning his wounded and of being "sick"—drunk—while in New Mexico. In Louisiana, it now appeared, Sibley had given a repeat performance. Taylor began drafting dispatches to try to save his army. One courier carried orders to General Mouton giving him command of all the forces south of Red River. Taylor sacked Sibley; he would soon place him under arrest.[9]

Taylor ordered Colonel Green to gather the remnants of the 4th, 5th, and 7th Texas Cavalries, the 13th Texas Cavalry Battalion, the Arizona Battalion, and the 2nd Louisiana Cavalry—in all, nearly one thousand veteran horsemen—to oppose the Yankee advance and cover the Rebel retreat. Green moved with alacrity, and in the following days he would display a native genius for rear-guard fighting that would make him famous.

Also that evening, at his headquarters in Franklin, Union General Banks sketched out his plans for pursuit. Already engineers were rebuilding and strengthening the bridge over Bayou Yokely to accommodate the passage of the 1st Indiana Heavy Artillery's mighty siege guns. Weitzel's men would lead the way up the New Iberia Road, screened in front by the combined cavalry commands from both fronts and now under the unified command of Major Harai Robinson. Altogether about 250 men were combined into an ersatz battalion. Grover would take his command the long way around, following the curves of Bayou Teche along the roads that flanked its banks. Emory would follow Weitzel down the cut-off, Harding Road.

Even though Taylor had slipped through the Federal trap, Banks still thought he could be captured. Even though they had failed to bag the entire Confederate army in southwestern Louisiana as hoped, the U.S. army had certainly dislodged and battered it. Now they simply had to run it down and finish the job.

In the predawn darkness of April 15 Major Robinson and his horsemen clattered across the new Bayou Yokely Bridge. His battalion, composed of his own 1st Louisiana Cavalry companies, Lieutenant Solon Perkins's men, and elements of the newly arrived 2nd Rhode Island Cavalry, just up from Brashear City, were a hard lot. Captain John Franklin Godfrey of the U.S. 1st Louisiana described Robinson as "a petty, small sort of man." He had similar harsh words for the New England newcomers. "This Rhode Island

Cavalry is a most miserable institution," Godfrey wrote. "They are continually deserting to the enemy, and seem to be a lawless, discontented set. They all received several hundred dollars bounty, and out of a regiment they have all run away, but about three hundred."[10]

The infantrymen in Weitzel's Brigade also moved out of their camps before sunrise. They faced a hard day's march. Lieutenant Elias P. Pellet of the 114th New York recalled that "at four o'clock a.m. . . . we were in motion. The weather was exceedingly hot, and the roads ankle deep with dust. We were barely allowed time to breathe and were hurried along at almost a double quick step." The pace and the weather began to wear down the troops. "Many, unaccustomed to marching, fell out, but a majority declared they would keep in the ranks," the major continued, "and pride alone kept the army together that day." Another officer described the misery of the troops. "The sun was scalding hot," he wrote, "dust almost thick enough to cut with a knife, and water mostly bad."[11]

With Weitzel and Emory underway on the New Iberia Road, Grover's Division moved out from their camps along the bayou. They learned that their flank would be secured by an old acquaintance on

USS *Clifton* moving up Bayou Teche. Dr. Daniel D. T. Nestell, acting assistant surgeon aboard the gunboat, sketched it heading up the Teche below Franklin, passing along heavily wooded banks.

Nestell Collection, Nimitz Library, U.S. Naval Academy, Annapolis, Maryland.

the waterway. "The camp was early astir," wrote Corporal Hosmer of the 53rd Massachusetts. "We bathed in the Teche, and watched the *Clifton,* our old, grim friend, which came steaming up. As soon as she had passed, it was time for us to go."[12]

The New York ferryboat appeared to be an invincible leviathan as it glided along the bayou on the army's right side. The *Clifton* was so wide abeam that it seemed to fill Bayou Teche from shore to shore. Lieutenant Root wrote home that "the strangest sight I have seen in a long time was the Clifton plowing her way up the stream, her sides almost touching the bank. The ground is a good deal higher than the stream and [from] a little way off the boat looked like a mammoth machine moving on the surface of the ground." Closer

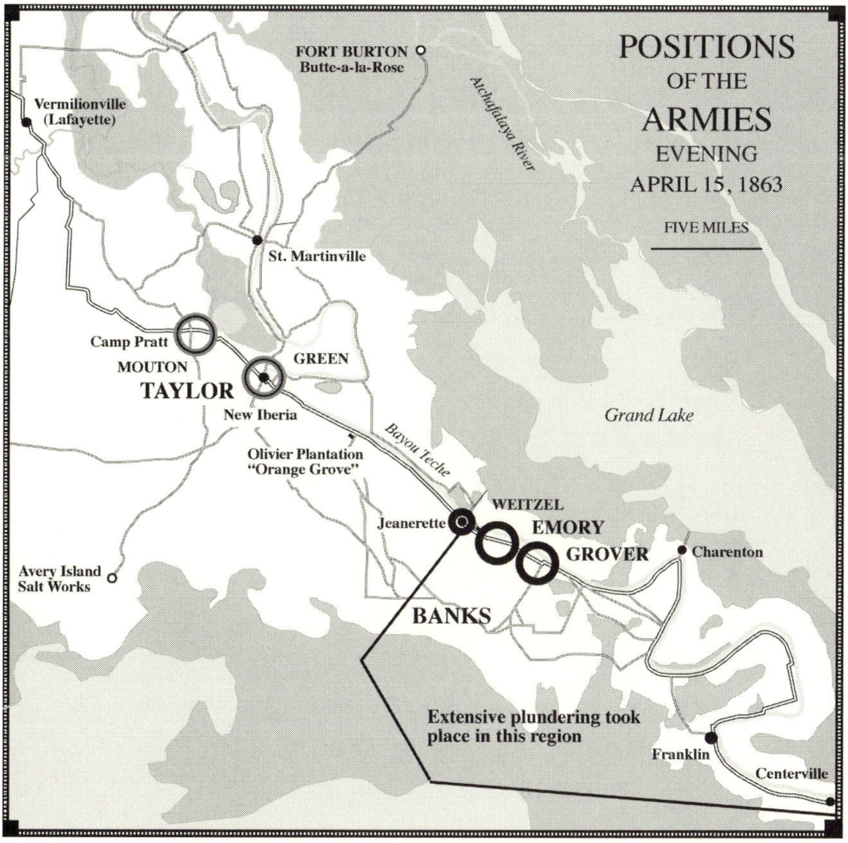

to the bayou, the men of the 52nd Massachusetts listened for the reassuring sound of the steamer's engine whenever trees obscured the view. "We could often hear the regular clank of the *Clifton*'s machinery, steadily keeping pace with us," Corporal Hosmer remembered, "as we plunged deeper and deeper into the heart of Rebeldom."[13]

When the pursuing Federals neared the rear of the Confederate column beyond Franklin, their scouts reported Colonel Green's delaying tactics. The Confederate veteran dismounted some of his rifle-armed command and a section of cannon to check the pursuing Yankee cavalry while sending mounted troops around to envelop the Union flanks. The Texan's Enfields, Springfields, and cannon outmatched the carbines, sabers, and pistols of the Union horse soldiers, forcing them to withdraw to the protection of their nearby infantry. When stronger formations of Federal foot soldiers arrived, bringing with them their supporting artillery, Green's men mounted their horses and galloped away only to repeat the process in a new location. For the next three days, the Texans would lay these traps at intervals to inflict casualties on the enemy and delay their pursuit. They had started what would become a running fight up the New Iberia Road and beyond.[14]

Green's command made its first ambush just short of Jeanerette. A salvo from Lieutenant T. K. Fauntleroy's masked battery of 6-pounders from the 1st Regular Battery scattered the column of pursuing Federal horsemen. The entire line of Texas and Louisiana cavalry then advanced in an impressive line, threatening to overwhelm the smaller Union advance. When Federal foot soldiers arrived to save their mounted comrades, the Rebel gunners limbered up their cannon and moved on, the cavalry following slowly behind. Private William Randolph Howell of the 5th Texas Cavalry described the tactics: "enemy soon commenced his advance, we as usual make stands. Skirmish awhile and as soon as their infantry arrives we fall back and take another position and so on during the day."[15]

As the frustrating pursuit continued, Federal officers discovered to their chagrin that their mixed army of veterans and newer New York and New England militia had become a little tattered over the last week, and committing them to another pitched battle might prove difficult. Despite good intentions and unit pride, many of the soldiers had drifted away from their regiments foraging for food, trophies, or some easier way to chase the Confederates. Some of the men left their places in the marching columns, weak from fatigue and heat. "Under every tree lay a group of panting men," one soldier remembered. When officers called the regiments into formation, they often met with disappointment. "General Banks . . . had made an important discovery," Dr. Beecher wrote. "In attempting to form his lines for an attack, he found that he had an almost unmanageable and demoralized army." The unrestrained looting and marauding of the day before continued. When the infantry tired of walking, they had pressed horses from the farms en route. When horseback travel grew tiresome, the infantry stole a carriage or wagon, one officer observed. "Every hour the army became more and more scattered into deplorable confusion," Beecher continued. "Company and regimental organizations lost their identity among the mass of horses, carts, and mules." Displaced slaves clustering around the column added to the confusion.[16]

Weitzel, whose brigade led the way, maintained the discipline of his command, but Emory's division behind him degenerated into a mob, dissipating its military power. "Such sights as were seen that afternoon, baffle all attempts at description," wrote Dr. Beecher. "Footmen and horsemen were mingled together. Horses without bridles or saddles were being conducted by rope halters, and loaded from ears to tails with chickens and turkeys. Oftentimes the road was blocked by kicking and plunging of obstinate mules and fractious horses." The variety of wheeled vehicles was staggering, and the novel uses the soldiers put them to showed great imagination. "In one instance, some officers were laid out at full length in a hearse, smoking their pipes, while an ugly mule and a ragged negro driver were conducting them along the road," Beecher continued. "An elegant barouche, conveying some officers with cigarettes, was drawn by a novel team composed of a cow and a mule. Had General Banks been vigorously attacked at that time, his army would no doubt have been utterly ruined."[17]

Some officers in the column, confident of victory and convinced the Confederate military threat had been eliminated, justified the plundering as war by other means. "It was my first peep into rebeldom," Lieutenant George H. Hepworth noted. "These very houses that were ransacked had, each of them, a representative in the army that we were chasing." Despite his clerical training, he would not censure the men for ravaging their enemies.[18]

The commander of the Army of the Gulf watched the shambling mass. "General Banks sat upon his horse near by observing the spectacle," a Union officer recorded, "while his face bore the evidence of mingled displeasure and chagrin. He decided to put an end to such evils by prompt and decided measures." Taking decisive action, the general called for a few companies of Weitzel's Brigade to fall out and to post themselves alongside the road. "A guard is posted over every house of more than two chimneys . . . to keep the soldiers from taking anything, though the smaller houses of the poor are left unguarded," complained Lieutenant Root. Staff officers established a checkpoint at a large fenced yard on the route of march. Riders passing by in unauthorized vehicles or riding without permission were to be arrested and their animals and wagons confiscated and parked in the makeshift pound. From this point forward, the army began to reassemble itself. By nightfall the U.S. troops had reached Jeanerette.[19]

The heroes of the Army of the Gulf began to grumble against their war chief. "The men say he cares more for the property of rebels than he does for the comfort of his own soldiers," Lieutenant Root groused. "He marches them very hard and then won't allow them to have what they want to eat. Yesterday our troops cheered Gen'l Banks when he passed along the lines, but tonight I don't think I could raise a cheer, [not] in the 75th [New York] at least."[20]

The day had been hard on the Confederates as well; the grueling pace required of a retreat in which they were closely pursued wore them down. Taylor's army—wounded over the last three days—bled men. While Green's mounted troops kept their plodding pursuers at a distance, each change of position resulted in confusion and disorganization. Many Confederates became lost or confused and separated from their commands. They ended up riding alone or in squads across the Attakapas Prairies. Fatigue, heat, and confusion clouded many soldiers' thinking. Mouton's infantry began to wear out, and dozens of exhausted foot soldiers simply surrendered. "Although we could not catch the Texan horsemen," Captain John William De Forest wrote, "we were marching the Louisiana infantry to tatters."[21]

Some Confederate units simply quit wholesale. "Nearly the whole of Lieutenant Colonel Fournet's battalion, passing through the country in which the men had lived before joining the army, deserted with their arms," Taylor reported. The men of Lieutenant Colonel Valsin Fournet's 10th Yellow Jacket Battalion were largely drawn from the St. Martinville and New Iberia region, and the lure of home proved too strong. "A very considerable number have voluntarily placed themselves within the reach of the enemy by stopping at their houses in the parishes through which we retreated, a very large proportion of our army being composed of conscripts, unwillingly put into service, and those who volunteered at a late date to avoid conscription."[22]

The remnant of the Louisiana Infantry and the army wagons reached New Iberia that same day—a little more than half a day's march ahead of Green's rearguard—and continued beyond the town. The foot soldiers bivouacked on the night of April 15 at Camp Pratt, "at the edge of the vast prairie that extends westwards for hundreds of miles and over whose surface is scattered little farms and large plantations," observed Major Silas T. Grisamore of the 18th Louisiana Infantry, "inhabited by a thrifty, frugal, and patriotic people, noted for genial hospitality and those social qualities which make life among the Southern people so agreeable and pleasant."[23]

That evening, at his headquarters in New Iberia, Taylor ordered the destruction of what was left of his Teche flotilla. Sailors moved the CSS *Stevens*—formerly the *Hart*—two miles downstream, maneuvered it across the width of the bayou, and sank the vessel. Despite its premature death, the boat's wreckage might still keep the USS *Clifton* at bay. Taylor ordered the New Iberia arsenal broken up and the matèriel of war loaded onto steamers. The *Darby*, *Uncle Tommy*, *Louise*, *Blue Hammock*, and *Cricket* moved upstream carrying beef, bacon, rum, sugar, uniforms, bulk cloth, commissary

New Iberia. A town of stately homes and wide boulevards, New Iberia occupied a strategic location on the edge of both the Attakapas Prairie to the west and the Atchafalaya Basin to the east.

Frank Leslie's Illustrated Newspaper.

stores, ammunition, salt, sabers, oil, and guns, in addition to the cannon once intended for the *Stevens.*

Amid the confusion of evacuation and defeat, Major J. D. Blair of the 2nd Louisiana Cavalry had reached his limit. After drinking a lunch of rum, he declared to his harried soldiers that he was through running and that he would turn and fight the Yankees, even if he had to do it singlehandedly. His comrades, aware of his impaired condition, instead convinced him to race his horse against them to St. Martinville, eight miles to the northeast, and to make his heroic stand there. They probably saved his life. The fifteen thousand soldiers of the Army of the Gulf would have been less charitable.[24]

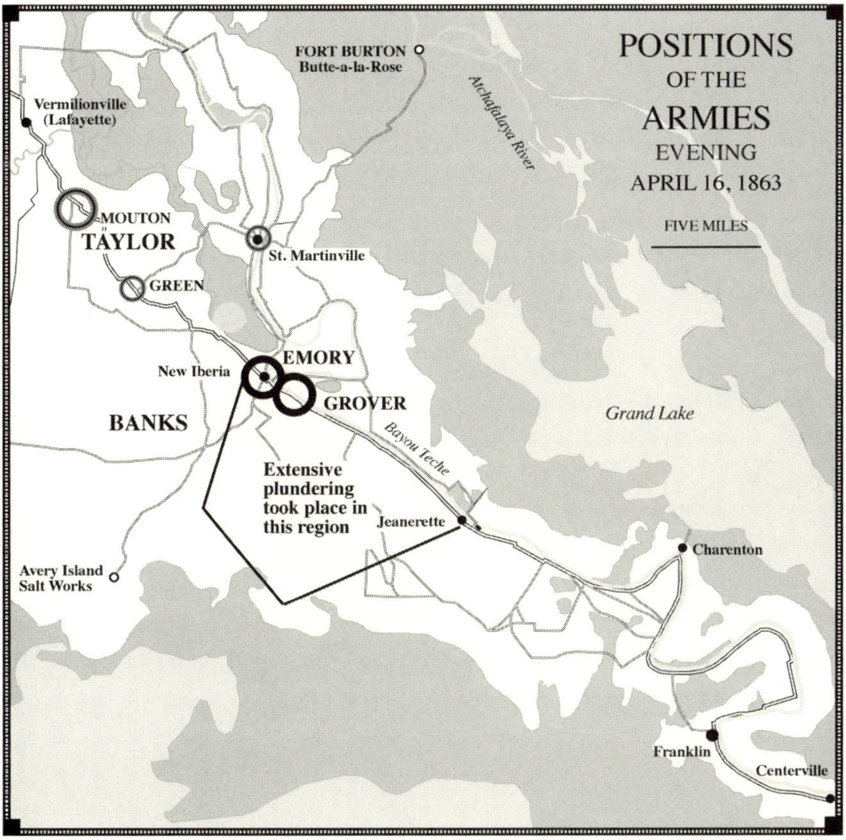

The next morning, April 16, the Confederates continued to evacuate to the north, Green's Texans laid their snares for the pursuing enemy. In one encounter, Captain Benton Bell Seat of Company F, 5th Texas Cavalry, made good use of the topography to once again ambush the Yankee cavalry. While the rest of the army continued northward, Seat positioned his men on the road two miles above New Iberia to begin the day's work. Sunken to six feet below the surrounding countryside, the road curved around an open field then made a hard left-hand turn at its northwestern edge. Seat's troopers moved out of the roadbed and lined the northern bank, dismounted, and sent their horses to the rear. "We had just taken our position when here they came, in full tilt, with banners flying," Seat wrote. "As they came to the corner I gave the orders to fire." The fast-moving Federals reeled in shock from the sudden volley, leaving several of their dead in the road as they retreated. Major Robinson and his Louisianans and Rhode Islanders routed several hundred yards back toward New Iberia.[25]

Captain Seat knew exactly what to do next. Instead of pursuing the Yankees, he ordered his men to mount as rapidly as possible and to leapfrog past Green's next position, using the temporary respite from pursuit to escape. "After mounting my horse, I gave him the spurs," he wrote. "He jumped down into the road, but he fell and threw me ten or fifteen feet away over his head." The stunned captain was now the closest Confederate to the agitated Yankee army, and as he regained his wits, he watched helplessly as his horse sped away toward enemy lines. "I turned and started to follow the company on foot," he wrote.[26]

As he trotted after his men, he had an unexpected encounter. "I had gone but a short distance when a tall Yankee emerged from the bushes on the right of the road," Seat recalled. The Texan made a prisoner of the unarmed Federal, urging him toward Confederate lines with his pistol. When Seat climbed the road bank to see if he could get his bearings, a soldier from his company, who had become confused in the skirmish, happened along. Seat mounted

Captain James Henry Tevis lived near El Paso, Texas, at the outbreak of the war and joined the Confederate army as part of the San Elizario Spy Company as a private. He took a lieutenant's commission in Company A, Arizona Battalion, and served on Colonel James Reily's mission to Mexico during the New Mexico Campaign. He retreated with the army and now found himself fighting Yankees far from his desert home.

William J. Kelly collection.

behind the man, and together they made their way to safety. "I don't know what became of the prisoner," Seat mused. "He probably went back into the bushes when he found I was not behind him."[27]

On the afternoon of April 16, Major Robinson and his Union cavalry had recovered sufficiently to retrace their movements, speed through New Iberia, and nip again at the Rebel heels. This time they caught Green's retreating Texans unprepared. "Our cavalry made a splendid charge," observed Lieutenant Henry Hill Goodell of the 25th Connecticut, "with bridles hanging loose and sabers drawn, waving, shouting at the top of their lungs, they galloped into the Texicans, hacking them helter-skilter. It was a grand sight and stirred my very blood." Green ordered his troops to face about and, fighting mounted this time, they boldly countercharged although they were at a great disadvantage. The ensuing melee checked the Federal horsemen, but at a price. Captain James Henry Tevis, commander of Company A, Arizona Battalion, reported that he lost more than a dozen men, "cut down by sabers." Green ordered his men to fall back, but he made certain that his officers prepared several more ambushes along his line of retreat so that the enemy would never again gained such an advantage.[28]

The lapse on the part of the Texas cavalry disgusted Captain Florian Cornay. A section of his St. Mary's Cannoneers had been assigned to help Green cover the retreat. "Colonel Green's command halted to quench their thirst," he wrote. Green ordered Cornay to take his two 12-pounder howitzers on up the road, as they had too short a range for rear-guard duty. "I obeyed as directed," he continued, "but when about half a mile in advance a few shots from fire arms were heard." Cornay turned to see what was happening and was quickly swamped by routing Texans. "The Cavalry . . . came on at full speed running over every thing in their way."[29]

The terror spread to the animals pulling his guns. "In this disorderly stampede in a narrow lane it be imagined that horses are easily stampeded, and my artillery horses did." A gunner who fell from one of the jostled limbers was run over and killed. Cornay regained control of his teams and did what he could to rally the Texans. "Myself riding . . . ahead I attempted to stop the stragglers at this point," he continued, "and some 10 or 15 stopped."[30]

The Federal infantry spent April 16 plodding relentlessly on, moving like a blue snake up the Teche. They marched for another twenty miles. "By this time they had learned to keep their places and move steadily without so much lameness and fatigue as at first," proudly proclaimed Dr. Beecher. "In many respects, a body of marching troops is a curiosity. Nowhere else can one see such a peculiar, swinging, shambling gait, as old soldiers always adopt." The officer also found the youthful levity of his young charges to be refreshing. "It is amusing, too, to hear the conversation carried on by different parties as they trudge along," Beecher continued. "Sometimes they get into a loud discussion; now and then they break into a patriotic song; again, they will imitate all manner of domestic or wild animals, thereby calling forth shouts of laughter from their comrades. Occasionally they will ask all kinds of queer questions to such persons as they observe near the road."[31]

After two days of pursuit, Union regiments encountered with greater frequency the flotsam from their defeated foes. More Rebel infantrymen surrendered in ones and twos. "It seemed like meeting old friends to come across the fellows of the Crescent regiment, whom we had encountered six months before at Labadieville or Georgia Landing," De Forest wrote. "They told us that their officers were driving the men on with drawn sabers, or the whole force would have gone to pieces under the exhaustion of the retreat." A few miles shy of New Iberia, the USS *Clifton* reached the limit of its travel as well—the scuttled wreck of the would-be ironclad CSS *Stevens* blocked its way. "The army lost the cooperation of the navy," a Union officer lamented. "The gunboats were unable to accompany them any further, for they found an impassible barrier to the navigation of the Teche."[32]

The fall of New Iberia on the afternoon of April 16 ushered in an orgy of looting and plunder in that picturesque town. Brigadier General William Dwight, upon reflection, felt horrified by the

USS *Clifton* prowling above Franklin. Lieutenant William H. Root of the 75th New York observed "the strangest sight I have seen in a long time was the Clifton plowing her way up the stream, her sides almost touching the bank. The ground is a good deal higher than the stream and [from] a little way off the boat looked like a mammoth machine moving on the surface of the ground."

Nestell Collection, Nimitz Library, U.S. Naval Academy, Annapolis, Maryland.

On the Bayou Tesche by David H. Strother was drawn on an 1857 visit to the region. War now roiled the peaceful waters he sketched.

West Virginia and Regional History Collection, West Virginia University Libraries Accession no.p.95.30.129.

conduct of the U.S. troops. "The scenes of disorder and pillage on these two days' march were disgraceful to civilized war," he spat. "Houses were entered and all in them destroyed in the most wanton manner. Ladies were frightened into delivering their jewels and valuables into the hands of the soldiers by threats of violence toward their husbands. Negro women were ravished in the presence of white women and children." Dwight fumed over army's poor behavior. "These disgusting scenes were due to the want of discipline . . . and to the utter incompetence of regimental officers."[33]

That evening Union hospitals in Brashear City, fifty miles to the southeast, received the products of the last few days' fights. Squads of stretcher bearers unloaded the human wreckage of the fights around Franklin. "Transport came in with about 200 of our own wounded, 14 died on the way down from Franklin," wrote Corporal Rufus Kinsley. His regiment, the 8th Vermont, had left him behind, sick. He now watched the medical wards fill with battlefield casualties. They joined nearly two hundred wounded Confederates who had been brought in from the *Cornie* the day before. "Not a woman in all this city to bring them water, or to make them tea or toast. In fact, no bread, 'no nothing,'" Kinsley reflected. The *Estrella* arrived, tied up at the docks, and offloaded another two hundred Confederate prisoners.[34]

Captain Julius Giesecke of the 4th Texas, who had been captured at Irish Bend, was one of the men who shuffled down the boat's gangplank. He was tired and hungry, having eaten only once since his capture and having been forced to march with the Federal column past Jeanerette before being marched back to Franklin and loaded onto the *Estrella* for transport to Brashear City. He found his captors surprisingly accommodating to defeated Confederate officers. "We met a really nice Yankee Doctor," the relieved German wrote, "who fed us almost all night with crackers, butter, whiskey, and his political views." The patients and prisoners would take the train to New Orleans the next day.[35]

18

Vermilion Bayou

"Fire a few more rounds and then . . . fall back slowly."

Colonel Tom Green
5th Texas Cavalry

After only two days of chasing the Confederates, the most immediate objective of the Federal campaign—the destruction of Major General Richard Taylor's army—seemed assured. Therefore, Major General Nathaniel P. Banks diverted some of his focus to more strategic aims. He divided his army in order to scour all the routes leading out of the road-hub town of New Iberia and detached some of his troops to strip the region of its resources. The Union army was to fan out on a number of roads that led into the interior of southern Louisiana. The next morning, April 17, Brigadier General Godfrey Weitzel's Brigade—with the army's cavalry attached—and most of Brigadier General William H. Emory's Division followed the road along the meandering Bayou Teche northeast to St. Martinville, entering that town behind the band of the 8th Vermont as it played "Yankee Doodle." Most of Weitzel's and Emory's commands then snaked back toward the northwest toward Brigadier General Cuvier Grover's main column on the road to Lafayette.

One of Weitzel's regiments peeled off and continued along Bayou Teche. At St. Martinville, the 173rd New York Infantry, with a dozen of its men mounted and in the lead, took a section of Battery F, 1st U.S. Artillery, and followed the Bayou Teche Road northward in a reconnaissance hunting Taylor's transports. Most pilots believed the Teche was impassable for steamers beyond St. Martinville, but Union troops had yet to discover any of the Confederate vessels. The New Yorkers continued the search, expecting to either find the Confederate paddle wheelers or run out of bayou in the process. After skirmishing with isolated groups of Rebels from the 2nd Louisiana Cavalry, the 173rd New York continued upriver. They reached Breaux Bridge and its famous span

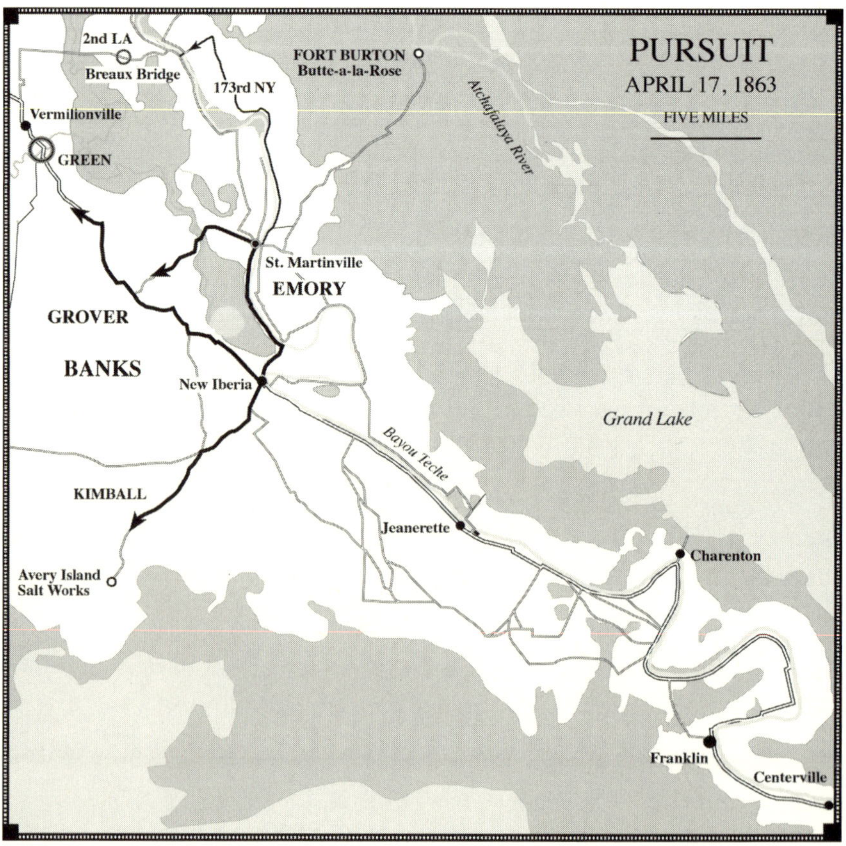

over the Teche too late to save that structure from the flames set by retreating Rebels. This small Federal detachment would cautiously travel north for the next five days on an isolated investigation in an unknown country.[1]

Banks dispatched another column southwest toward the salt works at Avery Island, a dozen miles away. Colonel William K. Kimball of Grover's 2nd Brigade took the 12th Maine, the 41st Massachusetts, a company of the 24th Connecticut, and a section of the 2nd Massachusetts Artillery on a day-long march to capture that valuable strategic prize.

The rest of Grover's men continued to follow Colonel Tom Green and the rest of the retreating Rebel army along the most direct route to Louisiana's interior. This Yankee Division, with the addition of Colonel Oliver P. Gooding's 3rd Brigade of Emory's Division, headed down the road to the crossing of the Vermilion River at Vermilionville (present-day Lafayette), following the most direct path to Opelousas, the capital of Confederate Louisiana. "Our army is rolling like a ball of fire through the finest portions of Louisiana," a Yankee newspaperman crowed. "When the rebels are thoroughly driven out of the Opelousas country, the backbone of the rebellion will be very much broken, so as the State is concerned." Emory and Weitzel would fall in behind Grover where the St. Martinsville Road rejoined the route to Opelousas. But the enemy remained just out of reach. The Union troops had been marching nearly two-dozen miles a day, observing "a great distant dust, showing how close we were to the Rebel flight," wrote Captain John William De Forest. "It is a solemn and menacing phenomenon, the dust of a marching enemy."[2]

There would also be casual violence as the tramping progressed. A soldier from the 53rd Massachusetts, stepping out of the ranks for a drink at a planter's well, lifted the water bucket to his lips but fell backwards, dead. Someone at the house had shot a bullet in his head. The soldier's comrades rushed the building, set it on fire, and watched as the structure burned and its occupants were consumed by the flames. "The man who shot him gave his life for his fool-hardiness," wrote Private Eldon D. Maddocks of the 26th Maine. "The man tried to make his escape from the back part of the house, but the boys fired at him and he did not make his appearance again."[3]

The speed and success of the Federal invasion had blindsided the Confederates. No one among the Southern high command on either side of the Mississippi River could make sense of what was happening. Signals and reports arrived with dizzying speed and often seemed to contradict each other. While the Confederate army tried to save itself in western Louisiana, the Rebels at Vicksburg under Major General Carter Stevenson lay inert, watching as the Federals across the river pushed west and south, and his superior, Lieutenant General John C. Pemberton, could only think about the defense of the state of Mississippi.

The Federals and the great river and beyond had been on the move. Admiral David Dixon Porter had run a dozen warships and transports past the batteries at Vicksburg on April 16. Likewise, Confederate strategists did not know that before the sun had set that evening, Union Colonel Benjamin Grierson left southwest Tennessee and launched a raid that would slash across Mississippi and cut the rest of the overland supply lines to Vicksburg. These moves terrified and confounded Confederates east of the river, adding to their paralysis.

Lieutenant General Edmund Kirby Smith, now keenly aware that Banks had savaged Taylor's army and was headed north, thought he had solved the strategic mystery. His aides scratched out dispatches heading in every direction, asking for reinforcements. Orders called for Major General John H. Walker's Division of Texas infantry to leave Arkansas and make its way south to Monroe. Kirby Smith wanted every spare regiment west of the Sabine sent as well. "It is probably the intention of the Federals to advance upon

Night Passage of Union Boats at Vicksburg. While Banks pushed Taylor's army northward into the heartland of Louisiana, Admiral David Dixon Porter's fleet moved south, down the Mississippi, and past the guns of Vicksburg. This painting by Samuel H. Lockett captures the difficult visibility of that night, with the Union gunboats silhouetted by bonfires on the Louisiana shore.

Courtesy of the collections of the Louisiana State Museum.

Opelousas and Alexandria and occupy Western Louisiana and thus cut off Texas from the rest of the Confederacy," read a message to Major General John Bankhead Magruder in Houston. The forces sent to Louisiana would be "returned . . . as soon as the necessity for their presence here ceases to exist." The great battle for the lower Mississippi River would be fought, he believed, as Union columns converged from the northeast and the south on Alexandria, Louisiana.[4]

The commander of the Confederate Trans-Mississippi demanded cooperation from his counterparts across the river. "The attack on Port Hudson and Vicksburg seems to have been abandoned," Kirby Smith wrote to his superiors in Richmond. "Re-enforcements should be promptly sent to General Taylor from across the Mississippi."

When Kirby Smith's dispatches reached him at his headquarters in Jackson, Mississippi, Lieutenant General Pemberton could not believe what he read. Did Kirby Smith not realize that eleven Union gunboats now controlled the river between Vicksburg and Port Hudson, and that the Federals controlled the west bank between Lake Providence and New Carthage, Louisiana—in force? Not only were Confederate supplies and troops no longer free to cross the Mississippi River, but also communications between Rebels commands remained unreliable. Additionally, Pemberton thought he had troubles of his own. "I have been compelled to withdraw 4,000 troops from Port Hudson," he wrote, "and could not therefore possibly send any forces from that point, severely threatened as it is now." Although the Confederate garrison left behind at the Louisiana stronghold with Brigadier General Franklin Gardner still outnumbered the Federals at Baton Rouge under Major General Christopher Columbus Augur, Pemberton believed his worries took precedence. Any Rebel troops available on the east side of the river would shuttle between the forts, not cross over to the west side.[5]

Another complication kept Pemberton from helping Kirby Smith. When the Confederates had broken the levees opposite Port Hudson to keep the Federals from bypassing the fort to the west, they had flooded the roads. With supreme confidence in Taylor's offensive capabilities, Southerners had used nature to forestall a Union advance east of the Atchafalaya. Now those flooded roads made it impossible for reinforcements from Port Hudson to travel to Opelousas, isolating the Rebel army in western Louisiana, in effect concluding the issue of sending help from east of the Mississippi.

In response to Kirby Smith's request, Pemberton issued demands of his own. He sent a directive insisting that Kirby Smith send all his troops gathering in the Trans-Mississippi against the Grant's Union forces sliding down the west bank of the Father of Waters. Perhaps the Texans and Louisianans could pin the Yankees at New

Carthage. Confederates on each side of the river, it seemed, would fight their own battles—and face their own fates—separately.[6]

The final act of the pursuit of Taylor's army would be played throughout the day of April 17. Before morning light the Confederate wagons and infantry trudged ahead and crossed Bayou Vermilion. They entered the town of Vermilionville at sunrise. Major Silas T. Grisamore discovered "the excited inhabitants in great confusion and consternation at the near approach of the enemy." The weary column pushed on until they reached Bayou Carencro, where they would rest for the night.[7]

Behind them, Major Joseph L. Brent, the Rebel chief of artillery, planned to slow the pursuers once again. He deployed a section of 12-pound howitzers from the Pelican Artillery and a 6-pounder from the Val Verde Battery on a wooded bluff overlooking Bayou Vermilion. At the same time, soldiers prepared the Pinhook Bridge for demolition. Because of a slight rise on the prairie opposite the crossing site, the Federals would almost certainly have to be close before discovering the trap.

Green's horsemen, meanwhile, had been carrying out orders to burn and destroy any valuable commodities in the region ahead of Banks and his horde. Columns of smoke from burning cotton bales, wagons, and other items that would have been useful or precious to the enemy marked the grim success of that mission. A Boston correspondent with the Union army described the destruction: "Last night in the distant horizon were numerous fires made of the late king [cotton]: the martyred monarch's funeral pyres."[8]

The raid up Bayou Teche had clearly routed the enemy and discredited the Confederacy among the inhabitants of the region. The success of the campaign made Banks and his staff giddy. The Union army had injured Taylor's command, perhaps mortally. Why not conquer this territory and hold it? Vicksburg and Port Hudson might now be irrelevant. "The General was in a high gale, swore he would hold the country and push on to Alexandria," offered Colonel Strother. "I urged it strongly." The belief among these officers was that Grant might be convinced to move away from Vicksburg for a moment and meet them in Alexandria—as Kirby Smith suspected. The junction of the two great Union armies would then doom the cause of secession west of the Mississippi. "I think Louisiana is settled for the war," Strother concluded. [9]

Banks and his staff officers moved into a plantation home on the broad prairie between St. Martinville and Vermilionville within easy sight of the passing blue army in the distance. "Our guard went immediately to work and the premises resounded with the outcries of pigs, sheep, and poultry." While his troopers cooked, Banks and his officers bathed in a nearby stream. "This refreshed us wonderfully and the Major General ran and rampaged up and down the green banks of the water in Adam's costume," Strother observed, "jumping like a young colt." Only a rider bearing dispatches from General Grover, reporting a likely fight ahead at Bayou Vermilion, interrupted the naked revelry.[10]

The Confederates were making yet another stand. When the vanguard of Grover's Division appeared in the distance, Rebel riders galloped out to gather in Green's troopers and move them across Bayou Vermilion and into position to contest the Federal crossing. "Came near being cut-off at Pinhook Bridge," Private William Randolph Howell of the 5th Texas Cavalry wrote, "but succeeded in getting across and . . . we take up positions to fight like the mischief until dark."[11]

Major Brent had crafted a cleaver ruse to bait his trap. A column of thirty wagons heading for the bridge lured the Yankees onward. A dozen men of the 6th New York Infantry, mounted as scouts, managed to cut out three wagons, but the balance escaped across the bridge, followed by a few Yankee cannon balls. Grover had no cavalry near him, and as a result, none of the Federals could follow the wagons into Brent's killing zone. Instead, at two o'clock that afternoon, the head of the Federal column arrived and deployed into line of battle, unsettled by the look of things ahead.

As the Yankees watched, the last of the mounted Texans clattered across the Pinhook Bridge before it exploded into a smoky, turpentine bonfire. "A detail . . . had saturated the bridge and built a fire on the opposite bank," wrote Private Felix Robert Collard of

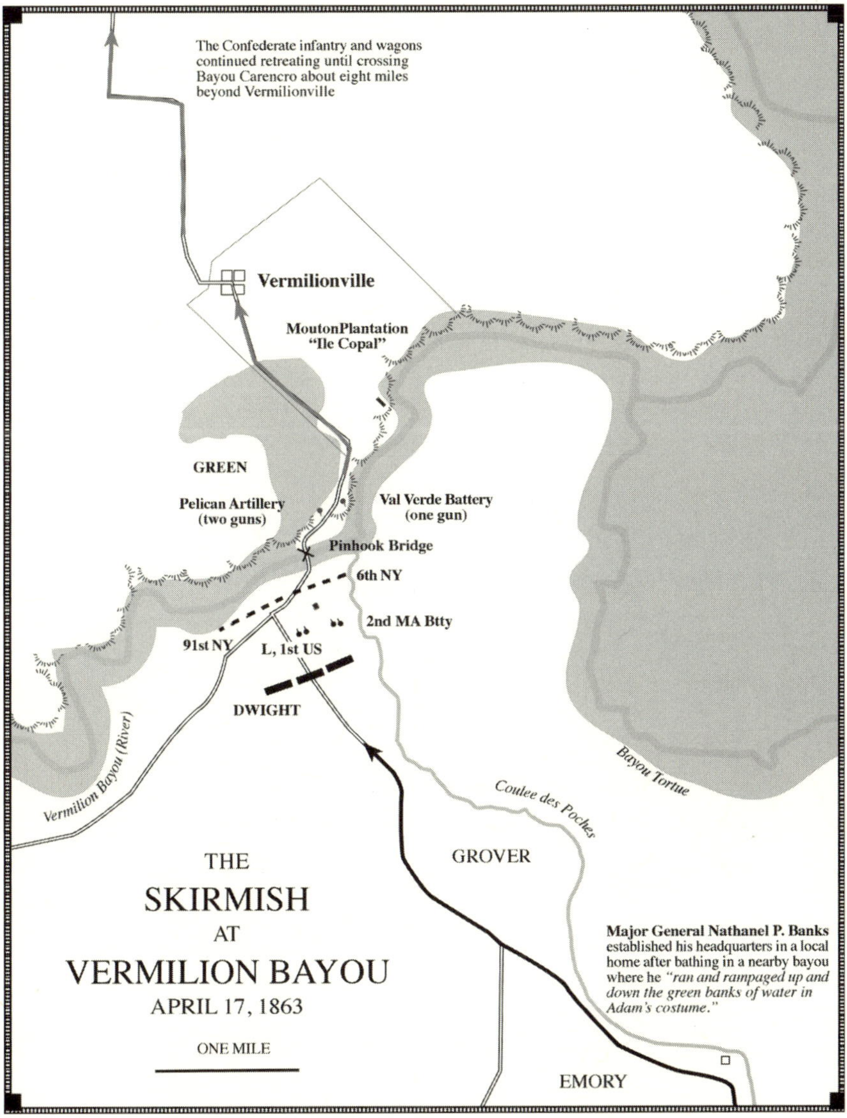

the 7th Texas. "When the cavalry crossed, this detail threw the fire on the bridge with long handled shovels. The flames shot up thirty feet high."[12]

The Confederate guns began their work at predetermined ranges and sites. One 12-pounder round slaughtered the wheel horses of a Union limber, and others skipped in amongst the infantry. "There was an old shanty out on the prairie some five hundred yards from the bayou," observed Collard. "On this, one piece loaded with a shell with fuse attached was trained. When the infantry came up the artillery treated them with a dose of grape." The Union troops took cover in and behind the presited building. "Then the shell dropped through the roof and exploded, setting the shanty on fire," Collard continued. "The enemy backed off." Grover ordered the

General Dwight at Vermilionville. A heroic painting showing General William Dwight advancing skirmishers to the banks of Bayou Vermilion. A dead Confederate lies in the foreground, a scruffy corpse compared to the fresh-faced youngsters of the Union army.

James E. Taylor, artist, in Rossiter Johnson, Campfires and Battlefields: An Illustrated History of the Campaigns and Conflicts of the Great Civil War *(New York: Bryan, Taylor and Company, 1894).*

6th and 91st New York Regiments of Brigadier General William Dwight's 1st Brigade to move forward as skirmishers while the rest of his infantry fell back. He then ordered his two artillery batteries to unlimber and return fire at a range of just under a mile.[13]

Unable to cross the bayou, the Federals contented themselves with shelling the Texans' position while their skirmishers traded bullets with the concealed Texans. The bombardment caused some anxiety for the Rebels. "Orders were that I should remain there until I was satisfied that the bridge was destroyed," wrote Lieutenant William Smith of the Val Verde Battery. "Soon after Col. Thomas Green of the 5th Tex. Mounted Vols., passing by, instructed me that so soon as the bridge was destroyed, and should the enemy press me too hard . . . to use my discretion in falling back a short distance, but to await further orders after so doing." As the shelling intensified, Smith rode to consult with nearby officers of the Pelican Battery and to report his instructions.[14]

Battle of Vermilionville. Artist James E. Taylor depicts the Union battle line fully engaged against Confederates on rising ground across the bayou. Notice the bridge is engulfed in flames and billowing smoke.

James E. Taylor, artist, in Rossiter Johnson, Campfires and Battlefields: An Illustrated History of the Campaigns and Conflicts of the Great Civil War *(New York: Bryan, Taylor and Company, 1894).*

When he returned to his guns, Smith found that the troops near him had already made up their minds, mounted up, and ridden off. "Finding my support from both right and left gone, and out of sight, with the enemy's sharpshooters bearing immediately on me from the front," he sent a sergeant to find Green and "report my situation and to know what I was to do." The colonel ordered Smith "to fire a few more rounds and then to fall back slowly."

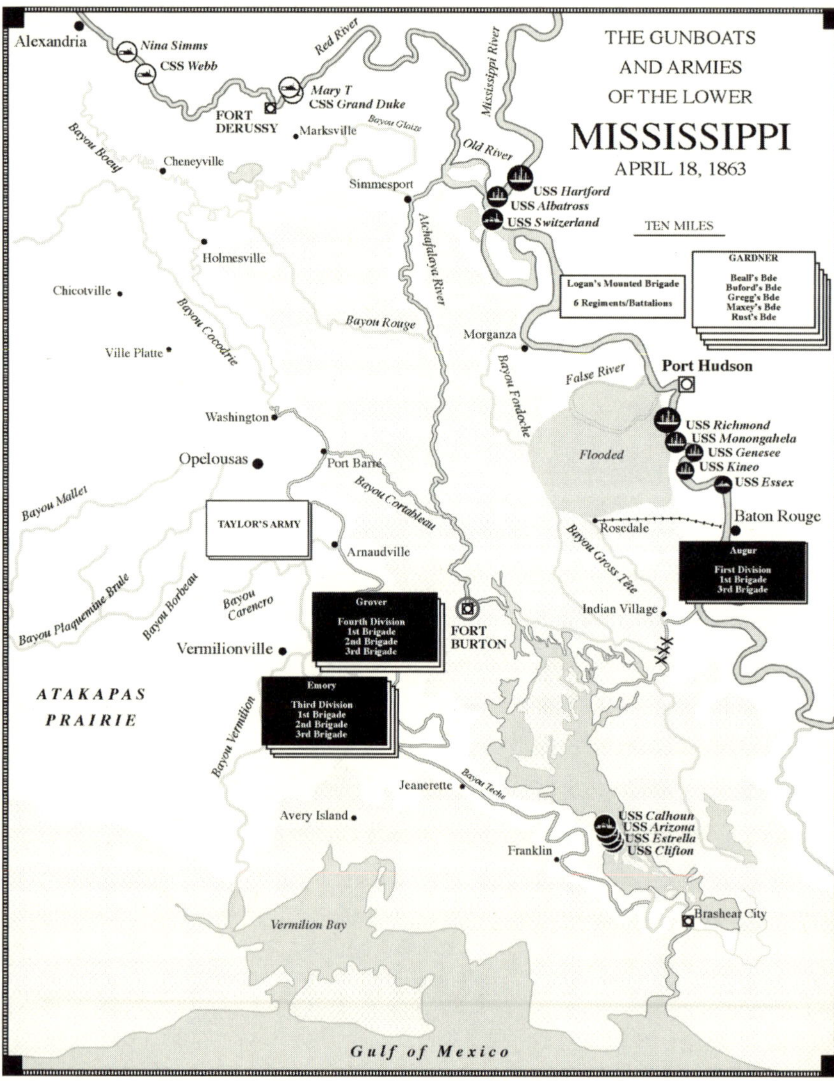

That was all Smith needed to hear. He ordered his guns out of action, and would have done so slowly, "except the fact that my leading driver . . . took up the trot and possibly the gallop." Green's and Brent's rear-guard efforts had finally stalled the Union advance; Banks and his army would not get across the Vermilion for another twenty-four hours.[15]

This was just the respite the Rebels needed after the constant dodging during the retreat. The day after the fight at Vermilion Bayou, the brigade remained in camp and received rations, their first in forty hours. Everyone was exhausted. "For five long days and nights our saddles were not removed from our horses," wrote Howell. "What sleeping was done was in the saddle; what cooking that was done was done for us by the noble and patriotic citizens, and what eating the boys did was done on the go." For one homesick German teenager in the 7th Texas, soldiering had lost all its charm. "This life is quite tiresome and the only pleasure I have is thinking of home," he scrawled in a letter to a friend. "You wrote that I might be home when the peaches ripen, but I believe the peaches will ripen a number of times before we get home."[16]

Although Banks did not realize it at the time, Taylor's army could now recover and fight again. The Confederate wagons and infantry, now safely beyond the range of the Federals, would not stop moving until reaching the town of Lecompte, twenty miles from Alexandria and eighty miles from danger. Green had given Taylor the time he had needed, and the general appreciated Green's success. "To his zeal, vigilance, and daring the extrication of our little army from its perilous position is indebted to a great extent," Taylor wrote. "In truth, he was the Ney of our retreat, and the shield and buckler of our little army."[17]

19

Limping to Victory

Oh, the horrors of marching on blistered feet."

Captain John William De Forest
12th Connecticut Infantryt

Although the Rebel wagons and the remnants of Major General Richard Taylor's army had passed beyond Yankee reach, Southern towns, farms, livestock, slaves, and cotton all remained. Major General Nathaniel P. Banks and his army would now rest and gather the spoils earned by the week-long hardship. Most of the Federal forces in southern Louisiana had been marching and fighting for more than a week, and many in the Army of the Gulf secretly thanked the Confederates for torching the bridge over Bayou Vermilion and turning Saturday, April 18, into a day of rest. The soldiers bivouacked on the prairies and lined the banks of the bayou to perform ablutions in its waters. "The boys eagerly embraced the opportunity to bathe themselves, and wash their underclothes in the bayou," remembered Dr. Harris Beecher of the 114th New York. "The heat of the past few days, which had been intense, caused the most copious perspiration, which, mingled with the flying dust, had been productive of the greatest uncleanliness." As the mixed grime of gunpowder, dirt, and sweat drifted with the current, the army symbolically purged itself of the pursuit of

Taylor's army. "Safely, kindly, has God brought us on our way," noted Private James Albert Osborne, enjoying his rest with his comrades in Company C, 38th Massachusetts. "Let us be thankful for his mercies."[1]

Many tasks remained. More than a dozen miles to the east of Banks, his army, and its large encampment, Union scouts continued to attempt to solve the mystery of Taylor's missing transports. Major Powers Gallway and his 173rd New York Infantry carried on with their push up Bayou Teche, snooping around for Rebel steamers.

Banks peeled off another regiment, the 114th New York, sending it back down the road toward Brashear City to scour the Teche region for horses, mules, cattle, wagons, cotton, sugar, and molasses. They were to drive their captures southward, all the way to Berwick Bay. "We bid *adieu* to our comrades," lamented Lieutenant Elias P. Pellet. "They to move up the country, perhaps to win victories and laurels; we to become cattle drivers and government horse-gobblers." They were also to escort slaves attached to the army into Union lines.[2]

More than one hundred miles to the south, at the burgeoning Federal base at Brashear City, Corporal Rufus Kinsley of the 8th Vermont got a close view of the men his comrades had captured during the great pursuit as additional gangs of sullen prisoners disembarked from a steamer. Of the nearly three hundred enemy soldiers, "not more than fifteen in the whole number dressed in uniform," Kinsley wrote. "Many have women's blankets, shawls, petticoats, and calico bed quilts rigged into coats," he sneered. "Some have hats, many none. One would think they had been robbing negro quarters . . . and had come out as escort to the Calathumpians." Additional clusters of defeated Rebels would almost daily at Brashear City over the course of the week.[3]

The navy did not rest on April 18. Tied up at the docks was the reassembled Federal gunboat flotilla—the *Arizona, Calhoun,*

Estrella, and *Clifton*—in preparation for a new expedition up the Atchafalaya River under Lieutenant Commander Augustus Paul Cooke. Garrison commanders had promised the men of the 16th New Hampshire that they would enjoy a leisurely time of garrison duty at Brashear City; instead, they found themselves relieved by the 4th Massachusetts, fresh from occupying Franklin. Stunned

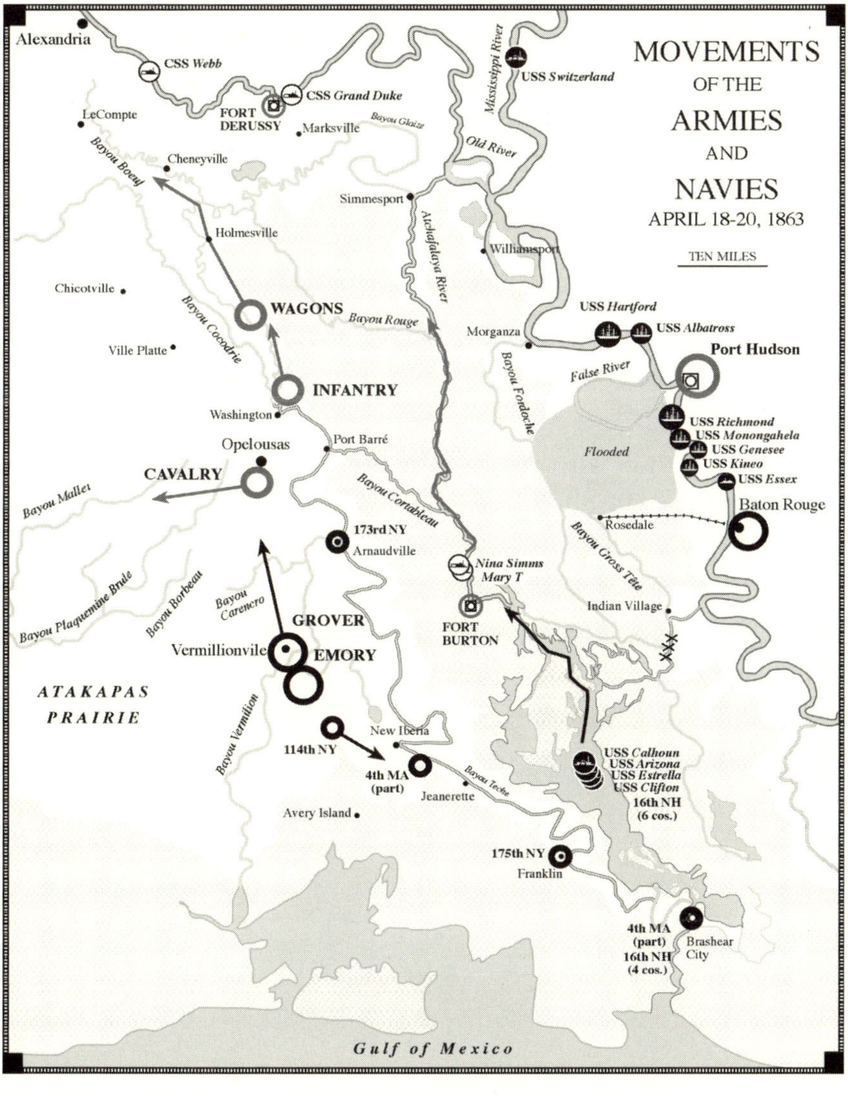

by the change in orders, six companies of the New Hampshire men broke into squads and loaded onto the steamers that same Saturday, equipped with one day's rations and one hundred rounds. The vessels splashed away from the docks late in the day and proceeded into Grand Lake for a specific mission. The Granite State troops were to keep watch against snipers on shore while the steamers made way for Fort Burton at Butte-a-la-Rose.[4]

The Yankees turned their attention toward the Rebel obstacle and the Southern gunboats they knew it sheltered. Once Commodore Cooke neutralized this last position, the way would be open to navigate to the head of the Atchafalaya, and from their by way of the mouth of the Red River to the Mississippi. He also understood that the Confederates had proven themselves daring and resourceful even with inferior equipment, and he took appropriate precautions. That night, halfway to the Rebel fort, he ordered his vessel, the *Estrella,* to drop its anchor. The other gunboats tied onto the *Estrella* with hemp hawsers. Should the Confederates try a night raid, the *Arizona, Calhoun,* and *Clifton* could slip their lines and be ready for action. To hide the flotilla as best he could, Cooke ordered that all lamps be extinguished or shaded. Dark and silent, the Union boats waited in the deep gloom of the Atchafalaya swamp, ready to surprise the Rebels should they come. They did not. Instead a loud, flashy thunderstorm rolled in, lashing southern Louisiana with a stinging rain.

On the morning of Sunday, April 19, the Union invasion continued along three lines. One column, Gallway's New Yorkers, tramped up the course of Bayou Teche; Cooke's naval flotilla renewed its ascent up the Atchafalaya. The main portion of Banks's army crossed the bayou on their newly built bridge at Vermilionville (present-day Lafayette) or used a ford upstream. "We formed our line at six o'clock and moved off," wrote Lieutenant Colonel Willoughby Babcock, commanding the 75th New York, "while Nims' Battery fired a salute in commemoration of the battle of

Lexington in the old time and the shedding of Massachusetts blood in the new."[5]

At Vermilionville the terrain changed dramatically from the swampy lowlands and expansive prairies they had just traversed. "We encountered, for the first time in the state, hills of respectable height," one soldier wrote. "It was pleasant to gallop up a hill after four months traveling over perfectly level ground. The country would hardly be called hilly in New England, but rolling, [with] fine light soil, plenty of timber and an occasional spring."[6]

Early that morning the troops entered the town, its streets still wet from its drenching the night before, as lighting flashed on the eastern horizon. "We entered and took possession," wrote one Yankee, "and all its hundred secesh and truce flags clinging in the wet to their various staffs [looked] mightily ashamed." Then the searches and confiscations began. In the course of their day Union officers placed the elderly statesman Alexandre Mouton under arrest at his mansion north of Vermilionville. In addition to being a former Louisiana governor and a retired U.S. senator, "this man," wrote a Northern newspaper man, "is one of the most wealthy men in the State, and a great secessionist." He was also the father of Brigadier General Alfred Mouton, the old nemesis of the Army of the Gulf. By the end of the day most of the Union army had proceeded northward on the Attakapas Prairies, crossed the

Governor Alexandre Mouton. A prewar photograph of the governor, senator, and Louisiana secessionist.

National Archives and Records Administration.

waist-high Bayou Carencro, and camped in line of battle within an easy march of Opelousas.[7]

Mouton, under guard, followed the army. "The road was filled with an indiscriminate mass of armed men, on horseback and on foot, with carts, wagons, cannon and caisson rolling along in a most tumultuous manner, while to the right and to the left, joining the mass, and detaching from it, singly and in groups, were hundreds going empty handed and returning laden," he testified. The soldiers gathered all they could carry, and employed nearby slaves, gawking at the spectacle, to aid them in their pillaging. "Disregarding the lanes and pathways, they broke through fields and enclosures, spreading in every direction that promised plunder or attracted their curiosity." Soldiers dragged, prodded, and herded horses, mules, cattle, and oxen "towards this seething torrent," and rejoined their column of march, Mouton continued, "with

Pig Catching. Lieutenant Colonel David Hunter Strother ("Porte Crayon") drew this comical scene of slaves catching a sow and her piglets while mounted figures watch. Notice the "razorback" profile of the hog, not unlike the millions of feral pigs that inhabit Louisiana and Texas today.

West Virginia and Regional History Collection, West Virginia University Libraries Accession no. 95.30.221a.

pigs, sheep, geese, ducks, and chickens swinging from their backs, fluttering, squealing, and quacking."[8]

Banks's rapacious army was limping to a victory purchased not only with blood but also with shoe leather. Most regiments had averaged between sixteen and twenty-four miles a day. After the seventy-five mile race to Vermilionville, Captain John William De Forest of the 12th Connecticut hobbled along like a cripple. He was not alone. "Oh, the horrors of marching on blistered feet," he wrote. "I do not mean a single blister, as big as a pea, but a series of blisters, each as large as a dollar, or, to judge from one's sensations, as large as a cart-wheel. I have had them one under the other, on the heel, behind the heel, on the ball of the foot, on every toe, a network, a labyrinth, an archipelago of agony." The captain compared it to standing on red-hot iron. "In the morning, the whole regiment starts limping, and by noon the best soldiers become nearly mutinous with suffering."[9]

Ile Copal. The country residence of the Mouton family, as painted by Adrien Persac.

State Library of Louisiana.

The exhausted soldiers sought solace wherever they could find it. At first, De Forest observed, the grouchy soldiers begin to fight with each other then grumble against their own officers for forcing them to march at this pace, then they cursed the enemy for not stopping and fighting. "They fling themselves down in the dust, refusing to move a step further," De Forest wrote. "Fevered with fatigue and pain, they are not actually themselves." The prospect of fighting again soon brought some relief. "It was curious to note how cheerful everyone became if cannon in front told of the proximity of the enemy," he added. "We were ready to fight the bloodiest of combats rather than march a mile further. We filed into line of battle delighted, and then resumed our pursuit heartsick." The plodding, stumbling soldiers had marched in pain for about a dozen miles before they camped that night near Bayou Carencro.[10]

To the east, on Bayou Teche, Major Gallway and his New Yorkers made a promising discovery that solved the mystery of the missing enemy transports. At the junction of Bayou Fusilier and Bayou Teche, at the town of Arnaudville, lay the wrecks of the steamers *Darby, Cricket, Blue Hammock,* and *Louise.* Only their smoke stacks and machinery poked above the brown water. The *Uncle Tommy* had met a flaming death a few miles further on; its name was still visible on its scorched siding. Spilled supplies and signs of hurried unloading littered the banks. "I found by the roadside empty musket boxes, and large quantities of shot, salt, some new cavalry sabers, and a few barrels of oil," he reported. Other spoils included a thousand barrels of salt and an equal load of corn. The last of Taylor's Teche fleet, and the hopes it had carried, lay charred and ruined.[11]

Only one major chore remained. In the heart of the Atchafalaya Basin, southeast of Gallway's New Yorkers, all that continued to deny free passage to a Union advance was Butte-a-la-Rose. Once they controlled that position and the fort on its banks, Yankee warships and supply vessels could move unmolested from the mouth of the Red River to Brashear City and beyond. For Commodore Cooke, closing the last few miles to his target proved troublesome due to low water and torturous navigation. About sixteen miles south this Rebel redoubt, Captain Luther Townsend of the 16th New Hampshire lamented his unexpected and tedious riverine duty. The view from the gunwales of the USS *Arizona* did little to cheer him. "The scenery along the margins of that bayou, as had been that along the shores of Grand Lake and other bayous the day before, was monotonous and uninspiring," he moaned. "The heavy foliage of the trees, the immense growth of moss, the dense undergrowth of vines, brushwood, and saplings afforded the fittest place in the world for the slimy pathway of moccasin and rattle snakes and for the stealthy creeping of numberless alligators, turtles, and other reptiles, but was a miserable place for men whose birthplace had been on the shores of the transparent streams and lakes and among the granite mountains of New Hampshire."[12]

The naval expedition encountered frequent trouble in the watery maze. The *Clifton,* in the lead, hit a tree about mid-morning and fell back in the column for repairs. The *Arizona* pushed ahead to scout the enemy position and came under fire from Rebel pickets. "These concealed enemies were especially dreaded by both our boys and marines," Townsend wrote. "These swamp devils as the boys called them took their stand behind some huge log or tree or among its branches, fired their deadly rifles and the next moment were in perfect hiding." In one ambush, Confederate bullets killed a gunner and wounded another sailor aboard the *Arizona,* within two miles of Confederate Fort Burton.[13]

The gunboat reversed its engines, glided to a stop, and tied to a tree to wait for the other steamers while its crew watched the banks for signs of Confederate snipers or gunboat foray. After several hours, Cooke and the rest of the flotilla still had not arrived, so the *Arizona* prudently backed down the stream, the boat's bow facing any potential enemy threat, as the soldiers on board peered back toward Butte-a-la-Rose. Distracted by moving in reverse, the pilot smashed the vessel into a tree. Crewmen untangled the *Arizona* from its branches, and the backward journey continued. "At length, in a somewhat dilapidated condition, she reached the remainder of the fleet at the head of Lake Chené," Townsend reported. No Rebel steamers had sallied out against the isolated Union warship, although the *Arizona* might have been easy prey in the narrow passage. Assuming that his enemies had either left the area or were completely cowed, Cooke prepared to go in boldly the next day, April 20. He ordered his gunboats to tie up again for the night. In the morning they would attack.[14]

During the night of April 19, most of the retreating Confederate army had moved on past Bayou Carencro to Bayou Bourbeaux, leaving behind volunteers from the various mounted commands to picket the enemy. One thirty-man detachment received instructions to spread out at thirty-yard intervals and to sidle toward a sluggish stream that flowed into the Carencro, thus anchoring the picket line. Under the light of a bright moon, the group's commander, Lieutenant John Shepherd of Company F, 5th Texas Cavalry, ordered two men to proceed down a road leading to the bayou, about three hundred yards in advance, and to take a position along its banks. "Going down to their stations, feeling certain that the enemy were not yet there, they were paying no attention," wrote Private Bill Davidson of the 5th Texas Cavalry.[15]

When they arrived at their destination, the pair looked to their right and in the silvery moonlight found to their surprise a Union line of battle stretching out into the fields, not fifty yards from them. The two had inadvertently ridden within hailing distance of the right of a regimental front. "The Yanks yelled 'Halt,'" remembered Davidson. Instead, the pair turned their horses and galloped back up the road. "They halted at the rate of two hundred miles an hour, right down that lane, and the Yankee bullets playing Dixie and Yankee Doodle both around their ears." The two pushed their mounts until one of the men jumped from his horse, hoping to provide less of a target. His companion bravely reined in his horse and convinced his comrade to remount. The pair of Rebels made it back to their detachment.[16]

The firing precipitated a night skirmish. The rest of the Confederate detachment moved in to fire at the Federal muzzle flashes in the far distance. "We would fire and fall back, and fire again," Davidson recalled. "We kept this up for about an hour." The shooting attracted more Confederates. Major Hannibal Honestus Boone arrived with the bulk of the 13th Texas Cavalry Battalion and took up the long-range harassment. "We left Boone there, and went to camp and went to sleep," Davidson wrote. "Boone nursed them all night and kept them quiet."[17]

At daybreak, Union captain Henry F. Williamson led his Company A, 1st Louisiana Cavalry, ahead of the army to renew contact with the Confederates, skirmishing all the while. "Our cavalry was itching for a charge," wrote Lieutenant George H. Hepworth, the chaplain who was along as an observer, "but it was concluded best not to risk anything." The Federal horsemen cautiously entered a patch of trees south of Opelousas; the Texans waited in a ditch within the woods. "Whiz, whiz, came the bullets singing around our heads," Hepworth wrote. A freedman guide and another trooper toppled from their saddles. The Massachusetts chaplain rode to where the men lay dead and watched as the soldier's more fortunate comrades passed by. "One in a while, I noticed a look of pity," he noted, "but generally the impulse to gaze was only curiosity."[18]

The conversation of two troopers especially fascinated the officer. Watching the Texans ride away in the distance, one soldier called out, "Look, Tom! There's one covey gone," then, turning to the corpse, yelled, "Say, they hit him right in the chops, didn't they?"[19]

The Texans had gone, this time for good. This unremarkable ambush would end the campaign for General Henry Hopkins Sibley's Texans. Colonel Tom Green, his rear-guard work completed, led most of these mounted troops to the west across the open prairies of the Attakapas country and toward the Sabine River and Texas, more than one hundred miles away. The troops were heading to Niblett's Bluff to rebuild their command, gather together wayward Texans who had scattered during the retreat, and join up with reinforcements from Houston. Green also needed supplies.

Taylor gave these departing Lone Star Rebels mixed marks. "From Sibley's Brigade . . . a very considerable number have straggled off and returned to their homes in Texas," he reported. "While those who participated in the engagements and the constant fighting on the retreat behaved with distinguished gallantry, it is to be regretted that a great lack of discipline pervades the brigade, which it is to be hoped will be corrected and the excellent material rendered of more efficient service to our cause." General Mouton went as well to oversee the regeneration of that part of the Confederate army. Major Boone stayed behind with his command, leading Colonel Edwin Waller's Battalion north past Opelousas to stay ahead of the enemy's advance and to report his movements to Taylor.[20]

In the warm morning haze of Monday, April 20, the Union horse soldiers in advance of the Army of the Gulf watched the Confederate horsemen leave. After passing Bayou Carencro, wrote one Northerner, "Our cavalry . . . saw, in the distance about 1500 of the enemy making rapid strides on fine horses, for their fatherland—Texas. I watched with much interest and regret their long column as it filed away to the South West, wondering if we were ever to catch them."[21]

Banks needed cavalry badly if he would ever counter the Confederate advantage in mobility. He could not be certain where Taylor's army had gone, and the disappearance of the Texas cavalry to the west made him nervous. With few horse soldiers of his own—250 men at best—he ordered the 4th Wisconsin mounted on captured mules and horses confiscated during the march from Franklin. The 41st Massachusetts quit the pedestrian life as well; Banks directed Lieutenant Solon A. Perkins's company of Massachusetts cavalry to merge with that regiment, and promoted him to captain. Meanwhile soldiers gathered a wide variety of Creole horses, prairie ponies, and farm mules to serve as their war-chargers. These two regiments, along with the two companies of the 1st Louisiana Cavalry and the remnants of the unruly 2nd Rhode Island Cavalry, would give him a small brigade of horse soldiers.[22]

Twenty five miles to the east that same morning, Commander Cooke launched his assault on Fort Burton at Butte-a-la-Rose. He ordered the *Arizona* and the *Clifton* to lead the way. Marine private Henry O. Gusley understood what was at stake—if this fort fell, the Atchafalaya would be open to the Red River. "The rebel stronghold," he wrote in his journal, "was a place of vast importance to the rebels at Port Hudson and Vicksburg." The soldiers and sailors of the expedition believed the Confederates would strongly contest their column. "Everybody then was in a state of expectancy," Townsend recalled. As the enemy fort came into view through the heavy woods, Union sailors and soldiers saw the shapes of two enemy gunboats hovering near the fort. "The guns of the fort and those of the two Confederate boats were trained on our slowly advancing fleet. We moved cautiously for no one knew but the Confederates had placed in the bayou dangerous obstructions and explosives." At 10:00 AM, when the *Clifton* came around the bend and at last had a clear shot at the Rebel redoubt, the gunners serving its 100-pounder Parrot on the bow sent a round screaming over Fort Burton's ramparts. Then all four of the vessels increased their steam and began their dash.[23]

The Confederates let fly when the Yankees came into range. The Louisianans behind the fort's 32-pounders and 24-pounders were deadly accurate. "The contrabands had told us correctly that 'De Loozy-anna Tigers in de fote done practice at de target off de p'int until dey can hit him in de bull's eye,'" wrote Acting Third Assistant Engineer George W. Baird aboard the *Calhoun.* "Sure enough, the *Clifton* and *Calhoun* were struck several times." Nevertheless, the Rebels were clearly outmatched, and they watched their gunboats give up the fight. The *Nina Simms* headed upstream to safety, and the *Mary T.* followed, abandoning Fort Burton to the onrushing enemy.[24]

The Federal gunboats fanned out. The *Arizona* closed on the fort, while the *Clifton* ran after the fleeing Confederate steamers. Sailors ran out broadside guns and swept the woods on the water's edge with grape shot on the chance that Southern riflemen might be waiting in ambush. Sailors and soldiers aboard the *Mary T.* fought

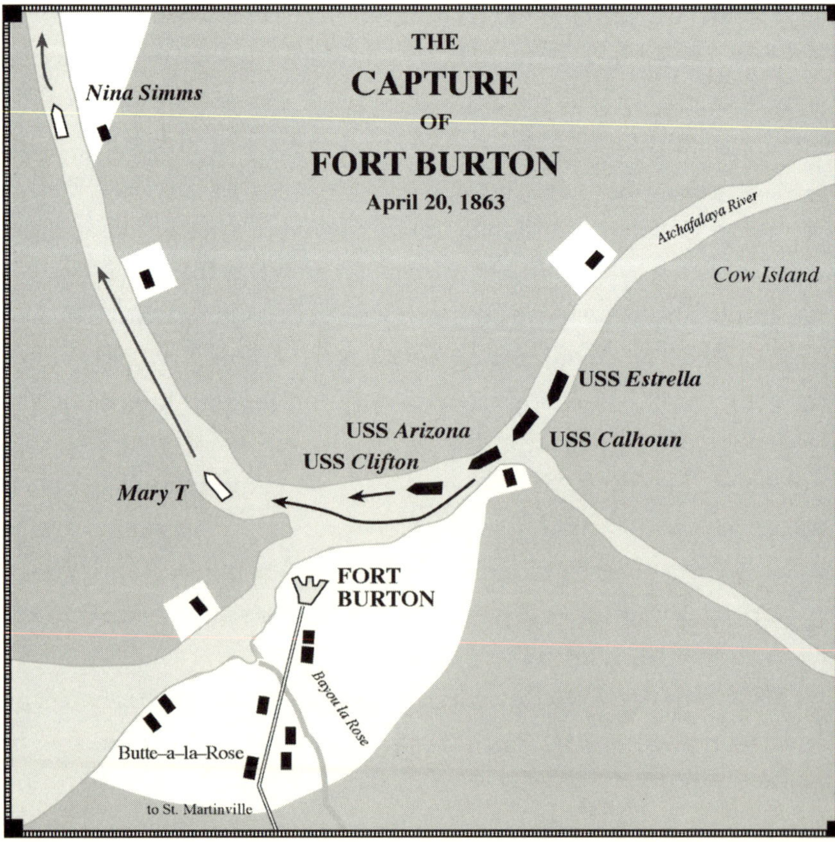

back against their pursuers from the stern, "but owing to a defective primer," wrote Lieutenant Edward T. King, "we only got one shot." It turned out to be a lucky one, careening off the walking beam of the *Clifton,* through the gunboat's wheelhouse and into the water, causing the vessel to temporarily lose power. The *Mary T.* steamed away, leaving behind its ship's boat, which had fallen off its davits. The *Arizona,* having sprinted past the Confederate fort, took up the chase on behalf of the wounded *Clifton.* The *Calhoun* and *Estrella* meanwhile blew blasts of grapeshot over the heads of the gunners in the fort. The onslaught convinced the Confederate defenders to raise the white flag. "The fight was short, sharp, and decisive," wrote Baird. "It was done after the style of Daddy Farragut; we rush in."[25]

For all the noise and excitement, Fort Burton yielded little reward. The Federals captured four guns and sixty men: Company E of the 24th Crescent Regiment under the command of Captain Eugene H. Holms of New Orleans. "They were well-dressed, neat, polite, and educated young men," Baird recorded. "The Tigers said the ships looked most formidable and appeared as if they would run right over or through the fort. We rushed right up to it and the four black vessels, all firing, made a savage appearance." The entire battle had cost Cooke two sailors killed and two others wounded. As the men of the 16th New Hampshire filed off the gunboats to garrison the fort, the Rebel captain remarked prophetically, "You are doubtless glad to get here, but you will be gladder when you leave."[26]

Upstream, the men aboard the *Mary T.* pushed their vessel in a run for its life. "We retreated up the Atchafalaya for fifteen miles, but fortunately none of their shot struck us and we escaped," Lieutenant King wrote. The paddle wheeler proceeded to Simmesport where another nasty surprise waited. Admiral David G. Farragut was nearby with the USS *Albatross,* USS *Switzerland,* and the USS *Hartford;* he lay anchored just five miles away at the

Battle of Butte-a-la-Rose. USS *Clifton* takes the lead against the CSS *Mary T.*, with USS *Arizona* coming on behind. USS *Calhoun* and the twin-funneled USS *Estrella* give Fort Burton some attention.

Naval Historical Center.

mouth of the Old River where it met the Mississippi. "No escape seemed possible, for we could see the smoke of a boat following us," King confessed. He believed he and his men were trapped between Federal fleets. "We determined to fight as long as possible and if we could not save her, to burn her and take to the woods and make our escape that way."[27]

As the Rebel crew held its breath, the pursuing vessel hove into view. "The boat that had been following us was not a gunboat, but a transport loaded with sugar molasses and rum, "making a run away from Farragut." The *Arizona* had apparently given up the chase. They had but to clear the three vessels ahead to make good their escape. At midnight that night, the men of the *Mary T.* moved up into the Old River, heading for the Red, hoping to slip by Farragut in the darkness. They fears proved unfounded. The *Harford* and *Albatross* had gone on some other errand and were well away in the Mississippi, and the *Switzerland* was gone as well. The *Mary T.* arrived safely at Fort DeRussy the next day and rejoined the *Nina Simms.*[28]

The edgy garrison at Fort DeRussy tried to make sense of their situation. The Texans slated for sharpshooter duty against Union shipping had already been hustled aboard the *Grand Duke* after word arrived that Federal flotillas would soon converge on them from both the Atchafalaya and the Mississippi. Braced for a naval onslaught, the garrison relaxed when they realized the columns of coal smoke coming upriver puffed from the funnels of the escaping *Mary T.* and *Nina Simms.* When other couriers arrived with reports that Banks was advancing toward the Red River, the troops moved off the *Grand Duke* and down the road leading from their fort toward the town of Evergreen, intending to contest any advance from that quarter. The soldiers occupied an earthwork at the bridge over Bayou Des Glaises, knowing their future looked gloomy. Either from an infantry assault from the rear or a naval battering from the river, Fort DeRussy would surely fall.

20

Opelousas

"Let me say that all my ideas on the subject have been changed by my experience in this campaign."

Major General Nathaniel P. Banks
Army of the Gulf

The Southern troops at Fort DeRussy had good reason to feel gloomy. The same day that the U.S. Navy and the 16th New Hampshire captured Butte-a-la-Rose, the Army of the Gulf's infantry left camp near Bayou Carencro and pushed on toward what had been the second capital of Confederate Louisiana. "We at length came in sight of Opelousas," wrote Lieutenant Colonel David Hunter Strother, "a steeple rising out of a grove." The Union cavalry made a dramatic entrance, charging into the town with their sabers drawn. Major General Nathaniel P. Banks and his staff followed closely behind in carefully staged military theater. The mayor approached the Federal cavalcade and surrendered the town on the afternoon of Monday, April 20; the Confederate government had long since fled. "This place in peace contains some 1800 people and for the past year has been the capital of Louisiana, but now that has again flown to Shrevesport on the Red river," heckled one soldier. "Really quite a traveling show." The triumphant infantry bivouacked in the fields south and west of town.[1]

The village of Opelousas presented an international air. A correspondent for the *Boston Morning Journal* wrote, "when our army entered this town, the French tri-color was found floating over a large proportion of the houses here. The original settlers were French, and that language is spoken here most entirely by the natives, many of whom cannot speak or understand English. The claim to French protection against the United States authorities is pleasingly absurd."[2]

Another reporter described what he took to be Rebel duplicity. "From their houses they hang out the white, red and blue of *La Belle France,* thereby indicating neutrality—though half the family may that moment be in the Confederate ranks. Indeed, I saw hardly a family but, on inquiry, I found some member of it was there," he wrote. "If the citizen unfortunately had no French colors to hang out, he would put out a white cloth, thus hoping to modify if not to prevent the destruction of his property and the violation of the females." The soldiers mostly ignored the effort. "Flags did not prevent our men from taking what poultry and fresh meat they wanted."[3]

Although happy to have arrived at this destination, most of the campaign's architects saw little long-term value to the town and its environs. "Opelousas, miles away from everything, in the heart of a vast prairie, presented in itself no object for an invading army," wrote Lieutenant Colonel Richard B. Irwin, assistant adjutant general of the Army of the Gulf. "Even the temptation of a good position was wanting. Banks meant merely to halt there a day or two for rest, and then, if it should be found practicable to obtain the necessary supplies, to push on rapidly to Alexandria, and dispose for the season of Taylor's disordered fragments."[4]

To many soldiers in the ranks, the stop seemed bewildering and the campaign seemed less than brilliant. "Much dissatisfaction prevailed at being so hurried along in pursuit of a foe who appeared to have out-generaled us and rendered nugatory our victories of Franklin, Irish Bend, and Vermilion Bayou," grumbled Captain

Captain Henry Upson served as the chaplain of the 13th Connecticut Infantry. After the Teche Campaign and the fight for Port Hudson, he had seen enough of war and General Nathaniel P. Banks. Upson resigned in July 1863 and returned home to Berlin, Connecticut.

US Army Military History Institute.

Homer B. Sprague of the 13th Connecticut. While on the march to Opelousas, Major General Banks had passed near the regiment and was met by a stony silence. When he had left, the unit's chaplain, Reverend Henry Upson, muttered to those within earshot, "what abominable mismanagement on the part of Banks!" Captain Sprague responded incredulously. "Why, Chaplain, who . . . could have done better?"

Reverend Upson sputtered out a quick answer. "Grover could have done better; Birge could have done better; Warner could have better; you could have done better; I could have done better!"

He turned to an Irish private nearby. "What's your name, boy?" the preacher asked.

"McDonough, your reverence," came the reply.

"Well, McDonough could have done better. Seriously, I'd rather be under McDonough than Banks!"[5]

Even so, some Union observers took pride in the suffering and humiliation they had inflicted upon the secessionist enemy. "Gen. Dick Taylor, son of the ex-President, and a degenerate son too, is getting disheartened," penned a writer for the *Boston Traveler.* "A few days ago he commanded all the country South of the Red River, and an army of 8000 or more of well appointed men. Now, driven from every spot, Sibley with his force gone home altogether, Mouton with his brigade of Louisianans, deserting daily and daily getting more weary, their leader sick and homesick, earnestly asking permission to remain at home with his father, at Vermilionville, that he might be *honorably* captured—this state of things would make any man disheartened." The reporter speculated that Major General Richard Taylor must have second thoughts about his support of the Confederacy. "He, whose father was so greatly honored by his country, and whose flag he had so proudly and successfully unfurled, fought and bled under . . . should sometimes wish he had not been so rash is not strange," the writer sneered. "But pride now keeps him what he is."[6]

The capture of Opelousas was largely symbolic, but a more strategic target lay just down the road. The cavalry continued their clattering advance and soon seized control of Washington, six miles to the north. The picturesque town boasted important steamer landings three miles below the confluence of Bayou Boeuf and Bayou Cocodrie, at the origins of the navigable portion of Bayou Courtableau. Downstream the Courtableau branched off where Bayou Teche and the inland shipping center, Port Barré, sat athwart this important junction of commerce arteries. Beyond that point Bayou Courtableau coursed its way southward for almost another twenty miles before emptying into the Atchafalaya. These three villages formed an almost equilateral triangle, with Opelousas as the southwest point, Washington as the northern point, and Port Barrè as the southeast point. Each side ranged between six and ten miles in length, and a boggy cypress thicket fill the area in the center.

Banks and his staff probably knew about the grumblers among the regiments, and they may have singled out the units that seemed to have the most malcontents. The men of the 13th Connecticut, already nestled for the night in a field near Opelousas, found themselves rousted from their blankets at 10:00 PM to escort a section of Battery C, 2nd U.S. Artillery, to strengthen the position of the horse soldiers up the road at Washington. The groggy soldiers put their shoes back on and continued their hike, not returning to their blankets until the early hours of April 21.[7]

Reminders that Confederate army had dribbled troops in its wake as it fled north abounded, including Private Theophilus Noel. The soldier lay collapsed in a home in Washington, unable to go further, when arriving Federal troops made him a prisoner. Elsewhere, Banks directed his Union doctors to do what they could for the enemy sick, wounded, and dying remaining in area homes. "I believe my life was saved thereby," Noel wrote. One medical officer proved to be a family friend who had visited his home in Seguin, Texas, before the war. "He recognized my name, having visited my folks," Noel remembered. "To him, and to General Banks, I owe all, and no man can accuse me of ever being ungrateful."[8]

The next day, Tuesday, April 21, another expedition headed east from Opelousas to Port Barrè. The soldiers of the 162nd New York, a section from the 1st Maine Battery, and a company from the 2nd Rhode Island Cavalry captured the hamlet on Bayou Courtableau. With it came a surprise: the sternwheel steamer *Ellen.*

Amid the good news pouring into the Union camps, that evening a visitor arrived to see Major General Banks at his headquarters. Lieutenant Joseph T. Tenney, from Colonel Nathan Augustus Monroe Dudley's Brigade of Major General Christopher Columbus Augur's Division at Baton Rouge, came bearing dispatches from Major General Ulysses S. Grant and Admiral David G. Farragut. The admiral's missive reported his complete control of the Mississippi River, the lower reaches of the Red River, and the upper reaches of the Atchafalaya River. The note from Grant, dated March 23, was a reply to Banks's March 13 letter, which had been sent north with Farragut before he had run the Port Hudson batteries. "Thus on either side began a correspondence clearly intended by both commanders to bring about an effective cooperation between the two armies, aided by the combined fleets of Farragut and Porter," Irwin explained. The problem was the time lag between the communications.[9]

Grant believed that the Army of the Gulf was determined to reduce Port Hudson by attacking from Baton Rouge, as had been the case when Banks had written his dispatch. Meanwhile Banks had written that he could not help Grant take Vicksburg until Port Hudson had fallen and that he needed additional troops. What Banks learned on April 21 was that the commander of the Army of the Tennessee had agreed to cooperate, offering to send him Major General John A. McClernand, the 13th Corps, and perhaps a fleet of transports. They would meet him at the junction of the Black River and the Red River on or about May 1. Together they would then turn and crush Port Hudson, and Vicksburg would be rendered irrelevant and would starve without rations from the Trans-Mississippi. That had been the state of matters in late March when Grant had penned his reply.[10]

But the intervening month had changed everything. Banks had bypassed Port Hudson to open communications with Grant via the Atchafalaya, Red, and Mississippi. To do so he had scattered Taylor's army, crushed his fleet, and seized his redoubts. But the great raid had allowed Banks to see Louisiana's potential, and he was growing captivated by it. After overrunning much the state, Banks apparently toyed with the idea of administering the *coup de grace* on the Confederate forces there and conquering Louisiana for the Union.

His thinking balanced on several critical possibilities. Was Port Hudson to remain the primary target of his operations? If so, was Taylor sufficiently chastened, and was his army rendered inert and powerless as a military threat? If Grant sent troops and transports—as it appeared he now would—they would arrive soon and force Banks to make a decision.

If the target remained Port Hudson, Banks would need to have his reinforced army ready to cross the Mississippi within days, allowing Taylor's remnants to escape. Banks had urged Grant to send his spare troops, and promised he would add them to his army then leave the Teche Country and head back to Baton Rouge to launch the siege of Port Hudson. That would simplify supply, transport, and logistical concerns, with beans and bullets coming upriver from New Orleans.

Now, from Opelousas, the strategic situation appeared differently. Banks hedged on the particulars of getting his and Grant's armies working together. "Let me say that all my ideas on the subject have been changed by my experience in this campaign," he wrote, signaling that Port Hudson might be fading as an objective to his Louisiana campaigning.[11]

The next morning, Wednesday, April 22, Banks ordered detachments from his army to shadow the retreating Confederates and try, if possible, to ascertain their intentions and their condition. Lieutenant Colonel Sidney Bean led his five hundred soldiers of the newly mounted 4th Wisconsin, a thirty-man squadron of the 2nd Rhode Island Cavalry, and a section of Battery F, 1st U.S. Artillery, to Plaquemine Brulè about a dozen miles to the southwest to search for the Texas cavalry. Bean reported that the enemy force—maybe as many as two thousand strong—had headed that direction from Bayou Carencro, had never been in Opelousas, and contained no infantry. They were apparently heading west in a hurry after stripping the country of what they could. "There are very few horses, mules, or negroes left," Bean reported, adding later "there is cotton here, but no transportation—no mules, carts, or harness." These Rebels appeared Texas bound and out of the fight for now.[12]

Even as the threat of mounted raiders faded into the distance, Banks's lines of communications improved on land and water. The capture of Port Barrè at last opened a riverine route to his base of supply at Brashear City, one hundred miles to the southeast. The *Cornie,* still under the command of Lieutenant Pickering

Dodge Allen and now armored with cotton bales and guarded by a detachment of the 4th Massachusetts, arrived at the landing on Thursday, April 23, bearing supplies and equipment for the worn-out army. At nearly the same time a wagon train of supplies arrived at Opelousas after traveling overland from New Iberia. "At sight of the white covered wagons winding over the plain, the men gave way to those demonstrations of delight so familiar to all who

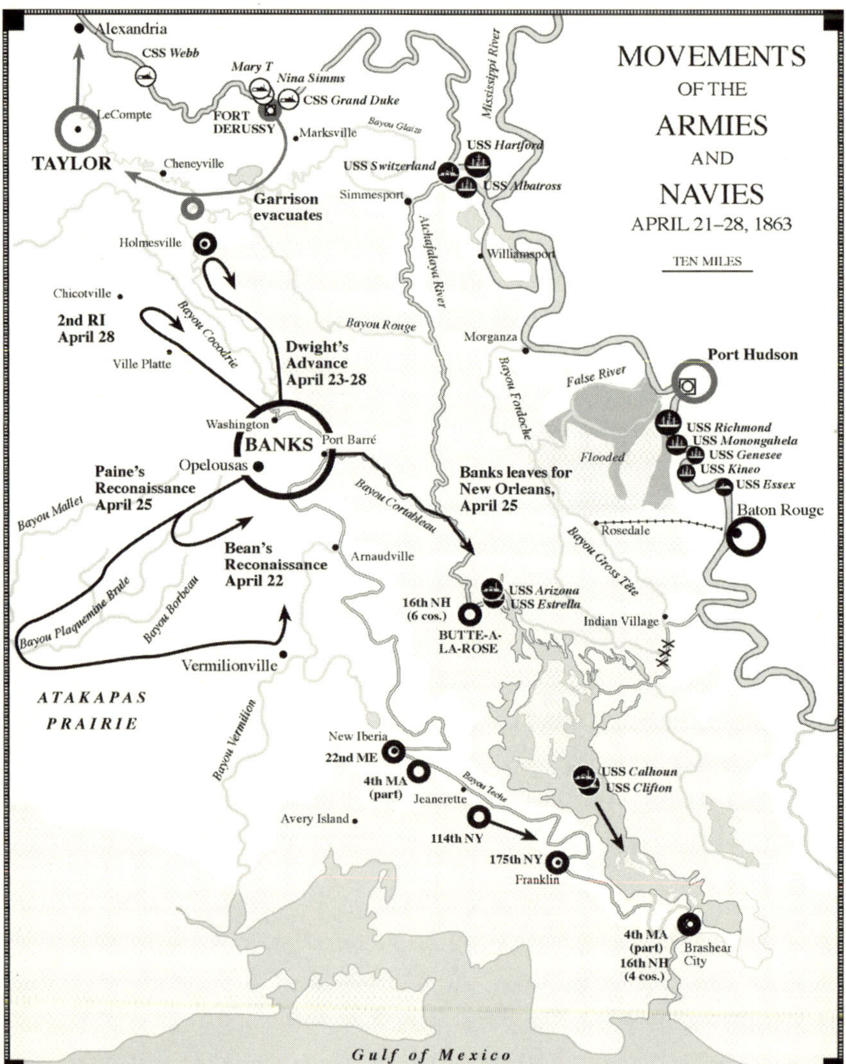

have ever seen soldiers rejoice," wrote Irwin. This train of wagons had moved unmolested across conquered Louisiana. They had been passed along in a relay of Union garrisons, with detachments from the 4th Massachusetts and 16th New Hampshire working the margins of Berwick Bay, troops from the 175th New York at Franklin, and the men of the 22nd Maine at New Iberia.[13]

The army delivery of salt pork and hard tack actually improved morale among the Federals. "For fifteen days they had been subsisting upon an uncertain issue of hard bread, coffee, and salt, eked out by levies . . . upon the countryside. They were sick of chickens and cornbread, and fairly loathed the very sight, to say nothing of the smell, of fresh-killed beef; tough at best, even in the heart of the tenderloin," recorded Irwin. "The flesh had to be eaten with the odor and the warmth of the blood still in it under penalty of finding it fly-blown before the next meal."[14]

The army, now on the mend, could return to the task at hand. In order to be as thorough as possible in harvesting the products and wealth of the region, Banks employed auxiliary foragers from among the local population living in the woods and prairies west of Opelousas. "For more than half a century this country has . . . been the refuge of the idle and depraved who have avoided the haunts of civilization," reported one Confederate official, horrified that these scofflaws had been summoned by Federal authorities. "With the same instincts that lead the vultures to gather around the carcass, these men flocked to General Banks at Opelousas." This area had been notorious for banditry and lawlessness for decades. Quartermasters handed these outriders guns and ammunition, and ordered them to spread out and gather the bounty of their neighbors and haul it in to Federal depots. Mostly they simply robbed and murdered as they saw fit. Banks had, in effect, mobilized dozens of jayhawkers—guerillas, bandits, and thieves—ostensibly working on behalf of the Union. They would plague the region for the rest of the war.[15]

Increased traffic on area roads testified to the success of the army's efforts. The supply wagons heading north toward Opelousas loaded with rations and ammunition, which had caused so much rejoicing in the ranks, passed other trains heading bearing cotton, sugar, and corn and trailing cattle and horses. The 114th New York tramped their way to Berwick Bay escorting one such herd, along with loaded wagons, freedmen in hacks and carts, and other spoils of war. The foragers, under directions from Banks, were to treat the human chattel that had once belonged to southern planters as implements of war, same as livestock. The marks of the recent campaign lay everywhere and showed the army's path. "It is a very easy matter to follow the trail of an army, for the way is well feathered, and skeletons of beeves, sheep and hogs mark its course with unerring fidelity," one Yankee wrote. The aftermath of the campaign along the Teche also carried on the wind. "If the army has been past a few days, the odors from decaying animals will be a sure guide."[16]

The soldiers of the 114th New York, like most of their comrades, had been thorough in their assigned job of gathering livestock. On April 28 the regiment arrived at Berwick Bay driving

Union Foragers. A cloud of plundering "foragers" fanned out from the edges of the Union army, including this mixed bunch of military and civilian scofflaws showing their booty.

Center for Louisiana Studies, University of Louisiana at Lafayette.

three thousand cattle and eight hundred horses before them. A trail of weak and doomed animals marked their progress. "From the prairies beyond New Iberia to Brashear city, the way is so thickly covered with dead and dying cattle, from the immense droves which are daily being driven down in execution of General Bank's order to sweep the whole country through which his army has passed, of cattle, horses, sheep, mules, cotton, corn, and sugar, that the stench is already intolerable," the writer continued, "for the stock is generally very thin and hundreds drop out from fatigue, and fall never to get up."[17]

Other signs abounded that told of Federal successes in the Teche Campaign. Confederate prisoners, by the hundreds, shuffled their way toward Federal pens and captivity. "We passed three droves of prisoners, in all 400; and a dirty ragged, squalid-looking set of fellows too," one Northerner wrote. The correspondent made a distinction between the enemies from the Pelican State and their Lone Star allies. "The Louisianans in Gen. Mouton's command are much better clad, and cleaner than Sibley's Texans, who are a wretched band of marauders," he wrote.[18]

Others noted similar distinction. The local population along Bayou Teche had come to distrust the soldiers from beyond the Sabine River. It was clearly a wedge between allies. "Every person on our line of march with whom I conversed on the subject, complained most bitterly of these Texan robbers," a reporter for a Boston newspaper wrote. "They stole all the planters horses and all the niggers they could, and then, if they had time before our advance came up, they set on fire the cotton and corn sheds, impoverishing and starving not us but the planter and the country. And the country is almost in a starving condition," he added, clearly overlooking the Northern army's contribution to the war-induced famine.[19]

Banks, satisfied with his progress thus far, consolidated his gains while pondering the future. Union troops transformed Washington into the forward base for Banks's army, in case he decided to lead the Army of the Gulf should continue north. Additional soldiers, Brigadier General William Dwight's Brigade of Brigadier General Cuvier Grover's Division, settled into camps around the town while commissary agents and staff officers commandeered its warehouses and homes.[20]

Dwight ordered patrols outside Washington to gather intelligence for the next phase of the campaign. Foot soldiers ascended the west bank of Bayou Courtableau on the bayou road before being hindered by the burned bridges at the confluence of Bayou Cocodrie and Bayou Boeuf. While his soldiers worked on repairing the structures, Dwight's cavalry forded the streams and continued the reconnaissance, blundering into an ambush a few miles down the road and losing two men. It was a small engagement, an affair of outposts. "The cavalry we encountered was a party of the enemy returning to ascertain our movements," he reported. Taylor, too, was planning for the future. "I do not expect to encounter them tomorrow," Dwight assured Irwin. He was wrong.[21]

The Union patrols had unexpectedly encountered the men of Colonel Edwin Waller's Battalion and other stragglers from General Henry Hopkins Sibley's Brigade who had missed the chance to head toward home. After repairing the bridges, Dwight ordered his infantry brigade to cross over and continue the march—a reconnaissance in force—along Bayou Boeuf's east bank, to see what hovered around his army. "I had in front of me during . . . a body of about 500 of the enemy's cavalry," he wrote. "They offered no resistance of any consequence, keeping about 30 or 40 men just out of our reach all the time." Dwight finally called a halt near Holmesville, twenty miles north of Washington, and arranged his brigade to be the advance for the army. He reported that the valley of Bayou Boeuf promised to yield enough supplies and cotton to make an advance worthwhile, as long as water transportation was available to haul it away. The Rebels, including those in his immediate vicinity, appeared to pose little threat. "There is no enemy before us, for that army cannot rally," he wrote with confidence. In addition, freed slaves brought news that the Confederates appeared to be gathering steamers and wagons at Alexandria for a massive evacuation. "The Rebel force is going to the Upper Red River and Texas," Dwight added. Despite the mounted nuisance in the neighborhood, Taylor and the whole Confederate command appeared to be beaten.[22]

Intentional or not, Dwight's advance also sealed the fate of Fort DeRussy. Finding themselves isolated, Confederates there felt certain the next blow would shortly fall on them. The Union brigade at Holmesville could head north toward Alexandria or northeast toward Bayou Des Glaizes and the rear approaches to Fort DeRussy via the hamlets of Evergreen and Mansura. Either route would cut off all overland avenues of retreat for the garrison. Meanwhile, Farragut, the *Hartford, Switzerland,* and the *Albatross* lurked nearby, likely in the Old River or the mouth of the Red River, and might come up at any time. The garrison slipped further into despair, certain Union gunboats and now Dwight's Brigade would pounce upon Taylor's Red River outpost from both the river and from behind.

News from Taylor's army fueled their fears. Private John W. Watkins of Company B, 5th Texas Cavalry, could hardly believe what he heard. Sibley's Brigade had not only been drubbed, losing hundreds of prisoners, but the rest of the army had routed before the enemy. His friends and neighbors, rumors alleged, had also plundered Louisiana farms of their horses to make a more speedy escape. "They have acted most dastardly," he confided to his wife. "They stole every horse they could lay hands on and acted like highwaymen." The 4th Texas came under particular criticism, and Watkins could not believe that this veteran regiment had bolted. "They stood up pretty well the first day, but on the morning of the second day's fight one half of that regiment ran, and some are in Texas now," he fumed. "Texas has always had the name of furnishing brave men, but when men act as some of Reily's regiment have done, I blush to think they are from Texas." Word arrived, too, of Sibley's censure after he "got drunk and was sent to Alexandria under arrest." Watkins concluded that Sibley's Brigade had shamed itself.[23]

Other news provided the abandoned Texans at Fort DeRussy a sliver of hope for the future: Colonel Tom Green now commanded Sibley's Brigade. "He has fought the enemy nearly every day and fell back at night," Watkins scrawled. "General Taylor asked Green to let him take command so that he might rest, but the brave old Colonel replied 'no, I can stand it as long as the enemy can.'" Watkins and his comrades yearned to rejoin their command, but as yet had received no orders from Green to do so. The brigade's officers, meanwhile, had assumed that the men loaned to Fort DeRussy had all been killed or captured. "[Green] would recall us," Watkins lamented, "but [he] is under the impression that we were on the gunboat *Queen of the West*."[24]

From where Watkins stood, the hopes for Confederate Louisiana looked as tenuous as their own. Peering over the makeshift parapets of the works guarding a bridge over the Bayou Des Glaizes, eight miles south of Fort DeRussy, Watkins continued a letter to his wife. "I don't think the enemy will attempt to cross here, they are already above us and we are nearly cut off," he scratched. "Major [Denman] Shannon received orders just now to burn the bridge and defend this place to the last." Nervous gossip rippled up the Rebel picket line as word arrived of an approaching U.S. gunboat, headed for the fort. "I am listening every minute for the guns at the fort to open," he continued. "Our horses are ready saddled and our guns are lying by ready for use. The enemy are reported within twenty miles of us. If they come in reach of us," he continued bravely, "we will give them a warm reception." While this soldier faced an uncertain future, he watched as refugees from the area plantations thronged the roads, eager to escape the Yankees, but like the garrison at DeRussy, uncertain which way to go.[25]

Remarkably, Union indecision kept the blow from falling. Banks remained unsure if he should order Dwight to continue toward Fort DeRussy. Without knowing exactly where Taylor's army had scattered, he remained unwilling to commit to a course of action. The appearance of Texas cavalry to his front might have unnerved him, since he had believed they were routed and retreating toward Texas. Dwight's men along Bayou Boeuf remained ready for the fight. Banks ordered additional patrols to head west and north of Opelousas to get a better handle on enemy whereabouts while he mulled larger strategic issues at his headquarters.

Banks decided to scrutinize his own army and judge its condition for future campaigning. On April 24 the general held a grand review on the open plains outside Opelousas. "The troops, not yet inured to the long and hard marches, were indeed greatly diminished in numbers by the unaccustomed toil and exposure, as well as the casualties of battle and the enervating effects of the climate," mused Lieutenant Colonel Irwin, part of the general staff. "Yet they presented a fine appearance and were in the best of spirits." Banks sized them up. Were they ready for the next phase of the campaign, whatever it might be?[26]

The labors of the last two weeks, he hoped, had seasoned his army. The soldiers, nearly half of whom were New England militia, had been very inexperienced heading into the fights at Fort Bisland and Irish Bend. Now they had been bloodied. Commanders had reconfigured other regiments that were still learning their new roles. The recently mounted 4th Wisconsin, for instance, remained a work in progress. Armed with a long .58-caliber Springfield rifle musket strapped across his back, the Wisconsin soldier look ungainly, as did the regiments' mounts and maneuvers. "When the order to face to the right was given, each man attempted to face to the right on his own ground," Colonel Halbert E. Paine observed.

This was how the infantry executed the move. But horses occupied longer ground, and confusion ensued. "The horses noses and tails got mixed up in inextricable confusion."[27]

That same day, just seventy miles north, Confederate lieutenant general Edmund Kirby Smith ordered the final evacuation of Alexandria and issued his final dispatches from that city. Newly arrived in Louisiana a month before, he was now abandoning the lower stretches of the state to the enemy. He ordered his headquarters moved to Shreveport and all his troops who had been scattered about to join the retreating column heading for Natchitoches. He praised Taylor's success in avoiding disaster but faulted Confederate national leadership and planning with what he believed would be the inevitable loss of the lower Mississippi. "Could General Taylor have drawn upon Port Hudson for reinforcements, or had the troops in East and West Louisiana been under one control," lamented Kirby Smith, "the force at Port Hudson might have been marched across to the Atchafalaya and rapidly transported to the scene of action in time to have defeated General Banks."[28]

The idea merited exploration. Brigadier General Franklin Gardner, who at one time had fourteen thousand men in and around the Confederate fort, faced about half that number under Major General Augur at Baton Rouge. Had some of these Southerners crossed the Mississippi and concentrated with all the troops headed to Louisiana from Arkansas and Texas, Banks would have faced an enemy army similar in size to, or larger, than his own. Even more dramatically, the Confederates would have a sizable force of infantry to his front and a significant force of cavalry on his flanks and rear and, most importantly, across his lines of supply and communications with Brashear City. An imaginative concentration of Rebel armies might have trapped Banks in central Louisiana. Confederate lieutenant general John C. Pemberton, commander of the Department of Mississippi and East Louisiana, instead used Gardner's troops as a reserve to support Vicksburg.

The opportunity, real or imagined, to force a decisive battle in the Trans-Mississippi and keep open the Texas supply lines passed.

Confederate commanders in western Louisiana knew it was time to give up Fort DeRussy. Taylor issued orders for the garrison to dismantle the bastion systematically, saving cannon, ammunition, and supplies. However, the garrison commander, Lieutenant Colonel Aristide Gérard, based on his scouts' information as well as camp rumors, believed the enemy would arrive momentarily. He thought he did not have enough time for a orderly retreat, so he ordered the destruction of the fort and its contents. Rations and ammunition went up in flames, and two of Fort DeRussy's battery of 32-pounders slid into the river while another glowed white hot in a bonfire of discarded gear and equipment.[29]

The soldiers at Fort DeRussy responded enthusiastically to the orders recalling them, and they moved quickly to vacate the premises. The more than one hundred horse marine volunteers from Sibley's Brigade and their allies in the 11th Louisiana Infantry Battalion gladly abandoned the garrison and started toward Alexandria. "Left our wagons and everything but the clothes we had on and one blanket and started for the enemy," Private Watkins wrote. "When we got there we found everything in confusion," he continued. The Yankees, reports claimed, were just twenty miles away from Alexandria. "We were ordered to saddle up and march to meet the enemy. I started with clothes I hadn't changed in a week and you can guess the plight I am in now."[30]

Up the Red River, the city of Alexandria had fallen into chaos. Civilians joined the throng leaving town, among them Richard Taylor's family—his wife, Marie, and their children, Richard, Zach, Louise, and Elizabeth. James Hewitt and his wife, Clarissa, vouched for their safety while their children played together aboard an awaiting steamer. "Accustomed to the gentlest care, my good wife had learned to take action for herself, insisting that she was unwilling to divert the smallest portion of my time from public duty," Taylor wrote. "A moment to say farewell, and she left with our four children, two girls and two boys, all pictures of vigorous health." As the paddle wheeler bearing his family churned the waters of Red River and headed north, Taylor led his troops out of Alexandria.[31]

Unknown to the general, illness stalked the refugee boat convoy heading toward Shreveport. Taylor's boys, Zach and Richard, both contracted scarlet fever shortly after the vessel left Alexandria. "One of the boys showed symptoms," Clarissa Hewitt wrote. "Before it was really known what was the matter with him, he died very suddenly. The younger died this morning."[32]

As General Taylor led his army up the road toward Natchitoches, a galloper arrived with the tragic news. "I was stunned by the intelligence, so unexpected, and it was well perhaps that the absorbing character of my duties left no time for the indulgence of private grief," he lamented. "It was sad to think of the afflicted mother, alone with her dead and dying, deprived of the consolation of my presence." Meanwhile, Marie Taylor thought of the boys' grieving father. "In the midst of her own overwhelming sorrow she is unselfishly thinking of her husband . . . fighting gallantly in defense of our country," Clarissa Hewitt observed. "The two little girls are a great comfort to their mother, as they are very sweet and attractive children."[33]

When Kirby Smith arrived in Shreveport, two hundred miles from the Union foe, he reorganized his headquarters and began planning his next move. He gave new officers their orders and changed the plans for the long-serving officers. Certain the Federals would attempt to clean out Louisiana while they could, he urged on John G. Walker's Division toward Monroe, and beckoned other regiments from Fort Smith, Arkansas, and northeast Texas, and instructed Major General John Bankhead Magruder to move his men from the eastern reaches of his district and rally them at Niblett's Bluff. Kirby Smith prepared himself and the Department of the

Trans-Mississippi for a showdown battle in northwest Louisiana that would determine the fate of the state and perhaps the department.

Refugees swelled into Shreveport. The Hewitts settled in with friends in the town, but James left immediately for Texas, locating property near Kaufman, thirty-five miles east of Dallas, where he could resettle his slaves. While she waited for his return, Clarissa found Shreveport refreshing. "It is a great temptation to linger on here," she wrote. "It is an attractive little city." Every house, it seemed, had boarders like her and her family. "It is hard to realize the dreadful war raging not far from us, the beautiful and happy homes that have been destroyed, the brokenhearted men and women who are in search of safety and peace," Clarissa Hewitt reflected. "God grant that it not last long."[34]

Refugee Family. The war displaced thousands of families, like the one pictured, who loaded up their belongings and tried to stay ahead of the armies.

National Archives and Records Administration.

Julia LeGrand, living in Federal-occupied New Orleans 350 miles away, echoed the sentiment. The war, she believed, unleashed evil forces on the nation. "It makes me miserable . . . to know that in thousands of hearts each day a hate is gathering volume and intensity, which will live, actuate, and work like a living principle," she wrote. "Children inherit what has grown into propensities in their progenitors, and so the wave—the blessed wave of civilization—is forever borne back." She had been an optimist in earlier days. Now, she feared for the future. "Progress seems the universal law," she observed. "I have believed so, hoped so, but we have leaped back, as it seems, thousands of dark and hopeless years." Future Americans, she predicted, would carry on the hostility of a conflict in which they never participated. "The young and vigorous will act upon this hate," she predicted, "it will live and taint the moral mind through generations to come."[35]

Back in Washington, Louisiana, roughly halfway between Shreveport and New Orleans, the chief war-bringer in Louisiana, Nathaniel P. Banks, lost his purpose. The dispatches from Grant he had received a few days before had clouded his thoughts. "To open communication with Grant and to dispose of Taylor had been the chief ends that Banks had proposed to himself in setting out on the campaign," wrote Lieutenant Colonel Irwin. "These ends he now held almost in his hand." Yet the general felt conflicted and unsure of Grant. Would he cooperate in a move against Port Hudson? Unable to decide whether to charge ahead and finish off Taylor or turn east and join up with Grant, Banks instead boarded the *Laurel Hill* at Port Barrè on Saturday night, April 25, and left for New Orleans via the Atchafalaya. Banks bore dispatches for Grant in which he urged him to hurry and send the 13th Army Corps toward Port Hudson. Meanwhile Banks would put into motion the necessary orders to reconcentrate his army at Baton Rouge. He had decided: he was done chasing Taylor.[36]

Banks put Brigadier General William H. Emory in charge of the army and appointed Colonel Thomas E. Chickering of the 41st

Massachusetts as the military governor of Opelousas, leaving them orders to continue stripping the local country of useful produce. "Business has improved in this place for the last two weeks, especially the cotton trade," wrote a Massachusetts soldier. "Cotton has been brought in large quantities from the plantations adjoining, and large numbers of 'loyal' men are waiting around the Provost Marshal's office to obtain receipts for their cotton that has been seized." Black laborers loaded wagons and forwarded the plundered bales to Port Barrè, where others stacked it for loading onto steamers for the trip the Brasher City. "Our officers have brought in about three thousand bales of cotton," the soldier continued, "and large quantities of corn, fodder, sugar and molasses have also been seized. This expedition has been evidently a paying one as Gen. Banks intended it should be, and his calculations are always correct."[37]

New officers in charge returned discipline to the Army of the Gulf. Brigadier General Emory, a regular soldier from antebellum days and a proponent of military discipline, summarized the lawlessness among his troops: "Grave disorders in our rear by bands of robbers, sometimes headed by stragglers from the ranks," he reported from his headquarters at Opelousas, "threatened for a moment to interrupt our communications, and even to disband and disperse into a band of robbers and thieves some of our less disciplined regiments." There were simply too many temptations, and passing out guns to the local banditti had only aggravated the situation. "The inducements for plunder in this country are so great that unless high-handed measures are taken many men will be lost to the ranks on the day of battle." Emory issued the necessary orders to curb the depredations.[38]

Squads of U.S. troops began to patrol the area, rounding up criminals, while others answered orders for execution details. "The orders that have been issued lately in regard to foraging and pillage are very stringent, death being the penalty for disobedience of orders," wrote one Yankee. On April 25 a firing squad executed the first transgressor when they shot a soldier from the 131st

New York, Dwight's Brigade. Others would follow. "Three men belonging to the 2d R. I. cavalry, and four negroes, have been arrested for pillaging," the writer continued. "They would enter the houses of planters for the ostensible purpose of searching for arms, demand the keys of their desks and wardrobes, and seize upon every article of value they could find."[39]

A sizable number of Banks's troops were the riffraff from impoverished Boston and New York neighborhoods, and many of the men had undoubtedly worked within the gang systems that ruled those urban jungles. The temptation to steal while performing government-sponsored plundering often proved too overwhelming to resist. "Quite a business has been carried on by a few ex-thieves from the Eastern penitentiaries, who have enlisted in the department under the impression that they would find a better field for plunder here than in the Eastern cities," wrote one newspaper correspondent with the *nom de plume* of Mattison. "They have brought reproach upon one of the best armies that ever marched, by their

Brashear City Depot. Lieutenant Colonel David Hunter Strother sketched a bustling military base on the shore of Berwick Bay on his way back to New Orleans and out of Louisiana. The steamboat *Kepper* is seen at the dock.

West Virginia and Regional History Collection, Accession no. p. 95.30.68.

lawless pillaging, and receive no sympathy from any one. The penalty for their misdeeds will doubtless be severe." The combination of eastern criminals, freed slaves, and Acadian jayhawkers had matured into bands of robbers, rapists, and murderers that compounded the miseries of war.[40]

One squad of criminals, when brought before the provost, yielded a bounty of loot. "They were thoroughly searched, and $800 in silver were found secreted in money belts, and in the lining of the waist-bands of their pants, in their boots, and in every conceivable place," wrote one indignant observer. "Besides the silver, some gold was found, and watches and jewelry." They faced a harsh future. "They will probably be sentenced to take a dose of blue pills," the soldier observed, using a euphemism for death by firing squad. The new rules had their intended affect, and the handful of executions actually carried out sent a clear signal. "I think if such examples are made, both officers and men will soon begin to find that they are not at a militia muster, playing soldier," a Northerner wrote home, "but are in the army where orders must be obeyed."[41]

By Sunday, April 26, the Army of the Gulf had sprawled across southwest Louisiana but had advanced no further. Stretching from Holmesville to Opelousas, with garrisons at intervals all the way to Brashear City, the command had covered southern Louisiana in a thin blue sheet. At the Methodist Church in Washington, even the pulpit had fallen to the Yankees. Captain Henry Upson, the chaplain of the 13th Connecticut, edging out their usual clergy, preached "the first Union sermon heard in that town for years," Captain Sprague recounted. "The text was 'Fight the good fight of Faith,' with special emphasis on the first word."[42]

Banks and members of his staff arrived in New Orleans on April 28. Lieutenant Colonel Strother, his capable aide whom he recruited from the garrison at Washington D.C., was transferring out of the Army of the Gulf and was heading north to receive promotion to colonel and command of a West Virginia regiment. The trip gave him time to visit with the general and his staff before leaving and the opportunity to encourage Banks to make a bold move. "We feared that Emory and others surrounding the General

The St. Charles Hotel.

Marshall Dunham Photograph Album, Mss. 3241, Louisiana and Lower Mississippi Valley Collections, LSU Libraries, Baton Rouge, La.

would check his career of victory by timid counsels," Strother penned. "We had advised him to go to Alexandria and thence to Shreveport, lick Kirby Smith if he showed himself, and clean out the whole country." Over the course of the three-day journey, through conversations in the smoky salons of a Louisiana bayou steamer and discussions in a swaying passenger car on the Opelousas and New Orleans Railroad, Banks's staff changed the general's mind; now the army would not be falling back to Baton Rouge and focusing on Port Hudson. The campaign on the Teche had evolved from a grand raid to a full-blown invasion. Banks would conquer and hold all of Louisiana. To do so, he would need more troops.[43]

Major General Henry W. Halleck, in faraway Washington, D.C., remained pleasantly ignorant of Banks's vacillations. The general-in-chief of Union armies, watching anxiously for good news from the Mississippi while keeping a wary eye on the show-down between General Joseph Hooker and General Robert E. Lee in Virginia, knew where this war would be won, and he believed Banks did too. "I agree with you," he wrote, "the Mississippi River is the all-important object of the present campaign. It is worth to us forty Richmonds." It remains unclear how Halleck would have measured the Mississippi against Alexandria and Shreveport. Had he known Banks had not followed his plans, he would likely have been apoplectic.[44]

In New Orleans Banks sent word for the five recently arrived companies of the 14th New York Cavalry to travel to Opelousas and lend a badly needed hand. He also sent Grant yet another dispatch: "It is of the utmost importance that you should send a force to the Red River immediately to cooperate with the army and navy now there. We have the Atchafalaya and the mouth of the Red River." Banks remained subtle about his new plans, writing "An addition to my force will give us the whole country west of the Mississippi."[45]

21

The Battle of Washington

"We will all get together tomorrow and give them another try."

Private John W. Watkins
Company B, 5th Texas Cavalry

While Major General Nathaniel P. Banks rethought his strategy in New Orleans, his subordinates managed his army around Opelousas. Like a hen gathering its chicks, Brigadier General William H. Emory ordered all of his scattered forces to come together in anticipation of Banks's return. The army's officers had last heard that the next move would be a withdrawal to Baton Rouge followed by an advance on Port Hudson. These orders disappointed his more war-like subalterns who were already hoping for a renewed advance against Major General Richard Taylor.

Skirmishing continued around the northern perimeter of the army as the advance elements prepared to strike deeper into the interior. Two companies of the Union 1st Louisiana Cavalry, working with Brigadier General William Dwight, had surprised and scattered some Confederates near Holmesville on Sunday, but the following Tuesday, April 28, the brigade received the surprising word to return to Washington. Dwight grudgingly complied, reporting that the Confederates were gathering nearby "because [they] are so much demoralized that they will disband unless they can fight us. They hope by a contest to call back to their ranks many who have deserted and many who insists on going to Texas." Dwight did not approve of the retrograde movement—he was ready to have another crack at the Confederates, despite believing a fight would rally them—but he followed the orders, abandoning his forward position at Holmesville and sending word that nearly six hundred Confederate cavalry lurked behind him and more were concentrating at Alexandria.[1]

Emory sent some of the 2nd Rhode Island Cavalry up a road toward Chicotville, at the edge of the Cocodrie Swamp, to verify the rumor. They returned empty handed except for a few enemy pickets they found along the way, reporting that the Rebels had burned the bridge over that Bayou Cocodrie and closed the road to Cheneyville.

The Confederates had remained just out of sight, anticipating another fight with the Federals as they moved toward Alexandria. When Waco, Texas, clerk-turned-private John W. Watkins left Alexandria, heading south toward Lecompte, he expected that he would run into the Federal vanguard within a few hours. After miles of anxious anticipation and hours spent scanning the horizon for the telltale signs of the coming enemy, the Texan felt baffled. The troops, including the remnants of Lieutenant Colonel Valsin Fournet's 10th Yellow Jacket Battalion mounted on mules and horses, passed through Cheneyville, and continued tentatively down Bayou Boeuf, past the road to Evergreen at Bayou Huffpower. When the four hundred or so Texans and Louisianans pushed on to Holmesville on Wednesday, April 29, they learned that the target of their expedition had withdrawn. The Rebels were perplexed. "The Yankees were advancing when we reached here," Watkins wrote, "but for some reason I can't understand they are getting back out of the country."[2]

That same Tuesday, Colonel Halbert E. Paine returned from a three-day scouting expedition southwest of Opelousas. Paine had led his entire brigade on a sixteen-mile reconnaissance in force to the two forks of the Plaquemine Brulè, and he had even pushed the mounted troops from the 4th Wisconsin twenty miles further, to Bayou Queue de Tortue and Bayou Mallet, to check for Rebels. They had wanted to make certain that the bogey men—Colonel Tom Green's Texans—had indeed left. Although Paine did not find the Confederates, he had encountered a growing crowd of nondescript desperados from the swamps and canebrakes who mingled with stragglers from the Union army. "These operations resulted in the capture of about forty guerillas," he reported, "with many arms and horses." On his way home, Paine dispatched his mounted troopers east to Vermilionville to escort another supply train to Opelousas while his foot soldiers tramped back the way they had come, bringing with then the suspicious locals. Paine and his men returned to Opelousas without incident.[3]

Confused by what seemed to be erractic movments by the Federals, the Confederate rallied at Holmesville to await developments. Rebel troops fanned out, gathered what stragglers they could, and directed them to fall in. "We staid there," Watkins continued, "and gathered up stragglers and other small bodies of men until our command numbered near 600 rank and file." This newly construed ersatz battalion would be under celebrity leadership. Colonel Eugene Waggaman, a New Orleans businessman who owned a sugar plantation in Jefferson Parish, had risen to command the 10th Louisiana Infantry in the Army of Northern Virginia. At Malvern Hill, less than a year before, he had been conspicuous at the head of his troops but fell prisoner during the Union counterattack. Authorities exchanged the officer after a period of imprisonment at Fort Warren in Boston Harbor. The Confederacy had already replaced him in his regiment, so Waggaman was sent back to Louisiana to work as a recruiting officer in Alexandria. As panic swept that city he had volunteered to lead a force to hold the Yankees at bay so that Taylor could escape with his guns and baggage. He was now heading into combat for the first time since his service in Virginia, and he assumed the mission was nearly hopeless.[4]

Colonel Eugene Waggaman led the 10th Louisiana Infantry in Virginia. He faced perhaps a greater challenge as he returned to combat, this time at the head of the leavings of Major General Richard Taylor's army.

US Army Military History Institute.

Instead, Dwight had withdrawn to Washington. With this gift of time, Waggaman mustered a respectable force. Colonel Edwin Waller's Battalion operated close by, giving the Confederates is essence a sizable brigade of mounted troops. The additions were mostly the leavings of various commands, including stragglers from Taylor's infantry. Feeling confident once again, the Southerners advanced. "We start again this morning to hunt them up," Watkins wrote to his wife on April 30. The Rebels pushed several miles down the east bank of Bayou Boeuf without finding their enemy, and they finally stopped in the late afternoon to cook supper among the buildings and trees at the Carritz farm. Here a muddy farm lane perpendicular to the bayou road headed northeast, through a soggy forest and cane brake, toward the settlement of Bayou Rouge.[5]

The short-lived respite at the crossroads was broken by the sounds of pistols and carbines echoing from the south. "Our advance guard came up with them and gave them a pretty close run for their quarters, but the Yankees being finely mounted made good their escape," Watkins wrote. The Confederates left their cooking fires to pursue the enemy, men from the 1st Louisiana and 2nd Rhode Island cavalries, and pressed on past sunset and through the night. The Confederates did not give up until 5:00 AM on May 1, when the Federals fell back through the hamlet of Moundville, at the junction of the two bayous, Boeuf and Cocodrie, that formed Bayou Courtableau. The sleepy Rebels unsaddled their horses and lay down for a few hours sleep in the fields just beyond this village.[6]

The hunt and skirmish resumed by midmorning. Private Felix Robert Collard of the 7th Texas Cavalry, who had been separated from his regiment since his escape at Fort Bisland and had fallen in with Waller's Battalion, trotted across plantation fields in open order with the enemy in sight. He watched as a Federal cavalryman lost his lunch in the running gun battle. "One man, at the crack of his gun, saw a haversack fly from a retreating enemy over a hundred and fifty yards away," he remembered. The fine shot at a distant target had missed its mark yet still yielded results. The successful marksman rode ahead and, slipping down the side of his trotting horse, recovered the prize. Collard wrote, "Inside was a cracker and a piece of pickled pork—it was the first bread and meat that had gone down that man's throat for weeks."[7]

This rolling scuffle continued until the Confederates approached Dwight's main encampment across Bayou Courtableau at Washington. Waggaman's battalion closed up on the mounted skirmishers. "After marching three miles firing commenced in our advance—we left the road at this point and went into a plantation so that we could see where the enemy lay," Watkins remembered. This combat was his first battle. The Federal cavalry screen fell back only to reveal the dismounted troopers of the 4th Wisconsin, five hundred strong, and a section of the 2nd Massachusetts Battery rumbling across the Courtableau Bridge. The units deployed and met the arriving Rebels with artillery salvos and rifle volleys. "[Major Hannibal Honestus] Boone showed himself and his men first here and then there on that farm," Collard wrote. "The artillery tried to follow them up, firing here and there. Boone, like a boy playing base, was apparently daring them to send a detachment after him." The men in Waggaman's command fell back to the cover of some woods, sending dismounted skirmishers to the front to continue the fight for the next few hours. "The air . . . was filled with messengers of death and I found I could see the cannonballs," Watkins wrote, describing his first time under fire. "But all passed over our heads doing no damage."[8]

A midafternoon lull in the fighting led the Confederates to believe the enemy planned to depart. Major Denman Shannon of the 5th Texas Cavalry led a squad of mounted Louisianans from Waggaman's battalion to the cover of a sugarhouse to see if the Federal guns had indeed left. "As soon as the Yanks found they were in there, they opened a battery on the house, completely riddling it but hurting no one," Watkins gasped. Shannon remounted his horse to retreat, and then a Union rifleman killed the animal but missed the man. The major, said Watkins, "took it as coolly as if nothing had happed."[9]

The pointlessness and indecision of the skirmish caused Dwight to rethink his approach. He ordered the mounted infantry of Lieutenant Colonel Sidney Bean's 4th Wisconsin to fall back for the time being so that they might rest, eat dinner, and reload their cartridge boxes. After their break the 4th Wisconsin was to push the Rebels again that evening with the aid of the two cannon. In the meantime he ordered Major Harai Robinson to use the remaining daylight hours to personally lead the 180 or so cavalrymen at hand on a circuitous route through heavy timber to the east. They were to gain the Rebel rear using the farm road, which would take them to the Carritz farm. Captain Richard Barrett, recently promoted commander of Company B, 1st Louisiana Cavalry, would lead the way. "He was furnished with a negro guide who was acquainted with the woods and paths," Dwight reported. "Major Robinson was told that if the negro guide did not show him the proper road . . . that he must shoot the negro and return to the command." The general planned for the 4th Wisconsin to drive the Rebels like a covey into Robinson's net. As Dwight planned his trap, the afternoon's battle petered out.[10]

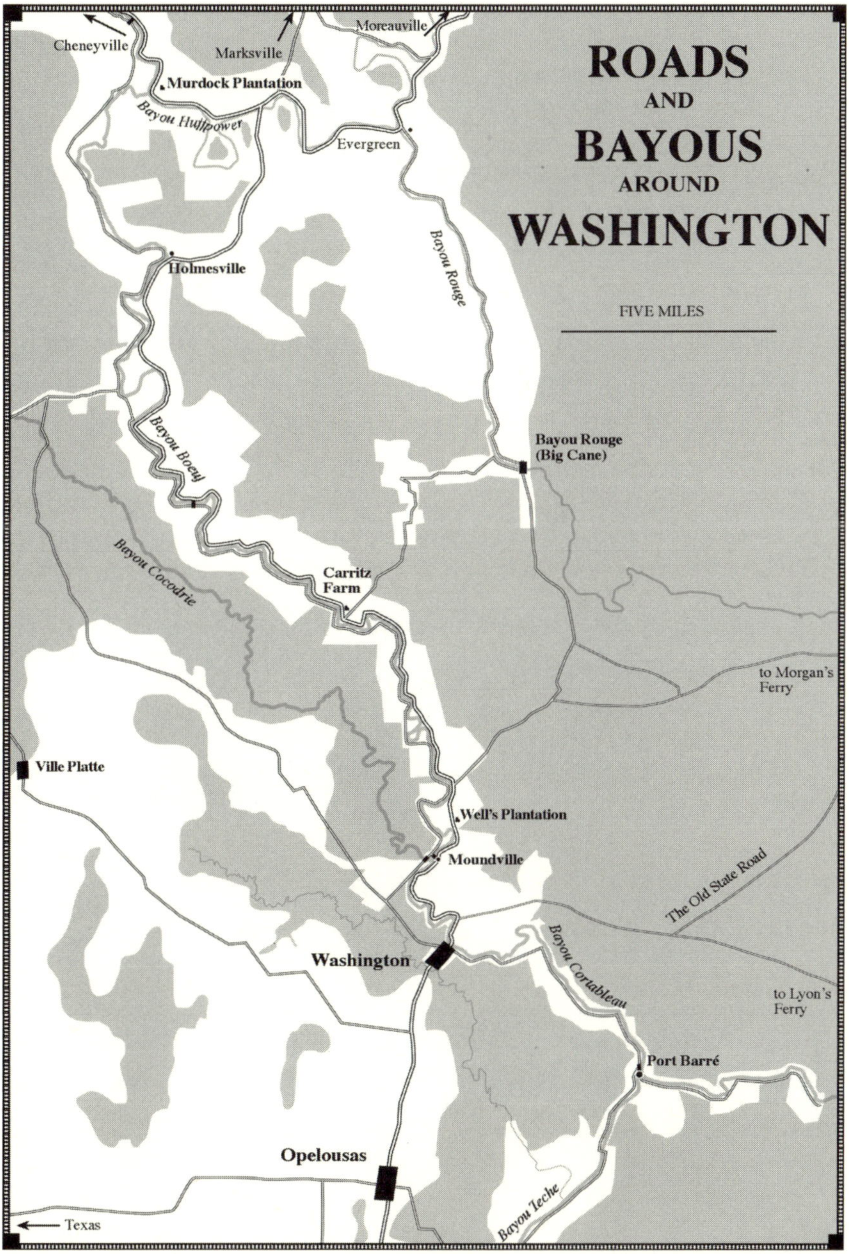

Major Robinson faced a challenging fifteen-mile ride. The plan was for his guide to lead him on cart paths and logging trails to the road that led from the Wells plantation through the swampy woods of Bayou Rouge toward the town of Big Cane. Once across that first obstacle, Robinson would intersect the Big Cane and Holmesville Road and turn left, heading northwest, paralleling Boone's line of retreat on the Bayou Boeuf Road, four miles away and beyond the intervening swamp. Robinson would then take the shortcut back across the swamp and fall upon the Confederate camps at the Carritz farm at about the time the 4th Wisconsin drove the enemy from the front.

Unaware that they were being stalked, Waggaman's Confederates withdrew that night, dropping back fifteen miles toward Holmesville to their camps at the Carritz farm. Boone and his battalion kept an eye on the Yankees in the three miles between Moundville and Washington while rooting around for food and

Asking Directions. Union cavalrymen get their bearing by asking the locals.

Library of Congress.

fodder. They discovered a huge cache of corn still in the husk. It had been intended for Southern forces before it had been captured by Dwight, and now the food was passed back to its original owners. "This was fine for the horses but rather a poor diet for hungry men," Collard reflected. The men passed the hours of early evening rustling their dinner, "the men tried to parch the corn in the ashes of the fire, others with iron gun sticks run into the pith of the cob were trying to roast it." Gunfire to their front interrupted their mediocre repast.[11]

"Suddenly there came a picket, under whip, warning his comrades to get from there and get ready to fight or run," described Collard. Boone chose to accept the challenge. He ordered his Texans, now remounted, to fall back, tie their horses out of range, and return to a stout fence at the edge of a field. He urged stealth—he wanted to shock these Yankees. "They . . . crept back to the fence sticking their rifles thru the cracks and let the enemy come on," Collard wrote. The shadowy forms of Federal skirmishers appeared in the distance as faint silhouettes in the light of a rising full moon. When the Federals came in range, the Texans fired a volley. The enemy continued their advance. The Texans fell back to their horses, remounted, fell back to another fence, and tried again, repeating the tactic for several miles. "Not stopping them . . . until after midnight," Collard recalled, "Boone bid them good-night and was going to run clear off to where his men could get something to eat." He led his column up the road to rejoin Waggaman.[12]

The Confederates failed to impress their adversaries. "The Rebels fought us a little while and then they would fall back and make another stand," Corporal Rufus Andrews of Company H, 4th Wisconsin, wrote to his wife. "They fired so high that they did not kill a man on our side."[13]

The hungry Rebels gladly yielded the field. Waggaman's command, by now rested and remounted, stood at the ready, anxious to learn the outcome of Boone's battle. The Union infantry, supported by artillery, still strode up the road, but the Texans had put a few miles between themselves and the blue coats. Boone decided that he had learned enough: Dwight had clearly consolidated his troops at Washington, ending the Union advance toward Alexandria for the moment—at least from that direction. There were others to scout. Boone's Texans assumed the lead in the retreat, heading up the Bayou Boeuf Road to a bridge about nine miles from Holmesville that would carry the Southern troops across to the bayou's west bank. Waggaman's troops brought up the rear. Once across the bayou, the Confederates could fall back toward Cheneyville while sending pickets to the west to see if the Yankees were heading north toward Alexandria on the Ville Platte Road.[14]

Captain Ormand Nims was a forty-two-year-old Boston druggist before the war but forged his 2nd Massachusetts Battery artillerymen into some of the finest in the army.

Caroline E. Whitcomb, History of the Second Massachusetts Battery (Nims' Battery) of Light Artillery, 1861–1865 *(Concord, New Hampshire: The Rumford Press, 1912).*

Dwight and his Federals, however, were one move ahead. Lieutenant Colonel Bean steadily advanced with the 4th Wisconsin. "It was a light moon, shiney night," Corporal Andrews wrote. "We followed them up until two o'clock in the morning." Meanwhile, the Massachusetts guns had pulled out of the fight. Dwight, believing he could not catch the elusive enemy, thought he might still be able to head them off and wisely consented to the request of a fast-thinking artilleryman. The new plan was to send the guns along a road that paralleled the Rebels' route from the opposite bank of the Boeuf. If the gunners hurried, they might cover the sixteen or so miles and be in position to rake the bridge the Confederates planned to cross. Dwight saw the potential for a double envelopment that would punish the enemy force: the artillery would block their path forward and the 4th Wisconsin and the cavalry would cut them up from their flank and rear. Perhaps he could destroy these enemies, or at least keep the Rebels on the other side of the Boeuf instead of blocking the Ville Platt Road to Alexandria.[15]

The Confederates' first inkling of trouble was a flash and the blast of canister whistling overhead from their front as they turned to cross over the Bayou Boeuf bridge. The head of the column, Captain Dan Ragsdale's South Texans of Company D, 5th Texas, used an old Ranger tactic: certain the blast had ruined the artillerymen's night vision, they spurred their horses directly at their adversaries and clattered across the bridge, past the baffled Union gunners who were in the process of reloading, and on to safety. Waggaman's Rebels, poor horsemen who were surprised and exhausted, began excitedly milling in the road, hemmed in by the bayou on their left, a stout fence fronting a field on their right, and the enemy ahead and behind. A second salvo from the guns of the 2nd Massachusetts landed two shells in the mob, killing or wounding nearly twenty-four Confederates.[16]

Major Boone rode back down the road to salvage the looming disaster. "Let down that fence and turn the head of the column

2nd Massachusetts Battery. All six of the battery's 3-inch Rodman Ordnance guns can be seen in this photograph.

Caroline E. Whitcomb, History of the Second Massachusetts Battery (Nims' Battery) of Light Artillery, 1861–1865 *(Concord, New Hampshire: The Rumford Press, 1912).*

Soldiers in the Swamp. An atmospheric image of bedraggled soldiers regrouping in a canebrake swamp. Notice the slaves cooking breakfast to the left and the half submerged sugar cooler to the right.

Harper's Weekly, *author's collection.*

through," he called out in the night air. His panicked troops used this release not only to flatten the fence but also to gallop across the narrow field and into the boggy woods.[17]

Union cavalry chief Robinson, hearing the sound of the guns, urged his men on through the blackness down the Carritz farm road. Arriving as if on cue to deliver the knockout blow, Robinson urged his men forward to fall upon the enemy he could barely see moving about in the moon light a few hundred yards to his front. Instead of attacking the Confederates and sealing off their retreat, however, he fell in on the rear of the 4th Wisconsin, which was crossing the fields of the Carritz farm. Robinson ordered his men to rein in. The cavalry had arrived too late. "Major Robinson made a thousand difficulties in the way of executing his orders," Dwight sputtered. "He accomplished nothing and . . . all hope was now lost of cutting off a portion of the enemy." Realizing that the enemy had slipped away, the Federals headed back to Washington. "We started back after making and drinking some coffee," Andrews recalled. "We got back [to camp] about 9 o'clock . . . after being up all night and riding all of the day before."[18]

For the odd collection of men fighting under Waggaman and Boone, it proved to be a long, uncomfortable night and morning. After the flight, "it was slush-slush-slush thru the swamp, thru green scummy ponds, rotten vines, palmettos, alligators, terrapins," Collard recalled. The scattered troops mucked through the swamp for five miles before emerging on the dry ground of the Bayou Rouge Prairie. They took a left at the first road they encountered and headed northwest toward Holmesville and safety, regrouping at the hamlet of Bayou Rouge. "We will all get together tomorrow and give them another try," penned Private Watkins optimistically.[19]

Back at his headquarters, Dwight dashed off a quick report of the battle near Washington that included his erroneous judgments about the enemy. He believed he had found Green, and he thought Banks should feel secure about the status of his lines of supply and communications back to Brashear City. "This reconnaissance shows that the enemy has a strong force in cavalry in our front; that all his cavalry is now concentrated on the left [east] bank of Bayou Boeuf; that his cavalry is composed of Sibley's Brigade, the enemy's [2nd] Louisiana cavalry, Clack's [12th Louisiana] Battalion, and Hubbard's [11th Louisiana] Battalion, in all about 3,000 mounted men," he stated. "While this force remained in its present position there is nothing to fear from attacks . . . from the plains leading toward Texas." The advance to Alexandria could continue, Dwight suggested, if Banks chose to carry on.[20]

22

Corps d'Afrique

"The Government makes use of mules, horses, uneducated and educated white men, in the defense of its institutions."

Major General Nathaniel P. Banks
Army of the Gulf

By the end of April, Brashear City thrummed with energy. The USS *Clifton* lay tied up at its docks for repairs. "The late fight at Butte-a-la-Rose has damaged us more than we at first thought," wrote Marine Henry O. Gusley. He did not mind. The crew had liberty of the town while they waited. "The weather is fine for such pastime and there is much ashore to enjoy and take away one's money." He shared the docks and streets with a growing throng. "Each day, too, brings us more evidence of the magnitude and completeness of our victories up the Teche," he continued. "Horses and cattle by the hundreds, and sugar, molasses, and cotton by boatloads, are continually coming in from the captured districts. Contrabands are also becoming plentiful around here."[1]

After his brief stay in New Orleans, Major General Nathaniel P. Banks returned to Brashear City at the end of April. Having decided to finish conquering western Louisiana, Banks ordered the USS *Arizona* to get up steam. He directed the gunboat to escort the transport *L. A. Sykes,* which he would board, up the Atchafalaya and into Grand Lake. "This expedition of the *Arizona* was one upon which Gen. Banks had put great stress. His brain had directed it and his heart was enlisted in its success, for much depended on its issue," wrote Mattison, the penname of a soldier in Banks's army who contributed regularly to the *Boston Morning Journal.* "He knew that danger threatened the expedition, for the enemy was known to have three gunboats somewhere between us and Alexandria, on the Red river; the rebels where known to have been at work a fortnight ago on an earthwork at Simmesport, and any sudden turn of the river might make us the envious mark of a masked battery, or behind any live oak trunk along the banks a gray-coated bandit might send his leaden compliments over—or *through*—our devoted heads."[2]

At the confluence of Bayou Courtableau, Banks, his staff, and the passengers aboard the *L. A. Sykes* parted company with the *Arizona.* The gunboat proceeded up the Atchafalaya with Captain Robert T. Dunham, assistant adjutant general of General Banks's staff carrying dispatches. Two dozen soldiers from the 16th New Hampshire guarded the *Arizona* against Rebel snipers. The steamer *L. A. Sykes* meanwhile returned Banks to Port Barrè and his army.[3]

The *Arizona* splashed ahead, heading deeper into the heart of the Atchafalaya Basin. "Through many miles of lowland swamp, untenanted save by the lazy alligators and their confreres of the slimy water, our course lay," Mattison gushed in a fountain of purple prose. "Now and then an inundated farm, once under a passable state of cultivation, we would leave behind us, the buildings drooping through with decay, and tenantless and deserted. Anon we would pass a fine estate, the crowded cotton gins showing through their broken sides the white edges of the cotton bales stowed away within. Grinning darkies congregated on the banks, nonplussed, perhaps, to see our little iron gunboat riding the waves so neatly, with the 'stars and stripes' hanging lazily at the mizzen—the first vessel that had carried our triumphant flag through the Atchafalaya since the secession of the State, and perhaps for many years before."[4]

Late on Friday afternoon, May 1, 1863, the *Arizona* passed Simmesport. "Here we expected to meet at least a rebel field battery, but not a soul was stirring," He continued, noting that two or three half-sunken flatboats lay below the town, and a hundred yards to the front on the river and on the right stretched along the expected earthwork, apparently abandoned in haste by the "gallant confederates," startled by the flight of the *Mary T.*, a week before. As

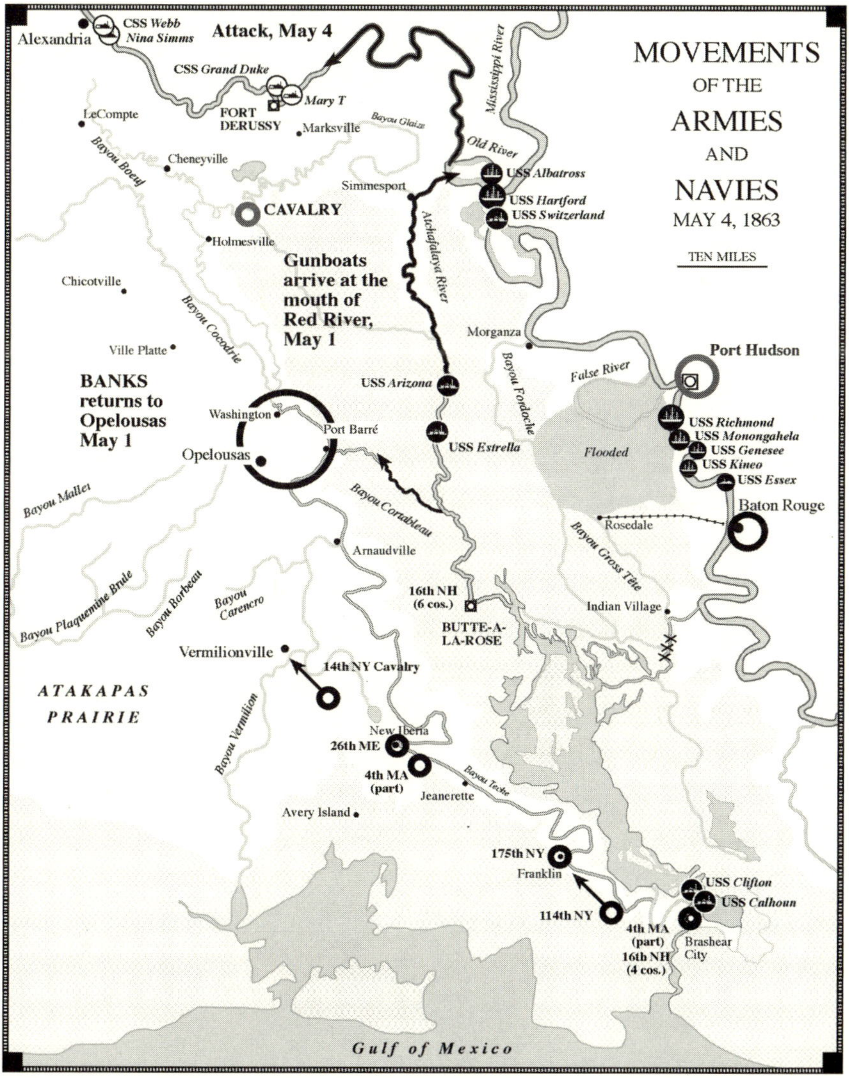

the sun set behind them, the *Arizona* cruised into the waters of Old River and headed eastward toward the Mississippi.[5]

In the darkness the *Arizona* faced its greatest danger, since it could be a target for friend or foe. "At about nine o'clock, over the low trees against our port bow, we suddenly came in sight of the three masts of the flag-ship *Hartford,*" Mattison wrote. "In an instant the word was passed, and a rocket sped skyward from our wheel-house. A few signal lights were burned in quick succession, and a signal lantern after a few minutes made its appearance on the spanker gaff of the *Hartford.* Soon we swept out in sight of the gray hull of the old leviathan." After identifying itself, the *Arizona* hove to near Admiral David G. Farragut's flagship and dropped its cutter as the crews of both ships raised a cheer. In five minutes the *Arizona*'s officers "were grasping the rough hand of the noble old Admiral. Congratulations were exchanged, dispatches were received, and in a few hours the *Arizona* was treading her way back again."[6]

"Yesterday was accomplished one of the handsomest events of the war, the junction of the fleet of Admiral Farragut and the army of Gen. Banks by means of the Atchafalaya River," crowed Mattison to the *Boston Morning Journal.* "This is a thing which has been for some time meditated, but it was left for the United States gunboat *Arizona.*" Aboard the steamer were important trophies of the recent naval victories—one of the charred deck beams of the *Queen of the West* as well as a misshapen lump of melted metal that had once been a silver service in that vessel's officer's mess.[7]

Despite the success of the mission, the dispatches carried by Captain Dunham and intended for Major General Ulysses S. Grant were now obsolete. The Army of the Tennessee had crossed over the Mississippi River that same day at Bruinsburg, Mississippi. Grant was heading for the interior and would not be in position to aid or cooperate with Banks for the foreseeable future. Niether the commander of the Army of the Gulf nor his aid, Captain Dunham, could have anticipated that daring move, however, and the event was so recent that the news had yet to spread.

Unburdened by this intelligence, Banks continued his journey back to his army, landing at Port Barrè, as the sounds of cannon fire rumbled in the distance beyond Washington, Banks returned to his headquarters at Opelousas on May 1 after nearly a week's absence. He was confident in his next course of action, expecting to be reinforced by an entire corps of rested troops, and fully aware of the military and political benefits waiting in his future. But as Banks settled in at Opelousas, he could not know that Grant and his army were pushing aside a Confederate force at Port Gibson, Mississippi.

Banks continued awaiting Grant's response. Ignorant of events east of the Mississippi, he turned his attention toward some long-neglected projects. One piece of business was the fate of the freed slaves who thronged the army and roamed the countryside. Banks used this respite from active campaigning to put in order his vision for the systematic recruitment of black soldiers in Louisiana. The army had never effectively dealt with this issue, although many officers had tried and several competing systems had emerged. To date in Louisiana, starting with Major General Benjamin Butler, army officers haphazardly employed most of the black men clustering around their commands as laborers or as informal guards at various Union-controlled plantations. Banks would use them to garrison the conquered state while he and his white regiments, along with those he anticipated getting from Grant, finished off Confederate resistance.

Would the freedmen fight? The 54th Massachusetts Regiment represented an experiment in using Northern black men, many of whom had been free for generations and were literate and politically savvy, to break the race barrier in the army. A similar unit was raised in Philadelphia. The Louisiana Native Guard regiments, mostly made up of educated free men of color from New Orleans, had been recruited around a cadre of free black militia who had a tradition dating back to the French colonial era. These educated soldiers were not representative of the vast majority of freed slaves following the wake of Northern armies.

Having signed the Emancipation Proclamation earlier in 1863, President Abraham Lincoln wanted to find a solution to the issue of what to do with the recently freed slaves. Brigadier General Daniel Ullmann, recently promoted after being captured at Cedar Mountain in Virginia and languishing at Libby Prison in Richmond, lobbied the government to allow him to experiment with the black men who had been liberated in Louisiana. The president gave his approval at the end of March, and by mid-April Ullmann traveled to New Orleans with two hundred white officers from the Army of the Potomac to raise a brigade of newly freed black men in southern Louisiana.[8]

It was an errand that confused jurisdictions. Ullmann worked within Banks's Department of the Gulf, but he remained semi-independent under the president's commission. "To now avail ourselves of this element of force is very important, if not indispensable," Lincoln wrote in his letter endorsing Ullmann to the department commander. "The necissity [sic] of this is palpable if, as I understand, you are now unable to effect anything with your present force; and which force is soon to be greatly diminished by the expiration of terms of service, as well as by ordinary causes." Lincoln knew that Banks needed the manpower, but he had lost confidence that Banks would accomplish much before his militia army left for home. Banks made a show of embracing the help, but Ullmann's commission threatened to disrupt the organization and recruitment of black labor for fieldwork and military needs, which Butler had started and Banks had inherited. This would especially affect the Lafourche District.[9]

Banks had his own plans for arming black men. He suggested through military channels that Ullmann should move his recruiting efforts away from the "pacified" parishes that had been occupied by Federal forces since the previous summer and fall and instead build his brigade at Brashear City, using some of the recently vacated camps and facilities left behind by his army. Banks also made clear that Ullmann need not bother taking workers from plantations in the LaFourche District or in the regions around Baton Rouge and New Orleans. Instead, Banks noted, he had picked up enough freedmen on his march up the Teche to fill Ullmann's ranks. "I believe I have that I have the men at hand, part of them already partially organized, for his entire brigade," Banks reported. "My belief is that Brashear City, on Berwick Bay, is in all respects the best position for the organization of his troops. He can organize his regiments in one week after establishing his headquarters from the men I have collected."[10]

Two Former Slaves. Young men like these would soon be forged into fighting regiments.

Library of Congress.

Banks never questioned the validity of using black men to fight the Rebels. "It is not established upon any dogma of equality or other theory, but as a practical and sensible matter of business," he directed. "The Government makes use of mules, horses, uneducated and educated white men, in the defense of its institutions. Why should not the negro contribute whatever is in his power to for the cause in which he is as deeply interested as other men? We may properly demand from him whatever service he can render."[11]

History, too, provided precedent. Black soldiers helped win the American Revolution, and Black sailors already served in the U.S. Navy, including among the crews of the gunboats supporting

Banks's campaign. Armies may be made of men, but valor came from training and discipline. "The European and American continents exhibit instances of this character, and the military prowess of every nation may be estimated by the centuries it has devoted to military contest, or the traditional passion of its people for military glory," Banks wrote. The Massachusetts general believed, however, that black people were "a race unaccustomed to military service." Perhaps, he posited, excellent officers—white men, of course—could train them to become warriors in the Anglo-Saxon tradition and give their men of "African" descent the benefit of centuries of "warlike habits and spirit" inherited from European bloodlines. Even so, Banks envisioned a largely guard, support, and garrison role for them in Louisiana.[12]

Despite Banks's reticence, by mid-April 1863 it was clear that black Federal soldiers would be in combat within months, if not weeks, somewhere in America. The commander of the Army of

Contraband Camp. This collection of old men, women, and children were bound for a different fate than that of able-bodied men.

State Library of Louisiana.

the Gulf proposed a grand vision for their effective training and employment: "The organization of a *Corps d'Armee* of colored troops, to be designated as the *Corps d'Afrique.*" With thousands of former slaves already being collected by his army, Banks was ready to employ a systematic approach that would ultimately render Ullmann's experiment redundant. Once employed, the Banks system would become the standard for employing black men as auxiliaries of the 19th Army Corps. He issued General Orders Number 40 on May 1, announcing the creation of the *Corps d'Afrique.*[13]

This organization would address the inefficiencies and challenges encountered so far. "The chief defect in organizations of this character has arisen from incorrect ideas of the officers in command," he wrote. "Their discipline has been lax, and in some cases the conduct of their regiments unsatisfactory and discreditable." Banks no doubt remembered the friction between the Louisiana Native Guards and the rest of his army near Port Hudson and Brigadier General Godfrey Weitzel's objections to arming freedmen after his successful invasion of the LaFourche country the previous year. Banks conceded that "controversies unnecessary and injurious to the service have arisen between them and other troops." But, he added, the Corps d'Afrique would "reconcile and avoid many of these troubles."[14]

The organization of this unit mirrored that of a regular army corps, but it was considerably smaller in size and strength. The Corps d'Afrique would have a total of eighteen regiments, including infantry, artillery, and cavalry, along with engineers and "flying hospitals" that would serve as mobile battlefield aid stations. These units would serve in two-regiment brigades, three of which would form a division. The entire corps would boast three divisions.

The new corps officers would all be white, and Banks hoped they would be among the best from his army. "With their aid," he wrote, "the corps will render important service to the army." For Banks, the issues of race were secondary to accomplishing the military task at hand. Talented leaders should look past the color of their recruits, he posited, and instead think of their nation. "Officers and soldiers will consider the exigencies of the service in this department and the absolute necessity of appropriating every element of power to the support of the Government," he wrote. "The prejudices or opinions of men are in nowise involved."[15]

Banks knew that his army was spread too thinly across southern Louisiana. He needed his white brigades concentrated once again for the effort to take the Red River; thus, he would pragmatically garrison the Corps d'Afrique in conquered Louisiana and allow his veterans to continue the war. With the reading of these new orders, officers and men at Opelousas marked off a camp for the freed slaves in the area, creating a stir among the Union regiments nearby. "It is understood that several negro regiments are to be organizes here, and the commission for officers will be given to the non-commissioned officers of white regiments who can bring recommendations from the Colonel of their own regiments," wrote a soldier from the 41st Massachusetts. Within days more than two thousand men, women, and children occupied the new facility. Once collected, troops would remove this population to Brashear City where white officers would sort them, sending the women, children, old, young, and men unsuited for military service to contraband camps and perhaps as labor to confiscated plantations. The officers would press the remainder—healthy young men—into the Corps d'Afrique.[16]

In arriving at his new plan for his campaign in Louisiana, Banks had simply decided to build upon his successes. It seemed inevitable that Port Hudson would eventually fall, so Banks would instead turn his attention to conquering, holding, and reconstructing the entire Pelican State. The domain he had sculpted with the Army of the Gulf was a tortured—but subdued—fiefdom. Behind the Federal army lay a wake of destruction that stretched all the way back to Brashear City, and Banks believed the population living in this area was ready for peace.

FRANK LESLIE'S ILLUSTRATED NEWSPAPER

Entered according to the Act of Congress in the year 1863, by Frank Leslie, in the Clerk's Office of the District Court for the Southern District of New York.

No. 388—Vol. XV.] NEW YORK, MARCH 7, 1863. [Price 8 Cents.

SCENES IN LOUISIANA.

Our Artist has sent us some sketches which illustrate, in a striking degree, the novel phases of life, both military and civil, which the present struggle is evolving. The fact of black regiments being actively employed is not a novelty, since they have been for some time part of the British military system, which, with its usual common sense, avails itself of every aid in the pursuit of its objects. Our Artist says that among the cypress swamps of Louisiana negro soldiers are invaluable, and accompanies his sketch of the pickets of the First Louisiana native troops, guarding the New Orleans, Opelousas and Great Western Railroad, with some remarks which we quote:

"In this swamp in the wilderness the 'nigger soldiers' are eminently useful. The melancholy solitude, with the spectral cypress trees, which seem to stand in silent despair, like nature's sentinels waving in the air wreaths of gray funereal moss, to warn all human beings of the latent pestilence around, though unendurable to our soldiers of the North, seems an elysium to these sable soldiers, for the swampy forest has no horrors to them. Impervious to miasma, they see only the home of the coon, the possum and the copperhead, so that with 'de gun dat Massa Sam gib 'em,' they have around them all the essential elements of colored happiness, except ladies' society."

The Old Slave Laws.

In strange forgetfulness of the use to which the colored race may be put, the new régime has empowered Provost Marshal Col. French to put in force the old Slave Laws of Louisiana. Our Artist says: "The first result of the Emancipation Proclamation has been attended with a paradoxical effect, namely, a revival of the old Slave Laws of Louisiana. On the evening in question, all the negroes found in the streets after nine o'clock wit-

The men of the **1st Louisiana Native Guard** appear as well-equipped soldiers in this popular account. Accepted into Federal service by Butler, under Banks's plan the regiment would be designated as the 1st Regiment, Corps d'Afrique, later the 73rd U.S. Colored Troops.

Library of Congress.

Banks had seized an agricultural empire and he intended to hold it. The great fields and fat farms from Vermilionville to Brashear staggered his soldiers from rocky lands in the North. "Indeed I have never seen a finer, richer or more productive section of country than the one we passed through," one argued. "The whole way—large plantations succeeding each other, with fine dwellings, immense brick sugar houses, and little villages of white cabins for their negroes, surrounded with the rich foliaged china and fig tree, and the grand old live oaks, evergreen, and bearing from its long and stretched branches large masses of . . . moss—all making a beautiful picturesque scene."[17]

The homes of these agricultural capitalists amazed the soldiers, most of whom claimed decidedly more humble origins. Each of the homes told a story. "Those dwellings were well stored with luxuries of this life, betokening wealth and education," a Northerner wrote. "Our first few days' march these houses and plantations [were] mostly deserted, but after leaving Franklin the inhabitants seemingly having found out that the Yankees were not cannibals, remained at home and thereby preserved their houses from pillage." Vacant dwellings were fair game for passing soldiers. "I am sorry to say, a deserted house is usually treated as being *pro bono - publico* by our soldiers."[18]

The agricultural bounty of Louisiana seemed limitless. "Another year and this State would almost have furnished corn enough for their whole army," one writer noted. "I never saw larger or finer looking fields of corn, now up about 18 inches, and doing finely."[19]

Banks believed this captured country could now sustain the Union war effort. The New Yorkers, Midwesterners, and New Englanders of Banks's army employed the region's produce and commodities in the cause of the Union. "Opelousas is just on the border of the vast cotton country of the west," one Northerner wrote. "From all I could infer, I think our army will not move, in force, much father, after these running rebels, but glean the country of all the cotton, sugar, cattle, &c., and leaving a good force there; try to most effectually cut off their supplies from the west the Mississippi. Their Texas cattle and corn no more coming [and] Louisiana sugar turned Yankeewards—these must nearly drive the rebels to starvation."[20]

Based on all he had surveyed, Banks believed he had essentially already conquered Louisiana. As soon as reinforcements from Grant's army arrived, he planned to sweep up the Red River to Shreveport and tidy up the loose ends. The tens of thousands of slaves his army had liberated would be transformed not only into a Corps d'Afrique but also into an army of occupation that held and pacified the country behind him. The Mississippi would be opened by ignoring Port Hudson for the moment. Once Vicksburg had fallen, as surely it must since its supply lines had been severed, then the combined Union forces of Grant and Banks could open the mighty river to Union commerce once again. The Mississippi Valley Campaign would close within months. Meanwhile, he would sweep the secessionists out of Louisiana and remake the state.

23

Niblett's Bluff, Fort DeRussy

"Big fish eat little fish."

Private Theophilus Noel
4th Texas Cavalry

By May 1863, a decisive Union victory seemed assured in Louisiana. Without a doubt, Major General Nathaniel P. Banks had thrashed Major General Richard Taylor. The small Confederate army had reeled from the repeated blows inflicted upon it by fifteen thousand Union soldiers. Other signs seemed more ambiguous. Colonel Halbert E. Paine had not found Colonel Tom Green lurking along Plaquemine Brulé, Bayou Queue de Tortue, and Bayou Mallet to the southwest, and Brigadier General William Dwight had reported these Texas phantoms between Washington and Alexandria. The truth, though, was that Green and his group of mounted Confederates had already reached the Texas-Louisiana border, a hundred miles away. At the same time Taylor and the remnants of Brigadier General Alfred Mouton's brigade, as well as the artillery and wagons, had dragged themselves out of danger, flushed from Lecompte by Dwight's advance to Holmesville, and then routed from Alexandria all the way to Natchitoches with the removal of Lieutenant General Edmund Kirby Smith's headquarters to Shreveport. "We are now in a regular race from the enemy," wrote Lieutenant Arthur W. Hyatt of the 24th Louisiana Infantry. "I shall remember this retreat as long as I live." Banks had cleared lower Louisiana of armed opposition, but the killing blow had yet to be struck.[1]

Green's Texans moved beyond the Federal reach. By May 1 the brigade of Texas horsemen lolled comfortably at Niblett's Bluff on the Sabine River, though it was "one of the meanest looking little places imaginable," according to Private William Randolph Howell of the 5th Texas Cavalry. They had passed through the Calcasieu country and Lake Charles en route, encountering "the poorest, jabbering lot of Frenchmen the world will ever see," Howell observed. They had drawn beef and flour from the reluctant Cajun population and had drifted in stages toward Texas. Now Niblett's Bluff bloomed into a bustling Rebel depot. The troops rested there for several days and received new underwear. As Howell put it, "after a couple of hours bathing . . . [I] come out a new man!"[2]

Safe from any Yankee threat, Green's Brigade counted heads and mourned their dead. Chief among their losses was the brigade's senior colonel, James Reily. His wife and daughter had been near the army at Franklin, where he had been killed, and they had seen the dead officer placed in a vault in the Franklin cemetery while Federal soldiers sneered at the funeral cortège. The bereaved women traveled through Niblett's Bluff on their way home to Texas, carrying with them Reily's sword, a last memento of husband and father.[3]

The city of Houston had already learned of the passing of this favorite son. "The death of Colonel James Reiley . . . near Franklin has created a profound reaction in this community," read an editorial in the *Houston Tri-Weekly Telegraph*. "He fell in the battle's front a hero of the war, and a noble sacrifice for the freedom of his country. His blood has helped win the freedom which the deserving man will enjoy." Reily joined a long list of dead Confederate Houstonians. "One by one has this, our city, laid upon the alter of liberty its noblest—best beloved. Who, alas, will step forward and fill their places?"[4]

As the days at Niblett's Bluff progressed and men compared experiences, they realized that the presumed losses of the brigade had been exaggerated. Unit cohesion had collapsed in the heat of combat and the strain of pursuit, but most of the missing were not dead or captured. In fact, they learned that General Henry Hopkins Sibley's old brigade lay strewn across a broad swath of the Pelican State. "We are yet far from our train, it being near Alexandria, and also more than half the brigade is with the train," reported a soldier in the 4th Texas Cavalry, writing from Niblett's Bluff. Once officers gathered the men again, the brigade, now under the command of Colonel Green, remained dangerously potent.[5]

Many of those feared dead among the rank and file proved to be quite alive. Some had fallen in with the 13th Texas Cavalry Battalion and were still in the field with Major Hannibal Honestus Boone or Colonel Eugene Waggaman. Others had fallen back with Taylor to Natchitoches. A few of the sick or injured had stayed behind in private homes, and others had made their own way through the tangles of south Louisiana to emerge unscathed. One of the returnees was Captain Jerome B. McCown of Company G, 5th Texas Cavalry, who many assumed to have been captured before the Battle of Fort Bisland after watching him fall off his horse in a drunken stupor. "The force is greatly diminished, but our men were continually coming in," Private Edmund Knowles of Company A, 5th Texas wrote home. "The enemy's pursuit was so close that our men scattered very much."[6]

Word of the Bayou Teche operations had also reached the Confederate garrison at Port Hudson. Texans serving there lamented the loss of communications with loved ones in the West with the closing of the Red River, but also reported other grim news. Captain Edward T. Broughton of Company C, 7th Texas Infantry, wrote his wife back in Kaufman County that Federal forces had clearly manhandled the Confederates in western Louisiana. "They . . . have succeeded in defeating our forces there under General Taylor and captured a considerable number of prisoners. Affairs on our side there have been doubtless badly managed, and I fear from the Yankees account that some of our troops have disgraced themselves," he wrote. "I . . . hope it will not be as bad as the Yankee's version."[7]

Bruised but healing quickly, the Texans at Niblett's Bluff understood how things might appear from afar, but they remained confident, even saucy. "People may say what they please about the battle, but when we come to take into consideration the overwhelming odds our little army fought, we cannot compare it to anything better that the 300 Spartans under Leonidas, at the pass of Thermopylae," one Lone Star Rebel crowed with classical superlative. "Had we one half the force to oppose the invaders they had against us, we should have driven them back to New Orleans." The men also knew they had hurt the enemy. Another Texan wrote, "our men seem conscious of having made the best fight of the war, and claim to have killed four to one."[8]

The Teche campaign had distilled the rough-and-tumble brigade, and its men had found a new leader—one they considered worthy of their sacrifices. "Col. Green, than whom a more gallant soldier never trod the field, is in immediate command of the Brigade (Sibley's)," one soldier reported. "He has fought the enemy almost every inch, until we have left the front and made a detour in their rear. He stubbornly resisted their advance at every step. He has doubly proved himself a hero from the firing of the first shell." Another soldier echoed the sentiment: "Had it not been for the gallantry of Green's regiment and Waller's Battalion, who covered the retreat, our army would have been entirely cut to pieces." The blood spilled in Louisiana had seemingly expunged the stain of New Mexico. "Green and his men have won laurels," a soldier boasted. They had also made a name for themselves in the Pantheon of Texas heroes. "The muse of the historian will point once again at them."[9]

Their former, and now twice disgraced, brigadier general received a mix of sympathy and censure. "We hear many reports in regard to the action of Gen. Sibley, but will not pass any opinion upon mere rumor," one soldier wrote to the Houston newspaper, adding "sufficient evidence is at our disposal to warrant us in saying that Sibley acted the coward on the field, and for which he is now under arrest in Shreveport." Private Theophilus Noel, a prisoner since falling into enemy hands on April 20 at Washington, gave more forgiving sentiments. "General Sibley was made to bear . . . all the blame of the unavoidable calamity. Big fish eat little fish," he wrote. A soldier in the 5th Texas took it more pragmatically: "Sibley . . . was treated badly; still, he was not liked by the brigade."[10]

By now, word of Banks and his sweep across Louisiana had rippled across the Trans-Mississippi Confederacy, and commanders gathered soldiers and supplies to forward to Taylor. At Galveston on May 3 the grumbling veterans of the recently dismounted 2nd Texas Cavalry headed for service east of the Sabine River. They made their way through the middle of town, a rag-tag martial spectacle. Colonel Arthur Fremantle, an English observer making his way across the Confederacy at the time, watched. "At 1:30 I saw Pyron's Regiment embark for Niblitt's Bluff to meet Banks," he wrote. "The procession was a droll one. First came eight or ten instruments braying discordantly, then an enormous Confederate flag followed by about four hundred men moving by fours—dressed in every variety of costume and armed with every variety of weapons. The men were a fine, determined-looking lot; and I saw amongst them a short stout boy of fourteen who had served through the Arizona campaign. This regiment is considered down here to be a very good one, and its colonel is spoken of as one of the bravest officers in the army." Two days later, Fremantle arrived at Crockett, Texas, and saw even more reinforcements heading east. "We passed through the encampment of Phillipps's regiment of Texas Rangers. And we underwent much chaff," he reported. "They were *en route* to resist Banks."[11]

For the troops back in Louisiana, the campaign continued unabated. On the Mississippi River, 150 miles east of Niblett's Bluff, the salts and sailors of Admiral David G. Farragut's squadron, now joined by Banks's little navy, were eager to continue hammering away at the enemy. They chafed at their secondary role while the army gathered laurels. The impatient admiral ordered a reconnaissance in force up the Red River on May 3, and three U.S. Navy ships—USS *Albatross,* USS *Arizona,* and USS *Estrella*—slipped away from the flotilla to clear out any residual Confederates along the river while investigating whether Taylor was receiving reinforcements. The expedition learned little from the civilians, slaves, and deserters they picked up, other than "there had been neither steamers nor troops passing for some time," according to Lieutenant Commander John E. Hart, skipper of the screw steamer USS *Albatross.* After probing the various major tributaries of the Red River, the small flotilla cautiously approached Fort DeRussy in the early light of May 4, tipped off by locals that the Rebels were preparing to leave.[12]

At around seven o'clock in the morning a lookout in the *Albatross*'s rigging reported seeing smoke from two steamers, and his news prodded the officers of the vessel into battle. "We gave the men breakfast and then cleared the ship for action, got everything in place, and everybody appeared to understand that a hard fight might possibly be in store for them," reported Hart. "It was indeed satisfying to see how willingly the officers and crew entered into the proper spirit." As part of his orders for the mission, Farragut had directed Hart to cautiously lob a few shells into Fort DeRussy to gauge the result, but the commander of the *Albatross* had another plan since he had sighted Confederate gunboats. "I thought it best that the attack on the steamers," he continued, "should be commenced quite suddenly with a view to surprise them if possible."[13]

The Confederates, unaware of the enemy lurking nearby, focused on their tasks. For the last two days crews had winched cannon out of the river, where they had been dumped in the panic to evacuate the post the week before. When the Federals had failed to advance beyond Washington, General Taylor had ordered crews back to Fort DeRussy to follow his directives this time and salvage all the useful parts that remained. Gangs of slave laborers had dismantled and stacked the railroad iron used to armor the fort's casemates while others had loaded the iron bars aboard a massive barge to be towed to the naval yard at Shreveport. The side-wheel steamer *Countess* idled nearby with a huge cable tied from its stern to the flatboat, ready to take the load upstream that morning. The *Mary T.* and *Grand Duke* lay near each other, tied to the bank near

USS *Albatross*. Confederate gunboats put in some hard licks on this vessel. In the fight against CSS *Grand Duke* and CSS *Mary T.*, the heroism of its quartermaster, James Brown, not only saved the ship, but it also earned him the Medal of Honor.

Naval Historical Center.

the fort's ramparts. Their bow guns were trained to fire downstream over a raft of logs that had been chained across the river to discourage any rushes by adventurous Yankee boat captains.

As the men continued their work, their routine was interrupted when a signal officer began wig-wagging a warning from a semaphore station downstream. Three enemy vessels were approaching. On board the *Grand Duke,* Captain John Kelso, commander of Taylor's gunboat flotilla, ordered the *Countess* to escape with its load while his gunners, the naval veterans of the Crescent Artillery, cleared for action. Nearby, the St. Martin's Rangers, led by Lieutenant Edward T. King, ran out the guns aboard the *Mary T.* The steamer and barge disappeared around a bend ten minutes after the first warning.[14]

The action began just before 9:00 AM. The *Albatross,* moving slowly ahead of the Federal battle line, cleared the point of land downstream of Fort DeRussy, exposing its broadsides. The *Grand Duke* fired at it, sending first one then another 32-pounder round spinning toward and over the *Albatross* as it moved steadily forward. Amid the shelling the *Albatross* hove into full view, following the far bank of the river, bringing its starboard guns to bear on the Rebel boats. Five hundred yards from the fort Lieutenant Commander Hart ordered his five guns to open fire while its engineers steadily reversed direction and advanced the ship into the opposite banks, holding its place abreast the river. The *Arizona* and *Estrella* lagged behind, firing over the bank from a more prudent, less-exposed position downriver.

The saltwater sailors on the *Albatross* quickly learned that they had picked a riverboat gun battle at close quarters. The brown-water dogfight roared along at close range. After twenty minutes a roiling cloud of smoke from eight broadsides against the Confederate gunboats and as many return salvos obscured the antagonists, slowing the combat. Both sides had been badly cut up. The *Grand Duke* was ablaze, and the *Albatross* was scarred from nearly a half-dozen hits.

When the smoke cleared, the gunners returned to work. The Rebels fired as fast as they could, and the Yankees fired in measured volleys every two and a half minutes. A 30-pound Parrott round from the bow pivot of the *Albatross* nearly ended the charmed career of the *Mary T.* The iron projectile blew through the cotton armor and clipped a steam pipe running to one of the wheels. Many crewmen, wounded and panicked by the scalding vapors, jumped off the boat and fell onto shore. "It was with great difficulty that Lieutenant Fogerty and I kept enough men aboard to serve our guns," remembered Lieutenant King. The crew of the *Grand Duke,* having doused the first fire aboard their vessel, now fought to squelch another as repeated shots from the *Albatross* tore the boat into shambles. "It was reported to me that all steering apparatuses of the flagship was shot away," Kelso wrote. "In fact, all the mechanical contrivances

Gunboat Battle at Fort DeRussy. A sketch attributed to sailor Helmuth Holtz shows the two Confederate vessels, CSS *Grand Duke* on the left and CSS *Mary T.* on the right near the unoccupied Fort DeRussy, gamely firing away at USS *Albatross* while USS *Arizona* and USS *Estrella* support from a less exposed position. Notice the raft obstructions located between the antagonists.

Spring Street Historical Museum, Shreveport, Louisiana.

by which communication is conveyed from one part of the boat to another, bell ropes, speaking tubes, etc., were shot to pieces." The pilot reported that the *Grand Duke* could not be steered. It was now little more than a floating battery.[15]

The Rebel guns had damaged the *Albatross* as well. The cannon of the burning *Grand Duke* and the hissing *Mary T.* had hit the Yankee combatant at least eleven times in the hull and repeatedly in the spars and rigging, and splintered wood and hanging ropes now draped the vessel. Rebel cannonballs had clipped the mainmast nearly flush with the deck and split off the foremast fifteen feet above the deck. The foreyard had been stowed along the railing to keep it from tangling with trees on the bank, but a cannonball had cut the pole in two and gouged a jagged groove across the deck. Smoke once again clouded visibility and brought about another lull in the battle. The *Albatross,* beaten severely on its starboard side and shipping water from a hit near the waterline, quickly turned around. The Yankees ran out the guns on the boat's port side and swung the pivots on the bow and the stern to renew the contest once the smoke cleared.

Captain Kelso believed he was losing the battle. Both of his ships lay immobilized, crippled, and splintered. His own *Grand Duke* was on fire for the third time; one of the Union gunboats downstream had found the range and hit the boat three times. To add to the captain's distress, the *Countess* had slipped off the cable connecting it to the barge to hasten its escape. The valuable treasures rescued from Fort DeRussy now drifted with the current, gliding by the battered Rebel steamers until the barge came to rest against the raft and chains downstream. Kelso could barely make out that the *Albatross* was turning around to bring its port guns to bear, and he directed his Crescent cannoneers to keep firing at their Yankee tormentor as it presented its stern to the Rebels.

The Rebels scored a lucky hit. A Confederate 32-pounder round shot tore through the bridge of the *Albatross.* Its wheel exploded in a shower of splinters, dowels, and handles as its wheelman and the nearby pilot flew apart in a mangled mess. The secondary pilot lunged forward from the wreckage and rolled across the deck, his hands shredded by splinters. The punch-drunk *Albatross* wobbled ahead toward the southern bank of the Red River, at almost the same location where the *Queen of the West* had met her fate a month and a half before. "As soon the wheel was gone came a critical time," Hart wrote, "scarcely a moment was to be lost." The ship's executive officer stepped forward and directed the recovery effort with "no pausing or wavering on his part," steering the ship with relieving tackles. "He received prompt attention," Hart continued, "both from those in charge of the engine and those in charge of the helm." The *Albatross* scraped the shoreline but moved back into safer water.[16]

After the close call, there would be no round three. Hart ordered his ship out of action, ending the battle forty minutes after it had started. "I could not require my brave crew to do any more than they had done, and I withdrew from my precarious position as deliberately as I had entered it, firing as I went," he reported, "having done all that lay in my power to disable the enemy." He had no idea how fortunate he was. Engineers below deck reported that the *Albatross,* in addition to shipping water, had a nice hole that ran completely through the boat and had neatly grazed the steam drum. The *Albatross* shuffled down the Red River with smoke pouring from its stack in three places—the top as intended, and from two holes made by the flight of a Rebel solid shot—until it rejoined the *Arizona* and *Estrella.* Chastened, the Federal flotilla headed back toward the Mississippi.[17]

Kelso did not realize how well his Crescent Artillery and St. Martin's Rangers gunners had done. "The leading gunboat of the enemy withdrew, apparently uninjured," he wrote. The Confederate commander consulted with his colleague on the next boat. Both feared that the Federals knew how extensively they had shot up the *Grand Duke* and the *Mary T.* and that they would destroy the gunboats from the enfilading position that the *Arizona* and *Estrella* had adopted. "It seeming to me clear that should the three boats select their positions," he wrote, "our destruction would be probable."[18]

The officers asked for damage reports, and the news proved grim. The crew had put out yet another fire on the *Grand Duke*—its fifth in less than an hour—and everything else had been knocked about. Kelso's crew determined that he could still propel his boat but would have to steer it by using the paddle wheels, relaying messages to the engine room via a verbal bucket brigade. He ordered the steamer to move upriver and out of range so that his sailors and gunners could splice together new cables and make other simple repairs while awaiting their destiny. The *Mary T.*, meanwhile, seemed finished. "The Captain of the *Grand Duke* left me with my boat disabled," King recalled. "I asked him what I should do with my boat, and he yelled to burn her."[19]

The commander of the *Mary T.* still had fight left in him, however, and he reckoned his boat did, too. "Seeing no immediate danger, I resolved if possible to save her," Lieutenant King continued. Some of his crew returned to the ship, and recommended that, if the steamer could get turned around to face upstream, they might be able to limp it up to Alexandria with one wheel. King agreed and pushed his vessel into the current, its good engine straining hard to bring it about. The current won, and the *Mary T.* drifted downstream and slid sideways against the raft and chains. King ordered the ship's boat dropped, and a crew climbed aboard it to row to the opposite side of the Red River, where they tried to manually drag the boat around with a tow line.[20]

The *Grand Duke,* crudely patched but at least under control, returned after about half an hour. Captain Kelso could not believe his good fortune. The *Mary T.* still lived, and the enemy had apparently left. "It was absolutely necessary to save the barge and her valuable freight," he wrote. The *Grand Duke* passed a line to the *Mary T.*, whose crew in turn passed a line to the barge. This bedraggled and ungainly caravan made its way up the Red River to safety.[21]

From the Red River to the Sabine, Confederate forces had survived to fight another day. The battered regiments resting at Niblett's Bluff and the splintered gunboats being hauled up at shipyards in Alexandria emerged as symbols of secessionist resilience against long odds. Taylor, itching for revenge, planned much mischief in the days ahead with the remnants of his army and navy.

24

Alexandria

"His officers have their baggage marked
'San Antonio, Texas'—and they bid fair to reach there
unless troops are sent to check their onward progress."

Private John W. Watkins
Company B, 5th Texas Cavalry

Back at Opelousas the newly energized Major General Nathaniel P. Banks ordered his army to renew the land offensive with a resolve to twist the knife they had jabbed into the heart of Rebel Louisiana. He had frittered away two weeks trying to decide his next move while his army idled at Opelousas. Now it was in motion again. Brigadier General William Dwight led the way north, marching his troops out of their camps at Washington on the afternoon of Monday, May 4, and rolling up the east bank of Bayou Boeuf toward Holmesville. Brigadier General Godfrey Weitzel led his troops on a parallel track out of Opelousas, heading toward Ville Platt to the north and a rendezvous with the other column marching out of Washington through Holmesville. "Everyone was in high spirits at the prospect of meeting the Army of the Tennessee," noted Lieutenant Colonel Richard B. Irwin, Banks's assistant adjutant general.[1]

What Banks had intended as simply a great raid up Bayou Teche had been very productive. "In round numbers, I may say that 20,000 beeves, mules, and horses have been forwarded to Brashear City, with 5,000 bales of cotton and many hogsheads of sugar," Banks crowed to Union leadership in Washington, D.C. This was just the beginning of what they could expect, he promised. His army would find more spoils on the road to the Red River.[2]

Amid the bustling excitement of the army's departure that afternoon, someone killed Captain Howard Dwight, a member of Banks's staff. Irwin described him as "brave and promising young officer and . . . a pleasant and always cheerful comrade." The soldier had received permission to leave headquarters at Opelousas to join his brother's brigade as it advanced. Traveling by carriage with the supply wagons, he abandoned that mode of transport in favor of riding swiftly ahead on horseback, leaving his orderlies

Contraband Camp. Freed slaves needed assistance through their bewildering change in circumstances, and Federal authorities organized collecting points for these displaced persons.

Massachusetts Comandery Military Order of the Loyal Legion and the US Army Military History Institute.

behind. Somewhere between Opelousas and the advance of the army on the east bank of Bayou Boeuf, he died from a bullet to the head.[3]

The Federals immediately blamed Rebel "guerillas." One report claimed Dwight was ambushed on the road along Bayou Boeuf by a party of armed men on the opposite bank. "Captain Dwight was quite alone," one officer recalled. "Armed only with his sword, and seeing his escape was hopeless, he instantly declared his readiness to surrender." Instead, the Rebels allegedly shouted "surrender be damned!" and shot him. His escorts from the 2nd Rhode Island Cavalry discovered the body three minutes later. Confederate private John W. Watkins reported the assailants as "two of our boys from Waller's Battalion" whom Dwight happened to surprise before they could fire. "But the bayou being between them and the Yankees [within] a hundred yards they couldn't take him and consequently they shot him."[4]

A newspaper correspondent at Opelousas told a slightly different story. He wrote that the captain "was shot and killed while on his way from Opelousas to Washington, a distance of six miles." The writer agreed that the officer had started with the wagons, but "he got out from the buggy and mounted his horse, and while proceeding along five men (guerillas) stopped him; they yelled out 'shoot the damned Yankee scoundrel.'" The captain attempted to surrender. "They cried out again to shoot him and shot at him, but did not kill him at the first fire. At the second fire a ball entered his head and killed him instantly." He had apparently ridden ahead of his orderlies. The only witnesses, according to official reports, were two "boys."[5]

A third account, in a New Orleans newspaper, also said a young boy was a witness. In this version Dwight rode to the Courtableau, "on the road from Alexandria to Franklin," where three men hailed him. He reined in his "beautiful black steed," asked who they were, and they drew down on him with pistols. He surrendered and dismounted, only to hear his captors say, "we don't want a prisoner, killed the damned Yankee." Bullets to the leg and head did the trick, and the men left Dwight's body lying in the road. A child watched over it until the arrival of Union cavalry. "The dastard bullet of the cowardly guerilla, in this instance, struck down one of the brightest and most promising of New England's sons," the article read. "He escaped the death-dealing shell and shot of the enemy . . . only to fall by the hands of an assassin."[6]

Captain Howard Dwight enlisted as a captain in the 4th Missouri Cavalry before joining the staff of his brother, Brigadier General William Dwight as assistant adjutant general in November 1862. He served in this capacity until one fateful day near Opelousas.

Massachusetts Comandery Military Order of the Loyal Legion and the US Army Military History Institute.

This story circulated widely among both armies. Federal authorities demanded the capture of the parties guilty of killing such a luminary. Banks directed hostages taken to ensure compliance. "The people of the neighborhood who harbor and feed these lawless men are even more directly responsible for the crimes which they commit," Banks wrote in his order. "It is by punishing them that this detestable practice will be stopped."[7]

Banks ordered that all the men living along Bayou Boeuf be rounded up. Soldiers arrested sixteen men, from young boys to a man in his eighties, and marched them back to Washington. After releasing their elderly captive, guards marched the remaining fifteen to Port Barré and loaded them onto a steamer loaded with confiscated cotton. The civilians traveled under armed escort to New Orleans for a three-month incarceration as hostages, pending a satisfactory outcome to the mystery. The government threatened to shoot them all.[8]

Evidence suggests that Howard Dwight's own men may have murdered him in a case of deliberate fratricide. He had died violently almost in the very heart of the fifteen-thousand-man Union army, with no witnesses except children. His death may have been a revenge murder. The dead man's brother, Brigadier General William Dwight, had punished looters the week before, broken up rings of thieves that included troops in the 2nd Rhode Island Cavalry, and ordered one New Yorker shot without benefit of a court-martial. Dwight's slain younger brother, in his role at headquarters, would have been involved in drawing up orders for the death sentence. On the day of Howard Dwight's demise, he may have fallen victim to his own orderlies or to a prearranged ambush. There may have been men lurking in the region more dangerous than the Confederate enemy.

Not surprisingly, scouts identified an alleged assailant. A company of the now notorious 2nd Rhode Island scoured the countryside and, according to a soldier in the 6th Massachusetts Battery, "succeeded in capturing the man who committed the deed." A military tribunal ordered the Rhode Islanders' Confederate sacrificial prisoner tried and shot as retribution. The doomed man was "not the one that fired the shot, but they were together so he had to die for it," wrote Lieutenant George G. Smith of the Union 1st Louisiana Infantry. A firing squad carried out the deed three days later. "Kneeling beside the grave, facing the firing party, the warrant was read, and the command given to fire. He fell forward on his face. I thought I heard some pistol shots afterward, but I had seen all I wanted to." There was no time to investigate such a trifling case in May 1863, and the story of the death of these two combatants—one famous, one anonymous—quickly faded.[9]

Despite small tragedies like the death of Captain Dwight and the execution of his alleged secessionist killer, the offensive up Bayou Teche had been a major achievement for Major General Banks, as he remained quick to remind those around him. "When I came here, [this department] was as bare of military supplies as it was at the date of the creation of the world," he huffed to Brigadier General Montgomery C. Meigs, quartermaster general of the army. Since leaving Brashear City a month before, Banks's soldiers had supplied their every want from the larder of Louisiana. "We have plenty of cattle, mules, and horses, and shall not ask any assistance from the Government in that respect." The army also had plenty of wagons.[10]

The Federals did not have enough steamboats, however. Banks could think of only a dozen or so suitable for navigating the streams of the region, and he thought he needed fifty. Banks believed he could build his own transport fleet. His troops had captured tons of lumber, and he had inventoried twenty steam engines in and around New Orleans that could be modified to drive a boat. "The singular formation of this country makes water and land transportation in equal strength necessary in all expeditions," he explained. The problem, Banks continued, was that the Rebels could crimp either an overland or a water supply line. His army needed a way to remain flexible when it came to feeding and equipping itself. He would ship the lumber to New Orleans and establish a shipyard to meet his transportation needs. He also planned to spend the summer repairing the vessels he had at hand.[11]

Banks also wrote letters and reports burnishing his reputation, defending his choices, and extolling his officers. "I hope I may be privileged to relieve myself of the almost unconquerable difficulties which have rested upon me from the moment of reaching New Orleans until now," he groused, "by supplying at the lowest possible expense to the Government these pressing and imperative demands." Gossips in Washington, D.C., complained that Banks accomplished little in Louisiana, and many actively pined for the return of Major

General Benjamin Butler. On the contrary, the commander of the Department of the Gulf asserted: he had inherited a mission and command left in complete disarray by his predecessor that he had in fact cleaned up. He believed the spoils of the Teche Campaign now set everything right.[12]

Colonel Thomas E. Chickering was famous as senior partner in a lucrative piano factory and distributor, Chickering and Sons of Boston. At thirty-eight years old, he set aside his business and accepted a commission as colonel of the 41st Massachusetts Infantry. Major General Banks added three independent companies of Bay State cavalry operating in Louisiana and converted the whole into the 3rd Massachusetts Cavalry and named Chickering as military governor of Opelousas with orders to strip the region of valuable commodities.

Massachusetts Comandery Military Order of the Loyal Legion and the US Army Military History Institute.

Nevertheless, Banks had not finished gleaning Louisiana. The second pulse of the renewed invasion followed on the morning of May 5. Brigadier General William H. Emory sent his division up the Ville Platt Road toward Alexandria. He returned to New Orleans ostensibly under doctor's orders; Colonel Halbert E. Paine took his command through the next phase of the campaign. Meanwhile Brigadier General Cuvier Grover marched out from Port Barré. As a closing curtain on the second act, Banks ordered that the army's depots be dismantled. Colonel Thomas E. Chickering would lead a four-regiment temporary brigade—a fifth of the available infantry—that would stay behind in Washington and Opelousas, shut down the various army operations, and then drive a plunder train and contraband caravan overland to Brashear City.

The Union troops would linger a few more days around Opelousas until they had stripped it bare of military contraband. At Port Barré Corporal James K. Hosmer witnessed the busy hum of an army on the move. "Steamers come from New Orleans and Brashear City to this remote landing, bringing supplies to the army, and go back loaded to the water's edge with cotton and sugar," he wrote. He justified the seizure of these commodities as being appropriate compensation for the efforts of the U.S. government in suppressing the rebellion and freeing the slaves. "It is right to take this, and use it in defraying our expenses in this war," he wrote, "for in our triumph is coming the time of jubilee to these unpaid blacks."[13]

Banks was fully committed to his vision of how to conquer the rest of Louisiana. First he would take Alexandria, where he was certain he would meet the reinforcements he had asked Major General Ulysses S. Grant to send—Major General John A. McClernand's 13th Corps. A few days before, he had entrusted this request to his aide-de-camp, a recent Harvard graduate-turned-volunteer lieutenant named Charles Sprague Sargent, sending him

Bringing in Contraband. Slaves were encouraged, and sometimes coerced into coming into the Federal camps where they could be processed for service to the republic—as free people.

John A. Kouwenhoven, Adventures of America, 1857–1900: A Pictorial Record from Harper's Weekly *(New York: Harper and Brothers Publishers, 1938).*

aboard the *Cornie* and down the Courtableau to the Atchafalaya to the mouth of the Red River. By now May 5, Banks reasoned, Sargent would have placed his dispatch into the care of Admiral David G. Farragut for delivery upstream to Grant. But just as Banks prepared to make a personal ride to the head of his conquering column, he received a confusing reply. Sargent arrived at headquarters, fresh from his errand but had failed to make contact with Admiral Farragut. Instead he had found Commander Selim E. Woodworth with the gunboats *Benton, Lafayette, Pittsburgh*; the rams *Price* and *Switzerland;* and the tug *Ivy.* Sargent reported the news that Grant had crossed the Mississippi on April 29 and had pushed inland toward Jackson with two of his three corps. Sargent also bore a letter from Admiral David Dixon Porter. "The taking of Vicksburg is a mere matter of time," the admiral boasted in his missive. The dispatch Sargent delivered to Banks also included Porter's promise to meet the army at Alexandria with some gunboats. None of the documents revealed any news on additional troops coming from Grant.[14]

USS *Benton*, an ironclad converted from a catamaran hulled, center wheel snag boat, was home for 175 men and housed sixteen guns and saw extensive service on the Mississippi River, from the attack on Fort Henry to passing the batteries at Vicksburg.

Naval Historical Center.

From the evidence Sargent presented, Grant had modified his plans as well, leaving Banks unsure what to do next. Remarkably, that same day, a courier galloped up to headquarters bearing a note from Grant, carried via the long route from New Orleans, and written in cipher. The military clerks at Opelousas could make out the words "Bayou Sara" and "25th." Banks now had his answer. Grant apparently still intended to send reinforcements, but instead of marching them overland he would send them on transports, which, like Porter's gunboats, had made it past Vicksburg. Grant would ship these men, presumably McClernand's 13th Corps, toward Port Hudson and have them in place north of that citadel by May 25. Banks sent the note by relays to New Iberia for a more thorough decoding and analysis at the army signal station there. Upon reflection, Banks decided that he had already gathered the meaning of the document; at any rate, Grant's coded message would not change Banks's immediate plans, since his army was already underway. Banks departed Opelousas on the morning of May 6, bound for Alexandria and, he hoped, for glory. Banks joined Grover's column as it passed through Washington on its way north. Once Banks arrived on the Red River he would decide what came next.[15]

USS *Lafayette* started life as a side wheel steamboat, *Aleck Scott*, in 1848. Purchased by the navy in May 1862, craftsmen in St. Louis converted the vessel into an impressive ironclad. The gunboat joined the Porter's Mississippi flotilla in early April, its heavy batteries of two 100-pounder Parrotts, two 11-inch Dahlgrens, and four 9-inch Dahlgrens a welcomed addition.

Naval Historical Center.

USS *Pittsburgh* first saw action against Fort Henry in February 1862 and served in every major riverine fight afterward. By the time the ironclad hove to at Alexandria, it was battle scarred and battle tested.

Naval Historical Center.

USS *General Price* had been the side wheel steamboat *Laurent Millaudon* before being converted by Confederate authorities into a gunboat ram for the defense of New Orleans and rechristened CSS *Sterling Price*. The vessel went to Memphis, Tennessee, in March 1862 and sparred with the Federal flotilla descending the river. On June 1, USS *Queen of the West* captured the *Price*, and, after repairs, it entered U.S. service.

Naval Historical Center.

USS *Switzerland* was one of Colonel Charles Ellet Jr.'s ram fleet and first saw action at Memphis. After it ran the Vicksburg batteries on March 25, 1863, it helped blockade the Red River.

Naval Historical Center.

The rapid Union advance nearly cut off the Confederate mounted forces operating between Holmesville and Evergreen. The bedraggled battalions of Colonel Eugene Waggaman and Colonel Edwin Waller hustled from their camps near Bayou Rouge and Bayou Huffpower to reach the Alexandria road ahead of the Union advance. They barely made it. "We saddled up . . . and got into it two miles ahead of the Yankees," Watkins told his wife. With the entire Union army now nearly within cannon range and closing, the Confederates prudently abandoned the main road to bypass the city on a circuitous route to the southwest. "When in twenty miles of Alexandria we . . . turned into the piney woods and came

through swamps and thickets traveling night and day," Watkins remembered. These Confederates made good their escape, emerging well to the northwest of town.[16]

These six hundred or so troopers continued their weary retreat up Bayou Rapides and on to Natchitoches where they rejoined the bulk of Major General Richard Taylor's army. Private Watkins of the 5th Texas Cavalry was especially glad to be reunited with the baggage wagons that he had parted from more than a month before. "I got a change of clothes, the first I had in four weeks," he wrote. "Our reinforcements are expected daily. Some have already arrived. The enemy [is] advancing rapidly and the tale will soon be told whether we are to give up this state and fall back to Texas or drive the Yankees back to the Gulf. If we ever get them started back we will use them pretty rough."[17]

For the first time since opening the campaign, the way toward Banks's objective lay free of enemy soldiers. "The roads were good, dry, and easy under foot," Lieutenant Colonel Irwin remarked, "the weather fine and the men were filled with a desire to push the march, and with an eager rivalry to be the first in Alexandria." The troops took the town without opposition late on the evening of Thursday, May 7, having covered an impressive eighty-seven road miles in three days. "God alone knows why we marched thus," griped Captain John William De Forest of the 12th Connecticut. "We had nothing more to boast of than we had accomplished thirty-four miles in one day, and eighty-seven miles in whole burst of seventy-six hours. That night I was too tired to eat, and went contentedly to sleep without supper."[18]

As the men of the Union 1st Louisiana passed through the streets, locals vented their anger at the invading troops. "In passing through the streets there was a house with a bright fire on the hearth," Lieutenant Smith recalled. "A girl was standing in the door, and I head her say, 'See the scabs.' I was too weary to reply, but I gathered from it that we were not very welcome."[19]

Banks and his army were not the first Federals to reach the city. Admiral Porter's promised flotilla arrived that morning with his gunboats as well as the *Estrella* and *Arizona.* They had passed Fort DeRussy on May 5, found it deserted and dismantled, and had pressed on upstream. They were as amazed as the infantry that the great campaign for Louisiana appeared to have been concluded without an additional shot fired.

Chaos roiled the city. Looters rifled stores and some residences while freed slaves flooded the streets to see the Federal soldiers to celebrate and take part in some of the pandemonium. Alexandria's fearful citizens sent an assembly of leading men to Banks, seeking assurance that the lawlessness would be checked. They were disappointed. "Believe it, gentlemen, as if you heard God himself speak it," the general boomed. "I will lay waste to your country, destroy your crops, stock, and agricultural implements, so that you shall never organize and maintain an army in this department." If the United States army did not hold this territory, Banks would see to it that the Rebels could not make use of it either.[20]

Banks Enters Alexandria. Lieutenant Colonel Richard Irwin remembered, "The roads were good, dry, and easy under foot, the weather fine and the men were filled with a desire . . . to be the first in Alexandria." They were not. The arrival of a gunboat flotilla preceded the triumphal entry of the army on May 7 by about eight hours.

Harper's Weekly, *June 20, 1863.*

Confederate planners hoped that the capture of this key city would mark another lull in the advance, but they were wrong. Couriers coming in to Taylor's headquarters reported that the Federals were still on the move, headed north. The brigades of Brigadier General Weitzel and Brigadier General Dwight alone continued the pursuit of Taylor's army. They moved beyond Alexandria for the next four days, pressing northwest up the Red River, catching a few of Waggaman's Battalion as they straggled out of the woods. Weitzel moved as far as the Cane River crossing at Monett's Ferry, his cavalry and mounted infantry hard on the enemy's heels. Weitzel's aggressive posture and desire to finish off the Rebels nearly succeeded, better than he could have hoped. His cavalry, pursuing whom they thought were merely Rebel scouts, nearly captured Taylor and an orderly who managed to outride the Yankees after a four-mile race. Federals scouts continued until thwarted by a sabotaged ferry, within a day's march of Natchitoches. They returned to the infantry columns convinced that Taylor had holed up just a few miles ahead, and might yet be brought to battle.[21]

Weitzel sent dispatches back to Banks asking permission to proceed on to Natchitoches and, if necessary, attack any Confederates there. Remarkably, he had advanced forty-one miles beyond Alexandria without any opposition. Yet, Weitzel wondered, where had Porter's gunboats had gone? "Why did not the gunboats come up and communicate with me?" the German general asked Banks. With their support, he was prepared to take Natchitoches and inflict one more defeat on Taylor—perhaps *the* defeat. "We probably could have captured all their artillery and wagon train," he suggested, which included more than three hundred vehicles—a potentially catastrophic loss to the Confederates.[22]

The answer was ominous: the navy had left. Porter detected that the water in the Red River was falling fast, and he wanted to move his heavy gunboats into deeper water. He certainly was not going to send them above the rocky falls at Alexandria to possibly become marooned in enemy territory. Banks trusted his judgments, wished the admiral well, and watched his flotilla steam downstream days around May 7, leaving only the ironclad *Lafayette* behind. Porter intended to complete a few tasks on his way back to the Mississippi. He ordered work crews from his fleet to finish dismantling Fort DeRussy, to keep the Rebels from reoccupying it anytime soon, and he sent four vessels up the Black River to the Ouachita in order to destroy Confederate Fort Beauregard at the bluffs of Harrisonburg.[23]

Clearly the Confederates in Louisiana faced a gloomy future. Weitzel and Dwight, poised to make a bold move might destroy them yet. "We couldn't muster at this place more than 3,000 men for duty," Watkins wrote. "Walker's Division from Arkansas is reported en route for this place. . . . I sometimes think they are not coming." Taylor's spies and scouts also reported that more Yankees were on the way. "Banks is said to have been reinforced until he has 60,000 men with him. His officers have their baggage marked 'San Antonio, Texas,'" Watkins worried, "and they bid fair to reach there unless troops are sent to check their onward progress."[24]

The panic that dogged Taylor's army also spread westward. Few believed the Federals would stop in Alexandria with a decisive victory so close at hand. As Colonel Arthur Fremantle of the British Coldstream Guards made his way by stagecoach toward Shreveport, he saw evidence of the alarm sweeping this portion of the Confederacy. "All the villages which we passed were deserted expect by women and very old men; their aspect was most melancholy," the officer reported. "We met several planters on the road, who with their families and negroes were taking refuge in Texas, after having abandoned their plantations in Louisiana on the approach of Banks." Among those leaving were James and Clarissa Hewitt, just starting west in refugee wagons toward their new home near Kaufman, Texas.[25]

Late in the afternoon on Friday, May 8, after a brutal and tiring ride from Galveston, the British soldier finally presented his credentials to Lieutenant General Edmund Kirby Smith at Shreveport. "He is a remarkably active man, and of very agreeable manners," Fremantle remarked. "He wears big spectacles and a black beard." The Floridian general showed little of the panic that seemed to be infecting the citizens of his domain. Instead, he was happy to have Fremantle's company and agreed to an evening's diversion. After dinner, Fremantle accompanied the general and his "extremely pretty" wife to the banks of the Red River to trap crawfish. "We . . . were most successful, the General displaying much energy on the occasion."[26]

While the Confederate commander of the Trans-Mississippi lured "mudbugs" into his snares and plantation owners streamed into Texas with their slaves, Banks paced the floor of his Alexandria headquarters, musing his options. Weitzel's scouts reported the final destruction of Taylor's army was within reach. Just one more aggressive push to Natchitoches and the chore might be finished. Then, on to Shreveport.

Should he allow his two brigades to pitch into them at Natchitoches? Banks could not give Weitzel an answer. He believed he needed the additional troops of the 13th Corps to finish the job. But where was Grant? Would his twenty thousand men be idling at Bayou Sara while Banks and his ten thousand road-weary troops chased Taylor? Perhaps he could send word via steamer to Grant so that he could divert the troops up the Red River. If Banks understood the ciphered message correctly, he still had a week to adjust Grant's timetable and movements.

At the same time, Banks understood that the march to Alexandria had again worn out his command, which combat, fatigue, disease, and detachments had already greatly diminished. If he pushed ahead now, as his most aggressive general suggested, he risked meeting a reinforced and fresh Confederate army while his army was weak and fatigued—rumors abounded that Rebel reinforcements were Louisiana bound. Had more Texans indeed arrived? Where were General Henry Hopkins Sibley and his brigade of veteran cavalry? Were they ahead of him, as Dwight had reported, or were they instead plotting against his supply lines stretching 150 miles back to Brashear City? Banks wrestled with the answer for two before finally ordering Weitzel to fall back from the approaches to Natchitoches. He needed Weitzel's men closer to Alexandria while he awaited word from Grant.

Banks's instincts proved correct; more Texans were indeed coming to Louisiana. To the north, Colonel Fremantle had continued on his journey and had headed east toward Monroe, writing that the road was "alive with negroes being 'run' into Texas out of Banks's way." The British officer would have to cross the Mississippi at some point, a goal that seemed increasingly problematic. Fremantle had taken Kirby Smith's advice and was heading toward the Ouachita River and then downstream toward Vidalia, Louisiana, and its cross-river counterpart, Natchez, Mississippi. Along the way he encountered the eight thousand Texans of General John G. Walker's Division on Sunday, May 10. "The division had embarked in steamers, and had already started down the 'Wachita' towards the Red River, when the news arrived of the fall of Alexandria, and of the presence of Federal gunboats." Banks, Farragut, Porter, and Grant had successfully scrambled the Confederate command and control in Louisiana, and the Southern armies seemed to flail about, unsure of their next move. When Fremantle arrived at a hotel in Monroe that night, he found chaos. "Universal confusion reigned there," he wrote. "It was full of officers and soldiers of Walker's Division, and no person would take the slightest notice of us."[27]

He eventually sought refuge at the headquarters of the area commander. The British officer awoke the next morning and spoke with his host, a veteran of the vicissitudes of the Confederate

Trans-Mississippi. "General Paul Octave Hébert is a good looking creole," Fremantle observed. "He used to hold Magruder's position as commander-in-chief in Texas, but he has now been shelved at Munroe." Hébert reported that the situation in the region looked grim. When Fremantle approached him for advice on how to continue his journey, the Confederate turned gloomy. Grant's troops had already approached to within forty miles of the town and had captured Delhi, Louisiana. No one among the Confederate leadership knew what the Federals were up to, but all feared that they were the targets. "[Hébert] expects to be taken prisoner every day; and from the present gloomy aspect of affairs about here, it seems extremely probable that he will not be disappointed in his expectations."[28]

Grant and his army were clearly on the move, but the Confederates in the Department of the Trans-Mississippi had not discerned his true intentions. Fremantle decided to avoid trouble if he could. U.S. authorities might take a dim view of his semi-official mission to observe the Confederate army on behalf of the British government. He took a steamer down the Ouachita the next morning, heading for the Confederate Fort Beauregard at Harrisonburg, about seventy-five miles away. Unknown to the frustrated British soldier, the USS *Pittsburgh, Arizona, General Price,* and *Switzerland* had just concluded an unsuccessful two-day bombardment of that Rebel outpost on their way back down from Alexandria. Fremantle would have to be careful as he threaded his way between the prowling Federals and their various raiders and outriders.[29]

Meanwhile, Federal mechanics at Brashear City had finished repairs to the engine of the *Clifton* during the first week in May. The gunboat had once again headed up the Atchafalaya to join the fleet operating on the Red River only to be smashed up by overhanging trees as it passed through the swamp, retarding its progress. While it was tied up to the bank and carpenters repaired the damage, the USS *Sachem,* on its way down stream from the mouth of the Red River to Brashear City, hailed the unlucky gunboat. Aboard was Admiral Farragut. "We were informed that our services were not needed up there, as Alexandria had already fallen into our hands without our aid," Marine private Henry O. Gusley wrote. The Clifton reversed its course, following the *Sachem* back to Brashear City, and Gusley returned to his old routine. "This place still presents a very business-like aspect," he observed from the streets of the once-quiet town that had blossomed into a major Union base. "Cotton, sugar, and livestock are still daily coming down the river."[30]

25

Indecision

"We shall watch with the greatest anxiety
the movements of yourself and General Grant."

Major General Henry W. Halleck
General-in-Chief, U.S. Army

Even as the Yankee movements confounded the Rebels, any answers regarding Major General Ulysses S. Grant's next move eluded many of the Federal commanders from Washington, D.C., to Alexandria, Louisiana, as well. On May 12, Major General Nathaniel P. Banks received the long-awaited dispatch from his counterpart operating against Vicksburg. Grant was not coming—ever—to meet him, nor was he sending the 13th Corps. He had accidentally been too successful against Lieutenant General John C. Pemberton. "It was my intention on gaining a foothold at Grand Gulf, to have sent a sufficient force to Port Hudson to have insured the fall of that place," the dispatch read. "Meeting the enemy, as I did, south of Port Gibson, I followed him . . . and could not afford to retrace my steps. Many days cannot elapse before the battle will begin which is to decide the fate of Vicksburg," wrote Grant. Instead, Grant wanted Banks to cease what he considered a wild goose chase and help him with his own rabbit hunt in Mississippi. "I urgently request therefore you join me," he wrote, "or send all the force you can spare." Even as Banks read the note in disbelief, Grant was fighting his way through a small Rebel force at Raymond, Mississippi.[1]

Banks rattled off an addled reply to Grant. "It is impossible for me to join you at Vicksburg in time or with force to be of service to you in any immediate attack," he dictated. "The only course for me, failing in cooperation with you, is to regain the Mississippi and attack Port Hudson or to move against the enemy at Shreveport. I regret very much my inability to join you."[2]

A startling realization dawned upon Major General Banks as he agonized at his Alexandria headquarters. The Army of the Gulf, although in unrestricted communication with the navy and now with Grant, had plunged deeply into enemy territory at nearly the exact moment his counterpart had done so in Mississippi. Either Pemberton or Major General Richard Taylor might soon be reinforced, if they had not been already. Grant or Banks might be surrounded in the interior, cut off from his supplies, and destroyed. This would clearly be a calamity to the nation. Banks now faced three options, and all were poor in his estimation. He could retreat toward Brashear City through a region he himself had ordered stripped of produce and supplies; he could abandon his territorial gains and retreat toward the Mississippi River at Simmesport; or he could surge deeper into Rebel Louisiana and finish off Taylor without knowing how many Rebels he might be facing. Whatever option he chose, he and his army would have to accomplish the move alone. Grant had abandoned him.

The Simmesport option appeared most appealing, since that would entail moving closer to friendly forces and away from the unknown. Dangers remained. If Banks managed to cross the great river—should transportation be at hand—he could be lodged between at least two Confederate armies, both of which had more men than he had, as well as the prospects of another Southern relief army sent from back east. If Grant met disaster—which seemed entirely possible given his unorthodox approach—Banks would be placing his tired and scattered command between the Confederate Scylla and Charybdis of Port Hudson and Vicksburg. If the navy's transportation was inadequate to move his army across the river, then a resuscitated Taylor might beset him while his men remained vulnerable and short of supplies.

After studying maps and listening to scouting reports, Banks declared the road to Simmesport to be inadequate. He simply could not be sure that he could get his army moving toward the Mississippi. If he bogged down on soggy Louisiana roads and was set upon by the Confederates, he would lose his guns, his wagons, and perhaps his army. Banks took counsel of his fears and directed his staff to draft orders reflecting what he believed was the safest choice: the Army of the Gulf would retreat to Brashear City the same way it had come, and the Teche Campaign would enter history as a massive raid with great territorial gains squandered by a lack of cooperation between Union commands. It was a grand opportunity lost.

Banks refused to take censure for this decision. "It would be utterly impossible for me to join General Grant before Vicksburg," he curtly wrote to Major General Henry W. Halleck in Washington. "I have not the transportation to do so, and if I had, to take my men to him would involve, besides the abandonment of our trains and all the negroes, horses, mules, cotton, and supplies that we have collected in this country, the probable loss of New Orleans in any event, and its certain fall in case of disaster above." Banks worked himself into a lather. "Had General Grant aided me to take Port Hudson, our forces united could have compelled the fall of Vicksburg sooner than I think he will be able to do it alone. I am reluctantly forced to the conclusion that there is now only one thing left to us—to retrace our steps to Baton Rouge . . . and to operate upon Port Hudson unaided."[3]

That afternoon, May 12, Brigadier General Godfrey Weitzel's soldiers drew back toward Alexandria, quitting their role as vanguard and now becoming the rear guard for Banks's retreating army. An ominous force shadowed their retreat. Behind them were some three hundred horsemen of the 1st Texas Partisan Rangers under the command of a feisty old warrior, Colonel Walter P. Lane. The regiment by itself was not much of a military threat, but it was a harbinger of the future. These mounted Texans, led by an Irish ex-Ranger, were the first reinforcements to answer Lieutenant General Edmund Kirby Smith's call. Almost immediately they started brushing up against Weitzel's withdrawing Federals, firing upon them as they tramped past McNutts Hill and Bayou Cotile on Bayou Rapides, northwest of Alexandria. Weitzel realized these were new men and that more Texans were certainly on their way. While Banks stewed about the course he should follow, Taylor bided his time at Natchitoches with a single purpose: destroying Yankees, the sooner the better. Little did he realize that he would have to hurry to catch the Yankee army.

On Wednesday, May 13, Banks changed his mind again. His engineers insisted that the road to Simmesport was better than anticipated and that it would support the passage of the army and its heavy artillery. Banks issued new orders, this time to withdraw the army to that point. There he could decide on his next move. He could use his own transports, plying the waters of the Atchafalaya to carry his army down that river, across the length of Grand Lake, and once again to its starting point at Brashear City. Or, depending on news from the Mississippi, Banks might yet find transportation to get him across the river. Once there, he might head north toward Grant or south to Port Hudson, depending on the situation and the location of Rebel armies and the successes of Union arms. Either way, now he was heading to Simmesport.

Perhaps to assuage his own frustrations, Banks declared that the Confederates in Louisiana were irrevocably beaten. The Union general settled his mind regarding Taylor. He had thrashed him soundly, Banks decided, and his tiny army no longer posed a threat.

Banks reported to his superiors that he had chased Taylor to Grand Ecore—forty miles further than even Weitzel had been—and the Confederates would not return any time soon. Banks ignored evidence to the contrary. Having convinced himself that he had ruined the Rebels in Louisiana, Banks directed that his army strip down to the essentials. Extra baggage, ammunition, and supplies would travel overland to Brashear City along with Colonel Thomas E. Chickering's column gathering at Opelousas, a safe trip by Banks's estimation, and would pick up the garrisons at New Iberia and Franklin along the way. These escorting regiments would then assume the defensive and serve as the principal force protecting the Lafourche District at the garrison of Brashear City. Unencumbered by extra baggage, Banks and the rest of the Army of the Gulf's fighting men would dash to the Mississippi.

Banks notified the navy that he was on his way and told them to stand fast until his arrival, so that he could keep his options open. "Our reconnaissances . . . show that it is practicable for us to join General Grant at Vicksburg," he wrote. "I shall make every sacrifice and hazard everything to effect this junction. My command will move to Simmesport . . . making that the base of our operations, and transport the army to Grand Gulf by transports and by such naval vessels as can assist us." Banks was certain he was not remaining in central Louisiana. Where he went next, however, neither he nor anyone else seemed to be sure, despite his professed interests in assisting Grant.[4]

Banks ended his great invasion of Louisiana in a cloud of second-guessing and confusion, but he hoped for the best. On Thursday, May 14, the first of the Union troops left Alexandria heading through Lecompte and Cheneyville before taking the left-hand fork toward the Mississippi via Evergreen. Brigadier General Cuvier Grover and his army led the column, followed by Colonel Halbert E. Paine leading Brigadier General William H. Emory's Division.

The Confederates watched him leave and closed in from behind. At the junction of Cotile Bayou and the Red River—fifteen miles upriver from Alexandria—men of the 1st Texas Partisan Rangers under Colonel Lane and probably Colonel Edwin Waller's

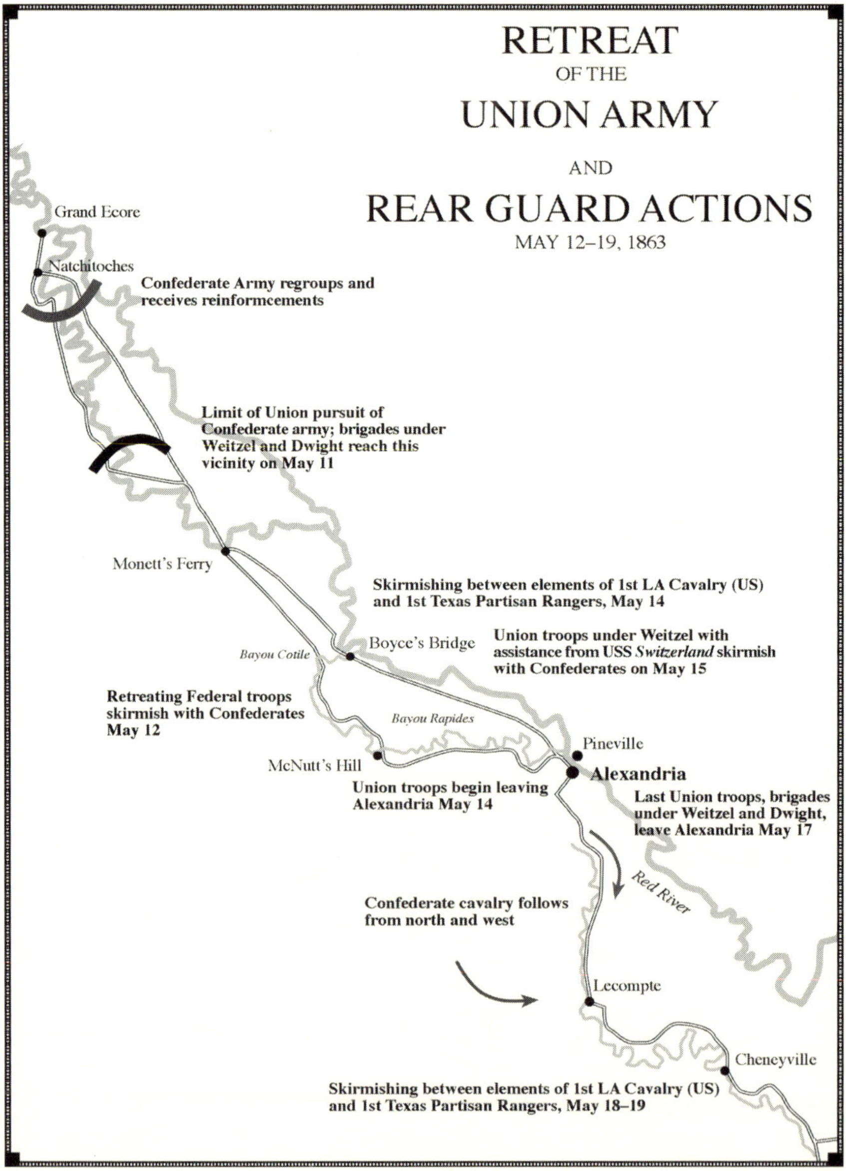

Colonel Walter P. Lane was a seasoned veteran of all of Texas's wars. Wounded as a youngster at the Battle of San Jacinto, he went on to serve in the army of the Republic of Texas. Wounded by Indians in 1838, he tried his hand at being a merchant in San Augustine, Texas, but found life with the Texas Rangers more to his liking and served with Jack Hays's hard-fighting regiment in the Mexican War. After rough luck for four years in the California gold fields, he gave up and settled in Marshall, Texas. At the beginning of the Civil War, Lane joined the 3rd Texas Cavalry as its lieutenant colonel and saw action in Missouri, Indian Territory, and Arkansas, then crossed the Mississippi with the regiment. He returned to Texas to raise the 1st Texas Partisan Rangers in 1862 and led that unit in the Battle of Prairie Grove, Arkansas, that December. By the time Lane and his troopers sparred with Yankees outside Alexandria, the grizzled soldier had survived numerous combat wounds and ten horses shot out from under him. This photo was taken near the end of his amazing life.

The Adventures and Recollections of General Walter P. Lane.

Battalion knocked together a makeshift cotton bale-and-earthwork fortification covering Boyce's Bridge, the main crossing on a principal road between the armies. Troopers from the Union 1st Louisiana Cavalry trotted up the road to investigate. After counting more than one thousand enemy soldiers backed by the 1st Regular artillery, the Federals left. Some of the Texans sallied out after them, only to have the Louisiana Unionists turn back and scatter them, killing or wounding a handful and bringing in a prisoner. The following day, May 15, Weitzel launched all of his cavalry and mounted infantry, nearly one thousand men, in a reconnaissance in force against the enemy position, accompanied by USS *Switzerland* with two hundred men of the 75th New York on board. The Confederates fled. Meanwhile, other patrols indicated additional Texas horsemen were heading toward Alexandria from the west.[5]

Clearly it was time for the Federals to leave. Brigadier

General William Dwight's and Wietzel's brigades—perhaps the two best in the army, quit Alexandria on Sunday, May 17. Between them and Paine were the extra wagons and supplies of the army, now a burden as Banks's wandering host crossed the great river. The two rear brigades would see this baggage safely on its way toward Colonel Chickering's command at Opelousas and Port Barré, and Chickering would then escort it back to Brashear City and into storage. Dwight and Weitzel would then double back toward the Mississippi. That same day, Grover crossed Bayou Des Glaize and pushed on to Simmesport. The Army of the Gulf stretched itself over sixty miles.

While Banks made his move, British colonel Arthur Fremantle finally crossed the Mississippi. He had reached Harrisonburg and Fort Beauregard soon after the withdrawal of the U.S. Navy. The steamer upon which he was a passenger ended up shadowing a half day behind the Federals, finally reaching Trinity, Louisiana. From

The Army Arrives at Simmesport. The steamers *St. Maurice* and *Empire Parish* appear to the left, taking on troops to ferry across the Mississippi. Harper's Weekly, *author's collection.*

Lieutenant Colonel Arthur Fremantle was an officer in the Coldstream Guards in the British Army and served as an administrator at Gibraltar in 1860. In that capacity, he met Captain Raphael Semmes, commander of the CSS *Sumter* and later, CSS *Alabama*. Fremantle, twenty-seven years old and spurred by tales of the U.S. Civil War, took a leave of absence and came to North America as something of a military tourist, entering Texas near Brownsville in early April 1863. He made it to Louisiana just in time to be caught up in the chaos following the near-destruction of Taylor's army. An image from later in his career.

Three Months in the Southern States.

here the British soldier went by pirogue through the swamps to Vidalia. "I crossed the father of rivers and landed on the Mississippi bank at 9 a.m.," he wrote on Friday, May 15. He had seen enough of operations in the western theater. He would continue eastward, passing through the Confederate armies of General Braxton Bragg and General Robert E. Lee and witnessing the Battle of Gettysburg from a tree-bough perch before concluding his tour of the Confederacy.[6]

The confusion of the past few weeks that had complicated Fremantle's travels had also confounded Union war planners. In Washington, General Halleck grew apoplectic. The great architect of Union military strategy could not believe what he was reading in the newspaper or the reports from his armies in the Mississippi valley. The two armies he had urged to support each other had moved in opposite directions and deeper into enemy territory. "I hear from the newspapers that you are in possession of Alexandria, and General Grant of Jackson," Halleck wrote to Banks. "This may be well enough so far, but these operations are too eccentric to be pursued."[7]

Halleck sensed a looming disaster. If the Confederates figured out that the two Union armies were flailing away in opposite directions, essentially independent of each other, they might defeat them in detail and still not risk losing their Mississippi River forts. "If these eccentric movements, with the main forces of the enemy on the Mississippi River, do not lead to some serious disaster, it will be because the enemy does not take full advantage of his opportunity. Your forces must be united at the earliest possible moment," he demanded. "We shall watch with the greatest anxiety the movements of yourself and General Grant."[8]

Weitzel worried as well. From his vantage at the rear of the army, he continued to hear reports that the Confederates dogged his heels. His Louisiana cavalry companies picked up some Texan pickets below Cheneyville who said the Southern army would soon coalesce again at Alexandria, carried south on the Red River aboard steamers. "Would it not be well to send some gunboats up the river to stop this," he queried Banks. He also worried that the Rebels would move around and ahead of him and block his route, preventing him from rejoining the main column. "Would it also not be well to keep a watch at Moreauville to prevent any cavalry making a raid along the mail road?" he asked. Intelligence from prisoners revealed around one thousand Texans hovering nearby—men from Waller's Battalion and Lane's 1st Texas Partisan Rangers along with fragments of General Henry Hopkins Sibley's regiments.[9]

General Taylor and his wounded army had started their move down from Natchitoches and the defiant Confederates felt their morale returning. After weeks running from a fight, Taylor shifted his thinking back toward an attack. The strength of his tiny force grew daily as the odd commands summoned from the corners of the Confederate Trans-Mississippi arrived and reorganized. Colonel Eugene Waggaman left his makeshift command and headed east, bound for greater glory with the Army of Northern Virginia, and the battalion he had led disbanded. Its troops joined other commands. Elements of the 11th Louisiana Battalion joined Brigadier General Alfred Mouton's old infantry brigade, now under command of Colonel Henry Gray, and an assortment of Texas horse marines from Fort DeRussy attached themselves to the 13th Texas Cavalry Battalion.

The Confederate commander wanted to find out where the Federals had gone. It seemed as though Banks had quit his campaign, driving his army back to the Gulf of Mexico. Colonel Lane's newly arrived 1st Texas Partisan Rangers, already bloodied near Alexandria, reported the enemy was on the move. Taylor ordered that his amalgam of Texas cavalry continue in that direction to confirm the news. West of Alexandria, Major Hannibal Honestus Boone led his troops through the piney hills and emerged in the vicinity of Lecompte. Lane's regiment and the detachment of Sibley's Brigade followed Bayou Rapides toward its junction with the Red River at Alexandria. Remarkably, their scouts reported the town was completely free of Union troops.

The Texans quickened their pace, noticing a bit of uneasiness on the part of Alexandria's citizens. Many residents had welcomed the Yankees' arrival a week before only to be abandoned to the Rebels. "I understand the citizens of Alexandria received them with open arms," wrote Private John W. Watkins, Company B, 5th Texas Cavalry, "hoisting the stars and stripes themselves and furnishing the guard to protect the flag. If they ever fall into our hands we will give them a hempen cravat that will last them their lifetime." The time for vengeance had arrived, and though the Texans were ready, civilians would have to wait. The Texans knew their true target lay southward, down the road that led to Cheneyville, where all these Southern horsemen soon congregated.[10]

Colonel Lane's newcomers picked up the Yankee trail heading toward Cheneyville and had pitched into Weitzel's cavalry—his second encounter with the Union 1st Louisiana since arriving—on the road south of Alexandria. Union major Harai Robinson merely reported that he had chased off some Texans who had moved too close to them. In Cheneyville the Federal horsemen fought the 1st Texas Partisan Rangers again, but they quickly disengaged and crossed to the east bank of Bayou Boeuf. Weitzel's rear guard kept moving until the entire brigade concentrated at Murdock's plantation, several miles down a stretch of road connecting Cheneyville to Evergreen, south by southeast. From there the road split. One route arced eastward and north, following Bayou Des Glaise before intersecting the Red River Road near Moreauville, between Marksville and Simmesport. The other fork turned generally south and passed through Holmesville and on to Washington and Opelousas.

Weitzel's anxiety about the pesky Texans had little effect on his commander. Banks left his army—again. By the time the last Federals left Alexandria, the general had already been journeying away from his command for two days. Banks traveled by steamer down the Atchafalaya on his way back to New Orleans. As his troops marched toward Simmesport, the commander of the Army of the Gulf returned to departmental headquarters to make sense of the new realities. He also needed to brief his remaining division commanders about the plan and to check on the progress of his Corps d'Afrique. With luck, he might still hold the vast swath of Louisiana he had conquered using the same men he had liberated.

While Banks was away, the Army of the Gulf neared a reunion with the brigades left at Baton Rouge. A mounted reconnaissance force left the Union base there, crossed over the Mississippi, and headed north across the flooded countryside toward False River, where they made an important discovery. Thousands of beeves and sheep had been collected near the small village of Waterloo and were ready to be taken across the Mississippi and into the Port Hudson. While the Federals watched, troops from the 1st Alabama Infantry crossed over the river from the east on skiffs, rowing to the mouth of False River. The Federals rode hard for the herds hoping to prevent them being swum across to feed the Rebel defenders, and both sides fed troops into a gun battle. Eventually the Federals made away with their captures. Rebel steamers serving Port Hudson sallied out of hiding and sent in additional troops, but the fight petered out. The next day, part of the mounted vanguard of the Federal army gathering upstream at Simmesport—Company C, 4th Wisconsin; Company F, 1st Louisiana; and companies A through E of the 14th New York "Metropolitan" Cavalry—tangled with these Confederates, who were estimated to consist of a brigade of two regiments and a battery of artillery.[11]

That same day, May 18, totally unbeknownst to Banks or Halleck, the leading elements of Major General Grant's Army of the Tennessee arrived at Vicksburg. They had Pemberton's Rebels on the run.

26

The Battle of Cheneyville

"All who are afraid to die now, drop out; the rest follow me!"

Major Hannibal Honestus Boone
13th Texas Cavalry Battalion

At the rear of Banks's extended column, the Federals kept a wary eye on Cheneyville, fearing the important crossroads village would soon harbor more Rebels who could fan out in a variety of directions. A main artery ran south from Cheneyville through Ville Platt to Opelousas. Another road headed northeast toward the Red River Road, the prairies around Marksville, and the now-ruined Fort DeRussy, but it was considered passable to vehicles only during very dry seasons. One bayou road led south along Bayou Boeuf, skirting the swampy wilderness of Bayou Cocodrie as it arced toward Washington via Holmesville. On the Boeuf's east bank another bayou road headed to the southeast, passing plantations and cane fields on its way to Evergreen. Nearly a dozen plantation bridges connected both banks of the Boeuf until the roads parted entirely at Bayou Huffpower.

This was a bountiful area, and farm buildings, slave quarters, and tasteful mansions lined the fenced and hedge-bordered roads. About a mile down the east bayou road from Cheneyville sat the Tanner plantation, one of the larger estates. Across from the farm headquarters, Walnut Grove, a plantation road bisected the sprawling acreage and made a perpendicular trace, almost due north away from the bayou road, connecting with the main northeast road from Cheneyville to Red River at the timbered, swampy margins of Bayou Du Lac. Tanner's Lane, as locals dubbed it, served as a utility road for this busy agricultural enterprise. Freight wagons loaded with oak timber felled in the dense forest, fuel for the large sugar-refining facility in the center of the plantation, frequently used the lane, and during the sugar harvest carts from the fields loaded with sugarcane clattered down its ruts.

Brigadier General Godfrey Weitzel had passed Tanner's farm on his way to Murdock's plantation, which sat at the junction of

Bayou Boeuf and Bayou Huffpower, but he took little notice of it. He had larger issues to consider. Two Union columns were leaving this country, and as commander of the rear guard, he had to guarantee the safety of both. The main body of the army was tramping in the same direction as the Red River, toward the Avoyelles Prairies and Marksville on the way to Simmesport. The pesky Texas horsemen might take the shortcut from Cheneyville to the river road, thus bypassing the rear guard to harass the rear of Major General Nathaniel P. Banks's army. Meanwhile, the other column, which contained the army's baggage and was a plump target itself, was heading down the Bayou Boeuf Road toward Colonel Thomas E. Chickering's command at Opelousas. Weitzel believed that at Murdock's plantation he could keep an eye on both columns and watch the enemy's movements. If he had a trusty scout to keep track of the Texans lurking nearby, Weitzel could then wait for word that the slow-trundling wagons had made it safely to Opelousas before he proceeded toward Evergreen on the way to Simmesport. Weitzel had an officer in mind who, he believed, would be capable of reporting on the Texans' schemes.[1]

Throughout the campaign Weitzel had leaned heavily on his small Louisiana Cavalry detachment, and they had showed themselves to be adroit at bloodying Texans. Its leader, New York major Harai Robinson, had earned promotion to chief of cavalry for the army operating in Louisiana. Among his officers, Captain Richard Barrett of Company B, 1st Louisiana Cavalry, showed clear evidence of his gifts. This Irish-born horse soldier had risen from a position as infantry sergeant in the 41st Massachusetts to the fore as an aggressive cavalry leader. He was so well known for his prowess that Major General Richard Taylor's men had marked him for vengeance. Barrett's specialties included picket skirmishing, hard drinking, and barroom brawling, and he and his men were proud of their ability to best Rebel horsemen and to bring in prisoners for interrogation. He had been responsible for flummoxing the

Confederate riders on many occasions, and he had embarrassed them more than once on the advance to Alexandria and the current retreat. "This officer and his company," a Lone Star officer noted, "were the especial boast and pride of the enemy."[2]

Meanwhile, as Confederate major Hannibal Honestus Boone rode into Cheneyville, couriers informed him and his officers of the Federal positions at Murdock's plantation. The wily Texan could have led his command toward either Banks on the Red River Road or the baggage train heading for Opelousas, but with two road-weary regiments and parts of a third, he did not have the numbers to pose much of a threat. Additionally, if he went after either Federal column, Weitzel and the rear guard could fall in behind him and sandwich him between larger Union forces. Boone opted to do what he could with what he had. Perhaps a move straight at Weitzel would bring the 1st Louisiana Federals out for another round. Besides, as Sergeant Keet McDade of the 13th Texas Cavalry Battalion wrote to his wife, the Texans "fought them wherever a chance presented itself." In the case of Captain Barrett, honor was at stake. If possible, Boone wanted Barrett's hide on the barn door like that of some pesky varmint.[3]

Boone's command arrived at Cheneyville and took over the pursuit from Colonel Walter P. Lane's tired soldiers. Scouts confirmed the Yankees were loitering at Murdock's plantation before leaving the region, and Boone sensed an opportunity to strike the enemy one last time in a violent send off. He knew well the enemy that waited at the junction of Bayou Boeuf and Bayou Huffpower; his troopers had seen the faces of these Federals through the v-and-blade sights of their Colt revolvers on nearly a daily basis for a month. "This regiment [the 1st Louisiana Cavalry] . . . and our battalion . . . frequently exchanged very warm compliments," remembered one Texan. "The frequency of these collisions had raised a spirit of rivalry among them, as to which were the better troops, and they were anxious to try each other on."[4]

Gathering as many men as he could on the morning of May 20, 1863, Boone decided to put his simple plan into action. He would draw the enemy out by worrying his picket line, then he would ambush the pursuers from concealed positions. Captain Alfred Sturgis Thurmond and his veteran Company A of the 7th Texas Cavalry would move down the west bank of Bayou Boeuf to engage the Union pickets there and keep them out of the fight on the east side. Boone sent Lieutenant J. R. Morris and Company B, 13th Texas Cavalry Battalion, and a squad from Company D with Thurmond. This one-hundred-man force would serve as a diversion.[5]

On the east side of Bayou Boeuf, Boone introduced a more elaborate plan. A few hundred yards away from the Federal camps,

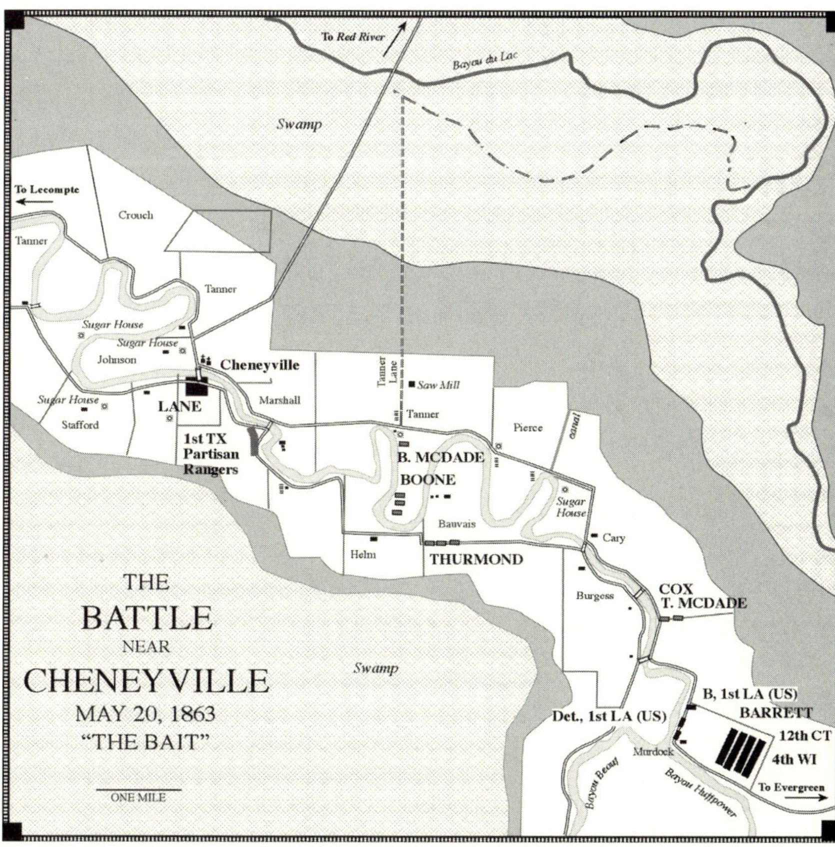

Lieutenant Tom McDade—one of three McDade brothers in the unit—and eleven men from Company C watched their Union counterparts moving among the fields of Murdock's plantation. Boone sent Captain C. C. Cox with the thirty Refugio, Calhoun, and San Patricio county men of Company E to reinforce the Rebel picket line, with orders to press the enemy troops back into their camps. "It was my appointment," recalled Captain Cox, "to bring on quite a serious fight." Meanwhile, at the Tanner plantation, the balance of the battalion, Companies A, D, and F, took positions south of the bayou road, concealed by a high hedge and fence, and into an orchard behind the buildings of Walnut Grove. Shielded by Tanner's sugarhouse, Captain Billy McDade, younger brother of the lieutenant on the picket line, kept the balance of Company C, twenty men, ready to dash down to aid his brother.[6]

The Texans relied on the vanity of their foe for the ambush to work. Boone reasoned that Robinson would not pass up such an obvious challenge when Captain Cox and Lieutenant McDade attacked his camp. The major also suspected that Barrett and his company would probably take the lead in any Union counterattack to drive the raiders away, and they would assume the Texans were very few in number. Furthermore, Boone suspected, Barrett would probably get carried away if the pursuit was somewhat close and would outpace any supporting troops. Accordingly, Boone had instructed Cox and Tom McDade to keep riding, as though in a panic, until they reached the Cheneyville Bridge. There, the horsemen would find the several hundred Texans of Lane's 1st Texas Partisan Rangers in prepared positions on the opposite bank. To ensure that the quarry rode into the snare, Billy McDade was to gallop out from behind the sugarhouse and fall in behind the Union troopers, cutting off their retreat. In the gap between Barrett's reckless company and the rest of Robinson's command, Boone would personally lead the one hundred men of his three remaining companies from the battalion in a charge that would stun the enemy long enough for Cox, the McDade brothers, and Lane's Texans to finish their work on Barrett. Any number of things could go wrong, Boone understood, but if these Union officers played their roles as scripted, the U.S. 1st Louisiana Cavalry would be well whipped.[7]

In the middle of the morning Boone's men could hear firing from the west bank, informing both sides that Thurmond's command had started the mischief as scheduled. The Federals would certainly respond, Boone believed, by ordering their men to prepare for a larger battle while strengthening the picket line. Captain Cox and his men rode down the Bayou Boeuf's east-bank road toward Evergreen and the enemy camps where, before long, the deep crack of Enfields and the shallow popping of pistols announced that he, too, had engaged the enemy. "After firing at the enemy some little time," Captain Cox recalled, "I heard the bugle call to Boots and Saddles." Inside the Union camp troops were mounting their horses to respond to the insolent Rebels.[8]

"The plan was a success," Cox continued. The sound of Texan gunfire soon slackened and was replaced by the yelps and hollers of men mounted on good horses being closely pursued. "A company of cavalry . . . marched out in our direction and when their purpose became sufficiently manifest," Cox wrote, "and they had gotten sufficiently near—we began to fall back." This only encouraged the blue coats, who kicked their mounts from a trot to a canter then into a gallop. "The enemy immediately brought out his force of cavalry," Boone reported, "and, as I expected he would do, made a rapid charge."[9]

Captain Cox's and Lieutenant McDade's troops emerged from down the road, galloping pell-mell, cutting through fields and funneling down the road to Cheneyville, their panic perhaps more genuine than feigned. "We of course regulated our gait by that of the pursuers," Cox remembered. As the Texans passed the ambush point, one of their number fell from his saddle, killed by a Federal carbine bullet. The Confederates concealed on both sides of the bayou road at the Tanner plantation watched their comrades scamper past them. Almost immediately some two dozen Union cavalrymen, on horses straining at the bits, rumbled down the road after their prey. Given the weeks of close encounters, many of the Texans recognized Captain Barrett at the head of this force.[10]

When the Federals passed him, Captain McDade knew it was time to save his older brother. After an initial volley from their rifles into the rear of Barrett's command, McDade and his men put spurs to flanks as they moved into the gap between the impetuous Barrett and the rest of the 1st Louisiana. Down the bayou road in the direction of Murdock's plantation, the Texans could clearly see some two hundred and fifty men, about two hundred yards behind them but moving quickly. Billy McDade boldly ignored this threat, turned his back on this enemy, and headed toward Cheneyville after Barrett, leaving an enemy closing in from behind. He trusted Major Boone to handle the Yankees.[11]

After Captain McDade started his chase, Major Boone knew it was his turn to act. "Boone took off his hat, ran his fingers through his hair, straightened himself in his stirrups, turned to the battalion," a Texan remembered. Boone addressed his command, "All who are afraid to die now, drop out; the rest follow me!" The major then spurred his horse, and the rest of his battalion trotted after him, filing through Tanner's gate and, turning right onto the bayou road, cantered toward their blue-clad enemy. The Louisiana Yankees, surprised by the appearance of so many more Rebels, reined in their steeds and spread out on the right and left to form a line of battle. Revolvers began snapping as the Union troopers began to fire into the onrushing Rebels, who, second by second, gathered momentum. "The enemy . . . halted and . . . stood their ground firmly, firing upon the head of my column," Boone reported. Lieutenant Reed Weisinger, of Victoria, Texas, charging on his mount at the head of the Confederate wedge, felt his horse's legs suddenly buckle. Man and animal tumbled into a great heap of blood and dust, and his troops galloped around the wreck and on toward the Federal ranks. The enemy gave way. "We had gotten within 30 feet of them," Boone added, "when they broke and fled in the utmost confusion."[12]

The men of the U.S. 1st Louisiana had not turned soon enough, and the impact of Boone's charge scrambled both commands. "It was like the meeting of two mighty engines, and the very earth trembled from the shock," a Texan wrote. "The front companies on each side were interlocked and entwined with each other, and the carnival of death commenced, each party determined to win or die." Lieutenant Weisinger struggled to his feet after his spectacular

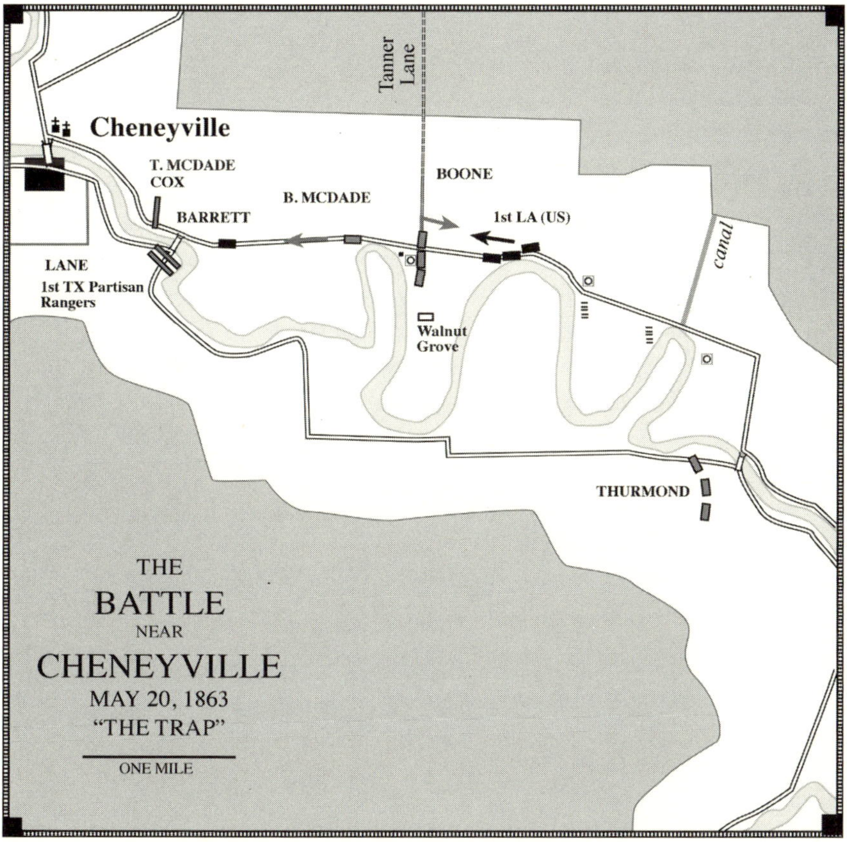

fall, and, amid the swirling chaos, scooped his pistol out of the dust and ran into the melee. He drew down on three mounted Federals, who quickly raised their hands in surrender.[13]

The fighting continued in similar fashion as both sides broke into individual duels. The Texans tumbled the 1st Louisiana Regiment down Tanner's Lane and the Bayou Boeuf's east-bank road toward Evergreen. "From Cheneyville [toward the] Mississippi is a long lane," remembered one Texan trooper. "In this lane occurred the most desperate fight of this, or any other, which for bravery, endurance, and tenacity of purpose, eclipses all other engagements."[14]

The battalion adjutant, Lieutenant D. C. Proctor, riding near Major Boone, threw his hands to his neck in shock after being struck by a bullet. "Major Boone, who was always as kind as he was brave, ran to his assistance," a Texan private remembered. Boone called out, "Proctor, are you badly hurt?" The stricken officer, the shock of the impact wearing off, began to probe the wound until his fingers emerged with a gory, flattened chunk of pistol lead. "Major Boone, there are three kinds of wounds," the wounded man replied. "The legislative, the judicial, and the executive wounds. I think that my wound will make me county judge."[15]

After pushing Robinson and his troops for almost half a mile, Boone and his Texans broke off contact so that they could turn about and participate in the final act of destroying Barrett and his company. "When still hearing firing in my rear, I ordered a halt and turned back to the assistance of McDade and Cox," Boone wrote. Behind him in the direction of Cheneyville, Captain Barrett's Yankees had sniffed out the trap laid by Cox and the McDade brothers and had yanked their horses around as well, just a few hundred yards short of the Cheneyville Bridge. They turned and easily rode through Captain McDade's twenty troopers, who found themselves turning their mounts left and right as the lathered horses of Barrett and his men sped by, heading back to safety. The Texans did what they could to slow the Yankees. "Captain McDade, with his company armed with Enfield rifles, not more than one forth of his men having pistols and none having sabers, successfully engaged a superior number of the enemy armed with Sharps rifles, six shooters, and sabers," Boone reported. Despite this brave account, Barrett and his men cut their way past everyone who opposed them.[16]

Now Boone, not Barrett, was in more danger. The clever Federal captain charged boldly into Boone's one-hundred-man column, threatening to push their way through the Texans and back into friendly lines. More importantly, Barrett's men tangled Boone's command, allowing the rest of the Federals retreating down the bayou road toward Evergreen to recover their composure, turn, and help thrash the Texans. Captain Cox and the McDade brothers, strung out over nearly a mile between Walnut Grove and the Cheneyville Bridge, would have to re-form and turn as well to pursue their escaping quarry lest Boone and his three companies be gobbled up by the reunited companies of the 1st Louisiana Cavalry.[17]

Boone's surprised Texans, caught unaware by this change in script, made a stand, firing their rifles from horseback in unsteady, ineffective, close-range desperation. "Several of the enemy had succeeded in cutting their way through," Boone wrote, "and were handling my rear very roughly with their sabers." The flashing Union blades stroked the air. "When my men had discharged their rifles, those who were without pistols clubbed their guns and used them against the sabers of the enemy," Boone reported proudly. Captain Joseph C. Terrell watched in horror as three of his Fort Worth boys fell beneath the Union swords: Private Sam Jefferson took a blade through the neck, Private H. G. Jennings fell from a blow to the head, and Private Dave Thomas was skewered through the lung. Writing after the war, this Rebel officer and veteran of a dozen battles remarked that "this is the only hand to hand fight I ever saw."[18]

In the mounted scuffle around the junction of Tanner's Lane and the bayou road, front, rear, and flank dissolved into individual battles. Texans galloping back from Cheneyville joined the fracas as they arrived. "It looked for a minute like pandemonium reigned in that road," reported Captain Cox. The swirling maelstrom of Federal and Confederate riders, astride their spinning mounts, raised clouds of dust and smoke. Bullets and sabers seemed to strike randomly amid the chaos.[19]

"The Federals exhausted their pistols, took to their swords, and cut many of our men down, while our boys continued the fight with their six shooters," a Rebel participant wrote. During the battle one Confederate, Private George Rose of Company E, 13th Texas Cavalry Battalion, fell from his mount into the dirt amid the stamping hooves of dozens of horses. A Texan officer, Lieutenant

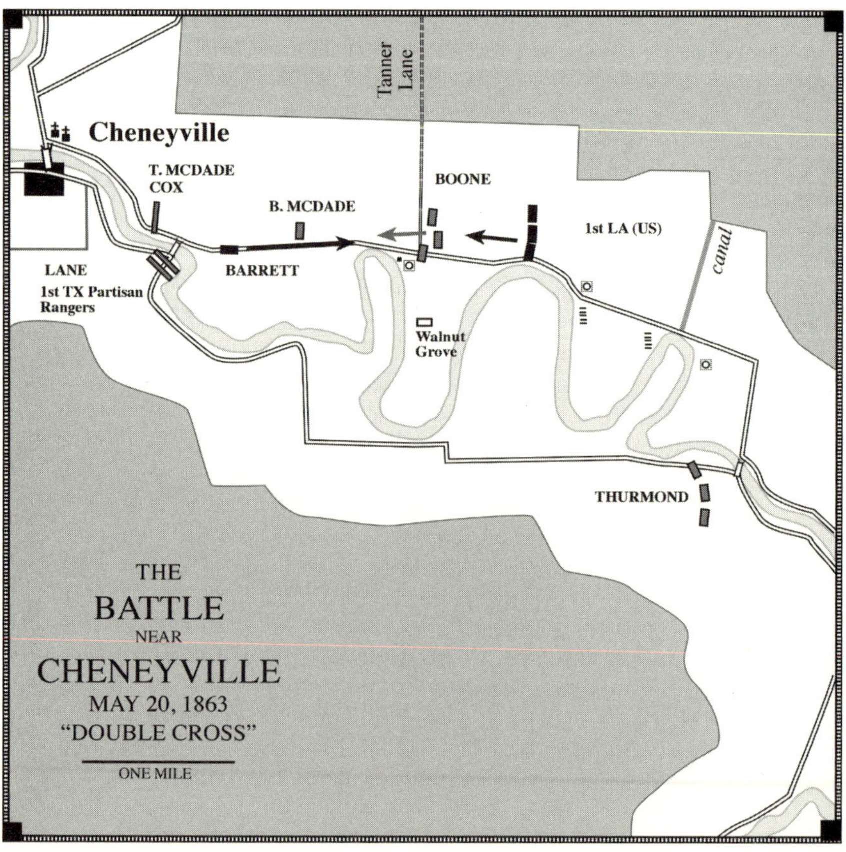

Pat Hughes of Company A, called out to another dismounted man, whom he described as a big fellow, to pull the stunned Rose out of the fray so that he would not be trampled. The big soldier was actually Federal Sergeant James Healey, and this Irishman's saber quickly stroked the air. "Instead of obeying the order, he attempted to amputate Pat's head with his sword, but missed him," a witness wrote. The Texan, jerking the reins on his spinning horse, tried to aim at his assailant. "Before Pat could shoot him, [the Yankee] made another lunge at him with his sword, striking him near the backbone and coming out at the point of his shoulder, making a terrible wound," recorded one of the Confederates.[20]

A half-dozen Texans, after witnessing the wounding of the lieutenant, focused their attention on this ferocious Federal. "This fellow was a fighter from fighterville," a Texan recalled. "After wounding Hughes he cut down several men, splitting the skull of one to the brain." The Confederates, mostly armed with rifles, had no effective way to parry the soldier's deftly wielded saber. A Texan later wrote, "He became such a fighter, that Boone concluded that to save his men from destruction, he must go down. So he worked his way towards him, until they met, and the big Federal went down."[21]

Sergeant Healey's tenacious stand created a pause in the fight, which allowed both sides, astride winded mounts, to break contact. The attention paid to the now-fallen Goliath had caused Boone to inadvertently regroup his command. The individual duels that had been occurring in the smoke and dust faded away, and the reunited Union cavalry at the far side of the Tanner fields continued its retreat back to camp instead of prolonging the fight. In the distance, down the bayou road, a column of dust announced that the mule-and-horse-borne 4th Wisconsin were belatedly jangling to their comrades' assistance. Boone prudently ordered his men back toward Cheneyville. His ambush was over, but he believed he had settled the score with Barrett.

General Weitzel gave a different view in his report to Banks's headquarters that evening. He did not acknowledge that Boone had bushwhacked his rear guard; instead, he simply dismissed the cavalry duel as a picket skirmish, nothing more than a simple attack on his outpost. "Colonel Bean (4th Wisconsin), in command of the advance guard, repulsed the enemy, and pursued him with his whole force, consisting of the cavalry (1st Louisiana), mounted infantry (4th Wisconsin), and the Twelfth Connecticut Volunteers," wrote Weitzel. He did report the embarrassment of the 1st Louisiana Cavalry as they had turned and pursued the harassing Texans. "When within about 1 ½ miles of Cheneyville, Major (Harai) Robinson, in command of the rest of the cavalry, halted the column. Captain

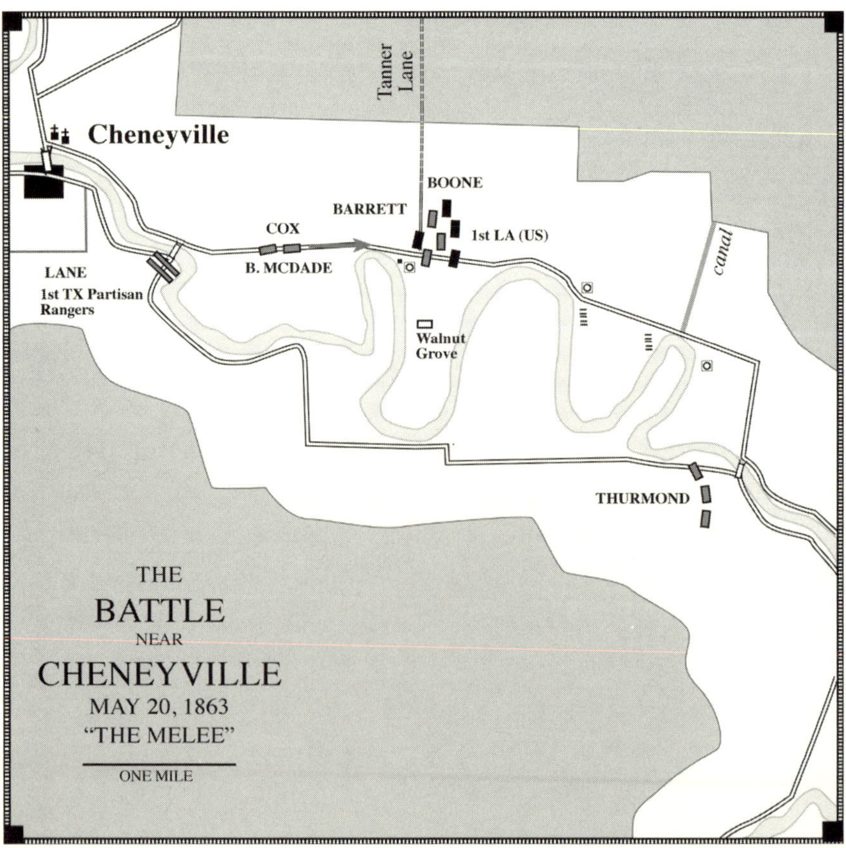

Barrett, rather too daringly, still continued to advance, and, after passing a sugar house, a force of about 150 Rebel cavalry jumped out, and cut him off from the rest of the command." Weitzel went on to inform Banks that Barrett and his command had all been killed or captured. On this last point, Weitzel was wrong.[22]

In the Rebel camps, officers were not sure who had won the fight or what had happened to the obnoxious Union officer in the smoke, dust, and chaos. The Texans had captured thirteen Federal soldiers while killing or wounding another seventeen. Most of the enemy casualties had come from Barrett's company, and one of his better sergeants—the "fighter from fighterville"—lay dead in the dust of Tanner's Lane. Despite Weitzel's report, though,

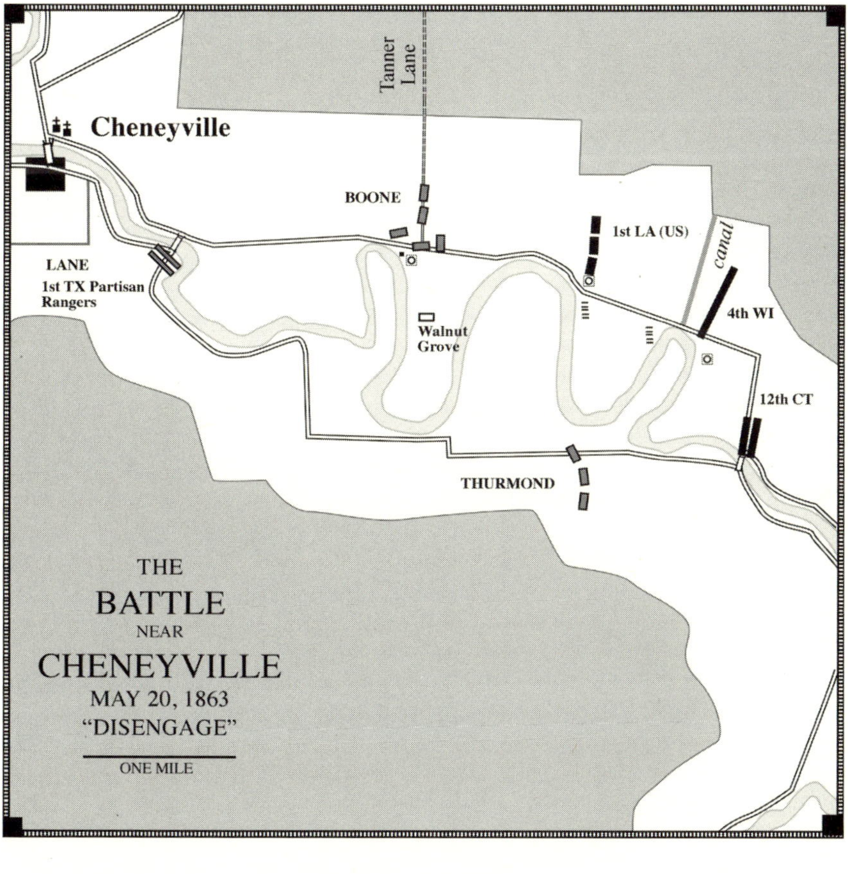

Captain Barrett was not among the slain or prisoners: he was simply missing. The ambush had cost Boone's command as well, with one Texan dead and eight others wounded, with two from the battalion missing as well. Others nursed nasty slashes and deep cuts from the enemy blades without reporting themselves as casualties. Confused about the battle's outcome, one Texan wrote, "Which whipped, you ask?"[23]

Boone figured he had won. In the following days, however, he learned his principal quarry had escaped. Barrett, once again, had personally bested the Texans. "I am sorry to say that this officer escaped," Boone wrote Major General Taylor, "but his escape was an ignominious one; he deserted his men in the dust and confusion, abandoned his arms and horse harness, leaped the fence and took refuge in the bayou." Boone's intelligence was correct. The morning after the skirmish, Weitzel awoke to learn that he had misled Banks as to the fate of the veteran cavalryman. Having spent the day and evening dodging stray Texans, Barrett had arrived back in camp at midnight, "sans hat, sans coat, sans boots and dripping wet."[24]

27

The Harvest

"It is a sort of retributive justice, I must confess I am not sorry to see."

Mattison
Correspondent, Boston Morning Journal

The weather in Boston remained cool at the beginning of May 1863, but spring was coming, lifting the spirits of the once snow-bound populace and bringing bright skies and warmer sea breezes to replace the winter gloom. Bostonians continued their routines, far removed from the dirt and blood of war in Louisiana. Those who perused the pages of the *Boston Herald* on May 2 may have noticed the following block of one-inch copy: "Funeral of an Officer: The obsequies over the remains of Capt. Samuel Gault, of Co. A, 38th Massachusetts—who was killed at one of the battles in Gen. Banks's late successful march, took place at St. Paul's Church at one o'clock this afternoon. Rev. Dr. Nicholson conducted the solemnities. The body was temporarily deposited in the receiving tomb, under the church." This brief announcement was one of the last echoes of the Army of the Gulf's great Teche Campaign.[1]

A funeral was held for another dead Bostonian soldier that week. A New Orleans hearse carried the embalmed body of Captain Howard Dwight from the corner of St. Philip and Magazine streets to Canal Street, then left to the Christ Church. "Escort of one hundred men, formed by detachments of Companies A, I and G, 47th Massachusetts Regiment," a newspaper reported, "with arms reversed, and followed by the splendid band of the 47th playing the Dead March." Inside the glass-sided wagon, Dwight's coffin lay festooned with a large U.S. flag and wreaths of intertwined magnolia flowers and cypress boughs. His black horse, with the captain's boots reversed in the stirrups, followed behind. At the front of the procession two white horses "ornamented with white plumes, indicating that the deceased was still in his youth and a batchelor," pulled the hearse. Brigadier General George F. Shepley,

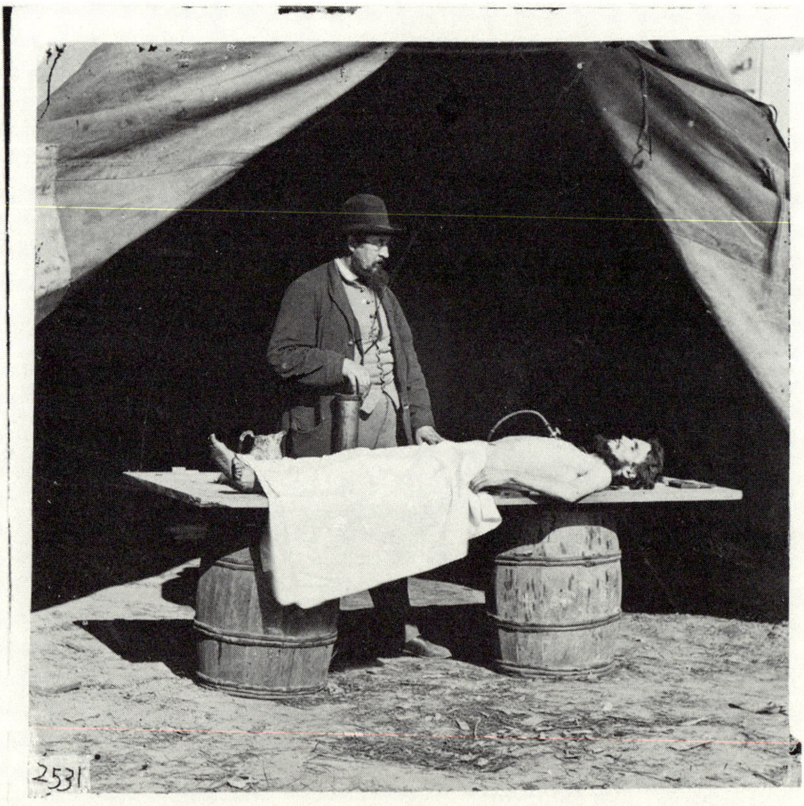

The Embalmer. The Union army in Louisiana clearly had access to an embalmer, judging from the number of officer corpses sent home to New England.

Library of Congress.

Union governor of Louisiana, and Colonel Benjamin Grierson sat among the mourners at the church.[2]

After an Episcopal funeral, Captain Dwight's boxed remains were loaded onto the steamship *George Peabody* for the trip to New England. "The directions on the coffin were 'To Wm. Dwight,

Christ Church. The principal Episcopalian church in New Orleans served frequently as the venue for the funerals of Union officers.

Marshall Dunham Photograph Album, Mss. 3241, Louisiana and Lower Mississippi Valley Collections, LSU Libraries, Baton Rouge, La.

Esq, 20 State Street, Boston. Remains of Capt. H. Dwight,'" the New Orleans newspaper recounted. "There will be mourning in the house of his father when the mangled body of the murdered son reaches State Street! When another of the Spartan Band is bourne to the arms of his mother, as it were, upon his shield."[3]

Despite these and other funerals, reporters tagging along with Major General Nathaniel P. Banks continued to send rosy dispatches to their readers in the eastern cities, reporting the progress of the Union cause in Louisiana. "I believe . . . that the little 'Iron man' is not to be defeated, and that with our nine months' troops, which are said by many to be good for nothing, he will be victorious; and succeed in cutting off the enemy's supplies, by reaching the Red River, opening the communication with Farragut, crossing the Mississippi and taking Port Hudson by an attack in the rear," wrote a Banks admirer. As the Army of the Gulf gathered at Simmesport, Northern observers anticipated great triumphs. "I believe that victory is to perch every where upon our banners, until the object of this expedition is accomplished, viz:—the opening of the Mississippi," the writer continued. "Gen. Banks is a judicious officer and one who keeps everything to himself, and plans his own campaigns without assistance from any one, and carries them out to a successful issue."[4]

If Banks was as certain as his admirers, he certainly kept his own counsel as advertised. He had hoped to meet Admiral David G. Farragut at Old River to seek his advice, but the grizzled naval veteran had left, having taken advantage of the all-water route to New Orleans to reunite with the rest of his fleet and staff. Banks followed Farragut's route south, giving no indication as to what he intended to do with his army.

From aboard the USS *Hartford* Commodore James Palmer sent dispatches downstream to Farragut, trying to make sense of what Banks, Major General Ulysses S. Grant, and their forces were doing. "Did you ever see such vacillation?" Palmer wrote. "I wrote you in my last [dispatch] that Grant had sent to Banks to come up and help him; at the same time Banks's messenger was on his way to ask of Grant to render him a similar favor." Now the conflicting orders had left the navy with a problem. Which plan were they to support? Palmer also wrote to Admiral David Dixon Porter upstream, signaling his frustrations. "I do not know what to make of this army," Palmer scribbled. "They have got the whole of them down at Simmesport, and the commanding general seems to be loitering down at New Orleans. I should be content if I could get these fellows to operate upon Port Hudson at once, but it requires patience when one has to do with a militia army."[5]

Banks arrived in New Orleans—his mind reeling from the constantly changing strategic situation—to seek counsel. Amid the chaotic hum and military bureaucracy of this captured city, Banks at last visited Farragut. The brief meeting invigorated Banks, and he emerged a resolute warrior. Port Hudson was to be the target after all. The commander of the Army of the Gulf issued immediate orders directing Brigadier General Thomas W. Sherman to move up to Baton Rouge, unite with the division under Major General Christopher Columbus Augur, and press against the Confederate fort from the south and east. Banks sent word to Brigadier General Cuvier Grover and Colonel Halbert E. Paine to move their troops across to Bayou Sara as soon as possible. Banks told them that he would be along shortly. First he wanted to tour the city and see how the experiment in reconstructing a new South was proceeding.

Banks viewed the fruits of two Massachusetts masterminds of Louisiana strategy. Major General Benjamin Butler had laid out the foundational principles that he had built upon, and their combined efforts had laid the cornerstone for a national transformation. The focus was on the status of chattel property and the freedmen's new role in a postwar South. Butler and Banks had also put into play political and economic measures for suppressing the rebellion in the state and for showing secession to have been a fraud inflicted upon a gullible electorate. The evidence of their work became increasingly obvious with each passing day. New Orleans was clearly and significantly changed from the city Butler had taken a year before. Now, two years after the fall of Fort Sumter, the great issues that had plagued the nation for so long were being worked out on the drill fields and barracks, the bayous and battlefields of Louisiana.

More and more Northerners, especially New Englanders, roamed the streets of New Orleans, glad to be part of a great crusade to overturn what they considered a clear evil. "I cannot wonder that with man's cupidity and love of power, slavery is attractive," one reporter wrote, feigning sympathy with Southerners. "In feudal times, lords were 'rich in some dozen paltry villages,' while here the proprietors are rich in lands and human souls—lords of villages, owners of their inhabitants, despots in power, and capricious as despotic." This Yankee self-righteousness tended to bloom enthusiastically in the Department of the Gulf. "Avarice glutted its capacious maw, gold filled their coffers; lust ravished the powerless, and unbridled licentiousness corrupted the land. This bane of our republic, conceived in sin, supported by power, and fostered by politics, shall be overthrown and its sufferings be avenged in blood. God speed the day!"[6]

Judgment Day had apparently arrived. One observer described occupied New Orleans as "almost deserted. Half her places of business are closed, all her places of amusement; her immense levee unoccupied; cotton presses empty; dwellings tenantless; grass growing in the streets; guns of our fleet frowning upon the rebellious city; marshal law proclaimed; and an army of occupation in her limits. Such are the fruits of secession."[7]

Despite this bitter harvest, an ember of Rebel New Orleans remained. "Still thousands of her inhabitants cherish the delusive phantom of a Southern Confederacy and wear the look of sullen submission. Ladies wear the white and red rose, and hide their faces with parasols whenever they meet a Union officer or soldier," a Boston-based reporter wrote. "The city is nevertheless well governed, quiet and orderly."[8]

The Union authorities in New Orleans had taken strict measures to quarantine the contagion of rebellion. One order compelled all "registered enemies" to leave the department by the middle of May. "The above is a 'genus' peculiar to New Orleans," wrote a soldier in the 38th Massachusetts. "They avow themselves to be enemies, but still claim our protection, and, manage to get along very well, indulging their little fancies unmolested; but this turns them out in the cold or rather compels them to join their chosen friends." One of those forced to leave was diarist Julia LeGrand. Authorities also ordered saloons and other notorious watering holes to close by 9:00 PM to discourage drunken would-be revolutionaries from getting out of hand.[9]

Federal authorities expected the residents of the Crescent City to behave. Orders issued by the military government levied harsh penalties including steep fines, "to be appropriated to the improvement of the City of New Orleans, and . . . for the benefit of the United Sates." Trafficking with the enemy could mean death. Yankee policemen had left their New York and Boston beats to reorganize the New Orleans force to mirror that of their home cities. Now the truncheon-toting veterans of those constabularies ran the streets of the Crescent City.[10]

The question of the status of freed slaves had vexed the nation since colonial times but had become acute as the reality of the matter clustered around the liberating Union armies. Brigadier General Daniel Ullmann had been to Opelousas and Port Barrè to view the camps of black men gathered there for transport back to the Union safe zone of the Lafourche District. "Able bodied men are to become soldiers," witnessed Corporal James K. Hosmer of the 52nd Massachusetts. "The women and older men, and all not fit for military duty, are to go on to plantations taken by the Government or loyal men. They are to receive wages." He noted that "no doubt, their condition will be most distressing in many cases. For them, it is a most momentous period of transition—a crises which they can hardly pass without suffering; but it will be temporary, and a bright future lies before them."[11]

Calls for the abolition of slavery had been a repeated rhythm in abolitionist New England, and soldiers in the garrison of New Orleans wondered if pesky politicians had lengthened the war by resisting the inclusion of freedmen in the army. "The query often arises in my mind . . . whether or no the war has been prolonged," one Yankee officer posited, "on account of public opinion as expressed by the ventilators of private opinion."[12]

By the time Banks arrived for his meeting with Farragut, black troops already defended New Orleans. "Capt. [Lorgen] Rygaard, commander of the colored artillery . . . afforded us an opportunity of witnessing the drilling of his men, first as heavy artillery, then as light artillery, and afterwards in the infantry manual of arms,"

The Sorting. An artist impression of the anguish of separation experienced by many recently freed slaves as men deemed militarily useful are pushed into the ranks of the army.

Harper's Weekly, *author's collection.*

wrote a correspondent who, with a party of Banks's officers, had ridden to the camps of these black troops. "We . . . were surprised to witness such wonderful proficiency and accuracy. With a natural reputation for dullness of comprehension, we found them quick motions and catching and obeying all orders with a promptness and alacrity, the truth compels me to admit, *far in advance* of almost any white troops I have seen in the volunteer service. This is a strong assertion, but I make it advisedly, and with thought." These men, recruited by Butler a half year before, would receive the designation of 1st Louisiana Colored Heavy Artillery, later the 1st Regiment Heavy Artillery, Corps d'Afrique.[13]

The observers reasoned that slavery had almost perfectly conditioned these men to be obedient troops. "The very fact of their former servitude leads them instinctively to a discipline such as it takes white soldiers long to obtain," he wrote. "The non-commissioned officers are blacks like the privates, and they appreciate their positions, and study constantly to be worthy of the confidence of their commander. There is no wrangling, nor discord. The boys all seem proud of their artillery jackets and blue pants, and get themselves neat and tidy. If, in the drill, they blunder, as is of course inevitable, they are firmly but kindly taught the right, and rarely need to be told twice the same thing." Among other men training at nearby Camp Parapet were the 1st Regiment of Louisiana Engineers, soon redesignated 1st Regiment Engineers, Corps d'Afrique.[14]

The Yankee observer recorded that the white officers treated the soldiers as men and not animals, and the troops loved them for it. "No officer addresses his men as 'you damned nigger,' but speaks to him kindly by his Christian name. Thus they are taught to have confidence in their superiors and respect for themselves."[15]

Activists back in Boston had long advocated letting black men fight. They had already begun raising a test unit, the all-black 54th Massachusetts, recruited from among the free blacks of Massachusetts and Pennsylvania and led by Colonel Robert Gould

Shaw, the son of wealthy abolitionist notables. An officer in the 48th Massachusetts remained skeptical. "I doubt the policy of spending $150,000 to raise a colored regiment in Massachusetts when the men can be had here for nothing and are ready to jump into the service at the first call."[16]

One of the problems with raising black regiments in the north, skeptics argued, was that the soldiers had already filled their heads with ideas counter to good discipline in an army. Free black men, they argued, were simply too free to be good soldiers. "Whatever difficulties may be in the way of recruiting colored soldiers in the North, where they have partaken of the white man's voices and nourished conceit and insolence, *here* it is a success," wrote a Union observer. "Coming, many of them, from the plantations, they are free from the vices of cities. The discipline of the army, while it is considered in a measure degrading to a white man, tends, under judicious officers, to the elevation of the black race. Here, where the experiment is being tried . . . the intelligent soldiery of the North always capable of speaking for themselves, are willing that the privations of the soldier's life . . . should be endured by those by birth and breeding fitted to such post of danger and disaster."[17]

Upriver in Baton Rouge one New England officer was also ready for the former slaves to lend a hand militarily. "I have seen enough here to convince me that the best course the Government can pursue is to make soldiers of the emancipated slaves," he wrote. "I have seen negro regiments at drill, on dress parade, and at work on entrenchments. I have been through their camps and conversed with officers and men. There are no troops in this department that appear better." Their years in bondage made them a quicker study on the manual of arms than white men, he contended. "This is due to their universal faculty of imitation," he opined. He was convinced that they would fight well when the day came and predicted that they would suffer fewer casualties from disease. "They are acclimated and can work here in the South," he added. "They are ready to enter the service and regiments can be raised just as fast as the Government can arm and equip them. This is the way to raise an army for this country, and to solve the question: What is to be done with the liberated slaves?"[18]

Many Federal soldiers, having been in the region for six months, were not convinced that Major General Banks had the correct idea regarding the use of free black labor on plantations. "I do not think it will succeed well at first," wrote an officer in the 48th Massachusetts. "The negro now is in a transition state; just free from the shackles, he has crude notions of freedom, which make him uncertain as a hired servant. He 'recokons' he can 'quit' at pleasure if he is not suited with his place or work. He wants discipline till his notions are worked out of him and he finds his true level as a free man." Therefore, the officer argued, "the army is the place to learn this; and into the army 300,000 of them ought to go, officered by whites at present, to hold this country and help clean it out."[19]

Additionally, argued another Northerner, arming and equipping the freed slaves would rub salt into the wounded Confederacy and serve the cause of poetic if not actual justice. "There is one class of people who do object to negro soldiers—these are the lordlings of the South—the devotees of King Cotton, and the fiery blooded chivalry of the rebel kingdom," he wrote. "Their talk . . . is malignant and venomous against the negro soldier. It humbles their ancient pride to have their slaves successful in arms against them. They feel no greater insult can be offered to their ragged and tattered pride than to be taken prisoners and placed under a negro guard. Such is sometimes among the chances of war, and it is a sort of retributive justice, I must confess I am not sorry to see."[20]

Other reminders of the course of the war in recent months also greeted Banks in New Orleans. Union authorities held captured Confederate officers in a vacant house at 25 Baron Street, away from their enlisted men. Among them were soldiers who had caused much of the trouble visited upon Banks and his army. "There were a few man of note among them, and one of them, Capt. Semmes, commander of a rebel battery, is a son of Capt. Semmes of the *Alabama,*" wrote a Massachusetts soldier. "He is about 23 years in age, small in stature, but a wiry and unusual man, with black eyes, and long black hair, which he wears brushed back over his forehead. It is unnecessary for me to say that he is a very smart, intelligent young man, and has the reputation of being a very accomplished officer." Another among the commissioned captives was Captain Julius Giesecke of the 4th Texas Cavalry, who had been captured at Irish Bend. "Our friends begin to bring us clothing and food, which made our position a little brighter," he wrote, adding that his accommodations were more than tolerable. "We are beginning to live right well, having also plenty of rooms."[21]

Prisoner in the Customs House. Union authorities held Confederates captured in the Teche Campaign in the New Orleans Customs House, "as is customary with all foreign goods" observed one Texan.

Harper's Weekly, *August 29, 1863, author's collection.*

After Banks finished his inspection, their captors changed the conditions of the Rebel officers' accommodations. Orders came for the twenty-five officers confined in the house to gather their gear and be ready to move. "We began to hope that we were to go on board a boat to be taken back to Dixie," Giesecke wrote. Instead, Federal infantry marched the Confederates to a cramped holding cell with a single barred window in the New Orleans Customs House, "as is customary with all foreign goods," quipped the captain. "The place was so small we could scarcely find room to lie down and the odor was terrible, so bad that we could not at first stand it," the German reported. "Rats were so bad they almost ate the hair from our heads."[22]

Nearly twelve hundred rank-and-file Rebel prisoners captured during the Teche Campaign languished in confinement at the Belleville Iron Works in Algiers, across the Mississippi from New Orleans. These Confederates became a source of curiosity for visitors from the North and Yankee soldiers who had not yet seen combat. Many crossed the river on the ferry to see for themselves the kind of men they were fighting. "The men looked remarkably well fresher than Southern men usually are," wrote a soldier in the 47th Massachusetts, "showing that their occupation as soldiers was not detrimental to their health."[23]

The first impression for most tourists was that these incarcerated Rebels represented a fairly well-equipped army—a testimony to the skills of Major General Richard Taylor's organization. "A greater part of the men wore soft, slouched hats, and Kentucky jean clothes of various colors, badly faded," one wrote, but "they all had good army shoes. This leads me to remark that we have just destroyed two shoe factories where five or six hundred pairs were turned out daily."[24]

For the most part the Rebels seemed to be glad to be out of the line of fire. "The men . . . seemed to be very cheerful and happy," wrote an observer. "There were a number who expressed the desire to take the oath of allegiance, and return North, saying that they had been pressed into the service by the Conscription Law." Observers remarked on the diversity of the group. "Some of the men where Frenchmen, who lived near the place where they were captured. Many were Texans, and these you could readily distinguish by their wild look. There were some from the different Southern States and one from Fall River, Mass. There were three who deliberately deserted from the rebels in front of the fortifications, and they appeared to be men who meant what they said."[25]

One Federal officer remained skeptical about the prisoners' lack of enthusiasm for the Rebel cause. "Boys, haven't you any patriotism?" he asked. "Aren't you willing to fight for the glorious South?"[26]

"We are not fighting for the South," shot back one cynical prisoner.

View from the Customs House. Union soldiers guarding Confederate officers in the New Orleans customs house could, from the roof, look out over the city toward the massive St. Charles Hotel in the French Quarter across Canal Street.

Marshall Dunham Photograph Album, Mss. 3241, Louisiana and Lower Mississippi Valley Collections, LSU Libraries, Baton Rouge, La.

"We are fighting for the niggers," another soldier snarled in disgust. "Their masters hire them to the government, to work on trenches, for eighteen dollars a month, while we slept out of doors and get nothing to eat and clothe ourselves for eleven dollars."

A third Confederate explained the Southern paradox: The planters "are terribly afraid a nigger will get killed and then they lose their [investment]. When there is prospect of a fight, they take all the niggers off out of harm's way, but they don't care for us, we didn't cost anything."[27]

Some of the prisoners quit their cause. "Many of the French, called Cagians, are taking the oath of allegiance to the U.S. and leaving the prison," observed Private William Henry King of Company B, 28th Louisiana. As the days passed, more of the defeated Confederates joined them and the numbers of Southern soldiers

Algiers Landing. A steamboat idles across the Mississippi from New Orleans at Algiers. This is the view prisoners taking the oath of allegiance would have had as they made their way to boats carrying them away from Confederate service.

Marshall Dunham Photograph Album, Mss. 3241, Louisiana and Lower Mississippi Valley Collections, LSU Libraries, Baton Rouge, La.

calling it quits grew. "Many are taking the oath," King wrote later. "I verily believe [half] of the 1200 prisoners brought to this place will have taken the oath before they are done," including "others beside the Cagians."[28]

Not everyone in the lockup had lost their zeal. Some among the Southerners remained convinced that Banks was headed for a disaster. "A non commissioned officer remarked . . . that Gen. Banks would undoubtedly have his own way until he met Gen. Kirby Smith, who, with a force of 11,000 men, was holding a place

Cajun Conscript. A Yankee view of Acadians conscripted into Confederate service. Notice how the bedraggled warrior is shackled to a tree. A soldier from northern Louisiana noted "many of the French, called Cagians, are taking the oath of allegiance to the U.S."

Center for Louisiana Studies Digital Archive, Louisiana State University, Lafayette.

strongly fortified, and as Gen. Banks would be obliged to leave a force in every place he passed," a Federal soldier wrote home. "This is his opinion."[29]

Indeed, to the Union veterans of the Teche Campaign who had made the march to Alexandria, the agricultural bounty of Louisiana—apparently limitless to northern soldiers—seemed to bear out the genuineness of this southern soldier's convictions. "Old sugar and cotton fields are now planted with corn," noted a soldier-correspondent for a Massachusetts newspaper as he passed through the Teche country. "These demonstrate that political life is more dear to them than money." The perceived willingness of the planters to shift from cash crops to staples impressed the journalist, and he gave a grudging compliment to the Confederates while scolding his fellow countrymen. "I sincerely think if the North fought with one tenth the 'fervency and zeal' that these rebels do, in thirty days we could conquer them of their treason."[30]

Wagons and Supplies by David Hunter Strother (aka Porte Crayon) gives an idea of the plunder being carried out of Louisiana by Union forces. Here lines of cotton bales await shipment to northern factories.

West Virginia and Regional History Collection, accession no. p.95.30.141.

Likewise, many of Banks's scattered men who had been left to complete the work remaining on Bayou Teche, grew nervous the longer they lingered in the area. The army that Banks had brought into the campaign had been spread out, and isolated outposts made tempting targets for Rebels who might return any day. These trips toiled on, nervously. At Port Barrè, Corporal Hosmer watched as workers loaded the wealth of south-central Louisiana onto steamers. "The pile of cotton is a mountain on the landing," he wrote. "All day long—everyday for weeks—teams have brought it in until it almost seems worth while to build here the factories that are to work it up into fabric; but since Mohomet will not come to the mountain . . . the mountain is going to Mahomet." The steady pattern of delivery and shipment proceeded unabated. "Down it goes, piecemeal," Hosmer continued, "through the bayou, on little steamers padded out like lank belles." He noted, though, that a white trail of this purloined wealth marked the passage of these spoils laden transports. From Port Barrè to the Atchafalaya, the branches of the trees overhanging Bayou Courtableau had brushed the passing boats, catching shreds of cotton in their boughs "as people carried into captivity by Indians, in old times," another soldier observed, "left pieces of their dress to mark a path for pursuing friends." The question remained: would there be a posse of pursuers coming to redeem the captive?[31]

28

The Wake of War

"It began in hope; it ended in fruition.
It began with bright anticipation; it ended in victory."

Private James K. Ewer
Company C, 3rd Massachusetts Cavalry

Major General Nathaniel P. Banks, awarded victor's laurels from the Teche Campaign, quit concerning himself with affairs west of the Mississippi, for he had moved on to his next great project. The principal elements of the Army of the Gulf had crossed the Mississippi energetically, and on Thursday, May 21, the 19th Army Corps reunited, more than fourteen thousand strong, as it circumvallated the Confederate works at Port Hudson. The corps continued to grow as the last parcels of Union troops made their way out of the Red River valley. Two days later Banks arrived at Port Hudson to personally take command of the reduction of the Rebel fort, and planned what he would do to Brigadier General Franklin Gardner and his seven thousand trapped Confederates.

Banks worried little about the conquered Teche Country because, in his mind, he had made arrangements for its security and exploitation. As the tempo of military activity at Port Hudson accelerated, Banks believed his anticipated army of African descent, the Corps d'Afrique, could soon be made operational and hold the ground that his white soldiers had taken in western Louisiana. With a little time, tens of thousands of former slaves would be wearing Union blue, performing patrols and garrison duty, and keeping the Rebels subdued.

Although Banks had turned his back on completing his conquest of Louisiana and had refocused his attention on Port Hudson, Major General Richard Taylor had not forgotten his directive to "baffle the enemy in his designs on the Mississippi" while harboring a desire to invade the Lafourche region and threaten New Orleans. As the Yankees who had pillaged his home state crossed the Mississippi River, the Confederate war chief began to phoenix-like regenerate his army. Banks had scattered Taylor's Rebels and killed many, but he had not destroyed them all. Now they would gather again—soon to be joined by thousands of their comrades from far afield—to renew the contest.

The Federal navy had throttled the Rebel lifeline of Trans-Mississippi beef, bacon, and corn that had helped sustained the forts at Port Hudson and Vicksburg for nearly a year. Taylor knew that the soldiers could not hold out for long without steady supplies and that he needed to strike, swiftly and with all the power he could muster, to retrieve the situation. His army, though growing, remained badly strewn from Shreveport to the Sabine; gathering it would rob him of precious time as the forts' supplies ran low.

One part of Taylor's army readied itself to sortie out of Niblett's Bluff. "The battles of Texas will be fought in Louisiana," trumpeted one Lone Star Rebel in a letter to the Houston newspaper. "There it behooves us to strike for our homes." Major General John Bankhead Magruder agreed with this assessment and continued sending all the troops from Texas that he could spare. Eventually some 2,500 men came from points stretching from the Neches River to the Brazos. The arrival of the 2nd Texas Cavalry at Niblett's Bluff in mid-May was followed the next day by the departure of the 2nd Louisiana Cavalry, heading east. Their mission was to scout the enemy near Vermilionville; determine the whereabouts of any remaining Federal forces; and scoop up Southern deserters, conscripts, and the timid and take them back to their Louisiana regiments. Jayhawkers, bandits, and guerillas also topped their list of targets. These steady Louisiana troopers swung into their saddles and headed their horses toward the east. They would serve as a vanguard for the gray flood that would slosh back into a region increasingly bereft of Federals.[1]

After the 2nd Louisiana Cavalry started on its mission, Texas Confederates continued to gather at Niblett's Bluff on the banks of the Sabine River. A five-gun artillery battery rumbled into camp led by Captain Thomas Gonzales, a wealthy Galveston merchant and native of Tampico in Vera Cruz, Mexico. This Hispanic officer had personally financed the unit and had played a prominent part in the Battle of Galveston. Now the *Tampiqueño* warrior would order his gunners to join the growing congregation; his four 6-pounders and single 12-pound howitzer were a welcome addition to the army.

The next arrivals were a curious bunch. Colonel George Wythe Baylor—one-time staff officer to General Albert Sidney Johnston, and a man who had listed his prewar profession as "Indian Killer"—led a mixed band of conscripts, desert dwellers, and Californians enrolled as the 2nd Arizona Cavalry. These troops had started out as part of the Arizona Brigade with an aim to conquer and hold the Southwest, but events in New Mexico had led Magruder to reorganize that wishful command and to redistribute the elements into small but workable regiments that might prove serviceable in Louisiana. Baylor counted no more than two hundred and fifty horsemen in his command.

Colonel Joseph Phillips, a Virginian who had traveled west with Magruder, rode at the head of the 3rd Arizona. This regiment, like Baylor's, was small and composed of men of mixed enthusiasm, but it had the added distinction of being nearly mutinous. Its slightly built commander, though, was extraordinarily brave and capable, and he managed to weld his command together through the judicious application of discipline and leadership by example—a quality Texans appreciated.

The son and namesake of one of the most famous Christian revivalists in America, Colonel Barton W. Stone, led the 2nd Texas Partisan Rangers. These Dallas-area troopers were mostly family men and reluctant warriors who had taken advantage of an act of the Confederate Congress to avoid being conscripted. Instead, they were guaranteed mounted service of an irregular nature. Having already seen action—they had been roughed up in a skirmish in Arkansas—the 2nd Texas reluctantly followed the orders taking them farther from their homes and into Louisiana.

Other troops headed to the Sabine River. The "Swamp Angels" of the 13th Texas Infantry headed east, broken into a strange collection of mounted, foot, and artillery units. These included Captain William Gibson's Battery, Major Lee C. Rountree's Mounted Battalion, and seven companies of infantry. Captain William Nichols's Texas Battery followed with four cannon, along with Lieutenant Colonel Ashley W. Spaight's peculiarly named 11th Texas Infantry-Cavalry Battalion, the defenders of Sabine Pass and Beaumont.

At Shreveport, Lieutenant General Edmund Kirby Smith watched an odd assortment of Texan troops from Arkansas and northeast Texas coming to the aid of Confederate Louisiana. As these units passed through town, Kirby Smith declared three shambling regiments to be unacceptable and ordered them into instruction camps. The sullen soldiers of the 22nd and 34th Texas Cavalries, dismounted, joined the Arkansas Post survivors—now cobbled together as the 17th Texas Consolidated Cavalry—in camps for drill and training approximately four miles west of Shreveport. They would be of no service to Taylor unless they knew how to soldier properly.

Other Lone Star reinforcements earned Kirby Smith's approval. Colonel Joseph Speight led a small brigade composed of the

31st Texas Dismounted Cavalry and the 15th Texas Infantry, and these seven hundred farmers from Waco and Milliken were ready to fight. The most anticipated arrival was Major General John G. Walker's hard-marching Texas division, still stalled around near Monroe. Walker's twelve regiments and accompanying artillery combined with the other Confederates who mustered at Niblett's Bluff might make a significant difference in Louisiana. Taylor was counting on them to be the shock troops that would lead his army to victory—and revenge.

At Natchitoches, Taylor watched the calendar nervously. If his entire army and the new reinforcements could concentrate in the next few weeks, he thought he might be able to save Port Hudson after all. He planned to avoid becoming entangled with the fighting at Port Hudson on the other side of the river. Instead, he would threaten New Orleans and interdict traffic on the Mississippi, which had always been his plan to baffle the enemy. In total, nine batteries of artillery, five brigades of infantry and dismounted cavalry, and the equivalent of three brigades of cavalry were coming to Louisiana—nearly ten thousand men—to join the nearly five thousand already there. An army of this size stood a reasonable chance of reversing Confederate fortunes in the state.

The longer Brigadier General Franklin Gardner held out at Port Hudson—and the more Yankees he killed—the more likely it was that Taylor could assemble a larger, more dangerous army than the Confederacy had ever seen in Louisiana and tip the strategic balance in the region. Lieutenant General John C. Pemberton, of course, would also have to hold on to Vicksburg as well. With Banks and Major General Ulysses S. Grant locked in sieges of Port Hudson and Vicksburg, swift columns of Confederates would be free to surge out of the Attakapas Prairies and the Red River valley to sweep away Union garrisons, dismantle the Federal work in protected areas like the Lafourche District, and reverse the Northern war effort. Taylor gambled that this distraction would force the Federals to give up their efforts at one or both of the Mississippi forts as they separated their force to again chase the Rebels. With a little luck, he would make his army impossible to ignore. Taylor hoped that Lieutenant General Kirby Smith embraced this strategic vision and would even mobilize Confederates in Arkansas to threaten the Union-held Mississippi at some strategic point there. A string of Union disasters on the Mississippi's west bank would certainly alarm Northern citizens and politicians.

To save Louisiana for the Confederacy, Taylor ordered his scattered command to rally at Opelousas and destroy the remaining Federals in the area. If his men responded promptly, the résumé of Union defeats in his new campaign might start with the destruction of Colonel Thomas E. Chickering's Brigade and the capture of Banks's baggage and plunder. Taylor moved his bruised Louisiana infantry regiments and supply train from Natchitoches to Opelousas while Tom Green, elevated to brigadier general to replace the disgraced general Henry Hopkins Sibley, led his cavalry brigade east from Niblett's Bluff on the Sabine, accompanied much of the way by his superior, Brigadier General Alfred Mouton. The other Texas and Arizona newcomers gathering to the north and west of the war zone would follow when armed, supplied, and ready.

On May 21, the same day the bulk of the Army of the Gulf encircled Port Hudson, Colonel Chickering of the 41st Massachusetts left Port Barrè with the booty from the Teche Campaign. "The long train . . . stretched for eight miles over the prairies, with a motley band of 5,000 negroes, 2,000 horses, and 1,500 beeves for a cumbrous accompaniment. With the possible exception of the herd that set out to follow Sherman's March through Georgia, this was perhaps the most curious column ever put in motion since that which defiled after Noah into the ark," remembered Lieutenant Colonel Richard B. Irwin. Chickering headed his menagerie for Brashear City, 125 miles away. Guarding this exodus was a brigade composed of the newly minted 3rd Massachusetts Cavalry (really the 41st infantry mounted on captured mules and horses);

52nd Massachusetts Infantry; 22nd and 26th Maine; 90th and 114th New York; Company E, 13th Connecticut; and one section of Captain Ormand French Nims's Massachusetts Battery. This small army of more than twenty-five hundred rifles could, Chickering believed, defend the column. He felt little concern about Major Hannibal Honestus Boone's and Colonel Walter P. Lane's Texans at Cheneyville, but the Yankee colonel did not know about other Southern storm clouds gathering just over the horizon to the north and west.[2]

Since the Union army was abandoning the region to the Confederates, Chickering enforced the policy of leaving little of value for the enemy to use. Directing his troops from inside a confiscated carriage, he continued his final sweep of the area as he led his column south. He divided his troops to cover both banks of Bayou Teche, with columns converging from Port Barrè and Opelousas, averaging eighteen miles a day. Soldiers ransacked the towns of Grand Coteau and St. Martinville while forcing all the slaves along their route to join the exodus. Terror at what might happen should they remain after the Union troops left convinced those slaves

Escaping out of Slavery.

Library of Congress.

who were reluctant to join the swelling mass of evacuees. "Haste! Haste! was the cry. Haste, the Rebels are coming. They are slaying the slaves as they advance. Fly! Fly!" wrote one observer. The retreat took on a panicky feel. "The flight down the Teche," reported observant Confederate officials, "was marked by visible disorder and despair. Children and infants were abandoned by the wayside, thrown from their mother's arms to perish. Smothered under a vague fear of impending calamity, the poor creatures fell upon everything within their reach which could convey them away."[3]

As the column headed south, the last remnant of the Federal army remained in Washington for a final task. The steamer *Louisiana Belle* pulled up to the town's landing to take on one last load of pilfered cotton. The fifty soldiers of Company B, 4th Massachusetts, fanned out, and some established a perimeter while others hauled seized commodities aboard the vessel. "Our forces had been entirely withdrawn from the town," noted Captain George S. Merrill, "and the inhabitants, in our limited intercourse, received us with evident lack of friendship." The Bay State infantrymen worked until midnight, nervously watching the mood turn darker among the townspeople as the night deepened. The last Federals in the region steamed away from the Washington landing in the early hours of May 22, 1863.[4]

For families living in remote farmsteads in the wilderness of western Louisiana and eastern Texas, the exact location of the contending armies continued to be sketchy. Some Texas Unionists traveled toward Louisiana, hoping to join Banks and help guide Federal troops to victory. Dennis Haynes was one such hopeful. A forty-three-year-old resident of Hardin County, Texas, and native of Dublin, Ireland, he figured the time was right to once again declare his allegiance to the United States. His home in the densely wooded and swampy region in East Texas known as the Big Thicket had allowed him to remain an unmolested spectator of the great national calamity breaking around him. "When General Banks whipped Dick Taylor on the Teche," he observed, "the Confederates broke, helter-skelter, in every direction; Taylor's army was demoralized." Now that he had seen the Confederate army weakened, Haynes would take an active part in the fight.[5]

He had cause to be optimistic. When Texas units from the Gulf Coast moved toward their rallying point at Niblett's Bluff, not everyone in the ranks obeyed orders. Haynes soon found himself at the head of a growing squad of deserters who hid in the Big Thicket. "Spaight's Battalion was ordered from Houston, Texas, to Louisiana to reinforce Taylor," Haynes continued. "This battalion was chiefly composed of Texians from the southeastern counties. Many deserted for their homes intending to remain with their families at all hazards." Called to a meeting at a secluded pond deep in the piney woods of East Texas, Haynes agreed to help the fifty or so men in attendance to organize and lead a resistance to Confederate authority in the region.[6]

The discontented soldiers complained that they had been duped by local planters and state officials into believing they had grievances

Bayou Teche. An Alfred R. Waud sketch of a bayou steamboat making its way toward Brashear City, not unlike the passage of *Louisiana Belle*.

Historic New Orleans Collection, Accession no. 1965.46.

against the Federal government. Once they threw their support to secession, promises that the state government would provide for their families never came to fruition, and instead Confederate commissary agents had seized corn, cattle, and hogs while offering only promises of payment. "Thus those cowardly vampires were fattening on the fat of the land, and enriching themselves on the misfortune of their country and miseries of the poor," Haynes hissed. The assembled men declared themselves determined to resist Confederate conscription officers and to ignore the authority of the Rebel officials. They also determined to outline in writing their grievances as well as their plan of action. Their resolution declared "the injustice of the rebellion and the incompetency of the Confederacy to gain its independence," Haynes reported, and "that the rebellion was uncalled for by any act of the United States Congress, and much less by the election of Abraham Lincoln."[7]

The group also intended to promote desertions among other men from the Big Thicket and to offer armed resistance to Confederate authorities trying to enforce their laws. They soon found their chance to act. Brigadier General George W. Van Vleck of Woodville, Texas, and commander of the local brigade of Texas state militia, heard about the seditious gathering, and he started a general roundup of the deserters and malcontents. Haynes and some of his companions headed toward Louisiana, hoping that Federal forces there might help them in their cause. "Before we quite got out of Texas," Haynes wrote, "we learned, to our great mortification, that Banks had evacuated Alexandria." Thus prematurely committed to assist the invading Union army, the roads into Louisiana turned dangerous for these dissenters, as Green and his one thousand mounted Confederates rattled down these same wooded lanes, as would hundreds more over the coming weeks. Haynes and his followers took to the forest.[8]

As the Confederate reinforcements surged across the prairies and the piney hills toward their rendezvous at Opelousas, they surveyed the impact of the passage of Banks's army. One effect quickly became evident: local brigands, jayhawkers, and militant runaway slaves had received arms and ammunition and would now conduct a small-scale but nagging resistance to the oncoming Rebels. The presence of the Federal forces had certainly given Unionists cause for optimism and bandits room to roam. Wagons and travelers were well advised to travel in convoy.

Troopers from Colonel Edwin Waller's Battalion, by now well acquainted with the neighborhood, were among the first Confederates returning to the Washington-Opelousas area. Already deployed to watch every road and waterway, locals reported that the *Louisiana Belle* had steamed past Port Barrè early on May 22. The Texans immediately made plans to intercept this last vestige of Banks's plundering expedition.

Down Bayou Courtableu, Federal lookouts on the *Louisiana Belle,* straining their eyes in the early light of morning, reported three riders, well-equipped, moving leisurely down the bayou road to their left. When the vessel came into view around a bend, the suspicious horsemen turned and quickly rode away, heading

downstream. After a few minutes passed, a civilian hailed the *Louisiana Belle* from the right bank, warning the men aboard of an imminent ambush. The Massachusetts soldiers grabbed their gear, took positions behind cover on deck, but when nothing happened immediately, they relaxed to eat breakfast.[9]

The Rebels struck at a little after 8:00 AM on a hairpin bend two miles from Port Barrè. "We were greeted with a murderous volley from the dense woods on the left bank," Captain Merrill reported. Bullets peppered the pilot house until it was "riddled by ball and buckshot," dropping one pilot, two deck hands, and ten soldiers. The boat's commander, standing exposed on the hurricane deck, fell grievously wounded when he was hit by bullets in his head and side. The *Louisiana Belle* clumsily plowed into a fallen tree on the left bank while its stern, pushed by the current, drifted broadside to the bayou and hit the right bank, and its paddlewheel entangled with overhanging branches. The attackers cheered wildly, assuming they had captured the Union vessel.[10]

They were wrong. Captain Merrill ordered his men to return fire while the crew freed the steamer. The Confederates, estimated to number around thirty, faded back into the trees, allowing the *Louisiana Belle* to swing once again into the current, bumping clumsily from bank to bank as its crew steered it from positions of safety below decks. For the next hour and a half the Southerners sniped at the paddle wheeler, but eventually the *Louisiana Belle* escaped the danger and proceeded with its cargo, its passengers, and its wounded, dead, and dying to Brashear City.[11]

Later that day, May 22 additional Texas cavalry arrived at Opelousas ready for more action against the Union invaders, but instead of confronting the enemy they faced some messy chores. The black people who had stayed behind or had been missed by the great Union roundup became a cause of extreme anxiety for the local population. Green's Texans moved quickly to smother any embers of insurrection by returning them to plantations still under strict control; this policing duty cost them another day. Then came word of the great Union spoils train working its way out of the region. Mouton ordered Green to pursue it.[12]

Confederate private William Randolph Howell, one of Green's troopers freshly arrived in Opelousas, turned his warhouse to the south and spent the next few days in the saddle. "We learn the thieves are three days ahead," he wrote from near a convent at Grand Coteau. The Texans could mark the path of the Union column by the dust, the smoke, and the litter of pillage along the way.[13]

Accompanying the hoof beats of these mounted Confederates came a new sound thundering across the swamps of central Louisiana, especially when the wind came from the east. At sunrise on May 23, 1863, the Army of the Gulf began shelling the Confederate trenches. Troops under Brigadier General Godfrey Weitzel, Colonel Halbert E. Paine, and Brigadier General Cuvier Grover launched an attack against the Confederate works at about ten o'clock that morning, but divisions under Brigadier General Thomas W. Sherman and Major General Christopher Columbus Augur failed to coordinate their movements and did not enter the battle until 2:00 PM. The attack ended in a brutal failure, a harbinger of just how hard it would be to take Port Hudson.

The Texas Unionist turned fugitive Haynes heard the guns as well. "Before we got within sixty miles of Alexandria, we could distinctly hear the Federal cannon battering at Port Hudson," he remembered. If there had even been any doubts that he and his comrades were on their own, they vanished. Haynes and other Unionists faded deeper into the forests and hills west of the Red River to plot their next move, alone and now unsupported by their government.[14]

That same day Colonel Chickering's responsibility for the eight-mile long plunder train weighed on him more heavily when scouts announced Confederates coming up fast from the rear. "Impelled by the alarm . . . that the rebels were on its track—thirsting for vengeance—the flying caravan went plunging through New Iberia with accelerated haste," an official reported. Chickering led his troops to the depot and signal station established the month before at the Olivier plantation four miles down the bayou and readied them to make a stand. The enemy horsemen vanished, however, and the Federals relaxed.[15]

But their peace would not last long. Reports of lurking Confederates caused Federal officers to signal an alarm that night. "There was a beat to arms in the dead of night, with the plantation bell pealing forth loud," an observer wrote, which also served as a "summons to the Negroes on the neighboring plantations." In the dark hours of Sunday morning, May 24, throngs of frightened slaves—those removed from Opelousas now joined by those

Sugar Factory. A sizable agricultural and industrial complex, the Olivier plantation, "Orange Grove," had a large house with long galleries, but also had a nearby refinery, or sugar house, and sizable storehouses making it a useful depot for both Confederate and Union forces operating in the Teche region.

Courtesy of the collections of the Louisiana State Museum.

Freed Slave. A man who made his way into Union lines, and who might soon be wearing a Federal uniform. *Library of Congress.*

from the local area—clustered around the depot, as Federal troops formed into ranks. Fear rippling through the mob of noncombatants, and soon, rowdies looted a cache of liquor, quickly fueling a near riot. "Soon their conduct knew no bounds," a southerner sneered. "In crowds they swayed . . . animated by a raving and incontrollable fury, and uttering shrieks of demoniacal rage. In a moment under Federal influence the Negroes had extinguished in their bosoms the civilized influences of a century."[16]

Chickering, eager to reach the Federal stronghold at Brashear City, and worried that he was losing control of the situation, ordered his command to form up and press on in the darkness. The regiments marched out, the wagon park uncoiled into a long column, and thousands of freed slaves, headed for the service of the United States either as soldiers in the Corps d'Afrique or as laborers on government-leased plantations, thronged the road. "It was a sight perhaps never witnessed before, and may never be again," one observer wrote. "The carts [in which the freed slaves rode] were those used to transport cane and cotton from the field, and would hold as much as a small canal boat. They were covered with awnings made of all kinds of material. Carpeting, clothing, reed mattings, dried cow hides, boards, and everything else which would serve to protect from the sun." Quite a few of the animals pulling these strange conveyances appeared unorthodox as well. "Some of the carts were drawn by oxen, some by horses, some by mules; and ox and a mule drawing at the same cart were not infrequent, and in one case a cow and a mule were harnessed together. The cooking utensils, clothing, bedding, and in fact all the traps of a negro cabin were loaded on, and the aged and the young were piled in promiscuously together."[17]

Potential Recruit. This image was taken in New Orleans. Banks considered men like him to be legitimate spoils of war.

Library of Congress.

The main force of Green's Confederate cavalry continued to reduce the distance between themselves and this motley caravan. Early on May 25, the Confederates arrived at New Iberia, where "the ladies seem much rejoiced at our return," Private Howell wrote. Green was now within a single day's march of the enemy, and he ordered his men to continue on quickly. He wanted to be in Franklin—and pitching into the Federal column—by dusk.[18]

At midday on Monday, May 25, Chickering and his command surged through Franklin, "the scene of Banks' recent triumph," crowed Private James K. Ewer of the 3rd Massachusetts Cavalry (formerly the 41st Infantry). "Here the men saw the remnants of Dick Taylor's camp. The ruins of Confederate gunboats and transports were on the river bank . . . among them was the famous gunboat [*Diana*]." Union soldiers from the 175th New York had just departed on the bullet-scarred steamer *Louisiana Belle,* heading for Brashear City with the remaining food and ammunition stockpiled at Franklin during the campaign. As the last of Chickering's caravan left the town, the end of Green's column had just left New Iberia. Now the Rebels were only six hours behind Chickering.[19]

That evening, Green's advance clattered across the Yankee-built Bayou Yokely Bridge and entered Franklin, nabbing a Federal major and four lieutenants from the 175th New York who had been left behind to tidy up government paperwork. His appetite whetted, Green ordered his soldiers to pause, check their gear, and get ready for a fight. "Our column arrives . . . at 8 p.m., ready and anxious for a dash into the trains," reported Howell. Within minutes the sounds of pistols, carbines, shotguns, and rifles crackled in the streets of town as the Confederates ran afoul of some of Chickering's mounted rear guards.[20]

The men of the 114th New York Infantry, who were marching in the rear of Chickering's command, found themselves overrun by excited riders, like so many rabbits fleeing a brush fire. "The day was beautiful, and just as the sun was setting we were marching leisurely along, hoping soon the halt for the night, when in our rear we heard shouting, and soon a mass, a mob, came dashing headlong, crying 'get out of the way, the Rebels are coming,'" wrote a newspaper correspondent with the troops. "At first we thought the mounted negroes and soldiers were running a race, but soon a cavalryman, dust-covered and bare-headed came dashing down, and said the rear-guard had been attacked and some killed." Panic rippled through the eight-mile long column.[21]

The scuffle at the edge of Franklin alerted Chickering's command to their imminent danger. At the far end of the Union column, the 26th Maine had gone into camp near Centerville for the evening. They had completed a twenty-one mile march that day and planned to lead the exodus to its conclusion the next. The

Confederates spoiled their timetable. "Just as we had got our coffee prepared," remembered Private Eldon D. Maddocks, "the bugle sounded and the Twenty-Sixth at once came into line and double quick, back four miles to assist our rear guard." Nearby the soldiers of the 52nd Massachusetts rolled out as well. "Silently, but with inward grumblings, we fall into line," wrote Sergeant Major Henry M. Whitney, "our silence broken only by an occasional expletive from one who does not see the fun of this all." Colonel Chickering sent couriers to Brashear City to alert the troops there and ordered rest of his mounted infantry and the two guns of Nims's battery to rush to the rear of the column. Masses of wagons, livestock, and freedmen passed south as Union soldiers pushed north. Three miles south of Franklin, a short Union battle line formed perpendicular to the road. It was the same ground where, a month before, Green had fought the first of a series of successful rear guard actions. Now road-weary Union soldiers peered into the darkness nervously, and Federal skirmishers stepped forward in the early-evening light and cautiously probed up the road toward town, searching for the Rebels.[22]

Officers interrogating a Confederate prisoner discovered that this was no ordinary dustup. "Colonel Chickering had learned somewhat of the plans of his pursuers," Ewer wrote. "The Confederate General Mouton . . . with Brigadier General Green, were preparing to attack the expedition and smash things generally." Part of the mounted forces would attack the rear of the Yankee train while the rest of the raiders would move around the flank of the retreating column. Then they would cut across the column's midsection and raise havoc among the wagons drivers, cattle herds, refugees, and freed slave families.[23]

Chickering had to save his command. He ordered his strengthened rear guard—which now included the 114th New York, the 26th Maine, and Nims's two guns—to hold off the Confederates as long as they could while he hurried the rest of the command to safety. The mounted 41st Massachusetts, now in their first fight as the 3rd Massachusetts Cavalry, fanned out toward Franklin, trotting ahead to find the enemy. The caravan behind them continued rumbling down the Bayou Teche road. "The train pushed forward with surprising rapidity," Ewer noted. "The crack of the whip could be heard on the backs of the horses and mules. The negroes were terribly excited. . . . That night was a long one to be remembered. No one slept," he added. "Eyes, ears, feet, and hands were in constant demand."[24]

Lieutenant Colonel Samuel R. Per Lee took command of the defensive line. He ordered his 114th New York into a column to advance toward Franklin, hoping to guard the rear of the Union

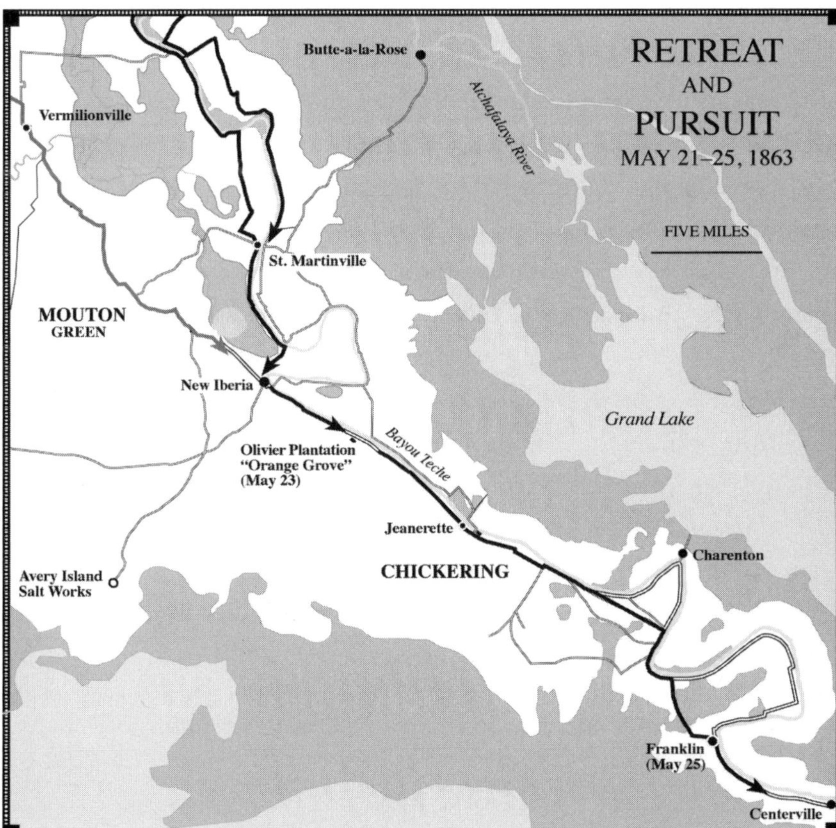

mass by pushing back against the Confederates. After two miles he ordered his troops to form a line of battle as clusters of mounted Federals from the 3rd Massachusetts retreated back from the streets of town just ahead. "We had hardly completed our formation, when several cavalrymen came rapidly down, and one of them gave his opinion as to the number and position of the enemy," Lieutenant Elias P. Pellet remembered. Lieutenant Colonel Per Lee ordered the horsemen to fall in with his command. When the soldier who had delivered the report did not respond, the officer grew impatient.

"My boy, are you not going?" Per Lee asked.

"I would go, Colonel, only for this," the rider responded, revealing a bullet wound to his side.[25]

The mixed command of Federal infantry and cavalry moved steadily back toward Franklin, gathering in stragglers, skirmishers, and soldiers wandering lost in the confusion, swelling their numbers. The gathering darkness combined with the dust made seeing nearly impossible. On the edge of town about one hundred Confederates opened fire, killing a New York lieutenant and wounding several soldiers. The Federals halted, and returned fire. Lieutenant Colonel Per Lee ordered his command into Franklin then, seeing how the buildings and fences broke up his formations, ordered his troops back out again, falling back a half mile, where they were once again into the open. Lieutenant Colonel Per Lee ordered his command to dress ranks, and he rode to the front. "Boys, there are a lot of those devils in there, and I am for going back and cleaning that town out!" he bellowed amid the cheering of his troops, their bloodlust high. Couriers ran down the road and returned with two additional companies of the 3rd Massachusetts Cavalry and Nims's two cannon. As a bright moon rose, Per Lee advanced his five hundred or so men toward Franklin, determined to assault the town and drive the Rebels from it.[26]

A night battle erupted within minutes. As the Federals came into range, firing again rippled through the streets and houses of Franklin. Bullets cut the air and whizzed overhead as the Yankees continued their approach. Dressing their ranks, they returned a volley into the town. Officers ordered their men to reload, and the rhythms of an infantry regiment at war took shape; behind the shooters, Nims's two 3-inch ordnance rifles began booming in cadence, blindly spinning shells among the houses of town suspected of sheltering Rebel riflemen.

Then, all was calm. The Federals ceased firing to once again register the location of their targets, but nothing moved in town. The Confederates had once again faded away. "We all hoped that the town might be burned," wrote Lieutenant Pellet. "We could distinctly see them firing from the windows of the houses, and yet this treacherous town was spared." Colonel Per Lee wisely decided

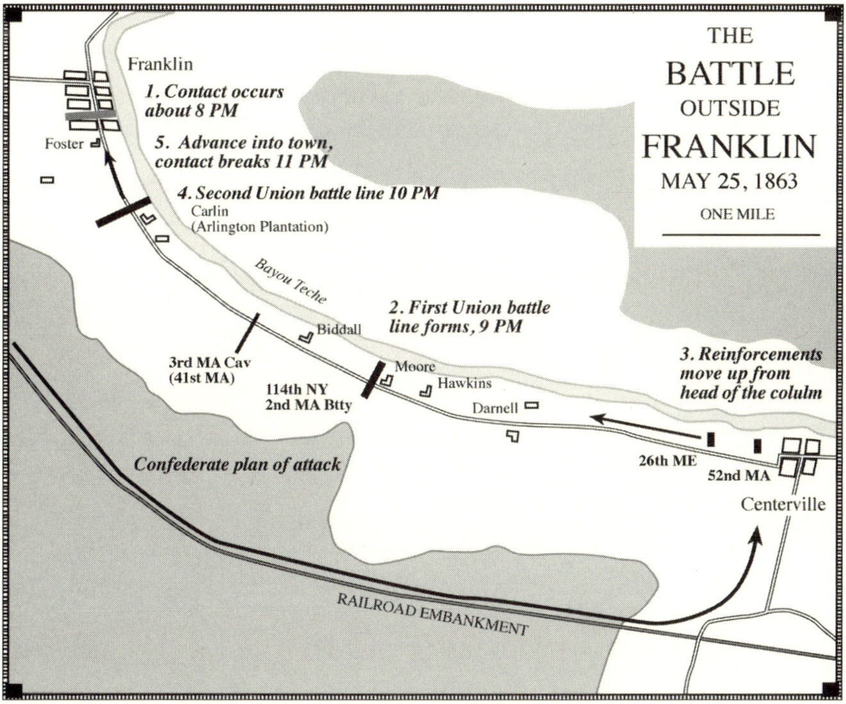

against reentering the town. The dust-up had already cost him about thirty men killed, wounded, and missing. A bushwhacking in the streets of Franklin might cost him his regiment. The New Yorkers and their allies once again fell back, confident that they had discouraged any renewed attacks from that quarter.[27]

They were correct; General Mouton had lost his nerve. The aggressive countermove by Lieutenant Colonel Per Lee had shaken Confederate confidence. "General Mouton deems it unsafe to go beyond Franklin to attack them," Private Howell wrote. "Consequently at 11 p.m. we are countermarched and greatly disappointed." In fact, Green and his troopers were fuming, ready to overrun the Yankees in the dark. "After a force march of about 150 miles, [Mouton] came up with their pickets," wrote Private John W. Watkins of the 5th Texas Cavalry to his wife. "After dilly dallying some time, [he] ordered a retreat from some cause I know not what. Colonel Green insisted on attacking them but was ordered to fall back by his superior officer and was bound to obey him, letting the Yankees off with over two hundred million dollars worth of property." After all they had been through in the last few weeks, these soldiers could not believe they would be denied a chance to punish the invaders. "Thus ended this part of the campaign," Watkins groused, "and I am afraid everyone will end likewise if we don't get more efficient Generals than we have."[28]

Chickering, meanwhile, marched his troops and the thousands of followers all night. At first light on May 26, the transport *Kepper* arrived at the mouth of Bayou Teche. It chaperoned the column on the last few miles of the retreat with two field pieces on its deck, keeping at a distance the Confederates scouts and skirmishers still hovering off the rear and flanks. "There appeared around the bend of the bayou one of the grandest sights that any body of troops ever looked upon," gushed Private Maddocks of the 26th Maine, "one of Uncle Sam's gunboats with that grand old flag flying." Chickering brought his command into Brashear City at 11:00 AM. "He had marched 110 miles in five days, and had made no mistake," wrote Pellet. "The authorities at Washington should have made him a brigadier." The tired and bedraggled column showed the rigors of the march. "A more dirty, dusty, ragged, and fatigued party of men never lived," Private Ewer concluded. "Thus ended the Teche Campaign. It began in hope; it ended in fruition. It began with bright anticipation; it ended in victory."[29]

Ewer was especially relieved to be back under the protection of the forts and gunboats at Berwick Bay, viewing the pandemonium with some satisfaction. "The braying of mules, the notes of bugles, the sound of drums, mingled with the oaths of the drivers and the shouts of soldiers. Wagons of all kinds covered the grounds; while in every direction roamed the emancipated contraband, whose first taste of freedom he was now enjoying. As for the soldiers," he added, "they were tired." A more practical-minded observer saw huge potential in this mass of humanity. "When we reached Brashear," Lieutenant Pellet wrote, "our crop of negroes was not less than twelve thousand strong." These former slaves would soon serve new masters for pay both as laborers and as soldiers.[30]

One last pocket of Union forces remained in the Teche region. Federal steamers finally retrieved the beleaguered 16th New Hampshire, which had been garrisoning the fort at Butte-a-la-Rose for the past six weeks. Low water in the Atchafalaya had prevented their recall before the end of May, but now the mission seemed more like a rescue. As the regiment left the captured Confederate fort on May 30, more than two hundred of its number lay buried in the Louisiana mud, victims of disease. The 16th New Hampshire was destined to never lose a man to hostile fire but to lose a quarter of its members to microbes.[31]

For the isolated Federal soldiers resting their weary feet at Brashear City, the days ahead looked dangerous. Until the Corps d'Afrique could be mobilized, equipped, trained, and brought to bear, their little band of three thousand white soldiers was all that defended the Lafourche District, that dearly won Union enclave behind them. While Banks bled his command at Port Hudson, these men would have to hold what had been won so far. The Confederates, they knew, would come.

They were already on their way. Along Bayou Teche and Bayou Courtebleau, from the Attakapas Prairies to the Atchafalaya Basin, Confederate forces were returning. The rumble of heavy guns in the distance reminded these troops that their comrades at Port Hudson were taking their turn whittling away at Banks and his army. The passage of time would reveal who would strike first—Taylor or Banks—and who would be the winner.

Sergeant Alfred B. Petticolas of the 4th Texas Cavalry, commissary agent for his command, was among the Confederates reassembling on the lower Teche. At the rear of the Rebel column, he passed through Opelousas at the end of May, noting a certain war

St. Maurice. Steamboats, including this one, were the backbone of Union operations on the Mississippi. Thousand of men and tons of supplies passed on and off its decks.

Marshall Dunham Photograph Album, Mss. 3241, Louisiana and Lower Mississippi Valley Collections, LSU Libraries, Baton Rouge, La.

weariness that lay upon the inhabitant of the town. "We . . . were warily welcomed by the citizens," he wrote. "No complaints now of our men committing depredations—no outcry about our having pressed horses when afoot to mount ourselves." The residents offered up flowers and even waved small Rebel flags as the Confederates passed.[32]

As Petticolas rode south, the condition of the country worsened. "The country from Opelousas down is a good deal devastated by the Federal visit," he penned. "Almost all the negroes are gone off with the Federals, and the horses that we left are taken and anything that the Feds desired to eat they took, and as a Yankee letter I saw expressed it, all they had to do was kill and eat."[33]

As the Texans returned to their battlefields of the month before, they, too, reflected on the war, their role in it, and the behavior of the people living on the lower Teche. Parson Lucius Jones,

Fleeing from the land of Bondage. Union soldiers herd these free people onto awaiting steamers to take them away from a familiar life of slavery into an unfamiliar world of freedom.

Massachusetts Comandery Military Order of the Loyal Legion and the US Army Military History Institute.

a thirty-five-year-old Episcopal preacher in the 4th Texas, led a harangue against these apparently reluctant Rebels in a Sunday sermon on May 31. "He is very much disgusted with the way the people of St. Mary's Parish have acted in the late raid by the Federals," Petticolas recalled. "The greater portion of the rich slave owners have taken the oath of allegiance to the U.S. Government to save their property." That act apparently did not help them much; marauding soldiers still ransacked their estates. "By sacrificing their principles," Petticolas continued, "they have lost both character and property."[34]

For this introspective soldier from Victoria, Texas, the behavior of these Louisianans brought him to a dilemma. Why, Petticolas wondered, had he left his home on the Texas frontier to put himself in danger on behalf of such a lukewarm population? Why should he fight so that people could keep their slaves? Maybe, Petticolas mused, he had been wrong to join the Confederate Army.

He asked Parson Jones for his views. "He says that if this is a war for the salvation of property, we will fail," Petticolas scribbled. Since that seemed to be the view of most of the gentry of Louisiana, the soldier believed, it really did little to justify his personal sacrifice. Petticolas was not sure he wanted to die on behalf of such folk.

"If it is a war for the right of self government," Parson Jones continued, sensing the conundrum facing his men, "we will succeed."

This buoyed the skeptical sergeant. "I am satisfied," he penned in his dairy, "that it is a war for freedom."[35]

Notes

Chapter 1

1. Samuel Amsler to his parents, brother, and sister, December 28, 1862, John Amsler Family Papers, Eugene C. Barker Texas History Collection, Dolph Briscoe Center for American History, University of Texas, Austin, hereafter cited as BTHC.
2. Ibid.
3. Ibid.
4. Ibid., January 18, 1863.
5. Ibid., January 6, 1863.
6. Ibid., January 18, 1863.
7. Julia LeGrand, *The Diary of Julia LeGrand, New Orleans 1862–1863,* edited by Kate Mason Rowland and Mrs. Morris L. Croxall (Richmond, VA: Everett Wadley, 1911), 66.
8. Jeffery S. Prushankin, *A Crisis in Confederate Command: Edmund Kirby Smith, Richard Taylor, and the Army of the Trans-Mississippi* (Baton Rouge: Louisiana State University Press, 2005), 20.
9. Jefferson Davis to Thomas Overton Moore, as quoted in Prushankin, *Crisis in Confederate Command,* 20.
10. J. H. Morrison to John C. Pemberton, November 6, 1862, in U.S. War Department, *The War of the Rebellion: A Compilation of the Official Records of the Union and Confederate Armies,* 128 vols. (Washington, DC: Government Printing Office, 1880–1901), Series I, vol. 15, 855; hereafter cited as *OR,* with all references to Series I unless otherwise stated.
11. Benjamin Butler to Henry Halleck, October 24, 1862, *OR,* vol. 15, 158–159.
12. George H. Hepworth, *The Whip, the Hoe, and Sword; or, the Gulf-Department in '63* (Boston: Walker and Wise, 1864), 83–84.
13. Prushankin, *Crisis in Confederate Command,* 21; *OR,* vol. 15, 859–861, 868.
14. Philip Caudill, *Moss Bluff Rebel: A Texas Pioneer in the Civil War* (College Station: Texas A & M University Press, 2009), 7–8; *Galveston Daily News,* December 2, 1856; Frank Vandiver, "Texas and the Confederate Army's Meat Problem," *Southwestern Historical Quarterly* 47, no. 3 (1944): 226.

15. Mansfield Lovell to Judah P. Benjamin, December 5, 1861, *OR,* vol. 6, 774–776; Lucius B. Northrop to George W. White, "White, George W.," April 2, 1862, Confederate Citizens File, 42, *Footnote.com,* http://www.footnote.com/image/#56376073 (accessed December 4, 2009).
16. Nathaniel P. Banks to Edwin M. Stanton, April 6, 1865, *OR,* vol. 26, pt. 1, 6–7; "Tod, John G.," October 4, 1861, Confederate Citizens File 18, *Footnote.com,* http://www.footnote.com/image/#54514332 (accessed December 4, 2009).
17. Abraham Lincoln to Edwin M. Stanton, January 23, 1863, in *The Collected Works of Abraham Lincoln,* ed. Roy P. Basler (New Brunswick, NJ: Rutgers University Press, 1953), 6:77–78.

Chapter 2

1. John B. Magruder to Richard Taylor, February 5, 1863, *OR,* vol. 15, 970; Magruder to James A. Seddon, February 5, 1862, *OR,* vol. 15, 967–968.
2. James Reily to Henry H. Sibley, January 31, 1863, *OR,* vol. 15, 968–970.
3. Ibid.; Reily to Magruder, January 31, 1863, *OR,* vol. 15, 970.
4. Taylor to Magruder, February 19, 1863, *OR,* vol. 15, 985.
5. LeGrand, *Diary,* 115–116.
6. Colonel Charles Rivers Ellet to Brigadier General Alfred W. Ellet, February 5, 1863, *OR,* vol. 24, pt. 1, 337.
7. Ibid., 337–338.
8. Sibley to Franklin Gardner, February 4, 1863, *OR,* vol. 24, pt. 1, 339; Gardner to J. R. Waddy, February 5, 1863, *OR,* vol. 24, pt. 1, 339.
9. Colonel Ellet to Brigadier General Ellet, February 5, 1863, *OR,* vol. 24, pt. 1, 337–338.
10. LeGrand, *Diary,* 104.
11. Nathaniel P. Banks to Henry Halleck, February 12, 1863, *OR,* vol. 15, 241.
12. Ibid., 240–241.
13. Banks to Halleck, February 16, 1863, *OR,* vol. 15, 242–243.
14. Halbert Paine to R. O. Ives, February 20, 1863, *OR,* vol. 15, 678; Banks to Halleck, February 26, 1863, *OR,* vol. 15, 1105.
15. Godfrey Weitzel to Christopher Columbus Augur, February 15, 1863, *OR,* vol. 15, 676–677.
16. Ibid., 676.
17. Ibid.
18. Cecil B. Eby Jr., ed. *A Virginia Yankee in the Civil War: The Diaries of David Hunter Strother* (Chapel Hill: University of North Carolina Press, 1989), 151.
19. Ibid., 150.

20. George H. Hepworth to Nathaniel P. Banks, March 24, 1863, as quoted in Susan Hayes Ward, *George H. Hepworth: Preacher, Journalist, Friend of the People, the Story of His Life Told to Susan Hayes Ward* (New York: E. P. Dutton, 1903), 78–79.
21. Colonel Ellet to David Dixon Porter, February 21, 1863, *OR,* vol. 24, pt. 1, 342.
22. Ron Brothers, "History of the 1st Texas Sharp Shooters Burnet's Battalion," http://gen.1starnet.com/civilwar/burnhist.htm (accessed June 2, 2010); "John Berrian Lindsley, ed., *The Military Annals of Tennessee: Confederate. First Series: Embracing a Review of Military Operations with Regimental Histories and Memorial Rolls* (Nashville: J. M. Lindsley, 1886), 463–469. Confederate officials redesignated the regiment as the 39th Tennessee Infantry on June 6, 1863.
23. George Brown to Porter, February 13, 1863, U.S. Naval War Records Office, *Official Records of the Union and Confederate Navies in the War of the Rebellion,* 27 vols. (Washington, DC: Government Printing Office, 1894–1922), vol. 24, 377–378; hereafter cited as *ORN.*
24. Colonel Ellet to Porter, February 21, 1863, *OR,* vol. 24, pt. 1, 342.
25. Taylor to Pemberton, February 20, 1863, *OR,* vol. 24, pt. 3, 636; Colonel Ellet to Porter, February 21, 1863, *OR,* vol. 24, pt. 1, 342–343.
26. Ellet to Porter, February 21, 1863, *OR,* vol. 24, pt. 1, 342–343.
27. Colonel Ellet to Porter, February 21, 1863, *OR,* vol. 24, pt. 1, 343.
28. Ibid.; Brown to Porter, May 28, 1863, *ORN,* vol. 24, 379–380.
29. Porter to Gideon Wells, February 22, 1863, *ORN*, vol. 24, 382–384.
30. Taylor to Pemberton, February 20, 1863, *OR,* vol. 24, pt. 3, 636.
31. Frank W. Loring to Weitzel, February 17, 1863, *OR,* vol. 15, 248.
32. Taylor to Pemberton, February 20, 1863, *OR,* vol. 24, pt. 3, 636.
33. Ibid.; Jefferson Davis to Joseph E. Johnson, *OR,* vol. 23, pt. 2, 641.
34. D. G. Farragut to Gideon Wells, February 23, 1863, *ORN,* vol. 19, 623; George Wiggin to A. P. Cooke, February 24, 1863, *ORN,* vol. 19, 623–624.

Chapter 3

1. Steven M. Mayeux, *Earthen Walls, Iron Men: Fort DeRussy, Louisiana, and the Defense of Red River* (Knoxville: University of Tennessee Press, 2007), 50; Joseph L. Brent, *Capture of the Ironclad "Indianola"* (New Orleans: Searcy and Pfaff, 1926), 13.
2. Richard Taylor, *Destruction and Reconstruction: Personal Experiences of the Late War* (New York: D. Appleton, 1879), 147; Mayeux, *Earthen Walls, Iron Men,* 50–51. The 31st Tennessee was also known as the "second" 31st Tennessee or Bradford's 31st Tennessee. Based on reports and muster rolls, Company B, C, and I appear to have been assigned to Fort DeRussy. The unit changed its designation June 6, 1863, to the 39th Tennessee Infantry.
3. Joseph L. Brent, as quoted in Mayeux, *Earthen Walls, Iron Men,* 50.

4. Mayeux, *Earthen Walls, Iron Men,* 56–57; Brent, *Capture,* 42.
5. Troops involved in this expedition were spread among five boats. On board the *Queen of the West* were twenty-six men from Maj. James Burnet's 1st Texas Sharpshooter Battalion under Adjutant R. S. Dulin; Around forty men from the 31st Tennessee under Capt. Elliot E. Carnes and Lt. Henry Miller, Company B; and a section of the 3rd Maryland Battery under Lt. W. Thompson Patten and Sergeant Edward Langly. Aboard the *Webb* were 2nd Lt. J. B. Pirtle and twenty men from the 1st Texas Sharpshooters and about twenty from Company I, 31st Tennessee under Lt. Hampton A. Rice and Lt. John M. Carson. The Tennessee troops under Capt. John D. Thomas, Company C, 31st, appear to have been aboard the *Grand Era*. Supporting the expedition were soldiers from Miles' Louisiana Legion from Port Hudson and Boone's Battery, aboard the steamer *Dr. Batey,* and 2nd Lt. W. R. Hale with eleven men of the 1st Texas Sharpshooters, on board the *Grand Era.* See "General Orders No. 20," *OR,* vol. 24, pt. 1, 362; Fredrick B. Brand to Lieutenant General Pemberton, February 25, 1863, *OR,* vol. 24, pt. 1, 362–363. The steamer *Dr. Batey,* spelled as shown in the *Official Records* and here, was spelled *Dr. Beaty* in Frederick Way Jr., *Way's Packet Directory, 1848–1994* (Athens: Ohio University Press, 1982), 130.
6. Taylor, *Destruction and Reconstruction,* 148.
7. George Brown to David Dixon Porter, May 28, 1863, *ORN,* vol. 24, 379–380; Joseph Brent to Edward Surget, February 25, 1863, *OR,* vol. 24, pt. 1, 364–369.
8. Taylor, *Destruction and Reconstruction,* 148.
9. Ibid.
10. George Brown to David Dixon Porter, May 28, 1863, *ORN,* vol. 24, 379–380. Brent to Surget, February 25, 1863, *OR*, vol. 24, pt. 1, 364–369; H. M. Mixer to Gideon Welles, April 26, 1863, *ORN,* vol. 24, 394.
11. Brown to Porter, May 28, 1863, *ORN,* vol. 24, 379–380; Brent to Surget, February 25, 1863, *OR,* vol. 24, pt. 1, 364–369; Mixer to Welles, April 26, 1863, *ORN,* vol. 24, 394.
12. Brent to Surget, February 25, 1863, *OR,* vol. 24, pt. 1, 364–369; Taylor, *Destruction and Reconstruction,* 148.
13. Mayeux, *Earthen Walls, Iron Men,* 64–65; Brent, *Capture,* 59.
14. Brent to Surget, February 25, 1863, *OR,* vol. 24, pt. 1, 364–369; Mayeux, *Earthen Walls, Iron Men,* 67; Brent, *Capture,* 62, 65; Taylor, *Destruction and Reconstruction,* 148.
15. Brent to Surget, February 25, 1863, *OR,* vol. 24, pt. 1, 364–369; Mayeux, *Earthen Walls, Iron Men,* 68.
16. Taylor, *Destruction and Reconstruction,* 149; Brent to Surget, February 25, 1863, *OR,* vol. 24, pt. 1, 364–369; Mayeux, *Earthen Walls, Iron Men,* 67–69; Brent, *Capture,* 61–65. Confederate reports listed Union casualties as one dead, one wounded. Among the men of the 39th Tennessee, Company B losses may have included Pvt. J. Wiley Wright, and Company C lost Pvt. Daniel F. Swan.

17. Jacod Austin Sperry, "Near Vicksburg, Mississippi," *The Dailey Register* (Knoxville, Tennessee), March 2, 1863; Taylor, *Destruction and Reconstruction,* 149; Brent to Surget, February 25, 1863, *OR,* vol. 24, pt. 1, 364–369; Mayeux, *Earthen Walls, Iron Men,* 67–69; Brent, *Capture,* 61–65.
18. Mayeux, *Earthen Walls, Iron Men,* 69–70; Brent, *Capture,* 66, 72.
19. S. Hassler to P. B. Stanberry, February 25, 1863, *ORN,* vol. 24, 395–396.
20. Mayeux, *Earthen Walls, Iron Men,* 72–79.
21. Edwin Cole Bearss, *Vicksburg is the Key,* vol. 1, *The Campaign for Vicksburg* (Dayton, OH: Morningside Press, 1985), 676–677.
22. Taylor, *Destruction and Reconstruction,* 149; John C. Pemberton to Samuel Cooper, *ORN,* vol. 24, 410; Pemberton to Taylor, *OR,* vol. 24, pt. 3, 650.
23. Edwin Cole Bearss, *Vicksburg is the Key,* 678.

Chapter 4

1. Edwin Cole Bearss, *The Vicksburg Campaign: Vicksburg is the Key* (Dayton, OH: Morningside Press, 1985), vol. I, 678.
2. Taylor, *Destruction and Reconstruction,* 127.
3. T. Michael Parrish, *Richard Taylor: Soldier Prince of Dixie* (Chapel Hill: University of North Carolina Press, 1992), 267; Taylor, *Destruction and Reconstruction,* 127.
4. Parrish, *Richard Taylor,* 267; Taylor, *Destruction and Reconstruction,* 127.
5. Richard B. Irwin, *History of the 19th Army Corps of the Union Army During the American Civil War* (New York: G. P. Putnam's Sons, 1893), 76.
6. Irwin, *History of the 19th Army Corps,* 76; Hepworth, *Whip, the Hoe, and Sword,* 246.
7. David G. Farragut to David Dixon Porter, March 20, 1863, *ORN,* vol. 20, 6.
8. Eby, *Virginia Yankee,* 161.
9. Ibid.
10. Donald S. Frazier, *Fire in the Cane Field: The Federal Invasion of Louisiana and Texas, January 1861–January 1863* (Buffalo Gap, TX: State House Press, 2009), 51; Francis Fearn, ed., *Diary of a Refugee* (New York: Moffat, Yard, 1910), 24–25.
11. Irwin, *History of the 19th Army Corps,* 77; Eby, *Virginia Yankee,* 154.
12. Eby, *Virginia Yankee,* 154.
13. Ibid., 155.
14. Irwin, *History of the 19th Army Corps,* 78–79; Eby, *Virginia Yankee,* 155.
15. Eby, *Virginia Yankee,* 156; Irwin, *History of the 19th Army Corps,* 81.
16. Nathaniel P. Banks to Henry Halleck, March 21, 1863, *OR,* vol. 15, 252; Irwin, *History of the 19th Army Corps,* 78–79; Lawrence Lee Hewitt, *Port Hudson, Confederate Bastion on the Mississippi* (Baton Rouge: Louisiana State University Press, 1987), 62–71.
17. Fearn, *Diary of a Refugee,* 24–25.

18. Ibid., 25–26.
19. Ibid.
20. Hewitt, *Port Hudson,* 82–83.
21. Eby, *Virginia Yankee,* 157.
22. Hewitt, *Port Hudson,* 84–90.
23. Eby, *Virginia Yankee,* 158–159.
24. Ibid., 158.
25. Banks to Halleck, March 21, 1863, *OR,* vol. 15, 254.
26. Eby, *Virginia Yankee,* 158.
27. Hepworth, *Whip, the Hoe, and Sword,* 92–94.
28. Ibid.
29. Eby, *Virginia Yankee,* 158–159.
30. Irwin, *History of the 19th Army Corps,* 76; Banks to Halleck, *OR,* vol. 15, 254; David C. Edmonds, *The Guns of Port Hudson,* vol. 1, *The River Campaign, February–May 1863* (Lafayette: Acadiana Press, 1983), 176.
31. *Boston Morning Journal,* April 9, 1863, p. 2, col. 2; Banks to Halleck, March 21, 1863, *OR,* vol. 15, 254; Banks to Halleck, March 27, 1863, *OR,* vol. 15, 257–258.
32. *Springfield (MA) Republican,* April 25, 1863, p. 1, col. 5.
33. Ibid.
34. Ibid.

Chapter 5

1. Bearss, *Vicksburg is the Key,* 603–613.
2. George L. Gillespie to Major W. H. Dameron, *OR,* vol. 24, pt. 3, 708.
3. Davis as quoted in Prushankin, *Crisis in Confederate Command,* 23–25.
4. Edward T. King to William Jones, June 27, 1910, William Jones Letters, Manuscript 524 (62), Special Collections, Howard-Tilton Memorial Library, Tulane University, New Orleans, Louisiana.
5. This list of boats was included in a correspondent's letter dated April 17, 1863, published first in the in the *New Orleans Era,* reprinted in the *Boston Journal,* and included in John Fisk Allen and George W. Briggs, *Memorial of Pickering Dodge Allen by His Father* (Boston: Henry W. Dutton and Son, 1867), 111–113.
6. Way, *Way's Packet Directory,* 196. For a thorough discussion of the "Block 66" naval yard at Shreveport, see Katherine Brash Jeter, ed., *A Man and His Boat: The Civil War Career and Correspondence of Lieutenant Jonathan H. Carter, CSN* (Lafayette: Center for Louisiana Studies, 1996).
7. James C. Cooley to Brigadier General James Bowen, February 25, 1863, *OR,* vol. 15, 1107; Irwin, *History of the 19th Army Corps,* 89.

8. Allen and Briggs, *Memorial of Pickering Dodge Allen,* 113.

9. Samuel Amsler to his parents, March 16, 1863, John Amsler Family Papers, BTHC; Robert Thompson Williams Diary, January 29–March 28, 1863, pp. 27–31, 4th Texas Cavalry File, Harold B. Simpson Confederate Research Center, Hillsboro, Texas.

10. James Reily to the editor, *Houston Tri-Weekly Telegraph,* April 7, 1863; Williams Diary, January 29–March 28, 1863, pp. 27–31.

11. William Randolph Howell to Sallie Patricks, May 4, 1863, William Randolph Howell Papers, BTHC.

12. Howell to Patricks, May 4, 1863, William Randolph Howell Papers.

13. J. W. Watkins to Irene, March 1, 1863, John W. Watkins Letters, Harold B. Simpson Confederate Research Center, Hillsboro, Texas.

14. Alfred B. Petticolas Diary, vol. 3, p. 157, private collection.

15. Ibid., 159–160.

16. Terry G. Jordan-Bychkov, et al., eds., translation by Irma Oglendorf Schwarz, "The Boesel Letters: Two Germans in Sibley's Brigade," *Southwestern Historical Quarterly* 102, No. 4 (April 1999): 457–486; Petticolas Diary, 163.

17. J. W. Watkins to Irene Watkins, March 20, 1863, John W. Watkins Letters.

18. Ibid.

19. Ibid., March 30, 1863.

20. Henry C. Wright, "Reminiscences of H. C. Wright of Austin," Wright Memoir, 56–57, BTHC.

21. J. W. Watkins to Irene Watkins, April 5, 1863, John W. Watkins Letters; Thomas Reade Rootes to Sarah A. Rootes, May 12, 1863, Sarah Rootes Correspondence, 1822–1884, Special Collections, Duke University, Durham, NC.

22. Howell to Patricks, January 19, 1863, William Randolph Howell Papers; Thomas Green to John M. Bronough, February 2, 1863, "Letter Book," John M. Bronough Papers, Texas Collection, Baylor University, Waco, TX; Theophilus Noel, *Autobiography and Reminiscences of Theophilus Noel* (Chicago: Theo. Noel Company Print, 1904), 89.

23. Sibley requested two thousand weapons and accoutrements for his command. See "Consolidated Report of Ordnance and Ordnance Stores in the Department of Southwestern Louisiana, March 26, 1863," J. L. Brent Papers, Group 55-B, Volume 41, Louisiana Historical Association Collection, Howard-Tilton Memorial Library, Tulane University, New Orleans (hereafter cited as LHA Collection, Tulane University); Howell to Patricks, May 4, 1863, William Randolph Howell Papers; William Randolph Howell Diary, April 8, 1863, William Randolph Howell Papers, BTHC; Petticolas Diary, April 27, 1863; Williams Diary, March 30 and April 4, 6, 7, 1863.

24. Wright Memoir, 57; Williams Diary, April 2, 3, 1863; Noel, *Autobiography and Reminiscences,* 90.

25. For a discussion of the various Louisiana units in the Teche Campaign, see Arthur W. Bergeron, *Guide to Louisiana Military Units, 1861–1865* (Baton Rouge: Louisiana State University Press, 1989); for a review of the Texas units service in New Mexico, see Donald S. Frazier, *Blood and Treasure: Confederate Empire in the Southwest* (College Station: Texas A&M University Press, 1995).

26. Williams Diary, April 2, 9, 1863; "Leila Robertson's Story" in Lucile Barbour Holmes, *Oaklawn Manor: Ante-bellum Plantation Home,* 4th ed. (Franklin, LA: printed by author, 1980), unmarked page; C. M. Horton Diary, April 6, 1863, Civil War Papers, Box 20, Folder 2, LHA Collection, Tulane University; Howell Diary, April 9, 1863; Noel, *Autobiography and Reminiscences,* 90.

27. Theophilus Noel, *A Campaign from Santa Fe to the Mississippi: Being a History of the Old Sibley Brigade from Its First Organization to the Present Time; Its Campaigns in New Mexico, Arizona, Texas, Louisiana and Arkansas in the Years 1861–2–3–4,* ed. by Martin Hardwick Hall and Edwin Adams Davis (Houston: Stagecoach Press, 1961), 78. For a biography of Henry Hopkins Sibley, see Jerry Thompson, *Henry Hopkins Sibley: Confederate General of the West* (Natchitoches, LA: Northwestern State University Press, 1987).

28. Taylor, *Destruction and Reconstruction,* 108, 165; Ezra Warner, *Generals in Gray: Lives of the Confederate Commanders* (Baton Rouge: Louisiana State University Press, 1959), 222–223; William Arceneaux, *Acadian General: Alfred Mouton and the Civil War* (Lafayette: Center for Louisiana Studies, University of Southwestern Louisiana, 1981), 10–11.

29. J. W. Watkins to Irene Watkins, April 17, 1863, John W. Watkins Papers.

30. Felix Robert Collard, "Reminiscences of a Private, Company G, 7th Texas Cavalry, Sibley Brigade, C.S.A.," private collection, 13; Alfred Mouton to Edward Surget, May 2, 1863, *OR,* vol. 15, 396–397; Horton Diary, April 11, 1863.

31. Men in the Crescent Regiment hailed almost entirely from New Orleans, where they had served in a prewar militia regiment. Oliver J. Semmes was the second son of Raphael Semmes of CSS *Alabama* fame. Men in the St. Mary's Cannoneers came from St. Mary's Parish and were organized at Franklin. Morris Raphael, *The Battle in the Bayou Country* (Detroit: Harlo Press, 1975), 80–82; Taylor, *Destruction and Reconstruction,* 108–109, 114.

32. Taylor, *Destruction and Reconstruction,* 113–115; "Consolidated Report of Ordnance."

33. The Val Verde guns were captured by frontal assault, an unusual feat for troops in their first battle. "Consolidated Report of Ordnance"; Taylor, *Destruction and Reconstruction,* 178–179; Joseph C. Terrell to "Ma" [Susan Kenerly Terrell], March 29, 1863, private collection. For a history of Waller's Battalion as told in the war journal of William J. Craig, see Charles Spurlin, ed., *West of the Mississippi with Waller's 13th Texas Cavalry Battalion CSA* (Hillsboro, TX: Hill Junior College Press, 1971).

34. Fearn, *Diary of a Refugee,* 28; Frazier, *Fire in the Cane Field,* 41.

35. Fearn, *Diary of a Refugee,* 28.

Chapter 6

1. David C. Rankin, ed., *Diary of a Christian Soldier: Rufus Kinsley and the Civil War* (New York: Cambridge University Press, 2003, 125.
2. Richard B. Irwin, "The Capture of Port Hudson," in Robert Underwood Johnson and Clarence Clough Buel, eds., *Battles and Leaders of the Civil War* (New York, 1887–1888. Reprint, Secaucus, NJ: Castle, 1987), 3:590; Raphael, *Battle in the Bayou Country,* 73–76.
3. Irwin, "Capture of Port Hudson," 586; Taylor, *Destruction and Reconstruction,* 120–121.
4. C. Peter Ripley, *Slaves and Freedmen in Civil War Louisiana* (Baton Rouge: Louisiana State University Press, 1976), 109–111.
5. Irwin, *History of the 19th Army Corps,* 89; Henry W. Morris to A. P. Cooke, March 27, 1863, *ORN,* vol. 20, 108.
6. John William De Forest, *A Volunteer's Adventures: A Union Captain's Record of the Civil War,* ed. James H. Croushore (Baton Rouge: Louisiana State University Press, 1996), 81; Henry W. Morris to Gideon Welles, March 28, 1863, *ORN,* vol. 20, 105–106.
7. Eby, *Virginia Yankee,* 165.
8. William Lott Davidson, "Capture of the Diana," *Overton (TX) Sharp-Shooter,* p. 1, July 12, 1888; Taylor, *Destruction and Reconstruction,* 118.
9. Davidson, "Capture of the Diana," *Overton (TX) Sharp-Shooter,* p. 1, July 12, 1888; Joseph C. Terrell, "Descriptive History Record, January 20, 1897," in Dora Davenport Jones, ed., "History of Julia Jackson Chapter #141, United Daughters of the Confederacy, Fort Worth, Texas, A Bicentennial City 1897–1976," typed manuscript, Fort Worth Public Library, Genealogy and Local History Section, Fort Worth, TX; George Ernest Bowman, comp., *Vital Records of Truro, Massachusetts to the year 1849* (Boston: Massachusetts Society of Mayflower Descendants, 1933), 239.
10. Davidson, "Capture of the Diana," *Overton (TX) Sharp-Shooter,* p. 1, July 12, 1888; Terrell, "Descriptive History Record," np.
11. C. C. Cox, "Reminiscences of C. C. Cox," *Southwestern Historical Quarterly* 6 (January 1903): 225. H. H. Boone, twenty-nine years old at the time of the Cheneyville fight, was a native of Tennessee who had lived in Texas for nine years before the Civil War began. He practiced law in Hempstead when he enlisted in the 2nd Texas Mounted Rifles in 1861. After his initial one-year enlistment, he joined Waller's Battalion as a second lieutenant, and rose through the ranks to major and second in command. He was seriously wounded at the Battle of the Fordoche (Sterling's plantation) on September 29, 1863, forcing his return to Texas as a semi-invalid. In 1876, the citizens of Texas elected Boone as attorney general, a position he held for one term. See "Hannibal Honestus Boone" in *The New Handbook of Texas* (Austin: Texas State Historical Association, 1996), 1:640.
12. Terrell, "Descriptive History Record."
13. Allen and Briggs, *Memorial of Pickering Dodge Allen,* 91. For an enthusiastic monograph about this incident, see Morris Raphael, *A Gunboat Named Diana* (New Iberia, LA: printed by author, 1993).

14. Allen and Briggs, *Memorial of Pickering Dodge Allen,* 91.
15. Ibid.
16. Ibid., 93.
17. Ibid., 99.
18. De Forest, *Volunteer's Adventures,* 83.
19. Allen and Briggs, *Memorial of Pickering Dodge Allen,* 93, 98.
20. Ibid., 103.
21. Henry Weston to Gideon Welles, March 28, 1865, *ORN,* vol. 20, 111–112.
22. J. M. Foltz to David G. Farragut, May 22, 1863, *ORN,* vol. 20, 110–111.
23. Terrell, "Descriptive History Record."
24. Allen and Briggs, *Memorial of Pickering Dodge Allen,* 103.
25. Godfrey Weitzel to Nathaniel P. Banks, March 28, 1863, *ORN,* vol. 20, 109; "Extract from Diary of Acting Third Assistant Engineer Baird, U.S. Navy, of the U.S.S. *Calhoun,*" *ORN,* vol. 20, 113.
26. A. P. Cooke to Henry W. Morris, March 30, 1863, *ORN,* vol. 20, 108–109.
27. Weitzel to Banks, March 28, 1863, *OR,* vol. 15, 290.
28. Allen and Briggs, *Memorial of Pickering Dodge Allen,* 97.
29. Augustine Joseph Hickey Duganne, *Camps and Prisons: Twenty Months in the Department of the Gulf* (New York: J. P. Robens, 1865), 199–201; Terrell, "Descriptive History Record."
30. Henry Weston to Gideon Welles, March 28, 1865, *ORN,* vol. 20, 112.
31. Terrell, "Descriptive History Record,"; Joseph C. Terrell, "Some Interesting Old Letters," Terrell Family Correspondence, Fort Worth Public Library, Genealogy and Local History Section, Fort Worth, TX.
32. Allen and Briggs, *Memorial of Pickering Dodge Allen,* 101.
33. Duganne, *Camps and Prisons,* 199–201; Terrell, "Descriptive History Record"; Allen and Briggs, *Memorial of Pickering Dodge Allen,* 103.
34. Davidson, "Capture of the Diana," *Overton (TX) Sharp-Shooter,* p. 1, July 12, 1888.
35. Duganne, *Camps and Prisons*, 199–201; Terrell, "Descriptive History Record."
36. James Reily to the editor, *Houston Tri-Weekly Telegraph,* April 7, 1863.
37. "Extract from Diary of Acting Third Assistant Engineer Baird, U.S. Navy, of the U.S.S. *Calhoun,*" *ORN,* vol. 20, 113.

Chapter 7

1. Bearss, *Vicksburg is the Key,* 694–695.
2. David Porter to David G. Farragut, March 22, 1863, *ORN,* vol. 20, 11.
3. Ibid.
4. Bearss, *Vicksburg is the Key,* 702–703.
5. J. W. Watkins to Irene Watkins, April 5, 1863, John W. Watkins Letters.
6. Ibid.; Noel, *Santa Fe to the Mississippi,* 68.

7. Bearss, *Vicksburg is the Key,* 703; *New York Times,* May 1, 1863.
8. Eby, *Virginia Yankee,* 164.
9. Hepworth, *Whip, the Hoe, and Sword,* 208.
10. LeGrand, *Diary,* 309–311.
11. Edward T. Cotham Jr., ed., *The Southern Journey of a Civil War Marine: The Illustrated Note-Book of Henry O. Gusley* (Austin: University of Texas Press, 2006), 149–150.
12. Edmund Miles to Elizabeth Miles, April 6, 1863, Edmund Miles Papers, MS N-378, Massachusetts Historical Society, Boston, MA.
13. Andrew M. Sherman, *In the Lowlands of Louisiana in 1863: An Address Delivered by Andrew M. Sherman at the Forty-Second Reunion of the Twenty-Third Connecticut* (Morristown, NJ: Howard Publishing, 1908), 17.
14. Eby, *Virginia Yankee,* 166.
15. Cotham, *Southern Journey,* 150.
16. Irwin, *History of the 19th Army Corps,* 89–90.
17. Hepworth, *Whip, the Hoe, and Sword,* 111–112; Frazier, *Fire in the Cane Field,* 91.
18. Irwin, *History of the 19th Army Corps,* 90.
19. L. Carroll Root, ed., "The Experiences of a Federal Soldier in Louisiana in 1863," *Louisiana Historical Quarterly* 19 (1936): 637.
20. De Forest, *Volunteer's Adventures,* 85–86.

Chapter 8

1. Richard Taylor to William Robertson Boggs, April 23, 1863, *OR*, vol. 15, 388.
2. Julius Giesecke, "The Diary of Julius Giesecke, 1863–1865," Oscar Haas, trans., *Military History of Texas and the Southwest* 18 (October 1988): 65; Petticolas Diary, April 9, 1863.
3. Taylor to Boggs, April 23, 1863, *OR,* vol. 15, 388; Frank M. Flinn, *Campaigning with Banks in Louisiana, '63 and '64, and with Sheridan in the Shenandoah Valley in '64 and '65* (Lynn, MA: Press of Thomas P. Nichols, 1887), 33; Samuel Gault Diary, April 9, 1863, MS 177, Historic New Orleans Collection, New Orleans, LA; Noel, *Santa Fe to the Mississippi,* 69.
4. Alfred Mouton to Edward Surget, May 2, 1863, *OR,* vol. 15, 396.
5. Taylor to Boggs, April 23, 1863, *OR,* vol. 15, 388; Davidson, "Capture of the Diana," *Overton (TX) Sharp-Shooter,* p. 1, July 12, 1888.
6. Eby, *Virginia Yankee,* 166.
7. Banks to U. S. Grant, April 10, 1863, *OR,* vol. 15, 296.
8. Taylor to Boggs, April 23, 1863, *OR,* vol. 15, 388; Davidson, "Capture of the Diana," *Overton (TX) Sharpshooter, Sharp-Shooter,* p. 1, July 12, 1888; Howell Diary, April 11, 1863.
9. L. Carroll Root, ed. "The Experiences of a Federal Soldier in Louisiana in 1863," *Louisiana Historical Quarterly* 19 (1936): 635

10. Howell Diary, April 11, 1863.
11. Flinn, *Campaigning with Banks,* 34; Harris H. Beecher, *Record of the 114th Regiment, N.Y.S.V.: Where It Went, What It Saw, and What It Did* (Norwich, NY: J. F. Hubbard Jr., 1866), 138.
12. Eby, *Virginia Yankee,* 166–167.
13. Williams Diary, April 11, 1863, pp. 27–31; Noel, *Santa Fe to the Mississippi,* 69; Giesecke, "Diary," 65–69; Howell Diary, April 11, 1862; Flinn, *Campaigning with Banks,* 33; Gault Diary, April 11, 1863.
14. Williams Diary, April 11, 1863; Noel, *Santa Fe to the Mississippi,* 69; Giesecke, "Diary," 65–69; Howell Diary, April 11, 1862; Flinn, *Campaigning with Banks,* 33; Gault Diary, April 11, 1863; Cotham, *Southern Journey,* 154.
15. Elias P. Pellet, *History of the 114th Regiment, New York State Volunteers* (Norwich, NY: Telegraph and Chronicle Power Press Printing, 1866), 64.
16. Beecher, *Record of the 114th Regiment,* 139.
17. Collard, "Reminiscences," 13; Lawrence Hewitt and Christopher Godwin, "The Battle of Bisland, Louisiana," *North and South: The Magazine of Civil War Conflict,* September 1998, 29–45.
18. Collard, "Reminiscences," 13; Mouton to Surget, May 2, 1863, *OR,* vol. 15, 396–397.
19. Collard, "Reminiscences," 13; Horton Diary, April 11, 1863.
20. On the far left, troops built an earthwork backed by a stockade and equipped with three gun platforms; on the extreme right, gunners from the Val Verde battery used large cypress, ash, and elm logs to construct an elevated emplacement that enabled the guns to direct fire over the heads of the infantry in front.
21. Collard, "Reminiscences," 13; Mouton to Surget, May 2, 1863, *OR,* vol. 15, 396–397.

Chapter 9

1. Cotham, *Southern Journey,* 154.
2. George N. Carpenter, *History of the Eighth Regiment Vermont Volunteers, 1861–1865* (Boston: Deland and Barta, 1886), 98.
3. Alfred Mouton to Edward Serget, May 2, 1863, *OR,* vol. 15, 397.
4. Davidson, "Movements of the Brigade in 1863," *Overton (TX) Sharp-Shooter,* pg.1, June 21, 1888.
5. Flinn, *Campaigning with Banks,* 37.
6. Carpenter, *Eighth Regiment Vermont Volunteers,* 98; Root, "Federal Soldier in Louisiana," 640.
7. Flinn, *Campaigning with Banks,* 36.
8. Ibid., 38.
9. Ibid.
10. Felix Robert Collard, "Personal Experiences at Battles of Bisland, Vermillion Prairie, and Vermillion Bayou," 1, private collection.

11. Ibid.
12. Davidson, "Movements of the Brigade in 1863," *Overton (TX) Sharp-Shooter,* pg.1, June 21, 1888; Giesecke, "Diary," 66; Williams Diary, April 12, 1863.
13. Flinn, *Campaigning with Banks,* 40.
14. Ibid., 40.
15. Pellet, *History of the 114th Regiment,* 65; Noel, *Santa Fe to the Mississippi,* 69; Flinn, *Campaigning with Banks,* 37.
16. Beecher, *Record of the 114th Regiment,* 139; Pellet, *History of the 114th Regiment,* 65–66; De Forest, *Volunteer's Adventures,* 87.
17. De Forest, *Volunteer's Adventures,* 87.
18. Beecher, *Record of the 114th Regiment,* 139; Pellet, *History of the 114th Regiment,* 65–66; De Forest, *Volunteer's Adventures,* 87.
19. Pellet, *History of the 114th Regiment,* 65–66.
20. De Forest, *A Volunteer's Adventures,* 88; Petticolas Diary, April 27, 1863; Howell Diary, April 12, 1863; Letter to the Editor, "In Camp on Bank of Sabine River, May 11, 1863," *Houston Tri-Weekly Telegraph,* May 18, 1863.
21. Noel, *Santa Fe to the Mississippi,* 70; Howell Diary, April 13, 1863.
22. Carpenter, *Eighth Regiment Vermont Volunteers,* 98–99.
23. Pellet, *History of the 114th Regiment,* 66.
24. De Forest, *Volunteer's Adventures,* 87–88.
25. Pellet, *History of the 114th Regiment,* 66.
26. Carpenter, *Eighth Regiment Vermont Volunteers,* 98–99.
27. De Forest, *Volunteer's Adventures,* 88.
28. Carpenter, *Eighth Regiment Vermont Volunteers,* 98–99.
29. Ibid.; Root, "Federal Soldier in Louisiana," 636.
30. E. C. Bainbridge to Richard Arnold, April 22, 1863, *OR,* vol. 15, 328; Frank H. Peck to J. D. Williams, April 22, 1863, *OR,* vol. 15, 328–329.
31. William Emory to Richard B. Irwin, April 21, 1863, *OR,* vol. 15, 330; De Forest, *Volunteer's Adventures,* 88.
32. Gault Diary, April 12, 1863.

Chapter 10

1. Cuvier Grover to Richard Irwin, *OR,* vol. 15, 358.
2. The description of Colonel Vincent comes from George C. Harding, *The Miscellaneous Writings of George C. Harding* (Indianapolis: Carlon and Hollenbeck,1882), 321.
3. Edward T. King to William Jones, June 27, 1910, *New Orleans Times Democrat,* William Jones Letters.
4. *Boston Herald,* p. 2, col. 1, April 28, 1863; King to Jones, June 27, 1910, William Jones Letters.
5. King to Jones, June 27, 1910, William Jones Letters.

6. James K. Hosmer, *The Color-Guard: Being a Corporal's Notes of Military Service in the Nineteenth Army Corps* (Boston: Walker and Wise, 1864), 125–126; George P. Bissell, Samuel K. Ellis, Thomas McManus, and Henry Hill Goodell, *The Twenty-Fifth Regiment Connecticut Volunteers in the War of the Rebellion: History, Description of Battle of Irish Bend, Carrying of Pay Roll, Roster* (Rockville, CT: Press of the Rockville Journal, 1913), 33–34.
7. Hosmer, *Color-Guard,* 125–126; Bissell et al., *Twenty-fifth Regiment Connecticut Volunteers,* 33–34.
8. Taylor, *Destruction and Reconstruction,* 130.
9. Thompson, *Henry Hopkins Sibley,* 325; Raphael, *Battle in the Bayou,* 94–95.
10. Alfred Mouton to Edward Serget, *OR,* vol. 15, 397.
11. Ibid.
12. Collard, "Reminiscences of a Private," 13.
13. Petticolas Diary, April 27, 1863; Gault Diary, April 12–13, 1863; Horton Diary, April 12, 1863; Howell Diary, April 12, 1863; De Forest, *Volunteer's Adventures,* 91.
14. Halbert Paine to Peter French, April 21, 1863, *OR,* vol. 15, 339.
15. Ibid., 339–340.
16. Ibid., 340
17. Horton Diary, April 12, 1863; Collard, "Reminiscences of a Private," 13.
18. Richard Taylor to Richard Boggs, April 23, 1863, *OR,* vol. 15, 389.

Chapter 11

1. Gault Diary, MS 177.
2. Collard, "Bisland, Vermillion Prairie, and Vermillion Bayou," 1.
3. Ibid.
4. Giesecke, "Diary," 66; Noel, *Santa Fe to the Mississippi,* 71; Howell Diary, April 13, 1863.
5. Judson Brinkerhoff, Six Miles Northwest of St. Martinsville, to Elizabeth Brinkerhoff, New York, New York, April 17, 1863, possession of Robert Brinkerhoff, Ada, Michigan.
6. Petticolas Diary, March 31 to April 27, 1863; "The Last Roll," *Confederate Veteran* IX, Number 1 (January 1901), 32.
7. Taylor, *Destruction and Reconstruction,* 131.
8. Ibid.
9. Davidson, "Capture of the *Diana,*" *Overton (TX) Sharp-Shooter.*
10. Collard, "Bisland, Vermillion Prairie, and Vermillion Bayou," 1.
11. Sioux (W. P. Doran), "In Camp on Bank of Sabine River," May 11, 1863, in *Houston Tri-Weekly Telegraph,* May 18, 1863.
12. De Forest, *Volunteer's Adventures,* 89.
13. Ibid.
14. Ibid.
15. Ibid.

16. Ibid.
17. "Consolidated Report of Ordnance and Ordnance Stores," J. L. Brent Papers, LHA Collection, Tulane University.
18. Arthur W. Bergeron Jr., ed., *Civil War Reminiscences of Major Silas T. Grisamore, CSA* (Baton Rouge: Louisiana State University Press, 1993), 113.
19. Ibid.
20. Hewitt and Godwin, "Battle of Bisland," 37.
21. Beecher, *Record of the 114th Regiment,* 143–144.
22. Root, "Federal Soldier in Louisiana," 642.
23. Ibid.
24. Beecher, *Record of the 114th Regiment,* 144.
25. Root, "Federal Soldier in Louisiana," 642.
26. Willam Emory to Richard Irwin, April 21, 1863, *OR,* vol. 15, 331; Carpenter, *Eighth Regiment Vermont Volunteers,* 103.
27. Halbert Eleazer Paine, *A Wisconsin Yankee in Confederate Bayou Country: The Civil War Reminiscences of a Union General,* edited by Samuel C. Hyde Jr. (Baton Rouge: Louisiana State University Press, 2009), 132–133.
28. Halbert Eleazer Paine, *A Wisconsin Yankee in Confederate Bayou Country: The Civil War Reminiscences of a Union General,* edited by Samuel C. Hyde Jr. (Baton Rouge: Louisiana State University Press, 2009), 132–133.
29. William Logan Rodman to Oliver P. Gooding, April 18, 1863, *OR,* vol. 15, 351–352.
30. Sioux (W. P. Doran), "In Camp on Bank of Sabine River," May 11, 1863, in *Houston Tri-Weekly Telegraph,* May 18, 1863; Flinn, *Campaigning with Banks,* 52; Rodman to Gooding, April 18, 1863, *OR,* vol. 15, 351–352.
31. Rodman to Gooding, April 18, 1863, *OR,* vol. 15, 351–352.
32. Sioux, "In Camp on Bank of Sabine River," May 11, 1863, in *Houston Tri-Weekly Telegraph,* May 18, 1863.
33. Collard, "Bisland, Vermillion Prairie, and Vermillion Bayou," 1.
34. Ibid.; J. W. C., 38th Massachusetts, Algiers, LA, May 1, 1863, to the editor, *Cambridge (MA) Chronicle,* p. 1, col. 5, May 30, 1863.
35. Hewitt and Godwin, "Battle of Bisland," 37.
36. Hewitt and Godwin, "Battle of Bisland," 37.
37. Ibid.
38. De Forest, *Volunteer's Adventures,* 89; Carpenter, *Eighth Regiment Vermont Volunteers,* 102–103.
39. Collard, "Bisland, Vermillion Prairie, and Vermillion Bayou," 2.
40. Ibid., 2–3.
41. Ibid., 3–4.
42. Thomas Faries to Joseph L. Brent, *OR,* volume 20, 1089–1093.
43. Paine, *Wisconsin Yankee,* 132.
44. Ibid.
45. Collard, "Bisland, Vermillion Prairie, and Vermillion Bayou," 3–4.

46. Hewitt and Godwin, "Battle of Bisland," 37.
47. Collard, "Bisland, Vermillion Prairie, and Vermillion Bayou," 3–4.
48. Ibid., 4; Oliver P. Gooding to Nathaniel P. Banks, April 21, 1863, *OR,* vol. 15, 347; Hewitt and Godwin, "Battle of Bisland," 37.
49. Taylor, *Destruction and Reconstruction,* 132.

Chapter 12

1. Cuvier Grover to Richard Irwin, May 2, 1863, *OR,* vol. 15, 358.
2. Richard E. Holcomb to William B. Hunt, April 28, 1863, *OR,* vol. 15, 377.
3. Holcomb to Hunt, April 28, 1863, *OR,* vol. 15, 377; Gouverneur Morris, *The History of a Volunteer Regiment, Being a Succinct Account of the Organization, Services, and Adventures of the Sixth Regiment, New York Volunteers, Infantry, Knows as Wilson's Zouaves: Where They Went, What They Did, and What They Saw in the War of the Rebellion, 1861–1865* (New York: Veteran Volunteer Publishing Company, 1891), 97.
4. Grover to Irwin, May 2, 1863, *OR,* vol. 15, 359.
5. James K. Ewer, *The Third Massachusetts Cavalry in the War for the Union* (n.p.: Historical Committee of the Regimental Association, 1903), 67.
6. Noel, *Santa Fe to the Mississippi,* 71–74.
7. Petticolas Diary, April 13, 1863; Nicholas Day to William Hunt, undated, *OR,* vol. 15, 381; J. Vann Zandt to William Hunt, undated, *OR,* vol. 15, 380; John I. Rodgers to Henry Clossen, April 21, 1863, *OR,* vol. 15, 366–367; Henry W. Clossen to Richard Arnold, April 21, 1863, *OR,* vol. 15, 365–366.
8. Giesecke, "Diary," 66; Holmes, *Oaklawn Manor,* unmarked page; Williams Diary, April 13, 1863; Petticolas Diary, April 13, 1863; Noel, *Santa Fe to the Mississippi,* 71–74.
9. Florian O. Cornay, to J. L. Brent, April 23, 1863, *OR,* vol. 53, 466.
10. Giesecke, "Diary," 66; Petticolas Diary, April 13, 1863; Noel, *Santa Fe to the Mississippi,* 71–74; Day to Hunt, undated, *OR,* vol. 15, 381.
11. Giesecke, "Diary," 66; Petticolas Diary, April 13, 1863; Noel, *Santa Fe to the Mississippi,* 71–74; Day to Hunt, undated, *OR,* vol. 15, 381.
12. A. P. Cooke to H. W. Morris, April 15, 1863, *ORN,* vol. 20, 134.
13. "G," 41st Regiment Massachusetts Volunteers, April 25, 1863, to the editor, *Boston Saturday Evening Gazette,* p. 1, cols. 2 and 3, May 30, 1863
14. Ibid.

Chapter 13

1. Giesecke, "Diary," 66; Williams Diary, April 13, 1863; Petticolas Diary, April 13, 1863; Noel, *Santa Fe to the Mississippi,* 71–74; Taylor, *Destruction and Reconstruction,* 132.
2. Taylor, *Destruction and Reconstruction,* 132.
3. Ibid.

4. Ibid.
5. Taylor, *Destruction and Reconstruction,* 133; Florian O. Cornay to James L. Brent, April 23, 1863, *OR,* vol. 53, 465–468; Noel, *Santa Fe to the Mississippi,* 71.
6. Horton Diary, April 14, 1863; Noel, *Santa Fe to the Mississippi,* 75; Howell Diary, April 14, 1863; Thompson, *Henry Hopkins Sibley,* 326; Cornay to Brent, April 23, 1863, *OR,* vol. 53, 469.
7. Richard Taylor to William R. Boggs, April 23, 1863, *OR,* vol. 15, 393.
8. "Letter from Above New Iberia" to the editor, *Boston Herald,* p. 2, col. 1, April 28, 1863.
9. Paine, *Wisconsin Yankee,* 133.
10. Bergeron, *Reminiscences of Major Silas T. Grisamore,* 113.
11. Petticolas Diary, April 13, 1863.
12. Ibid.
13. "Extract from the Diary of Acting Third Assistant Engineer Baird," April 14, 1863, *ORN,* vol. 20, 137.

Chapter 14

1. "Extract from the Diary of Acting Third Assistant Engineer Baird," April 14, 1863, *ORN,* vol. 20, 137.
2. Ibid., 138.
3. A. P. Cooke to H. W. Morris, April 15, 1863, *ORN,* vol. 20, 134–135.
4. Henry W. Morris to Gideon Welles, April 18, 1863, *ORN,* vol. 20, 135; "Diary of Acting Third Assistant Engineer Baird," April 14, 1863, *ORN,* vol. 20, 138; Edward T. King to William Jones, June 27, 1910, William Jones Letters; A. P. Cooke to H. W. Morris, April 15, 1863, *ORN,* vol. 20, 134–135.
5. *Boston Herald,* p. 2, col. 1, April 28, 1863.
6. Ibid.
7. "Diary of Acting Third Assistant Engineer Baird," April 14, 1863, *ORN,* vol. 20, 138.

Chapter 15

1. A. J. Scarborough to the editor, May 2, 1863, *Houston Telegraph,* published in *Houston Tri-Weekly Telegraph,* May 11, 1863.
2. Ibid.
3. Ibid.
4. Henry Hill Goodell, two miles from Vermilionville, to Dr. Prime, April 18, 1863, record group 73, accession number 1979.83.3-8, folder 6, Henry Hill Goodell Papers, 1852–1900, Louisiana State Museum, New Orleans, Louisiana; Elden B. Maddocks, *History of the Twenty-Sixth Maine Regiment* (Bangor, ME: Charles H. Glass, 1899), 28.

5. Noel, *Santa Fe to the Mississippi,* 74; Florian O. Cornay to J. L. Brent, April 23, 1863, *OR,* vol. 53, 467.
6. Noel, *Santa Fe to the Mississippi,* 74; Cornay to Brent, April 23, 1863, *OR,* vol. 53, 467; George Schubert to Sophia Schubert, April 18, 1863, George Schubert Letters, Schoff Civil War Collection, Soldiers Letters 11:18, Manuscripts Division, William L. Clements Library, University of Michigan, Ann Arbor, Michigan.
7. Maddocks, *Twenty-Sixth Maine Regiment,* 29
8. John I. Rodgers to Henry Clossen, April 21, 1863, *OR,* vol. 15, 366.
9. Maddocks, *Twenty-Sixth Maine Regiment,* 29.
10. Ibid., 30.
11. Hosmer, *Color-Guard,* 133–134.
12. Hosmer, *Color-Guard,* 132; John Farwell Moors, *History of the Fifty-Second Regiment, Massachusetts Volunteers* (Boston: G. H. Ellis, 1893), 117.
13. Cornay to Brent, April 23, 1863, *OR,* vol. 53, 467.
14. Edward Duffy, *History of the 159th Regiment, N.Y.S.V.* (New York: Hudson Gazette, 1890), 10.
15. Ibid.
16. Irwin, *History of the 19th Army Corps,* 112.
17. Henry Hill Goodell, two miles from Vermillionville, to Dr. Prime, April 18, 1863, Henry Hill Goodell Papers; George Schubert to Sophia Schubert, April 18, 1863, George Schubert Letters.
18. Duffy, *History of the 159th Regiment,* 10–11.
19. William Dwight to J. Hibbert Jr., April 27, 1863, *OR,* vol. 15, 372.
20. Diary of Homer B. Sprague, vol. 2, April 14, 1863, Papers of Homer B. Sprague, Manuscripts Division, Library of Congress.
21. Homer B. Sprague, *History of the 13th Infantry Regiment of Connecticut Volunteers during the Great Rebellion* (Hartford: Case, Lockwood, 1867), 113.
22. Ibid., 115.
23. Ibid.; Sprague Diary, April 14, 1863.
24. Sprague, *History of the 13th Infantry Regiment,* 115; Sprague Diary, April 14, 1863.
25. Ibid.
26. A. J. Scarborough to the editor, May 2, 1863, *Houston Telegraph,* published in *Houston Tri-Weekly Telegraph,* May 11, 1863.
27. Giesecke, "Diary," 66; Noel, *Autobiography and Reminiscences,* 92.
28. Sprague, *History of the 13th Infantry Regiment,* 115–117.
29. Ibid.
30. Noel, *Santa Fe to the Mississippi,* 71, 74–75; Giesecke, "Diary," 66.
31. Dwight to Hibbert, April 27, 1863, *OR,* vol. 15, 372.
32. Morris, *History of a Volunteer Regiment,* 99.
33. Sprague, *History of the 13th Infantry Regiment*, 115.

34. Ibid.; Sprague Diary, April 14, 1863.
35. Noel, *Autobiography and Reminiscences,* 90–91.
36. Sprague, *History of the 13th Infantry Regiment,* 115; Noel, *Autobiography and Reminiscences,* 92; Sprague Diary, April 14, Papers of Homer B. Sprague 1863.
37. Richard Taylor to William R. Boggs, April 23, 1863, *OR,* vol. 15, 392.
38. Rodgers to Clossen, April 21, 1863, *OR,* vol. 15, 366; Cuvier Grover to Richard Irwin, May 2, 1863, *OR,* vol. 15, 360–361; Morris, *History of a Volunteer Regiment,* 100; Maddocks, *Twenty-Sixth Maine Regiment,* 32.
39. Noel, *Autobiography and Reminiscences,* 93
40. Sioux (W. P. Doran), "In Camp on Bank of Sabine River," May 11, 1863, published in *Houston Tri-Weekly Telegraph,* May 18, 1863.
41. Morris, *History of a Volunteer Regiment,* 100.
42. Sprague Diary, April 14, 1863; Rodgers to Clossen, April 21, 1863, *OR,* vol. 15, 367; Cuvier Grover to Richard Irwin, May 2, 1863, *OR,* vol. 15, 360.
43. Henry Birge to J. Hibbert Jr., April 22, 1863, *OR,* vol. 15, 383–385.
44. E. H. Russell to George R. Herbert, July 28, 1863, *OR,* vol. 15, 327.
45. Sprague Diary, April 14,1863; Rodgers to Clossen, April 21, 1863, *OR,* vol. 15, 367.
46. Hosmer, *Color-Guard,* 134.
47. Ibid., 134–135.
48. Noel, *Santa Fe to the Mississippi,* 75.
49. Duffy, *History of the 159th Regiment,* 10; William Frank Tiemann to Edward Leslie Molineux, May 19, 1863, William Tiemann Collection, New York State Military Museum and Veterans Research Center, Saratoga Springs, New York; George Schubert, On the March, April 18, 1863, to Sophia Schubert, April 18, 1863, George Schubert Letters; Maddocks, *Twenty-Sixth Maine Regiment,* 32.
50. Sprague, *History of the 13th Infantry Regiment,* 120–121.
51. Sprague, *History of the 13th Infantry Regiment,* 117; Noel, *Santa Fe to the Mississippi,* 75–77.
52. A. J. Scarborough to the editor, May 2, 1863, *Houston Telegraph,* published in *Houston Tri-Weekly Telegraph,* May 11, 1863.
53. Maddocks, *Twenty-Sixth Maine Regiment,* 33.

Chapter 16

1. De Forest, *Volunteer's Adventures,* 91.
2. Ibid.
3. *Boston Herald,* p. 2, col. 1, April 28, 1863.
4. Ibid.
5. Beecher, *Record of the 114th Regiment,* 148.
6. Ibid.
7. Ibid., 149.

8. Ibid., 149–150.
9. Ibid., 150; Carpenter, *Eighth Regiment Vermont Volunteers,* 105; R. C. Duryea to Richard Arnold, April 21, 1863, *OR,* vol. 15, 337.
10. Beecher, *Record of the 114th Regiment,* 150.
11. John A. A. West to Joseph L. Brent, April 23, 1863, *OR,* vol. 53, 464–465
12. Ibid., 465.
13. Beecher, *Record of the 114th Regiment,* 101.
14. Richard Taylor to William R. Boggs, April 23, 1863, *OR,* vol. 15, 393.
15. Hosmer, *Color-Guard,* 134.
16. Allen and Briggs, *Memorial of Pickering Dodge Allen,* 106.
17. Noel, *Santa Fe to the Mississippi,* 75; Collard, "Bisland, Vermillion Prairie, and Vermillion Bayou," 27.
18. Root, "Federal Soldier in Louisiana," 643.
19. Alfred Mouton to Edward Surget, May 2, 1863, *OR,* vol. 15, 399.
20. Beecher, *Record of the 114th Regiment,* 150–151, 154.
21. Allen and Briggs, *Memorial of Pickering Dodge Allen,* 106, 112, 122.
22. Richard Taylor to William R. Boggs, April 23, 1863, *OR,* vol. 15, 393.

Chapter 17

1. Alfred Mouton to Edward Surget, May 2, 1863, *OR,* vol. 15, 399.
2. John W. Watkins to his wife, April 17, 1863, John W. Watkins Letters.
3. Thompson, *Henry Hopkins Sibley,* 326–332; Petticolas Diary, April 27, 1863; Noel, *Santa Fe to the Mississippi,* 75.
4. Richard Taylor to William R. Boggs, April 23, 1863, *OR,* vol. 15, 393.
5. Eby, *Virginia Yankee,* 168–169.
6. Beecher, *Record of the 114th Regiment,* 152–153; Root, "Federal Soldier in Louisiana," 635–637.
7. Hosmer, *Color-Guard,* 135–136; Maddocks, *Twenty-Sixth Maine Regiment,* 33–40.
8. Sprague, *History of the 13th Infantry Regiment,* 120.
9. Taylor to Boggs, April 23, 1863, *OR,* vol. 15, 388–396; Horton Diary, April 14–17, 1863; Noel, *Santa Fe to the Mississippi,* 75.
10. John Franklin Godfrey, *The Civil War Letters of Captain John Franklin Godfrey* (South Portland, ME: Ascensius Press, 1993), 46.
11. Pellet, *History of the 114th Regiment,* 66–75; John Farwell Moors, *History of the Fifty-Second Regiment, Massachusetts Volunteers* (Boston: G. H. Ellis, 1893), 113.
12. Hosmer, *Color-Guard,* 137.
13. Root, "Federal Soldier in Louisiana," 637; Hosmer, *Color-Guard,* 138.
14. Collard, "Bisland, Vermillion Prairie, and Vermillion Bayou," 3; Noel, *Santa Fe to the Mississippi,* 76.

15. Petticolas Diary, April 27, 1863; Noel, *Santa Fe to the Mississippi,* 75–76; Howell Diary, April 14–17, 1863; James Henry Tevis to the *Tucson Daily Citizen,* January 6, 1899. See also L. Boyd Finch, *Confederate Pathway to the Pacific: Major Sherod Hunter and Arizona Territory, C.S.A.* (Tucson: Arizona Historical Society, 1996), 181, and Robert P. Perkins, "Captain James Henry Tevis, Arizona Pioneer and Confederate Soldier," members.tripod.com/~azrebel/page23.html (accessed January 8, 2005).
16. Beecher, *Record of the 114th Regiment,* 153–154.
17. Ibid., 154.
18. Hepworth, *Whip, the Hoe, and Sword,* 273.
19. Root, "Federal Soldier in Louisiana," 644; Beecher, *Record of the 114th Regiment,* 154.
20. Root, "Federal Soldier in Louisiana," 644.
21. De Forest, *Volunteer's Adventures,* 92; Petticolas Diary, April 27, 1863; Horton Diary, April 14, 16, 1863.
22. Taylor to Boggs, April 23, 1863, *OR,* vol. 15, 394.
23. Bergeron, *Reminiscences of Major Silas T. Grisamore,* 114–115.
24. Raphael, *Battle in the Bayou Country,* 135.
25. Godfrey, *Civil War Letters,* 68; Benton Bell Seat, "Memoirs," 112–113, Special Collections, University of Arkansas Library, Fayetteville, AR.
26. Seat, "Memoirs," 112–113.
27. Ibid.
28. Calvin Stebbins, *Henry Hill Goodell: The Story of his Life, with Letters and a Few of his Addresses* (Cambridge, Mass: Riverside Press, 1911), 44; Petticolas Diary, April 27, 1863; Noel; *Santa Fe to the Mississippi,* 75–76; Howell Diary, April 14–17, 1863; James Henry Tevis to the *Tucson Daily Citizen,* January 6, 1899; Finch, *Confederate Pathway to the Pacific,* 181.
29. Headquarters, St. Mary Cannoneers Battery, Camp Winn, April 30, 1863, to Major Joseph L. Brent, J. L. Brent Collection, 55L–Correspondence, Reports, Orders, 1862–1865, LHA Collection, Tulane University.
30. Ibid.
31. Beecher, *Record of the 114th Regiment,* 155–156.
32. De Forest, *Volunteer's Adventures,* 92; Beecher, *Record of the 114th Regiment,* 156.
33. William Dwight to J. Hibbert, April 27, 1863, *OR,* vol. 15, 373.
34. Rankin, *Diary of a Christian Soldier,* 127.
35. Giesecke, "Diary," 67.

Chapter 18

1. A. Power Gallway to Peter French, April 21, 1863, *OR,* vol. 15, 343.
2. *Boston Herald,* p. 2, col. 1, April 28, 1863; De Forest, *Volunteer's Adventures,* 92.
3. Maddocks, *Twenty-Sixth Maine Regiment,* 41–45; H. M. P., "From Our Special Correspondent," April 26, 1863, in *Boston Traveler,* p. 2, col. 2, May 6, 1863.

4. J. F. Belton to John B. Magruder, April 16, 1863, *OR,* vol. 15, 1043; William R. Boggs to William R. Scurry, April 21, 1863, *OR,* vol. 15, 1043.
5. Edmund Kirby Smith to Samuel Cooper, April 18, 1863, *OR,* vol. 15, 1045; J. C. Pemberton to Kirby Smith, April 22, 1863, *OR,* vol. 15, 1049–1050.
6. Pemberton to Kirby Smith, April 22, 1863, *OR,* vol. 15, 1049.
7. Bergeron, *Reminiscences of Major Silas T. Grisamore,* 115.
8. *Boston Traveller,* p. 2, col. 2, May 5, 1863.
9. Eby, *Virginia Yankee,* 172.
10. Ibid.
11. Howell Diary, April 16–17, 1863.
12. Collard, "Reminiscences," 3–4.
13. Collard, "Reminiscences," 3–4; Cuvier Grover to Richard B. Irwin, May 2, 1863, *OR*, vol. 15, 361.
14. William Smith to Joseph L. Brent, April 29, 1863, J. L. Brent Collection, 55L–Correspondence, Reports, Orders, 1862–1865, LHA Collection, Tulane University.
15. Smith to Brent, April 29, 1863, J. L. Brent Collection; Williams Diary, April 17, 1863; Petticolas Diary, April 27, 1863; Howell Diary, April 17, 1863; Collard, "Reminiscences," 3–4; Noel, *Santa Fe to the Mississippi,* 76; Davidson, "The Retreat from Bisland," *Overton (TX) Sharp-Shooter,* pg. 1, June 28, 1888.
16. Joseph Faust to Herman Seele, May 13, 1863, Joseph Faust Papers; Howell Diary, April 17, 1863; Noel, *Santa Fe to the Mississippi,* 76.
17. Richard Taylor to Boggs, April 23, 1863, *OR,* vol. 15, 394–395.

Chapter 19

1. Beecher, *Record of the 114th Regiment,* 154–156; James Albert Osborne Diary, Saturday April 18, 1863, Massachusetts Historical Society, Boston, MA.
2. Pellet, *History of the 114th Regiment,* 73.
3. Rankin, *Diary of a Christian Soldier,* 127; Gary D. Joiner, Marilyn S. Joiner, and Clifton Cardin, eds., *No Pardons to Ask, nor Apologies to Make: The Journal of William Henry King, Gray's 28th Louisiana Infantry Regiment* (Knoxville: University of Tennessee Press, 2006), 94.
4. Luther Tracy Townsend, *History of the Sixteenth Regiment, New Hampshire Volunteers* (Washington, DC: Norman T. Elliot, 1897), 156.
5. Willoughby M. Babcock Jr., *Selections from the Letters and Diaries of Brevet-Brigadier General Willoughby Babcock of the Seventy-Fifth New York Volunteers: A Study of Camp Life in the Union Armies during the Civil War* (Albany: The University of the State of New York, 1922), 59.
6. H. M. P., "From Our Special Correspondent," April 18, 1863, in *Boston Traveler,* p. 2, col. 2, May 5, 1863.
7. H. M. P., "From Our Special Correspondent," April 26, 1863, in *Boston Traveler,* p. 2, col. 2, May 6, 1863; Babcock, *Selections from the Letters and Diaries,* 59.

8. Edmonds, David S., ed., *The Conduct of Federal Troops in Louisiana during the Invasions of 1863 and 1864: Official Report Compiled from the Sworn Testimony under Direction of Governor Henry W. Allen, Shreveport, April 1865* (Lafayette, LA: Acadiana Press, 1988), 7.
9. De Forest, *Volunteer's Adventures,* 92–93.
10. Ibid.
11. A. Power Gallway to Peter French, April 21, 1863, *OR,* vol. 15, 343–345.
12. Townsend, *History of the Sixteenth Regiment,* 156.
13. Ibid., 161–162.
14. Ibid.
15. Davidson, "The Retreat from Bisland," *Overton (TX) Sharp-Shooter,* pg. 1, June 28, 1888.
16. Ibid.
17. Ibid.
18. Hepworth, *Whip, the Hoe, and Sword,* 275–278.
19. Ibid.
20. Richard Taylor to William Boggs, April 23, 1863, *OR,* vol. 15, 394.
21. H. M. P., "From Our Special Correspondent," April 26, 1863, in *Boston Traveler,* p. 2, col. 2, May 6, 1863.
22. Ibid.; Paine, *Wisconsin Yankee,* 134.
23. Diary of Acting Third Assistant Engineer Baird, *ORN,* vol. 20, 154; Cotham, *Southern Journey,* 157–158.
24. Diary of Acting Third Assistant Engineer Baird, *ORN,* vol. 20, 154; Edward T. King to William Jones, June 27, 1910, William Jones Letters.
25. Diary of Acting Third Assistant Engineer Baird, *ORN,* vol. 20, 153–154; King to Jones, June 27, 1910, William Jones Letters; Diary of Acting Third Assistant Engineer Baird, *ORN,* vol. 20, 154.
26. Diary of Acting Third Assistant Engineer Baird, *ORN,* vol. 20, 154.
27. King to Jones, June 27, 1910, William Jones Letters.
28. Ibid.

Chapter 20

1. Eby, Virginia Yankee, 173; Sprague, *History of the 13th Infantry Regiment,* 125; H. M. P., "From Our Special Correspondent," April 26, 1863, in *Boston Traveler,* p. 2, col. 2, May 6, 1863.
2. Mattison, Headquarters, Department of the Gulf, Opelousas, LA, May 4, 1863, to the editor of the *Boston Morning Journal,* p. 2, col.2, May 23, 1863.
3. H. M. P., "From Our Special Correspondent," April 26, 1863, in *Boston Traveler,* p. 2, col. 2, May 6, 1863.
4. Irwin, *History of the 19th Army Corps,* 129.
5. Sprague, *History of the 13th Infantry,* 124–125.

6. H. M. P., "From Our Special Correspondent," April 26, 1863, in *Boston Traveler,* p. 2, col. 2, May 6, 1863.
7. Eby, *Virginia Yankee,* 173; Sprague, *History of the 13th Infantry,* 125.
8. Noel, *Autobiography and Reminiscences,* 93.
9. Irwin, *History of the 19th Army Corps,* 127–128.
10. Nathaniel P. Banks to Ulysses S. Grant, April 23, 1863, *OR,* vol. 24, pt. 3, 223–225.
11. Ibid., 225.
12. Sydney Bean to George L. Andrews, April 23, 1863, *OR,* vol. 15, 345.
13. Irwin, *History of the 19th Army Corps,* 127–128.
14. Ibid.
15. Edmonds, *Conduct of Federal Troops in Louisiana,* 45–46.
16. H. M. P., "From Our Special Correspondent," April 26, 1863, in *Boston Traveler,* p. 2, col. 2, May 6, 1863; as quoted in Robert L. Kerby, *Kirby Smith's Confederacy: The Trans-Mississippi South, 1863–1865* (Tuscaloosa: University of Alabama Press, 1991), 108.
17. H. M. P., "From Our Special Correspondent," April 26, 1863, in *Boston Traveler,* p. 2, col. 2, May 6, 1863.
18. Ibid.
19. Ibid.
20. Sprague, *History of the 13th Infantry Regiment,* 125.
21. William Dwight to Richard Irwin, April 22, 1863, *OR,* vol. 15, 367–368.
22. Dwight to Irwin, April 24, 1863, *OR,* vol. 15, 369; Dwight to Irwin, April 22, 1863, *OR,* vol. 15, 368; Dwight to Irwin, April 24, 1863, *OR,* vol. 15, 370.
23. John W. Watkins to his wife, April 23, 1863, John W. Watkins Letters.
24. Ibid.
25. Ibid.
26. Irwin, *History of the 19th Army Corps,* 128.
27. Paine, *Wisconsin Yankee,* 134.
28. Edmund Kirby Smith to Samuel Cooper, April 23, 1863, *OR,* vol. 15, 387.
29. Mayeux, *Earthen Walls, Iron Men,* 84–85.
30. John W. Watkins to his wife, April 30, 1863, John W. Watkins Letters.
31. Taylor, *Destruction and Reconstruction,* 136–137.
32. Fearn, *Diary of a Refugee,* 34.
33. Taylor, *Destruction and Reconstruction,* 136–137; Fearn, *Diary of a Refugee,* 34.
34. Fearn, *Diary of a Refugee,* 35.
35. LeGrand, *Diary,* 96–99.
36. Irwin, *History of the 19th Army Corps,* 129–135.
37. Showme, 41st Massachusetts, Opelousas, LA, May 5, 1863, to editor, *Boston Herald,* p. 4, col. 1, May 19, 1863.
38. William Emory to Richard Irwin, May 2, 1863, *OR,* vol. 15, 334; Hepworth, *Whip, the Hoe, and Sword,* 278–280.

39. Showme, 41st Massachusetts, Opelousas, LA, May 5, 1863, to editor, *Boston Herald,* p. 4, col. 1, May 19, 1863
40. Mattison, Headquarters, Department of the Gulf, Opelousas, LA, May 4, 1863, to the editor, *Boston Morning Journal,* p. 2, col. 2, May 23, 1863.
41. Showme, 41st Massachusetts, Opelousas, LA, May 5, 1863, to editor, *Boston Herald,* p. 4, col. 1, May 19, 1863.
42. Sprague, *History of the 13th Infantry Regiment,* 125.
43. Eby, *Virginia Yankee,* 177
44. Henry Halleck to Banks, May 11, 1863, *OR,* vol. 15, 725–726; Banks to Grant, April 23, 1863, *OR,* vol. 15, 303–315; Banks to Dwight, April 22, 1863, *OR,* vol. 15, 706–708; Banks to Halleck, April 29, 1863, *OR,* vol. 15, 1117–1119.
45. Eby, *Virginia Yankee,* 177.

Chapter 21

1. William Emory to Richard Irwin, May 2, 1863, *OR,* vol. 15, 333; William Dwight to Richard Irwin, April 27, 1863, *OR,* vol. 15, 375.
2. John W. Watkins to Irene Watkins, April 30, 1863, and May 2, 1863, John W. Watkins Letters.
3. Irwin, *History of the 19th Army Corps,* 127–134; Emory to Irwin, May 2, 1863, *OR,* vol. 15, 333–334; Paine, *Wisconsin Yankee,* 134–136.
4. John W. Watkins to Irene Watkins, April 30, 1863, and May 2, 1863, John W. Watkins Letters; "Colonel Eugene Waggaman, Who Led the Tenth Louisiana Regiment in the Famous Charge at Malvern Hill," *New Orleans Picayune,* February 10, 1889, reprinted in *Southern Historical Society Papers* 16 (1889): 446–451.
5. John W. Watkins to Irene Watkins, April 30, 1863, and May 2, 1863, John W. Watkins Letters.
6. John W. Watkins to Irene Watkins, April 30, 1863, John W. Watkins Letters.
7. Ibid.; Collard, "Memoir," 15.
8. Collard, "Memoir," 15–16; John W. Watkins to Irene Watkins, May 2, 1863, John W. Watkins Letters.
9. John W. Watkins to Irene Watkins, May 2, 1863, John W. Watkins Letters.
10. Dwight to Irwin, May 2, 1863, *OR,* vol. 15, 375.
11. Collard, "Memoir," 16.
12. Ibid., 14.
13. Rufus Andrews, *"Kiss Each Other for Me:" The Civil War Letters of Rufus Andrews* (Iron Mountain, MI: Mid-Peninsula Library Cooperative, 1979), 65–66.
14. Near present-day Beggs, Louisiana.
15. Andrews, *"Kiss Each Other for Me,"* 65–66.
16. Mattison, Headquarters, Department of the Gulf, Opelousas, LA, May 4, 1863, to the editor, *Boston Morning Journal,* p. 2, col. 2, May 23, 1863; John W. Watkins to Irene Watkins, May 2, 1863, John W. Watkins Letters; Collard, "Memoir," 16.

17. Collard, "Memoir," 16.
18. Dwight to Irwin, May 2, 1863, *OR,* vol. 15, 375–376; Andrews, *"Kiss Each Other for Me,"* 65–66.
19. Collard, "Memoir," 16; John W. Watkins to Irene Watkins, May 2, 1863, John W. Watkins Letters.
20. Dwight to Irwin, May 2, 1863, *OR,* vol. 15, 376.

Chapter 22

1. Cotham, *Southern Journey,* 158–159.
2. Mattison, Headquarters, Department of the Gulf, Near Opelousas, LA, May 2, 1863, to the editor, *Boston Morning Journal,* p. 2, col. 2, May 23, 1863.
3. Ibid.
4. Ibid.
5. Ibid.
6. Ibid.
7. Ibid.
8. James G. Hollandsworth,, Jr. *The Louisiana Native Guards: The Black Military Experience during the Civil War* (Baton Rouge: Louisiana State University Press, 1995), 66.
9. *New York Times,* September 21, 1892; Abraham Lincoln to Nathaniel P. Banks [Draft 1], March 29, 1863, Abraham Lincoln Papers, Library of Congress, transcribed and annotated by the Lincoln Studies Center, Knox College, Galesburg, IL.
10. Nathaniel P. Banks to Henry Halleck, May 1, 1863, *OR,* vol. 15, 716.
11. Nathaniel P. Banks, "General Order No. 40," May 1, 1863, *OR,* vol. 15, 717.
12. Ibid.; *New York Times,* May 18, 1863.
13. Nathaniel P. Banks, "General Order No. 40," May 1, 1863, *OR,* vol. 15, 716–717.
14. Ibid., 717.
15. Ibid.
16. Showme, 41st Massachusetts, Opelousas, LA, May 5, 1863, in *Boston Herald,* p. 4, col. 1, May 19, 1863.
17. H. M. P., "From Our Special Correspondent," April 26, 1863, in *Boston Traveler,* p. 2, col. 2, May 6, 1863.
18. Ibid.
19. Ibid.
20. Ibid.

Chapter 23

1. Arthur W. Hyatt, diaries, volume 2, p. 6, Arthur W. Hyatt Papers, Mss 180, Louisiana and Lower Mississippi Valley Collections, Special Collections, Louisiana State University, Baton Rouge, Louisiana, as quoted in Prushankin, *Crisis in Confederate Command,* 30.

2. Howell Diary, April 25–May 1, 1863.
3. A. W. McKee to W. R. Scurry, April 22, 24, 1863, in *Houston Tri-Weekly Telegraph,* April 23, 1863.
4. *Houston Tri-Weekly Telegraph,* April 22, 1863.
5. J. E. H. to the editor, April 30, 1863, in *Houston Tri-Weekly Telegraph,* May 1, 1863; J. E. H. to the editor, April 30, 1863, in *Houston Tri-Weekly Telegraph,* May 11, 1863
6. Edmund Knowles letter, in J. E. H. to the editor, April 30, 1863, in *Houston Tri-Weekly Telegraph,* May 11, 1863.
7. Edward Thomas Broughton, Port Hudson, Louisiana, to Mary Elizabeth Douglas Broughton, Kaufman County, Texas, April 27, 1863, "Letters to Molly," http://battleofraymond.org/history/letters.htm (accessed March 7, 2011).
8. Sioux (W. P. Doran), "In Camp on Bank of Sabine River," May 11, 1863, in *Houston Tri-Weekly Telegraph,* May 18, 1863; A. W. McKee to W. R. Scurry, April 22, 24, 1863, in *Houston Tri-Weekly Telegraph,* May 18, 1863.
9. J. E. H. to the editor, April 30, 1863, in *Houston Tri-Weekly Telegraph,* May 1, 1863; 11 May 1863; J. E. H. to the editor, April 30, 1863, in *Houston Tri-Weekly Telegraph,* May 11, 1863; Sioux (W. P. Doran), "In Camp on Bank of Sabine River," May 11, 1863, in *Houston Tri-Weekly Telegraph,* May 18, 1863.
10. Ibid.; Noel, *Santa Fe to the Mississippi,* 78; Davidson, "The Retreat from Bisland," *Overton (TX) Sharp-Shooter,* pg. 1, June 28, 1888.
11. Arthur Fremantle, *Three Months in the Southern States* (London: William Blackwood, 1863), 71–72, 75.
12. John E. Hart to David G. Farragut, May 6, 1863, *ORN,* vol. 20, 79.
13. Ibid., 80.
14. J. Kelso to Edward Surget, May 13, 1863, *ORN,* vol. 20, 91; Edward T. King to William Jones, June 27, 1910, William Jones Letters.
15. John E. Hart to David G. Farragut, May 6, 1863, *ORN,* vol. 20, 79; King to Jones, June 27, 1910, William Jones Letters; Kelso to Surget, May 13, 1863, *ORN,* vol. 20, 91.
16. John E. Hart to David G. Farragut, May 6, 1863, *ORN,* vol. 20, 79.
17. Ibid.
18. Kelso to Surget, May 13, 1863, *ORN,* vol. 20, 91.
19. King to Jones, June 27, 1910, William Jones Letters; Kelso to Surget, May 13, 1863, *ORN,* vol. 20, 91.
20. King to Jones, June 27, 1910, William Jones Letters.
21. Kelso to Surget, May 13, 1863, *ORN,* vol. 20, 91.

Chapter 24

1. Irwin, *History of the 19th Army Corps,* 145.
2. Nathaniel P. Banks to Henry Halleck, May 4, 1863, *OR,* vol. 15, 310.
3. Irwin, *History of the 19th Army Corps,* 145.

4. Ibid.; John W. Watkins to Irene Watkins, May 11, 1863, John W. Watkins Letters.
5. Showme, 41st Massachusetts, Opelousas, LA, May 5, 1863, in *Boston Herald,* p. 4, col. 1, May 19, 1863; Allen and Briggs, *Memorial of Pickering Dodge Allen,* 123.
6. *New Orleans Era,* p. 2, May 10, 1863; Hepworth, *Whip, the Hoe, and Sword,* 122.
7. Irwin, *History of the 19th Army Corps,* 145; Caroline Elizabeth Whitcomb, *History of the Second Massachusetts Battery of Light Artillery* (Concord, NH: Rumford Press, 1912), 47.
8. Edmonds, *Conduct of Federal Troops in Louisiana,* 57.
9. Irwin, *History of the 19th Army Corps,* 145; Whitcomb, *History of the Second Massachusetts Battery,* 47; George G. Smith, *Leaves from a Soldier's Diary: The Personal Record of Lieutenant George G. Smith, Co. C, 1st Louisiana Regiment Infantry Volunteers [White] During the War of Rebellion* (Putnam, CT: n.p., 1906), 51–52.
10. Nathaniel P. Banks to Montgomery C. Meigs, May 5, 1863, MSS 285, Historic New Orleans Collection.
11. Ibid.
12. Ibid.
13. Hosmer, *Color-Guard,* 154.
14. Kerby, *Kirby Smith's Confederacy,* 108; David Porter to Banks, May 4, 1863, *OR,* vol. 15, 312; Banks to Henry Halleck, May 5, 1863, *OR,* vol. 15, 311–312.
15. Irwin, *History of the 19th Army Corps,* 144–146.
16. John W. Watkins to Irene Watkins, May 11, 1863, John W. Watkins Letters.
17. Ibid.
18. De Forest, *Volunteer's Adventures,* 101–102; Irwin, *History of the 19th Army Corps,* 147.
19. Smith, *Leaves from a Soldier's Diary,* 52.
20. Edmonds, *Conduct of Federal Troops in Louisiana,* 145.
21. Godfrey Weitzel to Banks, May 11, 1863, *OR,* vol. 15, 325; Irwin, *History of the 19th Army Corps,* 149; Taylor, *Destruction and Reconstruction,* 137; Andrews, *"Kiss Each Other for Me,"* 69–73.
22. Weitzel to Banks, May 11, 1863, *OR,* vol. 15, 325; Irwin, *History of the 19th Army Corps,* 149; Taylor, *Destruction and Reconstruction,* 137.
23. Edwin Cole Bearss, *Unvexed to the Sea,* vol. 3, *The Campaign for Vicksburg* (Dayton, OH: Morningside Press, 1986), 699–707.
24. Taylor, *Destruction and Reconstruction,* 137; John W. Watkins to Irene Watkins, May 11, 1863, John W. Watkins Letters.
25. Fremantle, *Three Months in the Southern States,* 81; Fearn, *Diary of a Refugee,* 36.
26. Fremantle, *Three Months in the Southern States,* 81.
27. Ibid., 85.
28. Ibid., 87.
29. Ibid.
30. Cotham, *Southern Journey,* 154.

Chapter 25

1. Nathaniel P. Banks to Henry Halleck, May 12, 1863, *OR,* vol. 15, 314–315.
2. Banks to Ulysses S. Grant, May 12, 1863, *ORN,* vol. 20, 185.
3. Banks to Halleck, May 12, 1863, *OR,* vol. 15, 315.
4. Banks to Grant, May 13, 1863, *ORN,* vol. 20, 186.
5. S. A. Bean to Godfrey Weitzel, May 14, 1863, *OR,* vol. 15, 346; Weitzel to Richard Irwin, May 19, 1863, *OR,* vol. 26, pt. 1, 35–36.
6. Fremantle, *Three Months in the Southern States,* 97–98.
7. Halleck to Banks, May 23, 1863, *OR,* vol. 26, pt. 1, 500–501.
8. Irwin, *History of the 19th Army Corps,* 151; Halleck to Banks, May 19, 1863, *OR,* vol. 26, pt. 1, 494–495; Halleck to Banks, May 23, 1863, *OR,* vol. 26, pt. 1, 500–501.
9. Weitzel to Irwin, May 19, 1863, *OR,* vol. 26, pt. 1, 38; Weitzel to Irwin, May 20, 1863, *OR,* vol. 26, pt. 1, 39.
10. John W. Watkins to Irene Watkins, May 11, 1863, John W. Watkins Letters.
11. M. B. Locke to T. F. Wilson, May 18, 1863, *OR,* vol. 26, pt. 1, 36–37; Michael J. Martin, *A History of the 4th Wisconsin Infantry and Cavalry in the Civil War* (New York: Savas Beatie, 2006), 159–162; Frederick Phisterer, *New York in the War of the Rebellion, 1861–1865* (Albany: Weed and Parsons, 1890), 314.

Chapter 26

1. Godfrey Weitzel to Richard B. Irwin, May 19, 1863, *OR,* vol. 26, pt. 1, 38.
2. "Maj. Boone's Report," *Bellville (Texas) Countryman,* 2, August 8, 1863.
3. Keet McDade to Ann Cochran, May 9, 1863, Keet McDade Letters, private collection; Irwin, *History of the Nineteenth Army Corps,* 152–155.
4. Davidson, "The Retreat from Bisland," *Overton (TX) Sharp-Shooter,* pg. 1, June 28, 1888.
5. Boone, "Maj. Boone's Report," "*Bellville (Texas) Countryman,* 2, August 8, 1863. Alfred Sturgis Thurmond was one of the most experienced of Tom Green's captains, and he was fifty-three years old at the time of the fight at Cheneyville. He had arrived in Texas in 1836 but had missed any fighting in the revolution. During the Republic of Texas, however, he served in numerous campaigns with Ewen Cameron against the Mexicans. He was captured at Mier and imprisoned at Perote Castle, where his knowledge of Spanish made him a useful interpreter. When released, he learned that he had been elected Marshall of Victoria, Texas. He served in that capacity, and as sheriff of Victoria County, until the early 1850s. He read law and passed the bar by 1860, at which time he was ranching in Refugio County. Ironically, his younger brother, Zip Thurmond, was an ardent Unionists. See "Thurmond, Alfred Sturgis," in *The New Handbook of Texas* (Austin: Texas State Historical Association, 1996) 6:489. Company B, 13th Texas Cavalry Battalion hailed from Falls County, Company D came from Goliad County.

6. Cox, "Reminiscences of C. C. Cox," 225; Boone, "Maj. Boone's Report," *Bellville (Texas) Countryman,* 2, August 8, 1863. Company A came from Victoria County, Company C came from Austin County, and Company F had been raised in Fort Worth.
7. Boone, "Maj. Boone's Report," *Bellville (Texas) Countryman,* 2, August 8, 1863; Richard Barrett, *Compiled Service Records of Volunteer Soldiers Who Served in Organizations from the State of Louisiana,* M396, National Archives and Records Administration; Barrett originally enlisted in the 3rd Unattached Company, Massachusetts Cavalry and became Company B, 2nd Massachusetts Cavalry Battalion under General Benjamin Butler. He resigned from that unit to take a captain's commission in the new 1st Louisiana Cavalry in August 1862. The 1860 census indicates he was a native of Ireland, living in Boston, convicted of assault. In December 1862 he defended himself against charges of being drunk while on duty. In 1864 he would be discharged from the army for the same cause.
8. Cox, "Reminiscences of C. C. Cox," 225; Boone, "Maj. Boone's Report," *Bellville (Texas) Countryman,* 2, August 8, 1863.
9. Cox, "Reminiscences of C. C. Cox," 226; Boone, "Maj. Boone's Report," *Bellville (Texas) Countryman,* 2, August 8, 1863; Godfrey Weitzel to Richard Irwin, May 20, 1863, in "Report of Brigadier General Godfrey Weitzel, Skirmish near Cheneyville," May 20, 1863, *OR,* vol. 26, pt. 1, 39.
10. Cox, "Reminiscences of C. C. Cox," 225.
11. Cox, "Reminiscences of C. C. Cox," 225; Boone, "Maj. Boone's Report," *Bellville (Texas) Countryman,* 2, August 8, 1863.
12. Boone, "Maj. Boone's Report," *Bellville (Texas) Countryman,* 2, August 8, 1863; Davidson, "The Retreat from Bisland," *Overton (TX) Sharp-Shooter,* pg. 1, June 28, 1888.
13. Davidson, "The Retreat from Bisland," *Overton (TX) Sharp-Shooter,* pg. 1, June 28, 1888; Boone, "Maj. Boone's Report," *Bellville (Texas) Countryman,* p. 2, August 8, 1863.
14. Ibid.
15. Davidson, "The Retreat from Bisland," *Overton (TX) Sharp-Shooter,* pg. 1, June 28, 1888.
16. Boone, "Maj. Boone's Report," *Bellville (Texas) Countryman,* 2, August 8, 1863.
17. Boone, "Maj. Boone's Report," *Bellville (Texas) Countryman,* 2, August 8, 1863; Cox, "Reminiscences of C. C. Cox," 225.
18. Boone, "Maj. Boone's Report," *Bellville (Texas) Countryman,* 2, August 8, 1863; Joseph C. Terrell, "Descriptive History Record, January 20, 1897," in Dora Davenport Jones, ed., "History of Julia Jackson Chapter #141, United Daughters of the Confederacy, Fort Worth, Texas, A Bicentennial City, 1897–1976," n.p., typed manuscript, Fort Worth Public Library, Genealogy and Local History Section, Fort Worth, TX; J. C. Terrell to "Ma" (Susan Kennerly Terrell), June 28, 1863, Terrell Family Correspondence, Fort Worth Public Library.
19. Cox, "Reminiscences of C. C. Cox," 225.

20. Cox, "Reminiscences of C. C. Cox," 225; Davidson, "The Retreat from Bisland," *Overton (TX) Sharp-Shooter,* pg. 1, June 28, 1888.
21. Davidson, "The Retreat from Bisland," *Overton (TX) Sharp-Shooter,* pg. 1, June 28, 1888.
22. Godfrey Weitzel to Richard Irwin, May 20, 1863, *OR,* vol. 26, pt. 1, 39.
23. Davidson, "The Retreat from Bisland," *Overton (TX) Sharp-Shooter,* pg. 1, June 28, 1888; Boone, "Maj. Boone's Report," *Bellville (Texas) Countryman,* 2, August 8, 1863.
24. Boone, "Maj. Boone's Report," *Bellville (Texas) Countryman,* 2, August 8, 1863.

Chapter 27

1. *Boston Herald,* p. 1, col. 6, May 2, 1863.
2. "Honors to the Dead: Funeral of Captain Howard Dwight," *New Orleans Era,* p. 2, col. 4, May 10, 1863.
3. Ibid.
4. J. W. C., 38th Massachusetts, Algiers, LA, May 1, 1863, to the editor, *Cambridge (MA) Chronicle,* p. 1, col. 5, May 30, 1863.
5. James S. Palmer to David G. Farragut, May 14, 1863, *ORN,* vol. 20, 187; Palmer to Farragut, May 20, 1863, *ORN,* vol. 20, 203.
6. Dirigo, on board steamer *Mataneas,* New Orleans, April 24, 1863, to the editor, *Boston Morning Journal,* p. 4, col. 2, May 5, 1863.
7. Ibid.
8. Ibid.
9. J. W. C., 38th Massachusetts, Algiers, LA, May 1, 1863, to the editor, *Cambridge (MA) Chronicle,* p. 1, col. 5, May 30, 1863.
10. Ibid.
11. James K. Hosmer, *The Color-Guard*: Being a Corporal's Notes of Military Service in the Nineteenth Army Corps (Boston: Walker and Wise, 1864), 158.
12. J. W. C., 38th Massachusetts, Algiers, LA, May 1, 1863, to the editor, *Cambridge (MA) Chronicle,* p. 1, col. 5, May 30, 1863.
13. Mattison, New Orleans, April 28, 1863, to the editor, *Boston Morning Journal,* p. 2, col. 4, May 11, 1863.
14. Ibid.
15. Ibid.
16. Officer, 48th Massachusetts, Baton Rouge, April 22, 1863, in *Amesbury (MA) Villager,* p. 3, col. 1, May 16, 1863.
17. Mattison, New Orleans, April 28, 1863, to the editor, *Boston Morning Journal,* p. 2, col. 4, May 11, 1863.
18. Officer, 48th Massachusetts, Baton Rouge, April 22, 1863, in *Amesbury (MA) Villager,* p. 3, col. 1, May 16, 1863.
19. Ibid.

20. Mattison, New Orleans, April 28, 1863, to the editor, *Boston Morning Journal,* p. 2, col. 4, May 11, 1863.
21. J. W. C., 38th Massachusetts, Algiers, LA, May 1, 1863, to the editor, *Cambridge (MA) Chronicle,* p. 1, col. 5, May 30, 1863; THIRTY-EIGHTH MASSACHUSETTS, Algiers, Louisiana, May 1, 1863, to Editor, *Cambridge Chronicle,* published May 30 1863, pg. 1, col. 5; Giesecke, "Diary," 67.
22. Giesecke, "Diary," 68.
23. J. W. C., 38th Massachusetts, Algiers, LA, May 1, 1863, to the editor, *Cambridge (MA) Chronicle,* p. 1, col. 5, May 30, 1863.
24. Ibid.
25. Ibid.
26. Hepworth, *Whip, the Hoe, and Sword,* 110.
27. Ibid.
28. Gary D. Joiner, Marilyn S. Joiner, and Clifton Cardin, eds., *No Pardons to Ask, nor Apologies to Make: The Journal of William Henry King, Gray's 28th Louisiana Infantry Regiment* (Knoxville: University of Tennessee Press, 2006), 97–98.
29. Ibid.; J. W. C., 38th Massachusetts, Algiers, LA, May 1, 1863, to the editor, *Cambridge (MA) Chronicle,* p. 1, col. 5, May 30, 1863
30. Ibid.; J. W. C., 38th Massachusetts, Algiers, LA, May 1, 1863, to the editor, *Cambridge (MA) Chronicle,* p. 1, col. 5, May 30, 1863
31. Hosmer, *Color-Guard,* 158, 162.

Chapter 28

1. J. E. H., Nibletts Bluff, April 30, 1863, to the editor, *Houston Tri-Weekly Telegraph,* May 11, 1863.
2. Irwin, *History of the 19th Army,* 156–157.
3. Edmonds, *Conduct of Federal Troops in Louisiana,* 108; Moors, *History of the Fifty-Second Regiment,* 144.
4. George S. Merrill to E. T. Colby, May 23, 1863, *OR,* vol. 26, pt. 1, 183.
5. Haynes, *Thrilling Narrative,* 5.
6. Ibid., 5–6.
7. Ibid.
8. Ibid.
9. Merrill to Colby, May 23, 1863, *OR,* vol. 26, pt. 1, 183–184.
10. Ibid., 184.
11. Carl A. Brasseaux and Keith P. Fontenot, *Steamboats on Louisiana's Bayous: A History and Directory* (Baton Rouge: Louisiana State University Press, 2004), 101; Merrill to Colby, *OR,* vol. 26, pt. 1, 184–185.
12. Howell Diary, May 25, 1863; John W. Watkins to Irene Watkins, June 16, 1863, John W. Watkins Letters.
13. Howell Diary, May 25, 1863; John W. Watkins to Irene Watkins, June 16, 1863, John W. Watkins Letters.

14. Haynes, *Thrilling Narrative,* 5–6.
15. Edmonds, *Conduct of Federal Troops in Louisiana,* 111.
16. Ibid.
17. Pellet, *History of the 114th Regiment,* 83.
18. Howell Diary, May 25, 1863; John W. Watkins to Irene Watkins, June 16, 1863, John W. Watkins Letters.
19. Ewer, *Third Massachusetts Cavalry,* 85; *New York Irish American,* p. 1, col. 8, June 20, 1863.
20. Ewer, *Third Massachusetts Cavalry,* 85; *New York Irish American,* p. 1, col. 8, June 20, 1863. The soldiers were Major John Gray; Second Lieutenant Patrick E. Walsh, acting adjutant; Second Lieutenant Mathias Hayes, Company A; and First Lieutenant Richard Dunn, Company B.
21. Pellet, *History of the 114th Regiment,* 79–80.
22. Maddocks, *Twenty-Sixth Maine Regiment,* 36–37; Moors, *History of the Fifty-Second Regiment,* 144.
23. Ewer, *Third Massachusetts Cavalry,* 84; Maddocks, *Twenty-Sixth Maine Regiment,* 36–37.
24. Ewer, *Third Massachusetts Cavalry,* 85.
25. Pellet, *History of the 114th Regiment,* 80–81.
26. Ibid., 81.
27. Ibid., 81.
28. Howell Diary, May 25, 1863; John W. Watkins to Irene Watkins, June 16, 1863, John W. Watkins Letters.
29. Maddocks, *Twenty-Sixth Maine Regiment,* 37; Ewer, *Third Massachusetts Cavalry,* 85–86; Pellet, *History of the 114th Regiment,* 82–83.
30. Ewer, *Third Massachusetts Cavalry,* 86; Pellet, *History of the 114th Regiment,* 83.
31. Townsend, *History of the Sixteenth Regiment,* 203–209.
32. Petticolas Diary, May 31, 1863.
33. Ibid.
34. Ibid.
35. Ibid.

Bibliography

Unpublished Primary Sources

Manuscript Collections

Amsler, John. Family Papers. Eugene C. Barker Texas History Collection. Dolph Briscoe Center for American History. University of Texas, Austin.

Brent, J. L. Papers. Louisiana Historical Association Collection. Howard-Tilton Memorial Library. Tulane University, New Orleans, Louisiana.

Brinkerhoff, Judson. Letters. Private Collection.

Bronough, John M. Papers. Texas Collection. Baylor University, Waco, Texas.

Collard, Felix Robert. "Reminiscences of a Private, Company G, 7th Texas Cavalry, Sibley Brigade, C.S.A." Private Collection.

Collard, Felix Robert. "Personal Experiences at Battles of Bisland, Vermillion Prairie, and Vermillion Bayou." Private Collection.

"Consolidated Report of Ordnance and Ordnance Stores in the Department of Southwestern Louisiana, March 26, 1863." Tulane University, New Orleans, Louisiana.

Faust, Joseph. Papers. Eugene C. Barker Texas History Collection. Dolph Briscoe Center for American History. University of Texas, Austin.

Gault, Samuel. Diary. MS 177. Historic New Orleans Collection. New Orleans, Louisiana.

Goodell, Henry Hill. Papers, 1852–1900, Record Group 73, accession number 1979.83.3-8. Louisiana State Museum, New Orleans, Louisiana.

Horton, C. M. Diary. Civil War Papers. Louisiana Historical Association Collection. Howard-Tilton Memorial Library. Tulane University, New Orleans, Louisiana.

Howell, William Randolph. Papers and Diary. Eugene C. Barker Texas History Collection. Dolph Briscoe Center for American History. University of Texas, Austin.

Hyatt, Arthur W. Papers, Mss. 180. Louisiana and Lower Mississippi Valley Collection. LSU Libraries, Baton Rouge, Louisiana.

Jones, William. Letters, 1862–1863. Special Collections. Howard-Tilton Memorial Library. Tulane University, New Orleans, Louisiana.

Leonard, Orville W. Military Papers. Massachusetts Historical Society, Boston.

Lincoln, Abraham. Papers. Library of Congress, Washington, D.C. Transcribed and annotated by the Lincoln Studies Center, Knox College, Galesburg, IL

Maedgen, Moritz. Papers. Texas Collection. Baylor University, Waco, Texas.

McDade, Keet. Letters. Private Collection.

Miles, Edmund. Papers. Massachusetts Historical Society, Boston.

Osborne, James Albert. Diary. Massachusetts Historical Society, Boston.

Palfrey Family Papers. Louisiana and Lower Mississippi Valley Collection. LSU Libraries, Baton Rouge, Louisiana.

Petticolas, Alfred. Diary, Vol. 3. Private Collection.

Rainey, Green Jr. Papers. Eugene C. Barker Texas History Collection. Dolph Briscoe Center for American History. University of Texas, Austin.

Rootes, Sarah. Correspondence. Special Collections. Duke University Library, Durham, North Carolina.

Seat, Benton Bell. Memoir. Special Collections. University of Arkansas Library, Fayetteville, Arkansas.

Schubert, George. Letters. Schoff Civil War Collection. Manuscripts Division. William L. Clements Library. University of Michigan, Ann Arbor.

Sprague, Homer B. Papers. Library of Congress, Washington, D.C.

Terrell, Joseph C. "Descriptive History Record, January 20, 1897" in Jones, Dora Davenport, ed. "History of Julia Jackson Chapter #141, United Daughters of the Confederacy, Fort Worth, Texas, A Bicentennial City 1897–1976." Genealogy and Local History Section. Fort Worth Public Library, Texas.

Terrell, Joseph C. Letter. Private Collection.

Terrell Family Correspondence. Genealogy and Local History Section. Fort Worth Public Library, Texas.

Tiemann, William Frank Letter. Tiemann Collection. New York State Military Museum and Veterans Research Center, Saratoga Springs, New York.

Watkins, John W. Letters. Harold B. Simpson Confederate Research Center, Hillsboro, Texas.

Williams, Robert Thompson. Diary. 4th Texas Cavalry File. Harold B. Simpson Confederate Research Center, Hillsboro, Texas.

Wright, Henry C. Memoir. Eugene C. Barker Texas History Collection. Dolph Briscoe Center for American History. University of Texas, Austin.

Published Primary Sources

Government Documents

The National Archives and Record Administration. *Compiled Service Records of Volunteer Union Soldiers Who Served in Organizations from the State of Louisiana*, Record Group 94.

The National Archives and Record Administration. *Confederate Papers Relating to Citizens or Business Firms, compiled 1874–1899, documenting the period 1861–1865*, Record Group 109, Publication Number M346.

Naval Historical Center, Department of the Navy. *Dictionary of American Fighting Ships*. 8 vols. Washington, DC: Government Printing Office, 1975–1981.

U.S. Naval War Records Office. *Official Records of the Union and Confederate Navies in the War of the Rebellion*. 27 vols. Washington, DC: Government Printing Office, 1894–1922.

U.S. War Department. *The War of the Rebellion: A Compilation of the Official Records of the Union and Confederate Armies*. 128 vols. Washington, DC: Government Printing Office, 1880–1901.

Newspapers

Amesbury (MA) Villager

Austin Texas State Gazette

Bellville (TX) Countryman

Boston Herald

Boston Morning Journal

Boston Saturday Evening Gazette

Boston Traveler

Cambridge (MA) Chronicle

Galveston Daily News

Galveston Weekly News

Houston Tri-Weekly Telegraph

New Orleans Era

New Orleans Picayune

New York Irish American

New York Times

Overton (TX) Sharp–Shooter

Tucson Daily Citizen

Worcester (MA) National Aegis and Transcript

Books and Articles

Andrews, Rufus. *Kiss Each Other for Me: The Civil War Letters of Rufus Andrews.* Iron Mountain, MI: Mid-Peninsula Library Cooperative, 1979.

Alberts, Don E., ed. *Rebels on the Rio Grande: The Civil War Journal of A. B. Petticolas.* Albuquerque: University of New Mexico Press, 1984.

Allen, John Fisk, and George W. Briggs. *Memorial of Pickering Dodge Allen by His Father.* Boston: Henry W. Dutton, 1867.

Babcock, Willoughby M. Jr. *Selections from the Letters and Diaries of Brevet-Brigadier General Willoughby Babcock of the Seventy-Fifth New York Volunteers: A Study of Camp Life in the Union Armies During the Civil War.* Albany: University of the State of New York, 1922.

Bacon, Edward. *Among the Cotton Thieves.* Detroit: Freer Press Steam Book and Job Printing House, 1867.

Bergeron, Arthur W. Jr., ed. *A Thrilling Narrative: The Memoir of a Southern Unionist.* Fayetteville: University of Arkansas Press, 2006.

Beecher, Harris H. *Record of the 114th Regiment, N.Y.S.V.: Where It Went, What It Saw, and What It Did.* Norwich, NY: J. F. Hubbard Jr., 1866.

Bissell, George P., Samuel K. Ellis, Thomas McManus, and Henry Hill Goodell. *The Twenty-fifth Regiment Connecticut Volunteers in the War of the Rebellion: History, Description of Battle of Irish Bend, Carrying of Pay Roll, Roster.* Rockville, CT: Press of the Rockville Journal, 1913.

Carpenter, George N. *History of the Eighth Regiment Vermont Volunteers, 1861–1865.* Boston: Deland and Barta, 1886.

Cotham, Edward T. Jr., ed. *The Southern Journey of a Civil War Marine: The Illustrated Note-book of Henry O. Gusley.* Austin: University of Texas Press, 2006.

Cox, C. C. "Reminiscences of C. C. Cox." *Southwestern Historical Quarterly* 6 (January 1903): 204–235.

Crandall, Warren Daniel and Isaac Denison Newell. *History of the Ram Fleet and the Mississippi Marine Brigade in the War for the Union on the Mississippi and its Tributaries: The Story of the Ellets and their Men.* St. Louis: Society of Survivors, 1907.

De Forest, John William. *A Volunteer's Adventures: A Union Captain's Record of the Civil War.* Edited by James H. Croushore. Baton Rouge: Louisiana State University Press, 1996.

Doren, Carl Van, ed. *The Literary Works of Abraham Lincoln.* Norwalk, CT: Easton Press, 1980.

Duffy, Edward. *History of the 159th Regiment, N.Y.S.V.* New York: Hudson Gazette, 1890.

Duganne, Augustine Joseph Hickey. *Camps and Prisons: Twenty Months in the Department of the Gulf.* New York: J. P. Robens, Publisher, 1865.

Eby, Cecil B. Jr., ed. *A Virginia Yankee in the Civil War: The Diaries of David Hunter Strother.* Chapel Hill: University of North Carolina Press, 1989.

Edmonds, David S., ed. *The Conduct of Federal Troops in Louisiana during the Invasions of 1863 and 1864: Official Report Compiled from the Sworn Testimony under Direction of Governor Henry W. Allen, Shreveport, April 1865*. Lafayette, LA: Acadiana Press, 1988.

Ewer, James K. *The Third Massachusetts Cavalry in the War for the Union*. n.p.: Historical Committee of the Regimental Association, 1903.

Fearn, Francis, ed. *Diary of a Refugee*. New York: Moffat, Yard, 1910.

Flinn, Frank M. *Campaigning with Banks in Louisiana, '63 and '64, and with Sheridan in the Shenandoah Valley in '64 and '65*. Lynn, MA: Press of Thomas P. Nichols, 1887.

Fremantle, Arthur. *Three Months in the Southern States*. London: William Blackwood, 1863.

Giesecke, Julius. "The Diary of Julius Giesecke, 1863–1865." Translated by Oscar Haas. *Military History of Texas and the Southwest* 18 (October 1988): 65–92.

Godfrey, John Franklin. *The Civil War Letters of Captain John Franklin Godfrey*. South Portland, ME: Ascensius Press, 1993.

Goyne, Minetta Altgelt. *Lone Star and Double Eagle: Civil War Letters of a German-Texas Family*. Fort Worth: Texas Christian University Press, 1982.

Hall, Henry, and James Hall. *Cayuga in the Field: A Record of the 19th New York Volunteers, all the Batteries of the 3rd New York Artillery, and the 75th New York Volunteers, Comprising and Account of their Organization, Camp Life, Marches, Battles, Losses, Toils, and Triumphs in the War for the Union, with Complete Rolls of their Members*. Auburn, NY: Truair Smith, 1873.

Harding, George C. *The Miscellaneous Writings of George C. Harding*. Indianapolis: Carlon and Hollenbeck, 1882.

Haynes, Dennis E. *Civil War Reminiscences of Major Silas T. Grisamore, CSA*. Edited by Arthur W. Bergeron Jr. Baton Rouge: Louisiana State University Press, 1993.

Hepworth, George H. *The Whip, the Hoe, and Sword; or, the Gulf-Department in '63*. Boston: Walker and Wise, 1864.

Hosmer, James K. *The Color-Guard: Being a Corporal's Notes of Military Service in the Nineteenth Army Corps*. Boston: Walker and Wise, 1864.

Irwin, Richard B. *History of the 19th Army Corps of the Union Army During the American Civil War*. New York: G. P. Putnam's Sons, 1893. Reprint. Baton Rouge: Elliot's Book Shop Press, 1985.

Jeter, Katherine Brash, ed. *A Man and His Boat: The Civil War Career and Correspondence of Lieutenant Jonathan H. Carter, CSN*. Lafayette: Center for Louisiana Studies, 1996.

Johnson, Robert Underwood, and Clarence Clough Buel, eds. *Battles and Leaders of the Civil War*. 4 vols. New York, 1887–1888. Reprint. Secaucus, NJ: Castle, 1987.

Joiner, Gary D., Marilyn S. Joiner, and Clifton Cardin, eds. *No Pardons to Ask, nor Apologies to Make: The Journal of William Henry King, Gray's 28th Louisiana Infantry Regiment.* Knoxville: University of Tennessee Press, 2006.

Jordan-Bychkov, Terry G., et al., eds. "The Boesel Letters: Two Germans in Sibley's Brigade." Translated by Irma Oglendorf Schwarz. *Southwestern Historical Quarterly* 102, No. 4 (April 1999): 457–486.

LeGrand, Julia. *The Diary of Julia LeGrand, New Orleans 1862–1863.* Edited by Kate Mason Rowland and Mrs. Morris L. Croxall. Richmond, VA: Everett Wadley, 1911.

Lincoln, Abraham. *The Collected Works of Abraham Lincoln.* Edited by Roy P. Basler. 9 vols. New Brunswick, NJ: Rutgers University Press, 1953–1955.

Lubbock, Francis R. *Six Decades in Texas.* Austin: Ben C. Jones, 1900.

Maddocks, Elden B. *History of the Twenty-Sixth Maine Regiment.* Bangor, ME: Charles H. Glass, 1899.

Moors, John Farwell. *History of the Fifty-Second Regiment, Massachusetts Volunteers.* Boston: G. H. Ellis, 1893.

Morris, Gouverneur. *The History of a Volunteer Regiment, Being a Succinct Account of the Organization, Services, and Adventures of the Sixth Regiment, New York Volunteers, Infantry, Knows as Wilson's Zouaves: Where They Went, What They Did, and What They Saw in the War of the Rebellion, 1861–1865.* New York: Veteran Volunteer Publishing Company, 1891.

Noel, Theophilus. *A Campaign from Santa Fe to the Mississippi: Being a History of the Old Sibley Brigade from Its First Organization to the Present Time; Its Campaigns in New Mexico, Arizona, Texas, Louisiana and Arkansas in the Years 1861–2–3–4.* Edited by Martin Hardwick Hall and Edwin Adams Davis. Houston: Stagecoach Press, 1961.

Noel, Theophilus. *Autobiography and Reminiscences of Theophilus Noel.* Chicago: Theophilus Noel Company Print, 1904.

Paine, Halbert. *A Wisconsin Yankee in Confederate Bayou Country: The Civil War Reminiscences of a Union General.* Edited by Samuel C. Hyde Jr. Baton Rouge: Louisiana State University Press, 2009.

Pellet, Elias P. *History of the 114th Regiment, New York State Volunteers.* Norwich, NY: Telegraph and Chronicle Power Press Printing, 1866.

Rankin, David C., ed. *Diary of a Christian Soldier: Rufus Kinsley and the Civil War.* New York: Cambridge University Press, 2003.

Root, L. Carroll, ed. "The Experiences of a Federal Soldier in Louisiana in 1863." *Louisiana Historical Quarterly* 19 (1936): 635–667.

Sherman, Andrew M. *In the Lowlands of Louisiana in 1863: An Address Delivered by Andrew M. Sherman at the Forty-Second Reunion of the Twenty-Third Connecticut.* Morristown, NJ: Howard Publishing, 1908.

Smith, George G. *Leaves from a Soldier's Diary: The Personal Record of Lieutenant George G. Smith, Co. C, 1st Louisiana Regiment Infantry Volunteers [White] During the War of Rebellion.* Putnam, CT: n.p., 1906.

Southwood, Marion. *Beauty and Booty: The Watchword of New Orleans*. New York: M. Doolady, 1867.

Southern Historical Society Papers. 52 vols. Richmond, VA: 1876–1952.

Sprague, Homer B. *History of the 13th Infantry Regiment of Connecticut Volunteers during the Great Rebellion*. Hartford: Case, Lockwood, 1867.

Spurlin, Charles, ed. *West of the Mississippi with Waller's 13th Texas Cavalry Battalion CSA*. Hillsboro, TX: Hill Junior College Press, 1971.

Stanyan, John M. *A History of the Eighth Regiment of New Hampshire Volunteers*. Concord: Ira C. Evans, 1892.

Stebbins, Calvin. *Henry Hill Goodell: The Story of Hhis Life, with Letters and a Few of His Addresses*. Cambridge, MA: Riverside Press, 1911.

Taylor, Richard. *Destruction and Reconstruction: Personal Experiences of the Late War*. New York: D. Appleton, 1879.

Townsend, Luther Tracy. *History of the Sixteenth Regiment, New Hampshire Volunteers*. Washington, DC: Norman T. Elliot, 1897.

Whitcomb, Caroline Elizabeth. *History of the Second Massachusetts Battery of Light Artillery*. Concord, NH: Rumford Press, 1912.

Published Secondary Sources

Books and Articles

Arceneaux, William. *Acadian General: Alfred Mouton and the Civil War*. Lafayette: Center for Louisiana Studies, University of Southwestern Louisiana, 1981.

Bearss, Edwin Cole. *Grant Strikes a Fatal Blow*. Vol. 2 of *The Campaign for Vicksburg*. Dayton, OH: Morningside Press, 1986.

Bearss, Edwin Cole. *Unvexed to the Sea*. Vol. 3 of *The Campaign for Vicksburg*. Dayton, OH: Morningside Press, 1986.

Bearss, Edwin Cole. *Vicksburg is the Key*. Vol. 1 of *The Campaign for Vicksburg*. Dayton, OH: Morningside Press, 1985.

Bergeron, Arthur W. *Guide to Louisiana Confederate Military Units, 1861–1865*. Baton Rouge: Louisiana State University Press, 1989.

Bowman, George Ernest, comp. *Vital Records of Truro, Massachusetts to the year 1849*. Plymouth: Massachusetts Society of Mayflower Descendants, 1933.

Bragg, Jefferson Davis. *Louisiana in the Confederacy*. Baton Rouge: Louisiana State University Press, 1941.

Brasseaux, Carl A., and Keith P. Fontenot. *Steamboats on Louisiana's Bayous: A History and Directory*. Baton Rouge: Louisiana State University Press, 2004.

Brent, Joseph L. *Capture of the Ironclad "Indianola."* New Orleans: Searcy and Pfaff, 1926.

Caudill, Philip. *Moss Bluff Rebel: A Texas Pioneer in the Civil War*. College Station: Texas A & M University Press, 2009.

Clarke, James Freeman. *Memorial and Biographical Sketches*. Boston: Houghton, Osgood, 1878.

Coates, Earl J., and Dean S. Thomas. *An Introduction to Civil War Small Arms*. Gettysburg, PA: Thomas Publications, 1990.

Cotham, Edward T. Jr. *Battle on the Bay: The Civil War Struggle for Galveston* (Austin: University of Texas Press, 1998.

Current, Richard Nelson. *Lincoln's Loyalists: Union Soldiers from the Confederacy*. Boston: Northeastern University Press, 1992.

Davis, Edwin Adams. *Heroic Years: Louisiana in the War for Southern Independence*. Baton Rouge: Louisiana State University Press, 1964.

Dimitry, John. *Louisiana and Arkansas*. Vol. 10 of *Confederate Military History: A Library of Confederate States History, in Twelve Volumes, Written by Distinguished Men of the South, and Edited by Gen. Clement A. Evans of Georgia*. Edited by Clement A. Evans. Atlanta: Confederate Publishing Company, 1899.

Dufour, Charles L. *The Night the War Was Lost*. New York: Doubleday, 1960. Reprint, Lincoln: University of Nebraska Press, 1994.

Edmonds, David C. *The Guns of Port Hudson*. Vol. 1 of *The River Campaign, February–May 1863*. Lafayette, LA: Acadiana Press, 1983.

Finch, L. Boyd. *Confederate Pathway to the Pacific: Major Sherod Hunter and Arizona Territory, C.S.A.* Tucson: Arizona Historical Society, 1996.

Frazier, Donald S. *Blood and Treasure: Confederate Empire in the Southwest*. College Station: Texas A&M University Press, 1995.

Frazier, Donald S. *Fire in the Cane Field: The Federal Invasion of Louisiana and Texas, January 1861–January 1863*. Buffalo Gap, TX: State House Press, 2009.

Freeman, Douglas Southall. *Lee's Lieutenants*. 3 vols. New York: Charles Scribner's Sons, 1944.

Goodman, R. Christopher. Eric C. Poplin, and Lawrence L. Hewitt. *The Battle of Fort Bisland: Historical Research and Development of an Archeological Research Design*. New Orleans: U.S. Army Corps of Engineers, 1988.

Hall, Martin Hardwick. *The Confederate Army of New Mexico*. Austin: Presidial Press, 1978.

Hardee, William J. *Hardee's Rifle and Light Infantry Tactics, for the Instruction, Exercises and Manuevers of Riflemen and Light Infantry*. New York: J. O. Kane, 1862.

Hearn, Chester G. *When the Devil Came Down to Dixie: Ben Butler in New Orleans*. Baton Rouge: Louisiana State University Press, 1997.

Hewitt, Lawrence Lee. *Port Hudson: Confederate Bastion on the Mississippi*. Baton Rouge: Louisiana State University Press, 1994.

Hewitt, Lawrence Lee, and Christopher Godwin. "The Battle of Bisland, Louisiana." *North and South: The Magazine of Civil War Conflict*. September 1998.

Hollandsworth, James G. Jr. *Pretense of Glory: The Life of General Nathaniel P. Banks*. Baton Rouge: Louisiana State University Press, 1998.

Hollandsworth, James G. Jr. *The Louisiana Native Guards: The Black Military Experience during the Civil War*. Baton Rouge: Louisiana State University Press, 1995.

Holmes, Lucille Barbour. *Oaklawn Manor: Antebellum Plantation Home*. 4th ed. Franklin, LA: printed by author, 1980.

Holzman, Robert S. *Stormy Ben Butler*. New York: MacMillan, 1954. Reprint. New York: Collier Books, 1961.

Jones, Archer. *Civil War Command and Strategy: The Process of Victory and Defeat*. New York: Free Press, 1992.

Kerby, Robert L. *Kirby Smith's Confederacy: The Trans-Mississippi South, 1863–1865*. Tuscaloosa: University of Alabama Press, 1991.

Legan, Marshall Scott. "The Confederate Career of a Union Ram." *Louisiana History* 41 (2000): 277–300.

Lindsley, John B. *The Military Annals of Tennessee Confederate. First Series: Embracing a Review of Military Operations with Regimental Histories and Memorial Rolls*. Nashville: J. M. Lindsley, 1886.

Martin, Michael J. *A History of the 4th Wisconsin Infantry and Cavalry in the Civil War*. New York: Savas Beatie, 2006.

Mayeux, Steven M. *Earthen Walls, Iron Men: Fort DeRussy, Louisiana, and the Defense of Red River*. Knoxville: University of Tennessee Press, 2007.

McPherson, Edward. *The Political History of the United States of America during the Great Rebellion*. Washington, DC: Philip and Solomons, 1865.

Messner, William F. *Freedmen and the Ideology of Free Labor: Louisiana, 1862–1865*. Lafayette: Center for Louisiana Studies, 1978.

Millett, Allen R., and Peter Maslowski. *For the Common Defense: A Military History of the United States of America*. New York: Free Press, 1984.

The New Handbook of Texas. 6 vols. Austin: Texas State Historical Association, 1996.

Nolan, Dick. *Benjamin Franklin Butler: The Damnedest Yankee*. Novato, CA: Presidio Press, 1991.

Odom, Van D. "The Political Career of Thomas Overton Moore, Secession Governor of Louisiana." *Louisiana Historical Quarterly* 26 (October 1943): 975–1054.

Oltorf, Frank Calvert. *The Marlin Compound: Letters of a Singular Family*. Austin: University of Texas Press, 1968.

Pace, Robert F. "'It Was Bedlam Let Loose': The Louisiana Sugar Country and the Civil War." *Louisiana History* 39 (Fall 1998): 389–409.

Parrish, T. Michael. *Richard Taylor: Soldier Prince of Dixie*. Chapel Hill: University of North Carolina Press, 1992.

Peña, Christopher G. *Scarred by War: Civil War in Southeast Louisiana*. Bloomington, IN: Authorhouse, 2004.

Peña, Christopher G. *Touched by War: Battles Fought in the Lafourche District.* Thibodaux, LA: C. G. P. Press, 1998.

Phisterer, Frederick. *New York in the War of the Rebellion, 1861–1865.* Albany: Weed and Parsons, 1890.

Prichard, Walter. "The Effects of the Civil War on the Louisiana Sugar Industry." *The Journal of Southern History* 5 (August 1939): 315–332.

Prushankin, Jeffery S. *A Crisis in Confederate Command: Edmund Kirby Smith, Richard Taylor, and the Army of the Trans-Mississippi.* Baton Rouge: Louisiana State University Press, 2005.

Raphael, Morris. *The Battle in the Bayou Country.* Detroit: Harlo Press, 1975.

Raphael, Morris. *A Gunboat Named* Diana. New Iberia, Louisiana: Printed by the author, 1993.

Ripley, C. Peter. *Slaves and Freedmen in Civil War Louisiana.* Baton Rouge: Louisiana State University Press, 1976.

Roberts, O. M., and J. J. Dickison. *Texas and Florida.* Vol. 11 of *Confederate Military History: A Library of Confederate States History, in Twelve Volumes, Written by Distinguished Men of the South, and Edited by Gen. Clement A. Evans of Georgia.* Edited by Clement A. Evans. Atlanta: Confederate Publishing Company, 1899.

Roland, Charles P. *Louisiana Sugar Plantations During the Civil War.* 1957. Reprint. Baton Rouge: Louisiana State University Press, 1997.

Smith, George Winston "Some Northern Wartime Attitudes Toward the Post–Civil War South." *Journal of Southern History* 10, no. 3 (August 1944): 253–274.

Sutherland, Daniel E. "Abraham Lincoln, John Pope, and the Origins of Total War." *Journal of Military History* 56, no. 4 (October 1992): 568–574.

Thompson, Jerry. *Henry Hopkins Sibley: Confederate General of the West.* Natchitoches, LA: Northwestern State University Press, 1987.

Tunnell, Ted. *Crucible of Reconstruction: War, Radicalism, and Race in Louisiana, 1862–1877.* Baton Rouge: Louisiana State University Press, 1984.

Vandiver, Frank. "Texas and the Confederate Army's Meat Problem." *Southwestern Historical Quarterly* 47, no. 3 (January 1944): 225–233.

Ward, Susan Hayes. *George H. Hepworth: Preacher, Journalist, Friend of the People, the Story of His Life Told to Susan Hayes Ward.* New York: E. P. Dutton, 1903.

Warner, Ezra. *Generals in Gray: Lives of the Confederate Commanders.* Baton Rouge: Louisiana State University Press, 1959.

Way, Frederick Jr. *Way's Packet Directory, 1848–1994.* Athens: Ohio University Press, 1982.

Weaver, C. P. ed., *Thank God My Regiment an African One: The Civil War Diary of Colonel Nathan W. Daniels.* Baton Rouge: Louisiana State University Press, 1998.

Winschel, Terrence J. *Vicksburg: Fall of the Confederate Gibraltar.* Abilene, TX: McWhiney Foundation Press, 1999.

Winters, John D. *The Civil War in Louisiana*. Baton Rouge: Louisiana State University Press, 1987.
Wright, Marcus J. *Texas in the War, 1861–1865*. Edited by Harold B. Simpson. Hillsboro, TX: Hill Junior College Press, 1965.

Websites

Broughton, Thomas Edward. "Letters to Molly." http://battleofraymond.org/history/letters.htm (accessed March 7, 2011).
Brothers, Ron. "History of the 1st Texas Sharp Shooters Burnet's Battalion." http://gen.1starnet.com/civilwar/burnhist.htmhttp://gen.1starnet.com/civilwar/burnhist.htm (accessed June 2, 2010).
Perkins, Robert P. "Captain James Henry Tevis, Arizona Pioneer and Confederate Soldier," http://members.tripod.com/~azrebel/page23.html (accessed January 8, 2005)
"Tod, John G." October 4, 1861, Confederate Citizens File 18, http:// www.footnote.com/image/#54514332 (accessed December 4, 2009).
"White, George W." April 2, 1862, Confederate Citizens File 42, http://www.footnote.com/image/#56376073 (accessed December 4, 2009).

Index

D

G

H

M

N